THE WATCHER'S GUIDE 2

BY **NANCY HOLDER**

WITH **JEFF MARIOTTE** AND **MARYELIZABETH HART**

POCKET BOOKS
New York   London   Toronto   Sydney   Singapore

SPECIAL THANKS TO THE FOLLOWING PEOPLE:

Debbie Olshan and Caroline Kallas

Judith Curr, Nancy Pines, Patricia MacDonald, Kara Welsh, Donna O'Neill,
Penny Haynes, Jeanne Lee, Gina DiMarco, Anna Dorfman, Brian Blatz,
Lisa Feuer, Linda Dingler, Twisne Fan, Rodger Weinfeld,
Kathryn Briggs-Gordon, Margaret Clark, and Jennifer Robinson

An *Original* Publication of POCKET BOOKS

DESIGN BY: Lili Schwartz

EDITED BY: Lisa A. Clancy
EDITORIAL TEAM: Elizabeth Shiflett and Micol Ostow

Additional photography courtesy of Byron Cohen, Todd McIntosh and MVP Media.
Video grabs courtesy of OmniGraphic Solutions

POCKET BOOKS, a division of Simon & Schuster, Inc.
1230 Avenue of the Americas, New York, NY 10020

ISBN: 0-671-04260-2

First Pocket Books trade paperback printing November 2000

10 9 8 7 6 5 4 3 2 1

ACKNOWLEDGMENTS

We would like to thank the many people who helped in the writing and creation of this book. First and foremost, our gratitude to Joss Whedon and the cast, staff, and crew of *Buffy*, especially Caroline "Coy Woman" Kallas. It was a pleasure, as always, to visit your world. Kudos to Debbie Olshan at Fox, and to George Snyder at Mutant Enemy.

Many thanks to agent and friend Howard Morhaim and his thoughtful assistant, Lindsay Sagnette. Also, our deep appreciation and love to our Pocket family: our wonderful and nurturing editor, Lisa Clancy, her cheerful assistant, Micol Ostow, and the unflappable Liz Shiflett. Heartfelt thanks to Lili Schwartz for her beautiful work.

To the Mysterious Galaxy Book and Buffy Discussion Group, especially Christine and "Uncle" Carl, thank you. Thanks to Martha Modlin and Steve Carter, who helped us figure out what questions to ask. Many thanks to those who were there the first time out: Christopher Golden and Keith DeCandido.

Thanks also go to our support staff: Anne Cox, Shasta Dexter, Amy Dickens, Chris Dolan, Jean Jenkins, Lara Koljonen, and Bill Walker. We couldn't have done it without you!

To Angela Rienstra, many thanks for the research help, late-night support and generous offers of help above and beyond. You're great! And a very special acknowledgment to Allison "Little Willow" Costa, for her research, friendship, and most especially her writing contributions, consisting of sidebars and actor profiles. Allie, you rock!

To Matt Pallamary, for his computer expertise and comaraderie, muchas gracias. Thanks to Patrick "TMI" Heffernan and Elizabeth Baldwin. Thank-yous to the Monday Night Group at MHUMC. Karen Hackett, Elise Jones, and Lee Sigall, you're all terrific, and we thank you.

DEDICATIONS

To my daughter Belle, and to the members of our "Big Family": Jeff and Maryelizabeth and their children, Holly and David. You have blessed my child and me in so many lovely and loving ways. —N.H.

To my two wonderful cowriters, who did most of the work. Sleep now? —J.M.

To David ("To be, or not to be—that is the vampire!"), Belle ("yi yi yi yi yi yi yi!") and Holly, who missed many first-run episodes so we could watch in peace. —Me.H.

CONTENTS

FOREWORD

Over the past eight years Joss Whedon has transformed *Buffy the Vampire Slayer* from her original one-note movie incarnation of horror and comedy into a young woman any Watcher would be proud to be associated with. Since the television show first aired in 1997, Buffy Summers and her circle of family and friends have been shaped by fantastic expressions of the horrors every adolescent encounters in the growing process. Their demons manifest in the flesh, but the fears they bring with them are universal. Fear of isolation, of being an outsider. Fear of making the wrong choices in romance. Fear of losing a loved one.

In the time it has been on the air, *Buffy* has truly reached the status of "cultural phenomenon." This means more than appearing on refrigerator magnets and door hangers (although this edition of *The Watcher's Guide* covers that aspect as well). It means that Buffy and the other residents of Sunnydale have become a part of the world's vernacular. People who don't watch the show are at least acquainted with the premise. And people who do watch, embrace the characters and feel their trials and triumphs along with them.

In addition to fans' fascination with the characters, *Buffy* also has a strong element of metafiction. Viewers are both aware and appreciative that the situations and dialogue they view each week come from the minds of Joss and his fellow writers.

This book contains more information on both levels of the Buffyverse. It contains a complete episode guide for Seasons Three and Four, with cross-referenced continuity and in-depth character descriptions. It also contains more behind-the-scenes information—including a day-by-day look at the making of Season Four's pivotal episode, "The I in Team,"—than has ever been available before. We documented the process of turning ideas, words, photographs, and sketches into a televised episode in two weeks.

Our goal in assembling this material was to include everything we believe a true fan desires to know. We hope we have met that goal for you.

Nancy Holder
Jeff Mariotte
Maryelizabeth Hart

BUFFYVERSE

Buffy the Vampire Slayer

Though grounded in the very real emotions of growing up and finding one's way in the world, the universe of *Buffy the Vampire Slayer* deals just as seriously with fantasy and the supernatural—evil portents, alternate dimensions, ghosts, witches, spells, and prophetic dreams.

According to *Buffy* lore, demons were the first inhabitants of the planet Earth. Eventually they were forced into other dimensions or made into hybrid creatures by mingling in various ways with the human usurpers, who came after them. They have been trying to take back this world ever since. They are considered to be the forces of evil.

The champion of good is the Slayer: "In every generation there is a Chosen One. She and she alone will fight the demons, the vampires, and the forces of darkness. She is the Slayer." Her Watcher assists her, training and mentoring her, and providing information about how to combat the many different forms of evil she encounters. This system is "older than civilization," according to the Watchers Council.

Buffy Summers first learned about her destiny when she was fifteen. Her first Watcher, Merrick, approached her in Los Angeles, where she began her career fighting vampires. However, Merrick was killed, and Buffy was thrown out of Hemery High for, among other things, burning down the gym (to slay vampires, of course).

Her parents divorced, and Buffy and her mother moved to the small town of Sunnydale, two hours on the freeway from Los Angeles. Buffy thought her slaying days were over, and that she could return to the life of a normal teenager. However, her new Watcher, Rupert Giles, was already waiting for her. Sunnydale, it seems, is situated on a hellmouth—an opening into the demon dimensions—and its supernatural energy both draws and strengthens the forces of darkness. To Buffy's initial dismay, there was plenty of evil to fight in the deceptively boring "one-Starbucks town."

Though Buffy is technically the current Slayer, she does not fight alone. Through a fluke, Kendra, an additional Slayer, was called (Buffy drowned, but was revived with CPR). When Kendra died, Faith was called.

Buffy is also one of the only Slayers ever to have a band of friends help her with her battles. These are other students at Buffy's new school, Sunnydale High. Xander Harris and Willow Rosenberg came on board as fellow sophomores to fight the good fight. Cordelia Chase (reluctantly) joined soon after, followed by Oz. The group often refers to itself as the Slayerettes or the Scooby Gang.

Angel, a vampire "cursed" with his own human soul, had also arrived in Sunnydale with the intention of helping Buffy. She and he soon fell in love.

Dynamics within the group shifted with the mundane pressures of high school, romance, and the more arcane pressures of demon fighting as a lifestyle. Cordelia continued to help occasionally too, even after her falling out with Xander. Then, in Season Four, she left for Los Angeles after graduation. Angel also departed, forcing closure on a relationship with the only woman he has ever loved in over two hundred and forty years of life—Buffy.

By the end of Season Three, Buffy had quit the Watchers Council. Giles had already been fired for letting his "fatherly love" for Buffy override his objective use of her as a weapon in the Watchers' battle against evil. Buffy's new Watcher, Wesley Wyndam-Pryce, also eventually opted for fighting at Buffy's side on her own terms, over remaining within the Council.

In Season Four, Buffy found love with a new man—Riley Finn, a Teaching Assistant by day who was really a soldier with the super-secret Initiative, an antidemon military operation located beneath UC Sunnydale. Anyanka—introduced in Season Three as a demon dedicated to punishing men who cheat on their wives and girlfriends, and who was ultimately stripped of her powers—fell in love with Xander. She became a member of the Scooby Gang. Oz, who had been Willow's boyfriend, abandoned her in order to explore his werewolf nature. The blossoming Wiccan, Willow, discovered a deep and lasting bond with another witch, Tara, choosing her over Oz when faced with the decision.

At the end of Season Four, the Slayer continues to fight evil surrounded by her band of friends— Giles, Xander, Anya, Willow, and Tara. Spike the vampire is a most reluctant footsoldier in Buffy's small army. Faith wrought havoc, then fled to Los Angeles where Angel, Cordelia, and Wesley help the hopeless. With their help Faith regained some semblance of her conscience, and turned herself in to the authorities. Presumably she is still in jail, and her future is uncertain.

What does the future hold for the Slayer and her supporters?

Only time will tell. . .

THE SLAYER

"But, but that's who you are and stuff, right? I mean, you help people...." —LILY, IN "ANNE"

AS WE LEARNED IN SEASONS ONE AND TWO, the Slayer is the Chosen One, who will fight the forces of darkness. Though she has to work out to stay in shape, and trains with weapons, she possesses superhero strength, reflexes, and agility, and she heals faster than other human beings. All these facets of the Slayer's identity are reinforced during both Seasons Three and Four.

> **SUNDAY:** "This arm's not looking so good. It might have to come off."
> **BUFFY:** "You want to know the truth? I only need one."
> —"THE FRESHMAN"

RILEY: "No weapons. No backup. You don't go after a demon that size by yourself."

BUFFY: "I do." —"DOOMED"

We also learned that the Slayer has a mentor, called a Watcher, and that there is a federation of Watchers called the Watchers Council. When one Slayer dies, a new one is called to fight the forces of darkness. When Buffy drowned at the hands of the Master, Kendra was called. Drusilla killed Kendra and Faith was called:

BUFFY: "The only way you get a new Slayer is when the old one dies."

JOYCE: "That means you . . . when did you die, you never told me you died!"

BUFFY: "It was just for a few minutes." —"FAITH, HOPE & TRICK"

We discovered in Season Two that there is a *Slayer's Handbook*, and that Buffy had not been given it because Giles figured she was too unconventional to adhere to it. We also learned that there is no way to abdicate one's duty as the Slayer; i.e., she can't quit:

"I know you didn't choose this. I know it chose you. I've tried to march in the Slayer pride parade, but . . ." —JOYCE, IN "FAITH, HOPE & TRICK"

"It's an adventure, great, but for me it's destiny. It's something I can't escape, something I can't change. I'm stuck." —BUFFY, IN "DOOMED"

We have also known for two seasons now that Buffy yearns for a normal life:

"I thought, Homecoming Queen; I could open a yearbook someday and say, 'I was there. I went to high school and had friends and for just one minute, I got to live in the world.' And there'd be proof. Proof that I was chosen for something other than this." —BUFFY, IN "HOMECOMING"

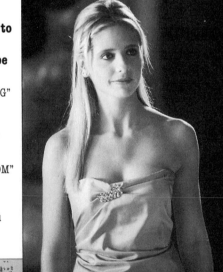

ANGEL: "But you have no idea how fast it goes, Buffy. Before you know it, you'll want it all—a normal life."

BUFFY: "I'll never have a normal life."

ANGEL: "Right. You'll always be a Slayer." —"THE PROM"

ANGEL: "Come on. Don't be that way."

BUFFY: ". . .I'm not being that way. I say 'prom' and you turn all grouchy."

ANGEL: "I'm sorry. I'm just worried that you're getting too. . .invested in this whole thing."

BUFFY: "In what 'whole thing'? This is the stuff I'm supposed to get invested in. Going to a formal. Graduating. Growing up." —"THE PROM"

But as wistful as Buffy is for more mundane teenage living, her life seemed full and rich compared to the far more restrictive existence Kendra experienced—one that was presented in Season Two as more in keeping with the traditions of the slaying life. Buffy found her Spartan existence and her suppression of all emotions—not to mention her supreme awkwardness around boys—to affect to her performance as a Slayer (after all, Buffy did outlive her). Then along comes Faith:

JOYCE: "So you're a Slayer, too. Isn't that interesting. Do you like it?"

FAITH: "I love it."

BUFFY: "Mom . . ."

JOYCE: "Just a sec, honey. Buffy never talks that way. Why do you love it?"

FAITH: "When I'm fighting, the whole world goes away and I know only one thing: I'm gonna win and they're gonna lose. I like that feeling."

BUFFY: "Well, sure, it's better than that dead feeling you get when they win and you lose."

FAITH: "I don't let that kind of negative thinking in."

JOYCE: "Right, right. That could get you hurt. Buffy can be awfully negative sometimes." —"FAITH, HOPE & TRICK"

Giles explains Faith's attitude:

"You yourself said she killed one of them. She's a plucky fighter who got a little carried away. Which is natural. She's focused on slaying. She doesn't have a whole other life here like you." —GILES, IN "FAITH, HOPE & TRICK"

Also new was the revelation that slaying brings with it certain side effects:

"God, I could eat a horse! Isn't it crazy? Slayin' always makes you just hungry and horny." —FAITH, IN "FAITH, HOPE & TRICK"

Buffy herself confirms the euphoria of slayage later in Season Three:

BUFFY: "It was intense. It was like I just let go, and became this force. I just didn't care anymore."

WILLOW: "Yeah, I know what that's like— "

BUFFY: "I don't think you can. It's kind of a Slayer thing. I don't even think I'm explaining it well." —"BAD GIRLS"

"Great thing about being a Slayer. Kicking ass is comfort food." —BUFFY, IN "THE PROM"

In Season Three it was reinforced that a Slayer may not take human life.

BUFFY: "A group of . . . human beings. Someone with a soul did this?"
GILES: "I'm afraid so."
BUFFY: "Okay, so while you're looking for the meaning of the squiggly mark, maybe you could turn up a loophole in the 'Slayers don't kill people' rule."   —"GINGERBREAD"

"Being a Slayer is not the same as being a killer."   —BUFFY, IN "BAD GIRLS"

Unfortunately, while patrolling, Faith accidentally stakes the deputy mayor, who was seeking them out to warn them about the evil Mayor. The cardinal rule has been broken. Buffy is stricken. But Faith, her "shadow self," the opposing viewpoint of life as a Slayer, shrugs off the killing as a mistake and nothing more.

BUFFY: "I know what you're feeling because I feel it too. . . . Dirty. Like something sick creeped inside you and you can't get it out. And you keep hoping what happened was just some nightmare. But it wasn't, Faith."
FAITH: "Is there gonna be an intermission in this?"   —"CONSEQUENCES"

FAITH: "Anyway, how many people do you think we've saved by now? Thousands? And didn't you stop the world from ending? In my book, that puts you and me firmly in the plus column."
BUFFY: "We help people. That doesn't mean we can do whatever we want."
FAITH: "Why not? This guy I offed was no Gandhi. We just saw. He was mixed up in dirty dealing."
BUFFY: "Maybe. But what if he was coming to us for help?"
FAITH: "What if he was? You're still not looking at the big picture, B. Something made us different. We're warriors. We were built to kill—"
BUFFY: "To kill demons. But it does not mean we get to pass judgment on people, like we're better than everybody else—"
FAITH: "We are better. That's right. Better. People need us to survive. In the balance? Nobody's gonna cry over some random bystander who got caught in the crossfire."
BUFFY: "I am."   —"CONSEQUENCES"

As Faith unravels, it's clear why the edict against killing humans is fundamental to the role of Slayer.

"See, you need me to toe the line because you're afraid you'll go over it, aren't you, B? You can't handle watching me living my own way and having a blast, because it tempts you. You know it could be you."
—FAITH, IN "CHOICES"

Faith is right. When Buffy learns that the blood of a Slayer will cure Angel, who is dying from a poisoned arrow shot by Faith, she goes after the renegade Slayer. But there is one important difference: Buffy has already quit the Council when she makes the decision to take a human life. She is no longer bound by their code of morality . . . only by her own.

Xander is concerned:

XANDER: "I don't mean to play devil's advocate here, but are you sure you're up for this?"

BUFFY: "It's time."

XANDER: "We're talking To The Death."

BUFFY: "I can't play kid games anymore. This is how she wants it."

XANDER: "I just don't want to lose you."

BUFFY: "I won't get hurt."

XANDER: "That's not what I meant." —"GRADUATION DAY, PART ONE"

Buffy makes the leap:

FAITH: "You know you're not gonna take me alive."

BUFFY: "That's not a problem."

FAITH: "Well, look at you, all dressed up in big sister's clothes."

BUFFY: "You told me I was just like you, Faith. That I was only holding it in."

FAITH: "You ready to cut loose?"

BUFFY: "Try me." —"GRADUATION DAY, PART ONE"

Buffy does indeed stab Faith. Faith manages to escape and does not die; she lapses into a coma. When she wakes up in Season Four she sums up Buffy's attempt to kill her from her point of view:

"I wake up to find out this blond chick isn't even dating the guy she was so nuts about before. She's moved on—to the first college beefstick she meets. Not only has she forgotten 'the love of her life,' she's forgotten all about the chick she nearly killed for him." —FAITH, IN "THIS YEAR'S GIRL"

With a magickal mechanism left for her by the Mayor, Faith switches bodies with Buffy. She intends to flee, but as Faith lives inside Buffy's skin, she moves from cynicism:

BUFFY: "Faith, these are innocent people."

FAITH: "No such animal." —"THIS YEAR'S GIRL"

... to a true Slayer. She's seen how people react to her, act with her, treat her as someone special while she has adopted Buffy's persona. How Buffy's own moral code and life choices gives her the respect from others she deserves. Airplane ticket in hand, her getaway assured, Faith chooses instead to risk her own life in order to save others:

FAITH: "You're not gonna kill these people."

BOONE: "Why not?"
FAITH: "Because it's wrong." —"WHO ARE YOU"

Confused by this turn of events, and disgusted to be back in her own body, Faith flees Sunnydale. (She turns up in L.A., where Angel finally sets her on the path to redemption—starting with what might be a first for the Council: a Slayer behind bars.)

Faith's departure for parts unknown leaves Buffy and company free to focus on a new threat—Adam, one of the Initiative's secret projects, a fighting machine made of various demon parts (and a computer processor). His strength and intelligence threaten everyone Buffy loves:

BUFFY: "I could barely fight him. It sounded like Maggie designed him to be the ultimate warrior. He's smart, and fast....He gave the commando guys the slip with no problem."
WILLOW (shaken)**:** "There's got to be a flaw—"
BUFFY: "I'd say the part where he's pure evil and kills randomly was an oversight...."
—"GOODBYE IOWA"

In "Primeval" and "Restless," the primal source of the Slayer is tapped, and Buffy becomes imbued with not only the strengths and abilities of her friends, Giles, Willow, and Xander, but also with that primal force. She becomes, according to the script, "ÜberBuffy," and she informs Adam, "You cannot hope to understand the source of our power." Once Adam is defeated, that source seeks retribution on Buffy, Willow, Xander, and Giles, by sending the First Slayer (also known as the Primitive) into their dreams to dispatch them. But Buffy thwarts the First Slayer, stating boldly, "You are not the source of me."

Tara murmurs to her in a voiceover as the season ends: "You think you know. What's to come, what you are. You haven't even begun."

· ·

THE SLAYERS: Buffy • Kendra • Faith
OTHER SLAYERS: The First Slayer • Korean slayer in the 1930s. • Two Slayers killed by Spike, one in China during the Boxer Rebellion between 1903–1904. • The Civil War Slayer mentioned in the series premiere (Virginia, 1866). • Chicago Gangland-era (1927) Slayer mentioned in the series premiere.

· ·

THE WATCHER

AS WE HAVE LEARNED IN SEASONS ONE AND TWO, each Slayer has a Watcher. Giles knew he was to be a Watcher by the time he was ten years old, and he rebelled by leaving Oxford and dabbling in the Black Arts. However, he eventually came around and spent his time waiting to be called—if called he would be—among the collections of the British Museum. Then he was sent to Sunnydale, in the guise of a librarian, to meet his new Slayer.

In Season Three, Giles continued on in his role as Watcher. He had become accustomed to the realities of Buffy's life as a Slayer, but that doesn't mean he didn't continue to face challenges posed by them. For example, he dealt with the resentment of Buffy's mother, Joyce, for being kept ignorant of her daughter's calling for so long:

> **JOYCE:** "I can hardly leave the house, I'm so afraid she'll call, that she'll...need help."
> **GILES:** "Buffy is the most capable child I have ever known. She may be confused, unhappy, but I honestly believe she's in no danger."
> **JOYCE:** "I just wish I could talk to her. The last thing we did was fight..."
> **GILES:** "Joyce, you mustn't blame yourself for Buffy's leaving. "
> **JOYCE:** "I don't . . . [looking him in the eye] I blame you."   —"ANNE"

Traditionally, Watchers exert control over Slayers. Despite the superhuman strength and healing powers of Slayers, they are, after all, still young girls, who need guidance and information to stay alive and do their jobs:

> **BUFFY:** "What if he's mad?"
> **XANDER:** "Mad? 'Cause you ran away and abandoned your post and your friends and your mother and made him lie awake every night worrying about you? Maybe we should wait out here."   —"DEAD MAN'S PARTY"

Xander raises an interesting point when Buffy returns to Sunnydale: If a Watcher has no Slayer to watch over, is he still a Watcher?

> **"Check it out. The Watcher is back on the clock. And just when you were thinking career change. Maybe becoming a 'Looker' or a 'seer.'"**
> —XANDER, WATCHING BUFFY AND GILES' REUNION, IN "DEAD MAN'S PARTY"

But when a Watcher is charged with the care of the Chosen One, he is *the* Watcher. And the Watcher is always on the clock:

GILES: "Buffy, good timing. I can use your help. I trust you remember the demon Acathla—"

BUFFY: "Giles, please, contain yourself. Yes, I'm finally back in school but you know how it embarrasses me when you gush so. Why don't we just skip all that and get right to work."   —"FAITH, HOPE & TRICK"

MRS. POST: "You wanted to see me, Mr. Giles?"

GILES: "Yes. I do apologize for bringing you in at this late hour."

MRS. POST: "Please. A good Watcher must be awake and alert at all hours."   —"REVELATIONS"

In "Faith, Hope & Trick," Willow celebrated the theme of Season Three: "It's the freedom!" A Watcherless Faith rolled into town to see Buffy, whom she assumed likewise would be Watcher-free. But Giles cannot be spared for the Watcher's retreat:

BUFFY: "Ow!"

GILES: "Sorry."

BUFFY: "Why do I put up with this?"

GILES: "Because it is your birthright and because I just bought twenty 'cocorific' candy bars."

BUFFY: "Okay, now you're just doing this to take funny pictures of me."

GILES: "I'm testing your awareness of an opponent's location during a fight in total darkness. You're to wait five seconds, then throw me the ball."

BUFFY: "You ran out of training ideas about a week ago, didn't you? Okay. Five, four, three-two-one." —JUST BEFORE BUFFY NAILS GILES WITH A KICKBALL, IN "BAND CANDY"

Still, despite his lot, Giles does maintain his sense of humor:

"We've got to find Buffy. Something terrible's happened. Just kidding. Thought I'd give you a scare. Are those finger sandwiches?"

—GILES, IN "HOMECOMING"

The Watcher—at least, this Watcher—watches out for the Slayer's morale. He must also maintain his authority, even when his mental state has reverted to that of a teenager:

"You're my Slayer. Knock those teeth down his throat!"

—GILES, IN "BAND CANDY"

Watchers are responsible for training their Slayers in the ways of, well, slayage:

MRS. POST: "You telegraph punches, leave blind sides open, and, for a school-night slaying, you both take entirely too much time. Which one of you is Faith?"

FAITH: "Depends. Who the hell are you?"
MRS. POST: "Gwendolyn Post. Mrs. Your New Watcher." ——"REVELATIONS"

MRS. POST: "I'm going to be very hard on you, Faith. I will not brook insolence, or laziness. I won't allow blunders like last night's attack. You will probably hate me a great deal of the time."
FAITH: "Ya think?"
MRS. POST: "But I will make you a better Slayer, and that will keep you alive. You have to trust that I'm right. God only knows what Mr. Giles has been filling your head with." ——"REVELATIONS"

GILES: "And this one?"
BUFFY: "Amethyst."
GILES: "Used for?"
BUFFY: "Breath mint?"
GILES: "For charm bags, money spells, and cleansing one's aura."
BUFFY: "Okay, so: How do you know when your aura's dirty? Somebody come by with a finger and write 'wash me' on it?"
GILES: "Buffy, I'm aware of your distaste for studying vibratory stones, but as it's part of your training, I'd appreciate your glib-free attention."
BUFFY: "Sorry. I just figure with Faith on one of her unannounced walkabouts someone should be out patrolling."
GILES: "Faith is not interested in proper training, so I rely on you to keep up with yours."
BUFFY: "I hate being the 'good' one." ——"GINGERBREAD"

You can take the Watcher out of the man, but it's hard to teach a former Watcher new tricks: After Giles reveals the nature of the Cruciamentum to Buffy (in "Helpless") he's relieved of his duties:

FAITH: "These babes were wicked rowdy. What's their deal?"
GILES: "I wish I knew. Most of my sources have dried up, since the Council has relieved me of my duties. I was aware that there was a nest here, but quite frankly I expected it to be vampires. These are new."
BUFFY: "And improved." ——"THE ZEPPO"

When Giles is replaced, the new Watcher, Wesley Wyndam-Pryce, apprises him of changes in the Watchers' training:

WESLEY: "Of course, training procedures have been updated quite a bit since your day. Much greater emphasis on field work."
GILES: "Really."
WESLEY: "Oh, yes. It's not all books and theory nowadays. I have in fact faced two vampires—under controlled circumstances, of course."
GILES: "Well, you're in no danger of finding any here."
WESLEY: "Vampires?"
GILES: "Controlled circumstances." ——"BAD GIRLS"

With Wesley "in charge," the gang is reminded of just how far Giles had come:

> **"Buffy, I must ask you to remember that I am your Watcher. From now on, anything you have to say about slaying, you say to me. The only thing you need discuss with Mr. Giles is overdue book fees. Understood?"** —WESLEY, IN "BAD GIRLS"

> **"One moment, girls. I am your commander now and on the matter of this murder, I am resolved. 'Natural' or 'super'— I want to know."**
>
> —WESLEY, IN "CONSEQUENCES"

WESLEY: "All right. Stop! I demand everyone stop this instant. I am in charge here! And I say this is all moving much too fast. We need time to fully analyze the situation and devise a proper and effective stratagem."
BUFFY: "Wes, hop on the train or get off the tracks." —"CHOICES"

A Watcher without a Slayer is jobless. When Buffy quits the Council for its refusal to cure Angel of Faith's poison, Wesley has no official reason for sticking around.

WESLEY: "You know that. . .when this is over. . ."
CORDELIA: "Yes?"
WESLEY: "Well, should we prevail, I'll be going back to England."
CORDELIA: "I know."
WESLEY: "With Buffy no longer working for the Council, there's really no place for me here." —"GRADUATION DAY, PART TWO"

This is the same conundrum facing Giles at the end of Season Three. Season Four is about redefining the formal role of Watcher into something more akin to a mentor, or friend, without any sense of vested authority.

However, it becomes clear that Watchers are the civilizing and guiding force of the power given to the Slayer, as shown in "Restless," when the First Slayer specifically cuts into Giles's skull (his intellect):

> **"Of course you underestimate me. You never had a Watcher."**
>
> —GILES, IN "RESTLESS"

ON EVERY WATCHER'S BEDSIDE TABLE: *Exploring Demon Dimensions* ("Faith, Hope & Trick") • *The Mystery of Acathla* ("Faith, Hope & Trick") • *Hume's Paranormal Encyclopedia* ("Revelations") • *Sir Robert Kane's Twilight Compendium* ("Revelations") • *The Labyrinth Maps of Malta* ("Revelations") • *Hebron's Almanac* ("Revelations") • *The Black Chronicles* ("Amends") • *The Diary of Lucius Temple* ("Amends") • *Twelfth Century Papal Encyclical* ("Gingerbread") • *Blood Rites and Sacrifices* ("Gingerbread") • *The Books of Pherian* ("The Zeppo") • *The Merenshtadt Text* ("Enemies") • The Books of Ascension (on Christmas list) ("Enemies") • *The Kippler Volumes* ("Graduation Day, Part Two") • *Oh, Jonathan!* ("Superstar")

XANDER: "I'm not enjoying this."
GILES: "Well, shelve them correctly and we can finish."
XANDER: "I don't get your crazy system."
GILES: "My system? It's called the alphabet."
XANDER: "Huh. Would you look at that."

—"THE HARSH LIGHT OF DAY"

THE WATCHERS COUNCIL

Before Season Three not much is known about the Watchers Council. Basically, there is a Council, and Watchers and potential Watchers keep in contact with one another. For example, Giles knew who Kendra's Watcher was.

Early in Season Three, in "Faith, Hope & Trick," it is revealed that there's an annual Watchers retreat in England. Faith uses it as the excuse to come to Sunnydale to pay a social call on the reigning Slayer. One might assume that Giles was not able to go because he is the reigning Watcher, but he's rather miffed about not having been invited:

> **"There is a Watcher retreat every year in the Cotswolds...lovely spot, very serene. They have horseback riding, river rafting, punting, lectures and discussions. Quite an honor to be invited. So I'm told..."**
>
> —GILES, IN "FAITH, HOPE & TRICK"

The Council also has the right to approve "transfers" of Watchers and Slayers:

BUFFY: "Um, maybe I should introduce you again. Faith, this is Giles."
FAITH: "I seen him. If I'da known they came this young and cute I'd've requested a transfer."
BUFFY: "Okay, raise your hand if 'ew.'"

—"FAITH, HOPE & TRICK"

FAITH: "I'm telling you, I don't need a new Watcher! No offense, lady, I just have this problem with authority figures. They end up kinda dead."

MRS. POST: "Duly noted, and fortunately, it's not up to you." —"REVELATIONS"

The Watchers Council is an ancient organization based in London, and appears to be comprised of men and women far removed from the actual battle between good and evil. Also, it can be rather disorganized:

BUFFY: "Let me guess. Gwendolyn Post, not a Watcher."

GILES: "Yes, she was. She was kicked out by the Council two years ago for misuses of dark power. They swear there was a memo." —"REVELATIONS"

"Yes, hello. I need Mr. Travers, Quentin Travers. Wesley Wyndam-Pryce calling. The code word? Monkey. M-O-N-K . . . just put him on, would you? This is an emergency." —WESLEY, IN "CONSEQUENCES"

In "Helpless," Buffy's knowledge of the Council's operations takes on a new dimension. As Buffy's eighteenth birthday approaches, Giles is forced to make her undergo a barbaric ritual called a "Cruciamentum." It's a rite of passage for Slayers—those who make it to the ripe old age of eighteen, that is—in which she is injected with drugs that make her temporarily lose her powers. Then, in a weakened and confused state, she is imprisoned with a supernatural adversary—in Buffy's case, a vampire named Zackary Kralik, who was criminally insane *before* he was changed.

Giles argued against the ritual, but Quentin Travers, who is his superior, overrules him:

GILES: "If any one of the Council still had actual contact with a Slayer, they'd see. But I'm the one in the thick of it."

TRAVERS: "Which is why you're not qualified to make this decision. You're too close."

GILES: "Not true."

TRAVERS: "I'm sorry. A Slayer must be more than physical prowess. She must have cunning, imagination. . .a confidence derived from self-reliance. Believe me, once this is all over, your Buffy will be stronger for it."

GILES: "Or she'll be dead for it." —"HELPLESS"

When Giles rebels against the edict of the Council and reveals the secret test to Buffy, there are consequences:

TRAVERS: "We're not in the business of 'fair,' Miss Summers. We're fighting a war."

GILES: "You're waging a war. She's fighting it. There is a difference."

TRAVERS: "Mr. Giles, if you don't mind—"

GILES: "The test is done. We're finished."

TRAVERS: "Not quite. She passed; you didn't. The Slayer isn't the only one who must perform in this situation. I have recommended to the Council, and they have agreed, that you be relieved of your duties as Watcher effective immediately. You're fired."   —"HELPLESS"

This heralds the arrival of Giles's replacement, Wesley Wyndam-Pryce. Wesley takes it for granted that once Buffy is assured of his identity, she will follow his orders without question.

BUFFY: "The last one was evil."

WESLEY: "Oh, yes. Gwendolyn Post. We all heard. A sad example of the seductive power of dark knowledge. No, Mr. Giles has checked my credentials rather thoroughly and phoned the Council, but I'm glad to see you're on the ball as well."   —"BAD GIRLS"

It takes Faith to make Buffy realize that she is, quite possibly, holding a few cards of her own. Also from "Bad Girls:"

WESLEY: "Are you perhaps not used to being given orders?"

BUFFY: "Whenever Giles sends me on a mission, he always says please. And afterwards, he gives me a cookie."

WESLEY: "I don't feel like we're getting off on quite the right foot—Ah! This is perhaps Faith?"

FAITH: "New Watcher?"

GILES/BUFFY: "New Watcher."

FAITH: "Screw that." [turns and walks out]

BUFFY: "Now, why didn't I say that?"

And

BUFFY: "I know this guy's a dork, but. . .I have nothing to follow that. He's just a dork."

FAITH: "You actually gonna take orders from him?"

BUFFY: "That's the job. What else can we do?"

FAITH: "Whatever we want! We're Slayers, girlfriend."   —"BAD GIRLS"

Then Faith mistakenly stabs the deputy mayor, figuring him for a vampire. She wants to sweep everything under the carpet and pretend it never happened, but Buffy is having trouble with that scenario. When she finally goes to Giles, he tells her—to her surprise—that of course there are procedures for this situation:

GILES: "Buffy, this is not the first time something like this has happened."

BUFFY: "It's not?"

GILES: "A Slayer is on the front lines of a nightly war, Buffy. It's tragic, but accidents have happened."

BUFFY: "What do you do?"

GILES: "The Council investigates, metes out punishment if punishment is due. I've no plan to involve them. That's the last thing Faith needs. She's unstable at the moment. She's utterly unable to accept responsibility."   —"CONSEQUENCES"

However, Wesley, the company man, phones home to England and obeys orders to capture Faith and return her to England:

> **"By the order of the Watchers Council of Britain, I am exercising my authority and removing you to England, where you will accept the judgment of the disciplinary committee."**

And

> **"Please believe, nobody is rushing to judgment. The first priority of both myself and the Council is to help you."**   —WESLEY, IN "CONSEQUENCES"

Giles, however, takes a more jaundiced view of the Council:

GILES: "Which means that Faith will soon be on her way to England to face the Watchers Council."

BUFFY: "And then what?"

GILES: "Most likely? They'll lock her away for a good, long while."   —"CONSEQUENCES"

Faith appears to see the error of her ways and the Council assesses her and Buffy both regarding fitness for duty:

> **"The Watchers Council shrink is heavily into tests. He's got tests for everything. T.A.T.'s, Rorschach, associative logic. . . .They even have that test to see if you're crazy that asks if you hear voices or have ever wanted to be a florist."**

And

> **"They've really got us running around on the physical side, too. A lot of precision training and reflex evaluation..."**   —BUFFY, IN "DOPPLEGANGLAND"

Faith manages to convince the Council that she's fit for duty ("Enemies"), and she and Buffy follow orders to the letter, only to discover it's Wesley who's now bending the rules:

GILES: "Perhaps I should contact the Council, run a search through the main branch—"

WESLEY: "No, I don't . . . it should be I that . . . the Council isn't entirely aware that I'm letting you work for me. With me. I don't think they'd be very happy with the idea of the two of us collaborating."

GILES: "I'm not about to burst into glorious song about it myself. But why don't you give them a call."

WESLEY: "I think the most expedient plan is to get the Books of Ascension themselves."

—"ENEMIES"

However, when Giles does something similar, Wesley is not amused:

WESLEY: "Well, I for one protest. You pitted Slayer against Slayer in a dangerous charade that could have gotten both killed. Without informing me. I'm telling the Council."

GILES: "Yes, I think you should. We have a rogue Slayer on our hands. I can't think of anything more dangerous."

—"ENEMIES"

Giles and Wesley do continue to work together, albeit not smoothly:

WESLEY: "Terribly sorry. I was detained. Official Council business. Giles, you were talking?"

GILES: "I was just filling Buffy in on my progress regarding the Ascension."

WESLEY: "Oh? And what took up the rest of the minute?"

GILES: "Touché. My work is, after all, unofficial, and my sources are limited. I'm sure, however, with the resources of the Council behind you, that you have something to add. We're all ears."

WESLEY: "Well, I...I am pleased to state with certainty that the demon Azorath will not be involved in—"

[Everyone is getting up, collecting their books]

WESLEY (calling after): "I'm sure we'll find out more soon."

—"EARSHOT"

The hold the Council has on Buffy is eroding, and Giles backs her every step of the way:

WESLEY: "You cannot leave Sunnydale. With the power invested in me by the Council, I forbid it."

BUFFY: [sighs]

GILES: "Oh, yes. That should settle it."

—"CHOICES"

Despite the Council's flaws, they've been around for a good, long time, and amassed a wealth of information about magic and other practices:

"The Council has all the known toxins on file, mystical or otherwise. I'll contact them immediately." —WESLEY, IN "GRADUATION DAY, PART ONE"

But they are unwilling to depart from established protocol to help the poisoned Angel:

GILES: "Did you reach the Council?"

WESLEY: "Yes. They, um. . .they couldn't help."

BUFFY: "Couldn't?"

WESLEY: "Wouldn't. It's not Council policy to cure vampires."

GILES: "Well, did you explain these were special—"

WESLEY: "Not under any circumstances, and yes, I did try to convince them."

BUFFY: "Try again."

WESLEY: "Buffy, they're very firm. We're talking about laws that have existed longer than civilization."

For Buffy, this is the last straw:

WESLEY: "The Council's orders are to—"

BUFFY: "Orders? I don't think I'm gonna be taking any more orders. Not from you. Not from them."

WESLEY: "You can't turn your back on the Council."

BUFFY: "They're in England! I don't think they can tell which way my back is facing."

WESLEY: "Giles, talk to her."

GILES: "I have nothing to say right now."

BUFFY: "Wesley, go back to your Council—"

WESLEY: "Don't you see what—"

BUFFY: "And tell them that until the next Slayer shows up they can close up shop. I'm not working for them anymore."   —"GRADUATION DAY, PART ONE"

Giles makes it official by announcing it to the group:

GILES: "Buffy has quit the Council. She'll not be working with Wesley from now on."

CORDELIA: "But he's her Watcher!"

GILES: "Buffy no longer needs a Watcher."   —"GRADUATION DAY, PART TWO"

Then it's Wesley's turn to graduate:

BUFFY: "The Council isn't welcome here. I got no time for orders. I need someone to scream like a woman, I'll give you a call."

WESLEY: "I'm not here for the Council. Just tell me how I can help."

—"GRADUATION DAY, PART TWO"

In Season Four's "This Year's Girl," once Faith awakes, the nurse who's been watching her calls the Watchers Council and tells them to "send the team." Someone calls Buffy at Giles's apartment to let her know that Faith has awakened and disappeared. Was it the Council? And once Buffy finds Faith, should she turn her over to the Council?

> **"Been there, tried that. Not unlike smothering a forest fire with napalm, as I recall."**   —XANDER, IN "THIS YEAR'S GIRL"

In the next episode, "Who Are You," the Watchers Council assassins (Collins, Smith, and Weatherby) hijack a police car and seize Buffy (who is trapped in Faith's body):

GILES: "They've sent a retrieval team to capture Faith."

FAITH (as Buffy): "Well, yeah. I mean, because that worked so well when Wesley tried it."

GILES: "This is a special operations unit. They handle the Council's trickier jobs. Smuggling, interrogation, wetworks."

WILLOW: "What's wetworks?"

XANDER: "Scuba type stuff."

ANYA: "I thought it was murder."

FAITH (as Buffy): "So the Watchers Council has assassins on the payroll? Sweet buncha guys."

GILES: "They've never had a contract on a human that I know of, but in the world of international sorcery, things get . . . complicated. It's not all pointy hats and purple cloaks, as I'm sure you well know." —DIALOGUE CUT DUE TO LENGTH, "WHO ARE YOU"

From their interactions with Buffy (in Faith's body), it's clear that the hardened assassins represent Council business as usual:

BUFFY: "You have to find Faith. Call Giles! Just get him here."

COLLINS: "Giles doesn't work for the Council anymore. For that matter, neither does Buffy Summers. What you are, Miss, is the package. I deliver the package. I don't much care what's inside. . . ."

WEATHERBY: "He may not care, but I do. The Watchers Council used to mean something. You perverted it. You trash. We should have killed you while you were asleep."

In the same episode, when Buffy tries to hold Smith hostage, she hits a wall in their assassin training:

BUFFY: "Now you unchain me, very slowly and politely, or I kill this guy."

COLLINS: "When we go on a job we always put our affairs in order first. In case of accident."

Buffy's escape plan thwarted, the assassins get the go-ahead to do what they came for:

COLLINS: "They can't get us passage. They've ordered the kill."

WEATHERBY: "Torch the place?"

COLLINS: "Get the gas."

SMITH: "She could've killed me. She didn't."

COLLINS: "Lucky you." —"WHO ARE YOU"

After Buffy affects the transfer back into her own body, Faith skips town. The assassins do, too. The ruthless men track her to L.A., where they run afoul of Angel and Wesley (whom they try to trick into helping them by promising to reinstate him on the Council). Angel and Wesley prevail.

THE WORLD, REAL AND NOT SO MUCH

SUNNYDALE THE TOWN

Season One revealed that Sunnydale is a town situated two hours on the freeway from Los Angeles. It sits on a hellmouth, which is a portal to the demon dimensions. The negative energy attracts demons, vampires, and other denizens of evil, some of whom have made concerted efforts to open the Hellmouth and overrun the human population with the Old Ones and their descendants.

Thus, Sunnydale is an obvious place for the current Slayer to live. However, both Buffy and her mother, Joyce, assumed that they independently chose to move to Sunnydale after Buffy was expelled from Hemery High School in Los Angeles. The divorced mom wanted to find a nice small town where she and her daughter could start a new life. She opened an art gallery in Sunnydale. Neither realized that Buffy's new Watcher, Rupert Giles, was awaiting their arrival so that he could guide her in the ongoing battle between good and evil.

Xander has described Sunnydale as "a one-Starbucks town," and various characters have bemoaned the lack of nightlife, decent shopping, or first-run movies. Sunnydale High School has the highest mortality rate in the nation, and bizarre events are blamed on "gangs on PCP" or "gas leaks." The city administration was behind these cover-ups, but as of the end of Season Two, we're not sure precisely who—or what—is in City Hall, nor why they're trying to hide all the nefarious goings-on of this not-so-fair city.

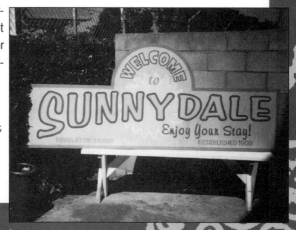

JOYCE: "Nothing's settled yet. I just wish you didn't have to be so secretive about things. I mean, it's not your fault you have a special circumstance. They should make allowances for you."

BUFFY: "Mom, I'm a Slayer. It's not like I have to ride the little bus to school."

JOYCE: "Couldn't you tell just a few people? Like Principal Snyder? And maybe the police? I'm sure they'd be happy to know that they have a superhero—is that the right term?"
— "DEAD MAN'S PARTY"

As Season Three begins, Willow, Xander, Oz, and Cordy have assumed the slayage duties (once Queen C returns from her wretched summer at a posh resort). Then Buffy, having fled town after killing Angel at the end of Season Two, returns and takes up her duties. Bad guys arrive. It's just another manic school year on the Hellmouth:

"Welcome to the Hellmouth petting zoo."
— BUFFY, RE: A DEAD ZOMBIE CAT, IN "DEAD MAN'S PARTY"

"Sunnydale. Town's got quaint, and the people: he called me sir. Don't you miss that? Admittedly not a haven for the brothers—strictly the Caucasian persuasion in the Dale—but you gotta stand up and salute their death rate. I ran a statistical analysis and Hello Darkness—makes D.C. look like Mayberry. And nobody sayin' boo about it. We could fit right in here. Have some fun."
— MR. TRICK, IN "FAITH, HOPE & TRICK"

"There's a big evil brewing. You'll never be bored here, Faith, 'cause this is Sunnydale, home of the big brewing evil."
— WILLOW, IN "FAITH, HOPE, AND TRICK"

"Get out of Sunnydale, that's a good thing! I mean, what kind of moron would ever want to come back here?"
— CORDELIA, IN "LOVER'S WALK"

"Once again—the Hellmouth puts the 'special' in special occasion."
— OZ, IN "THE PROM"

SUNNYDALE IS THE PROUD HOME OF: Happy Burger, located in the Sunset Ridge district • **The Buster Keaton film festival,** playing over on State Street • **Mr. Donut** • **Sunnydale Medical,** including an E.R. • A **retreat** up near the clearing in Breaker's Woods • **April Fool's** on Main • **Sun Cinema** on Main • **Espresso Pump** on Main • **The magic shop** on Main • **A bridal shop** on Main • **A liquor store** run by an Armenian man • **Willy's Place** • **A gun shop** on Main • A **sporting goods shop** on Main • **Sunnydale Arms** (abandoned inn) • **Mell's Butcher Shop** • **A bus station** ("Not the nicest part of town.") • **A**

beach • **Fire demon caves** near the beach • **The Sunnydale Motor Inn,** down by the freeway (a rattrap) • **UC Sunnydale** • **The Initiative Complex** (below Lowell House) • **The Sunnydale Mission** (also under UC Sunnydale) • **A bell tower**

"Check it out. This town—this very street—is wired for fiber optics. We jack in a T-4, hundred megs per, we got the whole world at our fingertips."
—MR. TRICK, IN "FAITH, HOPE & TRICK"

CITY ADMINISTRATION: Deputy Mayor Allan Finch (deceased) • **Mayor Richard Wilkins, III** (deceased) • **Chief of Police** • **Detective Paul Stein**

BIZARRO SUNNYDALE ("THE WISH")

WHAT IS COMMONLY REFERRED TO in the Buffyverse as "Bizarro Sunnydale" was established in "The Wish." Anyanka, patron demon of women scorned, created an alternate Sunnydale to satisfy the wish of Cordelia: "I wish Buffy Summers had never come to Sunnydale." (All quoted material taken from "The Wish.")

GILES: "She said the Slayer was supposed to be here. To have been here already."
OZ: "Well, that certainly would have been helpful."

"World is what it is. We fight and we die. Wishing doesn't change that."—BUFFY

VAMP WILLOW: "Buffy. Ooooh. Scary."
VAMP XANDER: "Someone has to talk to her people. That name is striking fear in nobody's heart."

WHITE HATS:
Rupert Giles, Librarian and former Watcher: **"Yes, I understand, but it's imperative that I see her. Here. Well, when will you. . .? You are her Watcher, I would think she'd at least check in to. . .Yes. I'm aware there is a great deal of demonic activity in Cleveland. It happens, you know, that Sunnydale is on a Hellmouth. It is so! Just give her the message, if you ever see her again."** ✦ Harmony ✦ Cordelia—dies: **"No. No way! I wished us into Bizarro Land and you guys are still together? I can not win!"** ✦ Ginger ✦ Ted Chervin ✦ John Lee ✦ Oz ✦ Larry ✦ Nancy—dies

ACTIVITIES:
Winterbrunch ◆ Monthly Memorial for dead students

VAMPIRES:
The Master, the evil vampire who reigns over Bizarro Sunnydale, previously defeated by Buffy in "real" Sunnydale: **"The plant goes into operation in less than twenty-four hours! You find that girl and kill her before she contacts the Slayer—or I'll see the both of you kissing daylight."** ◆ Xander Harris—vampire: **"Slap my hand, dead soul man."** ◆ Willow Rosenberg—vampire: **"Bored now."**

THE PUPPY:
Angel, prisoner of the Master, and tortured boytoy of Vamp Willow: **"The Master rose. He let me live, to punish me. I kept hoping maybe you'd come."**

THE BRONZE:
"Oh, the Bronze isn't cool in this reality. Gotta make these little adjustments."
—CORDELIA

THE PLANT:
Industrial processing plant for extracting the blood of live humans, assembly-line style

". . . Behold the technical wonder which is about to alter the very fabric of our society. Some have argued that such an advancement goes against our nature. They claim that death is our art. I say to them . . . well, I don't say anything to them because I kill them."
—THE MASTER

THE SLAYER—Buffy Summers, lives in Cleveland.

BUFFY: "Why don't I put a stake through her heart?"
GILES: "She's not a vampire."
BUFFY: "You'd be surprised how many things that'll kill."

UC SUNNYDALE:

In Season Four, Buffy, Willow, and Oz enter UC Sunnydale as freshmen.

BUFFY: "There's safer schools. There's safer prisons. I can't let you stay here because of me."

WILLOW: "Actually, this isn't about you. Although I'm fond, don't get me wrong, of you. The other night, being captured and all, facing off with Faith...things just got kind of clear. I mean, you've been fighting evil here for about three years, and I've been helping out some, and now we're supposed to be deciding what we wanna do with our lives and I realized that's what I want to do. Fight evil. Help people. I think it's worth doing, and I don't think you do it 'cause you have to. It's a good fight, Buffy, and I want in."

BUFFY: "I kind of love you."

WILLOW: "Besides, I have a shot at becoming a bad-ass Wicca, and what better place to learn?" —"CHOICES"

"It's gonna be fun. Will and I are gonna go visit the campus together on Saturday. I'm hoping Mom'll let me live on campus—it's too far to go home every night, plus the whole lack-of-cool factor . . ." —BUFFY, IN "CHOICES"

JOYCE: "That's not it. It's just—You should be at a good old-fashioned college, with keg parties and boys. Not here, with Hellmouths and vampires."

BUFFY: "Not really seeing a huge distinction there . . . ." —"LOVERS WALK"

COURSE LISTINGS:
Introduction to the Modern Novel ◆ **Introduction to Psychology** (105) taught by Dr. Maggie Walsh, who is world-renowned in the field of operant conditioning. Did a treatise on Dietrick's work. Riley Finn is her Teacher's Assistant. ◆ **Images of Pop Culture**, taught by Professor Riegert ◆ **Geology 101** ("where the football players are") ◆ **Modern Poetry** ◆ **Ethnomusicology** (West African drumming)

STUDENT ORGANIZATIONS:
FRATERNITIES: Alpha Delta—Oz's band is playing there first Thursday of the semester. Jell-O shots, and the site of Halloween's haunted house. Brothers include Edward, Chaz, and Josh. ◆ **Psi Theta**—lost their charter in 1982. Their frat house lies in ruins. Sunday's lair. ◆ **SORORITIES: Beta Delta Gamma**—Sisters include Paula and Melody.

UNHALLOWED HALLS AND HAUNTED HOUSES: Asian House ◆ Dunwirth—"Dead Eddie's" dorm ◆ **Fischer Hall** ◆ **Kresge Hall**—Parker Abrams (AKA "Stinky Parker Man") conducts his love life there, when his mother isn't visiting. ◆ **Lowell House**—the frat house that sits above the Initiative complex. Commandos Riley, Forrest, Mason, Graham, and A.J. live there (A.J. cuts the Dingoes song off the sound system for Riley when it upsets Willow). The house was once the Lowell Home for Children (1949–1960). The director of the Lowell Home for Children was Genevieve Holt, a religious wacko who tortured the 40-plus children in her care. When the house becomes saturated with poltergeist activity, Roy (of Black Frost Cro-Magnonhood) discovers the orgasmo-wall while showing off his French to Christy. Evan digs on the wall, too. At the same haunted party Xander flirts with Julie, who goes all Felicity shortly thereafter. ◆ **Porter Dorm**—the party dorm. Willow runs into Percy West and his snotty girlfriend, Laurie, at the Aftershock Party. Also, she finds a dead student with an apocalyptic sigil on his chest. ◆ **Richmond Hall**—next to the auditorium. They distribute work-study applications in the back of Richmond Hall at the beginning of the semester. ◆ **Stevenson Hall**—Buffy's dorm. She lives in Room 214. Her first roommate is Kathy Newman, a demon. Her second one is Willow, who nicks Buffy's sandwiches. Their dorm has a rec room, where Willow and Xander stage Buffy's surprise birthday party. ◆ **Weisman Hall**—ID cards provided there. ◆ **Wolf House**—parties there, including the one Buffy and Parker went to, running into Spike and Harmony.

OTHER BUILDINGS AND LOCATIONS:

The bike path—Buffy and Eddie get found near it. ◆ **The Bronze**—within walking distance of the dorms; Veruca's band, Shy, plays there; so does Dingoes. ◆ **Brookside Park**—site of Adam's cave. ◆ **The campus pub**—Black Frost beer on tap! Colm, Roy, Hunt, Kip and Caveslayer have a little too much Black Frost, thanks to vengeful Jack, who has been bartending there for twenty years. Xander is—briefly—employed there. ◆ **The dining hall**—Home of the Twinkie ◆ **The Grotto**—coffee hangout for studying and dozing off. Fire discovered there. ◆ **The main library and the science library**—big enough for the Nuremberg Rallies; open all night. ◆ **On-campus outdoor café**—where chicks ask if there's dressing on stuff (Veruca does <u>not</u>). ◆ **The Rocket Café**—local student hangout. ◆ **Ruggs Field**—a nice place to have a romantic picnic. ◆ **The Science Center**—home of the science lab, site of the death of Veruca wolf. ◆ **Sinkhole near campus**—You go, Spike! ◆ **The Sunnydale Cultural Partnership Center**—replacing the old Cultural Center. Professor Gerhardt of the Anthropology Deparament was the Curator. ◆ **The lost Sunnydale Mission**—discovered during the construction of the Sunnydale Cultural Partnership Center. It was buried during the Earthquake of 1812.

STUDENTS, DEAD AND ALIVE:

Alphabetical Roster (*The Scooby Core): A.J.—kills the music at a party when a Dingoes song depresses Willow ("The Initiative") ◆ **Buffy Summers*** ◆ **Chaz**—Alpha Delt brother ("Fear, Itself") ◆ **Cheryl**—Wicca group member ("Hush") ◆ **Chloe**—member of the Wicca group who rides a mountain bike to impress Justin ("Hush") ◆ **Christy**—Party guest who's chatted up by pretentious Roy ("Where the Wild Things Are") ◆ **Colm**—Neanderthal ("Beer Bad") ◆ **Dixon**—Initiative Soldier ("Primeval") ◆ **Eddie**—Freshman who is turned into a vampire, in Psych 105 with Buffy, Willow, and Oz ("The Freshman") ◆ **Edward**—Alpha Delt brother ("Fear, Itself") ◆ **Evan**—friend of Roy's who also experiences the wallgasm game ("Where the Wild Things Are") ◆ **Forrest**—Initiative soldier who hates Buffy—is killed and reanimated by Adam (first seen in "The Initiative") ◆ **Graham**—Initiative soldier (first seen in "The Initiative") ◆ **Hunt**—Neanderthal ("Beer Bad") ◆ **Josh**—Alpha Delt brother ("Fear, Itself") ◆ **Julie**—Partier who goes all Felicity ("Where the Wild Things Are") ◆ **Justin**—The object of mountain-biking Wicca Chloe's affections ("Hush") ◆ **Kathy Newman**—roommate from hell (well, a demon dimension, anyway—first seen in "The Freshman") ◆ **Kip**—Neanderthal ("Beer Bad") ◆ **Laurie**—Percy West's girlfriend ("Doomed") ◆ **Mason**—Initiative Soldier (first seen in "The I In Team") ◆ **Melody**—Beta Delta Gamma pledge ("Beer Bad") ◆ **Nicole**—Wicca group leader who favors bake sales ("Hush") ◆ **Paula**—barfly ("Beer Bad") ◆ **Paul**—AKA "Passing Student," who talks to Oz ("The Freshman") ◆ **Parker Abrams**—Buffy's brief crush whose intimacy problem is that he can't get enough of it (first seen in "Living Conditions") ◆ **Oz*** ◆ **Rachel**—Party guest who gets a fistful of eyeballs ("Fear, Itself") ◆ **Riley Finn**—Psych TA, Initiative Soldier, and Buffy's new man (first seen in "The Freshman") ◆ **Lisa Rosenberg**—Listed in the student directory ("The Initiative") ◆ **Cindy Rosenthal**—Listed in the student directory ("The Initiative") ◆ **Roy**—Neanderthal ("Beer Bad") ◆ **David Solomon**—Listed in the student directory ("The Initiative") ◆ **Tim Speed**—Listed in the student directory ("The Initiative") ◆ **Mike Starkey**—Listed in the student directory ("The Initiative") ◆ **Stavros**—Initiative Soldier ◆ **Bryan Sula**—Listed in the student directory ("The Initiative") ◆ **Tara**—Member of Willow's Wicca group and her new love interest (first seen in "Hush") ◆ **Tuck**—Initiative Soldier ◆ **Veruca**—Willow's werewolf rival for Oz's affections (first seen in "Beer Bad") ◆ **Willis**—Initiative soldier killed—but *not* by wolf-Oz ("New Moon Rising") ◆ **Willow***

THE INITIATIVE:

Deep beneath Lowell House, a historical frat house on the UC Sunnydale campus, sprawls the vast underground complex of the Initiative, a supersecret military operation. Its mission is best summed up by Buffy herself:

BUFFY: "...You're part of some military monster squad that rounds up demons, vampires—probably have official-sounding euphemisms for them like 'Unfriendlies' or 'Nonsapiens'...."

RILEY: "'Hostile Sub-Terrestrials.'"

BUFFY: "There you go. So you deliver these ... 'HST's' to a bunch of lab coats who perform experiments which, among other things, turn some into harmless bunnies. How am I doing so far?"

RILEY: "A little too well."
　　　　　　　　　　　　　　　　　　　　　　　　　　—"DOOMED"

Although the Initiative soldiers—eventually referred to as "Commandos"—are shown skulking around the UC Sunnydale campus and tasering a vampire in the fourth season opener, it is not until "Fear, Itself" that Buffy and the others actually lay eyes on them. The gang assumes they're guys dressed up for Halloween.

But when one of them gets in the way during Buffy's rescue of Willow from a werewolf attack, their presence takes on new significance.

GILES: "So this fellow in the woods—he was in military garb?"

BUFFY: "And he was toting some serious weaponry.... Thing is, I saw some other guys dressed exactly like him on Halloween night. I assumed they were in costume...."

GILES: "But maybe they were working."

BUFFY: "I want to know what's up. The guy got in my way; I almost didn't catch up to Oz in time."
　　　　　　　　　　　　　　　　　　　　　　　—"WILD AT HEART"

XANDER: "The latest in fall fascism, I like it. A little full in the hips for my taste, but ..."

GILES: "I think we can safely assume they're human. So, no need to research."
　　　　　　　　　　　　　　　　　　　　　　　—"THE INITIATIVE"

Meanwhile, Spike gets the "zap and trap" treatment. He's knocked unconscious, and when he awakens, in "The Initiative," he discovers he's been locked in a pristine cell. The vampire in the cell next to him befriends him, warning him off the blood packet that drops from the ceiling:

TOM: "They starve you. And when you're ready to bite your own arm, they shoot out one of those packets. You drink, and next thing you know—you're gone. That's when they do the experiments."

SPIKE: "And 'they' are...the government? Nazis? A major cosmetics company?"
　　　　　　　　　　　　　　　　　　　　　　　—"THE INITIATIVE"

Spike manages to escape. As the Initiative goes on full alert, we learn that Dr. Walsh is in charge there and that Buffy's new potential crush, Riley Finn, is one of the Commandos. So are the guys he hangs out with:

COMPUTER VOICE: "Retinal scan accepted."

GRAHAM: "I like her. I'm on your side here."

RILEY: "I know you are, Graham ... and that's what gives me the strength to put up with this comedian."

FORREST: "Dude—straight tip—I know about girls."

RILEY: "Exactly! 'Girls,' plural. I'm talking about one girl. One. Girl."

COMPUTER VOICE: "Initiative Vocal Code match complete. Special Agent Finn, Riley. Identity number seven-five-three-two-nine."

RILEY: "Problem is, what kind of girl's gonna go out with a guy who's acting all Joe Regular by day and then goes all Demon-Hunter by night?"

GRAHAM: "Maybe a peculiar one."

—"THE INITIATIVE"

The Commandos have military expertise and sophisticated anti-HST weaponry at their disposal. Plus, they're crack Special Ops guys:

FORREST: "I can tag a hostile at fifty yards."

And:

RILEY: "Tell me we're tracking."

GRAHAM: "Honing a signal . . . got it. Heading west."

RILEY: "It better be the hostile."

FORREST: "All units converge, all units converge, hard target sighted, heading one two alpha niner."

RILEY: "Let's bag it before this gets ugly."

And:

GRAHAM: "And . . . getting a picture. . .signature's locked."

RILEY: "What have we got?"

GRAHAM: "Humans of the freshman variety. Ninety-eight six, ninety-eight six, and. . . bingo. Got a cold one. Thermal output clocking in at exactly . . . room temperature."

FORREST: "Vampire."

RILEY: "Call in a standard triangle flanking maneuver. We're going in. I need a lockdown on grid six."   —"THE INITIATIVE"

And:

"I have a master key. Opens every shop on Main Street."

—RILEY, IN "A NEW MAN"

RILEY: "This is Agent Finn. I need a search. Local hotel registrations matching the name Ethan Rayne. R-A-Y-N-E. Call me back."
BUFFY: "You can do that?"
RILEY: "It'll take a couple minutes." —"A NEW MAN"

When the Commandos finally corner Spike during a blackout they've created, Buffy inadvertently rescues him when they try to take Willow as well.

FORREST: "Sir! Civilian. Could have turned."
RILEY: "Leave her."
FORREST: "We can't neglect quarantine, sir!"
GRAHAM: "Stop her!"
FORREST: "She's contained."
BUFFY: "Contain this." —"THE INITIATIVE"

The foiled operation leads Professor Walsh to an ironic, if accurate, conclusion. We also learn that she's done something to Spike:

PROFESSOR WALSH: "I'm sure you'll understand if I seem far from happy."
RILEY: "Yes, ma'am. If you read my report, you'll see—"
PROFESSOR WALSH: "Hostile Seventeen's found an accomplice who's smart, aggressive, and somehow escapes description."
FORREST: "Whoever he was, the guy was big."
GRAHAM: "Strong, too."
RILEY: "Whoever or whatever."
PROFESSOR WALSH: "I'm not interested in guesswork, gentlemen. Call me old-fashioned, I like results. This report reads like a children's riddle book. Agent Finn. Tell me something good. My implant?"
RILEY: "The implant works. Hostile Seventeen can't hurt any living creature, in any way, without intense neurological pain. Can't feed, can't hardly even hit anymore. We'll bag it."
PROFESSOR WALSH: "Yes, you will. Dismissed." —"THE INITIATIVE"

Meanwhile, Giles has not been idle:

"Now, I believe the commandos' installation is somewhere very close to, if not directly under, your school. And as such, I'm convinced one or more of them may be in your very midst—" —GILES, IN "DOOMED"

Riley pursues the knowledge in his own way:

RILEY: "What's a Slayer?"
FORREST: "Slayer? Thrash band. Anvil-heavy guitar rock with delusions of Black Sabbath."
RILEY: "No. A girl. With powers."

FORREST: "Oh, yeah, man. I've heard of the Slayer."

RILEY: "Fill me in."

FORREST: "Well, the way I got it figured, Slayer's like some kind of Bogeyman for the Sub-Terrestrials. Something they tell their little spawn to get them to eat their vegetables and clean up their slime pits."

RILEY: "You're telling me she doesn't exist."

FORREST: "Oh, wait a sec. Am I bursting somebody's bubble here? Maybe this is a bad time to tell you about Lara Croft. And the Easter bunny. Sorry. Sorry. It's a myth, Rye. All part of that medieval folklore garbage kooks dream up to explain the things we deal with everyday." —"THE INITIATIVE"

Buffy et. al have no trouble believing in the reality of a commando squad on campus, however, nor in confronting armed humans on their own terms:

XANDER: "Here we go. Gear for tonight. If some commando squad's out there, fully loaded, these babies might give us the edge we'll need."

GILES: "Very impressive. Where'd it all come from?"

XANDER: "Requisitioned it back when I was military guy."

GILES: "That was two years ago. Are you still a hundred percent?"

XANDER: "You kidding? I put the 'semper' in 'semper fi.' Maybe I can't assemble an M-16 blindfolded like I used to. Or pass weapons drill for the mobile infantry. . . . Might as well face it. Right now I don't have the technical skills to join the Swiss army. And all those guys make you do is uncork a couple of sassy cabernets." —"THE INITIATIVE"

Then, in "Hush," magic meets science. Both engaged in battling the Gentlemen, Buffy and Riley meet their secret identities face to face: The Slayer is armed with a crossbow, while the Special Forces agent carries a state-of-the-art blaster rifle.

The incongruity of their approaches to demon-fighting is underscored in "Doomed," as Buffy and company prepare to stop the end of the world ("again?!"):

GILES: "A Vahrall demon."

WILLOW: "Ew."

XANDER: "I second that revulsion."

GILES: "'Slick like gall, and gird in moonlight, father of portents and brother to blight. . .'"

BUFFY: " . . .'Limbs with talons, eyes like knives. Bane to the blameless, thief of lives'. . ."

         meanwhile:

RILEY: ". . . three hundred meters tall, approximately one hundred to one-twenty kilograms, based on my visual analysis."

GRAHAM: "Special hazards?"

RILEY: "Unknown, probably nothing we haven't handled before. There's no pattern that we can discern yet—got to assume he's on a basic 'Kill-crush-destroy.' So I want him bagged fast."

and back:

BUFFY: "Thing isn't digging up the bones of a child for fun."

XANDER: "Well, demons got some hilarious ideas about fun...."

WILLOW: "It has to be a spell of some kind. Something that uses blood and bones."

GILES: "There must be thousands of rituals like that. The Test of Gervail, a number of passion spells, death-pact bonding—"

On the other hand, science has its advantages. Indicating Riley's handheld device:

BUFFY: "Is this really the time for Donkey Kong?"

RILEY: "What? Oh. It takes trace readings of the creature's pheromones."

At the end of "Doomed," Slayer and Commando finally work together to stop the last of three demons from sacrificing itself to open the Hellmouth. Realizing the commonality of their missions (as well as their mutual attraction), Riley arranges for her to meet with his C.O., Professor Maggie Walsh:

MAGGIE: "Our goals are similar. We're each interested in curtailing the sub-terrestrial menace. It's only our methods that differ. We use the latest in scientific technology and state-of-the-art weaponry and you—if I understand this correctly—poke them with a sharp stick."

BUFFY: "It's more effective than it sounds."

MAGGIE: "Oh, I'm quite sure of that. As I'm just as sure we can learn much from each other. I'm working on getting you clearance to come into the Initiative. I think you'll find the results of our operation most impressive. Agent Finn here, alone, has captured or killed. . .how many is it?"

RILEY: "Seventeen. Eleven vampires. Six demons."

BUFFY: "Huh. Wow. Well, that is . . . I mean . . . seventeen."

MAGGIE: "What about you?"

BUFFY: "Me?"

MAGGIE: "How many hostiles would you say you've . . . slain?"   —"A NEW MAN"

Naturally, Professor Walsh and Riley are both suitably impressed with Buffy's answer. Things are looking good: the Slayer with additional support in her battle against evil, a new honey who knows everything about her, and yet adores her—what could go wrong?

Ethan Rayne, the British sorcerer who pops in from time to time, has information:

GILES: "What are they saying?"

ETHAN: "You know demons. It's all exaggeration and blank verse. 'Pain as bright as steel,' that kind of thing. They're scared. And there's something called three-fourteen's got 'em scared most of all. The kind of scared that turns to angry."

Ethan concludes:

"This new outfit, it's blundering into a place it doesn't belong. It's throwing the worlds out of balance and that's beyond chaos, mate. We're headed, quite literally, for one hell of a fight."

As they drink together, Giles lets down his hair:

"[Maggie's] the one putting the big scare on the demon world. Making a joke of my life's work. The demons...apparently the demons didn't even notice me. Didn't ruffle their routine one bit."

Drunker still, Giles grumbles:

"We're relics, mate. Dusty scraps of a world that doesn't exist anymore. I mean, the bleeding 'Initiative'—their methods may cause problems, but they're getting it done."

Giles is right, but on the other hand, there are advantages inherent in a new perspective:

BUFFY: "Now, why would I let you go?"

ETHAN: "Well, maybe 'cause you have no choice. I'm human. You can't kill me. What's a Slayer going to do to me?"

RILEY: "By the authority of the U.S. Military, you are being taken into custody pending a determination of your status. They'll take Mr. Rayne to a secret detention facility in the Nevada desert. I'm sure he'll be rehabilitated in no time." —"A NEW MAN"

So, the notion of something dangerous and scary that is called 314 has been brought into play . . . and at the end of "A New Man," we know (although Buffy doesn't) that Maggie has something to do with it.

Buffy is brought into the Initiative fold. Riley and Dr. Walsh give her the grand tour; Dr. Walsh points out Dr. Angleman:

MAGGIE: "He's head of our science team, a leader in the field of xenomorphic behavior modification."

BUFFY: "Behavior modification?"

MAGGIE: "We've made significant advancements reconditioning the sub-terrestrials. Bringing them to a point where they no longer pose a harmful threat."

—"THE I IN TEAM"

Buffy realizes that that's what they did to Spike—who has sought asylum with the Scooby Gang. She also notices the restricted research area. However, she remains mum on both topics.

Maggie Walsh is also keeping a few things to herself. After Buffy and Riley depart, Dr. Walsh lets herself into the secret area . . . and into a room marked "314." She confers with Dr. Angleman:

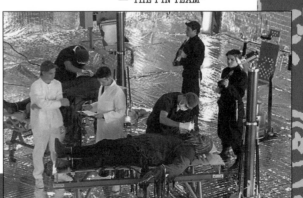

DR. ANGLEMAN: "How did the tour go?"
MAGGIE: "I'm not sure. She's . . . unpredictable."
DR. ANGLEMAN: "She's an unnecessary risk."
MAGGIE: "Possibly. And how's our baby doing today?" —"THE I IN TEAM"

It is then that we see that Dr. Angleman and Dr. Walsh are working on some kind of construct, a Frankenstein's monster of demon, human, and cyborg parts. His name is Adam, after the first man.

Buffy's so excited at being admitted into the Initiative that she lets her questions fall by the wayside. Buffy's friends, however, are not so sanguine.

WILLOW: "Like, what's their ultimate agenda? I mean, okay, they neuter vampires and demons. Then what? They're going to reintegrate them into society? Get them jobs as bagboys at Wal-Mart?"
BUFFY: "Does Wal-Mart have bagboys?"
WILLOW: "Plus, don't forget, there's that whole three-fourteen thing Ethan told Giles about."
BUFFY: "And I always say a man who worships chaos and tries to kill you is a man you can trust."
WILLOW: "Bad info or not, Buffy, I think you should be asking some questions before you go off to enlist." —"THE I IN TEAM"

When Buffy does ask a few questions—in the line of duty, as she joins the Commandos on a mission to capture a Polgara demon—she's the only one raising a hand:

DR. ANGLEMAN: "When threatened, bone skewers jut from the creature's forearms during battle. It's imperative, when ensnaring it, not to damage its arms. That's all you really need to—"
BUFFY: "Question."
MAGGIE: "Buffy?"
BUFFY: "Why exactly can't we damage this Polka thing's arms? Not that I want to. Just, in my experience, when you're fighting for your life, body parts get damaged. And better its bits than mine. Or ours."
DR. ANGLEMAN: "We wish to study the physiology of every sub-terrestrial's natural defenses. Part of the research we do here. Now—Yes?"
BUFFY: "What do they want?"
DR. ANGLEMAN: "Want?"
BUFFY: "Why are they here? Sacrifices, treasure, or are they just getting rampage-y? 'Cause it's easier to predict their responses if—"
DR. ANGLEMAN: "They're not sentient. Just destructive, I believe."

Buffy discusses the matter with Riley:

BUFFY: "Professor Walsh. The questions. An Initiative faux pas, yes?"
RILEY: "It's a little unusual. She's just not used to it." —"THE I IN TEAM"

Nevertheless Buffy keeps asking questions. After she and Riley defeat the Polgara demon by working together as a team, they make love for the first time. In the morning she starts asking again:

BUFFY: "You're quite the regimental soldier."

RILEY: "I am how they trained me."

BUFFY: "They? Who 'they'?"

RILEY: "You know, the government. Plucked me out of Special Ops training for this."

BUFFY: "What did they tell you it was for?"

RILEY: "Didn't. You learn in the military to follow orders, not ask questions."

BUFFY: "I don't understand. Aren't you curious about all this science and research stuff they're doing?"

RILEY: "I know all I need to know. We're doing good here. Protecting the public. Removing the Hostile Sub-terrestrial threat."

BUFFY: "What about three-fourteen?" —"THE I IN TEAM"

Little do they realize that Maggie Walsh is watching them during the entire conversation. All the rooms of the Lowell House, where the Commandos maintain their identities as frat boys, are hooked up to video cameras. Dr. Walsh calls Riley's room before he can answer. When he reports to her, she catches him trying to peer into the restricted area where 314 is located.

She sends him off after Hostile 17 (Spike). After he's out of the way, she consults with Dr. Angleman about Buffy. They agree she's too big a threat to their work. It's time to remove the problem, and the sooner the better—if only to ameliorate the effect it will certainly have on Agent Finn.

Maggie sends Buffy off on a "mission," which turns out to be a trap. Satisfied that the Slayer has been killed, she informs Riley that his girlfriend is dead.

But Buffy is alive after all, and Riley is faced with trying to fathom what his highly respected superior has attempted. After Riley stomps away, Maggie stumbles into Room 314, attempting to calm down. She rants to herself about Buffy. From "The I in Team":

> **"I've worked too long to let the little bitch threaten this project. Threaten me. She has no idea what she's dealing with. Once she's gone, Riley will come around. He'll understand. It was for the greater good. He'll see that. And if he doesn't, well . . . first things first. Remove the complication. She won't even see it coming. It'll happen right when she least expects."**
>
> —MAGGIE, IN "THE I IN TEAM"

Adam kills Maggie after this speech. Unaware of Dr. Walsh's death, Buffy warns the others that none of them is safe:

XANDER: "Right. I'm guessing the mad scientist isn't too keen on the fact that the entire Scooby Gang knows the Initiative is up to no good."

BUFFY: "Getting us back to the 'not safe for any of us' concept."

GILES: "What could've happened that would make Maggie want to kill you?"

BUFFY: "I don't know. She wasn't keen on the fact that I was asking a lot of questions, that's for sure."

ANYA: "So . . . you were getting too close to something."

GILES: "Clearly. I can only imagine what she was so desperate to hide."

Buffy goes on:

"All I know is that Maggie has it in for me. Which means the Initiative has it in for me."
—BUFFY, IN "GOODBYE IOWA"

Buffy rounds up her friends and they decide to hide in Xander's basement. Riley shows up almost as soon as they've arrived, and he's the target of everyone's suspicions except Buffy's. For his part, he simply can't believe that Professor Walsh would do such a thing:

RILEY: "Okay. Listen. I need you to go over everything. Step by step. There has to be some kind of mistake."

XANDER: "There's no mistake. And how do you know something happened? Where were you?"

RILEY: "I was on a mission, but I came back and . . . I'm not sure. Look, let's just keep our heads."

And

"Look, this isn't Professor Walsh. There must be something making her act this way. Something, I don't know, controlling her..."

Giles offers:

"I've heard rumors that The Initiative isn't all we've been told. That, secretly, they are working toward some darker purpose. Something that might harm us all . . ."
—"GOODBYE IOWA"

The situation is bad, when the men of the Initiative (Forrest in particular) conclude that Buffy must have killed Dr. Walsh, because of the manner of the doctor's death: She was run through with an object resembling a skewer. Or a stake.

As Buffy and the others continue to work on the mystery, Riley unravels before their eyes. He appears to be undergoing some kind of drug withdrawal. Desperate for answers, Buffy decides to infiltrate the Initiative. She and Xander go undercover, she as a scientist and he as a soldier.

"I have my clearance. I'm hoping Maggie never had time to revoke it."
—BUFFY, IN "GOODBYE IOWA"

Once in, this is what they overhear, also from "Goodbye Iowa":

DR. ANGLEMAN: "How many of the men are still out? The longer they go without their meds—"

SCIENTIST #1: "Everyone's off their schedules because of the professor's death."

DR. ANGLEMAN: "It's dangerous. I don't want to think about the damage our guys could do under the stress of withdrawal, especially since they won't understand what's happening to them. These guys don't know they've been getting meds through their food. So we'd better get them in here, stat."

SCIENTIST #1: "We've located all but a few. The last ones were in bad shape, but we've stabilized them."

DR. ANGLEMAN: "But Finn wasn't one of them, right?"

SCIENTIST #1: "No, but—"

DR. ANGLEMAN: "Find him. He's the one I care about. He's too important to the work to lose now."

When Buffy makes her presence known, Dr. Angleman struggles to spin the situation:

BUFFY: "Maggie wanted me dead, didn't she?"

DR. ANGLEMAN: "She did. But, understand, the Initiative has no interest in eliminating the Slayer. It was her own vendetta."

BUFFY: "Why? Spell it out for me. I feel an attack of dumb blond coming on . . . ."

DR. ANGLEMAN: "I don't know—"

BUFFY: "Think harder."

DR. ANGLEMAN: "It was the . . . project."

BUFFY: "Project? 314?"

DR. ANGLEMAN: "It escaped."

Shortly thereafter, Adam makes his appearance:

"I am a kinematically redundant, bio-mechanical demonoid. Designed by Maggie Walsh. She called me 'Adam,' and I called her 'Mother.'"
—"GOODBYE IOWA"

He goes on to explain that Maggie's done work on Riley, too. Before he can explain further, his "brother" attacks him, and Adam skewers Riley. Over Buffy's protests, the "Family" (as Forrest calls the Initiative Commandos) steps in and hauls Riley off to a military hospital. In "This Year's Girl," Buffy worries about what they might be doing to him:

WILLOW: "Maybe Giles has a point. Riley is kind of their top-gun guy. It doesn't make sense that they'd hurt him."

BUFFY: "But the Initiative has a whole branch of brain-washy, behavior modification guys."

WILLOW: "So?"

BUFFY: "So . . . what happens when they start not liking Riley's behavior?"

Buffy's right to worry. When Riley tries to leave his hospital room, the sentry stationed at his door will not stand down until Forrest tells him to. Forrest deeply resents Riley's attitude:

GRAHAM: "We all friends here, fellas?"

FORREST: "Absolutely. Riley here's just about to explain to us why he's leaving us so very quickly."

RILEY: "I don't explain, because I don't have to. I'm the one in charge."

FORREST: "Things change."

RILEY: "Do they?"

FORREST: "Hey. In case you failed to notice, we are in a world of hurt around here, and now is the time for us to band together, not go flying off our separate ways."

GRAHAM: "Forrest has a point, Rye."

FORREST: "We have a problem, we will deal with that problem, and you know the most important part of the equation right now is, we keep said problem within the family."

—"THIS YEAR'S GIRL"

Just as Buffy runs down a strategy for breaking Riley out of the Initiative, he arrives. Buffy's relief is palpable but not fully shared by all:

BUFFY: "How'd you get out?"

RILEY: "I walked."

WILLOW: "They didn't try to stop you?"

RILEY: "They did. Repeatedly. But then I told them they couldn't keep me without a major ass-kicking one way or another...and here I am."

XANDER: "That's great, Riley. And you know, there's no polite way to ask you this, but—did they put a chip in your brain?"   —"THIS YEAR'S GIRL"

Xander's question is not inappropriate, given Maggie Walsh's scorecard. However, the matter is dropped for the time being. More personally pressing issues arise with the return of Oz, who is misidentified as the perpetrator of a brutal attack on a Commando team while in wolf form. Riley assists Buffy and friends with his escape, resulting in the following exchanges, all from "New Moon Rising":

"Buffy, I leave now, I can't ever come back. [A beat. Is he going to stay?] Just wanted to hear it out loud."   —RILEY

GRAHAM: "This can't end well, man."

RILEY: "You gonna start killing people?"

FORREST: "I'm thinking just one."

RILEY: "You and me trained together from day one, Forrest. But I always outranked you. Come after me and you're going to find out why."

COLONEL McNAMARA: "You're a dead man, Finn."

RILEY: "No, sir. I'm an anarchist."

"Quite a day. Woke up to a big bowl of Wheaties, now you're a fugitive."

—BUFFY, IN "NEW MOON RISING"

Within the season's arc the dire shifts from the Initiative to the plans of Adam, who seeks an Armageddon-like battle between humans and demons, so that he will have plenty of raw material to create more beings like himself. The gang and the Initiative are as yet unaware of his dealings, mistrusting and confronting one another.

FORREST: "You killing humans now?"
BUFFY: "Not yet. Beating you senseless should do just fine."
FORREST: "I could have a patrol here in under a minute. So here's the plan: you go your way, and I'll go mine."
BUFFY: "I'm checking out that cave."
FORREST: "My orders exactly."
BUFFY: "Alone?"
FORREST: "We're spread a little thin right now, so yeah. Family's tearing apart—"
BUFFY: "Family? Last time I dropped by you put a gun to my head. What kind of family are you guys? The Corleones?"
FORREST: "Weren't until you showed up."   —"THE YOKO FACTOR"

Adam kills Forrest. The Initiative's cells are filled to overcapacity with demons; the friends are bickering; and Spike has slipped them a disk he claims to have stolen from the Initiative, but which he got directly from Adam, hoping to have his chip removed. Riley listens in agony as his Commando comrades on patrol engage the enemy—demons—over and over again, with results so very often not of the good.

Then, at the end of "The Yoko Factor," the final stunner: Riley presents himself to Adam:

ADAM: "I've been waiting for you."
RILEY: "And now I'm here."

In "Primeval," all comes clear: Adam has coopted the original plans of Maggie Walsh. In a secret lab behind Room 314, she planned to make more of Adam's kind. She had hoped to create a super-soldier; he wants to create a super-race of beings like himself. She implanted a chip in Riley, to be activated at a time of her choosing. But Adam has activated it himself, for his own purposes:

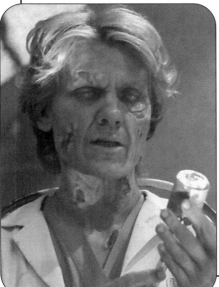

RILEY: "What have you done to me?"
ADAM: "Nothing. It was Mother—your Professor Walsh. She implanted the behavior modifier."
RILEY: "A chip in my head. She really did it."
ADAM: "There is no chip in your head."
RILEY: "Then what—"
ADAM: [He taps Riley's upper arm, near the shoulder] "The chip is here. Phase one of your preparation. Lying dormant until the time came. I simply activated it, brother."
RILEY: "Stop calling me that. I'm not your brother. You're a botched science experiment."   —"PRIMEVAL"

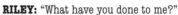

Adam has reanimated the dead Maggie Walsh, Dr. Angleman (Maggie died at the end of "Doomed"; Dr. Angelman died at the end of "Goodbye, Iowa"), and Forrest, supplementing and sustaining their decomposed flesh with mechanics and other...parts. He plans to turn Riley into something like himself. Adam has also convinced his demon followers to allow themselves to be captured, so that they would be inside the Initiative.

> **XANDER:** "Okay. Let me get this straight. The Initiative's about to get attacked by every demon this side of Helldonia. Nobody inside's going to believe us. Oh—and Riley can't help us. Wanna call the next move, Buff? 'Cause I'm stumped."
> **BUFFY:** "Simple. We attack Adam before he can attack them." —"PRIMEVAL"

Buffy and the gang sneak into the Initiative. Colonel McNamara, who's been brought in to mop up the mess left behind when Adam escaped, captures them:

> **BUFFY:** "This is not your business. It's mine. You, the Initiative, the boys at the Pentagon, you're all in way over your heads. You're all messing with primeval forces you have no comprehension of."
> **COLONEL McNAMARA:** "And you do."
> **BUFFY:** "I'm the Slayer." —"PRIMEVAL"

The battle begins. Lightning fast, it's "demon open house," in Xander's words. Mason is taken out. Zombie Forrest is incinerated. Buffy has become magically enhanced by Xander, Willow, and Giles, and Riley has freed himself from the power of the chip by digging it out of his arm. The carnage is unbelievable, but, as the military debrief the situation:

> **"Burn it down, gentlemen. Burn it, and salt the ground."**
> —BAKER, IN "PRIMEVAL"

So concludes the sorry business of the Initiative. Or does it? For the Slayer, the hits just keep on coming. . . .

VILLAINS:

(for more details on the monsters, please see Buffy the Vampire Slayer: The Monster Book*)*
SEASON THREE: Demon Ken—demon warden of a hellish dimension ("Anne") ◆ **Ovu Mobani**—Nigerian zombie demon ("Dead Man's Party") ◆ **Mr. Trick**—suave vampire ("Faith, Hope & Trick") ◆ **Kakistos**—vampire so ancient he has taken on demonic aspects ("Faith, Hope & Trick") ◆ **Lyle Gorch**—vampire, brother to Tector, whom Buffy killed in "Bad Eggs" ("Homecoming") ◆ **Candy Gorch**—Lyle's vampire bride. They're honeymooning at SlayerFest '98. ("Homecoming") ◆ **Kulak**—of the Miquot clan, in town for SlayerFest '98 ("Homecoming") ◆ **Mayor Richard Wilkins III**—used to be human, banking on Ascending and becoming the demon Olvikan (Season Three story arc, first appears in "Homecoming") ◆ **Lurconis**—demon snake who eats newborn humans every thirty years ("Band Candy") ◆ **Lagos**—a demon who comes to Sunnydale; Mrs. Post uses him as an excuse to find the Glove of Myhnegon

("Revelations") ◆ **Lenny**, a vampire who used to work for Spike, then for Mr. Trick ("Lovers Walk") ◆ **Spike**—the vampire we don't really hate ("Lovers Walk") ◆ **Anyanka**—patron demon of scorned women, becomes Anya, a twelfth grader ("The Wish") ◆ **The Master**—return appearance in the Bizarro Sunnydale ("The Wish") ◆ **The First**—an evil spiritual force, worshipped by the high priests, **The Harbringers** ("Amends") ◆ **D'Hoffryn**—one of the lower beings, has the power to elevate mortals to demons ("Doppelgangland," also appears in Season Four's "Something Blue") ◆ **Skyler**—demon peddling the Books of Ascension ("Enemies") ◆ **Shaman**—double-crosser hired by the Mayor to rob Angel of his soul—but hired by Giles to fake it instead ("Enemies") ◆ **Scabby Demons**—mouthless demons that infect Buffy with their telepathic "aspect" ("Earshot") ◆ **Hell Hounds**—killer canines brainwashed to destroy anything in formal wear ("The Prom") ◆ **Vamp Xander**—in the Bizarro World, Xander's like this bad-ass vampire ("The Wish") ◆ **Vamp Will**—Willow as an evil, skanky vampire ("The Wish" and "Doppelgangland") ◆ **The Hansel and Gretel demon** ("Gingerbread") ◆ **Zachary Kralick**—insane vampire who in life murdered his own mother ("Helpless") ◆ **Jack O'Toole**—resurrected leader of gang, pressures Xander to become their wheel man ("The Zeppo") ◆ **The Sisterhood of Jhe**—apocalyptic cult dedicated to bringing about world destruction ("The Zeppo") ◆ **Bob**—corpse raised by Jack O'Toole ("The Zeppo") ◆ **Dickie**—another corpse raised by Jack O'Toole ("The Zeppo") ◆ **Parker**—not Parker Abrams, but another corpse raised by Jack O'Toole ("The Zeppo") ◆ **The Hellmouth Creature**—bursting forth from the Hellmouth ("The Zeppo") ◆ **Balthazar**—hideous, bloated demon who lives in a vat, ancient enemy of the Mayor ("Bad Girls") ◆ **El Eliminati**—fifteenth-century vampire duelist cult, acolytes of Balthazar ("Bad Girls") ◆ **Vincent**—Mr. Trick's vampire henchman ("Bad Girls")

SEASON FOUR: Sunday—big vampire on campus at UC Sunnydale ("The Freshman") ◆ **Rookie**—Sunday's doper follower ("The Freshman") ◆ **Dav**—Sunday's redheaded follower ("The Freshman") ◆ **Kathy**—Buffy's demonic roommate ("The Freshman," "Living Conditions") ◆ **Spike**—still the vampire we love to hate (first appears in "The Harsh Light of Day") ◆ **Gachnar**—the fear demon—"Actual size" ("Fear, Itself") ◆ **Harmony**—former Cordette, became a vampire in Season Three finale (first appears in "The Harsh Light of Day") ◆ **Veruca**—Willow's werewolf rival (first appears in "Beer Bad") ◆ **Hus**—Chumash vengeance spirit warrior ("Pangs") ◆ **The Gentlemen**—fairy-tale monsters who steal voices and hearts ("Hush") ◆ **Vahrall demons**—three of them, trying to end the world by jumping into the Hellmouth ("Doomed") ◆ **Adam**—demon-human-robot hybrid (first appears in "The I In Team") ◆ **Jape**—Adam's vampire henchman (first appears in "Superstar") ◆ **The Monster**—nightmare creature created by Jonathan during his Augmentation spell ("Superstar") ◆ **Polgara demon**—monster with retractable skewers in its arms ("The I In Team") ◆ **Tapparich**—runaway Kathy Newman's demon father, who comes to Sunnydale to bring her back to their dimension ("Living Conditions") ◆ **Warrior Demons**—captured by the Initiative but later set loose on Buffy by Maggie Walsh ("The I In Team") ◆ **Boone**—Vampire and co-conspirator to Adam ("Who Are You") ◆ **The Primitive**—The first Slayer ("Restless")

HUMAN VILLAINS:

SEASON THREE: Faith—Slayer activated after Kendra's death, arrives in Sunnydale on the lam from the vampire Kakistos—loses her mind after accidentally killing a human, defects over to become Mayor McSleaze's right-hand woman (Season Three arc, first appears in "Faith, Hope & Trick," also appears in Season Four's "This Year's Girl," and "Who Are You") ◆ **Pete Clarner**—mucho mas macho student who kills his girlfriend in a rage-monster fit ("Beauty and the Beasts") ◆ **Hans and Frederick Gruenshtahler**—terrorists in town for SlayerFest '98 ("Homecoming") ◆ **Frawley**—a hunter enjoying SlayerFest '98, AKA "Jungle Bob" ("Homecoming") ◆ **"Old Man"**—also enjoying SlayerFest '98 ("Homecoming") ◆ **Ethan Rayne**—sorcerer and "old friend" of Rupert "Ripper" Giles, from the London days of Black Majick ("Band Candy") ◆ **Gwendolyn Post**—an ex-Watcher who comes to Sunnydale to retrieve the Glove of Myhnegon ("Revelations") ◆ **The Lunch Lady**—tries to kill the SHS students with rat poison ("Earshot") ◆ **Tucker Wells**—disgruntled SHS senior who trains Hell Hounds to attack kids at the prom ("The Prom")

SEASON FOUR: Professor Maggie Walsh—"Mother" of Adam (Season Four arc, first appears in "The Freshman") ◆ **Jack**—disgruntled bar owner whose bad beer transforms its drinkers into Neanderthals ("Beer Bad") ◆ **Ethan Rayne**—turns Giles into a Fyarl demon ("A New Man") ◆ **Dr. Angleman**—assisting Maggie Walsh in her plans to create a new demon-human-robot hybrid (first appears in "The I In Team") ◆ **Mrs. Holt**—twisted director of the Lowell Home for Children ("Where the Wild Things Are") ◆ **Colonel McNamara**—Initiative officer who wants Buffy out of the picture ("New Moon Rising," "The Yoko Factor," "Primeval") ◆ **Parker Abrams**—stinky man who trifles with Buffy's affections ("Living Conditions," "The Harsh Light of Day," "Beer Bad")

NUMEROLOGY IN THE BUFFYVERSE

2—Number of Slayers Spike has killed. ◆ **2**—Number of vampires Wesley had "faced" when he arrived in Sunnydale. ◆ **3**—Number of sacrifices required to end the world in "Doomed." ◆ **No. 4 Parkview**—Cordelia's address during high school. ◆ **"6 of 1"**—Nickname among the crew for Adam, who debuted in Episode Thirteen of Season Four (a reference to Seven of Nine, a character on Star Trek: Voyager, who is part of a collective. Adam is a collection of parts). ◆ **12**—Target episode number for Buffy's birthday scripts (beginning with Season Three) ◆ **Hostile 17**—Spike's code name, given to him by Maggie Walsh. ◆ **17**—Number of HST's Riley had killed when he brought Buffy to meet Maggie Walsh: 11 vampires and 6 demons. ◆ **54**—Number of the ambulance that takes Buffy away when she's in Faith's body. ◆ **126**—Spike's age ("The Initiative"). ◆ **214**, Stevenson Hall—Buffy and Willow's dorm room. ◆ **Room 217**—On the dorm hallway set, this is the door to another student dorm room. But if you actually walk through it, you will enter Giles's apartment; 217 is the number of the most extremely haunted room in Stephen King's novel The Shining. ◆ **Room 314**— Adam's room in the Restricted Area. ◆ **389**—The building number of the Bronze. ◆ **523 Oakpark Street, Apt. B, Sunnydale, CA 90211**—Giles's address. ◆ **1630** Revello Drive—Buffy's home address. ◆ **17619** Whiteoak Drive—Xander's address; he currently lives in the basement. ◆ **6305 Westminster Place**—Willow's home address. ◆ **75329**—Riley's Initiative Identity Number. ◆ **91423**—Buffy's Initiative Identity Number ◆ **ST67119**—The Polgara Demon's number. ◆ **7317204**—Restricted Research Area in the Initiative.

THE **CHARACTER GUIDE**

Buffy the vampire slayer

THERE HAVE BEEN a lot of changes in the lives of the characters we've loved and hated and loved to hate since <u>Buffy</u> first went on the air. For the basic first-and-second season background on the Slayerettes and those who run with and from them, please consult <u>The Watcher's Guide, Vol. 1</u>. This volume's character guide will include information about their lives beginning with "Anne," the premiere episode of Season Three.

Buffy Summers

At the end of Season Two, Buffy had been accused of murder, revealed herself as the Slayer to her mother, and sent a fully restored Angel to Hell. It was all too much for Buffy, and she exiled herself to another city, where she becomes Anne, a waitress at Helen's Kitchen. Figuring her Slaying days for over, Buffy fully intends to lose herself, just another runaway to add to the population of lost young people in the hellish town.

However, she is recognized by Lily, who once was Chanterelle back in Sunnydale (Season Two's "Lie to Me"). Buffy saved her then, and Chanterelle pleads with her to help her now: Rickie, her boyfriend, has gone missing.

A very reluctant Buffy consents. She and Lily fall through an interdimensional portal into Hell. The innocent-looking "Ken," who runs a sort of shelter for runaways, is actually a demon in charge of the human slaves he lures through the portal. He makes each of them announce that they are nobody, and that they will die nobodies.

But when challenged to deny herself, Buffy's dormant Slayer instincts are stirred, and she reclaims her heritage as the Chosen One. Inspiring Lily to defend herself, Buffy leads the others in rebellion. She, Lily, and the others return from Hell back into the world each of them tried so hard to escape.

Buffy goes home to assume her responsibilities, which have been taken up by the Slayerettes: Xander, Willow, Oz, and Cordelia. Things are clearly awkward all around. She and her mother are clumsy with each other. Buffy is banned from school, and the rest of the gang has compensated for the hole she left in their lives.

They have built up a lot of resentment over how Buffy has left them in the lurch, made no easier by Buffy's thoughts of running away again in "Dead Man's Party." Buffy tries to defend herself,

44

reminding her mother that it was she who told Buffy that if she left the house, not to come back ("Becoming, Part Two"). Joyce angrily reminds Buffy that she had just told her mother that she was the Slayer, a secret she had kept from her for years.

Buffy must deal with all the things she'd rather bury—figuratively and literally. She and Xander almost come to blows, and no one backs her up. However, when it's time to battle zombies that are invading the Summerses homes, the gang gets it together. They fight together as they once did, with the addition of Joyce joining them. For the first time, Joyce sees what it must be like for Buffy to fight the forces of darkness day in, day out...so to speak.

Buffy and her mother have prevailed upon the school board to force Principal Snyder's hand, (Giles has also threatened Snyder behind the scenes) and Buffy is readmitted to school. Then just as Buffy begins to reclaim her life, someone breezes to town intent upon sharing it: Faith.

Like Buffy, Faith is a Slayer. She was "activated" when Kendra died, at the hands of Spike's lover, Drusilla ("Becoming, Part One"). Just as Buffy's doing her best to shape up, Faith gets a lot of attention for being sassy and aggressive. The tough girl from Boston even flirts with Scott Hope, the boy Buffy has taken a liking to, and vice versa.

Giles has been pestering Buffy for details of her final battle with Angel "for a binding spell." Finally she is able to tell the gang what she has held in for so long: She sent Angel to Hell after he was cured. She knew he had regained his soul, and she still killed him, because it was the only way to save the world. Forced to share what has been an intolerable burden, she finds the courage deep within herself to tell him goodbye...not realizing that he then comes back....

In "Beauty and the Beasts," Buffy learns that Angel has returned. He's uncontrollable, animalistic, and clearly in great pain. She keeps it a secret, even though Oz is being tortured with the possibility that he has been savagely killing people while in wolf form.

Buffy does all she can to save a girl from her abusive boyfriend. She fails. Yet she continues to protect Angel, even though she has no guarantee that he won't harm either her or her loved ones if left to his own devices. Scott Hope sums up her dilemma:

"It's just...you never really know what's going on inside somebody, do you? You think if you care about them...but you never really do."

—SCOTT HOPE, IN "BEAUTY AND THE BEASTS"

Buffy certainly has no idea what's going on inside Scott. As soon as she tells the recovering Angel about her new boyfriend—to keep the distance between them—Scott dumps her. Buffy's disappointed, but she takes another stab at living a normal life when she runs against Cordelia for Homecoming Queen.

Unfortunately for both of them, Mr. Trick, a vampire who has stayed in town after the demise of his boss, Kakistos, is charging admission for SlayerFest '98. Buffy and Cordelia are targeted as the two Slayers of Sunnydale—leaving Faith to perform a tiny act of revenge for Buffy, by embarrassing Scott in front of his replacement Homecoming date. Buffy and Cordelia defeat their attackers, and Buffy, who was running against Cordelia for Homecoming Queen in an effort to make a mark, loses the contest and one more chance to be a normal teenager.

Buffy's (and Giles's) old enemy, Ethan Rayne, comes to town. Mr. Trick has subcontracted him to distract the people of Sunnydale so that four newborn babies can be sacrificed to the demon Lurconis.

Buffy and company are aghast when the adults in their lives "act like a bunch of us"—running amuck, crashing cars, looting, and singing "Louie Louie."

Joyce and Giles have sex. Twice. With handcuffs.

Things in Buffy's life take a turn for the deadly serious: her friends discover that Angel is back. Buffy incurs the hostility of her friends for lying, and though she assures them that Angel is his good self again, not even she can predict his future.

She is once again faced with the dilemma of what to do about him. She tells herself they're just friends, and that they can coexist as such. But Spike comes back to Sunnydale, drunk and grieving over Drusilla, who left him for a fungus demon. He sets them straight, and in her heart, Buffy knows he's right when he laughs at them for trying to have any kind of relationship.

> **"We're not friends. Never were. I can fool Giles, I can fool my friends, but I can't fool myself. Or Spike, for some reason. What I want from you, I can never have."**
> —BUFFY, IN "LOVERS WALK"

Heartbroken, she tells Angel that she's going to stay away from him from now on.

Meanwhile, a scorned Cordelia attracts the attention of Anyanka, a vengeance demon whose job it is to fulfill the wishes of women whose men have done them wrong. In a bizarre otherworld, Buffy is almost like Faith—very tough and battle-worn. She doesn't know Angel, and has no feeling for him; and in fact, she dies.

Giles breaks the spell. All is returned to normal, with no one the wiser…except Anyanka.

Then it's Christmas, and blazingly hot in Sunnydale. When Buffy bumps into Angel on the street, he's acting very strangely. Soon she's sharing his dreams of bloodlust and death. The First Evil, in the form of Giles's lost love, Jenny Calendar, seeks to convince Angel that his only purpose is to promote evil. If he cannot or *will* not, then his existence has no purpose. Unwilling to harm Buffy, he decides to commit suicide by waiting outside for the sun to rise, and Buffy must talk him out of it:

> **"Strong is fighting. It's hard and it's painful and it's every day. It's what we have to do and we can do it together…."**
> —BUFFY, IN "AMENDS"

Joyce wants to participate more in Buffy's life, and it is she who discovers two dead children, strangely marked, during patrol. Though it's not precisely clear at what point the "Hansel/Gretel demon" begins to exert its influence over Joyce, Buffy's mother organizes Mothers Opposed to the Occult (MOO). In her first public speech about MOO, Joyce equates slaying with all the other strange things wrong with Sunnydale, and Buffy's deeply hurt. She manages to save both herself and Willow from being burned at the stake, just as her mother regains her sanity.

Perhaps the pain of betrayal at the hands of a trusted adult lingers; in "Helpless," it is Giles who turns against Buffy. Council tradition requires that if a Slayer makes it to her eighteenth birthday, she must be rendered weak and helpless and forced to survive a battle to the death.

Ignorant of such a strange and barbaric custom, she is stunned to discover that Giles has been secretly injecting her with a drug to temporarily take away her powers.

Her test originally involved saving herself from a vampire who was already criminally insane before he was changed. But Kralik, the vampire, kidnaps Buffy's mother and plans on killing her. Giles abandons Buffy's test and helps her, earning the enmity of the Council, which fires him. His gesture doesn't come close to repairing the damage between Buffy and himself, but it is a start....

Meanwhile, the Mayor has been plotting for his Ascension. Richard Wilkins III is no friend to Slayers—although, at present, Buffy and Faith are unaware of his activities. Taking Faith's lead for a change, Buffy revels in her power as Slayer—"Want. Take. Have."—and she runs wild, like Faith. However, in their euphoria, they mistake the deputy mayor for a vampire. Buffy stops herself from staking him just in time, but Faith is not so lucky. She has violated the Slayer's code: Never kill humans.

Though Buffy's conscience torments her, Faith's does not. In fact, when she suspects that Buffy is going to come clean, she tries to frame her for the murder. She goes completely haywire, trying to kill Xander as well. (Angel saves him.) Buffy sees that—but for friends and support—she could be the same, and tries to do all she can to save Faith as she spirals downward.

But she fails, and Faith becomes her mortal enemy, joining forces with the Mayor.

In "Enemies," Buffy and Angel plot to trick Faith into revealing everything she knows about the Mayor's plans. Angel pretends that he has become evil again. He makes out with Faith in front of Buffy, and even knocks Buffy around. Once their plan is successfully carried out, Angel drops the act. But seeing him even acting evil, and having to watch him kiss Faith, have taken a toll on Buffy. She needs time apart, to think about their so very complicated relationship.

Buffy learns even more about the complexities of relationships in "Earshot." During battle with a demon, she develops telepathy. No thoughts are closed to her, save those of Angel. As with mirrors, his thoughts have no reflection. What she learns is that the people around her all have their own kind of pain, and that it occupies them so fully that they have little energy or compassion left for other people.

Knowing this, she feels she must take action to take care of her own life. With her excellent SAT scores, she gets accepted to several excellent colleges and begins lobbying for the right to go away to school. But after saving Willow from the Mayor, she faces facts: she is duty-bound to stay in Sunnydale.

There's light at the end of that tunnel, however, when she learns that Willow is going to stay in Sunnydale as well. She's going to go to UC Sunnydale, in fact. Buffy will have Willow, and Angel... or not. It's time to face facts: The relationship between Buffy and Angel is doomed. Spike knew it, the Mayor knows it, Joyce knows it, and Angel knows it. It is left to Angel to break Buffy's heart by ending the relationship just before her senior prom. When the Mayor is defeated, Angel will leave town. Buffy's determined, however, that her friends will have the most special moment of their lives—senior prom—and puts her own life on the line when a student unleashes Hell Hounds on the unsuspecting class.

Buffy destroys the hounds and arrives at the prom, alone, in her prom dress. Her friends all have dates—Xander has brought Anya, who is beginning to adjust to life as a human girl. Then, in a moving tribute, the class bestows an award on her: She is the Class Protector. Acknowledging all the evil that has been hushed up over the years, her contemporaries come forward to say they know she has saved them all time and again, and they are grateful beyond words.

So it's all been worth it…the sacrifices, the disappointments, and the heartbreak.

And then Angel shows, for one last dance, for one last moment. Buffy's prom is the thing that dreams—not real life—are made of.

But the prom is over, and graduation looms. The Mayor is scheduled to ascend at the graduation ceremony. During the total eclipse, he will turn into a full demon—not one of the hybrid demons Buffy is used to dealing with. Something much larger and deadlier.

In order to distract her, Faith has shot Angel with a poisoned arrow. When the Watchers Council refuses to help save him, Buffy turns her back on the Council. If the only other known cure is a Slayer's blood, then Buffy's ready to face Faith, to kill her if necessary. She fails, only putting Faith in a coma. Finally, she convinces the dying Angel to drink from her. He does, an experience that drains her, then leaves her remarkably clear-headed. In those moments of unconsciousness she met Faith in a dream world. And the girl she once tried to save gave her the key to stopping the Mayor and saving everyone.

In her capacity as Class Protector, Buffy masses the now-knowing students for war. Each is armed; each has a position; each does his best. Some live, some die.

The Mayor, as well as Sunnydale High School itself, is destroyed.

Angel bids Buffy a silent farewell, and disappears into the smoke, mixed with the blur of her tears.

At the start of Season Four, Buffy, Oz, and Willow are freshmen at UC Sunnydale. Willow is thriving, Oz knows everybody, and Buffy is completely overwhelmed. When the Big Vampire on Campus—Sunday—beats Buffy to a pulp during their first confrontation, Buffy wonders if she can hack the brave new world of college.

Enter Xander, who has been having challenges of his own, and reaches out to his old chum. Together they take on Sunday and her gang, with all the Scoobies arriving just in time to watch Buffy mop up the mess.

It's just like high school. Just like old times. "Which I can handle," Buffy announces.

Or so she thinks. For there's another element on campus—soldiers, or hunters—covertly bagging vampires and other assorted demons. And not so covertly, Parker Abrams goes for Buffy's heart. He's intense and charming, and before Buffy can say, "My roommate is an uptight, insufferable demon-girl from another dimension!" Buffy winds up in bed with Parker.

He immediately dumps her. Buffy is so

crushed she seeks solace in the campus bar, drowning her sorrows in magickal beer that turns her and her drinking buddies into Cro-Magnon people. However, even Caveslayer Buffy obeys her innate instinct to protect people—even if one of those people is stinky Parker man. She finds closure by bonking him on the head with her club as he soulfully apologizes to her.

Oz betrays Willow, and Buffy goes through that pain with her. She doesn't realize that the perfect guy for her—Riley Finn—is the one she keeps crashing into, in the bookstore, in the cafeteria, and even on patrol. Affable, good-looking, and "corn-fed," Riley is what Buffy wants—someone nice and normal.

Riley is the teaching assistant for the tough-as-nails psych instructor, Maggie Walsh. But Riley is also a Commando. He is with a covert operation warehoused in an enormous research facility beneath his fraternity house. Maggie Walsh is his leader supreme, and with his comrades, Forrest, Graham, and Mason, they "bag and tag" HSTs—Hostile Sub-terrestrials. Then Dr. Walsh experiments on them, placing a chip in their heads that prevents them from harming humans.

Buffy learns some of this from none other than Spike, who had originally returned to Sunnydale to hunt for the Gem of Amarra. It will make the vampire who wears it invincible, to the extent that he/she can survive stakings and sunlight. Spike eventually winds up with it, but Buffy takes it away from him and sends it to Angel in L.A.. Spike's out for revenge.

But after Dr. Walsh and the Initiative finish with Spike, he can't so much as bite anyone. However, he does escape from their secret laboratory, and for that reason alone, he's considered highly dangerous.

Eventually, Buffy puts two and two together when she sees Riley in full Commando gear. They are both battling the Gentlemen, evil fairy-tale monsters who steal the voices of everyone in Sunnydale, then butcher the innocent for their hearts. They see each other in action.

They both feel betrayed by the other for having a secret identity. Buffy requests distance; then she convinces herself that a relationship between them is doomed before it even begins. Riley is bewildered, figuring there could be no one more perfectly matched than he and Buffy. He calls Buffy on her pessimism and self-absorption. He begs her to take a chance on loving him. And she does.

Severe obstacles appear on their horizon: She is admitted into the Initiative, but she asks questions. Riley is a good soldier, used to obeying orders, but even he begins to wonder about "314" when Buffy prods him about it.

Then Maggie Walsh tries to kill her. Next thing, Maggie herself is dead…and Riley suspects her of doing it. He's not acting like himself; he's short-tempered and wildly out of control. This has happened to Buffy too many times—love someone, then he changes for the worst—but she persists in believing in Riley.

When it comes to light that Maggie Walsh has been trying to create a supersoldier, in part by drugging Riley and the others, Buffy can only keep vigil from a distance as Riley is spirited away from her. While he's locked away in a military hospital, she is powerless to help him.

Meanwhile, the monster Maggie created, named Adam, has gone on the rampage. Built out of parts of demons, humans, and machines, he is her legacy. He is killing and dissecting animals, demons, and humans, learning about the similarities between themselves and himself. He begins to build an army of followers—mainly vampires, at least at first—and sends some of them on a foray as a first strike.

While Adam launches his guerilla war, Faith awakens from her coma. Predictably, she comes after Buffy, and Buffy's ready for her. However, the Mayor left Faith a parting gift—a device that allows her to switch bodies with Buffy. Faith does so, and Buffy, not Faith, is hunted both by the police and by Watchers Council assassins.

Willow's new friend Tara is the one who realizes that Buffy isn't Buffy. With Willow, she creates a magickal device that allows Buffy to switch places with Faith once again...but not before some major damage has been done: Pretending to be Buffy, Faith has slept with Riley. It is an innocent betrayal on his part, but Buffy still has trouble handling it.

Then Jonathan Levenson, from Sunnydale High School, conjures up a fantasy life for himself in which he knows all, sees all, and does all. He is able to convince Buffy to give Riley one more chance—as Buffy gave Jonathan, in a way, up in the school bell tower ("Earshot"). When his fantasy fades away, Jonathan's good advice remains. Buffy takes it, and she and Riley are solid once more.

In fact, they become so self-absorbed that their sexual energy turns Lowell House into a prison haunted by guilt and repressed sensuality. Where most couples in the first flush of love metaphorically shut out the world, Buffy and Riley do so literally—until the gang, Tara included, unites to force them back into the real world.

Buffy's adaptability is tested yet again when Oz comes back for Willow. Riley is shocked to realize that Oz is a werewolf. For him, there are humans and there are demons. Demons are the bad guys. Always. There are no degrees of evil; no gray areas. But when confronted with the reality of Oz's innocence in the death of a Commando, Riley goes against everything he's learned to save him. Buffy supports him, reminding him that she quit the Council, and he can quit the Initiative. When he walks away from all that he had trained for, she understands how serious a stand he has taken. But she respects him all the more for it, and she's grateful for his new insight.

She can finally share her secrets with him.

She can finally tell him about Angel.

But she doesn't tell him everything: She leaves out the fact that the trigger for turning him bad was his having sex with her (Xander eventually spilled that). She pursues Faith to Los Angeles and faces a new, angry Angel, who is intent on putting her behind him while he redeems Faith. So when Angel follows her back to Sunnydale and starts throwing around Riley's fellow commandos, it's not hard to understand how Riley could make the mental leap that she slept with Angel in L.A. And there she is, ordering the two men who have been so important to her to stand down and cease hostilities.

When Angel apologizes for hitting her and saying cruel things back in Los Angeles, Buffy realizes that she and he have made the final break. She has a new life now, a new love. She will never stop loving Angel, but he is of the past. Riley represents the future.

Since Riley has been the focus of her life, she has neglected her old friends, and they are feeling that neglect. It's easy for Spike to exploit their resentments and insecurities, until none of them is speaking to Buffy. She makes a choice comment about understanding why Slayers traditionally have no friends, and it's not until she realizes that Spike duped them all into being angry with one another that she moves to apologize.

When her friends unite to imbue her with extra power in a magical ritual to defeat Adam, Buffy draws on a primal source of the Slayer's power, becoming more than she has ever been before (and easily defeating Adam). But the use of that force carries consequences: The First Slayer is called to destroy those who would dare to access it.

When confronted by the First Slayer, Buffy stands firm—she does not sleep on a bed of bones; she has a life; she is not a demon. She has friends. She walks in the world.

"Don't be too sure," Tara murmurs to Buffy as Season Four ends. *"You think you know, but you have no idea what you are, what's to come."*

Buffy is played by Sarah Michelle Gellar.

QUOTABLE
BUFFY

BUFFY: "Hey, Ken. Wanna see my impression of Gandhi?"

[Ken looks blearily at her. She swings the club down on his head with horrible force. We hear a wet sound that comes from inside his head.

Lily comes up to her, wide eyes on the corpse of Ken.]

LILY: "Gandhi?"

BUFFY: "Well, you know…if he was really pissed off." —"ANNE"

BUFFY: "Yeah, I just got in a few hours ago. Went to see Mom first."

GILES: "Of course. And how did you find her?"

BUFFY: "I pretty much remembered the address." —"DEAD MAN'S PARTY"

"Look, I'm sorry your honey was a demon, but most girls don't hop a Greyhound over boy trouble!"

—XANDER, TO BUFFY, IN "DEAD MAN'S PARTY"

OZ: "Hey, so, you're not wanted for murder anymore."

BUFFY: "Oh, good. That was such a drag." —"DEAD MAN'S PARTY"

"It's just pathetic. You're not even a loser anymore. You're a shell of a loser." —TO SPIKE, IN "LOVER'S WALK"

"Your logic does not resemble our Earth-logic."

—TO XANDER, IN "THE WISH"

"Is this a 'get in my pants' thing? You Sunnydale guys all talk like I'm the second coming."

—IN BIZARRO SUNNYDALE, IN "THE WISH"

"'The count of three' is not a plan. It's <u>Sesame Street</u>."

—TO FAITH, IN "BAD GIRLS"

"I hate it when they drown me."

—"BAD GIRLS"

"Yeah, he's some kind of demon looking for an all-powerful thingimibob and I've got to stop him before unholy havoc's unleashed and it's another Tuesday night in Sunnydale."

—BUFFY, TALKING ABOUT LAGOS, IN "REVELATIONS"

GILES: "Quite a couple of days."

BUFFY: "My brain hasn't processed everything yet. It's not really functioning at the higher levels. It's pretty much, 'fire bad, tree pretty.' Anything more complex . . . "

GILES: "Understandable. Well, when it starts working again, congratulate it on a good campaign. You did very well . . . . There is a certain dramatic irony in the way things turned out. A synchronicity that borders on predestination, one might say."

BUFFY: "Fire bad. Tree pretty."

—"GRADUATION DAY, PART TWO"

51

"I'm suffering the after-ness of a bad night of badness." —"BEER BAD"

FORREST: "Oh. Check her out. Is she hot or is she hot?"
RILEY: "She's Buffy."
FORREST: "Buffy. I like that. [trying it on] 'That girl's so hot, she's <u>Buffy</u>.'"
RILEY: "It's her name, Forrest."
—"THE INITIATIVE"

"Okay. You get fang. I'll get horny."
— PLANNING HER BATTLE STRATEGY WITH RILEY, IN "WHERE THE WILD THINGS ARE"

"This isn't your business. It's mine. You, the Initiative, the suits in the Pentagon....You're all messing with Primeval forces you can't begin to understand. I'm the Slayer. And you're playing on my turf."
—BUFFY, TELLING COLONEL McNAMARA AND THE INITIATIVE TO STAND DOWN, IN "PRIMEVAL"

"Judgmental? If I was any more open-minded about the choices you two make my entire brain would fall out."
—TO WILLOW AND XANDER, IN "THE YOKO FACTOR"

"But what else could I expect from a bunch of low-rent, no-account hood-lums like you—hoodlums! Yes, I mean you and your friends, your whole sex, throw 'em all in the sea for all I care, throw 'em in and wait for the bubbles. Men, with your groping and spitting, all-groin no-brain three billion of ya passin' around the same worn out urge. Men. With your . . . <u>sales</u>."
—BUFFY IN WILLOW'S NIGHTMARE PLAY OF <u>DEATH OF A SALESMAN</u>, IN "RESTLESS"

"You just have to get over the whole primal power thing. You're not the source of me."
—BUFFY, DREAMING OF THE FIRST SLAYER, IN "RESTLESS"

Alexander Lavelle Harris (Xander)

As the third season opens, Xander and Cordelia have made it through the summer together. Xander is "Nighthawk," part of the crack team of vampire hunters he, Willow, Oz, and Cordy have not exactly become since Buffy fled Sunnydale. It's all still there—the bickering, the kissage—except that the Slayer is missing.

Then she's back, and Xander doesn't exactly hide how angry he is with Buffy for "ruining our lives." She bailed, and he's not giving her any slack over it. They nearly come to blows at Buffy's welcome-back bash, except for the fact that they have to turn their attention to fighting zombies instead.

His ire is further raised when he discovers that she's been hiding Angel. He doesn't hesitate when Faith invites him to come along for the stakeout.

The fact remains, however, that he never told Buffy that Willow was trying to restore Angel's soul one more time, when he went with her to Angel's mansion at the end of Season Two. This is never addressed, not even when Buffy tells Giles and Willow that Angel was cured before she sent him to Hell, in "Faith, Hope & Trick."

There is also the matter of Xander and Willow's attraction to each other. Finally, after all the years of being best buddies, and landing sweeties of their own (and Xander getting over Buffy, sort of), they can barely keep their hands off each other. In "Homecoming," they finally kiss, and swear to each other they will never, ever do that again. It was…a fluke.

Then Spike, love's dog himself, imprisons them because he wants Willow to get Drusilla back for him. Xander and Willow both believe they're going to die. The heightened urgency of the moment combines with their ultra-intense passion, and things are getting very steamy when Cordelia and Oz arrive to save them. Blinded with hurt, Cordelia falls and is impaled on a rebar. Xander risks his life to stay with her, but she can't, won't forgive him for kissing Willow. Oz breaks up with Willow as well.

The happy is gone. Especially after Cordelia is approached by Anyanka, a vengeance demon whose specialty is fulfilling the wishes of women scorned. Cordelia wishes that Buffy had never come to Sunnydale…and suddenly Xander and Willow are a leather-clad vamp couple, the favorites of the Master and the keepers of "the puppy"—Angel. Vamp Willow's particular kink is to torture Angel. Vamp Xander's is to watch. Eventually all is put right, and no one remembers the strange alternate reality they've just been through…except for Anyanka, who is stripped of her powers. Now she is just Anya, a mortal girl, flunking math and bored to tears.

Xander's Christmas is a gloomy one. Cordelia has reverted to form, digging at him mercilessly before she goes off on an exotic ski vacation. Willow and Oz make up, which is as it should be, but Xander's increasingly aware that he is not cool. When Cordelia taunts him by calling him "The Zeppo," it hurts because he is already feeling very much like an appendage. He's the one who gets the supplies—the doughnuts—and he's the one asked to stay out of harm's way during demon battles. In fact, it's suggested he stay out of battles altogether!

Xander takes action. He quizzes Oz on the meaning of coolness and decides he needs a "thing." In his case, it's his uncle Roary's car. Cordelia mocks him…until one Lysette asks to be taken for a spin.

So begins a bizarre night for Xander, wherein he becomes wheelman for a gang of revenant hoods. He also rescues Faith from combat, and they have sex.

The newly risen good ol' dead boys decide to blow up the school, just for the fun of it. While Buffy and the others battle monsters crawling out of the Hellmouth, it is up to Xander to stop the dead guys from killing them all. He has a masterful moment, playing chicken with Jack, the leader of the pack, a bully in life and a bully now. Jack crumbles first, defusing the bomb that he and the others hid in the boiler room. Xander emerges triumphant…and aware that cool is as cool does. Cordelia's taunts don't bother him anymore…

…quite so much.

Xander's once more one of the heroes when he catches the insane lunch lady poisoning the mulligan stew in "Earshot."

Xander's black book has included an enormous praying mantis, a centuries-old mummy, and even Drusilla herself, when he forced Amy Madison, the school witch, to cast a love spell for him. Now Anya, former vengeance demon, asks him to go to the prom with her. Her reasoning:

"Well, you're not quite as obnoxious as most of the alpha males around here. Plus, I know you don't have a date." —"THE PROM"

Xander's big plan after graduation was to see America. But he got as far as Oxnard and ended up washing dishes at the Ladies' Night male strip club. He returns to Sunnydale the only member of the old high school gang still in town and not going to college. While everyone else has moved on campus (or, in Oz's case, to a house nearby), he's living in his parents' basement and paying rent for the dubious privilege.

He undertakes a series of jobs. What becomes clear is that while Xander is a sort of marginalized outsider as a "townie," the others come to him for advice and help. In "The Freshman" he helps Buffy research where Sunday the vampire may be living, and gathers the others to come to her rescue. In "Wild at Heart" Willow comes to him, worried that Oz is more interested in Veruca than in her. Xander repeatedly acts as backup in battle situations, such as going undercover with Buffy in the Initiative complex, in "Goodbye Iowa." Whatever the situation, Xander is now firmly loyal to Buffy:

"Buffy, I've gone through some fairly dark times in my life. Faced some scary things, among them the kitchen of the fabulous Ladies' Night Club. Let me tell you something. When it's dark and I'm all alone, and I'm scared or freaked out or whatever, I always think, 'What would Buffy do?' You're my hero." —"THE FRESHMAN"

Anya reappears in Xander's life in "The Harsh Light of Day." She makes it very clear that she now considers the two of them to be a dating couple. Then she escalates: she can't get Xander out of her mind, so she thinks they should have sex so she can put him behind her. "Not literally," she continues, matter-of-factly. "I was thinking face to face for the actual event itself."

Thus begins Xander's romance with Anya. She becomes a member of the gang and is a source of exasperation and amusement as she tries to absorb the complexities of relationships, discretion, and poker. Xander realizes that he loves her in "Hush," when he mistakenly beats up Spike for attacking her. He has clearly met his perfect match in terms of sexual, uuuh, interest. What will become of their relationship is unclear, but at the very least, Xander is living in interesting times.

Still, of all the group, Xander is most like Giles: he's not sure what he should be doing with his life. He's working to pay the rent on the basement in his parents' house. None of his jobs lasts very long, and he's nowhere near finding anything he could spend a lifetime doing. He's not getting an education. He has no plan, no magick gift or power to either

XANDER...
directionless loser OR sampler of the unknown?
YOU BE THE JUDGE:

- Dishwasher (and substitute dancer!) at a ladies-only strip club
- bartender
- Boost Bar distributor
- pizza delivery guy
- Starbucks worker
- sex phone line
- ice cream vendor

develop (like Willow) or overcome (like Oz). And, as usual, his girlfriend is a demon.

But Xander consistently underestimates how useful he is to the Slayer. He is the other one of the two, to paraphrase Willow. He is the heart of the group, the deep emotion.

As the season draws to a close, his fears about his future are not allayed. In Xander's "Restless" dream, he has a brief flirtation with Buffy's mother that seems to echo his proclivity toward unconventional attractions and relationships. Though he dashes off, he consistently finds himself back in his basement apartment as an unseen creature bangs at his door. Later, Spike tells Xander that Giles is priming him to be a Watcher, to which Xander responds, "I was into that for a while, but I got other stuff going on." What that other stuff might be, isn't clear, but there's a definite theme of fighting ("I'm a conquistador"). In a riff on *Apocalypse Now,* General Snyder tells Private Harris "You're a whipping boy raised by mongrels." Xander's father later seems to share this sentiment, shouting, "Line ends here, with us! You're not gonna change that. You haven't got the HEART." And with that, he yanks Xander's heart right out of his chest ending the dream. Big changes in store for the X-man as he moves to center stage in Season Five…

Xander is played by Nicholas Brendon.

QUOTABLE
XANDER

WILLOW: "I wonder what she's doing right now."
XANDER: "Oh, I know what she's doing. Gabbing to all her friends about her passionate affair with Pedro the cabana boy and laughing about me thinking she might still have feelings for me." [off Willow's look] "It's possible you were talking about Buffy." —"ANNE"

"You don't hide! You're bait! Go act baity." —TO CORDY, IN "ANNE"

FAITH: "—it was about a hundred and eighteen degrees, I'm sleepin' without a stitch on, suddenly I hear all this screamin'. I go tearin' outside—stark nude—this church bus has broke down and three vamps are feasting on half the Baptists in South Boston. So I waste the vamps and the preacher is hugging me like there's no tomorrow when the cops pull up. They arrested us both."
XANDER: "Wow. They should film that story and show it every Christmas."
 —"FAITH, HOPE & TRICK"

XANDER: "Angel? Weird? What are the odds?"
WILLOW: "Do you think there's something wrong? Should you maybe tell Giles?"
BUFFY: "I don't want to bug Giles. He's still twitchy about the subject of Angel."
XANDER: "Must be that whole Angel-killed-his-girlfriend-and-tortured-him thing. Giles is really petty about stuff like that."
 —"AMENDS"

FAITH: "She got me really wound up. A fight like that and no kill, I'm about ready to pop."

XANDER [the intimacy making him nervous]: "Really? Pop?"

FAITH: "You up for it?"

XANDER: "Oh, I'm up. I'm suddenly very up. It's just, um, I've never been up with people . . . before . . . ."

FAITH: "Just relax. And take your pants off."

XANDER: "Those two concepts are antithetical."

FAITH: "Don't worry. I'll steer you 'round the curves."

XANDER: "Did I mention that I'm having a very strange night?"   —"THE ZEPPO"

XANDER: "We know underground, there's a start. . . ."

BUFFY: "In a town with fourteen million square miles of sewer—"

XANDER: "Plus a lot of natural cave formations and a gateway to hell, yeah... [looking about him]. This does resemble square one."   —"AMENDS"

PARKER: "You wanna be in the gang, don't you?"

XANDER: "Yes, but I'm not dying to be in the gang...if you get the...the pun there...."

BOB: "What, are you too good to be dead? You got a problem with dead people?"

          —ZOMBIE PARKER, IN "THE ZEPPO"

JACK: "I'm not afraid to die. I'm already dead."

XANDER: "Yeah, but this is different. Being blowed up isn't walking around and drinking with your buddies dead. It's 'little bits swept up by the janitor' dead, and I don't think you're ready for that."

JACK "Are you?"

[Beat. Jack. Xander. Clock.]

XANDER (smiling calmly): "I like the quiet."
          —"THE ZEPPO"

CORDELIA: "Oh, look, it's Mister Excitement. On another life-or-death doughnut mis-

sion? Or are we cruising for bimbos again? Giving them lessons in lack of cool."

[He stops, looking at her. Little calm smile. He's little calm smile guy].

CORDELIA: "What?"

[He says nothing. Still with the smile.]

CORDELIA: "What?"

[Walks away.]

CORDELIA: "WHAT?"   —"THE ZEPPO"

XANDER: "Basically I got as far as Oxnard and the engine fell out of my car. And that was literally. So I ended up washing dishes at the fabulous Ladies' Night club for about a month and a half while I tried to pay for the repairs. Nobody really bothered me or even spoke to me there until one night one of the male strippers called in sick and no power on this Earth will make me tell you the rest of that story. Suffice to say I traded in my car for one that wasn't entirely made of rust and came trundling back home to the arms of my loving parents and everything was exactly as it was except I sleep in the basement and I have to pay rent. How's college?"

BUFFY: "Male strippers?"

XANDER: "No power on this earth."
          —"THE FRESHMAN"

"And nothing says 'thank you' like dollars in the waistband."

          —XANDER, IN "THE FRESHMAN"

"Just because you're better than us doesn't mean you can be all superior."

—XANDER TO BUFFY, IN "THE YOKO FACTOR"

"Sometimes I think about two women doing a spell...and then I do a spell by myself."

          —XANDER, RE: TARA AND WILLOW,
                    IN "RESTLESS"

XANDER: "It's all my fault."

GILES: "What makes you say that?"

XANDER: "I don't know. Statistical probability."

—XANDER, BLAMING HIMSELF FOR WILLOW'S DEATH, IN "DOPPELGANGLAND"

ANYA: "I think we should talk about it now!"

GILES: "Thank you for knocking—"

XANDER: "If you don't know how I feel—"

ANYA: "I don't! This isn't a relationship. You don't need me! All you care about is lots of orgasms!"

[bit of a beat there]

XANDER: "Okay, remember when we talked about private conversations? How they're less private when they're in front of my friends?"

SPIKE: "Oh, we're not your friends. Go on."

—"HUSH"

ANYA: "Look at him. Have you ever seen anything so masculine?"

BUFFY: "You mean Dean Guerrero, or his wife?"

WILLOW: "I think she means…" [indicates Xander]

BUFFY: "Oh right. Very manly. Not at all Village People."

ANYA: So much sexier than his last job. I'm imagining having sex with him right now. Ooh. Look at him."

WILLOW: "Very…diggy."

ANYA: "Soon he'll be sweating. I'm imagining having sex with him again."

BUFFY: "Imaginary Xander is quite the machine."

—"PANGS"

ANYA (to Spike): "I want to give you something for your new place."

XANDER: "That's my lamp!"

ANYA: "A gift is traditional. I read about it."

XANDER: "That's among friends. With bitter enemies, we don't give them my lamp."

—"A NEW MAN"

"Do you mind? I'm talking to my demon."

—XANDER, MEANING ANYA, IN HIS DREAM, IN "RESTLESS"

57

Willow Rosenberg

In Seasons One and Two, Willow blossomed in her relationship as best friend of the Slayer. Then she became the girlfriend of Daniel Osbourne—Oz—one of the coolest guys in school. She also stepped into the shoes of technopagan Jenny Calendar and has become a devoted student of Wicca. In "Anne," she's a pivotal member of the Slayerettes, substituting for the Slayer.

Over the summer Willow has been conducting experiments in witchcraft, keeping most of them from Giles, as she and the others battle the forces of darkness.

When Buffy comes back, Willow has some trouble forgiving her for running away right when she needed a best friend.

BUFFY: "Look, I'm sorry I had to leave, okay? You don't know what I was going through."

WILLOW: "What you were going through? Buffy…what about me?"

BUFFY: "Willow, I know you were worried, but—"

WILLOW: "No, I mean, what about me? My life. I have all sorts of—I'm dating, I'm having serious dating with a werewolf, and I've been studying witchcraft and killing vampires. I didn't have anyone to talk to about all this scary life stuff. And you were my <u>best friend</u>."
—"DEAD MAN'S PARTY"

Willow and Oz continue their relationship. Although she and Xander have admitted their attraction to each other, it's understood that their hearts belong to their sweethearts—Oz and Cordelia. There is no talk of breaking up and becoming a couple. This underscores another of Willow's big changes—pre-Buffy, Willow pined in silence for Xander. By the time Buffy came to town, Xander became attracted to Cordelia, and Willow finally moved on.

Her relationship with Oz is tested numerous times. In "Beauty and the Beasts" it's possible that Oz has gotten out and killed people. In "Lovers Walk" she and Xander betray Oz and Cordelia by having illicit smoothies together. Oz needs time to figure out how he feels about Willow now.

In "Amends" Oz makes up with Willow; and Willow, trying to prove that he is the most special guy in the world to her, puts on some Barry White and tries to seduce him. Oz reads her message loud and clear, and is moved. But Oz is a special guy, so he tells her he wants to wait until there's nothing left for her to prove.

Meanwhile, Willow's friendship with Buffy has taken some blows. During the Xander crisis, Willow wants very badly to confide in Buffy, but Buffy is distracted by the arrival of Faith. Buffy begins making comments such as "It's Slayer stuff. You wouldn't understand." In the past, Willow has shared the deepest secrets of Buffy's heart, and been there for her triumphs and her agonies. Probably no one on the planet understands Buffy as well as Willow. Time and again Willow has risked her life for Buffy. But Buffy doesn't tell Willow that Angel has returned.

As the school year progresses, Willow moves from helping Giles with magick spells (and getting in trouble for attempting them on her own) to thinking of herself as magickally powerful. In "Lovers Walk," her spellcasting abilities are called upon by none other than Spike. Her life and Xander's hang in the balance. In "Gingerbread" she creates a protection spell for Buffy's birthday. She tells her mother—or tries to—about her abilities.

Willow's clearly feeling more powerful than she did back in Season One, when she asked Buffy if she should move to make room for her at lunchtime. By third season she can confront Buffy directly, as she does when Buffy starts acting like a "Bad Girl" with Faith.

Shortly after that, Principal Snyder forces Willow to "tutor" Percy—which actually means that Willow's supposed to do his homework for him. Xander wants to know if she remembered to tape a TV show. Giles snaps at her to hop to and do some research. Buffy calls her "old reliable."

Willow's had just about enough. She eats her banana when she feels like it—lunchtime be damned!

Vamp Willow pops into this reality, and "our" Willow, masquerading as her, has this to say of herself:

"She bothered me. She's so weak, and accommodating. It's pathetic—she lets everyone walk all over her and then she gets cranky at her friends for no reason. I just couldn't let her live." —"DOPPELGANGLAND"

Then, at the end of the episode, Percy—having mistaken Vamp Willow for Willow—grovels. He has also done all his homework, on his own. Done more than he had to, in fact. Willow is bemused...and triumphant.

Magickally, Willow has progressed to where she can run "aural analyses" and asks Xander to go to the magick shop for her. When he says, "I'm a little low on cash," she replies, "Just tell them it's for me" ("Graduation Day, Part One").

The Mayor threatens to end the world, and Oz and Willow create their own: they make love for the first time. Willow glows; wonderingly, she tells Oz, "Well, things are just so terrible; everything's coming apart, and I'm just...in some ways it's the best night of my life" ("Graduation Day, Part Two").

When Season Four begins, Willow and Buffy have reversed roles. Willow thrives on the chaos and intellectual atmosphere. Buffy's wigged, awkward, and shy. Willow has an on-campus boyfriend whose band is already well known at UC Sunnydale. Buffy has Parker Abrams...or rather, he has her, and afterward, she goes into major moping.

Then the unthinkable happens: Oz is unfaithful to Willow.

It starts out slowly: Willow and Oz go to the Bronze when Shy is playing. Oz notices their lead singer, Veruca, and she clearly notices him back. In "Beer Bad" the stage directions say:

> Willow follows his gaze to the stage. She tenses—no way is this lost on her. She subtly eyes Oz. His attention to Veruca is a surprise to her.

It continues until Willow, very anxious, goes to Xander because Oz doesn't seem as interested in her as he should be. Her old friend tries to reassure her, but that's something only Oz can do. Then, on the second morning of his werewolf cycle, she brings breakfast for the two of them to his cage, only to find him lying asleep naked with Veruca.

What almost hurts as much as the betrayal is the fact that he didn't tell her about it. He denied there was anything wrong when obviously there was. He knew Veruca was a werewolf and that she liked to revel in it, even if it meant humans got hurt. His solution—to lock Veruca up with himself—is suspect at best: he already knows that she and he have mated while in wolf form.

Willow is beyond devastated. She's reeling, so lost in pain she steps in front of a speeding car without realizing it's there.

She decides to cast a spell of black magick that will harm both Veruca and Oz. But she can't do it. At the last moment she stops the spell . . . just as Veruca corners her in the school lab. As the sun's going down, she taunts Willow—"I have his scent on me." It's clear she's going to kill Willow. Oz shows. He and Veruca transform, and Oz kills her. He goes for Willow next, and only the tranquilizer gun in Buffy's hand saves Willow's life.

In the aftermath Oz decides he must leave. Willow is shattered.

Still, the plucky Willow stays in school, has Thanksgiving with Buffy and the gang, and tries to keep going. Then, in "Something Blue," she learns that Oz has written to Devon and asked him to send the rest of his things. There is no message for Willow. Nothing.

She gets drunk. She will do anything to stop feeling so awful. So she tries to cast a spell for her will to be done—and she wills for her heart to be healed. She wills a number of other things as well, exaggerating out of spite, and they come true. D'Hoffryn, the same demon who changed Anya into a vengeance demon eleven hundred and twenty years ago, is impressed by her skill, and offers to do the same to Willow. She tells him that she will try for a quiet rage. When all is put back to rights, she does seem better, baking cookies and trying to make amends with her friends.

In "Hush" she notices Tara, a shy girl who is a member of the disappointing Wicca group. They noticed each other, in fact; and when the Gentlemen steal all the voices in Sunnydale, Tara risks her life to seek out Willow, in order to try to reverse the spell. The two bond when they magickally barricade the door with a soda machine, their fingers laced together. After they've moved the machine, they continue to hold hands. Later, Willow is being self-effacing about her abilities, saying she's nothing special. Tara replies, with real sincerity, "No, you are."

Their connection grows. In "The I in Team" Tara sweetly tries to give Willow a family heirloom—a doll's-eye crystal—but Willow understands how valuable it is and tells Tara she can't accept it. However, having stayed the night at Tara's, she brings the crystal back to her dorm room. Later, she uses it to ionize the atmosphere when she's at Giles's and needs to block the transmitter embedded in Spike's back.

In the same episode Willow feels she has to exclude Tara from her date at the Bronze with the old gang, even though it's obvious she's hurting the other girl's feelings. Then Buffy shows up, an hour late, with half the Commandos—and Riley—in tow. Anya, who was invited, is so uncomfortable that she and Xander split. Willow's hurt, and somewhat peeved.

As time goes on, Tara and Willow continue to build a solid relationship. Willow grows as a witch and a person. Perhaps she's echoing her newfound understanding of Buffy's intense focus on Riley when she has the following exchange with Tara: .

> **WILLOW:** "Buffy's like my best friend, and she's really special, plus, you know, Slayer, that's a deal, and there's the whole bunch of us, and we have this group thing that kind of revolves around the slaying and I really want you to meet them and meet Buffy but I just sort of like having something that's just, you know, mine. I don't usually use that many words to say stuff that little. But do you get it at all?"
>
> **TARA:** "I do."
> **WILLOW:** "I should check in with Giles, get a situation update."
> **TARA:** "I am, you know."
> **WILLOW:** "What?"
> **TARA:** "Yours."   —"WHO ARE YOU"

In "New Moon Rising" Tara has been invited to sit in on a Scooby meeting. It has become standard *Buffy* convention that eventually, the boyfriends and girlfriends of the core gang become involved members of the inner circle themselves. The overt reason is that she's a very powerful witch. But it's clear that she and Willow are very comfortable in their relationship.

Without warning, Oz returns. Not only is he back, but he can control his transformation into wolf mode. It's better than Willow ever dreamed—except now she has Tara. She is faced with an impossible decision. And in discussing it with Buffy, she realizes the Slayer, her best friend, wasn't even aware of the nature of Willow's relationship with Tara, further underscoring the distance between Buffy and Willow this year.

Willow's choice is not made any easier by the fact that Oz is so upset by the realization that Willow is in love with Tara that he morphs. Tara gets word to the others that the Initiative has captured him, insuring the safety of her rival. And in the end, Willow chooses what her heart dictates:

WILLOW: "Tara, I have to tell you that—"
TARA: "I understand. You have to be with the person you love."
WILLOW: "I am."
TARA: "You mean—"
WILLOW: "I mean."
[Tara smiles—Willow returns it]
WILLOW: "Okay?"
TARA: "Oh, yes."

In Willow's "Restless" dream, she is reluctant to leave the comfort and safety of Tara's bed, but eventually must in order to attend her first drama class. (It is interesting that in "Primeval," as Willow and Tara are choosing classes for the fall semester, Willow decides to take drama—in direct counter-point to her fear of public performances that is demonstrated first in Season One's "Nightmares".) When she arrives at class, however, she finds an actual production just about to begin. All of her friends, including Riley, Buffy, and Harmony, are assembled and dressed for the play. Will's confused, but her friends seem unphased—and thankful that at least she's in costume.

"Okay, still needing to explain wherein this is just my outfit," she insists, but when Buffy rips her clothing off of her, Willow finds herself as viewers did, in "Welcome to the Hellmouth"—a much less evolved Willow.

Willow has always drawn strength from her relationships: first with Buffy, then Oz, and now Tara. Given Tara's secrecy about sabotaging Willow's demon-finding spell, and the major part she played in "Restless," one can only assume that their relationship will continue to develop.

Willow is played by Alyson Hannigan.

QUOTABLE
WILLOW

"Well, we try not to get killed. That's part of our whole mission statement. Don't get killed." —"ANNE"

"I tried to communicate with the spirit world and I so wasn't ready for that. It was like being pulled apart inside. Plus I blew the power for our whole block. Big scare."

—WILLOW, IN "DEAD MAN'S PARTY"

"I don't think so. He just needed to see you. Have you ever noticed when he _is_ mad but he's too English to say anything, he makes that weird 'cluck cluck' sound with his tongue—"

—ON GILES, IN "FAITH, HOPE & TRICK"

WILLOW: "Sage, love that smell…and Marnox root. Just a smidge of this mixed with a virgin's saliva— [off his look, drops root] —does something I know nothing about."

GILES: "These forces aren't something one plays around with, Willow. What have you been conjuring?"

WILLOW: "Nothing much. I mean, I tried that spell to cure Angel. I guess that was a bust, but after that just, you know, small stuff. Floating feather, fire out of ice, which next time I won't do on the bedspread—are you mad at me?"

GILES: "Of course not. If I were angry I believe I would be making a strange clucking sound with my tongue."

—WILLOW 'FESSING UP, IN "FAITH, HOPE & TRICK"

XANDER: "No worries. I can handle the Oz full monty. [quickly] I mean—not <u>handle</u>, handle—like 'hands to flesh' handle."

WILLOW: "It's not you I'm worried about. It's me. I'm still getting used to half a monty."

—"BEAUTY AND THE BEASTS"

"He saved me from a horrible flamey death. That sort of makes me like him again."

—DEFENDING ANGEL, IN "REVELATIONS"

WILLOW: "I worship Beelzebub! I do his bidding! Do you see any goats around? No! Because I sacrificed them! All bow before SATAN!"

MRS. ROSENBERG: "Willow, please. I'm not listening to this."

WILLOW: "Prince of Night, I summon you! Come fill me with your black, naughty evil!"

—WILLOW STRIVING FOR EFFECT, IN "GINGERBREAD"

"Buffy would never just take off. It's just not in her nature except that one time she disappeared for several months and changed her name but there were circumstances then."

—WILLOW, IN "THE FRESHMAN"

BUFFY: "Evil toenails. I took them off the floor when she was in the bathroom last night. She thought I was asleep."

WILLOW: "Good thinking. 'Cause, in the middle of the night, those toenails could have attacked you and left little half-moon marks all over your body."

—"LIVING CONDITIONS"

BUFFY: "And what are we, if not women up to a challenge?"

WILLOW: "Exactly. Did we not put the 'grrrr' in 'girl'?" —"LIVING CONDITIONS"

"You two are the two who are the two. I'm the other one."

—WILLOW EXPLAINS GROUP DYNAMICS TO XANDER AND BUFFY, "THE YOKO FACTOR"

"I used to just assume we'd be roomies through grad school and into little old ladyhood—you know, cheating at Bingo together and forgetting to take our pills." —"THE YOKO FACTOR"

WILLOW: "That wasn't just a temporal fold, that was some weird Hell place. I don't think you're telling me everything."

ANYA: "I swear, I'm just trying to find my necklace."

WILLOW: "Did you try looking inside the sofa in HELL?" —"DOPPELGANGLAND"

BUFFY: "It was you, Willow, in every detail. Except for your not being a dominatrix...as far as we know."

WILLOW: "Oh, right. Me and Oz play Mistress of Pain every night. Please."

XANDER: "Did anyone else just go to a scary visual place?" —"DOPPELGANGLAND"

"It's horrible. That's me as a vampire? I mean, I'm so evil, and skanky [softly, to Buffy] and I think I'm kind of gay."

—WILLOW, IN "DOPPELGANGLAND"

"I eat danger for breakfast."

—WILLOW, IN "CHOICES"

"Drowning your troubles over Parker, the mind-frying man! He deserves a torturous and slow death by spider bites. [beat] Well, for today, we'll just have to throw spit balls at the back of his neck in class."

—WILLOW, TRYING TO CHEER BUFFY UP, IN "BEER BAD"

WILLOW: "Why should I trust you?"

RILEY: "I was just sort of hoping you'd think I have an honest face."

WILLOW: "I've seen honest faces. They usually come attached to liars."

—"THE INITIATIVE"

"Then talk. Keep eye contact, funny is good, but don't be glib and remember: if you hurt her, I will beat you to death with a shovel. [off Riley's look] A vague disclaimer is nobody's friend. Have fun!"

—WILLOW, GIVING RILEY DATING ADVICE, IN "THE INITIATIVE"

Cordelia Chase

Cordelia's watchword for Season Three is disappointment. She begins senior year as Cordelia, with a twist: She's still Xander Harris's girlfriend, and liking it. She's also been helping with the demon busting, an entrenched member of the gang, when Buffy decides to return.

But she's still the queen of the honest statement:

WILLOW: "Maybe we shouldn't be too couply around Buffy."
CORDELIA: "Oh, you mean 'cause of how the only guy that ever liked her turned into a vicious killer and had to be put down like a dog?"
XANDER: "Can she cram complex issues into a nutshell or what?"　　　—"FAITH, HOPE & TRICK"

As usual, she is self-absorbed, forgetting to tell Buffy about school pictures while she campaigns for Homecoming Queen. Buffy's so furious that she decides to compete against Cordelia. But instead of being crowned queen, Cordelia is mistaken for Faith. She and Buffy are hunted as the quarry of SlayerFest '98, and by the time the two bedraggled (but victorious) girls show up at the Homecoming Dance, the tie for queen is being announced—it was won by the other two girls who were running, Holly Charleston and Michelle Blake.

School drags on. Then Spike comes to town and kidnaps Willow and Xander. Cordelia and Oz manage to rescue them, but they walk in on the two captives, kissing passionately. Cordelia flees, but is injured. Oz eventually forgives Willow, but it's over between Xander and Cordelia.

CORDELIA: (whispers) "Xander?"
XANDER: "Yeah?"
[Xander moves in close to her face.]
CORDELIA: (icy) "Stay away from me."
[He looks at her, then slowly moves from the bed. She looks back toward the window, pain etched on her face.]　　　—"LOVERS WALK"

She cuts up all her pictures of Xander, completely crushed, and returns to school a laughingstock. She tries to flirt with John Lee, a handsome, popular jock, but he's embarrassed to be seen with Xander Harris's "castoff." And Harmony, one of her Cordettes, completely humiliates her by suggesting she has just "the stallion" for Cordelia: "He's so you."

It's Jonathan, the class geek.

Her misery calls Anyanka, the vengeance demon. Cordelia wishes Buffy had never come to Sunnydale. The world becomes a terrible other-reality, in which Xander and Willow are a couple—of vampires—and they kill Cordelia.

So much for that.

Then—back in this reality—it comes out that her father has lost all his money. She can't afford to go to any of the top-notch colleges that accepted her. She's working in a dress shop, and she can't even afford the prom dress she put on layaway (Xander buys it for her).

Then the crowning blow: She and Wesley have ogled each other all year. Now that she's officially no longer a student, and the world might end with the Mayor's Ascension—plus he's going back to England!—this is what happens:

[Unable to contain themselves any longer, they come together in a passionate embrace, lips meeting...
...and lips not really getting along. It's a sad excuse for a kiss, and gives our lovers pause. They try again. Mouths incompatible, much effort, but no reward.
They stop, let go of each other. Puzzled and uncomfortable. A beat.]
CORDELIA: "Okay, so good luck in England."
WESLEY: "Yes, thanks. I'll drop a line sometime."
CORDELIA: "That'd be neat."

—"GRADUATION DAY, PART TWO"

Cordelia is played by Charisma Carpenter. After Season Three ended, she joined Angel in Los Angeles on his new show...as did Wesley Wyndam-Pryce.

QUOTABLE
CORDELIA

BUFFY: "Cordy, get out of my shoes!"
—THE GODDESS OF EMPATHY,
IN "DEAD MAN'S PARTY"

"He didn't meet anybody over the summer, did he? No, who's he gonna meet in Sunnydale besides monsters and stuff; then again, he's always kind of attracted to monsters.... How's my hair?"
—PRIORITIZING FOR THE BIG REUNION
WITH XANDER, IN "ANNE"

"Great. Now I'm going to be stuck with serious thoughts all day."
—"BEAUTY AND THE BEASTS"

BUFFY: "Do you really love Xander?"
CORDELIA: "Well, he just...grows on you, like a Chia Pet."   —"HOMECOMING"

CORDELIA: "Time out, Xand. I mean, put yourself in Buffy's shoes for a minute. I'm Buffy—freak of nature, right? Naturally, I pick a freak for a boyfriend. Then he's Mister Killing Spree, which is pretty much my fault, and—"

"The comedy stylings of Miss Cordelia Chase, everybody. Who incidentally won't be needing a higher education when she can just market her own very successful line of Hooker Wear."
—XANDER, IN "BAD GIRLS"

XANDER: "Oh, God, what'd you do to each other?"
BUFFY: "Long story."
CORDELIA: "Got hunted."
BUFFY: "Apparently not that long."

—"HOMECOMING"

"And I wish Xander Harris never again knows the touch of a woman. And that Willow wakes up tomorrow covered in monkey hair."

—"THE WISH"

CORDELIA: "First of all, 'posse?' Passe. Second, anyone with a teaspoon of brains would know not to take my flirting seriously. Especially with my extenuating circumstances."
GUY: "What circumstances?"
CORDELIA: "Rebound. Look it up."

—"HELPLESS"

"That's so cute, planning life as a loser. Most people just turn out that way, but you're really taking charge."

—TO XANDER (WHO ELSE?), IN "BAD GIRLS"

Angel

As Season Three begins, Angel, suffering in hell, appears as a dream lover in both Buffy's bittersweet night reveries and her nightmares. Just as she finally summons the will to tell him goodbye (in "Faith, Hope & Trick"), he returns from the equivalent of a century of torment in the demon realm.

He's a wild creature, and Buffy suspects him of some savage killings. Eventually he is exonerated. And he begins to come back, fully:

ANGEL: "Buffy?"
[They lock eyes. It's him. She sees the kindness returned there. The familiarity. She nods.]

—"BEAUTY AND THE BEASTS"

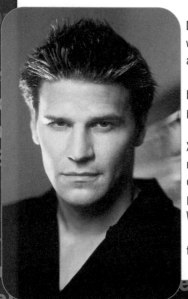

And with her affirmation, Angel falls to his knees at her feet. Despite the chains and the shackles, he wraps his arms around her waist, and begins to cry as he feels the first comfort he's known in a hundred years.

Buffy tells him she's moved on, and has a boyfriend. The news hurts, but he knows that's as it should be. Their attraction is palpable; they can barely keep their hands off each other.

Finally they give in and kiss passionately, in "Revelations." Xander sees them, and he and Faith try to kill Angel. Angel has retrieved the Glove of Myhnegon, and Mrs. Post, the false Watcher, dupes him into beginning the ritual that she needs to harness its power. Faith tries to kill him, but he proves his goodness by saving Willow from a fiery death.

Then, in "Lovers Walk," Buffy starts talking about going away to school. Of course the notion is agony to Angel, but he manages to encourage her "as a friend." But when it's time for honesty, it's Spike who provides it, reminding them they aren't just friends.

Buffy hears him.

> **ANGEL:** "I wondered when you were coming."
> **BUFFY:** "I'm not coming back."
> [He takes this in. Maybe it's not a total shock, but it still feels like a body blow.]
> **ANGEL:** "There must be some way we can still see each other."
> **BUFFY:** "There is. Just tell me you don't love me."
> [He is silent.]   —"LOVERS WALK"

In "The Wish" Angel tells a cynical, battle-toughened Buffy that he waited for her. That he was supposed to help her.

Even across dimensions, Angel loves Buffy.

Angel doesn't know why he was released from Hell and brought back to this dimension. In "Amends" his past haunts him—literally—in the form of the many he murdered, and of the loved ones his victims, left behind to grieve. Jenny Calendar taunts him, tempting him to make love to Buffy so that he will become evil again. It's what he was born for, built for: evil.

In this moving version of *A Christmas Carol,* he reviews his life and finds nothing redeeming about it. Buffy's faith in him saves him; the miraculous Christmas snow saves him. But still evil attacks him; in "Enemies" Faith tries to tempt him into sleeping with her to lose his soul. When that doesn't work, a shaman pretends to do the job. Buffy is forced to watch Angel as he was when he was Angelus: lustful, cruel, and hateful. It hurts her, and she needs a break.

Yet they can't stay apart; they keep telling themselves they'll stay friends, or find a way to be together. Even the Mayor tells them like it is:

> **MAYOR:** "Well, I wish you kids the best, I really do. But if you don't mind a bit of
>   fatherly advice, I, well, gosh, I don't see much of a future for you two. I don't sense a
>   lasting relationship, and not just because I plan to kill the both of you. You have a
>   bumpy road ahead."
> **BUFFY:** "I don't think we need to talk about this."
> **MAYOR:** "You kids, you don't like to think about the future, don't like to plan. But
>   unless you want Faith to gut your friend like a seabass, you'll show a little respect
>   for your elders."
> **ANGEL:** "You're not my elder. I've got a lot of years on you."
> **MAYOR:** "And that's just one of the things you're going to have to deal with. You're
>   immortal. She's not. It's not easy. I married my Edna Mae in aught three and I was
>   with her right until the end. Not a pretty scene. Wrinkled and senile and cursing me
>   for my youth. It wasn't our happiest time."
> [Buffy and Angel both stare steely-eyed at the Mayor, neither admitting that he is making sense. He moves slowly toward Angel.]
> **MAYOR:** "And let's forget the fact that any moment of true happiness will turn you
>   evil. What kind of life can you offer her? I don't see a lot of Sunday picnics in the
>   offing. Skulking in the shadows, hiding from the sun—she's a blossoming young
>   girl! You want to keep her from the life she should have till it's passed her by, and

67

by God I think that's a little selfish. Is that what you came back from Hell for? Is that your higher purpose?"
—"CHOICES"

Then Buffy's mother pays Angel a visit and says essentially the same thing. Angel finally finds the strength to do what he must. He is determined to leave after the Ascension, if they survive. Buffy is dashed, and he knows it. He can't help it.

But at the last moment, he goes to her prom, to take her in his arms one last time. After all, it's a big night for her.

The Ascension comes. The Mayor transforms. But Angel, Buffy, and the entire senior class prevail. And that means…Angel must leave. He must let Buffy go.

Angel leaves for Los Angeles where he sets about atoning, helping the hopeless. He does return to Sunnydale when he feels that Buffy is in trouble, such as in "Pangs." It is extremely painful for him to watch her from afar, never touching her, never letting her know he is there. But once he is sure she is safe, he melts away in the shadows again.

He isn't quite as subtle in "The Yoko Factor." After he and Buffy exchange words (and blows) in Los Angeles, he comes to Sunnydale to apologize. He finally meets Buffy's new love, Riley "I don't like him" Finn and they do come to blows. Significantly, he does not appear at all in Buffy's dream in "Restless." It appears that the Slayer has been able to seal him away in a private place in her heart…in essence, to lay her demon to rest.

Angel is played by David Boreanaz.

QUOTABLE
ANGEL

"Good to have the taste of a Slayer back in my mouth. It's like cigarettes, you know? Just when I thought I quit…"
—TO FAITH, IN "ENEMIES"

"Oh, it is good to be back in Sunnydale. Nice climate, plenty to eat, no tortured humanity to hold me down…"
—PSYCHING FAITH OUT, IN "ENEMIES"

"Will you dance with me?"
—ANGEL TO BUFFY, IN "THE PROM"

"You actually sleep with this guy?"
—RE: RILEY, IN "THE YOKO FACTOR"

XANDER: "One moment's happiness."
RILEY: "What about it?"
XANDER: "It's his trigger. Angel's an okay guy—so long as he's mopey and sad and brooding. But give him even one second of pure, real pleasure . . ."
RILEY: "And that sets him off."
XANDER: "Only in the big old kill-your-friends kind of way. And you know what makes Angel happiest? Give you a hint: It's not crème brulee."
—"THE YOKO FACTOR"

QUOTABLE
BUFFY-ANGEL

"I can't watch you die again!"

—BUFFY, IN "THE ZEPPO"

BUFFY: "That was…well, it was very artistic."

ANGEL: "Yeah . . . ."

BUFFY: Not quite what I'd expected. I'd never actually seen—well, from the title I thought it was about food."

ANGEL: "There was food . . . ."

BUFFY (remembering): "Right. The scene with the…the food. Do you feel like getting some hot chocolate? Or some cold shower?"

ANGEL: "I'm sorry. I wanted to take you out somewhere fun. It's been a while since I've been to the movies. They've changed."

BUFFY: "Little scary. [Angel nods.] And a little not, which is also scary.

[She has stopped, turned to him.]

BUFFY: "I'm just sorry to get you worked up like that. We can't do any of that stuff; you'd lose your soul, and besides, I don't even <u>own</u> a kimono."

ANGEL: "Buffy, you don't have to worry about me."

BUFFY: "I just don't like to rub your nose in it. [perplexed] Suddenly wondering where the phrase comes from . . ." —ENEMIES"

ANGEL: "I saw you called. It was a bright afternoon, out in front of your school, you walked down steps and I loved you."

BUFFY: "Why?"

ANGEL: "Because I could see your heart. You held it before you for everyone to see and I worried that it would be bruised or torn. More than anything in my life I wanted to keep it safe, to warm it with my own."

BUFFY: "That's beautiful. [a moment, as he holds her] Or, taken literally, incredibly gross."

ANGEL: "I was just thinking that too."

—"HELPLESS"

ANGEL: "Oh. And…Riley?"

BUFFY: "Yeah."

ANGEL (nods): "I don't like him."

—"THE YOKO FACTOR"

ANGEL: "You still my girl?"

BUFFY: "Always." —"ENEMIES"

69

Oz (Daniel Osbourne)

For years, Oz has been the definition of cool and composed. He's the lead singer of a cool band. His sweet girlfriend adores him. He's so cool that Xander holds him up as the standard:

XANDER: "But I mean, what is it? How do you get it? Who doesn't have it? And who decides who doesn't have it? What is the essence of cool?"

OZ: "Not sure."

XANDER: "I mean you yourself, Oz, are considered more or less cool. Why is that?"

OZ: "Am I?"

XANDER: "Is it about the talking? You know, the way you tend to express yourself in short, noncommittal phrases?"

OZ: "Could be."

XANDER: "No. No. It's the guitar thing. You're in a band, that's like a business class ticket to cool with a complimentary mojo after takeoff. I should play an instrument. Is it hard to play guitar?"

OZ: "Not the way I play it."

XANDER: "Okay, but on the other hand, eighth grade I'm taking flugelhorn and getting zero trim, so the instrument thing could be a mislead. But you need a thing. One thing nobody else has. What do I have?"

OZ: "An exciting new obsession—which I feel makes you very special."   —"THE ZEPPO"

But life is actually far more complicated for Oz. The lead singer of Dingoes Ate My Baby has not only failed senior year at Sunnydale High School, but failed to inform Willow, his girlfriend, of that fact. (Not even Xander or Buffy flunked a year of high school.)

Oz's big moments in his second senior year was times of stress and crisis. In "Beauty and the Beasts" he may have escaped his cage and horribly killed someone. Only the discovery that the ravaging monster kills in daylight gives him an alibi. But while he's under suspicion, he can hardly look Willow, the love of his life, in the eye.

Then, in "Lovers Walk," that love is betrayed. He and Cordelia come upon Willow and Xander in a passionate embrace. As he later says of it, "The thing is . . . seeing you with Xander, it was . . . well, I never felt that way before, when there wasn't a full moon."

Though he does reconcile with Willow, he keeps the physical relationship at bay a little longer, wanting them to be together only when neither has anything to forgive or prove.

But no one can mistake his evenness for unfeeling. When Willow is captured by the Mayor and Buffy and Wesley square off over a possible course of action, Oz settles the matter without words—by destroying the spell ingredients Wesley had hoped to use at Willow's expense.

Heading toward graduation, and the Ascension, Oz finally loses his cool, panicking as only he can: he and Willow make love. He leads a regiment of students in the fight against the Mayor's vamps, pauses a moment to reflect on their surviving high school, and moves on to college at UC Sunnydale with the appearance of no worries.

Obviously Oz's big fear is keeping—or failing to keep—control of his werewolf nature. In "Fear, Itself," when Gachnar, the fear demon, exploits everyone's deepest terror, Oz begins to change. But not only to change—to threaten Willow.

Given his intense love for Willow, it is doubly shocking when Oz falls for Veruca, a female werewolf at UC Sunnydale. She brings up a dilemma for Oz, which perhaps he's never before considered:

VERUCA: ". . . Maybe you want to pretend you're just a regular guy."

OZ: "I am. I'm only a wolf three nights a month."

VERUCA: "Or you're the wolf all the time, and your human face is just your disguise. Ever think of that?"   —"WILD AT HEART"

Oz mates with Veruca, twice, and cannot deny the animalistic attraction between the two of them.

When Oz decides the only thing to do is leave Sunnydale, he says:

> **"Veruca was right about something. The wolf is inside me all the time. And I don't know where the line is anymore, between me and it. Until I figure out what that means, I shouldn't be around you. Or anybody."**
>
> —OZ, IN "WILD AT HEART"

Oz leaves his beloved Willow. He searches the world for a cure to his werewolf's curse. He finally stays with some Tibetan monks, who teach him how to meditate, to keep his inner cool. He also takes "some herbs and stuff, some chanting, couple charms" ("New Moon Rising"). He returns to show Willow he can remain human during the night of a full moon.

He's learned how to soothe the savage beast.

But when he discovers that he has a rival in Tara, he loses his cool and does transform. In daylight he nearly kills Tara before the Initiative Commandos bring him down.

Willow—his beloved little Pez Witch—has a choice to make. And she makes it. She chooses Tara.

Oz leaves again, and no one knows if he will ever return. Willow still dreams of him; in "Restless," he appears to whisper with Tara when Willow is revealed as the same insecure person she was when Buffy first came to Sunnydale. But Tara holds the star role in her dream . . . and in everyone else's.

Oz is played by Seth Green.

QUOTABLE
OZ

WILLOW (proudly): "Oz is a werewolf."
BUFFY (to Faith): "Long story."
OZ: "Got bit."
BUFFY: "Apparently not that long."
　　　　　—"FAITH, HOPE, & TRICK"

WILLOW: "You came to visit me! [puzzled] You came with books." (brightening) "Are they books for me?"
OZ: "Actually, they're kind of for me."
WILLOW: "I don't get it."
OZ: "Well, it's sort of a funny story. [as they start up the hall] You remember when I didn't graduate?"
WILLOW: "Well, I know you had a lot of incompletes, but that's why you had summer school."
OZ: "Yeah. Remember when I didn't go?"
　　　　　—"ANNE"

> "Oz does not eat people. It's more, werewolf play. You know—I bat you around a little bit. Like a cat toy. I have harmless wolf fun. Is it Oz's fault that, you know, side effect, people get cut to ribbons and maybe then he takes a little nibble and I'm not helping, am I?"
>
> —THAT'D BE A NO, XANDER, IN "BEAUTY AND THE BEASTS"

> "Cordelia wished for something? If it was a long and healthy life, I think she should get her money back."
>
> —IN BIZARRO SUNNYDALE REALITY, IN "THE WISH"

> "There's something about you that's causing me to hug you. It's as if I have no will of my own."
>
> —HUGGING WILLOW, IN "DOPPELGANGLAND"

WILLOW: "Arrr! This is so frustrating!"
OZ "Nothing useful."
WILLOW: "No, it's great. If we want to make ferns invisible or communicate with shrimp, I've got the goods right here."
OZ: "Our lives are different than other peoples'."
> —"GRADUATION DAY, PART ONE"

WILLOW: "Oh, who am I kidding? I'm never gonna find a spell to stop the Ascension. I'm no witch; I can't even change poor Amy back to a person."
OZ: "But you got the swinging Habitrail goin'…I think Amy's in a good place emotionally."
> —"GRADUATION DAY, PART ONE"

CORDELIA: "Okay, well, I personally don't think it's possible to come up with a crazier plan."
OZ: "We attack the Mayor with hummus."
[a beat]
CORDELIA: "I stand corrected."
OZ: "Just keeping things in perspective."
> —"GRADUATION DAY, PART TWO"

OZ: "It was stupid to think you'd just be waiting."
WILLOW: "I was waiting. I feel like some part of me will always be waiting for you. Like, if I'm old and blue-haired and I turn a corner in Istanbul and there you are—I won't be surprised. Because you're with me—you know?"
OZ: "I know. But now's not that time."
WILLOW: "No. [then] What are you going to do?"
OZ: "I think I'd better take off."
WILLOW: "When?"
OZ: "Pretty much now."
> —AS OZ PREPARES TO LEAVE AGAIN, "NEW MOON RISING"

Riley Finn

Riley Finn is Buffy's boyfriend at UC Sunnydale, whom she gets together with after her disastrous "nonrelationship" with Parker Abrams.

His appearance in the Season Four opening script is described: "RILEY FINN is a junior, tall and good looking, with an open, honest face." Later, however, Buffy refers to him as a psych grad student, which is more in keeping with his true identity as a member of the military's elite.

There is no immediate sparkage between Riley and Buffy when they first meet. In fact, Willow captures his attention because of her intelligent questions about Dr. Walsh's psychology class, once he tells the girls he's the prof's teaching assistant.

Riley's relationship with Buffy grows gradually. When next seen in "Fear, Itself," he's friendly toward her, but nothing more. He's concerned about the downturn in her work and makes a casual attempt to offer her a sounding board about her life as a freshman. He also says something that will become a recurring theme with him:

> **"Look, I may be out of line here; it's not my business, but you seem like the kind of person who makes things really hard on themselves."**

Part of Riley's appeal is that he's optimistic. He's not a soulful brooder like Angel, or the falsely introspective Parker. Riley expects to make a difference. He's honest, straightforward, and patriotic. He's from Iowa. A nice, normal guy for a girl who's never had a boyfriend who's nice and normal. He strives to be the gentleman his father taught him to be. But he's also clever and composed, and he has the same kind of wry self-awareness that's a hallmark of Buffy's nearest and dearest.

Riley's stock continues to grow, but Buffy still doesn't think of him as boyfriend material. In "Wild at Heart" he saves Willow from being hit by a car, and Buffy murmurs, "Thank you. I was too far away…" implying that she, too, is a rescuer of people. He's direct and used to being in charge, suggesting to Buffy that she take Willow back to their dorm.

The first turning point in his relationship with Buffy comes in "The Initiative." Quizzed by Forrest, he finally concedes that yeah, Buffy's a hottie, then punches Parker out for being crude about his one-night stand with her. It finally dawns on him that he likes her, so in true Riley fashion, he goes on recon to find out how to woo her. "Work hard, apply yourself, get it done," is his motto, but when he sees her at a party at his frat house, he chokes.

We also learn in "The Initiative" that Riley is not all he seems: He's much, much more. Joe Regular by day, and a demon-hunter by night. Not only that, but a leader of demon-hunters:

[Riley takes center, speaks with total authority. Gone is the goofy, lovable college boy. This is SPECIAL AGENT FINN.] —SCRIPT NOTES FROM "THE INITIATIVE"

The sparks fly, figuratively, as Riley tries to persuade Buffy to leave a campus bench while the rest of his team searches for Hostile 17 (AKA Spike). As she accuses him of being Teutonic and tells *him* to shoo, they both leave in opposite directions when they hear a scream for help. Then later he unknowingly engages her, under smoky conditions, in fierce hand-to-hand combat, which ends in a draw. He must report to his C.O.—none other than Dr. Maggie Walsh—that Hostile 17 has an accomplice who's smart and aggressive.

But Riley does score a definite victory: The next day, he and Buffy meet up as civilians, very boy-meets-girl, and girl is definitely liking boy.

Girl even invites Riley to Thanksgiving, except he's going home to Iowa. His family always gets together at his grandparents' farm. There are dogs and walks by the river, and he clearly loves it.

He's helpful and open-minded, gently joking about being a lesbian when he helps the on-campus lesbian group with their banner. And he's disarming, admitting to Buffy that he practices the conversations he has with her because she's "tricky." And a mystery, and a beautiful girl.

He's unaware that a picnic in daylight is a different kind of first date. And he really doesn't know what to make of her joyful announcement that she's marrying some guy named Spike. Nor what to do about her amusement when she tells him that she was only joshing about getting married. So, though insane, she is still single....

In "Hush" Riley finally kisses Buffy, deeply and lovingly, during the crisis of silence. Their feelings about each other are revealed. Then later, when they come upon each other battling the Gentlemen, his secret is revealed...as is hers. Both of them are warriors in the battle against evil.

Awkwardness ensues. For all his demon-fighting, Riley has never heard of the Slayer. Even Dr. Walsh thought the Chosen One was a myth. Buffy has an easier time figuring out that Riley works for the government, but she raises enough questions about the mysterious "314" that even the solid soldier begins to question what's going on.

The key issue, however, is that Riley figures he and Buffy are a perfect match. But Buffy's hopes of having a nice, normal boyfriend are once again dashed. She asks for time, and he has no choice but to give her some space. But when she starts telling him they can't be together because "things fall apart" in her world, he has absolutely no use for her brand of doom and gloom. To Riley's chagrin, he pushes her too far.

But when she and he team up to save the world, she relents, and by "A New Man," they are very much a couple. He begins to realize the extent of her abilities. He doesn't mind that she's stronger than he is, nor that she's used to being in charge. He relishes it.

Eagerly he persuades Maggie Walsh to admit Buffy into the secret world of the Initiative. He and Buffy make love for the first time. Things are going well for Agent Finn.

Until he discovers that Maggie Walsh has tried to kill Buffy. And now Maggie is dead. "She was our mother," the monster Adam tells Riley. In Riley's case, figuratively; in Adam's, literally.

Riley's simple world of good and evil, black and white, changes forever. Shaken to his core, he suspects Buffy of having killed Dr. Walsh. He goes into severe withdrawal from the drugs Dr. Walsh was feeding him to turn him into a supersoldier. In a downward spiral, he loses control of himself and nearly shoots a civilian. After he's wounded, he's taken to a military hospital, clinging to Buffy's scarf as a symbol of his love for her. She is the one reality he can hold on to.

His relationship with Buffy is jeopardized when he unknowingly sleeps with Faith who is in Buffy's body and tells her he loves her. Buffy understands that he didn't know, but the damage is done. It takes Jonathan, in his fantasy capacity as God's gift, to untangle Buffy's confusion.

Riley and Buffy become obsessed with each other, manifesting the repressed sexual energy festering in Riley's frat house. And then more barriers between them are broken down, in "New Moon Rising," as Riley discovers there are still more gray areas in life…and Buffy can finally unburden herself to him about her past.

Riley Finn is played by Marc Blucas.

QUOTABLE
RILEY

"So, are you girls taking Intro Psych, or do you just want me dead?"

—"THE FRESHMAN"

"I'm sorry. I've forgotten my manners in all the concussion. I'm Riley."

—"THE FRESHMAN"

BUFFY: "How's your head?"
RILEY: "Fine. It just stung for a bit and I lost most of my basic motor functions. No biggie."

—"THE FRESHMAN"

RILEY: "These spells—they really work? I mean, can you really 'turn your enemies inside out?' Or 'learn to excrete gold coins?'"
ANYA: "That one's not so much fun."

—TRYING TO UNDO JONATHAN'S AUGMENTATION SPELL, IN "SUPERSTAR"

ANYA: "Alternate realities are neat."
XANDER: "You know what I'll always remember?"
RILEY: "Well, the swimsuit calendar's sticking in my mind. [off Buffy's look] Not in a good way."

—AFTER RETURNING FROM JONATHAN'S REALITY TO THE PROPER ONE, IN "SUPERSTAR"

BUFFY: "Then why with the crazy?"
RILEY: "Because I'm so in love with you I can't think straight."

—"THE YOKO FACTOR"

75

Spike

Spike came back to Sunnydale in Season Three's "Lovers Walk," drunkenly howling for Drusilla. He was devastated because Dru had left him *without* bothering to kill him. He kidnaps Willow to force her to make a love spell for him; then he takes Xander along for good measure. If Willow doesn't come up with a successful spell, he'll kill Xander.

While gathering supplies for the spell, Spike mocks Buffy and Angel for thinking they can be friends. With their help, he fends off a "welcoming committee" of vampires sent by the Mayor. Finally he has an epiphany:

"I'm glad I came here, you know? I been all wrongheaded about this.
Weeping, crawling, blaming everybody else. I want Dru back, I just have to

be the man I was. The man she loved. I'm gonna do what I shoulda done in the first place. I'll find her, wherever she is...and I'll tie her up and torture her until she likes me again...."

—SPIKE, IN "LOVERS WALK"

In "The Harsh Light of Day" Spike reappears in Sunnydale again on the outs with Dru. He's looking for the fabled Gem of Amarra. He's also picked up a new girlfriend: Harmony Kendall, who was changed during the battle at graduation.

His relationship with her is as twisted as the one he had with Dru, but in a different way:

HARMONY: "And if my heart's not beating, what are all these blue veins for? I'm simply covered in these blue veins. See?"

[Coquettishly, she traces a vein on her chest to where it disappears under her nightie. Spike looks at it hungrily, then traces it with his tongue. Harmony giggles. Spike rolls on top of her and pins her arms against the mattress. He licks along another vein. When he comes up for air:]

SPIKE: "We've got an extra set of chains."

HARMONY: "Eww. Just because Dorcas went in for that kind of stuff..."

[He grabs Harmony's hair, pulls her head back viciously.]

SPIKE: "Drusilla."

HARMONY: "Whatever."

[They're both getting excited.]

SPIKE: "Say her name."

HARMONY: "Dorcas."

SPIKE: "Bite your tongue."

HARMONY: "Do it for me."

[He crushes her mouth with his.]   —"THE HARSH LIGHT OF DAY"

Spike finally digs into the crypt where the gem is supposed to be buried. Harmony accidentally puts it on; she starts prattling endlessly about "sodding France," and Spike stakes her in frustration. Miraculously she heals. When she realizes what he's done, she tears off the ring and throws it at him, sobbing.

Emboldened by the powerful gem, Spike finds Buffy and taunts her. In broad daylight they have a knock-down, drag-out fight. He's too cocky by half—she grabs the ring off his finger; he starts to burn, and jumps to safety in a sewer entrance.

Spike then goes to Los Angeles to try to retrieve the gem (Buffy has sent it to Angel). He fails, and returns to Sunnydale (in "Wild at Heart") to exact revenge on Buffy.

But that's when things get very weird for Spike: he's captured by the Commandos and imprisoned inside the Initiative complex. He blames Buffy and swears he will get back at her for this. He manages to break out and escape. This causes enough concern at the Initiative that the Commandos begin to sweep-search for him. The fact that he knows they exist makes him very dangerous. Otherwise, they've rendered him harmless: They've put a chip in his head that creates tremendous pain if he tries to harm a human being. He learns this the hard way when he tries to bite Willow, in "The Initiative." He doesn't know what's happened to him, only that he can't harm her.

> **SPIKE:** "I don't understand. This sort of thing's never happened to me before."
> **WILLOW:** "Maybe you were nervous. You're probably just trying too hard. Doesn't this happen to every vampire?
> **SPIKE:** "Not to me, it doesn't!"

In "Pangs" Spike is wandering, hungry and alone. He returns to his lair, only to be thrown out by Harmony. She's been reading, she informs him, and he was mean to her. So out he goes.

He finds refuge (not that they want to give it to him) at Giles's apartment during the Thanksgiving feast preparations. He convinces them he's harmless. When the gang is attacked by Hus, the avenging spirit of the Chumash Indians, Spike is shot through several times. When it's over, Buffy tells him he can have gravy, as that has blood in it.

Spike realizes that his survival depends upon his ability to dole out just enough information about the Initiative to live another night...rather like a demonic Scherezade. Buffy is fast losing patience with him...until Willow conjures a spell in "Something Blue." Magickally, Buffy and Spike get engaged. They're two crazy kids, wildly in love.

Spike drinks blood through a straw (in a coffee mug that reads KISS THE LIBRARIAN) and gets hooked on soap operas. He moves in with Xander, then tries to stake himself out of desperation. In "Doomed" he realizes he can beat up demons. He's ecstatic. He gets to hit something. Anything evil. But when Giles suggests that this is a sign that Spike work for the side of good, Spike laughs at him. Renewed, he moves out of the basement and into a crypt, while staying out of the Commandos' way.

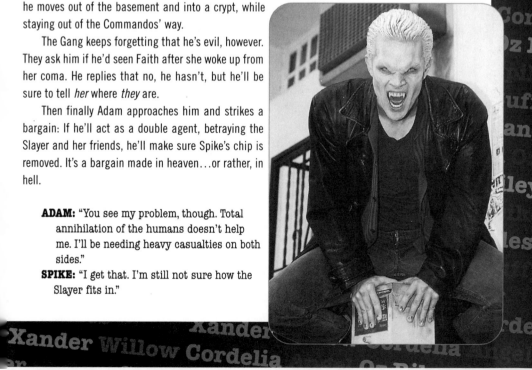

The Gang keeps forgetting that he's evil, however. They ask him if he'd seen Faith after she woke up from her coma. He replies that no, he hasn't, but he'll be sure to tell *her* where *they* are.

Then finally Adam approaches him and strikes a bargain: If he'll act as a double agent, betraying the Slayer and her friends, he'll make sure Spike's chip is removed. It's a bargain made in heaven...or rather, in hell.

> **ADAM:** "You see my problem, though. Total annihilation of the humans doesn't help me. I'll be needing heavy casualties on both sides."
> **SPIKE:** "I get that. I'm still not sure how the Slayer fits in."

ADAM: "The humans need a leader. A champion. The Slayer can do that—can even the odds. And she holds influence over Riley."

SPIKE: "Yeah. Thing about the Slayer is, she's a whiny little thing, but when it comes to fighting she does have a slight tendency to win."

ADAM: "Then I guess you should be on her side."

[Spike smiles.]

SPIKE: "This all goes down, the chip comes out, yeah? No tricks?"

ADAM [holds up hand]: "Scout's honor."

SPIKE: "You were a Boy Scout?"

ADAM: "Parts of me." —"THE YOKO FACTOR"

He manages to split the group apart, then realizes that by keeping Willow away from Buffy, Buffy won't receive the information he and Adam have planted that will entice the Slayer down into the Initiative. Poor Spike—Adam turns on him ("Hey, you're supposed to be so smart, and you let *me* plan this thing?") and Spike is forced to flee for his life. Again.

Along the way he rescues Giles, Willow, and Xander from a demon as they're performing the Enjoining Spell.

XANDER: "You probably just saved us so we wouldn't stake you right here."

SPIKE: "Well, yeah. Did it work? Well, then, everything's all right and we all get to be not staked through the heart. Good work, team!" —"PRIMEVAL"

Spike appears in "Restless" in conjunction with Giles. He tells Xander that Giles is going to teach him to become a Watcher; Giles says Spike's been like a son to him. Later, he vogues in scary vampire poses to make money. The puppy's still at the vet's, but he really likes to show his teeth and growl.

Spike is played by James Marsters, and he became a cast regular in Season Four beginning with "The Initiative."

- -

QUOTABLE
SPIKE

BUFFY: "What's the matter, Spike? Dru dump you again?"

[Buffy punches.]

SPIKE: "Maybe I dumped her."

[Spike punches back.]

HARMONY: "She left him for a fungus demon. It's all he talks about most days."

—"THE HARSH LIGHT OF DAY"

"Listen to me, you stupid bint. This gem is everything. I came back to Sunnydale for it. A place which has witnessed some truly spectacular kickings of my ass. Now, when I have the Gem, they all die, don't worry, but until then, stay inside. And, by the way, I would be insanely happy if, from this point on, I heard bugger all about sodding France!"

—SPIKE, TO FRANCO-PHILE VAMP HARMONY, IN "THE HARSH LIGHT OF DAY"

SPIKE: "Remember last year? You had on that fuzzy pink number with the lilac underneath. . . ." [nods knowingly]

WILLOW: "I never would have guessed. You play the blood-lust kind of cool."

SPIKE: "I hate being obvious. All fang-y and 'grrr.' [shrugs] Takes the mystery out."

— "THE INITIATIVE"

"Got to hand it to you, Goldilocks, you do have bleedin' tragic taste in men. I've got a cousin, married a regurgitating Frovlax demon, has better instincts than you."

— COMMENTING ON SECRET-AGENT MAN RILEY, IN "GOODBYE IOWA"

"You feel smothered. Trapped like an animal, pure in its ferocity, unable to actualize the urges within. . . . Clinging to one truth like a flame struggling to burn within an enclosed glass. . . . That a beast this powerful cannot be contained. Inevitably it will break free and savage the land again. I will make you whole again. Make you savage."

— ADAM, CHEERING SPIKE UP, IN "THE YOKO FACTOR"

"Say someone was to risk his life and limb—well, limb, anyway—to obtain said files, might be worth a little something..."

— SPIKE, NEGOTIATING WITH GILES, IN "THE YOKO FACTOR"

"Oh, who's the puffed-up manly man? All multicolored and possessive?"

— AND MORE OF THE NEEDLING, "WHERE THE WILD THINGS ARE"

"There's a plan. She's working solo, she won't have a chance to come after us when the wild rumpus begins. Plus it'll make her miserable, and I never get tired of that."

— SPIKE, PLOTTING WITH ADAM, IN "THE YOKO FACTOR"

79

Giles

In Seasons Three and Four, Giles is a man undergoing a search for identity. First he was fired from the Watchers Council; then he stayed on in an unofficial capacity to help Buffy—and because he had a job; now he has no job, and Buffy needs him less and less.

As Season Three opens, he is a Watcher who has spent the summer looking for his Slayer. Despite his assurances to Buffy's mother, he's obviously very worried about her. He follows each lead, no matter how minute. In a burst of honest anger Joyce reveals to him that she blames him for Buffy's disappearance—and for her slaying, too. From Joyce's point of view, he essentially took Buffy from her and ordered her to keep her life a secret from her own mother. While Giles can dispute the actual substance of Joyce's accusations, he cannot deny their tenor: he feels a heavy weight of blame for Buffy having run away.

The relationship between Buffy and Giles is very much one of child and parent. Her first concern when she goes to see Giles is whether or not he's angry with her. Just as her mother tries to persuade Snyder to admit her back into school, so does Buffy's surrogate father, taking it one step further and actually threatening the principal.

While Joyce cannot penetrate Buffy's defenses about running away (and in fact, focuses on the pain it caused her, not Buffy), Giles finds a way. By pretending to need information about Acathla, prodding ever so gently, at just the proper moments, he makes it possible for Buffy to unburden herself of the secret that she killed the restored Angel. Then, and only then, can she move on.

Giles, not Buffy's mother, waits for the outcome of her campaign to become Homecoming Queen. In "Band Candy" Giles and Joyce consummate their quasi-relationship as Buffy's "parents," and Buffy sees the rough, Cream-listening youth who became her Watcher. When Buffy's friends nail her for keeping Angel's return a secret, she can deal with their anger, and rather blithely ignores their concerns, until Giles privately voices his feelings:

> **"I won't remind you that the fate of the world often rests with the Slayer. What would be the point? Nor shall I remind you that you have jeopardized the lives of everyone you know by housing a known murderer. But sadly I must remind you that <u>Angel tortured me</u>. For hours. For pleasure. You should have told me he was alive. You didn't. You have no respect for me, or the job I perform."** —"REVELATIONS"

According to the script: "Buffy has nothing to say. She walks out, gutted." Giles's disapproval is the worst punishment she could have been given.

In "Helpless" it's Buffy's eighteenth birthday. Her biological father has bailed on their traditional trip to the ice show. Meanwhile, Giles has been ordered by the Watchers Council to secretly give Buffy a drug which temporarily takes away her powers. There is a time-honored tradition of putting a weakened Slayer through a trial by combat—essentially—to make her an even better Slayer. He must watch while she agonizes over what might be wrong with her. When the insane vampire she was to face escapes and kidnaps Joyce, Giles can no longer keep his terrible secret. Buffy is understandably shocked at this awful betrayal.

Perhaps even more shocking is that the Council fires Giles for telling her. The leader, Quentin Travers, puts it this way:

> **"Your affection for your charge has rendered you incapable of clear and impartial judgment. You have a father's love for the child and that is useless to the cause."** —"HELPLESS"

Giles does not leave her. Against the orders of the Council and the requests of the new Watcher—Wesley Wyndam-Pryce—Giles stays in Sunnydale and continues to guide Buffy.

While Joyce is the one to make Angel see that he must let Buffy go—a very parental moment—Giles is present at all her senior milestones. He is at her prom. It is he who hands her her signed diploma in the Season Three finale.

But now Sunnydale High School has blown up, and Giles has no job. In the beginning of Season Four, he is a "gentleman of leisure"—which, Buffy and company assume, is British for "slacker." He has time to jog, celebrate Halloween, and "entertain" an old flame, Olivia. In "The Freshman," when Buffy comes to him for help, he says:

> **"Officially, you no longer have a Watcher. Buffy, you know I will always be here when you need me. Your safety is more important to me than anything. But you are going to have to look after yourself. You're out of school now, and I can't always be there to guide you."**

Giles's little girl is growing up. But she insists that Thanksgiving dinner be at his house, as he is "the patriarch," and when she is bewitched into falling in love with Spike in "Something Blue," she asks Giles to give her away.

But on Buffy's nineteenth birthday Giles is only a guest at her surprise party. He didn't even know she had a boyfriend (Riley) until they're introduced. Since she speaks so often about Dr. Walsh, Giles goes to visit her:

GILES: ". . . Buffy isn't the typical student. Once you got to know her, you'd find out she's a very unique girl. I hope you're not going to push her too—"
MAGGIE: "I think I do know her. And I have found her to be a unique woman."
GILES: "Woman. Of course. How wrong of me to choose my own word."
MAGGIE: "She's very self-reliant, very independent..."
GILES: "Exactly—"
MAGGIE: "Which is not always a good thing. It can be unhealthy to take on adult roles too early. What I suspect I'm seeing is a reaction to the absence of a male role model."
GILES: "The absence of a—"
MAGGIE: "Buffy clearly lacks a strong father figure."
GILES: "I . . . I . . . I . . . "
MAGGIE: "I'm sorry. I have things to do. I'll tell Buffy her friend was looking for her."
—"A NEW MAN"

Giles subsequently discovers that Riley is a Commando, and that Dr. Walsh is in charge of all the Commandos. Buffy apologizes, saying she "forgot" to tell him. As Willow puts it, "He's feeling all neglected and out-of-the-loop-y."

Depressed Giles is lured out on the town with his ex-friend, Ethan Rayne, who turns Giles into a demon. Buffy believes that this demon is the demon who killed Giles, and she hunts him down with a special brand of hatred she hasn't shown before. As she stabs him with a (luckily) pewter letter opener—a silver one would have killed him—she realizes that he's Giles.

GILES: "How, how did you know it was me?"
BUFFY [quietly]: "Your eyes. There's only one person in the world that can look that annoyed with me."
—"A NEW MAN"

As the gang continues their various developments, Giles, too, has a year of personal growth. From the appearance of his long-distance girlfriend Olivia in the Season Four opener, "The Freshman," through his gig as a guitarist-singer at the coffee house in "Where the Wild Things Are," the stuffy Brit of the show's premiere is gone.

All of these searches for meaning and purpose come to a head in "The Yoko Factor," when a double-dealing Spike causes a rift between Slayer and ex-Watcher by telling Giles that he's useless to Buffy's work, and that Buffy knows this. Again, Giles seeks solace in drink, but he rallies when the gang realizes they've all been had by Spike. He rappels into the Initiative with Buffy, Xander, and Willow, and is an integral part of the empowering spell they perform to help Buffy defeat Adam.

Giles's "Restless" dream seems to be about making choices regarding his future. His girlfriend pushes a baby stroller; Buffy is his childlike charge. He reminds the others that he has a gig of his own, and even tells the First Slayer that the reason she doesn't know any better than to consider Buffy's friends as a valid source of power is because she never had a Watcher of her own. Is he really going to teach Spike to be a Watcher—or perhaps some other version of a fighter for the bright side? Only time will tell.

Giles is played by Anthony Stewart Head.

. . . .

QUOTABLE
GILES

"Unbelievable ... [as Joyce] do you like my mask? Isn't it pretty? It raises the dead! [himself] Americans!"

—GILES, IN "DEAD MAN'S PARTY"

BUFFY: "This is a bad time."
GILES: "You keep saying that."
BUFFY: "Well, it looks pretty bad! I think someone has just a little too much free time on their hands."
GILES: "I'm not supposed to have a private life?"
BUFFY: "No. Because you're very, very old and it's gross."
GILES: "Well, before I succumb to the ravages of age, why don't you tell me what brings you here." —"THE FRESHMAN"

"Buffy, I've been awake all night. I know I'm supposed to teach you self-reliance, but I can't leave you out there to fight alone. The hell with what's right! I'm ready to back you up. Let's find that evil and fight it together." —"THE FRESHMAN"

GILES: "Don't taunt the fear demon."
XANDER: "Why? Can he hurt me?"
GILES: "No, it's just...tacky."

—"FEAR, ITSELF"

BUFFY (to Willow): "I need you a lot. You're great with, with the computer. Usually."
GILES: "Right you are. And I'm great with the pacing and the saying of 'hmmm' and 'ahhhhh' and 'Good Lord.'"

—"THE YOKO FACTOR"

GILES (trying not to cry): "She was...truly the finest of all of us."
XANDER: "Way better than me...."
GILES (sadly nodding): "Much, much better."

—GRIEVING OVER WILLOW, WHO'S NOT DEAD, IN "DOPPELGANGLAND"

Parker Abrams

Parker is Buffy's first crush at UC Sunnydale. Gentle and seemingly introspective, he appears to be the kind of guy who would understand her loneliness and confusion. This is how he is described in "Living Conditions":

> [Buffy turns and finds herself staring up into the dreaminess that is PARKER ABRAMS. He's a few years older, very sweet and smart. And he makes girls go gaa-gaa with his eyes. Buffy tries to play it cool, despite the fact that she's a tad awed.]

Parker shields her from her roomie, Kathy, whom she is trying to avoid at all costs. He also explains the intricacies of squirreling away as much food as possible when going through the cafeteria line. Soon they're spending lots of time together.

Their conversations are deep and soulful, and Buffy shares a few secrets with him, such as the fact that she drowned. Talk of death leads to talk of seizing the moment, and Buffy does.

As soon as Buffy goes to bed with him, he dumps her and moves on. As Riley says in "Beer Bad," Parker "sets 'em up and knocks 'em down." But he does it so charmingly and without guile that Buffy can't quite bring herself to believe it's really over between them. She thinks he may have intimacy problems tied to the death of his father. But she finally has to admit the truth:

> **"It's just...Parker's problem with intimacy turns out to be that he can't get enough of it."** —BUFFY, TO XANDER, IN "BEER BAD"

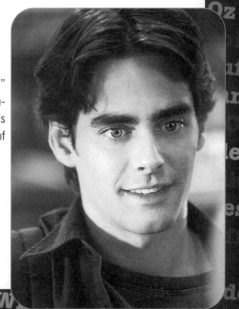

Even Willow is a bit taken in by Parker in "Beer Bad," though she has his number from the beginning of their conversation. She chastises him for hurting Buffy, and it seems at first that he is repentant as he explains to her the joys of casual sex:

> **"Some relationships center on a deep emotional tie or...a loyal friendship or something. But most are just two people passing through life, enriching or aggravating each other's lives briefly...just for one night."**

Can't two people who feel an attraction come together and create something wonderful? And then, go back to their lives the next day, better for it, but never overanalyzing it or wanting it to be more than it was?"

Ironically, Buffy has been daydreaming about Parker soulfully apologizing to her and asking for her forgiveness. CaveSlayer Buffy rescues him from the Grotto after the Cro-Magnon "Black Frost" beer drinkers have set it on fire. Once they're safe, Parker does apologize, using the exact same wording Buffy imagined he would. But her response this time is to grunt and bop him on the head with a club. "Parker...bad."

Parker Abrams is played by Adam Kaufman.

Larry Blaisedale

Larry, the gay football player who credits Xander with helping him come out of the closet, makes his first appearance of the third season in "Anne." In "The Wish" he has a substantial role alongside Oz as one of Giles's brave vampire hunters in the alternate reality willed into being by Anyanka.

Back in Sunnydale's normal reality, Larry's so grateful to Xander for helping him admit that he's gay that he tries to persuade Xander to do the same. Unfortunately, his courage proves the undoing of him during the battle at graduation...or does it? Larry's ultimate fate is not clear-cut. It's possible that he's survived to fight another day.

Larry is played by Larry Bagby, III.

Anya Emerson

Anya first appears in "The Wish" as Anyanka, the vengeance demon. Giles destroys her power center—her amulet—and her superiors—D'Hoffryn in particular—refuse to change her back. Anya is stuck in Sunnydale as a mortal.

"**For a thousand years I wielded the power of the wish. I brought ruin upon the heads of unfaithful men. I offered destruction and chaos for the pleasure of the lower beings. I was feared and worshipped across the mortal globe and now I'm stuck at Sunnydale High! A mortal! A child! And I'm flunking math.**" —"DOPPELGANGLAND"

Anya lies to Willow about her necklace, saying it's a family heirloom, and asks her to help her get it back with a magick spell. But something goes awry, and instead, the evil Vamp Willow who lived in the alternate reality of "The Wish" appears.

Anya now is stuck in this reality without her powers, so she begins to make adjustments. For one thing, she invites Xander to the prom. She regales him with tales of her exploits, including making men's heads explode and "parts fall off." She also shares with the others all she knows about the Ascension, having lived through one, including the fact that she, for one, is getting out of town as fast as is ex-demonically possible.

But she reappears in Season Four ("The Harsh Light of Day"), energetically ready to seduce Xander so she can get him out of her mind. Unfortunately, her plan doesn't work. So she and Xander begin dating. Their first date: the haunted frat house in "Fear, Itself." When Xander tells her to wear something scary, she shows up in an enormous pink bunny suit, because bunnies scare her.

Anya's lack of discretion makes for many diverting moments. When she announces that she has "three K-cards" in poker, Xander and Willow glumly fold. When Willow mentions that Buffy has a spanking-new boyfriend, she answers, "Yes, we've enjoyed spanking." Thanksgiving is "a ritual sacrifice. With pie." Olivia is Giles's "orgasm friend." ("Yes, that's exactly the most appalling thing you could have said.")

Thus far, Anya has been primarily an adjunct to Xander. She helps in rituals but does not initiate much action. Though she is not one of the Core Four (Xander, Willow, Buffy, and Giles), her appearance in "Restless" shows that she is much on everyone's minds, and has begun to be a character independent of Xander—viz., "Where the Wild Things Are" and her standup routine in "Restless"—and accepted as part of the new group (Though the Anya in Xander's "Restless" dream says she's thinking of getting back in the vengeance business....)

Anya is played by Emma Caulfield.

QUOTABLE
A N Y A

ANYA: "I'm eleven hundred and twenty years old! Just give me a friggin' BEER!"
[Beat.]
WAITER: "I.D."
ANYA: "Give me a Coke."
—"DOPPELGANGLAND"

"I'm just so tired of being around humans and all their baggage, I don't care if I ever get my power back. I think he should eat you."
—TO WILLOW, RE: A HUNGRY VAMPIRE, IN "DOPPELGANGLAND"

"Vampires. Always thinking with your teeth."
—IN "DOPPELGANGLAND"

ANYA: "I can't stop thinking about you. Sometimes in my dreams you're all naked."

XANDER: "Really? You know, if I'm in the check-out line at the Wal-Mart, I've had that same one."

ANYA: "So I can assume a standing Friday night date and a mutual recognition of prom night as our dating anniversary?"

XANDER: "Anya, slow down. In fact, come to a screeching halt."

— "THE HARSH LIGHT OF DAY"

ANYA: "At which point the matter is brought to a conclusion with both parties satisfied and able to move on with their separate lives and interests. To sum up, I think it's a workable plan."

XANDER: "So—so—so—the crux of this plan is…"

ANYA: "Sexual intercourse. I've said it like a dozen times."

XANDER: "Uh-huh. Just working through a little hysterical deafness here."

— "THE HARSH LIGHT OF DAY"

GILES: "This is rather like an activities room we had back at public school. One time I got up to a bit of a prank with the dartboard—"

ANYA (to Xander): "I'm bored. Let's eat."

XANDER: "Anya! We talked about this."

ANYA (to Giles): "I'm sorry. That was rude. Please continue your story. I hope it involves treacle and a headmaster."

— "A NEW MAN"

XANDER: "It happens that I'm good at lots of things! I help with all kinds of…stuff. I have…skills, and stratagems. I'm very…" (to Anya) Help me out."

ANYA (to Spike): "He's a Viking in the sack."

— "THE YOKO FACTOR"

"I've been keeping close tabs on cultural trends—a lot of men being unfaithful—very exciting things happening in the scorned women market. I don't wanna be left out."

— IN XANDERS DREAM, IN "RESTLESS"

Faith

In the mythology of the *Buffy* universe, when one Slayer dies, another is Chosen. At the end of Season One, Buffy was technically dead until Xander revived her with CPR. This activated Kendra, a Slayer who arrived in Sunnydale only to find her predecessor alive. They joined forces against Angelus, Spike, and Dru, and Kendra was killed.

The death of Kendra activated Faith. When the evil vampire Kakistos murdered her Watcher in front of her, Faith hightailed it to Sunnydale to look up the other Slayer. Breezing into town in "Faith, Hope & Trick," she lies to Buffy and Giles, saying that her Watcher went to the annual Watchers Retreat in England. Buffy's friends and her mother—and even her potential boyfriend, Scott!—are drawn to Faith. She's flirtatious and friendly, and has "rather a lot of zest," as Giles remarks. She tells exciting stories about her exploits. Everyone chalks up Buffy's concern about her to a mild case of jealousy. But Faith is also wild and undisciplined, and more than a little crazy. When she's fighting, she launches into a bloodlust that clouds her thinking and, on more than one occasion, puts Buffy at risk for her life.

She's also filled with self-condemnation for allowing her Watcher to be brutally murdered, right before her eyes. And it's not until she teams up with Buffy that she's able to destroy the murderer, the ages-old vampire, Kakistos.

Joss Whedon has been quoted as saying that Faith is Buffy's shadow self. Faith is what Buffy might have become, if she hadn't had friends and family to support her. Faith dropped out of high school. Her mother was trailer-park trash who wouldn't even let her have a puppy.

She doesn't trust men, insisting they're all animals out for the chase. In fact, she hardly trusts anybody, but she's game to be a good guy. It is she who risks her life to take down the wolfy Oz with a tranquilizer gun in "Beauty and the Beasts." When Scott Hope bails on Buffy just before Homecoming, Faith humiliates him in front of his date.

In "Revelations" she and Buffy have obviously become a team, working as partners to slay a bunch of vampires. They joke about the new Olympic category, "synchronized slaying." Faith tells Buffy about her bad luck with guys, and the fact that she's "a loser magnet."

When Faith's new Watcher arrives, she gives Faith her full attention—something Faith hasn't had in quite some time. She's furious, and deservedly so, to learn that Buffy's been shielding Angel. She doesn't hesitate to do what she thinks is right, which is to take the dangerous vampire out. But Faith's been hoodwinked by Mrs. Post, and Angel proves to be a good guy. Which goes to show what she's said all along—you can't trust people.

Buffy keeps reaching out to Faith. In "Amends" Faith is invited to Christmas with the Summers. She brings presents and ends up taking care of Joyce while Buffy leaves to deal with Angel.

Faith is hard because her emotional wounds have scarred her, but she's far from healed. Like Buffy, she's an unconventional Slayer, and like Buffy, she's honest. She loves slaying. She loves the battle. It makes her hungry and horny…something Buffy's never owned up to. Faith is sure she's going to win each time she goes up against an enemy…a positive attitude Buffy should adopt, Joyce tells her.

In "The Zeppo" she's part of the gang, fighting demons. She connects with Xander, having sex with him after he rescues her. She's aggressive but not too friendly.

Then things go terribly wrong. In "Bad Girls" she accidentally kills the Deputy Mayor. This is a direct violation of the Slayer's code. Buffy's devastated, but Faith goes more deeply into her shell, insisting she doesn't care. Sometimes the innocent get hurt or killed…but what's one life compared to the thousands they've saved?

Buffy's conscience won't let her rest. But Faith insists that because Slayers are different, they are better. Moreover, they are above the law. Buffy reaches out to her, as does Xander. She nearly kills him. The taste of killing is in her mouth now. Imprisoning her in a sort of intervention, Angel tells her she's got to let it go, or it will turn her into a monster. He knows whereof he speaks.

She is on the verge of trusting him, opening herself up to the possibility of redemption just a crack, when Wesley and his henchmen capture her. Her last remnant of trust is completely shattered, and Faith goes over to the dark side—she becomes the Mayor's personal Slayer.

He showers her with the attention and affection she has craved. She responds, doing everything he requires of her, including betraying her erstwhile friends. When she believes that Angel has turned bad and is going to help her torture Buffy to death, she unloads: Buffy is always the center of everyone's universe, even if Faith is the one who saves someone. Buffy is the good one, the decent one. While she, Faith, is trash.

The Mayor doesn't think so. And the good opinion of someone so evil propels Faith to commit more brutal crimes for him. She nearly kills Willow and Wesley, and she's looking forward to the Ascension, when the Mayor will put her at his right hand.

Then she poisons Angel to distract Buffy, and it turns out that the blood of a Slayer is required to save him. Draining a Slayer, in point of fact. She and Buffy square off. Their fight is long and brutal, and Buffy wins. She stabs Faith who escapes by jumping off the roof and ends up in a coma.

But even unconscious, Faith and Buffy share a bond. They communicate via dreams, and she tells Buffy how to defeat the Mayor.

> **"You wanna know the deal? Human weakness. It never goes away. Even his."**
> —"GRADUATION DAY, PART TWO"

By enraging him over her, Faith's, condition, Buffy defeats him in his new demon form.

In "This Year's Girl," when she awakens from her coma months later, none of her faith in humanity is restored: The Mayor, the only person who ever really cared for her, has left her a video and a device that will help her survive. But Buffy, who tried to kill her in order to save Angel, has moved on, and has a new boyfriend now. Buffy never came to visit her. No one did. They all conveniently forgot about her....

At the end of "This Year's Girl" she uses the Mayor's gift to switch bodies with Buffy. She discovers what it's like to have people genuinely and honestly care for her. To feel gratitude from someone whose life she's saved. To have tender love made to her by Riley, who tells her that he loves her...believing that he's said it to Buffy, of course.

It's too much for Faith. When she and Buffy battle, and she returns to her own body, she leaves town in a state of confusion. Things are not as she had assumed. She's not sure they ever were.

She arrives in L.A., where Angel and Wesley are helping the helpless....

Faith is played by Eliza Dushku.

QUOTABLE
FAITH

"How come Faith was a no show? I thought the mucussy demons were her favorites." —XANDER, IN "THE WISH"

"It's like fun, only boring."
—ON TRAINING AND TESTING, IN "DOPPELGANGLAND"

COP: "Now spread 'em!"
FAITH: "You wish."
COP: "Hands in the air where I can see 'em. Slow. Good. [to the other cop] Cuff 'em."
[The other cop begins cuffing the girls.]
FAITH: "I like him."
[She gives him a big, sexy wink.]
FAITH: "He's butch." —"BAD GIRLS"

WESLEY: "My. She's...cheeky. Isn't she?"
FAITH: "First word, jail, second word, bait."
—DISCUSSING CORDY, IN "CONSEQUENCES"

ANGEL: "You can't imagine the price for true evil."
FAITH: "Yeah? I hope evil takes MasterCard."
—"CONSEQUENCES"

WILLOW: "Competition is natural and healthy. And you'll definitely ace her on the psych tests. Just don't mark the box that says, 'I sometimes like to kill people.'"
BUFFY: "I know Faith isn't exactly on the cover of Sanity Fair, but she's had it rough. Different circumstances, that could be me."
—DISCUSSING SLAYER TESTING, IN "DOPPELGANGLAND"

GILES: "Nonetheless, keep watch. Faith has you at a disadvantage, Buffy."
BUFFY: "'Cause I'm not crazy or 'cause I don't kill people?"
GILES: "Both, actually."
—"GRADUATION DAY, PART ONE"

BUFFY: "There's no way around it. Faith is back, and like it or not, she's my responsibility."
WILLOW: "Yeah, too bad. [sighs] That was the funnest coma ever."
—"THIS YEAR'S GIRL"

Forrest

Forrest is Riley's second-in-command and one of his closest confidantes. He and Riley went through training together, but Forrest has always been second-best to the stellar Agent Finn. Like Riley, Forrest is also masquerading as a college student who lives at Lowell House. In his debut in "The Initiative" he is described:

[Riley is half-listening to his pal FORREST, an athletic-looking sophomore, who drops the suave guy talk.]

Forrest is uncomfortable when Buffy is admitted into the Initiative, and jealous when Riley gives her precedence on

missions. When Dr. Walsh is discovered killed, he assumes Buffy did it. In "Who Are You" he confronts her (although she is really Faith), telling her, in so many words, to give Riley some breathing room.

Forrest is concerned that the soldiers involved in the Initiative stick together as a family. Initially he refuses to allow Riley to leave the hospital, backing down only when Graham shows his support for Riley. And in "New Moon Rising," when Riley tries to help Oz escape, Forrest throws him in the brig. Their friendship is clearly over. From now on, Forrest and Riley are fighting on opposite sides. Though Buffy tried to save Forrest, Adam kills him in "The Yoko Factor," and rebuilds him into a demonoid in "Primeval." Riley realizes he must destroy him, and he does.

Forrest is played by Leonard Roberts.

· ·

Graham

Graham, Forrest, and Mason make up the small cadre of soldiers in Riley's circle. Usually acting as a strong, silent backup, Graham's loyalty lies with Riley, rather than the military. When the chips are down or the situation is ambiguous, Graham picks Riley every time. He is described in the stage directions in "The Intiative":

> [And a very fully loaded tray hits the table as GRAHAM joins the guys. Graham, a muscle-y mountain of a senior, sits, adjusts, and shovels forkloads of food in his face.]

Attacked by a wolflike creature in "New Moon Rising," Graham later fights with the Initiative against Adam. He survives to fight another day.

Graham is played by Bailey Chase.

· ·

Scott Hope

After Buffy returns to Sunnydale in Season Three, she catches the eye of Scott Hope. Scott wanted to ask Buffy out during junior year, but "you weren't ready then," Willow tells Buffy. But Scott is ready, and he makes a couple of attempts at connecting with her before he's successful. Just when it appears that they're finally connecting, Buffy panics at the sight of a friendship ring he wants to give her—a claddagh, like Angel's.

ANGEL

BUFFY

CORDELIA

XANDER

OZ

WILLOW

SPIKE

GILES

TARA

ANYA

RILEY

FAITH

"I see any more displays of testosterone poisoning...

...I will personally put you both in the hospital." —**BUFFY**

PRIMITIVE: "No...friends...just the kill...we are...*alone*."
BUFFY: "That's it. I'm waking up."

Eventually they do go out. Scott becomes her boyfriend, to the extent of in-school smoochies, but the two are "pre-posy."

Buffy and Scott bond when two of his friends tragically die: Pete, a rageaholic, beats his girlfriend, Debbie, to death. However, Angel's returned from Hell, and Buffy's heart still belongs to him. Scott senses that something is amiss with their relationship and breaks up with her even though they've just decided to go to the Homecoming Dance together.

Buffy is seriously disappointed, but rallies sufficiently to go for his sympathy vote when she runs for Homecoming Queen. And Faith, who at this point is still friendly with Buffy, commits a little private act of revenge on B.'s behalf when she sees Scott with another date at the dance.

("Scott, there you are honey. Good news—the doctor says the itching and the swelling *should* clear up, but we gotta keep using the ointment.")

In the script for "Faith, Hope & Trick," Scott is described as "nice guy senior."

Scott Hope is played by Fab Filippo.

● ●

Harmony Kendall

Harmony used to be one of Cordelia's Cordettes. In Season Three, she is still a mean, stuck-up airhead. In "The Wish," word gets out around Sunnydale High that "Queen C" Cordelia Chase's lame boyfriend, Xander Harris, has cheated on her. Cordy's stock plummets. This gossip is too delicious, and Harmony goes for the juglar. She embarrasses Cordy in front of their gaggle of friends, sarcastically suggesting that Jonathan Levenson is just the "stallion" to take Cordelia's mind off of "the temporary insanity that was Xander Harris." Harmony is a leading contender for Cordelia's crown as Queen of Mean. As the school year ends:

> **HARMONY:** "I hope we don't lose touch."
> **WILLOW:** "No. We'll hang out!"
> **HARMONY:** "Bye!"
> [She goes as Buffy approaches, having witnessed the exchange.]
> **WILLOW:** "Oh, I'm gonna miss her."
> **BUFFY:** "Don't you hate her?"
> **WILLOW** (with the same affectionate, wistful tone): "With a fiery vengeance. She picked on me for ten years, the vacuous tramp."
> —"GRADUATION DAY, PART ONE"

Harmony fights for her school (and her life) in the battle of Graduation Day, but ends up being bitten by vampires.

In "The Harsh Light of Day," Harmony, now a vampire, attacks Willow—unsuccessfully—and leaves with a parting shot: she's gonna get her boyfriend to beat up Willow for her.

Harmony's boyfriend is none other than Spike, who has returned to Sunnydale in search of the Gem of Amarra. To Spike, Harmony is petulant and demanding; she loves to push Spike's buttons, and—perhaps worst of all—baby-talks to him in front of other demons. However, as the script continues, "Life with Harmony has its kinky upside."

She has no sense of discretion, blabbing about the Gem to Buffy, telling her that Dru dumped Spike for a Fungus Demon. Later, when Harmoy prattles about going to France, it's too much for Spike: he stakes her. However, much to both of their shock, she does not dust. She's clearly, unwittingly, wearing the Gem of Amarra. When Harmony realizes what Spike has tried to do to her, she tears off the ring, throws it at him, and runs off, sobbing. She sums up her predicament when Giles, Willow, and Oz close in on her, demanding to know where Spike is, and if he has the Gem.

> **"He staked me and he took it. Tried to take it right off my finger. Like I wouldn't have just given it to him? I'd've given him anything he wanted. He was my platinum baby and I loved him."** —"THE HARSH LIGHT OF DAY"

The Initiative captures Spike. After he escapes (and tries to kill Willow) he returns to the lair:

[A vampire's lair. HARMONY unrolls a unicorn poster on the wall. Admires it. Hears a noise. Stops. Turns. Sees Spike, standing in the entrance, trying to look contrite.]
HARMONY: "Spike? Spike, is that really you?"
SPIKE: "It's me, baby. Your man is..."
[She slaps him hard across the face. He takes it.]
SPIKE: "...back."
HARMONY: "Bastard! You dumped me and staked me and hurt me and left me and..."
SPIKE: "I know, sugar, but you're forgetting one other thing I did.[sugary] I missed you." —"THE INITIATIVE"

But Spike's on a mission: he wants to kill the Slayer. And Harmony is finally fed up:

HARMONY (to Xander): "Can you believe him? Comes back with all these big promises, not that I believed him, but he could have spent one night. But no, everything was 'slayer this' and 'slayer that.' He probably already killed her but still I'm not taking him back. I just want to see why it is men always..."
[Harmony turns to see Xander is gone.]
HARMONY: "... leave." —"THE INITIATIVE"

Spike tries to pull off another reconciliation, because he's starving, but this time, Harmony has raised her consciousness—she's been reading self-help and she's not falling for his smooth talk again.

This time she stands firm.

Harmony is played by Mercedes McNab.

Jonathan Levenson

Scripted in as "the ubiquitous Jonathan" in "Dead Man's Party," Jonathan has increased in stature from his lowly days as "Student," "Freshman," and "Hostage Kid" in the early episodes of *Buffy* to guest starring in "Superstar." Often overlooked and/or mocked, Jonathan is the quintessential unpopular kid, and in pain because of it. It all becomes too much for him to handle, and he tries to commit suicide in "Earshot." Buffy stops him, and it is he who delivers the moving speech when she is honored as Class Protector at the prom.

Jonathan holds his own during the battle at graduation. He lives to fantasize another day in "Superstar," making it clear that while he did seek counseling after the events of "Earshot," perhaps he still needs to work on separating fantasy from reality. However, his relationship advice to Buffy, both as a superstar and as Jonathan, is crucial in getting her and Riley back on track after Faith, in Buffy's body, seduces Riley. And super-Jonathan does provide the necessary info—about Adam's power source—that the gang needs to defeat Adam. Proving that Jonathan—in any reality—has his place.

Jonathan is played by Danny Strong.

Devon MacLeish

Devon, the lead singer for Oz's band, Dingoes Ate My Baby, used to date Cordelia, as well as Harmony Kendall. He's at Buffy's house when the zombies invade in "Dead Man's Party" and he announces the names of the two Homecoming Queens in "Homecoming." He's looking for roadies in "Doppelgangland." (Angel refuses his offer.)

Since Oz continues playing with the Dingoes, Devon's still part of his world, appearing in "The Harsh Light of Day" when the Dingoes play at the Bronze, and sending Oz his stuff when the guitarist leaves school.

Devon is played by Jason Hall.

Olivia

Olivia is a long-distance girlfriend of Giles who's getting reacquainted with him now that he's job-free.

She is described in "The Freshman as" fairly striking, black, somewhat younger than Giles but old enough to see Buffy as nothing more than a child.

She's known him since his "Ripper" days, although she never believed all his talk of demons and dark forces—until she's in Sunnydale when the Gentlemen go on the rampage. After that experience, she's not certain she can continue in a relationship with Giles. When she reappears in his dreams in "Restless," she is Giles's pregnant wife or significant other…though he seems oblivious to her presence as he first follows the childlike Buffy, then chases his own thoughts as he tries to piece together the mystery of the First Slayer. Will she return to Sunnydale to stay?

Olivia is played by Phina Oruche.

Ethan Rayne

It seems that at least once a year, Ethan Rayne comes to town to foment chaos—which he worships. Ethan is an old sorcerer friend of Giles's, from the dark days in London.

In "Band Candy" he helps Mr. Trick and the Mayor distract the adults of Sunnydale from vigilance by turning them all into teenagers with magic chocolate bars. And in "A New Man" he poisons Giles's beer and turns him into a demon.

However, Riley takes him into custody and tells Buffy he'll be sent to a secret facility in Arizona. Is this the last we'll ever see of Ethan? Highly doubtful.

Ethan Rayne is played by Robin Sachs.

Sheila Rosenberg

Sheila Rosenberg is Willow's mother. As seen in "Gingerbread," an intellectual who spends more time theorizing about adolescent behavior and writing papers on the subject than she does with her own daughter. It takes her months to realize Willow's cut her hair, and she calls Willow's best friend "Bunny." She also initially assumes that Willow's announcement that she's a witch is mere adolescent rebellion.

During the MOO crisis, she's brainwashed by the Hansel/Gretel demon and tries to burn Willow at the stake. But when the demon is destroyed, she moves back into denial about Willow's occult gifts. Yet there's a shred of hope that she will begin paying more attention to her only daughter: Willow tells Buffy that her mom has insisted that she invite Oz over for dinner so she can meet him.

In the script for "Gingerbread" Mrs. Rosenberg is described as "sweet and well meaning—but definitely of the woolly intellectual variety."

Mrs. Rosenberg is played by Jordan Baker.

Principal Snyder

Principal Snyder arrived at Sunnydale High School after Principal Flutie was devoured by hyena people. Universally despised by Buffy and her friends, he does nothing to change their feelings toward him when he refuses to readmit Buffy after expelling her at the end of Season Two. Joyce Summers discovers for herself what a "nasty little horrid bigoted rodent man" he is when she locks horns with him. His reputation precedes him when he forces Willow to tutor Percy West, the school basketball hero.

But Snyder is at heart a little Napoleon who can be bullied, and who wants to belong. When Giles goes into Ripper mode to physically threaten him, he's truly frightened. When he is transformed back into a teenager in "Band Candy," he's beyond geekdom—no surprise to Buffy, who had his number as the dateless wonder long before then.

Snyder's in thick with the Mayor and City Hall. Though he's content to cover up many of the nefarious doings in the town, he joins in the witch hunt during "Gingerbread."

He wigs when he assumes he's breaking up a drug deal late at night in the cafeteria, only to find the Mayor involved and holding a box of very weird spiders. From then on, Snyder is unnerved by the Mayor. It becomes apparent that he's unaware of the mayoral plans for transformation into an indestructible demon, and the ultimate destruction of Sunnydale as Snyder knows and hates it.) He persists in his fascist devotion to order until he breathes his last. He finally pushes too far when he chastises the Mayor, who has turned into an enormous demonic snake, for turning the graduation ceremony into chaos. In reply, the Mayor devours him.

Principal Snyder reappears once in Season Four, when Xander dreams about *Apocalypse Now*. Snyder takes the role played by Marlon Brando in the film (Colonel Kurtz). He reveals, no surprise, that he has little faith in the next generation.

Principal Snyder is played by Armin Shimerman.

Joyce Summers

Buffy's mother is slowly letting go of her child. In "Anne" she has spent the summer worrying constantly about her daughter. She's been afraid to leave the house for even a moment, in case Buffy should call for help. But when Buffy returns, the tension does not ease up, and Joyce is very sorry for it.

Joyce and Giles get together to compare notes on Buffy's time management in "Band Candy," going so far as to chastise her for playing them against each other—as children are wont to do to their parents. Extending the parental symbolism, Joyce and Giles consummate their relationship.

Joyce also mothers Spike when he's whining about his breakup with Dru, making him hot chocolate (with the little marshmallows) and lending him an ear. She tries to strengthen her mother-daughter connection with Buffy, going so far as to pack a snack for the Slayer one night on patrol ("Gingerbread"). But when she discovers the bodies of two dead children in the playground, she comes unglued.

The children are actually two halves of a demon that "thrives on fostering persecution and hatred among the mortal animals." They foster that inside Joyce, who forms Mothers Opposed to the Occult (MOO) and proclaims, at a candlelight vigil for the dead children:

> **"For too long [our town has] been plagued by unnatural evils. It's not our town anymore. It belongs to the monsters, to the witches and Slayers."**
> [That hits Buffy hard, to hear Slaying lumped in with what's wrong with Sunnydale.]
> —"GINGERBREAD"

After this crisis is successfully concluded, Joyce makes what amounts to a mother's plea to the man she thinks is wrong for her daughter, asking Angel to make the break with Buffy because she knows Buffy can't.

Buffy sends her mother out of town for graduation, knowing that if her mom stays, she will be too distracted to fight the Mayor with everything she has.

And then it's a new school year, and Buffy is a freshman at UC Sunnydale. When she can't hack it, she returns home...only to discover that her mother has turned her bedroom into a temporary storage compartment. She visits again in "Fear Itself" to have her Halloween costume resewn, and Joyce can't help a trip down memory lane.

When Faith arrives, she goes to Buffy's house and taunts Joyce, trying to make her see that Buffy doesn't care about her, hasn't even shown up to protect her, when Buffy smashes through a window and throws a casual, "Hi, Mom" at her mother. To which Joyce, equally casually, replies, "Hi, honey."

Mom and Slayer know what they're about...at least until the last episode of the season, "Restless," in which, in Buffy's dream, Joyce is living in the walls, making lemonade and playing Mah Jong (a stereotypical retirement pastime.) When Buffy frets that Joyce shouldn't be living in the walls, Joyce ventures that Buffy could probably break it down. But as she speculates this, Buffy has spotted Xander in the distance, and has already wandered off—leaving her mother behind.

Joyce is played by Kristine Sutherland.

Tara

Tara is a member of Willow's on-campus Wicca group. She and Willow notice each other right away as the only two people in the group who are actually interested in spell-casting. When the Gentlemen steal the voices of Sunnydale, Tara tries to enlist Willow's aid in a spell that will give back the power of speech. Before she can, she is pursued by the Gentlemen. She and Willow unite in moving a heavy vending machine through the use of magick alone. When they can speak to each other, Tara tells Willow that she's been practicing magick all her life—her mother was quite powerful.

They begin practicing together, and their bond strengthens. With Buffy becoming so involved with Riley and the Initiative, Willow has more time and attention to share with Tara. She begins staying over in Tara's room, lying to Buffy about where she's been, wanting to keep her new relationship her own private treasure.

But one discordant note creeps into this new friendship: When Willow casts a spell to reveal the presence of demons throughout Sunnydale, Tara secretly sabotages it. And she's also a little hurt that Willow hasn't introduced her to her friends…until Willow does, not sensing that Faith is wearing Buffy's body. Faith is cruel to Tara, taunting her about her stammer and her relationship with Willow. But Tara figures out that something's wrong, and it is through her efforts, combined once more with Willow's, that Buffy is ultimately rescued.

Then Tara herself is nearly killed, by the monster Jonathan creates in "Superstar." Willow is beside herself with fear and anger, and the gang is galvanized into action: Tara has become one of their own. She's included in the Slayerettes' discussions in "Where the Wild Things Are," and she joins in the exorcism of Lowell House.

The romantic nature of her relationship with Willow is underscored in "Where the Wild Things Are," when the house's sexual energy affects her negatively during an innocent conversation with Willow about horses. But it is in "New Moon Rising" that the seriousness of their relationship is revealed. Tara's worst worry comes true when Oz comes back to Willow. He's been able to control his werewolf transformations, and he's ready to try again. Tara assumes Willow will cast her aside.

But Willow chooses Tara, affirming that she's with the person she loves. Their relationship takes on new dimensions in "The Yoko Factor," as they're outed to everyone. In "Primeval," she and Willow are now a couple (depicted as such in the same way that Xander and Anya are, with Willow as the main character and Tara as supporting).

However, in "Restless," Tara is brought into the spotlight as a character with her own knowledge of the future, someone (or something?) apart from Willow, limned so that she stands on her own. What she knows remains a mystery as Season Four concludes.

Tara's first appearance in "Hush" is described:

[As the girls are talking, we focus on one girl in particular. TARA sits on the floor, making herself as small as possible. When she speaks, it is hesitantly, with a slight stammer. When she doesn't, she seems to watch Willow most of the time.]

Tara is played by Amber Benson.

. . . .

Mr. Trick

Mr. Trick is a vamp who comes to town in the company of Faith's nemesis, Kakistos. Urbane and witty, he's also a survivor: As soon as he figures Kakistos for the loser in a battle against the Slayers, he decamps.

Next, for pure enjoyment and financial gain, he organizes SlayerFest '98. Employing the latest in technology, Mr. Trick charges several hunters—not all of them human—to hunt Buffy and Faith. That sort of initiative impresses Mayor Wilkins, who "invites" Trick to become a member of his team. Trick obliges.

One of Mr. Trick's first assignments is to help the Mayor pay his tribute to the demon Lurconis. He subcontracts the job to none other than Ethan Rayne, who has been a thorn in Giles and Buffy's side before. And as usual, when a Slayer gets the upper hand, Mr. Trick seizes the better part of valor and runs away.

Mr. Trick's next assignment involves keeping a demon named Balthazar at bay. (The disgusting demon is an ancient enemy of the Mayor's.) Buffy does the work for him. Mr. Trick survives to fight another night, serving as astonished witness to the Mayor's newly gained invincibility.

His stock grows when he realizes that a Slayer killed the Deputy Mayor. Both he and the Mayor are eager to see Buffy and/or Faith arrested for murder, and Trick moves into devious plan mode. But things go awry when the Slayers see Mayor Wilkins and Trick together, and realize that the Mayor is a bad guy.

Mr. Trick tries to take them both down. In a battle on the docks, he's just about to get his fangs into Buffy when Faith saves her. She dusts Mr. Trick, who has time for one last witty remark before he explodes into dust.

> **TRICK** (leaning in to bite Buffy): "I hear once you've tasted a Slayer? You never wanna go back."
> [Buffy struggles, but is clearly lost. TRICK'S FANGS GRAZE HER NECK....But he suddenly STOPS. Eyes wide. A look of indignation crossing his features.]
> **TRICK:** "Oh. No. No, this is no good at all—"
> [And HE GOES TO DUST.] —"CONSEQUENCES"

In the script for "Faith, Hope & Trick," Mr. Trick is described as: "young (20s), easygoing, and deadly. Speaks quickly and mellifluously, all charm."

Mr. Trick is played by K. Todd Freeman

● ●

Dr. Maggie Walsh

Maggie Walsh, a world-renowned psychologist, is famous for her work in operant conditioning. She's also a professor of psychology at UC Sunnydale by day, and the scientist-in-charge of a secret government research facility by night. Though Riley refers to her as "quite a character," she is described somewhat differently in the stage directions for "The Freshman":

> [As Buffy takes her seat, Professor MAGGIE WALSH sweeps into the room. She is a down-to-earth, likable woman in her fifties. As smart as she is strong willed. She peers at her students a moment as they quiet down.]

She eventually takes a liking to Buffy for standing up to her when she is unyielding to a heartbroken Willow, but she's also a harsh taskmistress who accepts no excuses for anything but top-level

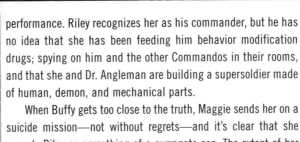

performance. Riley recognizes her as his commander, but he has no idea that she has been feeding him behavior modification drugs; spying on him and the other Commandos in their rooms, and that she and Dr. Angleman are building a supersoldier made of human, demon, and mechanical parts.

When Buffy gets too close to the truth, Maggie sends her on a suicide mission—not without regrets—and it's clear that she regards Riley as something of a surrogate son. The extent of her maniacal obsession with "the project" is revealed moments before her death, when she is muttering to herself that "no little bitch"—AKA Buffy—is going to jeopardize her years of effort.

Adam reanimates her to play her part in the creation of the new master race of demonoids, and the zombie Maggie comes at Buffy with the same whirring saw she was holding when she died the first time—an object that must signify bad luck for her, as the Slayer destroys her.

Maggie Walsh is played by Lindsay Crouse.

Mayor Richard Wilkins III

The Mayor of Sunnydale has been the mayor for a hundred years. He has paid tribute to numerous demons and dark gods in return for his power and long life. Though the chief of police and Principal Snyder alluded to cover-ups and conspiracies in Season Two, it's clear that Snyder, for one, had no idea that the Mayor had the long-range plan of becoming an indestructible demon-snake.

The Mayor debuted in "Homecoming." The script describes him thusly:

[As Allan talks, the Mayor takes the picture and we get our first good look at his face. It couldn't be more unassuming. One feels this man has not raised his voice in years, and although he is mild enough in demeanor, one hopes he won't.]

The Mayor is phobic about germs, and he doesn't like swearing. He is well connected to the demonic underground, and keeps tabs on the comings and goings of those who serve evil in his fair town. He has been aware of the Slayer—Snyder has reported in to him on a number of occasions about Buffy—but does not directly challenge her. When Mr. Trick initiates SlayerFest '98, the Mayor makes a point of contacting him. This is an important year for him, he tells Mr. Trick. He needs things to run smoothly.

His first assignment for his new vampire lieutenant is to find a way to distract the human denizens of Sunnydale so that His Honor can sacrifice four newborns to the demon Lurconis. Mr. Trick subcontracts the job to Ethan Rayne, and although Buffy thwarts them, she doesn't make the connection between Trick and the Mayor. She is still unaware of his evilness when he orders Deputy Mayor Allan Finch to take care of "the Spike problem" when the white-haired vampire plows into town and starts causing mischief. He appears only in his capacity as city father when Joyce forms Mothers Opposed to the Occult and holds a vigil at City Hall.

Finally, in "Bad Girls," the Mayor reveals his ultimate plan. After his dedication, he will be invincible for one hundred days. (His "To Do" list: "Greet Scouts, Plumber Union reschedule, call temp agency, become invincible"). After that, he will ascend to a higher plane—demonhood.

To ensure that all goes right, he needs to make sure both Slayers—Faith and Buffy—are out of the way. But there's another wrinkle—the followers of an old enemy of the Mayor's have come to town. It's Mayor Wilkins's understanding that the demon, Balthazar, was destroyed long ago. But just in case, he wants to make sure the Slayers go after Balthazar, not him—and that they and the demon kill each other. In the process, the deputy mayor is killed. However, the Mayor achieves his invincibility, and the "one hundred days" he has been talking about have officially begun.

Then, in "Consequences," Wesley orders the Slayers to investigate the murder of the Deputy Mayor. What he does not realize is that Faith is the killer. Mr. Trick and the Mayor, however, figure it out. The Mayor is delighted at the notion that one or both of the Slayers might be arrested and put away for Murder One.

As the Slayers pretend to investigate, however, they discover that Mr. Trick and the Mayor are in cahoots. This is the turning point, where Mayor Wilkins is finally uncovered as "a black hat." In a fierce battle Faith dusts Mr. Trick...and offers her services to the Mayor.

The Mayor becomes the father Faith never had. He truly dotes on her, giving her a lavish apartment and a Playstation. He lovingly admonishes her to drink her milk before she goes out to massacre his enemies.

He also gives her things to do, such as kill the demon that has the Books of Ascension and was offering to sell them to Buffy. Then he turns her loose on Angel, hoping she can seduce him so that Angel will lose his soul. When it's no go, he hires a shaman to do it.

It is at this point that Buffy and company figure out that the Mayor is more than a hundred years old. Also, that Faith is working for him. She spills the beans that he's going to transform into something that "might not have hands" on graduation day. But the Mayor pooh-poohs her worry that their plans are revealed and takes her miniature golfing.

Next, the Mayor sends Faith to retrieve the Box of Gavrok, required for his Ascension. Although Buffy and her friends manage to steal it, he captures Willow. A trade is made in the school cafeteria. He also gets to deal a severe blow to Buffy and Angel's hopes for their relationship, talking about his dead wife, Edna Mae. She hated him for never aging, and went to her grave cursing his name.

All seems well. Mayor Richard Wilkins is munching down the spiders inside the Box of Gavrok. His organs are shifting and merging, making way for his Ascension into a pure demon, not a hybrid such as walk the earth. Then he learns that Buffy has horribly wounded his Faith. Faith is in a coma, expected never to awaken. When the Mayor sees Buffy, also in the hospital, he attempts to kill her. Angel stops him, and rather than cause a scene, he leaves.

But finally the day arrives—graduation, and Ascension!

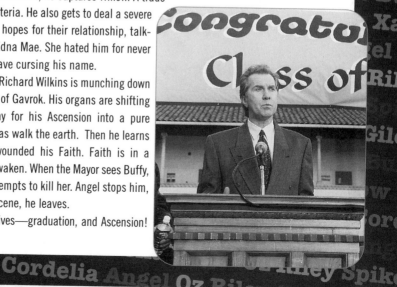

The Mayor has got an excellent speech about civic duty prepared, but as the sun is covered by a total eclipse, he cuts to the chase and changes into a huge snake-demon. After devouring the irritating Principal Snyder, he's distracted by Buffy, who taunts him with details of how she savaged Faith. Infuriated, he chases her, smashing the doors and walls of the school.

She lures him into the library, and Giles pushes the plunger: the entire school explodes, and the Mayor goes up with it.

He is destroyed.

But he has left a video for Faith, which she watches in "This Year's Girl," in Season Four. He explains that he has left her a device that will allow her to switch bodies with Buffy. It is the best he can do for the girl he has come to cherish and love as a daughter.

Mayor Wilkins is played by Harry Groener.

. . . .

Willy the Snitch

Willy is a double-dealing snitch who owns a bar frequented by demons, vampires, and low-life humans. Buffy and her friends have been pummeling information out of him for years. He has also been betraying them for years. He has a "spiritual experience" after some demons beat him up and nearly destroy his bar. He's classed up the joint; now it's "Willy's Place" and he's bought a deep fryer.

He does have a moment of the good when he tries to talk a drug-addled Riley from shooting an innocent customer. (Not that he has many innocent customers.)

Willy is played by Saverio Guerra.

. . . .

Wesley Wyndam-Pryce

Buffy's new British Watcher arrives in Sunnydale to less than a warm welcome. Gwendolyn Post, the evil Watcher who posed as Faith's new Watcher, has preceded him. And, of course, he's replacing Giles…or attempting to. Neither Buffy nor Faith will listen to him, although he "talks incessantly," according to the script of "Bad Girls."

The script continues: "Young, not bad looking, but a bit full of himself. Thinks he's Sean Connery when he's pretty much George Lazenby." He's book-learned in Watcher ways but lacking in experience, although he doesn't see himself that way. He's piqued, to say the least, at the way everyone pointedly ignores him.

When he and Giles are captured by the demon Balthazar, Wesley immediately caves and tells the demon everything he knows in order to save his life.

Nevertheless, Cordelia's quite taken with him, and he with her—despite the fact that she's a student, and not a teacher, as he first supposed.

When Faith kills the deputy mayor, Wesley takes matters into his own hands and informs the Council. His judgment and timing are both unfortunate, for just as it appears that Faith may open her heart to her friends, Wesley and his henchmen kidnap her. After she escapes, he takes responsibility for his error and offers his help in finding her.

However, he persists in his stuffy, by-the-book handling of the Slayers. Cordelia persists in finding him attractive. Under the pretext of asking him for help with her homework, she asks him out to dinner.

It comes to light that Wesley is beginning to unbend a little; he has not informed the Council that Giles is still in the picture. In fact, he begins to do Giles's bidding, rather than argue with him about who's in charge—until Giles excludes him from secret plans, such as Angel's pretending to lose his soul again. His crowning moment of authority comes when he overrules the gang's impulse to risk the lives of everyone in Sunnydale in order to save Willow (of course, they ignore him). At the prom, he cleans up nicely in a tux, and he and Cordelia make quite a pair.

He pushes Buffy too far, however, when the Council refuses to help cure Angel, and he stands by their rules. She quits the Council, leaving him nonplussed. And unemployed.

But when the chips are as down as they can be, Wesley rallies. He joins the fight to save Sunnydale without the backing of the Council. He also finally joins lips with Cordelia, and they discover, to their chagrin, that there's no real chemistry between them.

When last seen in Sunnydale, Wesley's being loaded into an ambulance after the graduation battle. He's begging for aspirin, or even to be knocked out, because he's in pain. But his "whining" is roundly ignored.

After this, he hits the road, imagining himself "a rogue demon hunter," eventually allying himself with Angel and Cordelia in Los Angeles, and is now a cast regular on *Angel*.

Wesley is played by Alexis Denisof.

QUOTABLE BIG NOISES:
AUTHORITY FIGURES

JOYCE: "But…you can't keep her out of school. You don't have the right."

PRINCIPAL SNYDER: "I have not only the right but also a nearly physical sensation of pleasure at the thought of keeping her out of school. I'd describe myself as tingly." —"DEAD MAN'S PARTY"

SNYDER: "I want you to tutor him. Percy is flunking history. Nothing seems to be able to motivate him."

PERCY: "Hey, I'm challenged."

SNYDER: "You're lazy, self-involved, and spoiled. That's quite the challenge. But we need a winning year, especially after last year's debacle with the swim team. Can't have our point guard benched."

—"DOPPELGANGLAND"

BUFFY: "So he threatened you? With what?"

WILLOW: "It wasn't anything exactly that he said. It was all in his eyes. I mean, there was some nostril work as well, but mostly eyes."

BUFFY: "Snyder needs me to kick his ass."

WILLOW: "Oh, no, Buffy, don't get yourself in trouble. I'll be okay. I just hate the way he bullies people. He just assumes their time is his."

GILES: "Willow, get on the computer. I want you to take another pass at accessing the Mayor's files."

WILLOW: "Okay." —"DOPPELGANGLAND"

GILES (to Wesley): "How did it go?"

WESLEY: "Faith…did quite well on the obstacle field. And her…reflexes are improving rapidly. Physically…[pointedly emphasized] she's in good shape. Still a little sloppy, though."

[He hands Giles a clipboard of times.]

GILES: "Do you feel up to taking Buffy out, or shall I?"

WESLEY: "No, I'll be fine. I just need a minute. And some difibulators, if it's not too much trouble." —"DOPPELGANGLAND"

THE MAYOR: "Now that Faith has brought you back, what are your intentions?"

ANGEL: "Well, gee, sir, I thought I'd find that Slayer who's giving you so much trouble and torture, maim, and kill her."

THE MAYOR: "Fine! Nice to hear you're not one of those 'slacker' types running around today." —"ENEMIES"

SNYDER: "I walked by your guidance counselor's office one time, a bunch of you were sitting there, waiting to be…shepherded, to be guided. You and the other problems, glassy-eyed, slack-jawed, I remember it smelled like dead flowers. Like decay, and it hit me, yes, that's what it is; the hope of our nation's future is a bunch of mulch."

XANDER: "You know, I never got the chance to tell you how glad I was you were eaten by a snake." —"RESTLESS"

QUOTABLE
HIGH SCHOOL LIFE

"How about home school? It's not just for scary religious people anymore."
—BUFFY TO JOYCE, IN "DEAD MAN'S PARTY"

"It's the freedom! As seniors we can go off campus now for lunch. It's no longer cutting, it's legal. Heck, it's expected. But also a big step forward, a Senior Moment.... "
—WILLOW TRIUMPHANT, IN "FAITH, HOPE & TRICK"

XANDER: "I hate that they make us take that thing. It's totally fascist, and personally, I think it discriminates against the uninformed."
CORDELIA: "Actually, I'm looking forward to it. I do well on standardized tests. [off their looks] What? I can't have layers?"
—DISCUSSING THE SATS, IN "BAND CANDY"

XANDER: "Oh, man. It's Nazi Germany and I have Playboys in my locker."
PRINCIPAL SNYDER: "This is a glorious day for principals everywhere. No pathetic whining about 'students' rights,' just a long row of lockers and a man with a key."
—"GINGERBREAD"

GILES: "This isn't over."
PRINCIPAL SNYDER: "Oh, I'd say it's just beginning. Fight it if you want—just remember: lift a finger against me, and you'll have to answer to MOO."
BUFFY: "Answer to MOO? Did that sentence make some sense that I'm just not in on?"
PRINCIPAL SNYDER: "Mothers Opposed to the Occult. A powerful new group."
BUFFY: "And who came up with that lame name?"
PRINCIPAL SNYDER: "That would be the founder. I believe you call her 'mom.'"
—"GINGERBREAD"

QUOTABLE
COLLEGE LIFE

105

XANDER: "What are these?"
WILLOW: "They're early-admission packets."
BUFFY: "Wow, Willow. Looks like early admission came early this year."
OZ: "Hence the name."
XANDER: "Harvard, Yale, Wesleyan, some German Polytechnical Institute whose name I can't pronounce... Is anyone else intimidated? Because I'm just expecting paper-thin slips with the words 'no way' written on them in crayon."
—"BAD GIRLS"

WILLOW: "'Images of Pop Culture.' This is good. They watch movies, shows, even commercials."
BUFFY: "For credit?"
WILLOW: "Isn't college cool?"
—"THE FRESHMAN"

Willow Cordelia
Cordelia Angel Oz Riley Giles Xander
Oz Riley
Xander
Willow
Oz Riley
Giles
lia Angel
Oz R

WILLOW: "It's my on-campus boyfriend!"
BUFFY: "Gee, I forgot to pick mine up. That line's probably really long now too."

—"THE FRESHMAN"

"Sorry, Miss 'I chose my major in play-group.'"

—BUFFY TO WILLOW, IN "THE FRESHMAN"

BUFFY: "I've been busy, you know? It's been a slay-heavy summer. I haven't had a lot of time to think about life at UC Sunnydale."
WILLOW: "It's exciting, though, huh?"
BUFFY: "Yeah. Gonna be an adjustment."
WILLOW: "Sure. It's like five miles away. Uncharted territory." —"THE FRESHMAN"

"I'm psyched for college, definitely. I'm just wondering how it's gonna work with my extracurricular activities. I've got to make sure it doesn't take the edge off my slaying."

—BUFFY, IN "THE FRESHMAN"

"It's just...in high school, knowledge was pretty much frowned upon. You really had to work to learn anything. But here, I mean, the energy, the collective intelligence, it's like this force, this penetrating force. I can feel my mind just opening up, you know, letting the place just thrust into it and...spurt knowledge... into...That sentence ended up in a different place than it started out in."

—WILLOW, IN "THE FRESHMAN"

RILEY: "I don't meet a lot of freshman that know that much about psychology."
WILLOW: "Well, it's fascinating."
BUFFY: "Yeah, 'cause, you know, everyone's got a brain...or, almost everyone."

—"THE FRESHMAN"

KATHY: "Are you excited for classes tomorrow?"
BUFFY: "Painfully."
KATHY: "I bet there's gonna be a lot of parties to go to this week, too. Not that I'm a crazy partier. And I'm not always this hyper, either. I'm just excited."
BUFFY: "Yeah. Me, too."
KATHY: "I'm really glad they put me with somebody cool. I can tell you're cool. I just know this whole year is gonna be super-fun!" —"THE FRESHMAN"

PROFESSOR RIEGERT: "You are sucking energy from everyone in this room. You are taking their time, their energy. They came here to learn. Get out."
BUFFY: "I didn't mean to...suck..."
PROFESSOR RIEGERT: "Leave!"

—"THE FRESHMAN"

EDDIE: "Did you, uh, lose your way?"
BUFFY: "No, no. I'm just heading to Fischer Hall. It's right, I know it's on the Earth Planet, I'm sure of that....['fessing up] Recently voted Most Pathetic, uh-huh."
EDDIE: "Well, I'm lost, and I have a map, so..."
BUFFY: "Oh! I come in second."

—"THE FRESHMAN"

SUNDAY: "Freshmen. Man, they're so predictable."
ROOKIE: "And you can never eat just one."

—"THE FRESHMAN"

BUFFY: "College is great."
XANDER: "Uh-huh. Once more with even less feeling."
BUFFY: "No, really. Willow's in heaven. Oz got this great off-campus house with the band—"
XANDER: "And you're sitting here alone at the Bronze looking like you were diagnosed with cancer of the puppy."

—"THE FRESHMAN"

BUFFY: "You freak of nature! Why didn't you call?"

XANDER: "I knew you guys were starting the whole college adventure and I didn't want to, you know, help you move."

—"THE FRESHMAN"

"This is so like them lately. It's all about them and the college life. You know what college is? It's high school without the actual going to class. Well, high school was sort of like that, too...."

—XANDER, TO ANYA, IN "THE YOKO FACTOR"

"Work with me here. I'm finally an essential part of your collegey life. No more 'looking down on the townie'— I'm the new bartender over at the pub. Got my lighter, my rag, my empathy face...."   —XANDER, IN "BEER BAD"

"I did actually attend university in the Mesozoic era. I do remember what it's like."   —GILES, WAXING NOSTALGIC, IN "WHERE THE WILD THINGS ARE"

"I'm Professor Walsh. Those of you who fall into my good graces will come to know me as Maggie. Those of you who don't will come to know me by the nickname my TA's use and don't think I know about: the Evil Bitch-Monster of Death. Make no mistake. I run a hard class. I assign a lot of work, I talk fast, and I expect you to keep up. If you're looking to coast, I recommend Geology 101. That's where the football players are."

—PROFESSOR MAGGIE WALSH, IN "THE FRESHMAN"

BUFFY: "I came to pick up today's assignments. I couldn't make it to class for personal reasons."

PROFESSOR WALSH: "Right. [looks her over] I count four limbs, a head, no visible scarring, so I assume your personal issue was not a life-threatening accident of any kind and am therefore uninterested. You got problems, solve them on your own time."   —"FEAR, ITSELF"

XANDER: "College not that scary after all, huh?"

BUFFY: "It's turning out to be a lot like high school. Which I can handle. You know, at least I know what to expect."

—"THE FRESHMAN"

QUOTABLE
FASHION

"It's a clothes fluke, and that's what it is, and there'll be no more fluking."

—XANDER, ON THE ALLURE OF PROM CLOTHES, IN "HOMECOMING"

"I've been looking for you. When we met this morning, I was like—thank God! There's one other person in town who actually reads W."

—ANYANKA, TO CORDELIA, IN "THE WISH"

CORDELIA: "The other part that totally weirded me out? That thing had good taste. I mean, he chucked Xander and went right for the formal wear."

XANDER: "That's right. He left behind his copy of Monster's Wear Daily."

—"THE PROM"

SPIKE: "I shrunk them. My bleeding shirt, trousers . . ."

XANDER: "Look at you. You have knees! Very white knees!"

107

SPIKE (sitting, as Xander's cut-offs ride up on his legs): "Damn things keep doing that."

XANDER: "You know I'm not any happier about you wearing my stuff than you are."

SPIKE: "That cannot be true."

—AFTER SPIKE IS FORCED TO BORROW XANDER CLOTHES, FOLLOWING A LAUNDRY DISASTER, IN "DOOMED"

"Seriously? That's a 'good' day? [off her nod] Well, there you go. Even when he's good he's all Mr. Billowy Coat King of Pain and girls really—"

—RILEY, FRETTING ABOUT ANGEL'S DUSTER, IN "THE YOKO FACTOR"

RILEY: "I got a little tired of sitting around waiting, so…"

BUFFY: "You joined the circus?"

[Cut back to show Riley is dressed in the brightly colored pants Xander left him earlier.]

RILEY (entering): "Xander took my clothes to clean them. Left me these. Does he hate me in some way I don't know about yet? I think I would've attracted less attention in my uniform." —"THE YOKO FACTOR"

"It's the pants, isn't it? It's okay. I couldn't take me seriously in these things, either."

—RILEY, IN "THE YOKO FACTOR"

BUFFY: "Well, at least now we've all got someone to go with. Some of us are going with demons, but I think that's a valid lifestyle choice. More importantly, I've got the kick dress."

WILLOW: "The pink one?"

BUFFY: "Oh, yeah. Angel's gonna lose it. [sudden worry] But not his soul. I mean just lose 'it.' His 'it.'" —"THE PROM"

QUOTABLE
FOOD

JOYCE: "Buffy, what would I do with forty chocolate bars?"

BUFFY: "You could give them out at the gallery. Buy something Pre-Colombian, get a free cavity." —"BAND CANDY"

BUFFY: "There is no problem that cannot be solved by chocolate."

WILLOW: "I think I'm gonna barf."

BUFFY: "'Cept that." —"FEAR, ITSELF"

GILES: "I don't really know what to say. I understand that this is the sort of thing that requires ice cream of some kind."

[She smiles ruefully.]

BUFFY: "Ice cream will come. First I feel like taking out psycho boy." —"THE PROM"

SNYDER: "Okay, what's in the bag?"

STUDENT (confused): "My lunch."

SNYDER: "Oh, is that the new drug lingo?"

STUDENT (still confused): "It's my lunch." —"CHOICES"

XANDER: "Kerouac. He's my teacher. The open road is my school."

BUFFY: "Making the open dumpster your cafeteria." —"CHOICES"

"I feel the need for more sugar than the human body can handle."

—BUFFY, IN "CHOICES"

"Ice water—do you want that on the rocks?" —XANDER, IN "BEER BAD"

"I wear the cheese. It does not wear me."

—THE CHEESEMAN, IN "RESTLESS"

"I'm not saying it's the key to her heart, but Buffy? She likes cheese."

—WILLOW TO RILEY, IN "THE INITIATIVE"

"To commemorate a past event you kill and eat an animal. It's a ritual sacrifice. With pie."

—ANYA, ON THANKSGIVING, IN "PANGS"

"It's a sham, but it's a sham with yams. A yam sham."

—BUFFY, ON THANKSGIVING, IN "PANGS"

"I like pancakes 'cause they're stackable. And waffles 'cause you could put stuff in the little holes if you wanted to."   —BUFFY, IN "A NEW MAN"

BUFFY: "But someone could wish the whole world to be different? That's possible?"

ANYA: "Sure. Alternate realities. You could have, like, a world without shrimp. Or with, you know, nothing but shrimp. You could even make a world where Jonathan's some kind of not-perfect mouth-breather if that's what's blowing your skirt up tonight. Just don't ask me to live there."   —"SUPERSTAR"

BUFFY: "Anya, tell them about the alternate universes."

ANYA: "Oh. Okay, well, say you really liked shrimp a lot. Or, we could say that you didn't like shrimp at all. 'Blah, I wish there weren't any shrimp,' you'd say to yourself—"

BUFFY: "No, no. She's not saying it right. I just think he did something so he's manipulating the world, and we're all, you know, like pawns."

ANYA (amusing herself): "Or prawns."

BUFFY (frustrated): "Stop with the shrimp! I'm trying to do something serious here!"

—"SUPERSTAR"

QUOTABLE
MAGIC

"Was Willow messing with her magic tricks again? Maybe they disappeared. Maybe she turned Xander into something ishy!"

—CORDY, IN "LOVERS WALK"

"I doubt your doubt. Everyone knows witches killed those kids. Amy is a witch. And Michael is whatever the boy of 'witch' is, plus being the poster child for yuck."

—CORDY, IN "GINGERBREAD"

WILLOW: "Aha! A curse on Slayers—oh, no, wait. It's 'lawyers.'"

XANDER: "Maybe we're on the wrong track with the spells, curses, and whammies. Maybe what we should be looking for is something like Slayer kryptonite."

OZ: "Faulty metaphor. Kryptonite kills."

XANDER (recovering comic book geek mode): "You're assuming I meant green kryptonite. I was referring, of course, to red kryptonite, which drains Superman of his powers."

OZ: "Wrong. The gold kryptonite's the power-sucker. Red kryptonite's the one that mutates Superman into some sort of weird—"

BUFFY: "Guys!"

[They turn and look at her. She indicates their environs.]

BUFFY: "Reality."   —"HELPLESS"

"Stinky? That's why I added the lavender. Give me time, and I could be the first Wicca to do all my conjuring in a pine-fresh scent."
—WILLOW, THE MARTHA STEWART OF MAGIC,
IN "BAD GIRLS"

GILES: "Where did you find that volume?"
WILLOW: "In the top of your book cabinet, with the stuff you try to keep hidden."
[Giles scowls, but goes to retrieve the book.]
XANDER: "Hidden? Any engravings I should know about? Frolicking nymphs of some kind?"
WILLOW: "No, just magic secrets Giles doesn't think I'm ready for." —"ENEMIES"

WILLOW: "I've got the basics down: levitation, charms, glamours...I just feel I've plateaued, wiccawise."
BUFFY: "What's the next level?"

WILLOW: "Transmutation, conjuring... Bringing forth something from nothing...It gets you pretty close to the primal forces. A little scary..."
BUFFY: "Will, no one's pushing. If it's too much, don't do it."
WILLOW: "'Don't do it?' What kind of encouragement is that?"
BUFFY: "This is an 'encourage me' talk? I thought it was a 'share my pain' talk."
—"FEAR, ITSELF"

WILLOW: "The coroner's office said she was missing an ear. So, I'm thinking maybe we're looking for a witch. There are some great spells that work much better with an ear in the mix."
BUFFY: "That's one fun little hobby you've got there, Will." —"PANGS"

THE PAIN

Buffy the vampire slayer

AS JOSS WHEDON AND THE *BUFFY* WRITING TEAM have often pointed out, the forces of darkness that embattle the Slayer and her friends are metaphors for the personal demons people face: fear, isolation, rejection, and the sad fact that most of us grow through suffering. In Whedon parlance this is "the Buffy" of any given episode: the pain a character must endure—or cause—in order to learn the next lesson on the hero's journey. In Seasons Three and Four there was plenty of "growing" to be spread around. Follow us, then, as we unwind the thread of pain through the labyrinth.

At the end of Season Two, Buffy has saved the world (again) by sacrificing the love of her life. After one single night of making love with the man she cherished, she woke up to find that her gift of herself had transformed Angel back into Angelus, one of the most depraved and evil creatures that ever walked the night. Deprived once more of his humanizing soul, he terrorized her friends and loved ones and viciously murdered Jenny Calendar once she discovered how to change him back.

Holding herself responsible for each heinous act Angel committed, Buffy kept hope alive that he would be restored. But Angelus had opened a portal to a hellish demon dimension, and the only way to close it was with his death. Bitterly, just at the last moment, Willow succeeded in returning his soul to his body through magic. Angel fully knew who he was, and that he was with Buffy, the only woman he had loved in 243 years.

Buffy had no choice but to carry through her mission to save the world from his apocalyptic plan. After kissing him deeply and telling him that she loved him, she rammed a sword through his heart, knowing full well that she was condemning an essentially innocent man to eternal torment. He would suffer for the wrongs committed by the demon inside him, and over which he, Angel, had no control.

This was an act far beyond Buffy's capacity to endure. Unable to feel such overwhelming pain, Buffy exiles herself to a place where the pain of the shattered dreams of many others—mostly young runaways—have transformed to numb hopelessness.

She abandons the battle, and simply exists, drifting in a state of deep depression. Her uselessness is juxtaposed against scenes of everyone else in her life continuing to fight the good fight: Her friends have taken over her Slayer duties, however ineptly; Giles searches for her; when Buffy comes home, her mother is fixing the dishwasher.

The relief of having Buffy safely back soon transforms to anger; her friends and her mother hold her accountable for all the tension and worry they suffered while she was missing. But one of the particular burdens of being the Slayer is that Buffy has developed the habit of depending first and foremost upon herself, despite the obvious fact that in the past she has been able to rely on her friends. When faced with insurmountable despair, she pulled up stakes and let no one in; that she could not connect, couldn't share, wounds the others so deeply that once again, she's unable to deal. The temptation is great to run away again.

BUFFY: "Okay, I screwed up! I know it, all right? But you have no idea. You have no idea what happened to me or what I was feeling—"

XANDER: "Did you even try talking to anybody?"

BUFFY: "What's the point? There was nothing anyone could do. I just had to deal on my own."

XANDER: "And you see how well that went. You can't just bury stuff, Buffy. It'll come right back up to get you." —"DEAD MAN'S PARTY"

Xander's right; Buffy is plagued by nightmares of killing Angel, and of his hating her for condemning him to eternal torment. Still she tells no one the root cause of her misery; she cannot bear to confess that Angel was cured when she killed him. The closest she comes is telling Giles that she has dreamed that he has come back. Giles shares his dreams of his dead love, Jenny Calendar, whom Angelus murdered:

"After Jenny was killed, I had dreams that she was still alive. That I saved her." —"BEAUTY AND THE BEASTS"

But Giles's pain is of a far more innocent sort: he had nothing to do with Jenny's death. Not only had Jenny lied about who she was but she herself had the means to prevent the tragedy that ensued: If she had warned Buffy and Angel of the Gypsy curse laid on Angel, they would not have slept together. Ignorant not only of her duplicity, but also of her secretive search for Angel's cure, Giles has nothing to regret. His relationship with Jenny was clearly on the mend when she died, and he is free to mourn. Pain such as his, though deep, is simple.

On the other hand, Buffy knowingly killed Angel; and for him, there were no flowers, no gravestone and a sweet melancholy sense of loss. For him there is only pain that will never stop. Buffy's loss of him is messy with its layers of guilt, remorse, betrayal, and shame.

Though Giles may not fully appreciate everything that Buffy is feeling, he realizes that she needs to talk about it to get through it. He invents the need for a binding spell that requires detailed information about her last moments with Angel. She resists, flippantly avoiding the issue, trying to be glib, be brusque, be anything but completely honest about what happened. But when she can finally confess, and tell her friends that Angel was cured when she killed him, and she had to kill him anyway, her pain becomes more bearable.

[She's not dancing and singing, but she's taken the first step in the long journey that will put him to rest and allow her to get on with her life.]
—FROM THE STAGE DIRECTIONS, IN "FAITH, HOPE & TRICK"

As Buffy has dreamed, Angel returns from Hell. But he is not her thoughtful, brooding lover; he is a feral vampire, more a marauding beast than anything remotely human. Buffy doesn't know how or why he's come back, and she keeps him a secret. Rather than reveal his presence, she allows Oz and Willow to endure the torment of wondering if Oz has committed a savage murder. Even though she's chained Angel in his mansion, there's no guarantee he will stay there; still she stays silent. She lets Xander take the rap for falling asleep while on Oz-duty, and Xander must agonize over whether he was an unwitting accomplice to a murder.

Buffy's out of control. Mr. Platt, the school counselor, gives it to her straight:

> **MR. PLATT:** "You know, lots of people lose themselves in love. It's no shame. They write songs 'bout it. The hitch is, you can't stay lost. Sooner or later, you have to get back to yourself."
>
> **BUFFY:** "And if you can't?"
>
> **MR. PLATT:** "If you can't, love becomes your master. And you're just its dog."
>
> —"BEAUTY AND THE BEASTS"

In the same episode, once Buffy realizes that Pete Clarner is beating his girlfriend, Debbie, she appeals to her:

> **BUFFY:** "You have to talk to us. We can't help you until you do."
>
> **DEBBIE:** "I didn't ask for your help."

Buffy is beginning to get a clue that it's easier to handle painful emotions when you let your friends fight them at your side. Sorrow and guilt are monsters that hunt down and overtake people when they're cut off from support. But during both seasons, she will continually forget this lesson, pulling away and drawing inward repeatedly, until the final catharsis of "Restless."

Buffy's new boyfriend, Scott Hope, echoes another recurring theme in Seasons Three and Four:

> **"It's just . . . you never really know what's going on inside somebody, do you? You think if you care about them . . . but you never really do."**
>
> —"BEAUTY AND THE BEASTS"

This has been proven time and again, most obviously by Buffy herself, when she ran away. Willow reminds Buffy that she was going through all kinds of confusing experiences herself while Buffy was gone, with no one to talk to. Buffy's mom turned to a flighty but well-meaning neighbor who spends her evenings going to social events—book clubs, empañada nights, and facial nights. Giles, apparently, had no one but Buffy's friends, yet even her closest friends at the time drifted off-topic from worrying about Buffy to more mundane high-school woes, such as Oz's repeating twelfth grade.

Prophetically, Scott dumps Buffy shortly after the above speech, and her friends help Cordelia run against her for Homecoming Queen. During their rivalry, Cordelia dishes out as much hurt as she can:

CORDELIA: "I don't see why your pathetic need to recapture your glory days gives you the right to splinter my vote!"

BUFFY: "How can you think it's okay to talk to people like that? Do you have parents?"

CORDELIA: "Yeah. <u>Two</u> of them. Unlike some people."
—"HOMECOMING"

It bears repeating that Cordelia is fully aware of the baggage that drove Buffy to run away. But when the Queen of Mean sets her sights on what she wants, hurting someone else's feelings is merely a form of inflicting some collateral damage.

Meanwhile, Willow and Xander are going through a private purgatory of their own: After years of misfiring, they have found each other and are madly in lust. As exhilarating as their racing hormones are, the amount of stress they're under while keeping their attraction a secret from Oz and Cordelia is turning them into nervous wrecks. Secrets hurt. Secrets are rarely of the good. It follows, therefore, that secret-keepers behave in a less than stellar manner—they are rife with the potential for inflicting a lot of harm.

WILLOW: "Because we felt so guilty about the fluke we overcompensated helping Cordelia—and spun the whole group dynamic out of orbit—we're a meteor storm heading for earth!"

XANDER: "Okay, calm down. Let's put our heads together. One of us is pretty darn smart and I'm . . . just in hell. I thought being a senior—at last—and having a girlfriend—at last—would be a good thing." —"HOMECOMING"

But the maze of senior year is twisted and filled with dead ends. Figuring out how to get out without a lot of psychic scars feels like an Advanced Placement–caliber class when something like Remedial Emotions is what's really called for.

The next episode of Season Three brings a different sort of discomfort to Buffy and the Scooby Gang—the pain of realizing just how immature they still are, when forced to watch "the grown-ups" around them turn into teenagers after eating chocolate bars. There is the "betrayal" perpetrated by Giles and Buffy's mom, who have sex—twice!—on the hood of a police car. Buffy watches in amazement as her Watcher and her mother

posture and bicker, even when the lives of four newborn infants are at stake. Damage to her car makes Joyce laugh at herself for buying such a geeky set of wheels in the first place. Can this possibly be the way Buffy herself acts—the Slayer who wanted to be a cheerleader and who has pouted on a number of occasions when patrol interfered with her social life?

Meanwhile, Buffy has been nursing Angel back to health. She let him live too long when he went bad (there is a moving speech in "Passions" when she apologizes to Giles for not killing Angel before he murdered Jenny), and she's pushing it again. Because she's involved with him (and her first attempt at trying to move on—Scott Hope—ended badly) she is once again holding off on dating. Cordelia sums up Buffy's situation succinctly, as she is wont to do:

"Excuse me. When your last steady kills half the class, and then your rebound guy sends you a dump-o-gram? It makes a girl shy."

— "REVELATIONS"

Buffy has told no one that Angel is back. That she has kept his return secret wounds Giles most of all. The thread unwinds. Secrets hurt. Secrets harm.

Meanwhile, Faith has appeared on the scene, and the gang comes to care for her, and to understand the hurts that have made her act hard. So it is even more painful when Gwendolyn Post, Faith's new Watcher, is believed to be a fraud and a villain, *and* Buffy didn't trust her enough to tell her that Angel was back.

BUFFY: "Look. Gwendolyn Post, or whoever she was, she fooled us all. Even Giles."
FAITH: "Yeah, well, you can't trust people. I shoulda learned that by now."
BUFFY: "This is gonna sound funny coming from someone who just spent a lot of time kicking your face, but you can trust me."
FAITH: "Is that right?"
BUFFY: "I know I've kept secrets, but I didn't have a choice. I'm on your side."
FAITH: "I'm on my side. And that's enough."
BUFFY: "It was wrong. I know that. And I know it can't happen again. But I—I'd never put you guys in danger. If I thought Angel was going to hurt anyone—"
XANDER: "You'd stop him. Like you did last time with Ms. Calendar."

— "REVELATIONS"

Nobody is trusting Buffy, and that hurts. She still doesn't believe she can share everything that's happening to her. There's always a line she can't, or won't cross, and she justifies it as Slayer business.

Pain continues to fan across the miserable town of Sunnydale as Spike returns, distraught because Drusilla has dumped him.

> "She wouldn't even kill me. She just left. She didn't even care enough to cut off my head, or set me on fire. I mean, was that so much to ask? You know, some little sign that she cared? It was that truce with Buffy that did it. Dru said I'd gone soft; wasn't demon enough for the likes of her. I told her it didn't mean anything, I was thinking of her the whole time. She didn't care. So we got to Brazil and she was just different. I gave her everything...beautiful jewels, beautiful dresses—with beautiful girls in them, but nothing made her happy. And she would flirt. I caught her on a park bench making out with a Chaos Demon. Have you ever seen a Chaos Demon? They're all slime and antlers, they're disgusting. She only did it to hurt me. So I said 'I'm not putting up with this anymore.' She said, 'Fine.' I said, 'Yeah, I've got an unlife, you know.' And she said...she said we could still be <u>friends</u>! God, I'm so <u>unhappy</u>!"   —SPIKE, IN "LOVERS WALK"

Meanwhile, Buffy's experiencing cognitive dissonance: With her high SAT scores, and Faith around to act as Slayer, she may actually get to leave Sunnydale to go to college. She's hurt when Angel encourages her to think about it, inferring that he doesn't care if she leaves town. She doesn't discuss it with him, but she broods about it. She reasons that she and he are only friends now. As a friend, he's speaking his mind when he tells her he thinks it's a good idea.

Then she's stabbed through the heart when Spike speaks his mind on her "friendship" with Angel.

> "You're not friends. You'll never be friends. You'll be in love till it kills you both. You'll fight, you'll shag, you'll hate each other till it makes you quiver, but you'll never be friends. Love isn't brains, children, it's blood, it's blood screaming inside you to work its will. I may be love's bitch, but at least I'm man enough to admit it."   —SPIKE, IN "LOVERS WALK"

When wanting is involved, it's obviously harder to be friends. The more people need from each other, the closer they want to be, the more opportunity there is to hurt each other, and to hurt others. Though Willow and Xander have been fighting their attraction, they give into their need for intimacy when sharing one of the most painful experiences there is: facing the probability of their deaths. Their lips touch, they embrace...and break the hearts of their loved ones, who are looking on in silent shock.

The secret has been revealed. Every glance, every touch, that was not shared with the person to whom Willow and Xander have pledged themselves is proven to be a lie. Willow understands the gravity of such dishonesty when Oz leaves her.

> "I never knew there was anything inside me that could feel this bad."
>
> —WILLOW, TO BUFFY, IN "LOVERS WALK"

Cordelia and Xander break up; Willow and Oz are apart; and Buffy tells Angel that they, too, must stop seeing each other. "Lovers Walk" ends with all the Scoobs in pain—and Spike gleefully resolved to find Dru and make her love him again.

Willow cannot apologize to Oz and agonize enough:

> **"Cordy belongs to the 'justified' camp. She should make us pay. And pay and pay and pay and pay . . . In fact, there's really not enough 'pay' to make up for—"**

Buffy tries to make a connection with Cordelia. She has learned part of the lesson:

> **"Please, Cordelia. I know what it's like to be hurt by someone. Hurt so much, you think you're not going to make it. The only thing that helped? I told my friends how I felt. And it got a little better."**

But it doesn't get better for Cordy. She's so hurt that she inadvertently summons Anyanka, the vengeance demon of women scorned. When the Bizarro Sunnydale Anyanka conjures is destroyed, Anyanka is forced to remain in Sunnydale and live life as a mortal. She can't help Cordelia; she can't help any woman who has been betrayed. Cordelia is left to get through the hurt by herself.

"Amends" begins with the holiday blues. "Everybody gets 'em," Willow tells the gang. "Especially when they're alone." Buffy's trying to steer clear of Angel. Xander will be sleeping outside to avoid his family's drunken Christmas fights. The glum loneliness of the holidays is underscored:

> **"Do you really want to let her [Faith] spend Christmas Eve all by herself in that dingy little motel room?"**   —JOYCE
>
> and
>
> **"Hey, what about Giles? He doesn't have family here."**   —BUFFY

Meanwhile, Angel is being tormented by visions of his past, and haunted by the truth of what he was as a young man.

> **MARGARET:** "A drunken, whoring layabout and a terrible disappointment to your parents."
> **ANGEL:** "I was...young....I never had the chance to—"
> **MARGARET:** "—to die of syphilis? You were a worthless being before you ever were a monster."

It's true; Angel's misery is past enduring. He thinks of all the terrible things he is responsible for—deaths, murders, tortures, and the glee he took in them, and his burden is too great to handle. Being returned from endless torment seems too much like forgiveness, and Angel is not ready to forgive himself. He suffers as Buffy has suffered, for events they both seem almost destined to have caused. Overwhelmed and in despair, Angel opts for the release of true death, trying to kill himself by waiting for the dawn.

> **"Because I want you so badly, I want to take comfort in you and I know it'll cost me my soul and a part of me doesn't care. I'm weak. I've never been**

anything else. It's not the demon in me that needs killing, Buffy. It's the man." —ANGEL, IN "AMENDS"

"What about me? What about—Angel, I love you so much—and I've tried to make you go away, I killed you and it didn't help. And I hate it. I hate that it's so hard...that you can hurt me so much. I know everything you've done because you did it to me. I wish I wished you dead. But I don't. I can't." —BUFFY, IN "AMENDS"

But the sun is covered by a miraculous Christmas snow, preventing Angel's self-immolation. The thread that ties him to this existence is too strong: the vampire with a soul has miles to go before he sleeps...if ever. He must continue to endure. And to suffer for his sins.

At the same time, Oz does forgive Willow, speaking of what it's like without her.

"This is what I do know. I miss you. Every second. It's like I've lost an arm. Worse. A torso. So I'm thinking I'd be willing to give it a shot."
—OZ, IN "AMENDS"

To prove herself to him, she tries to lift their relationship to the next level of intimacy—sex—connecting, literally, with the man she loves. Oz understands, and does not push. His kind and loving decision to wait mirrors the first time they were alone in his van, in "Innocence," and she asked him if wanted to make out with her. He was willing to wait for a time that didn't come tinged with bad feelings on her part. He's willing to wait again.

Überachiever Willow has another source of her own private pain: Her mother completely ignores her, to the point of not realizing that she's had a new haircut for at least four months, and she calls Buffy "Bunny." As Willow protests too much:

"Makes me glad my mother doesn't know about my extra-curricular activities. Or my curricular activities. Or the fact of my activeness in general"
—WILLOW, IN "GINGERBREAD"

When her mother does find out, Willow is hurt by Sheila Rosenberg's condescending attitude toward Willow's witchcraft.

At this point Joyce delivers Buffy a painful blow when she lumps slaying in with what's wrong with Sunnydale during a speech. Buffy is disheartened:

BUFFY: "My mom....She said some stuff to me. About being the Slayer. That it's fruitless. No fruit for Buffy."

ANGEL: "She's wrong."

BUFFY: "Was she? Is Sunnydale any better than when I came here? Okay, so I battle evil. But I don't really win. The bad keeps coming back and getting stronger. I'm like that kid in the story, the boy who stuck his finger in the duck."

ANGEL: "Dike. It's another word for a dam."

BUFFY: "Oh. Okay, that story makes a lot more sense now."

ANGEL: "Buffy, you know I'm still working things out; there's a lot I don't understand. But I know it's important to keep fighting and I learned that from you."

BUFFY: "But we never—"

ANGEL: "We never win."

BUFFY: "Not completely."

Just before she lights the fire to burn her own child at the stake, Joyce delivers another salvo:

> **"Since when does it matter what I want? I wanted a normal, happy daughter and instead I got a Slayer."**

When all is made right, Buffy can tell herself that her mother's betrayal of her was caused by a demon.

Buffy's father hurts her in much the same way when he cancels on their ritual birthday trip to the ice show. Joyce tries to excuse him, for Buffy's sake, saying that his quarterly projections were unraveling. She's implying that he's not responsible for hurting Buffy; his bad business situation is overpowering him and preventing him from doing the right thing by his daughter. When Buffy poignantly hints to Giles that he might take her to the show instead, he misses it altogether:

> **"I mean, if someone were free, they'd take their daughter or their . . . student . . . or their Slayer . . ."**
> —BUFFY, "HELPLESS"

Worse than missing this cue to do a kindness, Giles deliberately betrays Buffy and nearly causes the death of both the Slayer and her mother. Obeying orders from the Watchers Council, Giles weakens her with drugs and keeps from her the secret ritual called the Cruciamentum, an ancient rite of passage for any Slayer who makes it to eighteen. During the time that she's weakened, Buffy finds she must consider the very real possibility of life without her powers, and she has to make a difficult confession: like Angel, there was a certain...lack to Buffy Summers as a regular person:

> **"Before I became the Slayer I was...well, I don't want to say shallow, but let's just say a certain person who shall remain nameless, let's call**

her 'Spordelia,' looked like a classical philosopher next to me. Angel, if I'm not the Slayer...what do I have to offer? What do I do? Why would you like me?"

Angel reassures her, unknowingly adding to the pain they will undergo when forced to part ways:

"I watched you. I saw you called. It was a bright afternoon, out in front of your school. You walked down the steps and I loved you."

—ANGEL, IN "HELPLESS"

He fails her. Everyone fails her. The man who is charged with guiding and protecting her, whose worst nightmare was Buffy's death on his watch ("Nightmares"), passively stands by while the thread of Buffy's life unravels. When Giles confesses what he's been doing to her, Buffy is stunned:

BUFFY: "Who are you? How could you do this to me?"
GILES: "I'm deeply sorry, Buffy, you have to understand—"
BUFFY: "If you touch me, I'll kill you."

—"HELPLESS"

Once the crisis is past, Buffy concludes:

"Nothing's really gonna change. The important thing is, I kept up my special birthday tradition of gut-wrenching misery and horror."

One of the recurring hurts in Xander's life is that he doesn't feel appreciated—and he's worried that that's because he's not very important or useful. Cordelia, "Queen of Pain," knows this, and does everything she can to tie him in knots:

"It must be hard when all your friends have, like superpowers. Slayer, werewolves, witches, vampires, and you're like this little nothing. You must feel like Jimmy Olsen."

—"THE ZEPPO"

and she goes on:

XANDER: "I happen to be an integral part of that group and I happen to have a lot to offer."
CORDELIA: "Oh, please."
XANDER: "I do!"
CORDELIA: "Integral part of the group. Xander, you're the useless part of the group. You're the Zeppo. 'Cool.' Look it up. It's something a subliterate that's repeated twelfth grade three times has and you don't."

Although Xander has a moment in the sun in the end of "The Zeppo," he's still worried about his future:

"I feel your pain, Will. Like, right now? I'm torn between the fast-growing

industries of appliance repair and motel management. Of course, I'm still waiting to hear from the Corndog Emporium, so..." —XANDER, IN "BAD GIRLS"

But a more immediate source of pain plagues Buffy: Mistaking the deputy mayor for a vampire, Faith staked and killed him, in Buffy's presence. Buffy was unable to stop her, and Faith wants her to help with the cover-up. Buffy tries to reach her:

BUFFY: "Being a Slayer is not the same as being a killer. Please don't shut me out here. Faith. Sooner or later we both have to deal."

FAITH: "Wrong."

BUFFY: "I can help you."

FAITH: "I don't need it."

BUFFY: "Yeah? Who's wrong now? You can shut off all the emotions you want, but there's still the fact that sooner or later they have to find a body."

FAITH: "Okay. This is the last time we're having this conversation, and we're not even having it now, you understand me? There is no body. I took it, weighted it, and dumped it. The body does not exist."

BUFFY: "Getting rid of the evidence isn't making the problem go away."

FAITH: "It does for me."

BUFFY: "Faith. You don't get it. You killed a man."

FAITH: "No. You don't get it. I. Don't. Care."   —"BAD GIRLS"

Buffy can't buy that. She's awash in remorse, even though she didn't actually kill the deputy mayor herself. As usual, her personal sense of responsibility and accountability wars with her need to keep the death a secret. She's already kept so many, trying to save both herself and others from the consequences of various actions. But it's a tangled web that's woven when the truth is buried along with the body.

FAITH: "When you gonna learn, B.? It doesn't matter what kind of 'vibe' a person gives off. Nine times outta ten—the face they're showing you? It isn't the real one."

BUFFY: "I guess you know a lot about that."

FAITH: "What's that supposed to mean?"

BUFFY: "It's just...look at you, Faith. Less than twenty-four hours ago you killed a guy. And now it's all zipidee doo dah. That's not your real face, and I know it. I know what you're feeling because I feel it, too."

FAITH: "Do you? So, fill me in. I'd like to hear this."

BUFFY: "Dirty. Like something sick creeped inside you and you can't get it out. And you keep hoping what happened was just some nightmare. But it wasn't, Faith."

—"CONSEQUENCES"

Ever since Faith came to town, Willow has been feeling left out—another theme that will recur, especially in Season Four:

BUFFY: "I need to talk to you."

WILLOW: "Good. 'Cause I've been letting things fester. And I don't like it. I want to be fester-free."

BUFFY: "Yeah. Me, too—"

WILLOW: "I mean, don't get me wrong. I completely understand why you and Faith have been doing the bonding thing. You work together—you should get along."

BUFFY: "It's more complicated than that."

WILLOW: "But, see? It's that exact thing that's ticking me off. This whole 'Slayers only' attitude. Since when wouldn't I understand? You talk to me about everything! It's like—all of a sudden I'm not cool enough for you because I can't kill things with my bare hands!" —"CONSEQUENCES"

Despite being on the mend with Oz, Willow is further devastated when she realizes that Xander and Faith have slept together. Her first love has moved on. He has given his innocence to someone who didn't even appreciate it. Willow, whose own boyfriend rejected her offer of the same thing for love of her, mourns the severing of a connection that will never be made between her and Xander. She hides in the girls' room at school and sobs her heart out.

Believing, as Willow does, that he has some kind of tie to Faith, Xander tries to reach the murderous Slayer, and she does all she can to hurt him:

FAITH: "You'd dig that, wouldn't you? To get up in front of all your geek pals and go on record about how I made you my boy toy for a night—"

XANDER: "No. No, that's not it—"

FAITH: "I know what this all about. You just came here because you want another taste."

XANDER: "No…I mean, it was nice, it was <u>great</u>, well, it was kind of a blur, but, okay, someday, sure, yeah.…But not now, not like this."

FAITH: "More like how, then? Lights on or off? Kinks or vanilla?"

XANDER: "Faith, come on. I came here to help you. I thought we had a connection."

FAITH: "You want to feel our connection? It's just skin. I see. I want. I take. I forget." —"CONSEQUENCES"

123

Angel tries, too, and tragically, begins to make the longed-for connection between his pain and Faith's just as Wesley Wyndam-Pryce—her second, neglected Watcher—barges in and kidnaps her. Before that, the vampire frankly describes the joy he took in inflicting pain, in feeling the surge of power that hurting another creature can deliver:

"You and me, Faith, we're a lot alike. Time was, I thought humans existed just to hurt each other. But then I came here. And I found out that there were other kinds of people. People who genuinely wanted to do right. They still make mistakes. They fall down. But they keep caring. Keep trying. If you can trust us, Faith, this can all change. You don't have to disappear into the darkness."

—ANGEL, IN "CONSEQUENCES"

In "Doppelgangland," Willow is feeling like she is being taken for granted. Principal Snyder is forcing her to do Percy West's homework. Everyone else is calling her "Old Reliable." Though she gets a measure of satisfaction when a spell gone awry calls forth Vamp Willow from the bizarro dimension and Vamp Willow proceeds to assert herself in Willow's place, it's a problem that will recur for her as Seasons Three and Four move along. Faith oddly mirrors Willow's dilemma—she feels that nobody sees her true worth. Until she hooks up with the Mayor of Sunnydale. As a familial warmth develops between Faith and the Mayor, they concoct a scheme to steal Angel's soul; then Angelus and Faith will torture Buffy to death:

BUFFY: "Why, Faith? What's in it for you?"
FAITH: "What isn't? You know, I come to Sunnydale, I'm a Slayer, I do my job kicking ass better than anyone, and what do I hear about, everywhere I go? Buffy. So I slay. I behave. I do the good-little-girl routine, and who does everyone thank? Buffy."
BUFFY: "That's not my fault."
FAITH: "Everybody asks, 'Why can't you be more like Buffy?' but did anyone ever ask if you could be more like me?"   —"ENEMIES"

The charade succeeds, but it was too painful for Buffy to see Angel acting evil and kissing Faith. And Faith knows there's no going back:

MAYOR: "Well, you win some, you lose some. From where I'm sitting, it's batting average that counts. So you lost some friends."
FAITH: "Wouldn't exactly call them friends."
MAYOR: "So then, what are you worried about? Chin up. You don't see me looking disappointed, do you? Heck no. Know why? Because I know you'll always have me, Faith. I'm the best and most important friend you'll ever have. Besides, once the Ascension starts, that 'in crowd' you're so concerned about? Hoo! They'll be lucky if there's enough of 'em left to fill a pothole. Promise. Still unhappy? Okey-doke. I've got two words that are going to take all the pain away. Miniature. Golf."   —"ENEMIES"

For Faith, the pain translates into psychosis. In "Earshot" it translates into a suicide attempt by Jonathan Levenson. Buffy manages to talk him out of it by sharing what she's learned about pain from hearing the thoughts of everyone around her.

BUFFY: "No, I think you're in the clock tower with a high-powered rifle because you want to blend in. Believe it or not, Jonathan, I understand. About the pain."
JONATHAN: "Oh, right. 'Cause the burden of being beautiful and athletic, that's a crippler."
BUFFY: "You know what, I was wrong. You are an idiot. My life happens to on occasion suck beyond the telling of it. Sometimes more than I can handle. Every single person down there is ignoring your pain because they're too busy with their own. The beautiful ones, the popular ones, the guys that pick on you…everyone. If you could hear what they were feeling—the loneliness, the confusion…It looks quiet down there. It's not. It's deafening. . . . You know I could have taken that [the gun] by now."
JONATHAN: "I know."
BUFFY: "I'd rather do it this way."

JONATHAN: "I just wanted it to stop."

BUFFY: "Yeah, well, mass murder is not really doctor recommended for this kind of pain. And by the way, prison? A lot like high school, only instead of noogies—"

JONATHAN: "What are you talking about?"

BUFFY: "Actions having consequences, you know, stuff like that—"

JONATHAN: "I wouldn't ever hurt anybody. I came up here to kill <u>myself</u>."

In light of Buffy's heartfelt conversation with Jonathan, it's particularly touching that he is the one to give her the Class Protector award at the prom. But before the happiness of that moment, Buffy has to find her way down more dark corridors, without even a gossamer strand of hope to guide her. Her mother appeals to Angel to do the right thing by her:

"Because when it comes to you, Angel, she's just like any other young woman in love. You're all she can see of tomorrow. But I think we both know there are going to be some hard choices ahead. If she can't make them, you're going to have to. I know you care about her. I just hope you care enough."
— JOYCE, IN "THE PROM"

Angel does care enough.

ANGEL: "I'm sorry. Buffy, you know how much I love you. It kills me to say this—"

BUFFY: "Then don't! Who are you to tell me what's right for me? You think I haven't thought about this?"

ANGEL: "Have you? Rationally?"

BUFFY: "No, no, of course not. I'm just some swoony little schoolgirl, right?"

ANGEL: "I'm trying to do what's right here. I'm trying to think with my head instead of my heart."

BUFFY: "Heart? You have a heart? It isn't even beating."

ANGEL: "Don't."

BUFFY: "Don't what? Don't love you? I'm sorry. You know what, I didn't know I got a choice in that. I'm never going to change. I can't change. I want my life to be with you."

ANGEL: "I don't."

BUFFY: "You don't…want to be with me?"

ANGEL: "It doesn't mean that I don't—"

BUFFY: "How am I supposed to stay away from you?"

ANGEL: "I'm leaving. After the Ascension, after it's finished with the Mayor and Faith. If we survive, I'll go."
— "THE PROM"

For Buffy, no pain is greater. The loss of him again is more than she can take. But this time, she goes to friends for strength. Buffy has learned that much:

BUFFY: "Right now, I'm just trying to keep from dying."

WILLOW: "Oh, Buffy…"

BUFFY: "I can't breathe, Will. I feel like I can't breathe."

And

BUFFY: "Look. It's done. You want to go after them and tell them that they can't go? That all their planning and dreaming was for nothing? That they can't spend tonight of all nights with their honeys?"

GILES: "Angel's not taking you, is he?"

BUFFY: "Angel's leaving me. Leaving town."

Then Angel shows.

[They look at each other, their burdens lifted slightly, their pain not gone but mellowing. Worlds unsaid.]
                                    —(FROM STAGE DIRECTIONS) "THE PROM"

Meanwhile, Cordelia has some prom issues of her own: She's penniless. For Cordelia, this is probably worse than being cheated on by two school geeks. Her social standing, which meant everything to her, lies in ruins. Not only did she jeopardize her coolness factor by publicly dating Xander, but she had to suffer humiliation at the hands of her "friends" (formerly known as the Cordettes) when she caught him cheating on her. One solace lay in being accepted to good colleges, but now that she has no money, she stands square with Xander as far as her prospects go:

CORDELIA: "I have nothing! Okay? No dresses, no cell phone, no car. Everything has been taken away because Daddy made a little mistake on his taxes for the last twelve years. Satisfied? Are you a happy Xander now? I'm broke. I can't go to any of the colleges that accepted me and I can't stay home because we no longer have one."

XANDER: "Wow."

CORDELIA: "Yeah, neato. You can run along and tell all your friends how Cordy finally got hers, how she has to work part-time just to get a lousy prom dress on layaway. And how she has to wear a name tag. Oh, I'm a name tag person! Don't leave that out; the story just wouldn't have the same punch."   —"THE PROM"

The future lies before them, like the exit to the vast maze of high school. There is the bittersweet pain of facing graduation:

"It's like a sickness, Buffy. I'm just missing everything. I miss P.E.!"
                                    —WILLOW, IN "GRADUATION DAY, PART ONE"

And also, of facing death:

"When I think that something might happen to you, it feels bad. Inside. Like I might vomit."   —ANYA, TO XANDER, IN "GRADUATION DAY, PART ONE"

Then, worse than his simply leaving her, Buffy faces the possibility of Angel's death once more. Faith poisons him, and the only cure is another death: this time, of a Slayer. Pain and loss have hardened Buffy; love has given her resolve. She is willing to kill Faith to save him; when she fails in that, she is willing to sacrifice her own life in return for his:

"I won't let you die. I can't. Angel, the blood of a Slayer is the only cure."—"GRADUATION DAY, PART TWO"

After Buffy tries—and fails—to kill Faith for her blood, the Mayor reacts to Faith's apparently terminal condition by trying to suffocate Buffy. Such a violent demonstration of pain may just be the key they need to defeat the Mayor:

"At the hospital, he was grieving. Seriously crazed, and not just in a homicidal, I-wanna-be-a-demon way. She's his weak link." —ANGEL REPORTS TO THE GANG, IN "GRADUATION DAY, PART TWO"

For Buffy and Angel, their chemistry has defeated them. They, too, are each other's weak links. Their love for each other can damn both of them, make them responsible for more deaths, more destruction, more pain:

[She feels him before she sees him. Turns.
Angel stands some twenty yards away, looking at her. People coming and going in between.
They both stop. The noise fades away. They stare at each other.
Angel turns and walks away.
Buffy stands and watches him. After a moment, she goes in the opposite direction.]
—(FROM STAGE DIRECTIONS) "GRADUATION DAY, PART TWO"

The pain reasserts itself in college in "The Harsh Light of Day." Buffy crushes on Parker Abrams; moved by what she perceives as his depth, and their mutually shared pain (his father's death, her own death) she impulsively sleeps with him. What for her is a special experience turns out to be something less for Parker:

BUFFY: "Did I do something…something wrong?"
PARKER: "Something wrong? No, of course not. It was fun. Didn't you have fun? Watch out how you answer. My ego's fragile."
BUFFY: "I—you had fun. Is that all it was?"
PARKER: "What else was it supposed to be?"
BUFFY: "It seemed like you…liked me?"
PARKER: "I do. But I'm starting to feel like you thought that meant, what? Some kind of commitment? Is that really what you want right now?" —"THE HARSH LIGHT OF DAY"

In this episode Harmony Kendall appears as a vampire, whose new romance with Spike isn't going too well.

"He staked me." —HARMONY, IN "THE HARSH LIGHT OF DAY"

"Love hurts"—that's Spike's motto. And William the Bloody likes nothing more than to drive a few points home if they'll cause more than a little discomfort. Spike's vendetta with Buffy's going very nicely, as he makes a few cuts with the precision of a surgeon:

SPIKE: "So, you let Parker take a poke, eh? Didn't seem like you two knew each other that well. What exactly did it take to pry apart the Slayer's dimpled knees?"
BUFFY: "You're a pig, Spike."
SPIKE: "Did he play the sensitive lad and get <u>you</u> to seduce <u>him</u>? Good trick if the girl's thick enough to buy it. Wonder what you did wrong. Too strong? Did you bruise the boy? Whatever. Guess you're not worth a second go. Come to think of it, seems like someone told me as much. Who was that? Oh, yeah. Angel."
—"THE HARSH LIGHT OF DAY"

Buffy pines for Parker, imagining his begging her for forgiveness in windblown romance hero style. By the time it finally happens, she's past caring. En route, however, she's miserable, seeing him with other girls, forced to conclude:

BUFFY: "I know what he was, but…you know, if he were tied and gagged and left in a cave that vampires <u>happened</u> to frequent, it wouldn't really be like I killed him really.…"
XANDER: "Buffy…"
BUFFY: "I'm a slut." —"BEER BAD"

Meanwhile, Willow has begun to notice that Oz is noticing Veruca, the lead singer for Shy:

OZ: "Veruca's band. They asked me to sit in with them. Be cool if you were there.…"
WILLOW: "Two Veruca shows in two nights…Sure you want to share your groupie? I think I'm just gonna study. 'Cause of the fun."

She puts her unhappiness to good use, and chews out Parker:

"I'm tired of you men and your…man-ness. Buffy is really hurting right now. In fact, she's in need of a big mental tidy. Parker, how could you do this to her?" —WILLOW, IN "BEER BAD"

Parker has pretty much ripped the guts out of Buffy, much as she desultorily disembowels a pumpkin in "Fear, Itself." Then major pain catches up with Willow: Oz cheats on her with Veruca, who is also a werewolf. He tries to excuse his actions by saying that he had to keep an eye on Veruca, but he's not kidding anyone:

WILLOW: "Why didn't you talk to me? I knew. I knew, you jerk! And you sat there, telling me everything was fine? That's as bad as...as..."

OZ: "I know how it feels. I remember."

WILLOW: "Oh, so, what? This is payback? I had this coming?"

OZ: "No. That's not—"

WILLOW: "Because I thought that was behind us. And you know what happened with Xander—it doesn't compare. Not with what you and I had—and not with whatever you've been doing with her."

OZ: "I don't know what Veruca and I have done. When I change, it's like I'm gone and the wolf takes over."

WILLOW: "But before this, when you were just regular Oz, you had feelings for her, didn't you?"

OZ: "I could sense something, yes. But—"

WILLOW: "But—you wanted her. Like, in an animal way. Like...more than you wanted me." —"WILD AT HEART"

129

As painful as Oz's secret was; it's not as painful as what comes next. After he kills Veruca, he decides he must leave. Willow is bereft:

WILLOW: "Oz, don't you love me?"

OZ: "My whole life, I've never loved anything else." —"WILD AT HEART"

Oz does leave. Willow begins the mourning of the death of their relationship:

XANDER: "How's Will doing with the...?"

BUFFY: "With the black hole of despair she's lived in since Oz left? She's dealing. I'm helping. It's hard. Ergo, party." —"THE INITIATIVE"

Harmony is also still pining for her blondie bear, Spike, who has pretty much given in to the beast—or demon—inside him:

"Can you believe him? Comes back with all these big promises, not that I believed him, but he could have spent one night. But no, everything was 'Slayer this' and 'Slayer that.'" —HARMONY, TO XANDER, IN "THE INITIATIVE"

Angel comes to Sunnydale to watch over Buffy, based on a warning he received in Los Angeles. For him, it's no Thanksgiving picnic:

"Believe me, I'm not getting the good half of this deal. To be outside, looking in at what I can't...I'd forgotten how bad it feels."

—ANGEL, TO GILES, IN "PANGS"

Life moves on for Buffy and the others. Anya and Xander are by now official girlfriend and boyfriend, but Willow is stuck in her terrible grief. Oz has sent for the rest of his things, without even so much as a note for her:

WILLOW: "So I get punished 'cause I'm in pain."
GILES: "It's not punishment. I'm only saying this because—"
WILLOW: "You care. Right. Everybody cares. But nobody wants to be inconvenienced. You all want me to 'take the time to go through the pain' as long as you don't have to hear about it anymore!"
GILES: "That's not fair."
WILLOW: "Isn't it? 'Cause I'm doing the best I can—and that doesn't seem to be enough for you guys!"
GILES: "And I see how you could feel that way. I do—"
WILLOW: "No! You don't. You say that you do—but you don't see anything!"

—"SOMETHING BLUE"

She conjures, not realizing that her pain is affecting others, until Anya's old demon boss, D'Hoffryn, compliments her.

"You have much anger and pain. Your magic is strong, but your pain...it's like a scream that pierces dimensional walls. We heard your call."

And

"The pain and suffering you brought upon those you love has been inspired. You are ready to join us, here in Arashmaharr."

—D'HOFFRYN, IN "SOMETHING BLUE"

In moving on, Buffy has slowly gotten closer to a T.A. named Riley Finn:

BUFFY: "You've got a lot to learn about women."
[He reaches out and runs his hand through the back of her hair, cradling her head and bringing her close to him, firmly but entirely gently. She looks at him, startled but engaged. Their eyes close. He says simply:]
RILEY: "You're gonna teach me."

—"SOMETHING BLUE"

They eventually discover each other's secrets. Riley's delighted, and feels an even stronger connection between them. But Buffy's terrified of being hurt:

BUFFY: "There's too much risk—there's too much…It's just doomed, okay, and I can't do doomed again right now."

RILEY: "I don't understand where this is coming from. I know you like me. And it's not like we don't have anything in common."

BUFFY: "It's…"

RILEY: "Buffy. I'm thrown by this. I'm confused. But I can feel my skin humming—my hands, my …every inch of me. I've never been this excited by a girl and I'm not trying to scare you, not gonna force myself on you, but I am by God not gonna walk away because I think it might not work. I don't know what's happened in the past—"

BUFFY: "Death. Pain. Apocalypse—none of them fun. Do you know what the Hellmouth is? Do they have a fancy term for it? 'Cause I went to high school on top of it. For three years. We <u>don't</u> have that much in common. This is a job to you."

RILEY: "It's not just a job—"

BUFFY: "It's an adventure, great, but for me it's destiny. It's something I can't escape, something I can't change. I'm stuck."

RILEY: "You don't have to be. You're not in high school anymore. You can change things."

BUFFY: "Riley . . . no."

RILEY: "I know it seems like—"

BUFFY: "My answer is no."

—"DOOMED"

But they do connect—Buffy does risk the terrible pain of loving again—and they become lovers in every sense of the word.

Meanwhile, Giles must face the fact that he's not central in Buffy's life anymore. Giles and Ethan Rayne lament their obsolescence. But when push comes to shoving a pewter letter opener through his heart, Buffy shows that while she may not need him as much anymore, she does love him, and always will:

GILES: "Buffy, I don't know what to say. You know I'd never intentionally—"

BUFFY: "I know. And I'm so sorry about, you know, kicking your head—"

GILES: "How, how did you know it was me?"

BUFFY: "Your eyes."

GILES: "You recognized them."

BUFFY: "They looked…really exasperated. Knew it was you right away."   —"A NEW MAN"

Riley is in for pain next, as he learns the truth about Maggie Walsh, the woman who treated him practically like a son:

RILEY: "That's enough. You're making her sound like some psychopath. She wasn't like that. She was a brilliant woman."

DR. ANGLEMAN: "She was. It's not—"

RILEY: "All she was trying to do was help people...and this is how you want them to remember her?"

BUFFY: "Riley. Listen—I heard Angleman say that she was feeding you drugs—"

RILEY: "No! You're doing this to me, aren't you? This all started because of you."

BUFFY: "If you'll just listen. All I'm trying to do is help you get to the truth—"

RILEY: "You want truth? Then tell me! What did you do to her, Buffy."

—"GOODBYE IOWA"

Riley is eventually forced to confront the truth about Maggie Walsh: Not only did she have a terrible secret agenda in creating Adam but she was drugging Riley and all his "family" of Commandos in an effort to produce supersoldiers, and she tried to kill Buffy. Even "newborn" Adam can see the torment this causes Riley.

ADAM: "That's pain, isn't it? Why? Because your feeding schedule, the chemicals, have been interrupted? Or do you miss her? Tell me—"

RILEY: "I'll kill you."

ADAM: "You won't. You haven't been programmed to."

RILEY: "I can not be programmed. I'm a <u>man</u>."

ADAM: "It's here. The plan she had for us. How it ends."

RILEY: "No..."

ADAM: "Do you want to hear?"

RILEY: "No!"

—"GOODBYE IOWA"

Buffy's in for more pain, it appears:

WILLOW: "It'll be okay. Riley's just confused, that's all."

BUFFY: "I don't know. Seems like things could get heavier. I mean, his world's falling apart."

ANYA: "And after you went through all that stuff with Angel....You should get a boring boyfriend, like Xander. But you can't have Xander."

BUFFY: "That was the idea. Riley was supposed to be Mr. Joe Guy. We were supposed to do dumb stuff like hold hands through the daisies going, 'tra, la, la . . . .'"

WILLOW: "Poor Buffy. Your life resists all things average."

—"GOODBYE IOWA"

Buffy's right: things do get heavier. Without realizing it, Riley's going off his drugs cold turkey:

"I mean, who do you believe? First it sounds like lies. Then it sounds like truth...."

—RILEY, IN "GOODBYE IOWA"

Riley is taken away to recuperate in a military hospital. Buffy can do nothing to help him, echoing her near-helplessness when Faith poisoned Angel.

And speaking of This Year's Girl, pain of a new sort rears its lovely head: The rogue Slayer wakes up from the coma Buffy put her in. In a poignant scene, Faith discovers that the Mayor is dead, but that he thought of her to the end, communicating with her via a video he left her. The magical Katra device he left for her allows her to switch bodies with Buffy, and it is after the switch, in "Who Are You," that Faith's real pain surfaces. She discovers the level of contempt the Scoobs hold her in, and she has no idea how to react to the kindness and tenderness shown to her as Buffy. Her self-hatred wells up in their big battle, in which she pummels her own likeness, shrieking with hate:

"Shut up! You think I'm afraid of you? You're nothing! You're disgusting! A useless, murderous bitch! You're <u>nothing</u>!" —FAITH, IN "WHO ARE YOU"

Once their bodies are switched back, Faith makes her escape, but not before having wreaked havoc: While inside Buffy's body, Faith slept with Riley:

BUFFY: "It's all Faith's fault. She's like poison. No, worse, like acid that eats through everything. Or maybe a bomb. The point is, everything's going great with Riley and then she comes along and messes it all up."

JONATHAN: "Buffy, you know what I think? I don't think this is about you being angry with Faith. I think you're angry with Riley."

BUFFY: "Riley?"

JONATHAN: "Sure. I mean, you have this amazing connection with him. And then at the one moment when it matters most, he looks into your eyes and he doesn't even see it's not you looking back at him."

BUFFY: "Oh. But…but he couldn't have known. I mean, you don't just go, 'hey, that's not your body. Get out of that body with your hands up.'"

JONATHAN: "I know you <u>know</u> that. But you have to <u>believe</u> it. Buffy, if any part of you is blaming Riley for what happened, well, then, it seems like there's a part of you that needs to forgive him." —"SUPERSTAR"

Once Buffy sorts out the truth that Jonathan has altered reality so that he's popular, and restores the status quo, she and he have a talk that deals with the pain that both of them are feeling:

BUFFY: "Jonathan, you get why they're mad, right? Not just the Monster. People didn't like being, you know, the actors in your little sock puppet theater."

JONATHAN: "You weren't! You weren't socks! We were friends."

BUFFY: "Jonathan, you can't keep trying to make everything work out all at once, with some huge gesture. Things are complicated. They take time and work."

JONATHAN: "Yeah. Right. Hey…Buffy? You remember, I gave you some advice?"

BUFFY: "Um…Watch out for southpaws?"

JONATHAN: "No. About you and Riley. I mean, things are kinda starting to blur, but this cool thing I said, that I don't really remember, I think it was right. I think it was kinda the same thing you just said to me. About things taking work."

BUFFY: "I remember."

JONATHAN: "Good. Because it's true. What you have is really complicated, but it's worth it. I think that's what I said."

—"SUPERSTAR"

Then, Buffy and Riley reconcile and it's Anya's turn to be in pain.

ANYA: "I can't believe we're breaking up."

XANDER: "Breaking—? We're not! Are we?"

ANYA: "Of course we are. You've obviously grown tired of me. I've seen it happen to thousands of women over the centuries. I just never thought it would happen to me."

—"WHERE THE WILD THINGS ARE"

She's completely wrong. Xander truly loves her. But she doesn't understand why he's skipped having sex with her—twice!—and seeks solace with another demon who's lost his teeth, so to speak.

ANYA: "A year and a half ago, I could've eviscerated him with my thoughts. Things used to be so much simpler."

SPIKE: "You know, you take the killing for granted, and then it's gone and you're like, I wish I'd appreciated it more. Stopped and smelled the corpses, you know?"

ANYA: "Yeah. Now everything's complicated."

SPIKE: "Terrible thing, love is. Been there myself. Ended badly."

ANYA: "Of course it did. It always does. I've seen a thousand relationships. First there's the love and sex. Then there's nothing left but the vengeance. That's how it works."

SPIKE: "You and I, we should just go do the vengeance. Both of us. You eviscerate Xander, and I'll stake Dru. Like, a project."

ANYA: "I don't know...I just can't. But you can go do Dru though."

SPIKE: "Yeah. I will. Maybe later." —"WHERE THE WILD THINGS ARE"

In Lowell House, where the Commandos live, Buffy and Riley's nonstop lovemaking is fueling the pain of children who once lived there and were terribly abused by their caretaker. Willow, Tara, and Giles try to help them.

TARA: "We implore you. Be still."

GILES: "Find it in your hearts to leave our friends passage."

WILLOW: "Transform your pain. Release your past. And...uh...get over it."

—"WHERE THE WILD THINGS ARE"

But Willow herself has not gotten over "it." Oz returns, throwing Willow into intense confusion, and Tara into a lot of hurt:

WILLOW: "I don't want to hurt anyone, Buffy."
BUFFY: "No matter what happens, somebody's going to get hurt. The main thing is, you have to be honest—or it'll be a lot worse."
—"NEW MOON RISING"

Willow is deeply touched by Tara's love for her:

WILLOW: "I just wanted you to know, what you saw this morning, it wasn't—"
TARA: "It's okay. I always knew, if he came back—"
WILLOW: "We just talked. Nothing happened."
TARA: "Oh. Really?"
WILLOW: "But, you know, it was intense. Just talking. We have...a lot to talk about. I kind of feel like my head's going to explode."
TARA: "Whatever, you know, happens? I'll still be here. I mean, I'll still be your friend."
WILLOW: "Of course we'll be friends. That's not even a question."
TARA: "But, I'm saying, I know what Oz means to you."
WILLOW: "How can you, when I'm not even sure? I mean, I know what he meant to me. But he left. And everything changed. I changed. And then we..."
TARA: "It's okay."
WILLOW: "It's not okay. I mean, Tara, the time we spend together is..."
TARA: "What?"
WILLOW: "I don't know. It's just . . . life was starting to get so good again, and you're a big part of that. And here comes the thing I wanted most of all. And I don't know what to do. I want to know. But I don't."
TARA: "Do what makes you h-happy."
—"NEW MOON RISING"

Willow does, choosing Tara, but it doesn't lessen the pain of saying goodbye to Oz again.

"I missed you, Oz. I wrote you so many letters. But I didn't have any place to send them, you know? I couldn't live like that."
—WILLOW, IN "NEW MOON RISING"

Buffy is wrestling with questions about her own happiness, as Riley condemns Willow for having dated a demon—Oz, in werewolf form—forcing Buffy to refrain from telling him about Angel. For Riley, the matter is simple—demons are bad, and people are good. That is, until Oz is captured by the Initiative. Then Riley throws away his entire career to save him.

RILEY: "Still, I was in a totally black-and-white space. People versus monsters. Ain't like that. Especially when it comes to love."
BUFFY: "I gotta tell you some stuff. It's not all stuff you're gonna like."
RILEY: "You can tell me anything."
BUFFY: "I think so. I think I can." —"NEW MOON RISING"

Buffy does tell Riley that Angel is a vampire, and that she loved him. She tells him that he went bad, and then was cured. But she doesn't tell him what made Angel go bad. When she goes to Los Angeles to deal with Faith, Xander spills the beans she omitted: that it was having sex with her that took away Angel's soul. By the time Buffy returns, Riley's in bad shape and assumes Buffy and Angel have reconciled.

"Buffy, I feel like we've gotten really close. At least, I thought we had. I don't know much about Angel, or your relationship with him. But all I ask is, if you're gonna break my heart? Do it fast."
—"THE YOKO FACTOR"

She doesn't break his heart.

BUFFY: "Riley, have I ever given you reason to feel you couldn't trust me?"
RILEY: "No."
BUFFY: "Then why with the crazy?"
RILEY: "Because I'm so in love with you I can't think straight."
—"THE YOKO FACTOR"

When caught between Angel and Riley, Buffy clearly chooses Riley. And Angel moves on.
Playing Iago, Spike sets up a whispering campaign that pits Buffy, Giles, and the gang against one another, playing on their insecurities: Xander about his future prospects; Willow about her witchcraft and her involvement with Tara; and Giles, about the fact that Buffy no longer needs him. By the end of the episode, Spike's mission has been accomplished, and the ties of friendship have been sundered.

BUFFY: "No. You said you wanted to go. So let's go. All of us. We'll walk into that cave with you two attacking me and the funny drunk drooling on my shoes. Maybe that's the secret way to kill Adam."
XANDER: "Buffy—"

BUFFY: "Is that it? Is that how you can help? You're not answering. Go on. How can you possibly help? So . . . so I guess I'm on my own. I'm starting to get why there's no ancient prophecy about a Chosen One and her friends."　—"THE YOKO FACTOR"

The friends all make up after realizing that Spike manipulated them. As they rappel down the elevator shaft and into the Initiative complex, Buffy and Willow apologize to each other for keeping secrets from each other; they let Xander know they love him, too. Giles gets a few hugs, and the foursome— the original cast of characters when "Welcome to the Hellmouth" was first aired—are once more a family. Once unity is established, the three magically send their essence to Buffy in the great battle against Adam and the demons. Magic—and love—have triumphed over Dr. Walsh's evil science experiment—at the cost of many lives, including Riley's friend Forrest.

In the last episode of Season Four, Buffy faces down the First Slayer, summoned by the magical forces Giles, Willow, and Xander invoked to strengthen Buffy for her fight against Adam. "The Primitive," as she is called, stalks those the Slayer holds dear, outright rejecting the notion of friends:

> **TARA:** "The Slayer doesn't walk in the world."
> **BUFFY:** "I walk. I talk. I shop, I sneeze, I'm gonna be a fireman when the floods roll back. There's trees in the desert since you moved out, and I don't sleep on a bed of bones. Now <u>give me back my friends</u>."
> **PRIMITIVE:** "No…friends…just the kill…we are…<u>alone</u>."
> **BUFFY:** "That's it. I'm waking up."
> —"RESTLESS"

After a battle with the Primitive (the First Slayer), Buffy does wake up at home, surrounded by kith and kin. She's unsure of what lies ahead, but she does know this: She is not alone. The ties that bind—those of love and friendship, loyalty and trust—are strong enough to pull her and her friends along on their continuing journey. What destiny has joined together, no one may put asunder.

Pain is easier to handle that way.

EPISODE GUIDE

SEASON THREE

EPISODE NUMBER	EPISODE NAME	ORIGINAL U.S. AIRDATE
1	"Anne"	29-Sept. 1998
2	"Dead Man's Party"	6-Oct.
3	"Faith, Hope & Trick"	13-Oct.
4	"Beauty and the Beasts"	20-Oct.
5	"Homecoming"	3-Nov.
6	"Band Candy"	10-Nov.
7	"Revelations"	17-Nov.
8	"Lovers Walk"	24-Nov.
9	"The Wish"	8-Dec.
10	"Amends"	15-Dec.
11	"Gingerbread"	12-Jan. 1999
12	"Helpless"	19-Jan.
13	"The Zeppo"	26-Jan.
14	"Bad Girls"	9-Feb.
15	"Consequences"	16-Feb.
16	"Doppelgangland"	23-Feb.
17	"Enemies"	16-Mar.
18	"Earshot"	21-Sept.*
19	"Choices"	4-May
20	"The Prom"	11-May
21	"Graduation Day, Part One"	18-May
22	"Graduation Day, Part Two"	13-July*

STARRING

Sarah Michelle Gellar	**Buffy Summers**
Nicholas Brendon	**Xander Harris**
Alyson Hannigan	**Willow Rosenberg**
Charisma Carpenter	**Cordelia Chase**
David Boreanaz	**Angel**
Seth Green	**Oz**
Anthony Stewart Head	**Rupert Giles**

*Episodes aired out of order

THE END OF BUFFY SUMMERS'S junior year ("Becoming, Part One" and "Becoming, Part Two") at Sunnydale High was filled with significant events. Angel, free of the "curse" that restored his soul, worked with Drusilla to bring about Hell on Earth. Buffy and the Slayerettes were separated and sustained serious attacks, one of which resulted in Kendra's death at Drusilla's hand. The police suspected Buffy of murdering Kendra. The authorities conversed with Joyce, leading to a confrontation with Buffy and Joyce and the revelation that Buffy is the Slayer, followed by Principal Snyder kicking Buffy out of Sunnydale High. Spike, tired of sharing Drusilla's affections with Angel, assisted Buffy and departed the Hellmouth with Drusilla. A battered Willow worked to restore Angel's soul; ironically, Buffy still had to stab him and send him to Hell to close the gate he had opened in the demon Acathla. Having defied her mother, killed her lover and lost her school connection to her friends in the process of saving the world, an exhausted and grieving Slayer left a note and took a bus out of town.

WRITTEN AND DIRECTED BY: **Joss Whedon.** GUEST STARS: **Kristine Sutherland as Joyce Summers, Julia Lee as Lily, Carlos Jacott as Ken, Chad Todhunter as Rickie, Mary-Pat Green as Blood Bank Donor.**

ANNE

THE PLOT THICKENS

Willow, Xander, and Oz spend their last night of summer vacation gamely trying to cover the absent Slayer's patrol beat. Their quarry escapes . . . nothing new there.

Nothing new in another town either, where homeless girl Lily recognizes Buffy, who is working in a diner under her middle name, Anne. Lily was once known as Chantarelle, whom Buffy saved from

Spike and Dru back in Sunnydale (Season Two, "Lie to Me"). She begs Buffy to help locate her missing boyfriend, Rickie. Depressed and hopeless, Buffy wants nothing more to do with heroics, but she can't turn down the frantic girl.

Buffy eventually discovers Rickie's unnaturally aged corpse, recognizable only by his tattoo. She's been encountering other old people, who appear to be dazed and troubled. Her search leads her to the blood bank where Lily and Rickie used to donate, in exchange for a few bucks and cookies. A nurse has been providing the names of 'the healthy ones' to

Ken, a friendly adult who apparently offers hope at his shelter against street life and despair. Ken has lured Lily there with promises that she will see Rickie. In an attempt to save Lily, Buffy forces her way into the shelter, but tumbles through a portal into a hellish demon dimension.

Meanwhile, Giles has been searching for Buffy all summer. He painstakingly follows each lead, only to return to Sunnydale in frustration. The kids start school, and Willow is stunned to discover that Oz is a returning prodigal of sorts—he's the smartest kid ever to repeat senior year.

Buffy and Lily are rounded up with other human prisoners. Ken, his demonic nature revealed, explains the rules: They work until they drop. Then they will be returned to die in their own dimension. They will toil for years, but as time operates differently in this living hell, they will only be gone from the streets a few days.

Demon Ken and his henchmen force each new slave to announce that they are "no one." But when they prompt Buffy—"Who are you?"—a new kind of hell breaks loose. The enraged Slayer takes out the immediate threat, then motivates Lily and the other prisoners to escape. Lily reaches an epiphany of empowerment, and she and the others join in the battle. Ken is destroyed.

Victorious, Buffy and Lily seal the portal behind them, then part ways. The episode concludes with Buffy and Joyce embracing in the doorway of their home, in a reunion moving beyond words.

142

Stunt coordinator Jeff Pruitt is one of the thugs at the door of the Family Home; this is his second guest shot, as he played a vampire in "Ted."

QUOTE OF THE WEEK:

"Well, for God's sake, be careful. I mean, I appreciate your efforts to keep the vampire population down until Buffy returns, but if anything should happen to you, you should be hurt or killed, I shall take it somewhat amiss."

Giles, to Willow, Cordy, and Xander, who are subbing for Buffy.

THE AGONY AND THE ECSTASY:

Buffy is still agonizing over the loss of Angel. Giles and Joyce are concerned about their parenting skills and Buffy's absence. Willow is cautiously happy over Oz's failure to graduate from high school. Cordelia and Xander continue to be drawn together for reasons unknown. And Lily and Rickie experience true "till death do us part" love.

Jonathan Levenson was originally slated to give the "senior year" speech, not Larry.

POP-CULTURE IQ:

"Anne" works in Helen's Kitchen, a subtle reference to Hell's Kitchen, a once-dangerous neighborhood of New York.

"If I can suggest . . . 'this time it's personal'? I mean, there's a reason it's a classic."
Oz quotes the fourth *Jaws* movie for Willow's personal arsenal of Slayer quips.

CONTINUITY:

Time moving differently in Hell is established—foreshadowing Angel's experience in "Beauty and the Beasts," etc. Lily recognized Buffy from their encounters in "Lie to Me"; at the time she was a member of the vampire club, and called herself "Chanterelle."

FROM THE ORIGINAL TELEPLAY:

The following line of Willow's was cut from this episode for length:

"Oh! That reminds me. I asked around about Andrew Hoelick, our gymnastic vampire, and apparently he used to like to hang out in Hammersmith Park and pick up grilles! Or, okay, that could be girls."

The original stage directions for the main chamber of Hell include "Carey [Carey Meyer, Production Designer] and David K [David Koneff, Set Decorator] blow their entire budgets for the year, and Gareth [Davies, Producer] can be seen in the corner weeping." In other words, *très* elaborate.

WRITTEN BY: **Marti Noxon**; DIRECTED BY: **James Whitmore, Jr.**
GUEST STARS: **Kristine Sutherland as Joyce Summers, Nancy Lenehan as Pat, Armin Shimerman as Principal Snyder; with Co-stars Danny Strong as Jonathan Levenson, Jason Hall as Devon MacLeish.**

DEAD MAN'S PARTY

143

THE PLOT THICKENS

The Slayer is back in Sunnydale, but Joyce and Buffy can't seem to relax around each other, and Xander nearly stakes Buffy when she interrupts a Team Slayer staking in an alley. The group is all tricked out in soldiering gear and carrying walkie-talkies. Xander is "Nighthawk."

At least Giles's welcome is heartfelt.

Equally genuine is Principal Snyder's smirk and "tingly sensations" as he defeats Buffy and Joyce's first attempt at getting Buffy reinstated. A dejected Buffy heads home, where she meets Pat, Joyce's new book group friend. Buffy begins to grasp just how difficult her mother's life was while she, Buffy, was gone.

Joyce is determined to get Buffy back in the swim; she invites Giles and the Scoobs over for dinner. Sent to retrieve the good plates from the basement, Buffy discovers a cat's moldering corpse. She and Joyce bury it in the yard; after dark the eyes of a Nigerian mask in Joyce's bedroom glow, and the cat emerges from its grave.

The zombie cat gets back into the house. The next day, while helping to trap the cat, Giles notices the mask and makes a mental note to research it.

Later that evening, at Casa Summers, Buffy's small party spirals out of control. The Dingoes play and Joyce and Pat stay in the kitchen, discussing how difficult it is to have Buffy back. Wounded, Buffy can't manage to reconnect with Willow, Xander, or even Cordelia.

It's too much. She decides to leave again.

Joyce and Willow bust her. Everyone gets a chance to express a summer's worth of concern and anger. Meanwhile, Giles figures out that Joyce's mask is inhabited by Ovu Moboni, a Nigerian demon. As a result of its majick, the dead will walk . . . and they do. Right into Buffy's party.

Buffy, Xander, Willow, and Joyce barricade themselves in Joyce's bedroom with Pat, who doesn't survive her encounter with a zombie. Ovu Moboni possesses her dead body; when Buffy destroys Zombie Pat, Moboni is destroyed, and all the zombies with it.

The next morning Giles lets a bit of the Ripper rip into Principal Snyder. Buffy had better be readmitted, or there will be consequences.

QUOTE OF THE WEEK:

"You can't just bury stuff, Buffy! It'll come right back up to get you...."

Xander backs up Joyce, who wants to clear the air with her yet-again running-away daughter.

THE AGONY AND THE ECSTASY:

Buffy dreams of standing on a sunlit beach with Angel. Her dream turns to nightmare as he reminds her that she killed him. She also dreams of him at Sunnydale High, which is deserted except for the two of them. The ecstasy of being home is dimmed for Buffy and replaced by the agonies varying from the outright rejection of Principal Snyder to the distance her friends maintain. Running away accomplished nothing. No one is able to keep the past dead and buried, not even the Slayer.

POP-CULTURE IQ:

"Sorry. He's not here. You got the wrong <u>casa</u>, Mr. Belvedere."
Partygoer's dismissal of Giles on the telephone, mistaking him for a fictional TV Brit butler.

The episode title is a reference to an Oingo Boingo song of the same name, while the zombies obviously watched Philadelphia filmmaker George Romero's classic movies to learn how to do the zombie shuffle.

CONTINUITY:

The Slayer and parties are destined not to mix well ("Reptile Boy"), a trait which will continue into college ("A New Man"). Xander has no comprehension of the irony in his comment about Buffy's associating with "kindly old people" during her summer absence. Giles's familiarity with hot wiring cars is a reminder of his wilder days ("The Dark Age" and "Band Candy").

FROM THE ORIGINAL TELEPLAY:

Joyce's descriptive venting about Snyder was cut from the episode due to length:

"Have you ever noticed his teeth? They're like tiny, little rodent teeth—horrible gnashing little teeth. You just want to pull them out with pliers."

FAITH, HOPE & TRICK

WRITTEN BY: David Greenwalt; **DIRECTED BY:** James A. Contner. **GUEST STARS:** Kristine Sutherland as Joyce Summers, K. Todd Freeman as Mr. Trick, Fab Filippo as Scott Hope, Jeremy Roberts as Kakistos, Eliza Dushku as Faith, Armin Shimerman as Principal Snyder.

THE PLOT THICKENS

Buffy, still *persona non grata* on the Sunnydale High campus, shares a picnic lunch off campus with the Scooby Gang and mildly flirts with "nice guy senior" Scott Hope. The arrival of suave vampire Mr. Trick and the ancient Kakistos, who has been a vampire so long his demonic aspect has over-

whelmed his original human form, promises to disrupt her idyllic attempt at enjoying girlie stuff. When Snyder reluctantly read-mits Buffy, she and Willow think Giles will celebrate. Instead, he is preoccupied with a protective spell to make sure Acathla is bound. He asks a number of probing ques-tions about how Buffy killed Angel, leaving her somewhat shaken.

Later at the Bronze, Scott Hope asks Buffy to dance. She is distracted by one of the dancers, whose extroverted personality looks doomed to meet an untimely end by an obvious vamp-face (AKA "Slut-o-rama and Disco Dave" in Cordy-speak). Buffy and the gang ride to the girl's rescue in time to witness a spectacular vamp dusting by said girl. Oz appraises the sit-uation quickly: "I'm going to go out on a limb here and say we've got a new Slayer in town."

They do. She is Faith, visiting from Boston while her Watcher is on the annual Watchers' Retreat. Sassy and fetching, she quickly assimilates into life in Sunnydale. Her stories and lust for the slay-ing life appeal to everyone except Buffy, including Joyce and Buffy's "not boyfriend" Scott.

Mr. Trick and Kakistos plot to kill the Slayers, while Buffy and Faith experiment with the concept of duo-patrolling. But Faith's slaying style is of the bad: she loses herself in a frenzy of violence rather than efficiently staking her opponents. She's also impulsive, rushing into dangerous situa-tions without a plan.

Then Giles finds out that Faith's lying: Her Watcher isn't at the annual Watchers' Retreat; she's dead. Buffy also reports a run-in with Kakistos's henchvamps. Giles knows who Kakistos is, and he's plenty alarmed by the ancient vampire's arrival in Sunnydale. Could it possibly have something to do with Faith's arrival?

Buffy goes to Faith's hotel to get some answers. Turns out Kakistos killed Faith's Watcher brutally. Faith was there and saw it all. She's terrified of Kakistos.

Then Mr. Trick, Kakistos, and his minions arrive. Faith nearly abandons hope, but once more the tag team of Faith and Buffy gains the upper hand. The pragmatic Mr. Trick abandons Kakistos to his death. Giles assumes temporary Watcher duty for Faith as well as Buffy.

Faith has been freed of the thing that haunts her: Now it's Buffy's turn. She tells Giles and the others that Angel was cured before she killed him. Knowing full well that his soul had been restored, she still sent him to Hell.

Alone, Buffy goes to Angel's mansion and sadly takes off the Claddagh ring he gave her. Scott Hope wants to date her; it's time to move on. She whispers her goodbye.

As soon as she leaves, Angel drops into this dimension, naked and trembling. He is back.

QUOTE OF THE WEEK:

WILLOW: "Maybe we shouldn't be too couply around Buffy."
CORDELIA: "Oh, you mean 'cause of how the only guy that ever liked her turned into a vicious killer and had to be put down like a dog?"
XANDER: "Can she cram complex issues into a nutshell or what?"
The couples Xander and Cordy, Willow and Oz try to spare off-campus Buffy's feelings.

THE AGONY AND THE ECSTASY:

Giles's paternal heartstrings are tugged by Buffy's inability to heal the emotional wounds inflicted by her killing Angel. Buffy, just recently returned to Sunnydale, is not comfortable with how well Faith "gets along with my friends, my Watcher, my mom—look! Now she's getting along with my fries!" Faith's thrill for the kill and suppressed emotions over the death of her Watcher at Kakistos's cloven hands are just the tip of her unstable emotional iceberg. Scott Hope wants to date Buffy; she takes off the ring Angel gave her for her birthday, the night they made love.

> "All I'm sayin' is, we stay local—where the humans are jumpin' and the cotton is high—but we live global." Mr. Trick mutates George Gershwin's *Porgy & Bess* for his own benefit

POP-CULTURE IQ:

"I'm the one getting Single White Femaled here."
Buffy, referring to *Single White Female,* a 1992 film starring Bridget Fonda and Jennifer Jason Leigh. Nobody knew the new roomie was psycho. There's a comparison to be made with Faith.

With lots of time on her hands, Buffy surpasses Martha Stewart, homemaker extraordinaire, with the picnic lunch she provides for her friends.

CONTINUITY:

Faith's deceased Watcher is the first mention of a contemporary female (Giles's grandmother shared his vocation), setting the stage for Mrs. Post in "Revelations." Buffy is uncomfortable from the very start by Faith's enthusiasm for slayage. Faith demonstrates her hunger for food, sensuality and slaying—shades of "The Zeppo"—and Buffy worries about Faith's stepping into her shoes ("Who Am I?"). We are reminded of both Buffy's death ("Prophecy Girl") and Kendra's ("Becoming, Part One"), with Joyce learning of the former for the first time, and the fact that a new Slayer is called when the current one dies. Giles tricked Buffy into admitting that Willow's spell worked; he'll "trick" her again—

with grave repercussions—in "Helpless." Xander has never told Buffy that Willow was trying the spell again ("Becoming, Part Two").

Buffy and Mr. Trick's exchange from their battle was cut due to length:
MR. TRICK: "I believe this dance is mine."
BUFFY: "The music stopped."
MR. TRICK: "But the beat goes on. Gimme whatchya got."

WRITTEN BY: **Marti Noxon;** DIRECTED BY: **James Whitmore, Jr.**
GUEST STARS: **Fab Filippo as Scott Hope, John Patrick White as Pete Clarner, Danielle Weeks as Debbie Foley, Phill Lewis as Stephen Platt, Eliza Dushku as Faith.**

BEAUTY AND THE BEASTS

THE PLOT THICKENS

Readings from *The Call of the Wild,* Jack London's classic examination about the nature of the beast, frames this episode. Buffy and Faith discuss Faith's theory that "Every guy—from 'Manimal' right on down to 'Mr. I Loved *The English Patient*'—has beast in him." Buffy's not sure of that; she's got her own issues to deal with, and Snyder has made visits to the school counselor, Mr. Platt, part of her conditions for readmittance. Scott's friend Debbie can relate—she sees Mr. Platt as well.

The routine of locking Oz up in the library during his three wolf nights a month was established in Season Two. Now there's bad news: A student has been mutilated and killed, and there's evidence that Oz got out of the cage. This distressing situation brings Buffy down from her good initial meeting with Mr. Platt.

That night, patrolling, Buffy collides with Angel. He's feral and savage, completely out of his mind. She clocks him and chains him to the mansion wall. Could it have been Angel who killed the student?

Anxious to clear her boyfriend, Willow collects forensic evidence. It's frustratingly inconclusive. Oz and Willow are distraught, but Buffy does not share the fact of Angel's return, and that he might have been the killer. After she relieves Faith of Oz-watching, she spends the night searching library tomes for information on Angel's return.

When Debbie and Pete duck into a garden shed for a quick makeout session, it becomes clear that Pete concocted some kind of Jekyll/Hyde potion that has transformed him into some kind of rage demon. When he becomes angry, he turns into a horrifying creature with throbbing veins. Debbie knows, but she has told no one, just as she has never shared the fact that he beats her.

The discovery of the viciously slain-in-broad-daylight Mr. Platt clears Oz. Buffy and Willow question Debbie, the remaining common denominator among the slain. She is willing to defend Pete to the death.

Pete discovers Oz locked in the book cage. Jealous over the guitarist's friendship with Debbie, Pete attacks Oz in Rage Monster mode mere moments before Oz wolfs out. In the ensuing chaos Giles gets shot with a tranquilizer dart, and both beast boys are on the run. Pete's run ends in the garden shed, where he kills Debbie, then turns on Buffy. A slightly less feral Angel joins Buffy's fight with Pete, strangling him with the chains from the still-attached shackles, then falling at her feet, whispering her name.

QUOTE OF THE WEEK:

GILES: "Clearly we're looking for a depraved, sadistic animal."
OZ: "Present. Hey, I may be a cold-blooded jelly doughnut—but my timing's impeccable."
Oz walks in on a conversation dissing a local brutal killer who, fortunately for the werewolf, kills during the day.

THE AGONY AND THE ECSTASY:

Just as it looks as if talking to Mr. Platt may help Buffy resolve her Angel issues, Mr. Platt is killed, and Angel's back in her life and a murder suspect. Willow's concern for Oz and Debbie's for Pete parallel the Buffy/Angel angst. Each girl is torn between wanting the murderous rampage to stop and fear that her boyfriend is behind it. Scott Hope and Buffy have become a couple, and bond over the deaths of Debbie and Pete.

POP-CULTURE IQ:

"I can handle the Oz Full Monty."
The Full Monty was a 1997 British film about a group of men who decide to give the Chippendales a run for their money. Xander's talking about Oz's naked state after he de-wolfs.

> Willow uses a Scooby Doo lunchbox for her forensic tools, perfect for a member of the "Scooby Gang."

CONTINUITY:

The fact that Oz is repeating his senior year ("Dead Man's Party") is revisited with his offer to assist Debbie with biology notes. Giles refers to Jenny Calendar's death ("Passion"). Buffy remembers her time in the demon dimension ("Anne"). For once Willow supplies doughnuts, usually Xander's job ("The Zeppo"). When Buffy enters the mansion wearing a leather jacket, it is reminiscent of the jacket Angel lent her early in the relationship ("Angel").

148

FROM THE ORIGINAL TELEPLAY:

Scott advises Buffy before her visit to Mr. Platt in this exchange cut due to length:

SCOTT: "Stable. Okay. Topics to avoid. The little men that live in your teeth…your compulsion to paint circus clowns…"

BUFFY: "But if God keeps telling me to kill— it just seems snotty not to, you know?"

HOMECOMING

WRITTEN BY: **David Greenwalt;** DIRECTED BY: **David Greenwalt.**
GUEST STARS: **K. Todd Freeman as Mr. Trick, Jeremy Ratchford as Lyle Gorch, Fab Filippo as Scott Hope, Ian Abercrombie as Old Man, Harry Groener as Mayor Richard Wilkins III, Eliza Dushku as Faith;** with Co-stars **Danny Strong as Jonathan Levenson, Joseph Daube as Hans Gruenshtahler, Jermyn Daube as Frederick Gruenshtahler, Lee Everett as Candy, Chad Stahelski as Kulak.**

THE PLOT THICKENS:

Limo and partner plans are made for the Homecoming Dance. Scott invites Buffy, and she's in. Buffy secretly takes off to the mansion to check on a recovering Angel, practically flinging the fact of Scott Hope in his face to maintain distance between the two of them. A distracted Cordelia, working the room in her campaign to be elected Homecoming Queen, completely forgets to tell Buffy that it's yearbook picture day. Buffy's pissed: this time it really is personal, and she throws down the gauntlet. The school's only big enough for one Homecoming Queen, and Buffy is going to be it.

Meanwhile, Willow and Xander are putting on a formal-wear fashion show for each other, in hopes of stunning their respective sweeties, when their lips lock into passionate mutual kissage. They are overcome with guilt . . . and really wanna do it again.

Meanwhile, Scott has broken up with Buffy. Buffy, suddenly datelesss goes for the crown with a vengeance.

Mr. Trick is keeping busy, too. He has organized SlayerFest '98, promising some out-of-town hunters some exotic prey—two Slayers to bag. German psychos Hans and Fredrick Gruenshtahler, demon Kulak of the Miquot Clan, "The Most Dangerous Game" hunter Frawley, and Texas vamp Lyle Gorch and wife Candy show up with lots of weapons and enthusiasm. And money.

The competition heats up on both the Homecoming and SlayerFest fronts, as the competitors bring a variety of weapons from muffin baskets to bear traps into play. Buffy is chagrined to find her best friend, Xander, and Oz working for Cordelia. Guilt-ridden, Willow and Xander arrange for the gang's limo to pick up Cordelia and Buffy only, so they can have a good, long talk.

Hans is the chauffeur; while the two girls argue over who should get which corsage, he transports them to Miller's Woods instead of the prom. SlayerFest is on!

While Buffy and Cordelia battle for their lives in the woods, a mopey Willow and Xander make small talk with Giles, and Faith, angry with Scott for hurting Buffy, deliberately humiliates him in front of his date.

Buffy and Cordelia make a pretty good team; they remove Frawley and Kulak in the woods, with a little help from a German grenade launcher. They flee to the library, where the Gorches have trussed Giles like a rodeo calf. Buffy stakes Candy with a spatula but is temporarily knocked out, while the Queen of Mean, seemingly defenseless, scares the wits out of Lyle. He runs fleeing into the night.

Buffy realizes they are being tracked via their corsages and, with a little strategy and judicious use of a spitball, arranges for the Germans to fire on each other. Cordelia, Buffy, and Giles arrive at the dance just in time to hear the announcement of two queens sharing the crown: competitors Holly and Michelle.

QUOTE OF THE WEEK:

"I thought, Homecoming Queen, I could open a yearbook someday and say, 'I was there, I went to high school and had friends and for just one minute I got to live in the world.' And there'd be proof. Proof I was chosen for something other than this. Besides, I look cute in a tiara." Buffy explains it all to Cordelia, who still doesn't care.

Buffy stunt-man Chad Stahelski is in the Kulak suit.

THE AGONY AND THE ECSTASY:

An increasingly sentient Angel hears about Scott Hope from Buffy for the first time; the next day Scott breaks off his relationship with Buffy. Willow and Xander are guilty enough over their kiss to support Cordelia's campaign over Buffy's. Cordelia sums up her affection for Xander: "He just . . . grows on you, like a Chia Pet."

POP-CULTURE IQ:

"Are you kidding? I've been doing the Vulcan death grip since I was four." Cordelia strives to get the Trekkie vote during her Queen campaign.

CONTINUITY:

Blood from Mel's Butcher Shop will appear again when Spike needs sustenance in Season Four. At Hemery High, Buffy was not only a cheerleader, but also the Prom Princess and the Fiesta Queen— at Sunnydale, she may not even make the class photo section of the yearbook. The loss of some of Sunnydale's students at the "Dead Man's Party" is mentioned. Lyle Gorch seems to be the Energizer Bunny of vampires—he keeps coming after the Slayer, then winds up retreating (Buffy killed his brother, Tector, in "Bad Eggs"). Mayor Richard Wilkins III is introduced; he "invites" Mr. Trick to his office for a dressing down. His true nature is partially revealed, but there have been hints that he's

Willow claims "She Knows," played by Dingoes Ate My Baby (Four Star Mary), was written for her by Oz.

not exactly Mr. Civic Responsibility based on Snyder's calls to and from city hall ("Some Assembly Required," "Becoming, Part Two," "Dead Man's Party"). "School Hard" is the first episode where we know Snyder is working with the Mayor. Cordelia's two-word "long story" of their evening is a parallel to Oz's story of his werewolf history from "Faith, Hope & Trick:" Buffy: "Long story." Oz: "Got bit." Buffy: "Long story." Cordy: "Got hunted."

FROM THE ORIGINAL TELEPLAY:

The following exchange was cut due to length:
Buffy: "Okay, how 'bout . . . you vote for me and I don't beat the living crap out of you."
Jonathan: "That works good for me."
Buffy: "Tell your friends!"
Had this encounter played as originally written, Buffy and Jonathan's interactions in "Earshot" and "The Prom" would've been very different.

WRITTEN BY: **Jane Espenson**; DIRECTED BY: **Michael Lange**.
GUEST STARS: **Kristine Sutherland as Joyce Summers, K. Todd Freeman as Mr. Trick, Robin Sachs as Ethan Rayne, Harry Groener as Mayor Richard Wilkins III, Armin Shimerman as Principal Snyder.**

BAND CANDY

THE PLOT THICKENS:

It's a late night in Sunnydale: among the gravestones in the cemetery Buffy uses her number two pencil for SAT preparation and vampire staking, and the Mayor solicits Mr. Trick's assistance procuring outside talent for a project of his. It's an important year for the Mayor; one of his demon sponsors is due for some tribute. "And I keep my campaign promises."

The gang's SAT-studying bitch fest ends as Principal Snyder forcibly distributes boxes of band candy to sell. Buffy cuts short her interactions with both Joyce and Giles (after forcing purchases of multiple candy bars) to duck out to visit Angel, who is still recovering. Joyce and Giles bust her for using each other as excuses, then disappearing altogether. Weary from the burdens of parenthood, they set to consoling themselves with the chocolate band candy.

Ethan Rayne, the sorcerer who worships chaos and a former friend of Giles, is presiding over the production of the bars. This is Ethan's third trip to Sunnydale ("Halloween" and "The Dark Age").

The students notice the staff at Sunnydale High behaving in an unusually irresponsible manner, while the chocolate bars seem to sell themselves. An oddly relaxed Joyce and Giles grant Buffy the joy of driving Joyce's car—which she does, extraordinarily badly. Willow and Buffy drive to the Bronze, which has been overtaken by Sunnydale's adults, now behaving like teenagers. Mr. Trick and Ethan supervise production and distribution of more candy.

Spazball teen Snyder joins Willow, Buffy, and Oz as they head to Giles's. Joyce and Giles cruise downtown, where Giles liberates a coat for an adoring Joyce from a window display; when a police officer objects, the Ripper disarms him. Joyce is transported . . . right on top of the hood of the police car.

Once Buffy realizes the link between the band candy and the adults abandoning their responsibilities, she makes Snyder lead them to the source. Buffy stops her march on Ethan's warehouse only long enough to break up a smooching Giles and Joyce. Ethan rats out Mr. Trick (but not the Mayor) when

Buffy and Giles trap him in a "talk or bleed" situation. Ethan reveals that the purpose of the candy is to distract Sunnydale's adult population while a demon "tribute" is collected. Oz discovers the tribute is a ritual feeding of newborns to the demon Lurconis. Buffy secures Ethan with the handcuffs Joyce contributes, then uses a recovering Giles's knowledge to track Lurconis to the sewers. Buffy leads Giles and Joyce to Mr. Trick's sacrificial area in time to rescue the babies and toast Lurconis. The Mayor warns Mr. Trick to be careful in his future interactions with the Slayer.

QUOTE OF THE WEEK:

"I don't get this. The candy's supposed to make you all immature and stuff, but I ate a ton and I don't feel any dif—never mind."

Xander has a moment of revelation regarding his maturity—i.e., he has none.

THE AGONY AND THE ECSTASY:

Buffy keeps Angel's return a secret, especially from Xander and Giles. Willow and Xander continue to battle being attracted to each other despite their feelings for Oz and Cordelia. Willow, swamped with guilt, momentarily believes she's busted when Cordelia inquires "Wanna swap?" during research time. Buffy believes Giles and Joyce did not progress beyond the smooching stage when they were wild and crazy sweeties ("Earshot").

POP-CULTURE IQ:

"I'm supervised twenty-four seven. It's like living in The Real World house, only real."
Buffy compares her life to the MTV "reality TV" program in which a group of young people, previously unknown to one another, live in a house provided by MTV. In return they allow the MTV cameras to film their daily activities and to interview them periodically.

"Um, as much as I'm sure we all love the idea of going all Willy Loman . . . we're not in the band."
Willy Loman is the tragic main character in the Arthur Miller play *Death of a Salesman*. Buffy is not loving the idea of selling candy bars. (Nor salesman in general—"Restless")

"Call me Snyder. Just a last name. Like Barbarino."
Striving for coolness, Principal Snyder refers to John Travolta's character on the TV series *Welcome Back, Kotter*.

> **"So let's just sit quietly...and pretend to read or something until we're sure Commandant Snyder is gone, and then we're all out of here."**

Commandant Snyder is a reference to the '60s TV comedy show *Hogan's Heroes,* about a group of Allied POWs in a Nazi prison camp. Ms. Barton has been affected by the magic candy.

> **"Do you like Seals and Croft?"**

Seals and Croft is a classic '70s group; their most recognizable song is "Summer Breeze." Joyce is looking for common ground with her crush, Giles.

> **"Kiss rocks? Why would anyone want to kiss—? Oh, wait. I get it."**

Kiss was a rock group founded in 1972. Willow and company are being put on graffiti-removal detail.

> Angel's smoothly performed T'ai Chi Ch'uan exercises provide a nice contrast to Snyder's "I took Tae Kwon Do at the Y."

> **"You are so cool. You're like Burt Reynolds."**

Joyce tries to cozy up to Ripper by comparing him to the actor who was once considered one of the hottest men in Hollywood.

> **"That's cool. Kind of Juice Newton."**

Joyce compares a coat in a store window to the style of the Grammy-award-winning country/pop singer who became popular in the 1980s.

CONTINUITY:

Joyce calls Giles "Ripper," harkening back to "The Dark Age." Buffy elaborates: "Giles at sixteen. Less 'together guy.' More 'bad magic, hates the world, ticking-time-bomb' kind of guy." Buffy has her first face-to-face encounter with Mr. Trick—"You and me, girl. There's high times ahead" (at least until "Consequences"). The Mayor's habit of paying tribute to demons is established. Buffy's ongoing lack of success with cars and their brakepads is punctuated by a pretty neat car crash.

FROM THE ORIGINAL TELEPLAY:

Buffy cracks wise at the robed figures before availing herself of a gas pipe and their lighting system in this comment cut for length:

> **"I love that you guys love torches."**

A chant by the Lurconis summoners was also cut due to length.

WRITTEN BY: **Douglas Petrie;** DIRECTED BY: **James A. Contner.**
GUEST STARS: **Serena Scott Thomas as Gwendolyn Post, Eliza Dushku as Faith; with Co-stars Jason Hall as Devon MacLeish, Kate Rodger as Paramedic.**

THE PLOT THICKENS:

Xander and Willow are at the Bronze with their honeys; desperate to distract Cordelia and Oz from noticing their mutual attraction, Willow and Xander turn the conversation to Buffy's atypical absences of late and speculate she may have a new boyfriend. Buffy plays along for a moment, but her actual plans for the evening are for synchronized slaying with Faith. The Slayers and Giles are satisfied with their performance, but Faith's new Watcher, Mrs. Gwendolyn Post, is critical.

Yes, Mrs. Gwendolyn Post has arrived, all spit and polish, ready to criticize Giles for essentially "going native." He's positively American, by her standards, implying his research methods are inadequate, as is his occult library. And his Slayer is not getting the regimented training one requires.

Mrs. Post informs them that not only is she in Sunnydale for Faith, but also to bring them news about Lagos, a demon seeking a powerful occult weapon, the Glove of Myhnegon. Initially her cold, disdainful demeanor fails to win over Giles, Buffy, or Faith.

Buffy continues to visit Angel. She still hasn't told anyone he's back. She doesn't know why he was allowed to return, and he's still quite weak. Hyperaware of each other, she and he finish their Tai Chi practice with a near embrace. Their love can never be fulfilled again—one moment of true happiness and Angel would lose his soul again.

A nervous Buffy shares the news of Lagos with Angel; then the frustrated pair go their separate ways. Giles continues in research mode in the library with the surprisingly unwilling assistance of Willow and Xander. Interrupting their naughty kissing in the stacks, Giles informs them that the Glove of Myhnegon is likely to be in the Restfield Cemetery in the Von Hauptman family crypt.

Faith and Buffy search one of the other dozen or so cemeteries in Sunnydale. Faith is sharing notes on her so very unromantic past, but Buffy isn't forthcoming with any details about Angel. They split up, and Faith heads for Shady Hill Cemetery solo, where her confrontation with Lagos ends with him still on the loose and her on the ground. Xander is shaken when he discovers the back-from-beyond Angel exiting the Von Hauptman crypt with a bundle under his arm, but not so much as when he tracks him to the mansion where he spies Buffy and Angel passionately embracing.

Buffy and Angel separate, and Angel shows the Glove to Buffy; he agrees to store it at the mansion for safekeeping. Mrs. Post and Giles explore various magick tomes for more information about the Glove while she tweaks him about his influence—or lack thereof—on Buffy. As he is reassuring her that he has his Slayer firmly under control, Xander bursts in, urgently exclaiming, "Giles. We have a big problem. It's Buffy."

Later Buffy enters the library with triumphant news about the Glove, only to find Xander, Cordelia, Willow, Oz, and Giles hostile and freaked out about the revelation that Angel is still alive and that she's been hiding him. The conversation heats up; Giles ends the angry confrontation, but when Buffy privately thanks him, he reveals how deeply her betrayal of his trust has hurt him.

Mrs. Post visits Faith in her Spartan motel room, and encourages Faith to trust and rely on her by reinforcing the distance Faith feels from Buffy and the gang. Xander tells Faith that Angel is back and has the Glove, and she's off to slay. Xander wants a piece of Dead Boy, too, and they decide to go to the library to gather weapons.

Giles invites Mrs. Post to his office to share the whereabouts of the Glove and the method of destroying it; once he's told her all he knows, she knocks him unconscious.

Willow verges on sharing her Xander secret with Buffy but backs off when Lagos attacks and Buffy decapitates him. Xander and Faith arrive to arm themselves in the library; when they discover the badly injured Giles, Xander remains with him and Faith leaves, believing she has one more reason to kill Angel. Not that she needed any more. . . .

Buffy and Willow intercept Giles's ambulance, and Xander tells them Faith has headed for the mansion. Mrs. Post reaches the mansion first, and Angel's rewarded for showing her the Glove's location with a blow to the back of the head. Angel rises from the floor in vampface and is battling Mrs. Post when Faith arrives. Mrs. Post instructs Faith to take Angel out.

Faith is inches from successfully dusting Angel when Buffy intervenes. Willow and Xander bring the ingredients for the Living Flame to the mansion and try to stop the battling Slayers. Mrs. Post takes the opportunity to model the Glove as her very dangerous fashion accessory. It was the Glove she wanted all along. When Faith realizes she's been played, she works with Buffy to fight Mrs. Post. Buffy, knowing the Glove is now permanently attached to Mrs. Post's arm, throws a shard of glass at her and slices off her arm. Mrs. Post is dispatched in a blaze of electric glory. They successfully destroy the Glove and tentatively mend bridges between friends. Faith rebuffs Buffy's overtures, preferring to remain a lone wolf.

QUOTE OF THE WEEK:

"Ronnie. Deadbeat. Steve. Klepto. Kenny. <u>Drummer</u>. Eventually I had to face up to my destiny as a loser magnet. Now it's strictly get some and get gone. You can't trust guys."   Faith sets the foundation for her romantic relationships.

THE AGONY AND THE ECSTASY:

Almost everyone suffers from Buffy's keeping Angel's return a secret, especially Giles. Xander and Willow bring their own issues to their responses to Angel and Buffy: Willow decides perhaps secret romances might be all right, and Xander channels his frustrations at his situation with Cordelia and Willow into anger at Angel and Buffy. Buffy reminds Xander of his previous romantic interest in her, to Cordelia's annoyance. Angel and Buffy continue to walk a fine balance in their relationship, not wanting to resurrect Angelus. Faith's feeling of isolation from Buffy and her friends grows.

POP-CULTURE IQ:

> Buffy's comment "It's another Tuesday night in Sunnydale" alludes to the show's regular Tuesday night schedule.

"Excuse me, Mary Poppins, you're not listening...."
Faith envisions the stuffy new Watcher, Mrs. Post, as P. L. Travers's British nanny

BUFFY (re: Giles): "How long do you think he can stay angry at me anyway?"
WILLOW: "The emotional Marathon Man?"
Willow attributes Giles with the psychological prowess of William Goldman's 1974 title character.

CONTINUITY:

It is established that there are twelve cemeteries in Sunnydale. Xander mentions Buffy's killing zombies in "Dead Man's Party" and torching Lurconis in "Band Candy" (and, in the original script, her "freeing the enslaved populace of a parallel dimension" à la "Anne"). Faith mentions the death of her previous Watcher ("Faith, Hope & Trick"). The wrapped glove parallels the Judge's arm in "Surprise." The "Demons Anonymous" intervention for Buffy regarding Angel will be replayed in a different form for Willow in "Something Blue." Angel's attacks on Buffy and her friends while Angelus in Season Two are painfully remembered ("Innocence" through "Becoming, Part Two"). Buffy's betrayal of Giles's feelings will be reversed when he betrays her trust in "Helpless." Mrs. Post's evil intentions affect Wesley's reception in "Bad Girls." Willow's willingness to keep romantic relations a secret will resurface with Tara in Season Four. Willow mentions her own slaying ability, notably in "Anne." Faith somewhat surprisingly forgoes the crossbow when she and Xander are choosing weapons to use against Angel ("Choices" and "Graduation Day, Part One"). Faith and Buffy have their first face off in Angel's mansion, but not their last ("Enemies").

> **Guest star Serena Scott Thomas and "I-Loved-*The-English Patient*"actress Kristen Scott Thomas are sisters.**

FROM THE ORIGINAL TELEPLAY:

Cordelia is not convinced Angel has reformed in this exchange cut due to length:
CORDELIA: "Okay, but when there's a big massacre, who gets the I-told-you-so?"
XANDER: "You get the I-told-you-so."
CORDELIA: "Just so we're clear..."

Faith's comment on the interior design of her hotel room was also cut for length:
"The decorator just left. Cost me a pretty penny—but a motif like this don't come cheap."

156

WRITTEN BY: **Dan Vebber;** DIRECTED BY: **David Semel.**
GUEST STARS: **Kristine Sutherland as Joyce Summers, Harry Groener as Mayor Richard Wilkins III, James Marsters as Spike; with Co-stars Jack Plotnick as Deputy Mayor Allan Finch, Mark Burnham as Lenny, Suzanne Krull as Clerk.**

THE PLOT THICKENS

Xander comforts Willow, who is devastated by her self-perceived poor performance on the SATs. Buffy's unanticipated high scores are a shock to all, causing her to reevaluate her thoughts on her future. Cordelia points out that non-Hellmouth options are a good thing, asking, "What kind of moron would want to come back here?" Spike's drunken arrival answers that.

Spike mopes for Drusilla in the abandoned factory. Cordelia, Xander, Willow, and Oz plan a double date for bowling. Cordy actually has photos of Xander in her locker, and Oz gifts Willow with a Pez candy-dispenser witch—true love! Buffy shares Joyce's enthusiastic response to her high test scores with Giles, on his way to a retreat. He unexpectedly responds in the positive when Buffy mentions the idea of school outside of Sunnydale. Willow decides to solve her romantic dilemma through an anti-love spell. Spike is in the majick shop looking for a curse to torment Angel; when Willow enters, he gets a better idea.

The Mayor authorizes Deputy Mayor Allan Finch to seek Mr. Trick's assistance in ridding Sunnydale of Spike. Angel endorses Buffy's tentative plan to leave Sunnydale, much to her chagrin. Willow tries to perform her de-lusting spell on an unknowing Xander, but he refuses to cooperate. Spike ends their debate by kidnapping both of them, knocking Xander unconscious, and informing Willow she is to perform a spell to draw Drusilla back to him—or they're both dead, Xander first. She persuades him she can't possibly cast a successful spell without more ingredients and a spell book. Oz and Cordelia alert Buffy about Xander and Willow's disappearance; she sets them on the road to retrieve Giles and is phoning Joyce when she hears Spike greet Joyce on the other end of the line.

Joyce is lending Spike a sympathetic ear when Angel spots them over their cocoa. Spike is so delighted by Angel's impotent attempts to convince Joyce to invite him in, he doesn't notice Buffy until she knocks him to the ground. While Joyce watches in confusion, Buffy invites Angel in and prepares to dust Spike, halting only when he reveals he is holding hostages. Oz and Cordelia are diverted from their frantic Giles retrieval by Oz's detecting Willow's scent. Spike, Buffy, and Angel search the magick shop for spell components. Spike decides misery loves company and spells out Buffy and Angel's romantic contradictions, leaving them "comeback deficient." Willow comforts a revived Xander; they rationalize the comfort's turn to romance through invoking their dire situation. A situation that is dire in new ways, as Oz and Cordelia arrive to rescue them, only to discover them kissing. Cordelia's hasty exit from the warehouse is cut short as she falls through a rotten stair, impaling herself on a sharp spike. While an anxious Willow watches, Xander descends to check her condition. Oz goes for help.

Buffy, Angel, and Spike's return to the warehouse is interrupted by the appearance of ten vampires sent by Mr. Trick, led by Lenny, an old acquaintance of Spike's. It takes a while, but the ten-to-three odds aren't in the vampires' favor, especially when Buffy and Angel discover an assortment of bottles of holy water. Spike finds the rush of the battle improves his spirits to such a degree he no longer feels the need for Willow or her spell. Revived, he heads off to Brazil to "tie [Drusilla] up and torture her" until she cares for him again. Buffy consoles Willow, grieving over Oz. Xander attempts to make peace with the hospitalized Cordelia, who summons her strength just long enough to dismiss him absolutely. Buffy tells Angel she can't continue their relationship, that she has to be honest with herself. The episode closes with "a series of images: the kids in misery," as Willow, Oz, Xander, Cordelia, and Buffy all face the future with sadness and uncertainty.

QUOTE OF THE WEEK:

BUFFY: "She saw these scores and her head spun around and exploded."
GILES: "I've been on the Hellmouth too long. That was metaphorical, yes?"
Giles worries Joyce has had an *Exorcist* moment over Buffy's high SAT scores.

157

THE AGONY AND THE ECSTASY:

Everyone in this episode is "love's bitch" in one way or another. Willow and Xander struggle with the opposing desires to act on their attractions and be faithful to their chosen partners. Buffy and Angel struggle with admitting their continued love, as they've been cloaking it in the guise of her playing nursemaid to a friend in need. Cordelia makes the momentous leap of publicly displaying Xander's photo in her locker, only to find herself cuckolded, as does Oz. Spike pines for Drusilla the fickle (Angel/Chaos Demon/Fungus Demon). Joyce continues to struggle with Buffy being a Slayer, her enthusiasm for the SATs a reflection of her continued desire for Buffy to have a normal life.

POP-CULTURE IQ:

"I'm Cletus the Slack-Jawed Yokel."
Bemoaning her "low" SAT scores, Willow compares herself to the stereotypically idiotic character from *The Simpsons*.

"Be kind. Rewind."
Buffy implores Giles to back up during his discussion of her leaving Sunnydale to go to college. She's using video store vernacular.

"I'm thinking Weird Science."
Buffy may mean either the 1985 film or the 1994 television show as she inspects Willow's abandoned spell ingredients after Spike abducted her.

Angel's long life and international experiences allow him to read philosopher Jean-Paul Sarte's *Nausea* in the original French (*La Nausée*).

CONTINUITY:

Spike's return is a fractured mirror of his original arrival in "School Hard" (see below), and a reverse of his departure in "Becoming, Part Two." Buffy's comment "Faith could be Miss Sunnydale in the Slayer pageant" evokes "Homecoming." The Mayor knew of Spike's activities in Sunnydale during the second season but didn't take exception to them before. Xander is nervous about Willow's "de-lusting" spell after Amy's love spell misfired in "Bewitched, Bothered, and Bewildered." Drusilla leaves Spike for a Chaos Demon this time; in "The Harsh Light of Day" Harmony reports that she left him for a Fungus Demon instead. Spike nuzzles Willow's neck, a moment they'll relive when he unsuccessfully attacks her in "The Initiative." Joyce has no reason to fear Spike, introduced to her as a singer in a band in "Becoming, Part Two." Joyce hears in passing that Willow is a witch, but doesn't take it seriously until "Gingerbread." Oz's were-abilities manifesting when he's human are a pivotal plot point in "New Moon Rising." The events of "The Wish," "Doppelgangland" and Anya/Anyanaka's presence in Sunnydale are all consequences of Xander and Willow's factory embrace. Spike's speech about how impossible Buffy and Angel's relationship is will be echoed by the Mayor ("Choices") and Joyce ("The Prom"), eventually resulting in Angel's departure.

FROM THE ORIGINAL TELEPLAY:

Script directions for the teaser:

[A shot-by-shot recreation of Spike's arrival in "School Hard." There's that "Welcome to Sunnydale" sign. And here comes Spike's car, crashing into it as it screeches to a stop. Growling rock cue as the door opens. Except instead of one boot, an entire Spike falls bodily out of the car. A clatter of empties, beer bottles and cans, accompanies him. Our boy's bombed.]

SPIKE: "Home sweet . . . home."

[A moment of looking blearily around, then his head drops back and hits pavement.]

THE WISH

WRITTEN BY: **Marti Noxon**; DIRECTED BY: **David Greenwalt**.
GUEST STARS: **Mark Metcalf as the Master, Emma Caulfield as Anyanaka/Anya, Larry Bagby III as Larry Blaisdell, Mercedes McNab as Harmony Kendall**; with Co-star **Danny Strong as Jonathan Levenson**.

THE PLOT THICKENS

Xander and Willow help Buffy slay as a distraction from their broken hearts. Cordelia, mending physically, burns Xander's photos. On Cordelia's first day back at school, fashion-aware new girl Anya doesn't harass her for having dated Xander like the other Cordettes do. Evening at the Bronze finds Buffy, Willow, and Xander moping over chocolate while Cordelia shows Xander she's moved on. Cordelia heads home when her rebar wound cuts her demonstration short. Buffy tries to intervene with her on Xander's behalf. A random vamp attack ends their debate, and Buffy's successful vamp staking dumps Cordelia in the trash. The next day a sympathetic Anya lends a furiously venting Cordelia her necklace, and Cordelia speaks the fateful words "I wish Buffy Summers had never come to Sunnydale." Anya reveals her demonic visage, and Sunnydale transforms.

Sunnydale High with no Buffy Summers has a series of deceased principals, monthly memorial services, and students uniformly choosing to dress in subdued, nonvampire-attracting colors. Cordelia makes several adjustments in her new reality: curfew, no car, and a vamp-infested Bronze. Harmony tells Cordelia that Xander and Willow are dead; actually, they're undead vampires. Cordelia, desperate for someone called the Slayer, is rescued from Vamp Willow and Vamp Xander by Giles, Oz, and Larry. Vamp Willow and Vamp Xander visit the Master at the Bronze, who rep-

rimands them for not killing Cordelia outright when she mentioned the Slayer. They cruise to the library, cage Giles, and drain Cordy.

The white hats report other losses to Giles and remove Cordelia's body. Giles retains Anyanaka's amulet. The Master rewards Xander and Willow, granting Willow permission to "play with the puppy." Translation: torturing a captive Angel for sexual entertainment. Giles makes progress researching Anya and her pendant. He stops to battle vampires who are rounding up citizens, and is losing when Slayer Buffy Summers arrives from Cleveland.

This scarred Buffy has little patience with Giles's research, preferring to find something to stake to solve their problems. When Giles reveals that the Master inhabits the Bronze, she is on the hunt. Angel manages to overcome Buffy's mistrust of him and lead her to the Master and Co. at the factory, where the Master has perfected a technique to harvest blood from Sunnydale's remaining human population. Giles invokes Anya and takes steps to destroy her power center as Buffy and Angel lead an attack on the Master and his minions. Just as the Master kills Buffy, Giles succeeds in reversing Cordelia's wish by destroying the amulet, leaving Anya powerless and bewildered.

QUOTE OF THE WEEK:

"Okay, the entire world sucks because some dead ditz made a wish? I just want to be clear." Larry in Bizarro Sunnydale delivers the eulogy for dead Bizarro Cordelia, recently killed by Vamp Willow and Vamp Xander.

THE AGONY AND THE ECSTASY:

Demon Anyanka grants wishes for women scorned. Death as a metaphor is at work for almost every character with a broken heart in this episode. Vamp Willow and Vamp Xander drain Cordelia. Vamp Xander dusts Angel. Buffy stakes Vamp Xander. Oz slays Vamp Willow. Giles grieves for the Slayer he never Watched, who dies at the hands of the Master (again).

"Cordette #1"— Nicole Bilderback— played opposite Seth Green in the 1998 film *Can't Hardly Wait.*

POP-CULTURE IQ:

"Most people can't tell Prada from . . . Payless."
Bonding with Anya, Cordelia separates the Italian designer from inexpensive retail.

"Look at her. Tears of a clown, baby."
Xander, watching Cordelia not missing him, quotes Smokey Robinson and the Miracles.

"You're taking a lot on faith here, Jeeves."
In Bizarro Sunnydale, Buffy mistakes Giles for P. D. Wodehouse's creation.

"I had no idea her wish would be so exciting. Brave new world."
Anya's old enough to be quoting both William Shakespeare's play *The Tempest* and Aldous Huxley's novel *Brave New World* in this reference to Cordelia's wish that Buffy had never come to Sunnydale.

Wicca girl Amy Madison doesn't appear in this episode, but tells Willow offscreen she saw the recovering, betrayed Cordy at the mall. Cordelia and Anya bond over distaste for everything Harmony. In regular continuity, Oz rebuffs Willow's overtures and Buffy advises Xander and Willow about doomed romance. Anya tries to reverse events and regain her powers in "Doppelgangland."

Even in the alternate reality Angel has been summoned to Sunnydale to assist Buffy the Slayer. The Master emerges victorious over Buffy, reversing the events of "Prophecy Girl."

FROM THE ORIGINAL TELEPLAY:

Giles's exposition was changed:

"Anyanka raised a demon to ruin her unfaithful lover. The demon did her bidding—but then cursed her and turned her into a sort of patron saint for scorned women. Apparently the cry of a wronged woman is like a siren's call to Anyanka."

WRITTEN AND DIRECTED BY: **Joss Whedon**. GUEST STARS:
Kristine Sutherland as Joyce Summers, Saverio Guerra as Willy the Snitch, Shane Barach as Daniel, Edward Edwards as Travis, Cornelia Hayes O'Herlihy as Margaret, Robia LaMorte as Jenny Calendar, Eliza Dushku as Faith.

AMENDS   161

THE PLOT THICKENS

It's a typical balmy Southern California Christmas season. No one seems to have the proper spirit except for Cordelia, headed for the slopes of Aspen and "actual snow." Willow's Jewish and still Oz-

less. Xander plans to sleep outside, away from family battles. Joyce guilt-trips Buffy into inviting Faith to join their festivities. Giles is somber, despite the "Mr. Giles" stocking hanging from the library door. And the apparitions of three of his victims, including Jenny Calendar, are haunting Angel.

Buffy and Joyce shop for a tree, avoiding the large circle of unpleasantly dead ones in the tree lot. Angel tries to get information from a wary Giles about his nightmarish visitors but flees when Jenny's apparition appears in Giles's apartment. He dreams of another victim, and this time shares his dream with Buffy, who also appears in it. Angel is still tormented by Jenny and the others even when he awakens. Buffy seeks Giles's help, sharing the research load with Xander and Willow. The apparitions remind Angel he lacked integrity in life, and whisper to him of the evil he is capable of, with or without his demon. Buffy and Angel share a nightmare, which ends with Angel vamping out and biting her. Jenny appears and taunts Angel by telling him the dream reflects his true desires.

Buffy and Giles's research pays off with info on the three Harbingers, eyeless priests who draw on the power of an unimaginably ancient evil, the First. Even the powers of the Slayer won't be able to affect the First, so Buffy's tactic is to try to find its priests. Willy imparts that the priests are rumored to be somewhere underground—not much of a lead in tunnel-infested Sunnydale. Buffy and Joyce decorate their tree in front of an unnecessary but cheery fire. Faith accepts the Summerses' invitation, and Buffy heads upstairs to retrieve presents. Angel waits in her room and delivers an incoherent warning to stay away from him. Buffy leaves Faith to guard Joyce. The spirit of Jenny continues to torment Angel, encouraging him to kill Buffy.

The passage "the harbingers of death, nothing shall grow above or below" tips Buffy off to the Harbingers' location. Buffy takes out all three priests almost effortlessly but cannot physically assault the First, who, in the guise of Jenny, promises her that Angel will be dead by sunrise, when he plans to end his torment and hers. Just before dawn Buffy tracks Angel to an exposed bluff. Unable to persuade Angel to continue to be undead, Buffy moves from pleading to anger. As they prepare for sunrise, an unprecedented snow falls on them from the sun-obscuring cloud cover. Buffy and a rescued, stronger Angel walk silently through the snowy streets. "Not saying a word. Not needing to" [from the stage directions].

QUOTE OF THE WEEK:

"Strong is fighting. It's hard and it's painful and it's every day. It's what we have to do, and we can do it together, but if you're too much of a coward for that, then burn."
> Buffy, trying to talk Angel into coming in out of the sun before it rises.

> The weatherman who appears on a TV screen in the episode, discussing the freak snowstorm, is actually KTLA weatherman Mark Kriski, who reports for the Los Angeles WB affiliate. His colleague, KTLA anchorman Carlos Amezcua, appears in "Hush."

THE AGONY AND THE ECSTASY:

Oz and Willow reunite, but Oz gently puts Willow's adorable attempted seduction of him on hold. When a guilty but needy Angel approaches him for help, Giles strives to forget "that whole Angel-killed-his-girlfriend-and-tortured-him thing." Buffy and Angel have a chance to air all the unspoken feelings that have been simmering between them since his return from Hell.

POP-CULTURE IQ:

"Tree. Nog. Roast Beast."
Buffy envisions Christmas dinner with *The Grinch Who Stole Christmas*, written in 1957 by Dr. Seuss.

"And you got the Barry working for you."
During Willow's planned seduction of Oz, he appreciates fellow musician Barry White, the "King of Love," who began performing in the '60s.

> Ironically "Amends," billed by the network as "A Buffy Christmas," began filming 10/31/98—Halloween—although it did air 12/15/98, during the holiday season.

CONTINUITY:

Angel killed Jenny Calendar in "Passion." She also appeared in "Becoming, Part Two" as part of Drusilla's spell to ensnare Giles. However, the script makes clear that this is not the vengeful ghost of

Jenny, but simply a form the First Evil has taken in order to provoke guilt in Angel. The scenes from 1753 Ireland and 1838 Romania establish more of the timeline of Angel's past. Xander provides research snacks, a theme echoed in "The Zeppo." Joyce is not anxious to invite Giles to Christmas dinner following the events of "Band Candy."

> The Mutant Enemy logo monster gets in the seasonal spirit with a Santa cap and jingle bells in the background. He was also altered in "Becoming, Part Two," when he requested a hug, and "Graduation Day," when he wore a graduation cap.

FROM THE ORIGINAL TELEPLAY:

Buffy's response to Joyce is more prophetic in the original version:

JOYCE: "You know, honey, I was thinking—maybe we should invite Faith to spend Christmas Eve with us."

BUFFY: "I'll ask her. Worst she can do is—well, the worst she can do is serious bodily harm, but she'll probably just say no."

TELEPLAY BY: **Jane Espenson** STORY BY: **Thania St. John & Jane Espenson**; DIRECTED BY: **James Whitmore, Jr.** GUEST STARS: **Kristine Sutherland as Joyce Summers, Elizabeth Anne Allen as Amy Madison, Harry Groener as Mayor Richard Wilkins III, Jordan Baker as Sheila Rosenberg, Armin Shimerman as Principal Snyder.**

GINGERBREAD

163

THE PLOT THICKENS

Joyce decides to bond with Buffy on patrol and discovers the slain bodies of two children with a mysterious arcane symbol on their hands. She is devastated by the children's deaths, and Buffy has extra incentive to slay whoever's behind it because of Joyce's distress. Giles suggests that the killer may be a human rather than a demon. Buffy brings Oz, Xander, Willow, and Amy up to speed in the

cafeteria. Joyce reacts very negatively to the idea of humans, especially students, practicing occult rituals, to Amy and Willow's discomfort. Joyce garners support for a town meeting, where Willow and "Bunny," as Mrs. Rosenberg refers to Buffy, are surprised to also encounter Willow's absentminded academic mom. Joyce rallies her supporters, even "outing" the concept of Slayers.

At school, students are harassing suspected witches as Buffy tracks down one of Giles's books that Willow borrowed. Buffy finds the same arcane symbol on one of Willow's notebooks, and Willow confesses it's a protective symbol for a spell cast by her, Amy, and Michael. A gleeful Snyder leads a raid on student lockers, and then Giles's books are confiscated by order of the Mothers Opposed to the Occult (MOO). Willow confronts her mother, and Buffy confronts Joyce, the organizing force behind MOO, with unsatisfactory results. The ghosts of the slain children appear to Joyce and urge her to avenge their deaths.

Without books or Willow's computer expertise, the Scooby Gang labors to discover any background on the two dead children. The various computer hits reveal a pattern of similar occasions about every fifty years—leading back to Hansel and Gretel. A demon has struck. It assumes the guise of two slain children—Hans and Greta Strauss—and feeds on "fostering persecution and hatred among the mortal animals" as the children's killer is sought for punishment. Willow, Buffy, and Amy are all targets for the mob led by Joyce and Mrs. Rosenberg. The girls are bound to stakes and surrounded by books for burning. Cordelia and Giles team to mount an attack on the demon as Xander and Oz try to rescue the girls from the mob. Amy escapes by turning herself into a rat, leaving Willow and Buffy to try to reason with their mothers. Giles reverses the demon's illusion, causing the two children to morph into one big nasty demon. It attacks Buffy, who snaps the pole she is still bound to and drives it through the charging demon's neck like a super stake.

QUOTE OF THE WEEK:

"This is not a good town. How many of us have lost someone who just...disappeared or got skinned or suffered 'neck rupture'?! And how many of us have been too afraid to speak out? I was supposed to lead us in a moment of silence. But silence is this town's disease. For too long it's been plagued by unnatural evils. It's not our town anymore. It belongs to the monsters, to the witches and Slayers." —Joyce at the rally as leader of MOO (Mothers Opposed to the Occult).

THE AGONY AND THE ECSTASY:

Joyce and Giles remain uncomfortable together following the events in "Band Candy." Buffy reminds Xander of being busted with Willow in "Lovers Walk." Buffy and Giles discuss the "Slayers don't kill people" rule, foreshadowing the death of Deputy Mayor Finch in "Bad Girls." Buffy is discouraged by her mom's observation that she is fighting symptoms, not curing the world of evil. She is rejuvenated by Angel's giving her a pep talk along the lines of the one she gave him in "Amends." Her mother, under the influence of a spell, betrays Buffy; Giles will betray her in "Helpless."

POP-CULTURE IQ:

"Ah, I love the smell of desperate librarian in the morning."
Snyder brings *Apocalypse Now* to the stacks after he takes away Giles's research books.

GILES: "Ordinarily I would say we widen our research...."
BUFFY: "Using what, a dictionary and <u>My Friend Flicka</u>?"
Buffy believes the book-banning MOO would approve of Mary O'Hara's 1941 horse novel.

WILLOW: "The last time we had a conversation over three minutes it was about the patriarchal bias of the <u>Mister Rogers</u>' show."
SHEILA ROSENBERG: "Well, with King Friday lording it over all the lesser puppets..."
Willow and her mom don't want to live in *Mr. Rogers' Neighborhood*, and Shelia doesn't want to pay attention to what Willow's really trying to say.

> Willow's protective symbol is stitched on the stuffed Willow bean bag bear!

"I don't know about you, but I'm going to go trade my cow in for some beans. No one else is seeing the funny here?"
Xander gets into the spirit of things during a discussion about a demon straight out of *Hansel and Gretel*.

"What's with the grim? We're here to join you guys."
Xander's pun on the Brothers Grimm, delivered to extremely grim MOO rally attendees.

CONTINUITY:

Buffy's tough rep with the jocks is solid, in marked contrast to "Helpless." The "skinned" victims from "Go Fish" are mentioned in Joyce's speech. Willow says the protective spell is for Buffy's birthday, which is in the immediate future. Amy the rat makes frequent appearances in later episodes as Willow's replacement pet, but remains vermin when Willow takes her to college . . . until Willow accidentally (and very briefly) conjures her in human form in "Something Blue."

FROM THE ORIGINAL TELEPLAY:

Amy and Willow have more in common than Wicca in this exchange cut due to length:
AMY: "Oh, God, and Mr. Nyman that thing he does with his face..."
WILLOW: "The thing with the face! When he makes a point, the—I always think he's going to sneeze!"
AMY: "I thought I was the only one who saw it."

Excerpts from the Call Sheets for Season Three:

EPISODE ONE: Anne

In a memo from Joss "to the cast, crew, and staff of *Buffy*," he expressed his gratitude for all their hard work on "Anne," the Season Three premiere, and set up a sundae bar for them "as an entirely inadequate thank-you."

EPISODE TWO: Dead Man's Party

Special Notes:
Notify SPCA. Livestock—1 Zombie Cat.

EPISODE THREE: Faith, Hope & Trick

Special Notes:
SFX: E Fan, Atmos Smoke, Ring vibrates; Smoke flame from carpet

EPISODE FOUR: Beauty and the Beasts

Special Notes:
PROPS: 3 kinds of Jell-O with marshmallows

EPISODE FIVE: Homecoming

Special notes:
PROPS: Quart of Blood and Corsages
COSTUMES—Buffy and Cordy a mess

EPISODE SIX: Band Candy

STAND-INS AND ATMOSPHERE: 6 Newborns
PROPS: Dbl dummies for Oz, Snyder, Willow. Band candy bars.

EPISODE SEVEN: Revelations

Special Notes:
ART DEPT.: Additional Greens, Leaves, Contents of Tomb

EPISODE EIGHT: Lovers Walk

Special Notes:
Rig for Skewered Cordy (Rebar)

EPISODE NINE: The Wish

STAGE 1: "New" Bronze, "New" Library
Special notes:
MU [makeup]: Blood, Buffy's scar, Master MU.

EPISODE TEN: Amends

Dress warmly for nite work!
Special Notes:
Barry White Album

EPISODE ELEVEN: Gingerbread

Special Notes:
TRANSPO: Hot Water in Star Trailers
Thanksgiving off Company Idle

EPISODE TWELVE: Helpless

Special Notes:
Door for Kralik to bust

EPISODE THIRTEEN: The Zeppo

Special Notes:
OPTIC NERVE: Tentacles, Good, Mr. Hellmouth

EPISODE FOURTEEN: Bad Girls

Begin Holiday Hiatus 12-18—1-4-99.
Merry Xmas—Happy Hannukah—Joyous Kwaanza—Happy New Year
Special Notes:
SFX: Torches, warm water, breakaway door & window

EPISODE FIFTEEN: Consequences

Special Notes:
Water Safety Personnel
Baywatch Tank

EPISODE SIXTEEN: Doppelgangland

Special Notes:
MU: Alyson—prosthetic vamp mu.

EPISODE SEVENTEEN: Enemies

Special Notes:
Stand-in and Atmos: 35 students (20 with change)
(include 6 kissing couples)

EPISODE EIGHTEEN: Earshot

Special Notes:
Steadicam, Scissor Lift

EPISODE NINETEEN: Choices

Special Notes:
Optic Nerve: Mech. spiders, pull-apart squishing spider, stunt spider,
spider on wire

EPISODE TWENTY: The Prom

Special Notes:
PROPS: Dummy to Burn
SET DRESSING: Hanging Slabs of Meat

HELPLESS

WRITTEN BY: **David Fury;** DIRECTED BY: **James A. Contner.**
GUEST STARS: **Kristine Sutherland as Joyce Summers, Jeff Kober as Zackary Kralik, Harris Yulin as Quentin Travers.**

THE PLOT THICKENS:

Buffy and Angel's workout sublimates the energy between them into Slayer practice. Buffy studies crystals with Giles. She is surprised when her responses are abnormally slow when confronting a vampire on patrol, and later with knife practice in the library. She discusses her birthday ice-show plans with her dad with the Scooby Gang, then heads home to discover that Dad has canceled. Buffy tries subtly to persuade Giles to substitute for her dad at the ice show, but he focuses her on her crystal studies. When a certain crystal hypnotizes her, he injects her with a mysterious substance.

Buffy tries to separate an oaf from Cordelia, but gets smashed to the ground for her efforts. Giles promises her an answer for her weakened condition, but his conversation with Watchers Council representative Quentin Travers reveals she is facing the Cruciamentum, a ritual test administered by the Watchers Council to all Slayers who achieve the age of eighteen. The preparations for the test involve setting a diminished Slayer against a captive vampire. But their vampire, Kralik, turns out to be insane. Restrained by Council members and dependent on the pills they dole out to him, he outsmarts his keepers and sires one into vampdom. Then they drain the other Council worker together.

Giles visits the test-site boardinghouse in search of Travers, discovering the changed circumstances. Kralik chases Buffy as she leaves Angel's, and nabs her red jacket as the powerless Slayer runs for her life. Giles and his Citroen rescue Buffy from Kralik's progeny. When Giles reveals the plan for the Cruciamentum and his part in it, Buffy is shocked to the core of her being. Kralik torments a bound and gagged Joyce in the basement, and Buffy tracks them to rescue her mom. Giles defies Travers and the Council's authority to go to Buffy's aid. Buffy manages to defeat Kralik through cunning rather than superior strength after a prolonged chase. Travers congratulates Buffy on passing the test, but fires Giles from his Watcher post because of his violating the test rules because of his fatherly love for Buffy. Buffy's response to Travers: "Bite me."

QUOTE OF THE WEEK:

"She's dead to me now. Mostly 'cause I killed and ate her."
Psycho vamp Kralik describes his dysfunctional relationship with his mother to a captive Joyce.

THE AGONY AND THE ECSTASY:

Buffy's issues with her parents and parental figures continue: Joyce nearly burned her at the stake in "Gingerbread," her dad now bails on their special birthday engagement. And father figure Giles deceives and "poisons" her. Buffy receives a copy of *Sonnets from the Portuguese* by Elizabeth Barrett Browning, inscribed simply "Always" from Angel. *Sonnets* was deliberately misquoted by Amy in "The Witch," which is also the episode in which Xander gave Buffy a bracelet inscribed "Yours, always." Angel tells Buffy for the first time that he saw her before she was called to be a Slayer, and fell in love with her on the spot. (Since this was shown in a flashback in "Becoming, Part One," the audience has known that he saw her in Los Angeles, although she did not.)

169

POP-CULTURE IQ:

XANDER: "Maybe what we should be looking for is something like Slayer kryptonite."
OZ: "Faulty metaphor. Kryptonite kills."
The boys debate the various forms of Superman's rocky nemesis while trying to figure out why Buffy's powers have left the building.

"I saw Snoopy on Ice once when I was little. My dad took me backstage and I got scared and threw up on Woodstock."
Like Willow, who wants to make sure Buffy really enjoys the ice show, Charles Shultz's little yellow bird suffers from a nervous stomach.

"Brian Boitano doing Carmen, it's a life changer."
Buffy's sophisticated tastes include Olympic medalists performing opera on the ice; Giles is still not moved to accompany her in her absent father's stead.

CONTINUITY:

Buffy's birthdays have been bad in the past ("Surprise") and continue to suck in the future ("A New Man"). "Maybe it's time to call a moratorium on parties in my honor. They tend to go badly. Monsters crash, people die...." ("Surprise" and "Dead Man's Party"). Angel reminds her she received the Judge's arm in a box in "Surprise." The Claddagh ring she wears was his gift to her on her seventeenth birthday. When Buffy patrols the playground, the shrine to the false children from "Gingerbread" is gone. Buffy's love of ice-skating was first revealed in "What's My Line? Part One," and her fear of abandonment by her father in "Nightmares" Willow is still trying to reverse Amy the rat's spell ("Gingerbread").

Buffy lists the merits of becoming a non-Slayer in this exchange cut due to length:

BUFFY: "I mean, there's a plus side to being a regular girl. The whole not-bleeding-and-killing-and-dying experience."

WILLOW: "As for example."

BUFFY: "Then there's buying outfits without worrying if they're good for bleeding-and-killing-and-dying in. There's a lot of good to it."

THE ZEPPO

WRITTEN BY: Dan Vebber; DIRECTED BY: James Whitmore, Jr.
GUEST STARS: Saverio Guerra as Willy the Snitch, Channon Roe as Jack, Michael Cudlitz as Bob, Eliza Dushku as Faith; with Co-stars Darin Heames as Parker, Scott Torrence as Dickie, Whitney Dylan as Lysette.

THE PLOT THICKENS

Buffy and Faith slay several of the Sisterhood of Jhe, with the assistance of Willow and Giles. Concerned for his safety, they all suggest the badly beaten Xander should stay out of future battles. He doesn't fare any better the next day at school, when he misses catching a football that hits Jack O'Toole ("A subliterate that's repeated twelfth grade three times," according to Cordelia) and gives Cordelia ample opportunity for Xander bashing. Xander develops what Oz describes as "an exciting new obsession"—how to define and achieve coolness. He starts by driving his uncle Roary's 1957 Chevy Bel Aire, which attracts the attention of both car fan Lysette Torchio, and his new best friend Jack. The rest of the gang tries to find ways to stop the Sisterhood of Jhe from opening the Hellmouth and bringing about the end of the world, asking Xander to remain out of the way except for the occasional doughnut run.

Xander finds himself "having a very strange night." Under duress, he travels with Jack to three cemeteries to revive Jack's gang members. He discovers that Jack is also recently dead and revived, although prior to that he was a living, breathing high school bully. They decide to follow Dickie's plan to "bake a cake." Xander's attempts to get Angel, Giles, or Willow to rescue him from his predicament are rebuffed. He flees for his life when Jack threatens to make him the fifth dead member of the gang.

Xander assists Faith by slamming into a member of the Sisterhood of Jhe with the car. Back in her hotel room she assists him in losing his virginity. She then tosses him out, pants in hand, and as he climbs back in the car, he realizes "baking a cake" is a euphemism for building a bomb. A new man, he drives past the gang and persuades one of the gang members to divulge the location of the bomb before he loses his head. Everyone ends up back at Sunnydale High, with Xander and his zombie buddies chasing one another through the halls as the rest of the Scooby Gang battle the demons emerging from the Hellmouth. Xander faces his final opponent, Jack, over the bomb as it ticks down its final seconds. Xander convinces Jack to pull the plug on it, then departs, with nothing more to prove. A surly Jack chooses the other exit, running into Wolf Oz. The next day the library warriors gather to examine their wounds, and Xander gives Cordelia the Teflon treatment, secure in his role in the universe.

QUOTE OF THE WEEK:

"I brought marshmallows! Occasionally I am callous and strange."

Willow suggests a use for burning demons after Buffy and gang toast the Sisterhood of Jhe.

THE AGONY AND THE ECSTASY:

Xander and Cordelia's relationship is still strained and bitter following "Lovers Walk" and "The Wish." Xander's attempts to lose his virginity have been around since "Teacher's Pet." Buffy and Angel pledge to love each other even beyond death, with shades of both "Becoming, Part Two" and "Amends."

POP-CULTURE IQ:

"But, gee, Mr. White, if Clark and Lois get all the big stories I'll never be a good reporter."

Xander, feeling useless, makes a Jimmy Olsen reference, which is lost on Giles.

"It must be hard when all your friends here have, like, superpowers. Slayer, werewolves, witches, vampires, and you're like this little nothing. You must feel like...Jimmy Olsen."

Cordelia gets *Superman* references and isn't afraid to use them if it will give Xander pain.

"You're the useless part of the group. You're the Zeppo."

The Queen of Mean compares Xander to the fifth Marx brother, who may or may not also have been sent to get the doughnuts.

"Walker, Texas Ranger. You been tapin' 'em?"

When he rises from the grave, Dead Bob needs his Chuck Norris fix.

"It's just, um, I've never been up with people...before...."

Xander chooses the All-American singing group as a euphemism...or is it a metaphor?...to describe his currently virgin state.

"Hello, Nasty."

And the musical references keep coming as Xander quotes the Beastie Boys at the bomb. The Beastie Boys were originally a punk-rock group founded in 1981; they have since become known for their hip-hop sound.

Giles continues to assist his Slayer, despite being "unofficial." The gang re-explores the concept of "cool," also discussed in "Gingerbread." The book cage has once again been deemed secure enough for Wolf Oz ("Beauty and the Beasts") and proven otherwise. Giles and Buffy mention her dying at the hands of the Master the last time the Hellmouth opened, complete with demon now returning. Faith has returned from her "walkabout" activities in "Helpless" to actively slay with Buffy. The theft from the hardware store echoes both "Band Candy" and "Bad Girls." Rival gang the Jackals is mentioned, perhaps cousins to the hyena kids in "The Pack." Giles works to keep Willow safe, Angel acts to keep Buffy safe, Willow tries to keep Oz safe, and everyone acts to keep the world safe.

FROM THE ORIGINAL TELEPLAY:

Jack changes his mind about Xander's coolness factor in this comment cut due to length:
"That's it. No way am I bringing him back after I kill him."

BAD GIRLS

WRITTEN BY: Douglas Petrie; DIRECTED BY: Michael Lange. GUEST STARS: Kristine Sutherland as Joyce Summers, Harry Groener as Mayor Richard Wilkins III, K. Todd Freeman as Mr. Trick, Jack Plotnick as Deputy Mayor Allan Finch, Alexis Denisof as Wesley Wyndam-Pryce, Christian Clemenson as Balthazar, Eliza Dushku as Faith.

THE PLOT THICKENS

Faith and Buffy share girl talk and dust three vampires, one of whom has some impressive swords that disappear; the swords reappear in the Mayor's office. The Mayor suggests setting the vampire cult against the Slayers to keep both from interfering with his imminent dedication. Once this occurs, he will be invincible for the 100 days before his Ascension. The gang discusses life after high school, and Buffy pays a visit to Giles to discover that her new Watcher, Wesley Wyndam-Pryce, has arrived. Buffy learns the sword-bearing vampires are probably acolytes of the purportedly deceased demon Balthazar and may be seeking his amulet. Buffy shares her info with Faith, who suggests Buffy take slaying and Council-assigned Watchers less seriously and enjoy the power of being one of the Chosen more. Her arguments grow more persuasive as they battle the vampires, and Buffy begins to agree.

She reports to Giles the next morning, to the annoyance of Wesley. Buffy is distracting Willow and Xander from their chem test when Faith appears in the window. The Slayers play hooky, dusting vampires and showering a group of guys with pheromones on the Bronze dance floor. Angel extracts Buffy and tells her Balthazar is alive and in Sunnydale. Buffy and Faith track Balthazar to his warehouse lair and break into a sporting goods store in search of weapons. The police nab

them, but they escape custody (a trick which will come in handy on future occasions). Vincent, one of Balthazar's vampire minions, assaults the Mayor in his office but is captured and disarmed by an unimpressed Mr. Trick.

A subdued Buffy and Faith stake vamps; Buffy realizes Deputy Mayor Finch isn't a vamp just a heartbeat before Faith stakes him and he dies. Apparently he was coming to warn the Slayers about the Mayor and Mr. Trick. They flee the police again and head for the warehouse where Balthazar prepares to torture his two captive Watchers. Balthazar and his crew are slain, but not before he passes on the warning "when he rises . . . you'll wish I had killed you all." The Mayor completes the dedication ceremony and tests his new invulnerability against a killing stroke from Vincent, who is then dispatched by Trick. Faith tells Buffy that as far as she's concerned, Finch's murder never occurred—she weighted and dumped his body, and shows no remorse for taking the life of an innocent.

173

Regular "watchers" of the TV series *Highlander* saw Anthony Stewart Head and Alexis Denisof in guest appearances. Beheading one's opponents with swords was a regular activity.

THE AGONY AND THE ECSTASY:

Xander and Cordelia's sniping battle rages on, despite his newfound self-confidence in "The Zeppo." Buffy's resentment toward the Watchers' Council and their dismissal of Giles is turned on Wesley. Buffy and Willow's relationship suffers, as Buffy grows closer to Faith, although it will be repaired in "Consequences" and solid again by "Choices." Xander's eye twitches every time Faith is mentioned following their encounter in "The Zeppo." Buffy sees in Faith the consequences of the "Want. Take. Have." approach to life.

POP-CULTURE IQ:

"This isn't a Tupperware party. It's a little hard to plan."
Faith compares slaying and dinnerware events after her enthusiasm for product demonstration nearly gets Buffy killed.

"The count of three isn't a plan. It's Sesame Street."
Buffy mentions the children's television show but not its resident vampire, the counting Count. Faith's tactics included ignoring Buffy in distress so she could wail on her target.

"I just love the 'Family Circus.' That P.J. He's getting to be quite a handful."

The Mayor is a Bil Keane comic-strip fan, and woe betide a deputy mayor who confesses he prefers "Cathy."

"I like 'Marmaduke'. . . . nobody's telling Marmaduke what to do. That's my kind of dog."

Brad Anderson's independent Great Dane appeals to Mr. Trick, who scores points for a comeback during the Mayor's discussion of good comics.

"I like to read 'Cathy.'"

Deputy Mayor Finch is fond of Cathy Guisewite's career gal, losing valuable "cool" points

"Tell you what. Let Captain Courageous here go, and I'll tell you what you need to know."

Giles compares Wesley, who caves and tells Balthazar who has his amulet, to Rudyard Kipling's riches to rags protagonist in a mocking, ironic way. Kipling was a British writer (1865–1936) and his novel *Captains Courageous* was published in 1897.

CONTINUITY:

Willow's academic qualities are reinforced by the stellar caliber of the colleges sending her early acceptance forms. Xander predicts his nonacademic career in Season Four. Cordelia mocks Xander for his father's lack of a job, which will be ironic by the time of "The Prom." Wesley's boasting about hand-to-hand vampire combat and bumbling stance foreshadow his activities as a "rogue demon hunter" in the *Angel* spinoff. The evil Gwendolyn Post from "Revelations" is mentioned. Buffy's hiding under a corpse in the crypt will be echoed by Spike in "The I in Team." When Balthazar's minion tries to drown Buffy, she mentions the events of "Prophecy Girl." Buffy and Faith break into a sporting goods store (between them, Jack and his gang in "The Zeppo," and Giles and Joyce in "Band Candy," retail insurance in Sunnydale must be a bear.) Buffy and Faith are handcuffed but not sharing one set ("Graduation Day, Part One"). Faith lays claim to the longbow as her new weapon of choice ("Choices" and "Graduation Day, Part One"). Angel sees Buffy's bloody hand but won't know the whole story until "Consequences." Cordelia and Wesley are instantly attracted to each other; his presence draws her back into the Scooby Corps. Their lives will further intertwine when they both start working for Angel in Los Angeles.

FROM THE ORIGINAL TELEPLAY:

Buffy reaches out to Faith a little more in this last scene, which was cut due to length:

"I know you think you can handle this. And you've gotten used to being on your own. You've got your tough loner act down pretty well."

174

WRITTEN BY: **Marti Noxon**; DIRECTED BY: **Michael Gershman.**
GUEST STARS: **Kristine Sutherland as Joyce Summers, Harry Groener as Mayor Richard Wilkins III, K. Todd Freeman as Mr. Trick, Jack Plotnick as Deputy Mayor Allan Finch, Alexis Denisof as Wesley Wyndam-Pryce, James MacDonald as Detective Paul Stein, Eliza Dushku as Faith.**

THE PLOT THICKENS

Buffy awakens from a nightmare of being pulled underwater by the corpse of Deputy Mayor Finch to find Joyce watching a news report on the discovery of his body. In the library Wesley asks Buffy and Faith to investigate the murder. Privately Buffy protests the hypocrisy of their actions to Faith, who reacts in anger. The Mayor receives the police report on the murder, including the discovery of wood splinters in the wound to the heart. Faith and Buffy rifle Finch's office but only discover empty files.

They also see Mr. Trick and the Mayor together. They separate, divided about the right action to take. Detective Stein, who already questioned Buffy about the death of her mother's boyfriend in "Ted," says a witness placed them near the scene. He interviews both of them, getting fairly similar stories that do not allay his suspicions.

Buffy makes peace with Willow and confesses, then goes to Giles's office to do the same. Faith has beaten her there and blamed *her* for Finch's death. Giles dismisses Faith and reassures Buffy he knows the truth. They work with Xander and Willow to save Faith from herself and the authorities, while continuing to investigate why Wilkins and Mr. Trick were together. Xander tries talking with Faith one on one and almost dies at her hands. Angel intervenes in time to knock Faith out with a baseball bat, and she awakens chained to the wall of the mansion. Angel tells Buffy he'll work with, Faith but cautions her against getting her hopes up. Before Angel can make a successful breakthrough, Wesley and other Watchers Council members remove Faith from his care.

A beaten Wesley tells Buffy and the others Faith has slipped his grasp, and Buffy heads for the docks to look for her. She is successful but unable to contain her anger when Faith taunts her. They have just come to blows when Buffy is pinned to the docks by a cargo crate released by Mr. Trick. Faith and Buffy dispose of his three hench vamps, and Faith dusts Mr. Trick with his fangs scant inches from Buffy's throat. With Mr. Trick gone, Faith crosses firmly to the dark side and takes his job assisting the Mayor.

QUOTE OF THE WEEK:

WESLEY: "Does everyone know about you?"
BUFFY: "She's a friend."
CORDELIA: "Let's not exaggerate."
Cordelia clarifies her relationship to the gang, while Wesley gets to know his new Slayer and her lack of a secret identity.

THE AGONY AND THE ECSTASY:

Despite her tough persona, Faith is hurt when Buffy is reluctant to lie to protect her, even though she spent months lying about Angel's return ("Revelations"). Willow meets with fellow witch Michael to attempt to "de-rat" the still-enchanted Amy. Buffy actually thinks Giles might believe Faith for a moment, as their relationship mends ("Helpless"). Willow is heartbroken to discover Xander has joined the ranks of Faith's one-night boy toys. Angel's chains continue to get a workout—he was chained in "Beauty and the Beasts," Buffy is chained there in "Enemies."

POP-CULTURE IQ:

"Check out Giles, the next generation. What's your deal?"
Cordy sees Wesley as Picard to Giles's Kirk when she meets him for the first time.

"Look at you, Faith. Less than twenty-four hours ago you killed a guy. And now you're all 'zipidee doo dah.'"
Buffy quotes the cheerful song from *The Song of the South*.

"This guy I offed was no Gandhi."
Faith the warrior mentions the personification of passive resistance, reminding Buffy that Deputy Mayor Finch had some dirty laundry (and of her mistaken Ghandi refrence to Ken in "Anne").

CONTINUITY:

Another rare occasion where Cordelia requests nonsupernatural books from the library ("Helpless"). Wesley and Cordelia's attraction for each other will zoom up the charts in "The Prom," then fail to make the top ten when they kiss in "Graduation Day, Part One." Faith's comment about the good she's done canceling her misdeed is a dark counterpart to Angel's redemptive goal on his show. Willow and Buffy discuss another definition of "cool," as applied to Slayers. Giles reveals that other innocents have occasionally been lost in the long war between Slayers and evil. More: that it happens and that the Watchers Council understands. Buffy mentions the intervention the gang did for her in "Revelations." Wesley calls Travers ("Helpless") to report the Faith problem to the Watchers Council. Faith's "I see. I want. I take. I forget." is a repetition of her "Bad Girls" philosophy. Detective Stein interviewed Buffy and Joyce in the wake of Kendra's death ("Becoming, Part Two"). The Watchers Council Disciplinary Committee is introduced. Faith is chained in the Watchers Council van; Buffy in Faith's body will be in the same position in "Who Are You?" Faith betrayed everyone; she always perceives herself in Buffy's shadow. She is the mirror of Buffy.

FROM THE ORIGINAL TELEPLAY:

Faith appeals to Angel's practical side while chained in this exchange cut due to length:
ANGEL: "You and me, Faith, we're a lot alike."
FAITH: "Well, you're kind of dead..."
ANGEL: "Like I said. A lot alike."
FAITH: "Sorry, buddy. I'm alive and kicking. In fact, I've got a bodily function that needs attending to pretty quick here."
ANGEL: "You're not alive. You're just running. Afraid to feel. Afraid to be touched. . . ."
FAITH: "Save it for Hallmark. I have to pee."

WRITTEN AND DIRECTED BY: **Joss Whedon.** GUEST STARS: **Harry Groener as Mayor Richard Wilkins III, Alexis Denisof as Wesley Wyndam-Pryce, Emma Caulfield as Anya, Ethan Erickson as Percy West, Eliza Dushku as Faith, Armin Shimerman as Principal Snyder; with Co-stars Danny Strong as Jonathan Levenson, Andy Umberger as D'Hoffryn.**

DOPPELGANGLAND

THE PLOT THICKENS

The still-mortal-bound Anya/Anyanka pleads unsuccessfully with superior demon D'Hoffryn to restore her powers. Dissatisfied with being just a twelfth grader, she decides to try other methods. Buffy and Willow discuss emotional control and Faith's upcoming tests for reinstatement by the Watchers Council. Snyder forces Willow to tutor Percy West, a star athlete used to academic perks. Faith, now leading a double life, and a winded Wesley return from the physical portion of her test to find Giles asking Willow to hack into the Mayor's system. Willow rebels at being a "reliable dog geyser person." She jumps at the chance to assist Anya in a spell. Anya tries to use their combined powers to bring her amulet back, but somehow Willow's involvement causes a misfire. The result: Vamp Willow from "The Wish" is brought to this Sunnydale.

Vamp Willow wanders into the Bronze and terrorizes Percy when he inquires about the state of his homework. Xander intervenes on her behalf, and he and Buffy are stunned by her evident self-transformation, especially when she reveals her vampiric nature. The Mayor's thugs attack Vamp Willow by mistake and are converted to *her* hench vamps. One of them is Alphonse. Buffy and Xander break the bad news to Giles, when Willow enters the library to explain that the rumors of her death are greatly exaggerated. Back at the Bronze Anya sits morosely at the bar and Dingoes Ate My Baby set up on the stage. Alphonse enters and claims the Bronze for Vamp Willow. Angel exits in search of Buffy while a stunned Oz regards Vamp Willow. Anya realizes Willow is from the alternate Sunnydale, the one she wants to get to as well.

Vamp Willow and Willow clash in the library, and Willow emerges the victor. With an unconscious Vamp Willow locked in the book cage, Willow dons her clothes to infiltrate the Bronze. Vamp Willow awakens in Willow's fuzzy outfit and tries to convince an unsuspecting Cordelia to release her. Thinking this is Willow, Cordelia lectures her captive audience about boyfriend-stealing (viz., "Lovers Walk"), then relents. Vamp Willow steps from the cage and gives chase to Cordelia until intercepted by Wesley. Anya "outs" Willow in the Bronze, and Buffy and the gang charge in to her rescue. Hench vamps are slain, and Anya and Vamp Willow are both subdued. Anya conducts a ritual to return Vamp Willow to her own reality, and Willow enjoys the new respect paid to her by Percy.

QUOTE OF THE WEEK:

WILLOW: "Old Reliable? Yeah, great! There's a sexy nickname."
BUFFY: "Oh, Will, I didn't mean..."

WILLOW: "No, it's fine. I'm Old Reliable."

XANDER: "She just meant, you know, the geyser. You're like a geyser of fun that goes off at regular intervals."

WILLOW: "That's Old Faithful."

XANDER: "Isn't that the dog that the guy has to shoot...."

WILLOW: "That's Old Yeller."

BUFFY: "Xander, I beg you not to help me."

Xander fails the Pop Culture references portion of trying to cheer up Willow.

THE AGONY AND THE ECSTASY:

Willow's negative feelings about Faith remain in the wake of the events of "Bad Girls" and "Consequences." Xander's reaction to Vamp Willow's "naughty touching" is based on their history from "Homecoming" through "Lovers Walk."

POP-CULTURE IQ:

"I know Faith isn't exactly on the cover of <u>Sanity Fair</u>, but she's had it rough."
Buffy plays on the well-known fashion magazine when discussing Faith with Willow.

"If she's a vampire, then I'm the <u>Creature from the Black Lagoon</u>!"
Anya outs Willow when she's masquerading as her evil twin, not knowing that Xander, her future boyfriend, almost *was* a fish creature.

CONTINUITY:

The events of "The Wish" provide the base for this whole episode. Willow practices pencil floating, a very handy skill to have in "Choices," and a precursor to the rose floating with Tara in Season Four. Snyder is eager for a winning basketball team after the poor outcome of the swim team in "Go Fish." The Mayor moves Faith from her shabby hotel room to a nice new apartment, to be seen, then trashed, in "Graduation Day, Part One." Giles is keeping Faith out of battles around civilians for the time being ("Bad Girls"). Willow shoots Vamp Willow with the tranquilizer gun kept in the library for Oz ("Beauty and the Beasts," and "The Zeppo"). Buffy stifles Angel when he disagrees with her observation that "a vampire's personality has nothing to do with the person it was," as Willow's attraction to Tara will emerge in her college days, harkening to Vamp Willow's attraction to Willow in this episode. Despite her disclaimers, Willow's bravery is growing ("Choices"). It looks like Vamp Will may get to bite Cordelia in this reality as well as her own, after being submitted to her lecture on "her" behavior in "Lovers Walk."

FROM THE ORIGINAL TELEPLAY:

Devon offers Angel a different career track in this exchange cut due to length:

DEVON: "Hey, man, how'd you like to be our roadie?"

ANGEL: "Less than you'd think."

Xander takes responsibility in an exchange with Giles also cut for length:

XANDER: "It's all my fault."

GILES: "What makes you say that?"

XANDER: "I don't know.....Statistical probability."

WRITTEN BY: **Douglas Petrie;** DIRECTED BY: **David Grossman.**
GUEST STARS: **Kristine Sutherland as Joyce Summers, Harry
Groener as Mayor Richard Wilkins III, Alexis Denisof as Wesley
Wyndam-Pryce, Michael Manasseri as Skyler, Gary Bullock as
Shaman, Eliza Dushku as Faith.**

ENEMIES

THE PLOT THICKENS

Buffy and Angel exit an arousing movie and are necking when Faith nabs Buffy for patrol. Buffy is
declining to discuss her romance with Faith when they are interrupted by something most unusual—a
demon looking to cut a deal. Skyler the demon offers the Slayers the five Books of Ascension for a price.

Faith reports this activity to the Mayor, who
seems fairly unconcerned. Wesley suggests
investigating Skyler more thoroughly. Faith is
already on the assignment, although on the
Mayor's payroll, and murders Skyler and removes
the books. After the kill she tries to seduce
Angel, who gently rebuffs her; Buffy only sees
them sharing an intimate moment. Faith and
the Mayor proceed to Plan B for removing Angel's
soul. The Watchers send the Slayers to Skyler's
apartment after the books and information.
Buffy is distressed by Skyler's corpse, the

absence of the Books of Ascension, and Faith's poorly-concealed familiarity with the apartment.
Buffy confesses her concerns about Angel and Faith to Willow. Faith returns to the mansion where
she and a Shaman appear to rip Angel's soul from him, returning him to Angelus. Angelus kisses
and strikes Faith with equal passion, and she battles him to the ground to relay the Mayor's pro-
posal to him. The Mayor gives Angelus and Faith the task of killing Buffy.

Angel and Faith pick up Buffy from Casa Summers and head to the mansion on the pretext of
getting the books. They turn on her, knocking her unconscious and chaining her to Angel's wall.
Xander, punched out by Angel, rouses himself to report the bad news to the others. Buffy awakens
to find Faith and Angel planning her slow torturous death. Faith lets all her resentment for Buffy
flow forth in a fit of rage, including sharing details of the Mayor's plan. Buffy and Angel reveal
they've been duping Faith just as the rest of Team Slayer arrives. Buffy and Faith fight to a draw,
and Faith departs into the night. Giles thanks the Shaman for his services and the gang absorbs
the news that Angel is good, and Faith is bad.

QUOTE OF THE WEEK:

**"Demons after money. Whatever happened to the still beating heart of a virgin?
No one has standards anymore...."**

Giles is dismayed by Skyler's lack of class when trying to buy the Books of Ascension off him.

THE AGONY AND THE ECSTASY:

Cordelia asks Wesley for a dinner date in the guise of assistance on her English paper, making Xander see red. Buffy suspects Angel is attracted to Faith's kindred nature even before they conduct their charade. Willow points out that while Faith would make a move on Buffy's man, Angel would not respond. New day, same chains: Buffy is secured where Angel was chained in "Beauty and the Beasts," and Faith was chained in "Consequences." Xander remains threatened by Angel, as evidenced by his self-righteous tone when he believes Angel has lost his soul again. When a doubtful Buffy decides to take a break from Angel, he asks, "You still my girl?" She answers with the affirmation he wrote in her birthday book ("Helpless"): "Always."

> "You have the greatest voice. Have you ever thought of doing books on tape?" Cordelia's character inquires of Wesley. In the real world, Charisma Carpenter did the audio book of *Immortal*, the first *Buffy* hardcover novel.

POP-CULTURE IQ:

"Then Buffy and the Superfriends are gonna—"
Faith draws another DC comics comparison while fretting to the Mayor.

"And all your little lame-ass friends are gonna be Kibbles 'n Bits."
According to Faith, the Ascension doesn't just mean dog food, it means *name-brand* dog food!

CONTINUITY:

The next time Buffy, Angel, and Faith are assembled by the Sun Cinema will be in "Graduation Day, Part One," when Faith shoots Angel. Faith's bloody hands are a reminder of Finch's murder in "Bad Girls." The Watchers Council is surprisingly short on references to Ascensions, making the pages Willow obtains from the books in "Choices" very important. The Scooby Gang's research suggests a previous Ascension obliterated an entire town. Unable to intimidate him, Xander bribes Willy the Snitch for Skyler's address. The Mayor is willing to seek outside help again in the Shaman, despite the negative outcome with Ethan Rayne ("Band Candy"). The Mayor is as indifferent to Angel's letter-opener attack as he was to Vincent's sword attack ("Bad Girls"). Angel kisses Buffy on the forehead in the bedroom: Faith kisses Buffy on the forehead before fleeing the mansion, a kiss Buffy will return in "Graduation Day, Part Two." Angel mentions that Buffy "looks so cute when she's sleeping"; he sketched her in her vulnerable state in "Passion." The Mayor is not only more than a hundred years old but also built Sunnydale on the Hellmouth for the demons he pays tribute to. Faith has developed the habit of calling Buffy "B," begun in "Faith, Hope & Trick," and her habit of saying "five by five" was established then, too—a giveaway when she switches bodies with Buffy in Season Four.

> Fans of science-fiction TV may have ecognized Skyler's voice, if not his face. Michael Manasseri also performed in TV's *Weird Science*.

FROM THE ORIGINAL TELEPLAY:

Buffy and Willow get a little graphic in an exchange cut due to length:
BUFFY: "I can't stop thinking about that demon."
WILLOW: "'Cause of him being chopped up into little bits and all?"
BUFFY: "Yeah, Will, let's keep bringing on the visuals."
Wesley assays humor in a line also cut for length:

"You failed in last night's mission because you lacked faith. If you had simply…'Lacked Faith.' A pun. From me! Well. Bet you never thought I had the funny in me, eh?"

WRITTEN BY: Jane Espenson; DIRECTED BY: Regis B. Kimble.
GUEST STARS: Kristine Sutherland as Joyce Summers, Alexis Denisof as Wesley Wyndam-Pryce, Ethan Erickson as Percy West, Danny Strong as Jonathan Levenson; with Co-stars Larry Bagby III as Larry Blaisdell, Karem Malicki-Sánchez as Freddy, Justin Doran as Hogan, Lauren Roman as Nancy, Wendy Worthington as Lunch Lady, Robert Arce as Mr. Beach, Molly Bryant as Ms. Murray.

EARSHOT

THE PLOT THICKENS

Buffy slays several mouthless demons in the park, getting demon goo on her hand in the process. Giles finds out Buffy will manifest "an aspect of the demon" after being infected with its body fluids. The gang attends a pep rally: Willow to support Percy, and Xander to watch the cheerleaders. Buffy patrols solo on game night and tries not to feel left out of the recap the next day. She catches Xander's jealous thought about Cordelia and Wesley, and realizes what her aspect must be: telepathy.

Buffy informs Giles of the aspect, and shines in the class discussion of *Othello* by building on Ms. Murray's thoughts of her own dissertation. She also catches jealous thoughts from Nancy Doyle, and "sardonic" thoughts from Freddy Iverson, editor of the school paper. The gang has varied uncomfortable reactions to Buffy's new talent. Buffy's ability to be selective about the telepathic input diminishes. In the midst of a jumble of voices in the cafeteria, one stands out: "This time tomorrow, I'll kill you all."

Buffy is highly stressed by all the voices in her head; if a cure isn't found soon, Giles predicts she'll go insane. Isolated from as much input as possible at home in bed, Buffy twists in torment. Willow provides Xander, Oz, and Cordelia with interview forms to help narrow down the suspect list. Oz is unable to locate a hiding Freddy. Angel brings the Watchers the heart of the last demon, which

is part of Buffy's cure. She drinks the potion made from it and rushes back to school.

A trapped Freddy finally reveals he hid from Oz simply because he gave the Dingoes a trash review. Cordelia finds a note from Jonathan, and they figure out he's the potential shooter. They search the school as Jonathan assembles a rifle in the bell tower. Buffy spots the gun in the tower, and does a Xena, Warrior Princess, routine to the roof. She disarms Jonathan by speaking with him honestly about the pain everyone suffers in isolation. It turns out that Jonathan was planning to kill only himself. He had no plans to harm anyone else. He hands over the gun, no longer intent on suicide. The lunch lady confirms Xander's paranoid fantasy when he finds her pouring rat poison in the mulligan stew. She was the person bent on taking out as many students as possible. Her evil plan is averted when Buffy fights her.

QUOTE OF THE WEEK:

"My life happens on occasion to suck beyond the telling of it."

Up in the bell tower, Buffy tries to reassure Jonathan that life is nevertheless worth living.

THE AGONY AND THE ECSTASY:

Buffy is still disquieted by Angel's interactions with Faith in "Enemies," and sees her aspect of the demon as a chance to read his mind, not knowing vampires are immune. Xander's proprietary interest in Cordelia continues, inflamed by her obvious attraction to Wesley. The attraction is mutual, but Wesley is constrained by their student-teacher relationship. The jealousy themes of *Othello* provide a counterpoint to Buffy's readiness to believe Angel is attracted to Faith.

POP-CULTURE IQ:

"He's looking at her. He's got his filthy, Pierce Brosnan-y eyeballs all over my Cordy."
Xander compares Wesley to Agent 007 at the school basketball game.

"Principal Snyder has 'Walk Like an Egyptian' stuck in his head."
During her mind-reading phase, Buffy discovers Snyder is a Bangles fan.

> Cordelia reads the Sunnydale High newspaper for mention of the cheerleading squad. Oz reads it for the obituaries.

CONTINUITY:

Giles continues to be a "cross-referencing fool" in search of information about the Mayor's Ascension, but he and Wesley meet with limited success. Percy's respect for Willow as Vamp Willow in "Doppelgangland" is undiminished. *Othello* in the classroom underscores the episode's jealousy theme as well as the dark/light Faith/Buffy relationship. An earlier similar use of Shakespeare appeared in "Out of Mind, Out of Sight," and many of Maggie Walsh's lectures are thematic in Season Four. Buffy cuts school again ("Bad Girls"), this time to visit Angel. Joyce is unable to avoid Buffy's discovery that she and Giles had sex during "Band Candy." Giles now also knows that Buffy knows about him and her mother. Willow's interrogation of Jonathan is déjà vu from "Go Fish," and a precursor to "Superstar." Larry and Xander's discussion parallels "Phases." Oz's ability to track a human by scent seems just to apply to Willow ("Lovers Walk" and "New Moon Rising"). Xander should just stay out of the Sunnydale High cafeteria ("I Only Have Eyes for You" and "Go Fish").

FROM THE ORIGINAL TELEPLAY:

Freddy Iverson was originally Freddy Munson.

More snappy Slayer dialogue as Buffy speaks to the mouthless demons, in this line cut for length:
"Say 'Uncle.' Oops. No mouth."

WRITTEN BY: **David Fury**; DIRECTED BY: **James A. Contner.**
GUEST STARS: **Kristine Sutherland as Joyce Summers, Harry Groener as Mayor Richard Wilkins III, Alexis Denisof as Wesley Wyndam-Pryce, Eliza Dushku as Faith, Armin Shimerman as Principal Snyder; with Co-stars Keith Brunsmann as Vamp-Lackey, Jason Reed as Vamp-Guard.**

THE PLOT THICKENS

The Mayor gives Faith a wicked knife as a present and asks her to retrieve a package from the airport. Buffy, inspired by thoughts of leaving Sunnydale after graduation, suggests initiating a confrontation with the Mayor instead of waiting on his actions. Faith kills the courier and brings his mysterious package to the Mayor. Buffy gets the lowdown on the Box of Gavrok and its location at city hall. The gang makes plans to retrieve the box and invoke the necessary ritual magick to neutralize any protection on it.

Buffy, Willow, and Angel stage a calculated assault on city hall, while Giles and Wesley provide a necessary diversion, and Xander and Oz prepare the magick ritual to Willow's specific actions. Willow neutralizes the magical protective field and departs. Angel fastens Buffy into her *Mission Impossible* gear and lowers her through the skylight. She lifts the box, triggering an alarm. As Angel tries to lift her and the box, the rigging jams. A couple of vampire guards appear. Buffy and Angel battle them and escape with the box. The Mayor surveys the room with disapproval, until Faith appears with their consolation prize: Willow.

Wesley has all the others set against him as he argues that destroying the box and stopping the Mayor is more important than trading it for Willow. Oz settles the debate by destroying the ritual items. Willow searches the room she is imprisoned in for weapons; thanks to her Wiccan skills, a levitating pencil serves as an improvised stake for her vamp guard. She enters the Mayor's office and is absorbed in the Books of Ascension when Faith ends her reading at knifepoint. The Mayor orders Willow kept alive as a bargaining tool, and the black-and-white hats meet in the Sunnydale High cafeteria. Snyder arrives with security guards as the hostage exchange is completed, and confiscates the box. Several black spidery creatures emerge to be dispatched by members of both sides. The Mayor eats one. Faith skewers one with her knife, saving Wesley, and reluctantly leaves it in the wall as the Mayor's party exits. Willow cheers her side by sharing several significant pages she removed from the Books of Ascension.

Willow and Buffy discuss college, and Willow tells Buffy she's going to join Buffy at U.C. Sunnydale. Later, alone in the graveyard, Buffy and Angel try to refute the Mayor's comments about their relationship. They really can't.

"Raise your hand if you're invulnerable. . . ."

The Mayor taunts the Scooby Gang during his collection of his magic box of spiders.

THE AGONY AND THE ECSTASY:

Angel and Buffy's casual opening discussion about their future has a far different tone from the closing one after the Mayor's dissection of their relationship. Xander's comments to Cordelia in the dress shop suggest he is still vulnerable to her caustic comments, even with his increased confidence ("The Zeppo"). Angel and Buffy choose to face an uncertain future together, but their already difficult romance is further shaken by the Mayor's comments.

> According to the prop department, the cross bow is Joss's favorite weapon for Buffy.

POP-CULTURE IQ:

"I'm tired of waiting for Mayor McSleaze to make his move, while we sit on our hands counting down to Ascension Day."

Buffy diminishes the Mayor to a McDonald's character gone bad.

"You just can't stop Nancy Drew-ing, can you?"

Faith asks Willow if she detects some of Carolyn Keene's famous red-headed detective in herself.

CONTINUITY:

The Mayor gives Faith *the knife,* which will play such a significant role in "Graduation Day." Xander's fascination with the open road won't actually take him very far ("The Freshmen"). Faith's shooting the courier with her new bow ("Bad Girls") from the roof is practice for shooting Angel in "Graduation Day." Buffy interrogates the limo vamp with Kendra's "Mr. Pointy" stake. Willow's control over her levitating pencils has improved ("Gingerbread"). Willow and Buffy choose to remain in Sunnydale and fight the battles they can, even if they cannot win the war ("Gingerbread"). Buffy's conflicts with Wesley and the dictates of the Watchers Council escalate. Buffy retrieves Faith's knife from the cafeteria wall for future use ("Graduation Day").

FROM THE ORIGINAL TELEPLAY:

Script directions for sounding the alarm:
[She grips the box, lifts it off the table and . . .
WHOOP WHOOP WHOOP (there it is) AN ALARM BLARES!]

THE PROM

WRITTEN BY: **Marti Noxon**; DIRECTED BY: **David Solomon**. GUEST STARS: **Kristine Sutherland as Joyce Summers, Alexis Denisof as Wesley Wyndam-Pryce, Brad Kane as Tucker, Emma Caulfield as Anya; with Co-stars Danny Strong as Jonathan Levenson and Mike Kimmel as Harv.**

THE PLOT THICKENS

Buffy discusses prom and housekeeping plans with a reluctant Angel. Anya asks Xander to the prom. Joyce visits Angel and tells him if he loves Buffy, he should end their relationship. Prom plans are discussed in the library as Giles tries to focus everyone on the Ascension. Angel and Buffy are on patrol in the sewers when she brings up the prom again. He not only turns her down for the prom, he tells her they have no future. If they survive the Ascension, he will leave Sunnydale. Willow con-

soles Buffy as Buffy faces her heartbreak and going stag to the prom.

Xander enters the dress shop to tease Cordelia until he discovers that she has been reduced to a working girl trying to earn her prom dress. As they bicker, a Hell Hound bursts through the window and savages a youth in a tux before disappearing as abruptly as it appeared. The gang views the shop's videotape of the incident and realizes the Hell Hound was drawn to the victim by his formal attire. They also spot Tucker, apparent master of the hound. Buffy squashes any thoughts of the gang miss-

ing the prom to assist her in Hell Hound roundup. Buffy and Angel have an uncomfortable run-in at the meat-packing plant, where Buffy gets Tucker's address. Buffy sends the others off to the prom; Giles remains behind to offer sympathy.

At the dance Willow and Oz, Xander and Anya, Cordelia, and Wesley mingle and keep an eye out for disaster. Buffy subdues Tucker only to find he has already released three of his Hell Hounds. Buffy manages to take them out one at a time before they can enter the dance floor. She changes into her "kick" pink prom dress. The Class Awards are given, including a new and unexpected one: "Buffy Summers, Class Protector." Giles and Buffy quietly contemplate the significance of her work being appreciated by her peers while the others dance. Angel arrives in his tuxedo to help Buffy capture at least one "perfect high school moment."

QUOTE OF THE WEEK:

"I will be wearing pink taffeta as the chenille does nothing for my complexion and can we PLEASE talk about the Ascension?"

Giles prefers slaying to shopping, though Willow and Buffy would rather discuss what to wear to the prom.

185

THE AGONY AND THE ECSTASY:

Buffy sleeps in Angel's bedroom. Anya is drawn to Xander despite blaming him for her mortality ("The Wish"). Angel dreams of wedding Buffy, then seeing her destroyed as their life together tries to withstand the harsh light of day. He makes the hard choice to leave her rather than see their relationship ruin her chance for a normal romantic life. Wesley is jealous when he sees Xander and Cordelia together on the tape. Xander rises to the occasion by not revealing Cordelia's "shame," and by dipping into his road fund to purchase her dress. Wesley asks Cordelia to dance at the prom, one more step in their mutual attraction. Willow and Oz's romance continues to blossom.

> Variations of "Hell Hounds" abound in world mythology. The most famous is Cerberus from Greek mythology. Ray Harryhausen depicted a fierce two-headed Cerberus in 1981's *Clash of the Titans.*

POP-CULTURE IQ:

"I bet you'd look way 'double oh seven' in a tux."
Cordelia compares Wesley to James Bond, prompting him to volunteer for chaperone duty at the prom.

"Giles, we got it. Miles to go before we sleep."
Buffy quotes Robert Frost's "Stopping by Woods on a Snowy Evening," meaning that she has lots to do before she can fully appreciate the fashion choices associated with prom worthiness.

"Or check and see who's been stocking up on Hell Hound snausages."
Xander believes in pet treats for Hell Hounds, and wants to employ a clever strategy to find same.

"I mean—where did I think you got your blood? McPlasma's?"
Buffy conjures visions of bloody dripping golden arches when she finds Angel with some takeout down at the butcher's dock.

"I've got to stop a crazy from pulling a Carrie at the prom."
Buffy refers to Stephen King's 1974 debut novel, comparing the imminent attack on promgoers to the carnage that psychokinetic Carrie caused after being humiliated at the prom.

"I'm going to lock you up in here, and then I'm going to party like it's. . ."
Buffy remembers when The Artist was known as Prince—the first time—when confronting Tucker.

CONTINUITY:

Xander reminds everyone of Willow's brave acquisition of key parts of the Books of Ascension ("Choices"). Joyce's conversation with Angel is a kinder version of the Mayor's ("Choices"). Angel refers to his post-sex reversion to Angelus in "Surprise" and "Innocence." Willow's low opinion of guys who break up with their girlfriends and leave town will be heard again ("Pangs"). Jonathan has special reason to think of Buffy as the Class Protector ("Earshot"). Other students refer to incidents with zombies ("Dead Man's Party") and hyena people ("The Pack"). Buffy takes her umbrella to UC Sunnydale with her, where it is mistreated by Sunday ("The Freshman").

> During the days when the actual prom scene was shot, the weather varied from drizzle to pouring rain, making makeup, hair, and costumes that much more difficult.

Stage directions indicate the process Tucker uses to train his Hell Hounds: [His eyes held open with metal clamps (à la <u>A Clockwork Orange</u>).]

Giles endeavors to comprehend adolescence in this exchange cut due to length:

GILES: "Fine. You're all suffering from a touch of spring madness, if you ask me."

OZ: "Mine is more space madness. But I'll feel better once I get used to the weightlessness."

WILLOW (to Oz): "Promise me you'll never be linear."

OZ (a pledge): "On my trout."

WRITTEN AND DIRECTED BY: **Joss Whedon.** GUEST STARS: **Kristine Sutherland as Joyce Summers, Harry Groener as Mayor Richard Wilkins III, Alexis Denisof as Wesley Wyndam-Pryce, Mercedes McNab as Harmony, Ethan Erickson as Percy West, Emma Caulfield as Anya, Eliza Dushku as Faith, Armin Shimerman as Principal Snyder; with Co-stars James Lurie as Mr. Miller, Hal Robinson as Lester Worth**.

THE PLOT THICKENS

Xander is facing graduation day and the Mayor's Ascension with a sense of certain doom. Buffy tells Willow she doesn't find the graduation ceremony significant and may not attend. She changes her mind upon hearing that the Mayor will be the commencement speaker. Faith pays a fatal call on the seemingly innocuous geology professor, Lester Worth, and steals his papers, which have details of the last Ascension. Buffy recognizes her MO from the news report and decides to investigate. Xander learns Anya witnessed an Ascension in the past. Anya recalls the devastation that resulted when a human became a demon in pure, not hybrid, form. She is striving to contribute specifics when the Mayor braves "the inner sanctum" of the library. The Mayor's threat to Buffy goads Giles into stabbing him, to no avail.

Buffy packs up Joyce and sends her safely out of town. Giles sends Angel to help Buffy look for clues at Professor Worth's. As they argue on the street, Faith shoots Angel in the chest with an arrow. Giles and Buffy do first aid on Angel's wound as Wesley reads Professor Worth's papers. They learn an eruption killed an earlier demon. Angel collapses from the poisoned arrow, distracting Buffy per Faith's plan. Anya makes plans to leave town pre-Ascension and invites Xander to join her. The Watchers Council will not share information on healing Angel. Buffy reaches her breaking point and disassociates herself from the organization. Oz succeeds in tracking down a cure for Angel: "to drain the blood of a Slayer." Buffy heads out to sacrifice Faith to the cause.

Faith is chillin' when Buffy enters her apartment and informs her of both Angel's cure and her intent to see he gets it. They fight, no holds barred, with everything they value at stake. The fight extends violently through the window to the rooftop, where a determined Buffy handcuffs herself to her dark counterpart. Faith has enough energy to break the cuffs but is tiring as Buffy draws a familiar knife. Buffy stabs Faith. Faith knocks Buffy back from the edge of the roof, then falls out of reach onto the bed of a passing truck, denying Buffy her hard-won victory.

QUOTE Of THE WEEK:

XANDER: "The Mayor's going to kill us all during graduation."
CORDELIA: "Oh. [beat] Are you gonna go to fifth period?"
XANDER: "I'm thinking I might skip it."
What's a little hooky compared to the end of the world?

THE AGONY AND THE ECSTASY:

The Mayor and Faith continue to bond in their own mega-dysfunctional family manner; she responds to his praise and assurances he will still need her even after his Ascension. Anya strives to better understand herself and her attraction to Xander, despite her centuries of anti-male actions. Joyce hates leaving Buffy in Sunnydale to face danger without her, but recognizes she is a liability. Willow and Oz make love for the first time, seeking comfort in the face of danger. After their breakup Buffy can't stand being with Angel or separated from him. Either way she is not willing to let Faith or anyone else take the choice away from her. Xander's mature concern for Buffy's emotional well-being if she kills Faith is a mark of his growth.

> Faith shoots Angel from atop the Sunnydale cinema, proving once again "The Sun" is bad for vampires.

POP-CULTURE IQ:

"Siegfried? Roy? One of their tigers?"
Willow's dream commencement speakers are Las Vegas headliners, but no such luck: They're getting the Mayor.

"We're gonna need a bigger boat."
Xander references *Jaws* yet again when he sees a picture of what the Mayor plans to transform into.

CONTINUITY:

Willow and Harmony pledge to keep in touch; the undead Harmony returns in "The Harsh Light of Day." Percy thanks Willow for refraining from assaulting him again ("Doppelgangland"). Amy is still a rat, but with a "swinging habitrail" ("Gingerbread"). Buffy tells Angel he's her "last office romance" but changes her mind for Riley in Season Four. Faith shoots Angel from a rooftop with her longbow, the same MO she used for the courier ("Choices"). Anya questions Xander's contributions to the group efforts, echoing Cordelia's taunts in "The Zeppo." Buffy collected Faith's knife in the cafeteria after Faith killed an escapee from the Box of Gavrok ("Choices"). Anya and the death of

Professor Worth provide essential clues to the demon's destruction, and Anya clarifies pure vs. "hybrid" (tainted) demons.

fROM THE ORIGINAL TELEPLAY:

In the opening dialogue Cordelia has lobbied for red graduation robes, and Xander prefers blue. Buffy later describes her gown as dark blue. The robes ended up being Sunnydale's maroon color.

WRITTEN AND DIRECTED BY: **Joss Whedon.** GUEST STARS: **Harry Groener as Mayor Richard Wilkins III, Alexis Denisof as Wesley Wyndam-Pryce, Danny Strong as Jonathan Levenson, Larry Bagby III as Larry Blaisdell, Mercedes McNab as Harmony, Ethan Erickson as Percy West, Eliza Dushku as Faith, Armin Shimerman as Principal Snyder; with Co-stars Paulo Andres as Dr. Powell, Tom Bellin as Dr. Gold.**

GRADUATION DAY, *PART TWO*

THE PLOT THICKENS

The Mayor's confidence is shaken by Faith's empty post-battle apartment. Cordelia gets the skinny on Buffy's quitting the Council from research fiends Giles and Xander. Buffy relieves Oz and Willow from Angel watch. She forces Angel to drink her blood so that he can recover from the "Killer of the Dead" poison. Angel rushes the unconscious Buffy to the hospital, where she is treated just a few rooms down from the comatose Faith. The Mayor tries to suffocate Buffy, but Angel and the hospital staff rescue her. Angel assures the arriving Scooby Gang that Buffy will recover and will not turn into a vampire, but they're angry with him for nearly killing Buffy. Buffy and Faith share a dream, and a subdued Faith tells Buffy to use the Mayor's human weakness to destroy him. Buffy visits the recumbent Faith, then leads her team into preparations for war.

The gang meets in the library to formulate their attack plans. Suggestions include attacking the Mayor with hummus and a fake Ebola virus. Wesley joins them in a non-Watcher capacity, and they

make do-it-yourself volcano arrangements. A scheduled eclipse means both Angel and the Mayor's hench vamps can join in the battle. Xander and Willow spearhead the effort to recruit other students.

The graduation ceremony begins. Snyder gives a completely uninspiring intro to the Mayor, who lectures his captive, about-to-be-devoured audience on Sunnydale history. The eclipse occurs, and he transforms into an "unholy big-ass snake thing." Snyder's dismay at this chaos is brief, as the Mayor swallows him. The students drop their robes to reveal an assortment of weapons, the Mayor's vampires attack from the flank, and the battle is joined. Casualties are inflicted on both sides, as Larry is slammed by the Mayor's tail, and Harmony is bitten by a vampire. Buffy engages the Mayor in some David and Goliath action, taunting him with

Faith's knife, then fleeing for her life and everyone else's. She charges through the school halls and into the library with the Mayor demon-snake in hot—and destructive—pursuit. She bursts out of the library's rear window, and as the Mayor enters the library, Giles detonates the explosives filling the library. As the survivors survey the wreckage, Giles presents Buffy with her charred diploma. Buffy, Willow, Xander, Oz, and Cordelia contemplate the fact that they have a post-high school future. The final shot is of a yearbook lying on the ground, captioned "Sunnydale High '99—The Future Is Ours."

QUOTE OF THE WEEK:

GILES: "Buffy no longer needs a Watcher."
CORDELIA: "Well, does [Wesley] have to leave the country? I mean, you got fired and you still hang around like a big loser, why can't he?"
Cordelia employs her usual tact when discussing Wesley's planned departure for England.

THE AGONY AND THE ECSTASY:

Willow and Oz are glowing with romantic contentment despite the arrival of the Ascension. Giles and Willow both show compassion for Angel, despite the harm done to them by Angelus ("Passion" and "Becoming, Parts One & Two"). Buffy is willing to risk her life to save Angel, even knowing they have no future together. Cordelia and Wesley get a chance to act on their attraction but the resulting kiss is really, really bad. Angel tells Buffy he won't prolong their goodbyes—in some ways they've been saying goodbye since "Choices." After the destruction of Sunnydale High and the Mayor, Buffy and Angel confirm each other's physical well-being with a look, then he departs without another word.

> It's graduation time for everyone as the Mutant Enemy logo monster dons his mortarboard as well.

POP-CULTURE IQ:

"Oh, yeah. Miles to go. Little Miss Muffet counting down from seven three oh."

Faith's dream speech refers to both Robert Frost and Mother Goose.

CONTINUITY:

Angel's vampiric nature rising in response to pain parallels Oz's wolf nature responding to emotional pain in "New Moon Rising." Buffy kisses the comatose Faith on the forehead in unconscious imitation of Faith's gesture in "Enemies." The battle plan discussions include a reference to Xander's psuedo-military knowledge ("Halloween") and Buffy's use of a rocket launcher against the Judge ("Innocence"). Wesley and Cordelia box the library books, which were recently returned after being removed in "Gingerbread." Buffy retrieves the knife she used on Faith ("Graduation Day, Part One"), which was originally a gift from the Mayor ("Choices"), and uses it as the bait to lure the Mayor. Oz and Willow have sex again right before the graduation ceremony. Buffy's post-explosion verbal skills—"fire bad, tree pretty"—will resurface in "Beer Bad."

FROM THE ORIGINAL TELEPLAY:

"Guys, we blew up the school! It's the best day ever!"
Xander fails to be politically correct in this line cut for length.

ARTIST	SONG TITLE	EPISODE NAME
BELLYLOVE Bad Boy Kitty Records—1998's *bellylove*	"Back to Freedom"	"ANNE"
FOUR STAR MARY MSG Records—1999's *Thrown to the Wolves*	"Never Mind"	"DEAD MAN'S PARTY"
FOUR STAR MARY For more information see Web site: msgrecords.com/FSM	"Sway"	"DEAD MAN'S PARTY"
FOUR STAR MARY MSG Records—1997's *Four Star Mary*	"Pain"	"DEAD MAN'S PARTY"
THE BRIAN JONESTOWN MASSACRE TVT—1998's *Strung Out in Heaven*	"Going To Hell"	"FAITH, HOPE & TRICK"
DARLING VIOLETTA Opaline Records—1997's *BathWaterFlowers*	"Blue Sun"	"FAITH, HOPE & TRICK"
DARLING VIOLETTA Opaline Records—2000's *The Kill You* EP	"Cure"	"FAITH, HOPE & TRICK"
THIRD EYE BLIND Elektra Entertainment—1997's *Third Eye Blind*	"The Background"	"FAITH, HOPE & TRICK"
LORI CARSON BMG/Restless—1995's *Where It Goes*	"Fell Into the Loneliness"	"HOMECOMING"
THE PINEHURST KIDS Four Alarm—1999's *Minnesota Hotel*	"Jodie Foster"	"HOMECOMING"
LISA LOEB Uni/Geffen—1997's *Firecracker*	"How"	"HOMECOMING"
FOUR STAR MARY MSG Records—1999's *Thrown to the Wolves*	"She Knows"	"HOMECOMING"
FASTBALL Uni/Hollywood—1998's *All the Pain Money Can Buy*	"Fire Escape"	"HOMECOMING"

SONGLIST

ARTIST	SONG TITLE	EPISODE NAME
MAD COW Label—*Eureka*	"Blas"	"BAND CANDY"
FOUR STAR MARY MSG Records—1999's *Thrown to the Wolves*	"Violent"	"BAND CANDY"
EVERY BIT OF NOTHING Label—*Austamosta*	"Slip Jimmy"	"BAND CANDY"
CREAM Uni/Polydor—1998's remastered *Disraeli Gears*	"Tales of Brave Ulysses"	"BAND CANDY"
FOUR STAR MARY MSG Records—1999's *Thrown to the Wolves*	"Run"	"REVELATIONS"
LOTION SpinArt Records—1998's *The Telephone Album*	"West of Here"	"REVELATIONS"
LOLLY Available online	"Silver Dollar"	"REVELATIONS"
GARY OLDMAN MCA Records—1986's *Sid and Nancy* Soundtrack	"My Way"	"LOVERS WALK"
THE SPIES Fig Records—*Toy Surprise Inside*	"Tired of Being Alone"	"THE WISH"
PLASTIC (Information not available)	"Dedicated to Pain"	"THE WISH"
GINGERSOL Dental Records—1996's *Extended Play*	"Never Noticed"	"THE WISH"
BARRY WHITE Mercury/Polygram—1994's *All-Time Greatest Hits*	"Can't Get Enough of Your Love, Babe"	"AMENDS"
SUPERGRASS EMI/Capitol—1997's *In It for the Money*	"G-Song"	"THE ZEPPO"
TRICKY WOO Sonic Unyon—1998's *Enemy is Real*	"Easy"	"THE ZEPPO"

ARTIST	SONG TITLE	EPISODE NAME
CURVE Universal Records/EMI—1998's *Come Clean*	**"Chinese Burn"**	"BAD GIRLS"
KATHLEEN WILHOITE BMG/Gee Street—1998's *Pitch Like a Girl*	**"Wish We Never Met"**	"CONSEQUENCES"
K'S CHOICE Twentieth Century Fox—1999's *Buffy the Vampire Slayer: The Album*	**"Virgin State of Mind"**	"DOPPELGANGLAND"
SPECTATOR PUMP Trik Magik Records—1998's *Styrofoam Archives*	**"Priced 2 Move"**	"DOPPELGANGLAND"
FATBOY SLIM Virgin—1998's *You've Come a Long Way, Baby*	**"Praise You"**	"THE PROM"
KOOL & THE GANG Mercury Records—1994's *Celebration: Best of Kool & the Gang*	**"Celebration"**	"THE PROM"
CRACKER Virgin—1998's *Gentleman's Blues*	**"The Good Life"**	"THE PROM"
THE LASSIE FOUNDATION Shogun Sounds—1999's *Pacifico*	**"El Rey"**	"THE PROM"
THE SUNDAYS Geffen—1992's *Blind*	**"Wild Horses"**	"THE PROM"
SPECTATOR PUMP Trik Magik Records—1998's *Styrofoam Archives*	**"Sunday Mail"**	"GRADUATION DAY, PART ONE"

SONGLIST

SEASON FOUR

EPISODE NUMBER	EPISODE NAME	ORIGINAL U.S. AIRDATE
1	"The Freshman"	5-Oct. 1999
2	"Living Conditions"	12-Oct.
3	"The Harsh Light of Day"	19-Oct.
4	"Fear, Itself"	26-Oct.
5	"Beer Bad"	2-Nov.
6	"Wild at Heart"	9-Nov.
7	"The Initiative"	16-Nov.
8	"Pangs"	23-Nov.
9	"Something Blue"	30-Nov.
10	"Hush"	14-Dec.
11	"Doomed"	18-Jan. 2000
12	"A New Man"	25-Jan.
13	"The I in Team"	8-Feb.
14	"Goodbye, Iowa"	15-Feb.
15	"This Year's Girl"	22-Feb.
16	"Who Are You"	29-Feb.
17	"Superstar"	4-Apr.
18	"Where the Wild Things Are"	25-Apr.
19	"New Moon Rising"	2-May
20	"The Yoko Factor"	9-May
21	"Primeval"	16-May
22	"Restless"	23-May

STARRING

Sarah Michelle Gellar .... **Buffy Summers**
Nicholas Brendon .... **Xander Harris**
Alyson Hannigan .... **Willow Rosenberg**
Anthony Stewart Head .... **Rupert Giles**
Seth Green .... **Oz [Through "Wild at Heart"]**
James Marsters .... **Spike [Beginning with "The Initiative"]**
Marc Blucas .... **Riley Finn [Beginning with "Doomed"]**

THE FRESHMAN

WRITTEN AND DIRECTED BY: Joss Whedon. **GUEST STARS:** Kristine Sutherland as Joyce, Marc Blucas as Riley Finn, Dagney Kerr as Kathy, Pedro Balmaceda as Eddie, Katharine Towne as Sunday, Lindsay Crouse as Professor Maggie Walsh; with Co-stars Mike Rad as Rookie, Shannon Hillary as Dav, Phina Oruche as Olivia.

THE PLOT THICKENS:

The season opener begins with Buffy and Willow talking about course selections while waiting for a new vampire to rise from its grave. Willow insists that Buffy take Dr. Walsh's psychology class—a decision that will have far-reaching consequences.

Buffy suffers major culture shock on the first day of school at UC Sunnydale. Willow, fully prepared and with an on-campus boyfriend, is filled with excitement. Oz, whose band Dingoes Ate My Baby has played at the university many times, is likewise at ease.

Buffy and Willow check out the enormous library, and then the bookstore. When Buffy tries to reach their psychology texts, she accidentally conks a nice-looking guy on the head with them. He is Riley Finn, their psychology teaching assistant. Willow chats comfortably with him about operant conditioning while Buffy fumbles and grows more and more socially awkward.

Buffy meets her roommate Kathy, who is far too perky for Buffy's taste, and snores to boot. The first day of school goes downhill from there, as Buffy is thrown out of Pop Culture, a class she had hoped to crash, for talking.

Buffy begins to wonder if she's the only person on the planet reeling from all the newness, until she meets another freshman named Eddie, who admits to freshman jitters of his own. He tells her that he has a security blanket that he takes wherever he goes, and shows her his well-worn copy of the novel, *Of Human Bondage*. They part company, and Eddie runs into a pack of vampires led by a blond vampire dressed like a punked-out school girl.

In class the next day Buffy notices that Eddie's absent. She goes to his dorm room, to discover that all his stuff is missing. The Resident Adviser shows her a note Eddie left in which he says he can't handle university life after all. The RA tells Buffy that a number of freshmen leave unexpectedly every year. Buffy spots Eddie's copy of *Of Human Bondage* in a drawer.

Meanwhile, the punked-out vampire and her followers are going through Eddie's stuff in their lair. Eddie is dead in the corner, and just as the vampires get ready to hunt, he awakens.

Buffy's suspicious about Eddie's disappearance. She visits Giles at his apartment to ask for help. But her former Watcher—who's entertaining "an old friend," Olivia, reminds her that she's got to be more self-reliant.

During patrol, newly vamped Eddie lures her into a confrontation with the Big Vampire on Campus, who introduces herself as Sunday. Sunday and her followers are itching for a fight with the newly matriculated Slayer. Buffy takes Sunday on, and barely escapes.

Shaken by her defeat, she goes to the Bronze to mope and discovers that Xander has returned from his disappointing trip to find America. He got as far as Oxnard and ended up working in a male strip club, washing dishes . . . most of the time.

Together they do the research and locate Sunday's lair—an old frat house. Sunday and her groupies murder the occasional freshman and steal his/her stuff. Now it's Buffy's turn. When she and Xander locate the lair, Buffy discovers that all her possessions have been taken.

Thinking Buffy's safely waiting for him to return with weapons, Xander assures Willow and Oz that Buffy's fine for the moment. But Buffy falls through the ceiling skylight into the lair. She does battle once more with the vampire, emerging triumphant just as her loyal Scooby Gang arrives to help. The episode concludes with Buffy realizing college is something she can handle after all, now that she knows what to expect . . . followed by a brief teaser in which Sunday's sole surviving hench vamp is captured by three mysterious figures dressed in military gear.

QUOTE OF THE WEEK:

"Some friends of Buffy's played a funny joke. They took her stuff, and now she wants us to help get it back from her friends who sleep all day and have no tans."
Xander sums up Buffy's predicament in front of Kathy, who isn't supposed to know about vampires.

THE AGONY AND THE ECSTASY:

In a wrenching role reversal from the first-ever episode of *Buffy*, Willow is the confident girl while Buffy feels insecure and lonely. Willow has an on-campus boyfriend who's in a band, no less, and Riley Finn, destined to become Buffy's love interest, only remembers Buffy as "Willow's friend." Meanwhile, the plaintive notes of Buffy and Angel's love song play over a phone call Buffy answers—no reply on the other end—and the world stops when she thinks she sees Angel at the Bronze. In a moment of great tenderness Xander confesses to the Slayer that she's his hero. Giles is seeing Olivia, who "couldn't pass through Sunny Cal without looking up old Ripper."

Of Human Bondage by W. Somerset Maugham: Eddie's security blanket is an autobiographical novel written in 1915. It chronicles a young man's struggle for independence and identity, and is considered Maugham's finest literary achievement.

POP-CULTURE IQ:

"Okay, remember before you became Hugh Hefner, when you were a Watcher?"
Buffy's referring to the founder of *Playboy* magazine, usually photographed surrounded by beautiful women and wearing a bathrobe or smoking jacket. She comes upon Giles similarly attired and alone with a beautiful woman apparently wearing nothing but an oversized chambray shirt.

"...Hate leads to anger ... no, wait ... Fear leads to hate, hate leads to the dark side ...."

Xander delivers a convoluted homage to the Jedi code from *Star Wars* to Buffy, in his attempt to explain away her freshman jitters.

"Avengers assemble!"

Xander suggests to Buffy that they call the group together to fight Sunday and her gang. The Avengers are a group of comic-book superheroes; the commercial for their cartoon show carries the tag line.

"This is great if we ever need a place for the Nuremberg rallies."

Buffy's referring to the immense size of the UC Sunnydale library. In the 1930s German dictator Adolf Hitler held huge rallies in cities such as Nuremberg to incite the masses to support his genocidal reign of terror.

"This is pretty much a madhouse, a madhouse."

Oz's deadpan delivery of Charleton Heston's line in *Planet of the Apes*. Xander also uses it in a "guess the movie" contest with Willow in the opening scene of "When She Was Bad."

> **"Monet still well in the lead, but look out for team Klimt coming from behind."** The posters the vampires routinely steal from the walls of freshman dorm rooms are Monet's *Water Lilies* and Gustave Klimt's *The Kiss*, referring to the most common dorm decorations freshmen buy.

CONTINUITY:

There's bad stuff at UC Sunnydale, just as there was at Sunnydale High. Giles reminds Buffy that she has resigned from working for the Watcher's Council and that he is no longer her Watcher. His address is established as 523 Oakpark Street, Apt. B, Sunnydale, CA 90211. Professor Maggie Walsh, who really *is* the "evil bitch monster of death," makes her first appearance. Riley Finn, masquerading as Maggie's teaching assistant, meets Buffy for the first time. The three paramilitary figures foreshadow the emergence of the Initiative. Buffy's problems with her roommate, Kathy, escalate in "Living Conditions." Olivia will reappear in "Hush" and "Restless." Xander's and Giles's uncertain futures provide storylines concerning Xander's frequently changing jobs and Giles's feeling increasingly superfluous. Buffy refers to "Mr. Pointy," a gift from the Slayer, Kendra, who was murdered at the end of Season Two. Sunday dares to toy with Mr. Gordo, Buffy's stuffed piggy, who was first-ever mentioned in "What's My Line? Part One." Willow also mentions the beloved Mr. G. to Riley in "The Initiative." Sunday asks for death when she breaks Buffy's Class Protector umbrella, given to her in "The Prom."

> Originally, Buffy's roommate Kathy was supposed to put up a Backstreet Boys poster to display her lack of coolness. It was later changed to a poster of Celine Dion.

FROM THE ORIGINAL TELEPLAY:

"What better way to say, 'I am the very most of geek.'"

Sunday, dissing Buffy's Class Protector umbrella in a line cut for length.

The script describes the UC Sunnydale library (in reality, UCLA's Powell Library) as "unbelievably gigantoid."

Riley Finn is described in the script as "a junior, tall and good-looking, with an open, honest face."

When Buffy falters during the initial small talk with Riley, the script reads:

[Riley smiles politely at this lamest of comments. Buffy trails behind the other two, awed by her own ineptitude.]

Buffy's line: "I'm Betty Louise Plotnick of East Cupcake, Illinois" originally read, "I'm Betty Louise Plotnick of Blue Falls, Missouri."

WRITTEN BY: **Marti Noxon**; DIRECTED BY: **David Grossman**. GUEST STARS: **Dagney Kerr as Kathy, Adam Kaufman as Parker;** with Co-star Roger Morrissey as Tapparich.

LIVING CONDITIONS

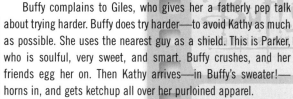

THE PLOT THICKENS:

Buffy has been having a lot of trouble adjusting to life with her roommate, Kathy Newman. Kathy's a neat freak, a control freak, and a perky freak. She wants to log every phone call, she labels every piece of food in the refrigerator, and she tries to tag along when Buffy goes on patrol.

On said patrol, a cloaked demon attacks the girls; before Kathy can realize what's happening, Buffy shoves her out of harm's way. Kathy's reaction is to criticize her for taking on a mugger and to whine about her ruined sweater.

The demon joins his fellows and they talk in creepy demon speak, discussing the fact that "she may be the one" and agreeing that they'd better follow her.

Buffy complains to Giles, who gives her a fatherly pep talk about trying harder. Buffy does try harder—to avoid Kathy as much as possible. She uses the nearest guy as a shield. This is Parker, who is soulful, very sweet, and smart. Buffy crushes, and her friends egg her on. Then Kathy arrives—in Buffy's sweater!—horns in, and gets ketchup all over her purloined apparel.

Things get more and more tense between the roommates. Then Buffy has a terrible dream that involves an ugly demon force-feeding Buffy some blood, a scorpion, and chanting. When Buffy tells Giles about it, it turns out that Kathy had the same dream.

The other demons summon their leader, Tapparich. Kathy horns in on Buffy's "territory" when Parker stops by. Their irritation with each other escalates until Buffy is gulping down Kathy's labeled milk from the fridge, letting it pour maniacally down the front of her pajamas.

Buffy's definitely going over the edge. Her friends try to keep an eye on her. Oz patrols with her, noticing Veruca for the first time.

The nightmares continue. Buffy seems more and more irrational.

The gang lures her to Giles's apartment to keep her from hurting anyone until they figure out what's wrong with her. She's screaming at them that Kathy is a demon. She's got proof—Kathy cut her toenails and Buffy collected them clippings. They're growing after being cut, a sure sign of someone being demonic!

Buffy knocks Xander's and Oz's heads together and goes after Kathy. She unmasks the demonic girl just as Giles realizes she was telling the truth. Kathy is an interdimensional demon—a Mok'tagar who has escaped her own dimension in order to go to college. To hide from her father's bounty hunters, Kathy has been using a ritual on Buffy every night in order to steal the Slayer's soul a little bit at a time. Their species has no soul, and "Kathy" is counting on the fact that when her father's minions arrive to take her home, they'll mistake Buffy for the missing daughter of their great leader, Tapparich.

As with the script of Episode One where the annoying poster was changed between the script and shooting, Mariah Carey's "Butterfly" was the song Buffy found irritating in the script. It was changed in the show to Cher's "Believe," which was nominated for a Grammy for Best Record. Later, the script calls for Celine Dion "blaring."

Giles and Willow begin a ritual to return the portion of Buffy's soul that's been stolen back into her body while she and Kathy engage in a knock-down, drag-out battle of the stressed-out roommates. Just as all the bits of Buffy's soul reenters her body, Kathy's father, Tapparich, appears in the dorm room. He chastises his errant child and flings her into a dimensional portal, leaping in after her.

Big remorse from everyone. The happy ending: Willow moves in with Buffy. All will be well now...or will it? For it appears that Willow has a few bad habits that may eventually get on the Slayer's nerves....

200

QUOTE OF THE WEEK:

"Wish me monsters."

Buffy to Willow, as Buffy goes on patrol and Willow goes to see Oz.

The plot line concerning Oz and Veruca was originally conceived for a longer run. Seth Green's leave of absence from the show cut it short.

THE AGONY AND THE ECSTASY:

Buffy meets the handsome and charming Parker Abrams, who will later break her heart. Jealousy rears when Kathy flirts with him. Xander is trying to deal with the fact that he's not in college with the others. Oz sees or senses Veruca for the first time.

POP-CULTURE IQ:

"Kathy's nice and everything, but she's sort of like—I don't know—Mini-Mom of Momdonia."

Buffy's trying to explain her irritation with her roommate to Willow. Mini-Me is a miniature "clone" of Dr. Evil in *Austin Powers: The Spy Who Shagged Me*.

"You're saying Buffy's been doing a Linda Blair on us because Kathy's been sucking her soul?"

Xander's reference to the actress who played Regan, a young girl possessed by a demon, in the film *The Exorcist*.

"That's because he got hit by the Buffinator."
Xander's assuring Buffy that Parker is smitten with her—a reference to Arnold Schwarzenegger's relentless robot assassin in the films *The Terminator* and *Terminator 2: Judgment Day*.

CONTINUITY:

Oz and Veruca notice each other for the first time. Oz is bemused by her, but Willow is the only apple of his eye at this time. This is the first time in the new season that the magic shop is visited. Willow says of Buffy, "I mean, she was bordering on Cordelia-esque." This is a reference to their sharp, sarcastic high school chum, Cordelia, who wound up working with Angel in Los Angeles.

> Clayton Barber, who played "Demon 1," has also been a stunt double for Angel. Walt Borchert, who played "Demon 2," was a vampire in "The Freshman." Roger Morrissey, who played Tapparich, was also the "Gingerbread" demon.

From stage directions: "Kathy reaches in and produces MR. POINTY." [A reminder of Kendra, the Slayer who was killed in Season Two by Drusilla.] In the show as it was broadcast, Kathy instead picks up a crossbow and a cross.

FROM THE ORIGINAL TELEPLAY:

In a line cut for length, when Buffy is complaining early on to Giles about Kathy, she says:

"I mean, she'd make anybody nuts. She has her outfits written up on index cards, and she gives them names like 'Easter at the White House.' I find that deeply, deeply disturbed. Don't you?"

Also cut for length, from Oz's dialogue:
"I'm pretty sure the next part is about fava beans and a nice Chianti."

And the following dialogue was cut due to length, after Buffy crows, "I knew it! I know you were one of those demon things."
KATHY: "I'm not. Those guys are after me."
BUFFY: "Funny. I'm seeing the skin, the eyes. . . ."
KATHY: "So, I'm from the same dimension. But I'm not like them. They're disgusting."
BUFFY: "What, they don't live by the Kathy 'system'?"

Also cut for length, during the argument between Kathy and Tapparich, after Kathy whines, "I'm 3000 years old! When are you going to stop treating me like I'm 900?!"
TAPPARICH [subtitled]: "When you stop acting that way. I can't tell you how much you've upset your mother."
[Xander and Oz arrive. Xander presses his ear to the door.]
XANDER: "I only hear talking. Maybe we got here in time."
KATHY [subtitled]: "You never let me do anything."

THE **HARSH** LIGHT OF DAY

WRITTEN BY: Jane Espenson; **DIRECTED BY:** James A. Contner.
GUEST STARS: Emma Caulfield as Anya, Mercedes McNab as
Harmony Kendall, Adam Kaufman as Parker, James Marsters as
Spike; with Co-Star Jason Hall as Devon MacLeish of the Dingoes.

THE PLOT THICKENS:

This is the first of three *Buffy/Angel* "crossovers," which are
episodes in which characters from one show visit the other
show. The other fourth season crossovers are "Pangs" and
"The Yoko Factor."

Buffy and Willow are happy at the Bronze. Buffy is crush-
ing on Parker, and Willow is reveling in the fact that her guy,
Oz, and his band are playing. Parker offers to take Buffy
home. While Willow's waiting for Oz and the Dingoes to finish
packing up, Harmony Kendall, one of the snooty "Cordettes"
from Sunnydale High School days, reveals that she's a vampire and attacks her. Willow and Oz fend her off, but she
assures them that her boyfriend will get them back for being
mean to her.

As Buffy and Parker stroll home, Parker moves Buffy
with his thoughtful conversations about death and making
his life mean something. He seems to be someone who
understands what her life is like, even though she can't tell him about her secret life as the Slayer.
Their good night kiss is interrupted by the arrival of Willow and Oz, revealing—carefully—that
Willow has been bitten by a vampire. Parker has time to invite Buffy to a party the next evening
before Buffy goes to help Willow.

Harmony had planned a post-graduation trip to France. Instead, she got changed into a vampire during the Mayor's thwarted Ascension in "Graduation Day, Part Two." Now she's hooked up with
Spike, who has returned to Sunnydale to find the fabled Gem of Amarra. She's bored and he promises
to take her to a nice party.

Anya unexpectedly shows at Giles's flat to demand of Xander where their relationship is going.
Xander is flabbergasted, unaware that the two of them had a relationship. She confesses that
"sometimes in my dreams you're all naked," and Xander can't help but be charmed.

At the party, Buffy and Parker run into Harmony and Spike as they are dragging off a victim.
Spike splits and Buffy gives chase. While they're battling, Harmony tells Buffy that Spike's looking
for the Gem.

Meanwhile, Anya goes to Xander's basement and takes off her clothes.

Buffy phones Giles from the party to tell him about the Gem. The Gem is like the Holy Grail for
vampires, Giles explains, and no wonder—its wearer can walk in daylight and cannot be killed.

Buffy hies back to the party. Parker is warm and deep and mysterious; he seduces her, and they
make tender love. In the morning, he says he can't spend the day with her because his mother is
coming to see him, but he'll call soon.

Anya announces to Xander that she's over him, but neither of them looks very happy about that. Harmony, meanwhile, is still bored, bored, bored.

Longingly, Buffy waits for Parker's call. It becomes heartbreakingly clear that Parker considers their "fun" one-night stand over and done with. Spike, who "loves syphilis" more than Harmony, discovers that she is wearing the Gem when, in a fit of rage, he stakes her. When she doesn't turn to dust, he knows the ring she's slipped on her finger is his "Holy Grail." He takes the ring from her and seeks out the Slayer. Laughing at her for trusting Parker, he engages her in a wild battle in broad daylight. Eventually she subdues him and yanks the ring off his finger. Spike dives into a service tunnel to escape the burning sunlight.

Later, Buffy's friends assemble to discuss what's happened and how to destroy the ring. But Buffy has other plans for the magical object. Oz and the Dingoes are going to Los Angeles, and Buffy asks Oz to deliver the ring to Angel.

QUOTE OF THE WEEK:

"Buffy's looking at Parker. Who, it turns out, has a reflection. So, big plus there."
—Willow sums up Parker's attributes to Oz; turns out this is the only one.

THE AGONY AND THE ECSTASY:

Buffy and Parker's tender lovemaking turns out to be nothing but a one-night stand. Humiliated and heartbroken, Buffy wonders by show's end if a) all men become evil once you sleep with them, and b) if she's repulsive. Harmony and Spike's *affaire de kink* may be over. Spike not only tries to kill Harmony in a fit of rage, but he deserts her after she gives him the Gem of Amarra. Harmony sums up her disappointment: "Being a vampire sucks." Anya, who assumes she has a relationship with Xander because of their prom date last spring, asks him to go to bed with her so she can get him behind her...not literally. "I'm thinking face to face for the actual event." An astonished Xander complies. To her consternation, Anya finds that she's more in love with Xander now that she's had sex with him. She's unaware that Xander is likewise awash in confusion.

> Here are some of the sweet things Spike and Harmony call each other during their Season of Love:
>
> baby ♥ sugar ♥ my little foam latte ♥ my blondey-bear ♥ *mon petite crème brulee* ♥ my little mentholated pack of smokes ♥ Spikey ♥ my platinum baby

POP-CULTURE IQ:

"I'm going to regret being too nervous to ask you to the party at Wolf House tomorrow night."
Parker is inviting Buffy to a frat house bearing the name of author Jack London's home in the San Francisco bay area.

Giles chastises Oz for looking through his record collection in a time of crisis. In response, Oz holds up a copy of the album *Loaded* by the Velvet Underground. Joyce also admired his collection in "Band Candy."

"Is Antonio Banderas a vampire?"

Spike tells Harmony—who's asking—that the actor isn't a vampire, he just played "Armand" in *Interview with the Vampire*.

CONTINUITY:

This is Spike's first appearance since "Lover's Walk." Buffy and Harmony both mention Dru, the love of Spike's eternal life, who has dumped him for a Fungus Demon. Parker continues to cut his swath through the freshman girls, now that the Buffy notch is on his bedpost. The events of graduation day are mentioned in passing with the reappearance of both Harmony and Anya. Oz mentions that Devon used to date Harmony. Xander makes reference to his sexual encounter with Faith, which took place in "The Zeppo," just before he and the ex-demon Anya make love: "And the amazing thing? Still more romantic than Faith." Xander summarizes his and Anya's past: "Second date called on account of snake, remember? And there's the whole you-used-to-be-a-man-killing demon thing, which, to be fair, is as much my issue as it is yours...." There are several references to Angel. Willow indirectly speaks of him when she notes that Parker has a reflection. Spike is crueler, taunting Buffy for going to bed with Parker so quickly. He tells her that Angel also said she wasn't worth a second go. Parker notices the scar Angel left on Buffy's neck when he nearly drained her dry in "Graduation Day, Part Two."

FROM THE ORIGINAL TELEPLAY

The following lines were cut due to length:

WILLOW: "You know what else I love about college? How when the professor comes in, the class gets all quiet."
BUFFY: "Oh, I hate that. I'm always like, what? Did something scary come in? Do I have to kill it?"

DEVON: "Man, that looked like Harmony. Weird. I saw her get bit at graduation. [off their looks] I didn't tell you?"

After Buffy tells Parker she drowned:
PARKER: "Wow, I mean, you hear about stuff like that."
BUFFY: "Yeah, well, pool safety, important. Anyway..."

and

PARKER: "Buffy? When you . . . drowned, whoever brought you back? They're getting a big kiss from me."
BUFFY: "Xander will be so happy."

When Anya is propositioning Xander:
XANDER: "This is just, I'd say out of nowhere, but that doesn't really capture the amount of nowhere which it's out of."

When Buffy runs into Harmony and Spike at the Wolf House party:
BUFFY: "I think you two should go."
SPIKE: "But the fun's just starting: old friends, lots to drink . . . ." [Spike jiggles the victim as he says, 'lots to drink'.]

Anya visits Xander's basement for the first time:
"So...you're my first guest at Casa del Xander—not the final name, still working on it."

Buffy and Giles discuss Spike's surprising hookup with Harmony:

BUFFY: "I mean, I thought Spike and Dru were a forever kind of deal, didn't you? Where's the commitment?"

GILES (get on with it): "I'm disillusioned. I shall never love again."

Parker and Buffy, discussing his view that everyone has a choice with everything they do:

BUFFY: "It doesn't feel like it. To me, a lot of the time, it feels like stuff's just coming at me, you know, and I'm reacting as fast as I can, just trying to keep going. Just—just trying to be on my feet before the next thing hits."

PARKER: "That sounds exhausting."

BUFFY: "It really is."

From when Buffy confronts Parker:

PARKER: "Okay, I'm a little confused now. I mean, I definitely got the idea you'd done it before. You were the one who was all over me. It was fun."

Buffy and Willow debrief after Buffy asks Oz to take the ring to Angel. Buffy is wondering if the way of the world is that a girl sleeps with a guy and then he goes all evil.

WILLOW: "Well, from what I understand, pretty much. But it won't always be like that. You've just had some really bad luck."

BUFFY: "I don't know, Will. Bad luck just happens. I made this happen."

WILLOW: "Well, why shouldn't you, if it's what you want? I mean, as long as it's safe. Oh, Buffy, it was safe, wasn't it?"

BUFFY: "It was safe. It's not that. It's that the whole time, I kept thinking, hey, look at me with someone who isn't Angel. Look how much I'm not hung up on Angel anymore. Look how this is not <u>all</u> about Angel. God, how come I didn't see it?"

Here is an interesting stage direction from the episode:

When Spike and Harmony enter the crypt containing the treasure and the Gem of Amarra:

[There is a dead demon here, withered and decayed and brown and crunchy, arrayed in finery on a carved wooden bier.]

written by: **David Fury**; directed by: **Tucker Gates**. GUEST STARS: **Kristine Sutherland as Joyce, Marc Blucas as Riley, Emma Caulfield as Anya, Adam Kaufman as Parker, Lindsay Crouse as Professor Maggie Walsh**; with Co-stars **Marc Rose as Josh, Sulo Williams as Chaz, Adam Bitterman as Gachnar, Michele Nordin as Rachel.**

THE PLOT THICKENS:

It's the night before Halloween, the traditional slow night for slayage. Glum Buffy, still pining over Parker, neglects her pumpkin-carving duties and agrees to accompany Willow, Oz, and Xander to the Alpha Delta haunted house on the big night itself. Xander's a little hurt that they forgot to mention it to him—also he tried to rent *Phantasm,* but ended up with *Fantasia* by mistake. So it's all to the good that there's an alternate plan.

Giles is dressed for the happy evening in a ridiculous sombrero and a poncho. He assures Buffy that she may have the night off and enjoy herself.

Before the horrors begin, the frat brothers prevail upon Oz to help them with their sound system. Oz cuts himself, dripping blood onto the mystical rune fratboy Chaz is busily painting on the floor for decoration. No one realizes that this rune calls forth Gachnar, the fear demon.

Anya wants to be with Xander, so he invites her to the haunted house party. She's not sure what kind of costume constitutes a "scary" one, but Xander has faith in her. She will join them at the party later, once she figures out a costume. Buffy decides to go after all, and her mother lets out her Little Red Riding Hood costume.

Meanwhile, hell has broken loose at the frat house. Fake eyeballs in a dish have turned into real ones; zombies and ghouls are chasing the students. There's complete panic; people are dying. But the house is mysteriously quiet when Buffy and company walk up the front door. They have just seen some guys in pretty cool soldier outfits, and their minds are more on that.

During the episode, the unseen demon exploits each of the fears of all the party guests, which include Buffy, Willow, Xander, and Oz, to feed himself. Buffy has confessed to her mother that she's afraid of being vulnerable: "Open your heart to someone and he...he bails on you." Gachnar uses Willow's spider phobia, as well as the fear of using magic that's too strong for her (shared by the others). Xander, the only townie among the gang, fears becoming invisible to his friends. Oz, afraid of the beast inside himself, begins to wolf.

Anya, not scary at all in an enormous bunny suit, fetches Giles when the front door disappears. Giles arrives with the knowledge (and a chainsaw). Despite his attempts to tell Buffy how to destroy the demon, Gachnar appears. Turns out he's about three inches tall, as is Buffy's fear: "They're all going to leave you, you know," he squawks at Buffy. Her blase reply—"Yeah, yeah"—is the last thing Gachnar hears before she squashes him like a bug with her sneaker.

QUOTE OF THE WEEK:

"You know, maybe it's 'cause of all the horrific things we've seen, but hippos wearing tutus just don't unnerve me like they used to."
—Oz waxes nostalgic on the notion of watching *Fantasia* on Halloween.

THE AGONY AND THE ECSTASY:

Buffy's mother opens up to Buffy about her loneliness and initial reluctance to make new friends in Sunnydale. Buffy reveals her fear that every time she loves someone, they bail on her. Parker continues cutting a swath, with Buffy an unwilling spectator. Willow is moved by Oz's concern over her magic experimentation. Anya admits that she's not over Xander after all, and Xander invites her to go to the haunted house as a date. Oz flees from Willow to protect her from his wolf-nature, she cries, "Oz, don't leave me!" He leaves anyway.

In the second season Halloween episode, our intrepid heroes became:

BUFFY: an eighteenth-century noblewoman
WILLLOW: a ghost (and a very sexy one! She caught Oz's eye.)
XANDER: a soldier
CORDELIA: remained Cordelia
LARRY: a pirate

In the fourth season their Halloween costumes were:

BUFFY: Little Red Riding-Hood, with a basket full of weapons
WILLLOW: Joan of Arc
XANDER: James Bond (or a headwaiter)
OZ: God
ANYA: A big pink bunny—a revenge demon's version of scary
GILES: Mexican caballero bearing chocolatey goodness

POP-CULTURE IQ:

"Prepare to have your spines tingled and gooses bumped by the terrifying... Fantasia?!"

Xander is shocked and appalled to see that he has rented *Fantasia,* a mild-mannered animation film produced by Disney.

"Phantasm! This was supposed to be Phantasm! Stupid video store."

Xander planned a Halloween fright night viewing of a horror movie written and directed by Don Coscarelli.

"Sensing a disturbance in the Force, Master?"

Xander's riff on *Star Wars* to Oz, as Oz frowns at the left speaker.

"It's alive!"

Giles's riff on the 1931 film version of *Frankenstein,* as his animated Frankenstein's monster Halloween decoration jiggles.

CONTINUITY:

All Buffy's friends are sympathetic to Buffy's post-Parker depression. Giles is still a "gentleman of leisure," with enough time on his hands for observing the traditions of Halloween (including wearing a ridiculous sombrero) for the first time since Buffy's known him. Joyce mentions Buffy's father,

> The title of the episode "Fear, Itself" refers to a famous speech given by President Franklin Delano Roosevelt as the United States entered WWII.

who lives in Los Angeles, and Ted (played by John Ritter), her first serious Sunnydale boyfriend, who turned out to be a homicidal robot. The gang makes reference to the previous Halloween episode, in which Ethan Rayne's spell caused them to become a representation of their costume. Anya and Xander's relationship progresses to dating mode. They discuss Uncle Roary's (mentioned in "The Zeppo") aroma of schnapps. Willow presses forward with her explorations into magic, referring back to "Gingerbread" in Season Three, in which her mother and Joyce Summers almost burned her, Amy, and Buffy at the stake for being witches. Professor Walsh continues to be a harsh taskmistress; Riley is sympathetic and warm toward Buffy. Buffy and friends see some Commandos for the first time but assume they are students dressed up for Halloween.

FROM THE ORIGINAL TELEPLAY:

WILLOW: "Oz!"
XANDER: "Will!"
[She appears, moving down the hall.]
XANDER: "We've got trouble. There's something terribly wrong with Buffy. She can't even tell that I'm—"

WILLOW (calling out): "Oz!"

[Xander stops, defeated. She can't see him, either. She looks around, upset.]

WILLOW: "Oh, God . . . . Okay, guiding spell. Okay. Yeah. I can do it."

[She takes off. Xander turns back and, with a mounting frustration, knocks a small pumpkin off a side table. Exits at a good clip.]

WRITTEN BY: **Tracey Forbes;** DIRECTED BY: **David Solomon.** GUEST STARS: **Marc Blucas as Riley, Adam Kaufman as Parker, Paige Moss as Veruca, Eric Matheny as Colm, Stephen M. Porter as Jack, Lindsay Crouse as Professor Maggie Walsh; with Co-stars Kal Penn as Hunt, Jake Phillips as Kip, Bryan Cuprill as Roy, Lisa Johnson as Paula.**

BEER BAD

THE PLOT THICKENS:

Professor Walsh explains the pleasure principal to Buffy's psych class while Buffy sadly daydreams about Parker. Her romantic fantasies, in which he thanks her profusely for saving his life from vampires, and begs her to forgive her, are rudely interrupted by reality as Parker makes another conquest of a classmate.

Meanwhile, Xander has landed a job as a bartender at the campus pub. On his first (chaotic!) night on the job, Xander is humiliated by Colm, a college guy who throws big words and big concepts his way. Colm and his fellow academic snobs drink vast quantities of Black Frost beer.

Enter Buffy. Distracted by yet more proof of Parker's manipulativeness, she collides with Riley. Riley mortifies her when he tosses off a comment on Parker's well-known seduction techniques. She decides to bail but is waylaid by Colm and his drinking buddies. They invite her to have a beer. Pretty soon she's a wee bit...goofy.

But what Xander mistakes for simple drunkenness is actually the result of potent magic. Jack, Xander's bar-owner boss, has been brewing up the Black Frost with a recipe provided by his warlock brother-in-law. The beer turns those who guzzle it into Cro-Magnons...literally. Said guzzlers: Colm, his friends, and their new gal pal, Buffy.

Buffy's fellow "questers for fire" drag females into the Grotto and accidentally set the place on fire. "Parker, bad," she announces, lumbering across campus in search of him. Parker is also in the Grotto, talking with Willow, who has been highly astonished by his ability to turn on the charm like a faucet. Buffy arrives in time to save them all. Then the moment she has been dreaming of arrives, as Parker soulfully apologizes and begs her forgiveness. With a grunt, Caveslayer smacks him with her club and Stinky Parker Man is down for the count.

QUOTE OF THE WEEK:

The Grotto is the name of a student hangout specializing in studying and coffee beverages; in "Go Fish" a set called "the grotto" was built. Producer Gareth Davies loved the grotto set. The company held a party in/on it.

XANDER: "And was there a lesson in all this? What have we learned about beer?"
BUFFY: "Foamy."

Xander, making sure that Buffy has learned her lesson about drinking.

THE AGONY AND THE ECSTASY:

Buffy's finally over Parker, but now Willow has Veruca to worry about. Seen first in "Living Conditions," the sexy lead singer of the band Shy is clearly interested in Oz…and vice versa.

POP-CULTURE IQ:

"Uh, how much beer would you say a person would need to consume before they started seriously questing for fire?"
Worried about the increasingly erratic behavior of Buffy and her new friends, Xander references *Quest for Fire,* a 1981 film about three prehistoric men searching for a new fire source.

"I've seen <u>Cocktail</u>. I can do the hippy-hippy shake."
Xander's talking about the film *Cocktail,* starring Tom Cruise as a bartender who had all the right moves.

"Mr. I-spent-the-sixties-in-an-electric-Kool-Aid-funky-Satan-groove."
Xander is riffing off the work of influential New Journalism author Tom Wolfe. Wolfe chronicled the hippie movement in several books and essays with "psychedelic" titles such as *The Electric Kool-Aid Acid Test* (1968). In the seventies, Giles rebelled against his destiny to become a Watcher and experimented with Black Majik. There's also a contemporary cocktail called an "electric Kool-Aid."

CONTINUITY:

More friendly encounters for Buffy with nice Riley. Xander continues his string of jobs. Willow tells Buffy that Veruca "dresses like Faith," reminding the viewer of the renegade Slayer of the third season, currently off-camera in a coma. She'll show back up in "This Year's Girl" and "Who Are You."

FROM THE ORIGINAL TELEPLAY:

These stage directions appeared in the script for this episode:
[The Vamps drop Parker. And they engage in a fast and intense slugfest. Buffy is even sharper than usual, if that's possible. And to finish them off, a spectacular flip-toss, STAKING both vamps who SCREAM all their merry way to Hell.]
INSERT – FAKE I.D. showing Xander with a big Tom Selleck mustache.

WILD AT HEART

**WRITTEN BY: Marti Noxon; DIRECTED BY: David Grossman.
GUEST STARS: Marc Blucas as Riley, Paige Moss as Veruca, James
Marsters as Spike, Lindsay Crouse as Professor Maggie Walsh.**

THE PLOT THICKENS:

Unbeknownst to Buffy, Spike has returned from Los
Angeles. In the teaser he's bagged by the mysterious Commandos, and at this point we know nothing more of his fate. Meanwhile, Oz is fascinated
by the sexy singer Veruca, much to the consternation of Willow. Willow attends a campus Wicca
meeting while Oz locks himself in his cage. Once
transformed, he breaks out—and mates with
Veruca, likewise transformed.

Oz is beyond upset by his animalistic betrayal
of Willow. Willow senses that something is amiss,
and when he rebuffs her invitations to make love,
she goes to Xander to ask for a guy perspective on
what's going on.

Giles is in his apartment with little to do but watch quiz shows. He's delighted to see Buffy and
they discuss the possibility of two new werewolves roaming Sunnydale. When Buffy goes to talk to
Oz, she finds him welding a new hasp lock on his cage. He tells her he got out but does not tell her
about Veruca.

Night begins to fall. Oz has called Veruca, and they rendezvous at his cage, He is kidding only
himself when he insists that the usually free-roaming werewolf spend the night of the full moon
alone with him, in his cage. The inevitable occurs (again), but this time Willow finds out about it
when she brings Oz some breakfast.

Heartbroken, Willow prepares to do in the illicit lovers with Black Majik. She terminates her
spell, however, just as Veruca appears in the deserted classroom lab and makes it clear that she's
going to kill Willow. Buffy and Oz have figured this out and are racing to save Willow, when Buffy is
waylaid by a figure in military commando garb.

Oz reaches the lab first and faces off with Veruca. After the sun sets, they change into werewolves, he savagely kills her, then mindlessly goes after Willow. Buffy arrives in the nick of time
and stops him. Seeing now that he must find out if he's a man who turns into a beast, or a beast
who wears the form of a man, he leaves a heartbroken Willow and departs Sunnydale. Buffy and
Giles puzzle over the identity of the soldier who slowed Buffy up, nearly causing Willow's death.

QUOTE OF THE WEEK:

WILLOW (desperate): "Oz...don't you love me...?"
OZ: "My whole life, I've never loved anything else."
Oz leaves Sunnydale to figure things out.

THE AGONY AND THE ECSTASY:

As has become a pattern, Xander provides advice and support when one of his friends (Willow, in this case) is troubled. As werewolves, Veruca and Oz consummate their lust. Oz tries to tell himself—and others—that he had no choice but to lock the two of them inside his cage, but no one buys it, especially not Willow. Distraught over his infidelity, she's overwhelmed when he kills Veruca and almost kills her; then completely crushed when he leaves town to learn about the wolf inside himself.

POP-CULTURE IQ:

"But it's your cutting edge 8-tracks that keep you ahead of the scene."
Buffy's teasing Giles about his insistence that he's musically "with it." 8-track tapes were the ancient predecessor of cassette tapes.

"If the Stones are still rolling, why can't Giles?"
Buffy, making some points with Giles in the Bronze when he shows to attend the "gig."

"She's quell Fiona."
Buffy on Veruca. Fiona Apple is considered a very strange eccentric by some reviewers and a talented singer by others. The title of her current album is ninety words long.

"I don't know about tonight. Unless the extreme Jerry Garcia look turns you on."
Oz is referring to the fact that he's going to wolf out. Jerry Garcia—leader of the Grateful Dead, and sadly, dead—had big, frizzy hair and a heavy beard.

OZ: "Number one? I gotta go with Hound Dog."
WILLOW: "Me, too. That was a great song. I mean, Elvis—what a guy."
Actually Oz is talking about amps, not the song made famous by singer Elvis Presley.

"Wild monkey love or tender Sarah McLachlan love?"
Xander's trying to define the terms of lovemaking in a conversation with Willow. Sarah McLachlan is a popular singer and the creator of the Lilith Fair, a showcase for women singers. Her song, "Full of Grace," was playing when Buffy left Sunnydale at the end of "Becoming, Part Two."

CONTINUITY:

Oz has a Cibo Matto poster in his room (they played in "When She Was Bad"); also a Widespread Panic poster. Could this be the work of set dresser Johnny Youngblood?

Buffy is still in Dr. Walsh's psych class and doing significantly better— an oblique reference to the fact that she's over Parker. Willow mentions that she's going to look into the Wicca group that meets on campus. Later she will notice and hook up with Tara, a member of the group. When Willow catches Oz with Veruca, they touch on the fact that Willow and Xander cheated on Oz and Cordy in "Lovers Walk." The werewolves attack Professor Walsh. Riley rescues a distraught Willow from being run over by a car. When Buffy and Oz are trying to save Willow from Veruca, a "commando guy" gets in Buffy's way. She and Giles begin to wonder who the commando guys are. The Commandos have captured Spike, who has returned from Los Angeles *sans* the Gem of Amarra.

FROM THE ORIGINAL TELEPLAY:

Willow and Buffy discuss Veruca:

WILLOW: "And I don't want to be the kind of girl who freaks every time my boyfriend notices somebody else [Then the following lines were cut for length]—even if she is throwing herself at him like a twenty dollar ho."

BUFFY [also cut for length]: "Please. Ten dollar ho. Fifteen, max."

The following lines were also cut due to length:
Maggie is telling Buffy and Riley about the "two wild dogs" that attacked her:

"I know how it sounds. But crazy is my specialty. And I definitely saw what I saw."

Buffy has gone to discuss Maggie's "wild dog" attack with Giles:

"Clearly we need to get you kicking some monster bootie, stat."

VERUCA: "Go ahead and cry—but you should have seen this coming. You can't tame a wild thing. He's not yours any more. He's in you, he'd be thinking about me. No. Not thinking. It's deeper than that. Why don't you just try to relax now? In a minute or two it'll all be over."

XANDER: "Love. It's a logic blocker."

THE INITIATIVE

WRITTEN BY: **Douglas Petrie;** DIRECTED BY: **James A. Contner.** GUEST STARS: **Marc Blucas as Riley Finn, Mercedes McNab as Harmony Kendall, Adam Kaufman as Parker, Bailey Chase as Graham, Leonard Roberts as Forrest, Lindsay Crouse as Professor Maggie Walsh; with Co-star Mace Lombard as Tom.**

THE PLOT THICKENS:

Riley finally figures out that he's interested in Buffy, after decking Parker for making insulting comments about her. Meanwhile, the secret of the Commandos is revealed, at least to us: Riley, Forrest, and Graham are actually U.S. military soldiers (occasionally referred to as "Marines") on secret assignment. Below Lowell House—their frat house—a vast underground complex called the Initiative is run by none other than Professor Maggie Walsh. Their mission: to bag the demons and vampires rampant in Sunnydale. The government is experimenting on them...although at this point, we don't know why. But we do know that Riley is worried that his double life as a college student by day, demon hunter by night, will pose problems for his romance with Buffy.

Spike was captured and classified as Hostile 17. Tom, the sole-surviving vampire from Sunday's posse ("The Freshman") is cowering in the holding cell next to him. He warns Spike not to drink the

drugged blood delivered to him like food pellets. When Spike breaks out, he uses Tom as a shield during his escape.

Spike returns to Harmony, but she's "been reading" and throws him out. Meanwhile, Riley begins his courtship of Buffy, first asking Willow for help, and then choking—twice—when the target of his affections comes within range. While at the party, Riley nervously offers Buffy a little cocktail snack of cheese. Spike attacks Willow in her dorm room, but when he tries to hurt her he gets incredible blinding pain in his head. His failure to achieve penetration (!) is remarked upon by both of them, with Willow offering sympathy and rationalization ("maybe you're trying too hard").

Tracking Spike, the Commandos—Riley, Forrest, and Graham—raid Stevenson Hall. They turn off the power and throw tear gas; grappling with Spike, they're just about to leave when Buffy arrives. Not understanding what the chaos is all about, she kicks Commando butt. Spike escapes again. The next day Buffy and Riley meet up, unaware of their secret identities. Their courtship begins with a pleasant walk in the sunshine.

QUOTE OF THE WEEK:

"You know, for someone who teaches human behavior? You might try showing some."
—Buffy lets Maggie Walsh have it after the professor wounds Willow deeply.

THE AGONY AND THE ECSTASY:

Willow is still shattered over Oz's departure. Harmony has had enough of Spike and his—ew!—Sex Pistols CDs. Riley finally realizes he's attracted to Buffy, and the tone of their romance is set—both of them ignorant of each other's secret missions, both of them kind and pleasant to each other.

POP-CULTURE IQ:

"Like I'd ever listen to the Sex Pistols."
Harmony, informing Xander that the stuff she's about to burn belongs to Spike, not her. The Sex Pistols were a founding group of Britain's punk movement. The character of Spike is patterned after bassist Sid Vicious. At the end of Season Two, when Spike is barreling out of town with Drusilla, he is singing "My Way," a song by Paul Anka which Sid Vicious recorded for the Sex Pistols' 1980 film, *The Great Rock 'n 'Roll Swindle.* However, the version Spike is actually singing along with is sung by Gary Oldman, for the 1986 film *Sid and Nancy.*

"Who died and made you John Wayne?"
Buffy, not loving the fact that Riley is trying to protect her from being alone on campus at night. John Wayne was a famous film actor, most noted for his heroic roles.

CONTINUITY:

Spike's prisonmate, Tom, is the vampire who survived Buffy's attack on Sunday's lair in "The Freshman." Stinky Parker Man, last detested in "Beer Bad," reveals himself as extremely stinky when he says rotten stuff about Buffy. The Commando mystery continues. Spike returns to Sunnydale. Willow winces at Dingoes music, but her Dingoes poster is still on the wall. Also in this episode, Oz's full name is revealed as Daniel Osbourne. Giles and Xander are disappointed that the Commandos are human; there doesn't seem to be much for them to do. Still, Xander remembers some of what he knew when he was turned into a soldier by Ethan Rayne, two years before. The Initiative's work with vampires makes them unable to bite.

FROM THE ORIGINAL TELEPLAY:

The bolded section was cut for length:

BUFFY: "Giles, I live in a dorm now. **Filled with what the young people these days call 'the young people.'**"

WRITTEN BY: Jane Espenson; DIRECTED BY: Michael Lange. GUEST STARS: Marc Blucas as Riley, Mercedes McNab as Harmony, Emma Caulfield as Anya, Leonard Roberts as Forrest, Bailey Chase as Graham, Tod Thawley as Hus, David Boreanaz as Angel; with Co-stars Margaret Easley as Curator (Professor Gerhardt), William Vogt as Jamie, Mark Ankeny as Dean Guerrero.

PANGS

214

THE PLOT THICKENS:

It's Thanksgiving break. Alerted that Buffy may be in danger, Angel has returned to Sunnydale. He's decided it would both hurt and distract Buffy if she saw him, so he lurks in the shadows and keeps watch over her. But the Slayer's spidery-sense is tingling; she knows something is different about this picture.

Meanwhile, at the ground-breaking ceremony for the UC Sunnydale Cultural Partnership Center, Xander falls through said ground and lands in the ruins of the old Sunnydale Mission. The mission was buried during the earthquake of 1812.

Buried with the mission was the undying rage of the local Chumash tribe for vengeance. The European conquerors subjected them to horrible atrocities. Hus, a spirit released when Xander fell into the mission, begins to recreate the wrongs committed upon his people. First he slashes the throat of Professor Gerhardt, who was to be curator of the new Cultural Partnership Center, and cuts off her ear. He hangs a priest. When Buffy starts to attack him, he turns into a flock of birds. Xander falls prey to syphilis, smallpox, malaria—diseases the Chumash contracted from their oppressors.

Willow, who is morally opposed to Thanksgiving, is also opposed to destroying Hus. Buffy—who has been busily orchestrating the group's Thanksgiving feast—is uncertain. It is left to Spike, who has escaped the Commandos and seeks refuge with Buffy and friends, to remind them that all this PC stuff is well and good, but their lives are at stake. Giles, Xander, and Willow all know Angel is in Sunnydale and at various times speak to him without telling Buffy.

Willow, Xander, and Anya rush to Dean Guerrero's on-campus home to warn him that he may be in danger. Hus is clearly going after authority figures. While they're leaving—with pie, Anya happily notes—Angel approaches them to talk about the situation. They figure out that Hus will attack Giles's condo, because Buffy's there and she's the strongest warrior of her tribe, hence, a leader. The four cavalry snatch bicycles and head back to the fort with all due haste.

Hus calls up more spirit warriors, and they move in for the attack on Giles's apartment. Unseen by Buffy, Angel pitches in. When Buffy slashes Hus, he turns into a bear. She gets his own stone knife away from him, and when she stabs him with it, all the warriors instantly vanish. Angel, satisfied that Buffy is out of danger, leaves as silently as he came.

Buffy presides over her turkey dinner. Spike complains bitterly because he's hungry; Buffy suggests he have some gravy, as there's blood in it. At the conclusion of dinner Xander lets slip that Angel was in Sunnydale. Buffy is stunned. This provides the opportunity for another *Buffy/Angel* crossover, as Buffy goes to Los Angeles to ask Angel why he came to Sunnydale in "I Will Remember You."

QUOTE OF THE WEEK:

"I'm saying Spike had a little trip to the vet, and now he doesn't chase the other puppies anymore."
—Spike, lamenting the job the Initiative did on him.

THE AGONY AND THE ECSTASY:

It is hell for Angel to observe Buffy, and not speak to her. Equally hurtful is seeing her with another guy. Xander and Anya move to boyfriend-girlfriend mode. Harmony, the reader, dumps Spike.

POP-CULTURE IQ:

"And they say one person can't make a difference."
Buffy's riff to a vampire on President George Bush's "one thousand points of light."

"Very manly. Not at all Village People."
Buffy's making a joke about Xander's sexy construction-worker look at the ceremonial groundbreaking for the new Cultural Center. The Village People were a disco band.

"It was more like a riot than a Ralph's."
Buffy's been shopping at a prominent grocery store chain for her Thanksgiving recipe ingredients.

"And there's...trees, and I know what you're thinking, it's like I grew up in a Grant Wood painting."
Riley's discussing his Thanksgiving plans to Buffy. Grant Wood was an American painter best known for capturing the vistas and people of his native Iowa. His most famous work is *American Gothic.*

"The thing is, I like my evil like I like my men: evil. You know, straight up, black hat, tie you to the railroad tracks, soon-my-electro-ray-will-destroy-Metropolis bad."
Buffy reads DC's *Superman* comics; she is angsting about killing Hus, the Chumash vengeance warrior, who's only trying to even out the score.

"Hey!, Gentle Ben! Over here!"
Xander is baiting the ferocious bear Hus has transformed into; *Gentle Ben* was a television series that ran from 1967–1969.

CONTINUITY:

We learn that Riley is from Iowa. Willow's anti-Thanksgiving sentiments harken back to her mom's pop-pysch theories ("Gingerbread"). Angel returns to Sunnydale. His presence calls up old memories of his hopeless love for Buffy. The gang is initially a bit skittish around him, trying to ensure that he hasn't become evil again. When Giles points out that it's not Angel's job to protect Buffy, Angel counters that it's not Giles's job anymore, either. He's no longer her Watcher. Forrest coughs "Mama's boy" into his fist, not realizing that Maggie Walsh does think of Riley as her son. The beloved Mr. Gordo is mentioned, as is Buffy's love for the Ice Capades (last mentioned in "Helpless").

FROM THE ORIGINAL TELEPLAY:

The following exchange was cut due to length:
XANDER: "I didn't mean—you're an EX-vengeance demon. It's totally different."
ANYA (very hurt): "Sure. It's okay."

There is an appended note in the script, which gives the full text of the Curator's speech delivered in Act One. The parts that are bolded are in theory what's actually heard by the viewer:

When I first realized we were outgrowing the current Cultural Center, I was concerned. Then I realized it was like seeing one's child grow up, and move on to better things. In this case, a spacious new facility to be built on this site. . . . . Give your dream room to grow and it will fill the largest palace. And of course, it isn't just space that makes a collection of this kind valuable, it's accessibility. I want this to be a place that students visit on their own, because they want to. Because what they've seen here has connected them with other peoples and other times and given them a basis for understanding something in their own lives. This collection isn't about dusty relics from some past, irrelevant lives. It's about a direct line to the past, a lifeline, if you will. That's why...**it's appropriate that the UC Sunnydale Cultural Partnership Center is taking place so soon before Thanksgiving. Because**

that's what the **Melting Pot is about, contributions from all cultures making our culture stronger.** Some of you will see artifacts that may have been handled by your own ancestors. All of you will recognize in our displays a common thread of humanity, whether it is in the tools that speak of our relationship with the land, or in the clothing and art that speak of our need to improve and to express. But of course, history is not just about the past. I like to think that our breaking ground here today is also part of history. It is the start of something that doesn't just look backward, but also forward into your lives and lives of future generations. **And thus . . . a symbolic beginning!**

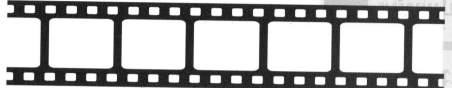

WRITTEN BY: Tracey Forbes; DIRECTED BY: Nick Marck.
GUEST STARS: Marc Blucas as Riley, Emma Caulfield as Anya, Elizabeth Anne Allen as Amy; with Co-star Andy Umberger as D'Hoffryn.

THE PLOT THICKENS:

Riley is friendly and affable and known around school. He helps the Lesbian group hang their banner. When he sees Buffy, he invites her on a picnic in a rather roundabout way, confessing that she makes him nervous and that he practices their conversations before they have them.

Buffy tells Willow about the upcoming date, musing that while Riley's nice, she's not particularly attracted to nice. She's gotten pretty much hooked on danger guys. As she absently stakes a vampire, she muses, "I wonder where I get that from?"

Speaking of danger guys and not-danger guys, Spike is still around. At Thanksgiving he bought his way into sanctuary at Giles's by promising to give Buffy information about the Initiative. As far as Buffy's concerned, Spike has been living on borrowed time ever since. Chained in Giles's bathtub, sipping pig's blood from a mug, his memories about the Initiative and the Commandos remain "vague." She taunts him, offering her neck for biting, which he cannot do, and generally makes his life miserable. Willow suggests they perform a truth spell, and plans are made for the following morning.

Then Willow stops by Oz's former room, to discover that it has been stripped bare. Oz asked Devon for all his belongs to be sent on, but included no note for Willow. Not one single word. She's crushed beyond the telling of it.

Buffy and Riley are picnicking when Willow tries to tell Buffy what has happened. By that evening, Buffy has heard and is clueing in Xander and Anya as they watch Willow dance at the Bronze. It turns out that Willow's been drinking, and the others jump on her case for it, out of honest concern. She lashes back defensively.

She's had enough. She has sunk into a black pit of despair over Oz, and it seems that everyone's tired of listening to how much she hurts. She tiptoes into the women's bathroom and casts a spell to make the world respond to her. Flames rise up and it's scary, but she can't even unbend a Q-tip, much less heal her heart, so she thinks the spell has failed.

Later, Giles comes by, irritated because she forgot to do the truth spell with him. Giles expresses his concern about her spellcasting, as her emotions are unfocused. She chastises him, saying, "You don't see anything!" and Giles's eyesight begins to dim. Spike takes advantage of Giles's failing vision—morphing into total blindness—by getting the keys to his handcuffs and escaping.

In another conversation with Buffy, Willow changes Amy rat back into a human for about two seconds. Buffy's off to look for Spike, and Willow bitterly (and rhetorically) grumbles to Xander, "Why doesn't she just go marry him?" So be it! The Slayer and Hostile 17 are engaged to be married. Willow tells Xander he's a demon magnet, and soon enough, demons of all sorts are trying to kill him.

Buffy breaks the news to Riley of her impending nuptials with sweet regret and he stumbles off, totally stunned. Then Buffy's attention is diverted once more as demons stream after Xander, forcing everyone into a crypt for a huge battle.

D'Hoffryn, the demon who turned Anya into a vengeance demon more than eleven hundred years ago, brings Willow to his dimension to offer her the same opportunity; she's got a penchant for creating pain in other people's lives. Once Willow realizes all the damage she's done, she thanks D'Hoffryn for his kind offer, turns him down, and asks him to help her friends. She appears in the crypt as demons pour into it and Buffy and Spike kiss for one final time, anticipating death at the hands of the invaders. Then poof! everything returns to normal...or what passes for normal in Sunnydale...and Riley is even more entranced by Buffy, who, though obviously insane, is blessedly single.

QUOTE OF THE WEEK:

"Honey, we have to talk about invitations. Do you want to be 'William the Bloody' or just 'Spike?'"
    —Buffy, the eager bride-to-be, plans her dream wedding when Willow's spell goes awry.

THE AGONY AND THE ECSTASY:

Willow is in terrible pain over Oz. Just when it seems it can't get any more unbearable, Oz contacts Devon and asks him to send him the rest of his belongings. She lashes out at her friends because no one seems to understand how miserable she is. Buffy finds true love...with Spike? The evil, neutered vampire is likewise smitten. Bewitched, Buffy happily informs Riley that she's getting married. Riley is not pleased, to say the least. Though all is set right once Willow's spell is broken, Riley's fascination with Buffy is compounded by her strange behavior.

POP-CULTURE IQ:

"'Cause you've got your hands full with the undead English patient."
Willow is referring to Spike, who is staying in Giles's bathtub. Giles waits on him as if he were an invalid. *The English Patient* is a romantic movie about a nurse devoted to caring for her dying patient.

"Passions is on!"
Passions is a soap opera with supernatural overtones; Spike's become an avid viewer.

"And now for something completely different."
A quote in the stage directions originated by the comedy group Monty Python.

"I believe that is the dance of a brave little toaster."
The Brave Little Toaster is a series of children's books by Thomas M. Disch about a plucky little toaster and his appliance friends. The toaster is very cute and tries very hard to be courageous, just like Willow when she gets drunk at the Bronze.

BUFFY: "Anybody remember when Buffy had a fun beer fest and went One Million Years B.C.?"
XANDER: "Sadly, without the fuzzy bikini."
One Million Years B.C. is a SF/fantasy film about prehistoric cave love. Raquel Welch wore the bikini.

"Oh, not with the girl power bit."
During their engagement, Spike mocks Buffy's insistence on taking care of herself; "girl power" is a term popularized by the Spice Girls, a British all-female singing group.

"Yeah, well, I'm not the one who wanted 'Wind Beneath My Wings' for the first dance."
Spike's recalling Buffy's wedding preparations; "Wind Beneath My Wings" is a sentimental song sung by Bette Midler in the 1988 movie *Beaches*.

"I figured, seeing as how I'm kinda grievey, we could have a girl night. You know— eat sundaes and then watch Steel Magnolias, and you could tell me how at least I don't have diabetes."
Willow's talking about a 1989 chick flick starring Julia Roberts.

CONTINUITY:

Buffy joins in admonishing Willow about drinking beer by reminding her of the events in "Beer Bad." Witch Amy briefly becomes human again, then reverts to rat form. (She changed herself into a rat in "Gingerbread.") Willow counts down Xander's various demon girlfriends: Mummy Girl ("Inca Mummy Girl"); Preying Mantis ("Teacher's Pet"); and Anya.

FROM THE ORIGINAL TELEPLAY:

The following line of Buffy's was cut due to length:
"So she did a good spell—but the plan kind of sucked. I mean, she's the one stuck eating pellets out of a plastic cup."

HUSH

WRITTEN AND DIRECTED BY: Joss Whedon.
GUEST STARS: Marc Blucas as Riley, Emma Caulfield as Anya, Leonard Roberts as Forrest, Phina Oruche as Olivia, Amber Benson as Tara, Brooke Bloom as Cheryl, Jessica Townsend as Nicole, Lindsay Crouse as Maggie; with Co-stars Doug Jones as a Gentleman, Camden Toy as a Gentleman, Don W. Lewis as a Gentleman, Charlie Brumbly as a Gentleman.

> "Hush" is considered a ground-breaking piece of television in that it's almost completely silent. Many other directors have dreamed of making silent episodes; Joss Whedon achieved it. It has been nominated for an Emmy®.

THE PLOT THICKENS:

Buffy dozes off during Professor Walsh's lecture on communication. Her dream is a curious mixture of kissing Riley and of a young girl reciting a strange nursery rhyme about The Gentlemen. The girl is holding a mystical-looking box. Riley wants to analyze the dream, but Buffy shares it with Giles instead. Neither he nor his Weetabix-hogging housemate, Spike, has ever heard of The Gentlemen.

Anya drills Xander about the nature of their relationship, and any resolution is deferred by Giles's request that Xander take care of Spike for a few days while Olivia comes to visit. The campus Wicca group is a major disappointment to

Willow, but she does notice a shy young woman there named Tara.

That night, as everyone sleeps, the evil Gentlemen come to town and magically steal all their voices. Confusion reigns. Riley and the Commandos don civvies, intending to help keep order in the Dale. Buffy and Willow walk through the town, stunned by the silence.

That night The Gentlemen glide eerily through the town. Olivia sees them and is able to sketch one of them for Giles the next morning. They take their first victim, a young male college student, who shrieks in silent terror as they slice open his chest and extract his heart.

Giles finally realizes that The Gentlemen are part of a fairy tale. To kill them, the Princess must scream. But he has no idea how to give Buffy back her voice.

Tara goes in search of Willow, intending (we later learn) to do a spell with her. She is nearly captured by The Gentlemen. She and Willow escape together and for the first time join forces to create magic. Buffy and Riley also join forces, coming upon each other as they battle The Gentlemen at the clock tower. Riley smashes the box containing all the voices of Sunnydale, and Buffy (the Princess) screams. The Gentlemen's heads explode. The horror is over.

In the morning Riley comes to Buffy's dorm room. They have to talk, he tells her. She agrees...and they sit facing each other in uncomfortable silence.

> **Revelation 15:1**
> A minister and his flock are silently reading from the Bible. This is the verse written on the congregates' signboard: "Then I saw another portent in heaven, great and wonderful, seven angels with seven plagues, which are the last, for with them the wrath of God is ended."

QUOTE OF THE WEEK:

Xander has scribbled on a pad, holds up for all to see: HOW DO YOU KILL THEM?
Buffy snorts contemptuously, then circles her fist around an imaginary stake, plunges it down repeatedly.
Everybody looks at her, a little thrown: the gesture doesn't read the way she intended.
Realizing it, Buffy hurriedly and sheepishly grabs a stake from her purse, repeats the gesture.
Buffy accidentally makes an obscene gesture as described in the stage directions

THE AGONY AND THE ECSTASY:

Despite their soulful first kiss, Riley and Buffy founder just when the moment for honesty arrives. Willow still misses Oz terribly. And Anya is thrilled when Xander attacks Spike when Xander thinks that the vampire has bitten her. Olivia and Rupert must decide if she can handle knowing that the things that go bump in the night are real.

POP-CULTURE IQ:

"He'd better have cable 'cause I'm not missing Passions."
Spike's doesn't want to miss a single moment of the soap opera with supernatural overtones (first mentioned in "Something Blue") when he's bunking at Xander's.

"We have a gig that would inevitably cause any girl living to think we are cool upon cool, yet we must Clark Kent our way through the dating scene and never use this unfair advantage."
Clark Kent is the shy, doltish alter-ego of Superman. Riley is not loving keeping his commando life a secret from Buffy. Forrest gets it.

"Well, no, I wasn't actually one of the original members of Pink Floyd."
British psychedelic band formed in 1965. Giles is confessing to Olivia that while monsters are real, his rock fame is not.

CONTINUITY:

There is an oblique reference to Angel when Buffy dreams of kissing Riley: He tells her he will make the sun go down. Buffy and Riley do kiss, in the street during the silence that has spread all over town. Xander and Giles continue to work together on matters arcane. Willow floated a pencil in "Doppelgangland," and in "Choices" she staked a vampire with a pencil. She mentions she would like to float some-thing bigger than a pencil in "Hush"; then she and Tara together use their powers to slam a soda machine against a door.

The following dialogue was cut for length from the Wicca group scene:

CHERYL: "Well, you missed last week. We did a healing chant for Chloe's ankle. She said the swelling went right down."

NICOLE: "What's she doing on a mountain bike anyway?"

CHERYL: "She was trying to impress Justin."

WILLOW: "I was actually talking more about real spells."

Here are descriptions from the shooting script of two scenes:

INT. TARA'S ROOM—CONTINUING

Her room is wicca-y and also painted black and depressed-y.

EXT. CLOCK TOWER—NIGHT

From up here we can see the whole town—or possibly much less than all of it, but I can hope—and the collective breaths snake all across the town heading here.

Description of one of The Gentlemen

He's old, bone white, bald—Nosferatu meets Hellraiser by way of the Joker. Actually, he looks kind of like Mr. Burns, except that he can't stop his rictus-grin, and his teeth are gleaming metal.

> "Danse Macabre," the classical music Giles plays during his presentation on The Gentlemen, was also used as the theme song for the UK production *Jonathan Creek*, which Anthony Stewart Head also appeared in.

DOOMED

WRITTEN BY: **Marti Noxon & David Fury & Jane Espenson**; DIRECTED BY: **James A. Contner.** GUEST STARS: **Leonard Roberts as Forrest, Bailey Chase as Graham, Ethan Erickson as Percy; with Co-stars Anastasia Horne as Laurie, Anthony Anselmi as Partyer.**

THE PLOT THICKENS:

Buffy and Riley are still seated facing each other in silence, as they were at the end of "Hush." Buffy finally breaks the silence. Both of them are edgy, forced to admit they've been less than honest with each other about who and what they really are. Buffy offers a wicked-accurate summation of Riley's military mission—"You're part of some military monster squad that rounds up demons, vampires, probably has some official-sounding euphemisms for them like 'Unfriendlies' or 'Non-sapiens'"—but Riley has never heard of the Slayer. That surprises Buffy.

Their conversation is interrupted by an earthquake. Worried, Buffy goes to Giles, who reminds her that in Southern California, earthquakes are common. He suggests that they concentrate on the presence of the Commandos. Buffy does not share information.

Willow is doing her best to get down at Porter Dorm, which is hosting a post-earthquake party. But she's crushed when Percy, the jock she tutored in high school, makes fun of her behind her back. Looking for a place to compose herself, she discovers the corpse of a male student. The guy has been drained of blood and an arcane symbol carved into his chest.

Giles tells the gang that the symbol portends the end of the world. Everyone groans, "Again?" Buffy investigates a mausoleum with the identical symbol carved on its wall, and battles a Vahrall demon that's collecting the child-size bones of a little skeleton. It gets away, but Buffy runs into Riley also tracking it. She tells him she can't be with him; it wouldn't work out.

Meanwhile, Xander, who is paying the rent (to his parents!) by delivering pizzas, is fed up with his unwelcome houseguest, Spike. Spike's completely demoralized and eventually tries to commit suicide by falling on a stake. Willow insists they bring him along as they try to stop the end of the world.

Giles is attacked by demons, who take a talisman from him. They now have all the ingredients they need to make the world end. Their destination: the Hellmouth, located beneath the ruins of the Sunnydale High School library.

Buffy and company hurry back to their alma mater. Riley shows in full Commando gear. A huge battle ensues, during which Spike realizes he can hurt demons. Buffy leaps into the Hellmouth to avert the apocalypse, aided by Riley, who pulls her out.

Once the crisis has been averted, Buffy visits Riley. Making up ensues.

Porter is also a UC-Santa Cruz college.

QUOTE OF THE WEEK:

"Of course, the Percy thing isn't really important. It's the dead guy on the bed." —Willow gets her priorities straight after Percy called her a nerd.

THE AGONY AND THE ECSTASY:

Willow still misses Oz terribly, including the cachet of dating a guy in a band. Buffy's heartsick at telling Riley they can't be together, and definitely perks up when she decides to go for it.

POP-CULTURE IQ:

"Slayer? Thrash band. Anvil-heavy guitar rock with delusions of Black Sabbath."
Slayer was formed in the 1980s. Black Sabbath was a heavy metal band formed in 1968. Ozzy Osbourne was the original front man. Forrest is discussing the *other* Slayer with Riley.

"Maybe this is a bad time to tell you about Lara Croft."
Lara Croft is the fictional heroine of Tomb Raider video games and comic books. Forrest is assuring Riley that the Slayer is only a legend.

"Granted, a little rarer than the ones you grew up with on that little farm in Smallville, but—"
Riley's from Iowa; Smallville is the small town in the Midwest where Superman grew up. Forrest is explaining that demons are just fancy animals and nothing more.

223

"Ground control to Major Finn."

As Riley moons over Buffy, Forrest riffs on a song by David Bowie; his original lyric was "Ground control to Major Tom."

"It's kind of like the CBS logo. Could this be the handiwork of one Mr. Morley Safer?"

Morley Safer appears on the CBS-TV program *60 Minutes;* Xander is seeing a connection to the mark carved into a dead student's chest.

CONTINUITY:

This is Percy's first appearance in Season Four. Willow tutored him at the command of Principal Snyder in "Doppelgangland." He was also in "Earshot" and both parts of "Graduation Day." Xander continues to work at menial jobs. The gang returns to the ruins of Sunnydale High, and Xander steps on "Mayor meat, extra crispy," referring to the thwarted ascension of Mayor Richard Wilkins III. "Snake jerky" is mentioned in "New Moon Rising." The high school has not been rebuilt. Faith will stare at it in stunned silence in "This Year's Girl," and Buffy and Riley will hide out there in "New Moon Rising" and "The Yoko Factor." Spike taunts Willow and Xander about being useless to the Slayer; he will revisit this theme in "The Yoko Factor." Amy rat freaks out during the earthquake; she became a rat in "Gingerbread" and briefly appeared in human form in "Something Blue." Buffy and earthquakes go way back: The Master (from Season One) was trapped underground during an earthquake, and in "Prophecy Girl," earthquakes foretold the death of the Slayer at his hands. Spike learns that he can fight demons, and everyone except Giles learns of Riley's secret identity.

> **Previous End of the World scripts:** "The Harvest"; "Prophecy Girl"; "Becoming, Part Two"; and "The Zeppo."

Buffy is "Capricorn on the cusp of Aquarius," with a birthday between January 17 and 20. This is usually when her birthday episodes appear. The show's new convention is that the twelfth episode of each season is her birthday episode. "A New Man" aired on 1/25/2000.

FROM THE ORIGINAL TELEPLAY:

The following dialogue between Xander and Spike was cut due to length:

XANDER: "Look at you! You have knees! Very white knees!"

SPIKE: "Damn things keep doing that."

XANDER: "You know I'm not any happier about you wearing my stuff than you are."

SPIKE: "That cannot be true. Don't know how you let yourself be seen in this . . . wanker-wear."

> Forrest tells Riley, "You don't got game, son." Leonard Roberts, who plays Forrest, appeared in the film *He Got Game* in 1998.

WRITTEN BY: **Jane Espenson**; DIRECTED BY: **Michael Gershman**.
GUEST STARS: **Robin Sachs as Ethan Rayne, Amber Benson as Tara, Emma Caulfield as Anya, Lindsay Crouse as Maggie Walsh.**

THE PLOT THICKENS:

It's Episode Twelve, and time for Buffy's birthday party. This time it's a surprise party, and Giles is there as the only guest over twenty-five years of age. He's startled to discover that Buffy has a new boyfriend, and stunned when Willow and Xander casually mention that Riley's in the Initiative, both of them assuming that he already knew...since they, Anya, and Spike know. Add to that Maggie

Walsh's dismissive attitude toward him, and her opinion that Buffy has lacked a strong male role model, and it's time for a midlife depression for Giles.

Ethan Rayne, a sorcerer who practices Black Majik and worships chaos, is back in town. Not seen in Sunnydale since "Band Candy," he commiserates with Giles in the Lucky Pint, a Sunnydale watering hole, about feeling old and useless. He also tells Giles that rumors are flying fast and furious about something called "314," which has demons quaking in their boots.

The two become quite drunk together, and in the morning Giles suffers from more than a hangover. Ethan slipped him something that has turned him into a Fyarl demon. He's hideous, with huge, curved horns, and his speech consists of Fyarl grunts and growls. When he goes to Xander's house and tries to tell him what's happened, Xander reacts violently and defends himself with pots and pans. Giles escapes, running through Xander's neighborhood, prompting a 911 call.

While on the run, Giles runs into Spike. It turns out that Spike speaks Fyarl, and therefore, can communicate with him. Spike agrees to help him...if Giles will pay. Meanwhile, Buffy, Riley, and the rest of the gang assume that the demon has either kidnapped Giles or killed him—in which case, Buffy promises vengeance. She takes from Giles's desk what she believes to be a silver letter opener; silver is what can kill the Fyarl demon. With great glee Giles chases Maggie Walsh down the street—payback to "the fishwife" for her insults.

Buffy and Riley go to the magic shop to look for clues. Buffy finds a receipt signed by Ethan Rayne, and with Riley's help traces Ethan to his crummy motel. Riley tries to tell Buffy that the Initiative will take it from here, but Buffy insists that this is her battle. Together, they go to the motel and discover that Giles (still a demon) is already there, in full demon rage, about to kill the duplicitous sorcerer. Buffy attacks Giles. Only after she has dealt him a death blow does she recognize him...by his eyes. It turns out that the letter opener is made of pewter, not silver. Giles's life is spared.

After changing Giles back into his human form, Ethan is taken into custody by the military police. When Giles and Buffy talk about what's happened, he realizes that she loves him like a father and always will. Riley tells Buffy that he likes her strength and her take-charge attitude. Much mutual admiration takes place.

The episode ends with Dr. Walsh's entering a room...room number 314—the same arcane number that is terrifying the demons of Sunnydale.

QUOTE OF THE WEEK:

"She's good at what she does. And she has the truest soul I've ever known."

Riley loves Buffy, and he doesn't care if Maggie Walsh knows it.

THE AGONY AND THE ECSTASY:

Buffy holds back a bit when she spars with Riley, anxious that he'll be put off by her strength. She also soft-pedals how many demons and vampires she's slain. It turns out that Riley is not threatened by her superior strength and fighting ability. Much joy. Willow and Tara get together and bond through their magic experimentation.

POP-CULTURE IQ:

"You're really strong. Like, Spiderman strong."

Spiderman is a Marvel comic book hero. Buffy is Riley's hero, as he assures her after they nab Ethan Rayne.

CONTINUITY:

Ethan Rayne first appeared in "Halloween." Next came "The Dark Age" and then "Band Candy." Giles recalls his days at public school in England, reminding us of his upper-class roots. Buffy's previous birthday episodes were "Surprise" and "Helpless." Giles has been hit on the head in at least half a dozen previous episodes and has been unconscious more than a dozen times. Maggie Walsh implies that Giles has been a bad influence on Buffy. We get our first glimpse of Room 314.

FROM THE ORIGINAL TELEPLAY:

The following line of Riley's was cut for length:

"My dad was out of work for a while back. He sells farm equipment. It was rough."

And this exchange between Ethan and the waitress at the Lucky Pint was also cut due to length:

WAITRESS (off napkin): "You're not Roger Moore."

ETHAN: "God's truth. Tell her, Ripper."

GILES: "What? Oh. He's not Roger Moore."

This line of Buffy's was also cut for length:

"I'm so sorry about, you know, stabbing you in the heart."

WRITTEN BY: **David Fury**; DIRECTED BY: **James A. Contner.**
GUEST STARS: **Amber Benson as Tara, George Hertzberg as Adam,
Leonard Roberts as Forrest, Bailey Chase as Graham, Jack Stehlin as
Dr. Angleman, Emma Caulfield as Anya, Lindsay Crouse as Professor
Maggie Walsh; with Co-star Neil Daly as Mason.**

THE *I* IN TEAM

THE PLOT THICKENS:

While Xander and Willow teach Anya how to play poker, Xander voices his concerns about the Initiative. Secret organizations aren't high on his list, even if Buffy's new boyfriend, Riley, is fairly high on Willow's. And Anya's not happy about their anti-demon attitude. Meanwhile, Xander has become the new distributor of Boost Bars, which, judging from the expressions on the faces of Xander's few customers, are dreadful.

Buffy does her best in various tests to impress Maggie Walsh. She succeeds, and Maggie invites her to join the Initiative. Buffy gets the grand tour, and she's suitably impressed. But she's so wrapped up in her new adventure that she gives short shrift to her old friends, bringing Riley and some other Commandos to a long-awaited "Scoobies Only" gathering at the Bronze, and ignoring Willow's stories in the campus dining hall in favor of watching Riley buy something to eat.

Hurt, Willow spends more time with Tara, a shy, socially awkward girl from her Wicca group. As Willow began to assume in "Hush," Tara is a powerful witch in her own right. She owns a beautiful doll's-eye crystal, which she shyly offers to Willow as a gift. At that time, in the commons, Willow says she can't accept such a valuable thing, but later—after she's been with Tara all night—she brings it back to the dorm room.

"The lab coats" send the Commandos—Buffy included—to capture a dangerous Polgara demon. Buffy and Riley battle it together, then make passionate love. Unknown to them, Maggie Walsh has cameras in Riley's room and watches them. In the morning, after Riley takes his regi-

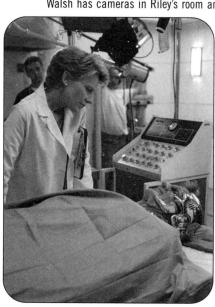

mental vitamin, Buffy asks Riley what 314 is. Maggie Walsh interrupts their conversation with a phone call.

Dr. Walsh and her associate, Dr. Angleman, decide that Buffy's too much of a liability. Riley and the others are sent to track Hostile 17—otherwise known as Spike. They succeed in shooting a homing beacon into him, and Spike goes to Giles for help. After Giles makes Spike pay him, Giles, Willow, Xander, and Anya manage to dig it out of him and flush it down the toilet.

While the Commandos are distracted looking for Spike, Maggie puts her plan for murdering Buffy into action. She sends the Slayer alone into the tunnels to investigate a blip—assuring Buffy it could be a rather weak species of demon, or even a raccoon. But Buffy is ambushed instead by two huge Warrior Demons. The weapon Dr. Walsh gave her proves faulty. And as she turns to retreat, her way is barred as the tunnel gate comes crashing down.

Dr. Walsh, assuming Buffy is dead because her Communications Control monitor flatlines, delivers the bad news to Riley. But Buffy's alive and kicking...and promises Dr. Walsh, in full view of Riley on the monitor screens, that she'll be seeing her real soon.

In a panic Dr. Walsh goes into Room 314. Her creation, a monster built from demon, human, and electronic parts, rises from his slab and kills her, uttering his first word: "Mommy."

QUOTE OF THE WEEK:

"Yes, we've enjoyed spanking."

Anya gives Willow too much information during a poker game with her and Xander.

THE AGONY AND THE ECSTASY:

Xander and Anya continue their strange courtship. Willow and Xander are hurt that Buffy's blowing them off. Buffy and Riley sleep together for the first time. Tara and Willow are also together all night.

POP-CULTURE IQ:

"And I don't want you crawling back here, knocking on my door, pleading for help the second teen witch's magic goes all wonky or Little Xander cuts a new tooth."

Spike is referring to Willow; *Teen Witch* is a 1989 film about a young girl who discovers that she's a witch shortly before her sixteenth birthday. It's also a current book about witchcraft.

"Probably off living the life of Riley."

Xander's riffing off Riley's name; *The Life of Riley* was a 1940s radio and TV show.

"Thought about it, but on me it's going to look all Private Benjamin."

Buffy's referring to the film starring Goldie Hawn as a blond bimbo who joins the army, and all her uniforms are oversized. It spawned a TV series with the same name.

"I don't care if it's playing 'Rockin' the Casbah' on the bloody Jew's harp."

Spike referencing "Rock the Casbah," a song by the British band the Clash. Inspired by the Sex Pistols (Spike's favorite band), the Clash formed in 1976.

CONTINUITY:

Willow reminds Buffy that Ethan Rayne warned Giles about the number 314 in "A New Man." The Commandos have been searching for "Hostile 17" (Spike) ever since he escaped in "The Initiative." Adam, the new villain for the rest of the season, is introduced. Spike comes back for help, for which he must pay; he would only help Giles for money in "A New Man." Adam uses his Polgara demon skewer arm to kill Maggie, and this casts suspicion on Buffy in "Goodbye, Iowa" as the murderer—the Slayer often stakes her quarry.

FROM THE ORIGINAL TELEPLAY:

Buffy's accidental creation of her password to get into the Initiative was cut due to length:

RILEY: "That panel—say something into it"

[Buffy crosses to it, is about to speak, then stops.]

BUFFY: "My mind's a blank."

The following line of Buffy's was also cut for length:

"Slick trap you set for me. Sorry to disappoint you, but I killed your two pets. There's a couple of research grants down the drain. Oh, and about you trying to kill me? I'd say that's an issue you and I need to discuss. So get ready. I'll be paying you a visit. Real soon."

Excerpts from the Call Sheets for Season Four:*

EPISODE ONE: The Freshman

Special Notes and instructions:
PROPS: Klimt poster, Bleu cheese, *Of Human Bondage*

EPISODE TWO: Living Conditions

Special Notes and instructions:
LIVESTOCK: Madagascar Beetle, Scorpion
PROPS: Ketchup gag, dental floss
COSTUMES: Sc—Ketchup on Kathy's (Buffy's) sweater (Dbls)

EPISODE THREE: The Harsh Light of Day

Special Notes and instructions:
Keg of beer; need couples to make out; bottles for juggler

EPISODE FOUR: Fear, Itself

Special Notes and instructions:
PROPS: Hellcome mat, chainsaw, fake skeleton

EPISODE FIVE: Beer Bad

Special Notes and instructions:
PROPS: Black Frost keg, Bag of Spiders
LABOR: Lns Tech,
SPEQ: Lightning Strikes

*as far as they'd shot when the writers visited

EPISODE SIX: Wild at Heart

Special Notes and instructions:
Wolf suits for Oz and Veruca, hand doubles. Permit for pumpkin flames.

EPISODE SEVEN: The Initiative

There will be atmo smoke on Set today!

EPISODE EIGHT: Pangs

MU/HAIR: Sc. 18—priest to look quite dead
Memo from Locations Manager Ed Duffy about a wedding rehearsal in the chapel from 6 PM to 7 PM on October 14, 1999.
LIVE ANIMAL ON SET TODAY: "BONKERS" THE BEAR & A COYOTE

EPISODE NINE: Something Blue

Special Notes and instructions:
ART DEPT./SET DRESSING: Wedding dresses in window
Complimentary flu shots October 21 from 2–5 PM

EPISODE TEN: Hush

STAND-INS AND ATMO: Giles Hand Dbl, Olivia Hand Dbl, Riley Photo Dbl, Studio Teacher
MEMO: "Wed., Nov 10 & 11, we will be filming at Universal Studios on Colonial Drive. Another company will be filming on the residential portion of Colonial Drive on Friday, Nov. 12, 1999. As a result, our official strike day will be Monday, Nov. 15, 1999. Please wrap all equipment/sets from the residential area on the evening of Thursday, Nov. 11, 1999, and stage it off the road in the town portion/cul-de-sac area of Colonial Drive for pickup on Monday."

EPISODE ELEVEN: Doomed

Special Notes and instructions:
LIVESTOCK: SC: 1 Handler with Rat (Amy, the rat)
There will be atmo smoke and dust in int. library unit; please use respirators!
Animal Handling Rules for the Motion Picture Industry

EPISODE TWELVE: A New Man

Form included for Secret Santa participants

EPISODE THIRTEEN: The I in Team

DAY 1 OF 8 DAYS: Secret Santa Memo.
Special Notes:
STAND-IN AND ATMOS: 62 Bronze Patrons

WRITTEN BY: Marti Noxon; **DIRECTED BY:** David Solomon.
GUEST STARS: Amber Benson as Tara, George Hertzberg as Adam,
Leonard Roberts as Forrest, Bailey Chase as Graham, Jack Stehlin as
Dr. Angleman, JB Gaynor as Boy, Saverio Guerra as Willy the Snitch,
Emma Caulfield as Anya.

GOODBYE, IOWA

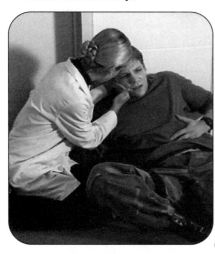

THE PLOT THICKENS:

While Buffy is explaining that Dr. Walsh tried to kill her, Spike voices the suspicion the others have secretly harbored: Did Riley have something to do with the attempt on Buffy's life? Buffy is adamant that Riley couldn't do such a thing. Her belief in him is tested when he recognizes Spike as Hostile 17 and realizes that Buffy's been protecting Spike from the Initiative.

Adam, the Frankenstein's monster that Maggie Walsh created, walks the earth. In a scene reminiscent of the original film *Frankenstein,* (1931) he comes upon a young child. Later, the child's brutal death is announced on TV. Buffy, in search of Adam, observes the removal of the little boy's body, Riley approaches her and tells her that Maggie Walsh is dead. Dr. Angleman discovered her body. "Happy now?" he asks her cruelly.

Buffy continues her search, which leads her to Willy the snitch, the bar owner who has renamed the Alibi to Willy's Place. Riley has been following her, and in the bar his behavior becomes alarmingly erratic. He draws his pistol on a bar patron, then nearly collapses. Buffy realizes he's ill and brings him to Xander's basement, where everyone is hiding out from the Initiative.

Meanwhile, Willow asks Tara to perform a spell with her, having already assured her that she doesn't come to Tara's room only to do spells. The spell's purpose is to pinpoint the locations of all the demons in Sunnydale. But when Willow's eyes are closed, Tara deliberately sabotages the spell.

Spike walks into Willy's and orders a double shot of O' Neg, only to be summarily thrown out and beaten up by a demon. Word is out that Spike's been making war on the demon world and helping out the Slayer. The demon who beats him tells him not to come around Willy's anymore.

Buffy and Xander infiltrate the Initiative complex. They learn that Dr. Walsh was giving the soldiers some kind of behavior modification drugs. They'll suffer withdrawal if they don't take their daily allowance. Riley hasn't been taking his, and that's what's happening to him.

Adam reveals himself and confronts Riley, who has once again followed Buffy. Then Adam kills Dr. Angleman. The created monster tells Riley that Maggie Walsh was essentially their mother. Furious, Riley attacks Adam. In the struggle that ensues, Adam skewers Riley in the side with the same Polgara demon arm he used to kill Maggie Walsh. Forrest orders that Riley be taken to their military hospital and has Buffy and Xander escorted out.

Buffy is left to worry about Riley…who is barely hanging on to his sanity in his dreary military hospital room. The only thing that's keeping him going is Buffy's scarf, tied around his knuckles….

QUOTE OF THE WEEK:

"I totally get it now. Can I have sex with Riley, too?"

Xander sees the Initiative complex for the first time.

THE AGONY AND THE ECSTASY:

Buffy's love for Riley is severely tested, and vice versa. Then they are separated, and Buffy doesn't even know if he's alive. Anya frets for Xander's safety, which touches him. Willow and Tara move closer to each other, Spike continues to talk about Buffy's love life.

POP-CULTURE IQ:

BUFFY: "Next thing I know, it's raining monsters—"
XANDER: "Hallelujah."
Sunnydale variant on the Weather Girls' song "It's Raining Men."

From the stage directions:
[Morning breaks, and our gang has spent a restless night in Xander's basement. We see that the room has been DIVIDED BY A BLANKET THAT HANGS ON A ROPE into a section for the boys and a section for the girls (à la It Happened One Night.)]
It Happened One Night is a 1934 film starring Clark Gable and Claudette Colbert. Directed by Frank Capra, it received five Academy Awards.

The gang watches a Roadrunner and Wile E. Coyote cartoon—"a wonderful Warner Brothers cartoon!" (according to the script).

CONTINUITY:

After a couple of previous chance encounters, Riley finally recognizes Spike. Spike stayed in Xander's basement for the first time in "Hush." Riley saw him in the ruins of Sunnydale High School in "Doomed." Spike disses Buffy again on her poor taste in men, including Angel and Parker. He started in on her about it in "The Harsh Light of Day." Willy's back for the first time since "The Zeppo." Anya refers to Xander's single night as a soldier, in "Halloween."

This was added to the conversation Dr. Angleman has with "Scientist #1," probably for the sake of clarity: "These guys don't know they've been getting meds through their food. So we'd better get them in here, stat."

FROM THE ORIGINAL TELEPLAY:

The following exchange was cut due to length:
WILLOW (encouraging): "I bet you will."
BUFFY: "No. No bet. I will make it work."
[This came out a tad more strident than she planned.]

WRITTEN BY: **Douglas Petrie**; DIRECTED BY: **Michael Gershman.**
GUEST STARS: **Kristine Sutherland as Joyce, Amber Benson as Tara, Leonard Roberts as Forrest, Bailey Chase as Graham, Chet Grissom as Detective Clark, Alastair Duncan as Collins, Harry Groener as Mayor Wilkins, Eliza Dushku as Faith;** with **Jeff Ricketts as Weatherby, Kevin Owers as Smith.**

THIS YEAR'S GIRL

THE PLOT THICKENS:

Faith lies in her hospital bed in the basement of Sunnydale Hospital, dreaming of a cold-hearted, murderous Buffy and a warm and caring Mayor Wilkins. When at last she defeats Buffy in one of her nightmares, she awakens from her coma to discover that Graduation Day has come and gone. She beats up a woman and takes her clothes. Her nurse alerts someone by phone and tells him to "send the team." Making her way to the ruins of Sunnydale High, Faith faces the truth: the Mayor is dead.

Riley also rises from his hospital bed and has to pull rank to leave the Initiative complex. He has kicked the meds Maggie Walsh was feeding him, but the wound Adam dealt him is still troublesome. Buffy is filled with joy at the sight of him, and their reunion is tender. She reminds him that he has choices, despite the fact that he's been trained to obey orders.

Someone contacts Buffy (we don't know who) to tell her that Faith has escaped, while Faith seeks Buffy out. Faith is enraged that Buffy seems to have forgotten all about her. She goads Buffy, reminding her rival that Buffy tried to kill her for her Slayer's blood, in order to save Angel. And now Buffy's boinking some *other* guy....Their fight is brutal, but inconclusive, as the police arrive and Faith disappears onto the streets.

233

Meanwhile, "the team" arrives: three nasty-looking men who make themselves at home in Giles's condo and greet him familiarly.

Willow and Tara are more of a couple now, Willow acting protectively toward Tara as she explains to her about Faith. Meanwhile, Faith is moved by the Mayor's love for her—he made a farewell video for her. He also left her a magical device, a Draconian Katra, which will allow her to switch bodies with Buffy. She goes to Buffy's house and terrorizes Joyce, assuming that Buffy will come rescue her mother. Buffy crashes into the bedroom, rescuing her mother, and she and Faith have a battle royal all over the Summers's home. The police sirens blare in the background—Joyce has called 911—and at the last possible moment, Faith makes the switch, with no one the wiser.

QUOTE OF THE WEEK:

"I'd hate to see the pursuit of a homicidal lunatic get in the way of pursuing a homicidal lunatic." Xander talking strategy with the gang on who to go after first, Faith or Adam.

THE AGONY AND THE ECSTASY:

Faith knows how to hurt Buffy—by reminding her of Angel. Buffy hurt Faith by destroying the Mayor. But Buffy and Riley's love appears very strong as they reunite. Tara and Willow are close and affectionate, clearly happy to have each other.

POP-CULTURE IQ:

"Now if it was called 'The Orgasminator,' I'd be the first to try your basic button-press approach."

Word play we have known and loved: Trey Parker's film, *Orgazmo,* which was executive-produced by Fran Rubel Kuzui and Kaz Kuzui. The Kuzuis also executive-produce *Buffy.* Woody Allen's 1973 film *Sleeper* and Roger Vadim's *Barbarella* also featured Orgasmatrons. However, Xander is talking about an Initiative blaster.

"He's the Terminator without the bashful charm."

Buffy, referring to the character played by Arnold Schwarzenegger in *The Terminator* (1984) and *Terminator 2: Judgment Day* (1991). Both were directed by James Cameron.

"Riley is kind of their top-gun guy."

Top Gun is a 1986 film about ace fighter pilots starring Tom Cruise, Val Kilmer, and *ER*'s Anthony Edwards. Willow's reassuring Buffy, who is worried the Initiative will hurt him.

[It is strung up like Hannibal Lecter's cell guard in <u>The Silence of the Lambs</u>.]

Script directions for a scene in which Adam has killed a demon. Thomas Harris wrote *The Silence of the Lambs* in 1988; it was made into an Academy Award-winning film in 1991.

"She's my wacky identical cousin from England, and every time she visits, hijinks ensue."

Buffy's referring to *The Patty Duke Show,* which ran from 1963–1966. It starred Patty Duke as look-alike cousins.

"If I were her, I'd get out of Dodge post-hasty."

"Marshal Dillon" Summers wants Faith gone from Sunnydale in this reference to the city in *Gunsmoke,* a popular TV western series.

"In <u>The World According to Joyce</u>, Buffy's gonna come crashing through that door any minute."

Faith's referring to *The World According to Garp,* a novel by John Irving, made into a film in 1982.

> Faith asks a hospital visitor for the date. In the original script the answer was Tuesday, February eighth. It was changed to Friday, February twenty-fifth.

CONTINUITY:

The blaster Xander is trying to repair is the faulty one Maggie Walsh gave Buffy when she tried to kill her in "The I in Team." The duplicity of Maggie Walsh and the murky ethical status of the Initiative are kept in focus. The past with Faith—"Faith, Hope & Trick," "Revelations," "Bad Girls," "Enemies," and "Consequences"—is partially spelled out. Spike still has the chip in his head, which prevents him from hurting any human being—no matter how much he might like to. Buffy tells Riley about the Watchers Council and about Faith.

fROM THE ORIGINAL TELEPLAY:

"Explosives, tear gas, grappling hooks."
Buffy explains what kind of force she plans to use to get into the Initiative, in this line cut for length.

Stage directions for one of Faith's dreams:
[We cut back to the Mayor. He's being horribly, brutally HACKED APART by Buffy with her knife. He's real dead real fast. Finished with this prey, Buffy whips her gaze to Faith, impatient and peeved.]

WRITTEN AND DIRECTED BY: **Joss Whedon.** GUEST STARS: **Kristine Sutherland as Joyce Summers, Amber Benson as Tara, Leonard Roberts as Forrest, George Hertzberg as Adam, Chet Grissom as Detective Clark, Alastair Duncan as Collins, Emma Caulfield as Anya, Eliza Dushku as Faith; with Rick Stear as Boone, Jeff Ricketts as Weatherby, Kevin Owers as Smith.**

THE PLOT THICKENS

Trapped inside Faith's body, Buffy is strapped to a gurney and loaded into an ambulance as Joyce and Faith, in Buffy's body, observe. Faith is able to fool Joyce as she mimics Buffy's speech patterns and movements, and extricates herself from an uncomfortable moment of tenderness in which Joyce hugs her, by announcing that she's going to take a bath. Alone, she luxuriates in her new body, and she mocks Buffy's goody-goody attitude in front of the mirror.

Meanwhile, in the hospital, Buffy frantically tries to get free of the doctors, nurses, and cops holding her down long enough to sedate her. She tries to explain that Faith has taken her body and is alone with her mother, but she finally succumbs to unconsciousness.

Willow and Tara are in Tara's room, and Willow is frightened that Faith will come after her. Tara reminds her that since no one knows she, Tara, exists, Willow ought to be safe with her. It's clear she's hurt that Willow hasn't introduced her to her friends. Willow tries to explain that she's being possessive of Tara, rather than ashamed, and Tara glows with understanding.

Faith buys a plane ticket with Joyce's credit card. While Buffy is being transported from the hospital to jail, a van deliberately pulls into the path of the police car, causing a crash. The men of "the team" drag Buffy into the van. They are the Watchers Council operatives.

Faith as Buffy goes on over to Giles's house "to kill time"

before her flight by chatting with them about the capture of "Faith." Giles informs them all that the Watchers Council team has gotten hold of her. Faith is delighted. She's also having psychotic delusions of gutting Willow, but she manages to keep her psychotic interludes hidden from the others.

Pretending to be the good little soldier, she informs the others that she's going to go patrolling for Adam. Instead, she goes to the Bronze to party. There, she runs into Spike, whom she's never met before. Once she realizes who he is, she baits him mercilessly, coming on to him and then laughing in his face.

Adam has taken over the lair of Boone, a young vampire. He kills one of Boone's homeys to get the attention of the others, then offers them some interesting perspectives on their existence, and on his own personal mission.

Buffy wakes up shackled in the Watchers Council van. The assassins are not loving her, and they are not believing her story that she's really Buffy Summers inside Faith's body.

Back at the Bronze, Willow brings Tara to the club for the first time. They're holding hands, clearly a couple. Willow spies "Buffy," chugalugging and flirting with a bunch of guys in a most unBuffylike way. She introduces Faith to Tara; while she goes off for drinks, Faith verbally savages Tara, making fun of her stammer and making sure poor Tara knows just how much Willow loves Oz.

But Faith begins to experience what it's like to be well regarded: After she dusts a vamp, the girl he was feeding on shakes Faith with the depth of her gratitude. When she seeks out Riley and tries to work her sexual wiles on him, going for the kink, he stops her and makes tender love to her. Believing he's with his Buffy, he tells her for the first time that he loves her.

Buffy manages to escape from the assassins, and Tara tells Willow that Buffy's not herself. Willow and she work intense magic, sending Willow to the nether realms. They conjure a Katra for Buffy, to switch her back into her own body, and find her at Giles's condo. They tell her that for it to work, she must make physical contact with Faith.

Adam has launched his assault against humanity by sending Boone and the other vampires to a church. Faith, still masquerading as Buffy, charges to the rescue. She accidentally meets up with Riley, who's on the scene because he was going to church. The real Buffy and company show up.

Buffy and Faith fight the vampires, and then each other. Buffy manages to clasp hands with her, and they switch back into their own bodies. Buffy is left to deal with the aftermath of Faith's escapades—including Riley's having slept with her—while Faith catches a train out of town, trying to process everything that's happened.

QUOTE OF THE WEEK:

FAITH: "You're not gonna kill these people."
BOONE: "Why not?"
FAITH: "Because it's wrong."
Facing down Adam's vampires, Faith rises to the occasion.

THE AGONY AND THE ECSTASY:

Faith experiences tenderness and kindness for perhaps the first time in her life; her lovemaking with Riley, followed by his declaration of love, throws her into a panic. Willow tries to explain her intense feelings to Tara, who clearly reciprocates. Tara and Willow bond ever closer as they work magic together. Buffy's devastated when she discovers that Riley—unknowingly—slept with Faith.

POP-CULTURE IQ:

"On her way to the big house."
Faith's riffing off prison movies; Buffy's on her way to jail.

CONTINUITY:

This is part two of a two-part episode. Faith is unimpressed when the Watchers Council sends someone to retrieve the rogue Slayer "because that worked so well when Wesley tried it" (in "Consequences"). They discuss Adam, who's still at large. Spike brings Faith up to date on the chip in his head. Boone, the vampire, becomes Adam's mouthpiece in the church confrontation. One of the assassins reminds Faith that Buffy and Giles are no longer part of the Council. Willow tells Tara that she, Xander, and Buffy used to live at the Bronze. Faith has switched bodies with Buffy and goes after Riley, the same as she did with Angel. Willow mentions hyena possession, which occurred to Xander in "The Pack." Riley mentions the drugs Maggie Walsh had been giving him. Buffy's still a bad driver, which has been a recurring joke in many episodes, including "Band Candy." In trying to convince Giles that she's who she insists she is, she makes reference to his being a demon ("A New Man") and Olivia ("Hush"), blowing up Sunnydale High ("Graduation Day, Part Two"), and his having had sex with her mother ("Band Candy").

> There were six drafts of the script for "Who Are You," the first draft delivered on January 24, 2000, and the final pages distributed to the cast, staff, and crew on February 2, 2000.

FROM THE ORIGINAL TELEPLAY:

The following line of Adam's was cut due to length:
"You are here to be my first. To let them know I'm coming. I am the end of all life, of all magic. I'm the war between man and demon, the war that no one can win. You're a part of that now. You have to show me you're ready."

WRITTEN BY: Jane Espenson; **DIRECTED BY:** David Grossman.
GUEST STARS: Danny Strong as Jonathan, Amber Benson as Tara, Bailey Chase as Graham, Robert Patrick Benedict as Jape, John Saint Ryan as Colonel Haviland, George Hertzberg as Adam; with Erica Luttrell as Karen, Adam Clark as Sergeant, Chanie Costello as Inga, Julie Costello as Ilsa.

SUPERSTAR

THE PLOT THICKENS:

Who ya gonna call? Jonathan!

Jonathan Levenson, former Sunnydale High classmate of Buffy and company, is the coolest, most important person in the world. Jonathan is stronger and more agile than the Slayer; a computer hacker cleverer than Willow; idolized by everyone, and the inventor of everything.

Buffy and Riley are feeling very awkward around each other; while Riley didn't realize it was Faith he slept with, nevertheless he did sleep with her. The two concentrate on finding Adam, who is still on the loose. Jonathan gets to the heart of the problem for Buffy: when it mattered most, Riley didn't look into her eyes and realize she wasn't looking back at him.

Colonel Haviland, the new head of the Initiative, reviews the troops and explains that he's there while the government conducts a facility review. Their primary mission remains the recovery of Adam. To that end, Colonel Haviland asks the aid of their tactical consultant…Jonathan. He has detected Adam's internal power source: a small reservoir of Uranium 235 encased in lead.

While Jonathan is briefing Riley and the other Commandos, Karen, a fan of his, is attacked by a hideous monster with a distinctive symbol on his forehead.

Jonathan offers Riley advice on how to get back together with Buffy; at the Bronze, Xander accuses Anya of murmuring "Jonathan" during a critical private moment. All is forgotten as Jonathan takes the stage and begins singing. Then Karen enters, bloodied and weeping.

It seems she was attacked on his property; Buffy, Riley, Jonathan, and Karen go to investigate. When she sketches the symbol that was on the monster, something registers with Jonathan. Buffy notices, but he quickly recovers and insists it was nothing. He assures her that he'll take care of the monster himself.

But Adam knows it's something. He knows that Jonathan has cast some sort of spell, because he himself is impervious to it.

Shortly after that, Tara is attacked by the monster. Buffy's faith in Jonathan is badly shaken. It occurs to her that some of Jonathan's accomplishments don't add up: He's only eighteen, yet he's graduated from medical school. He starred in *The Matrix*, but he never left town.

Then she realizes Jonathan sports the identical mark as the monster, and she pressures him to go on recon with her to find it. While the two of them search, the others research the mark. It turns out that Jonathan did an Augmentation spell on himself to make everyone idolize him. But he also created the monster. Kill the monster, and the spell is broken.

With Jonathan's help, Buffy prevails. The world becomes as it should be, with Jonathan something of a nebbish. However, the advice he gave Buffy and Riley sticks…and they reunite.

QUOTE OF THE WEEK:

WILLOW [trying it out]: "Buffy was right. Buffy was right."
ANYA: "Doesn't sound very likely, does it?"
> Controlled by Jonathan's spell, the gang's not used to Buffy's leadership skills.

The Jonathan comic features a brown-eyed super-Jonathan, but his eyes are actually crystal blue.

THE AGONY AND THE ECSTASY:

Buffy and Riley are having a lot of trouble dealing with the fact that Riley slept with Faith. Xander's jealous of Jonathan. In the end Buffy and Riley are able to put the past behind them, and Xander and Anya are solid again. Willow and Tara are still very much in the honeymoon stage.

POP-CULTURE IQ:

"The Nimzowitsch Defense. Let's see if I remember...."
Aron Nimzowitsch is one of the pioneers of hypermodern chess. In his magical world, Jonathan is a chess master.

"He got a perfect score, and then he recreated the original proof of Fermat's last theorem in the margins around the answer bubbles."
This famous theorem was not proven for more than 350 years after Fermat first described it; Willow's talking about Jonathan, who solved it, of course.

"I was just at the part where he invents the Internet!"
Gentle poke at Vice President Al Gore, who is reputed to have made the same claim. Anya's reading Jonathan's autobiography.

"He starred in <u>The Matrix</u>, but he never left town?"
Buffy's seeing the illogic in all the things she and others believe about Jonathan. Joss Whedon has said the film, starring Keanu Reeves, is one of his favorites.

> "Superstar" author Jane Espenson also wrote "Earshot." She and Danny Strong have become friends.

CONTINUITY:

Spike is still defanged; Adam is still at large. In this reality Buffy gave Jonathan the Class Protector Award at the Prom. Once the jig is up, Jonathan refers to the events in "Earshot," when Buffy stopped him from committing suicide in the bell tower. Anya's past as a vengeance demon is discussed.

FROM THE ORIGINAL TELEPLAY:

The following line of Spike's was cut due to length:

"You're a bleeding idiot, you are, Jonathan. 'Cuz you'll be the first victim and you'll be stone dead before you hit the ground. [then, to himself, proudly] The <u>worst</u> kind of scum."

WRITTEN BY: **Tracey Forbes**; DIRECTED BY: **David Solomon.**
GUEST STARS: **Amber Benson as Tara, Leonard Roberts as Forrest, Bailey Chase as Graham, Kathryn Joosten as Mrs. Holt, Emma Caulfield as Anya; with Casey McCarthy as Julie, Neil Daly as Mason, Jeff Wilson as Evan, Bryan Cuprill as Roy.**

WHERE THE WILD THINGS ARE

THE PLOT THICKENS:

Adam's been recruiting soldiers: Vampires and demons are working together, which is unusual. Giles should be informed...soon...tomorrow....

Buffy and Riley can't get enough of each other. Every chance they have, they steal away to Riley's room to make love. Spooky sounds of dripping water in the bathroom foreshadow ensuing…spookiness. But when Riley goes to investigate, he finds nothing out of the ordinary.

Anya and Xander are having relationship woes: Anya's positive the fun part of their relationship has ended because they didn't have sex the night before; now comes the breakup and, in her day, the vengeance.

Riley and Buffy continue their trips to Riley's bedroom, unaware that Lowell House has become extremely cold, and nothing can heat it. Mason is badly burned by the fire the Commandos build in the fireplace.

Meanwhile, Riley has called for a party at Lowell House to build troop morale. Adam's threat has got his boys feeling blue. Anya's down in the dumps, too. So is Spike, feeling ineffectual and missing Dru. Anya decides to take him to the party. Xander is rebound-bound with one Julie. Some of the partiers (including Roy of "Beer Bad") discover that touching a particular wall in the frat house gives feelings of intense sexual pleasure.

Buffy and Riley can't seem to stop making love. They're becoming more and more isolated from the rest of the house; needier, and insatiable.

Tara rebuffs Willow's gesture of affection, and during a spin-the-bottle kiss, Julie practically swallows Xander's face, then freaks out and hides under the stairs. She begins to hack off her hair, sobbing that she's dirty. Willow has a ghostly encounter in the bathroom: A young boy is bound hand and foot, and is nearly drowning in the bathtub. The spin-the-bottle game has gotten out of control; the bottle explodes and everyone runs, screaming.

When Tara, Xander, and Willow try to alert Buffy, they can't get the door open. In fact, the door fuses into the wall. The house shakes violently and people flee. Once outside, however, no one can get back in.

Giles is tracked down: He's singing unplugged at the Espresso Pump, a local hangout. The dumbfounded Slayerettes break up his set, and together they track down the former director of the Lowell Home for Children. Lowell House was once a sort of orphanage for disadvantaged kids.

It turns out that the director, Mrs. Holt, is an emotionally ill woman obsessed with sin; she tortured the children to conquer any traces of lust within them. Their repressed rage has created a sort of group poltergeist, and the lust between Buffy and Riley is feeding it. If the poltergeist is not exorcised, Buffy and Riley will die.

Willow, Tara, and Giles perform the exorcism while Anya and Xander return to the house. Xander is nearly drowned. Eventually Buffy and Riley are freed and the house is cleansed.

And everyone now knows that Giles is the god of the acoustic guitar….

QUOTE OF THE WEEK:

"We're fresh out of super-people and somebody's got to go back in there. Now who's with me?" Xander plans to go back into the possessed Lowell House.

THE AGONY AND THE ECSTASY:

Anya's convinced Xander doesn't love her anymore; she briefly hooks up with Spike, two formerly dangerous demonic types unlucky in love. Riley and Buffy shut everyone else out—literally—until they are rescued. Tara and Willow are solid, after the initial freakout in Lowell House, caused by the poltergeist influences. Willow reveals that she had a crush on Giles for quite some time. Xander and Anya get back together.

POP-CULTURE IQ:

"Who says we can't all get along?"
Replay of a statement by Rodney King, who was beaten by L.A. police officers. The case went to trial in 1992; the officers were acquitted, setting off violent riots throughout Los Angeles. Buffy's talking about vamps and demons working together—highly unusual.

"There's ghosts and shaking and people going all Felicity with their hair."
Keri Russell, star of the WB's *Felicity,* cut her beautiful, wild hair very short. So did Julie, the girl who passionately kissed Xander during a game of "Spin the Possessed Bottle."

"Like Martin Luther King."
Famous civil rights activist and leader; he gave the speech "I have a dream." Willow's commenting on the fact that demons that are usually enemies are joining Adam's army.

CONTINUITY:

The Uninvited—Stella Starlight was named for the song, "Stella by Starlight," written by Hoagy Carmichael for this scary film about a haunted house.
Other famous Haunted House movies:
The Haunting ● *The House* series ● *The Poltergeist* series

Spike still has a chip on his shoulder about having a chip in his head. He speaks sadly of Dru, last seen in "Becoming, Part Two"; mourned over in "Lover's Walk," and mocked in "The Harsh Light of Day." Anya reminisces about the good old days when she could kill men in brutal ways. Xander's series of minimum-wage jobs continues. Adam is building an army. Xander starts calling Spike "Hostile 17" in a loud voice at the Lowell House party, recalling Spike's status as a fugitive from the Initiative. Tara and Willow continue to work magic together.

FROM THE ORIGINAL TELEPLAY:

The following line of Willow's was cut for length:
"But probably a lot less eloquent...and with the...evil...so, different than Martin Luther King. Let's move on."

NEW MOON RISING

WRITTEN BY: **Marti Noxon;** DIRECTED BY: **James A. Contner.**
GUEST STARS: **Amber Benson as Tara, Leonard Roberts as Forrest, Bailey Chase as Graham, Robert Patrick Benedict as Jape, Conor O'Farrell as Colonel McNamara, George Hertzberg as Adam, Emma Caulfield as Anya, Seth Green as Oz.**

THE PLOT THICKENS:

It's finally happened: Oz has returned. Not only that, but he has learned how to control his werewolf transformations.

This is the moment Willow used to dream about. Now she's conflicted beyond the telling: She also loves Tara.

She confides in Buffy, who didn't realize the nature of her close friendship with Tara. Poor Willow has no idea what she's going to do, and Tara is suffering terribly.

Riley is shocked to discover that the guy Willow's been pining for is a werewolf; to the soldier, werewolves are on the same level as demons: bad. Buffy, thinking of Angel, rallies to Oz's defense, stating that there are degrees of evil. Riley can't go anywhere near there in his thinking, and Buffy pulls away, defensive because of her past relationship with the vampire who has a soul.

Adam approaches Spike and informs him that he will be acting as a double agent for him. If he cooperates and foments chaos among the humans, Adam will take Spike's antiviolence chip out.

One of the Commandos is killed by a demon during patrol; Graham's blurry look at the killer vaguely fits the description of a werewolf. When Oz realizes that Tara is his rival for Willow, he loses control and the wolf comes out. The Commandos capture him.

Spike leads Buffy, Willow, and Xander into the Initiative to rescue Oz. Riley has been watching the scientists experimenting on Oz; Oz manages to stop his transformation each time. Riley joins in liberating him, decking his commanding officer and essentially going AWOL.

Buffy and he hide out in the ruins of Sunnydale High School. There's no going back now for Riley. For Buffy a world is opening up: She finally finds the courage to tell Riley about Angel.

Willow chooses Tara, and Oz leaves Sunnydale again.

Maybe forever.

QUOTE OF THE WEEK:

"I feel like some part of me will always be waiting for you. Like, if I'm old and blue-haired and I turn a corner in Istanbul and there you are, I won't be surprised. Because you're with me, you know?" —Willow, to Oz, as they part.

THE AGONY AND THE ECSTASY:

Buffy's secret about having loved a demon with a soul—Angel—isolates her from Riley, who feels her smoldering defensiveness keenly. Tara waits in agony while Willow decides between her and Oz;

her sincere desire for Willow's happiness is heartbreaking. Oz loses, and he and Willow grieve for what was, and what might have been. Willow promises Tara she will make up for the pain she has caused her.

POP-CULTURE IQ:

"A woman in Tibet traded it to me for a Radiohead CD."
Radiohead is a British music group: Oz is telling Willow about his travels.

"Stay back or I'll do a William Burroughs on your leader here!"
William S. Burroughs (1914–1997) was an American author who was a prominent member of the Beat Generation. During a drunken game of William Tell in Mexico, he tried to shoot a shot glass off his wife's head. He missed and killed her. Buffy is holding Colonel MacNamara hostage.

CONTINUITY:

Adam continues to pose a threat. Spike agrees to work for him. The Initiative has been "bagging and tagging" demons at a significantly high rate, and their containment facilities are overcrowded. Oz and Willow's past history includes his leaving her without warning, never writing, and not informing her of his imminent return. Buffy makes an allusion to Angel—the vampire with a soul. Riley and Buffy return to the ruins of Sunnydale High School, last seen in "This Year's Girl." Buffy points out the dubious benefits of the presence of "snake jerky"— the Mayor turned into a demon snake during his Ascension. He was blown to bits, and pieces of him are still lying around. The campus is blacked out because of Oz's wolf transformation and the presence, according to Colonel McNamara, of "anarchists" (Buffy and company).

FROM THE ORIGINAL TELEPLAY:

The character of Jape was cut from this episode due to length. Some of his dialogue:
"Yeah! Count me in for the crazy fun plan! I'm gonna feed the minions."

WRITTEN BY: **Douglas Petrie**; DIRECTED BY: **David Grossman.**
GUEST STARS: **Amber Benson as Tara, Leonard Roberts as Forrest, Conor O'Farrell as Colonel McNamara, George Hertzberg as Adam, Emma Caulfield as Anya, David Boreanaz as Angel.**

THE YOKO FACTOR

THE PLOT THICKENS:

Hearing that Faith had been seen in Los Angeles, Buffy went there and discovered her with Angel, in the *Angel* series crossover episode, "Sanctuary." The visit was a disaster, with the two former lovers yelling and hitting each other.

Meanwhile, Buffy is searching for Adam. She encounters Forrest on the way to Adam's cave. They exchange very hostile words—Forrest has never cared for Buffy, and blames her for Riley's becoming a traitor—and very reluctantly end up going into the cave together. Adam is there, and he kills Forrest during the ensuing battle. Buffy barely gets out alive.

Meanwhile, Adam and Spike continue plotting to separate the Slayer from her friends. Spike pretends that he has infiltrated the Initiative and stolen a disk containing information about Adam. Willow sets to work on its encryption code. Spike begins dropping hints and spreading innuendo that suggests that the friends have been gossiping about one another. He pinpoints each of their vulnerable spots. He lets Xander think that Willow and Buffy have been saying how stupid he is, that all he's good for is joining the army. He plays on Willow's insecurity about her relationship with Tara through the metaphor of her having forsaken her computer skills in favor of her "Wicca thing." He takes advantage of Giles's feeling of uselessness, and soon Giles has finished off one bottle of Scotch and begun another. By the time Spike is finished with them, the friends are not speaking to one another and Giles is drunk.

Angel has arrived in Sunnydale, intent on finding Buffy to apologize to her. Some Commandos attack him and Riley arrives on the scene as Angel's defending himself. He assumes that Angel has gone bad once more, having only recently learned from Xander that Angel lost his soul when he slept with Buffy. They come to major blows. Angel gets to Buffy's dorm room only seconds before Riley catches up with him. Buffy makes them stop fighting, promising to land them both in the hospital if they don't.

Buffy and Angel go out into the hall to talk; in a touching scene between the two of them, Buffy acknowledges that what Angel said in Los Angels is right: They don't live in each other's worlds any more. Their time together is over. Then she goes in to Riley, to reassure him that she loves him and only him. He admits that he's so in love with her he can't think straight.

After Buffy, Willow, Xander and Giles have one last major confrontation, Buffy storms off to find the only person she can trust to help her fight Adam...but at episode's end, Riley presents himself to Adam, who's been expecting him....

QUOTE OF THE WEEK:

"Xander. He is the deadest man in Deadonia."

Buffy, fuming at Xander for spilling the beans about the fact that it's not crème brûlée that makes Angel go bad...

THE AGONY AND THE ECSTASY:

Tara adopts a kitten, and "Miss Kitty Fantastico" quickly becomes her and Willow's surrogate baby; they begin circling the idea of living together. Anya and Xander are still solid; she gives him a proprietary swat when Spike indicates there's a rumor going around that Xander is joining the army. Riley and Buffy confess that they're so in love with each other they can't think straight. When Buffy speaks privately with Angel, it's clear that he accepts that she has moved on, and why.

POP-CULTURE IQ:

"You're like Tony Robbins if he was a big, scary Frankenstein-looking . . . You're exactly like Tony Robbins."
Spike is complimenting Adam on his inspirational speaking while they are plotting the demise of both human and demon races. Tony Robbins is an internationally renowned "peak performance coach"—i.e., motivational speaker and author.

"L.A. Woman?"
Xander refers to Buffy this way when talking to Riley because Buffy's been in Los Angeles tracking down Faith. "L.A. Woman" is the title track on an album released by the rock band the Doors in April, 1971.

"So you don't have to be G.I. Joe while your civvies are getting washed."
Xander has brought Riley some clothing to wear in lieu of his military uniform. First sold in 1964, G. I. Joe was the first "action figure," a term coined to make it acceptable for boys to play with dolls.

"Oh, okay. You and Will go do the superpower thing. I'll stay behind and putter around the batcave [indicates Giles] with crusty old Alfred here."
Xander is being sarcastic about superhero Batman and his British butler, Alfred, and the fact that Buffy is dismissing him in the plan to save Oz.

CONTINUITY:

The military is investigating the Initiative: They're looking for Riley and the Slayer both. Spike continues to plot with Adam, in return for getting the chip out of his head. Buffy's trip to Los Angeles to deal with Faith is referenced. Adam kills Forrest. Riley and Xander discuss Angel's curse, referring back to "Surprise" and "Innocence," when Buffy made love to Angel on her seventeenth birthday. Spike reminds us that Giles used to be Buffy's Watcher, but is now only a retired librarian. Spike also plays on Xander's insecurity about not being as smart as the others and the fact that he's drifting from job to job. Tara and Willow's relationship keeps growing, as does Willow's interest in Wicca; the estrangement that has been developing all season among the original core characters (Xander, Willow, Giles, and Buffy) is emphasized.

FROM THE ORIGINAL TELEPLAY:

"Now that you've turned Super Wicca and you're damn near Amish. All candles and hand-ground herbs..."
Spike baits Willow in this line cut due to length.

PRIMEVAL

WRITTEN BY: David Fury; DIRECTED BY: James A. Contner.
GUEST STARS: Leonard Roberts as Forrest, Amber Benson as Tara,
Bailey Chase as Graham, Jack Stehlin as Dr. Angleman, Conor
O'Farrell as Colonel McNamara, George Hertzberg as Adam, Emma
Caulfield as Anya, Lindsay Crouse as Professor Maggie Walsh.

THE PLOT THICKENS:

Adam reveals to Riley that he has activated a chip in Riley's arm, placed there by Maggie Walsh. He controls Riley's movements and actions now, even to speak or to be silent. He reveals the master plan, to create "demonoids" like himself, amalgams of demons and humans. Spike shows, enjoying watching Riley's frustration, but is frustrated himself when Adam refuses to take out Spike's chip...just yet. Spike didn't quite think through his plan to separate the Slayer from her friends—Willow is decrypting the disks he "smuggled" from the Initiative, but she's not speaking to Buffy now, and vice versa.

Willow forgot her laptop at Giles's condo. She and Tara go back for it, and Giles is extremely hung over. They leave awkwardly, with no resolution. Anya tries to cheer up Xander, who is worried that his friends are right and that he is a directionless loser. Adam introduces Riley to the reanimated Maggie Walsh and Dr. Angleman, who will help Adam create demonoid creatures for the new world order. Dead Forrest is there as well. He is sentient and actually quite pleased about his transformation.

Buffy is searching for Adam back at the cave where she last saw him. Spike is there, pretending that he's looking for "a little weekend getaway place." He's awkward in his attempts to encourage Buffy to go down into the Initiative all by herself, and she grows suspicious of his motives. As the discs decrypt themselves, Buffy calls Willow and gets the four—Xander, Giles, Willow, and Buffy herself—to meet and clear the air. Tara and Anya sit out the peace talks.

The four realize that Spike deliberately set them against each other. They also acknowledge that he was able to do so only because they had grown apart. As they talk, they compare notes and figure out Adam's plan to build a new race from dead humans and dead demons in an all-out war between Initiative commandos and captured HSTs.

Buffy, Xander, Willow, and Giles sneak into the Initiative via the elevator shaft and have a teary make-up session at the bottom, but Colonel McNamara and his men are waiting for them. Buffy demands that he listen to her but he's already convinced she and the others are anarchists; his opinion isn't changed when Giles explains that the object he's holding is a magic gourd. The power grid goes down and backup doesn't respond. Adam releases all the demons and the carnage begins.

Buffy tries to get McNamara to let her fight, but he orders two of his men to lock up the lot of them. As soon as McNamara is out of the room, Buffy clocks both of the guards left in charge of them. She leads the way and they battle their everything in their paths. Spike is wailing on demons as he looks for an escape route.

Willow jacks in, searching for Adam. She discovers evidence of a secret lab behind 314. That's where Buffy expects to battle Adam. Spike is now fighting the demons (and Adam) because he didn't deliver Buffy alone, so Adam won't take his chip out.

Xander, Willow, and Giles magically imbue Buffy with supernatural gifts surpassing her current Slayer abilities. Once he digs the chip out of his arm, Riley joins in, battling Maggie, Dr. Angleman, and Forrest. Speaking in Sumerian, Buffy is able to rip the power center—the heart—right out of Adam. The battle rages all around them, and Spike protects the Scooby Gang as they finish up.

Colonel McNamara is killed, but many other commandos get out, thanks to Buffy, Riley, and the others. After a debriefing about the incident, the military brass decide to "erase" the Initiative: one suit goes so far as to suggest they sow the ground with salt.

> Lindsay Crouse was disappointed when she discovered Maggie Walsh was going to be killed before the end of the season. As often happens on *Buffy,* that didn't prevent her return to the show.

QUOTE OF THE WEEK:

"This isn't your business. It's mine. You, the Initiative, the suits in the Pentagon... you're all messing with primeval forces you can't begin to understand. I'm the Slayer. And you're playing on my turf."

—Buffy, explaining the way things are to Colonel MacNamara.

THE AGONY AND THE ECSTASY:

Anya reassures Xander that no matter what, she loves him; Willow and Buffy tell each other that they love each other, then shower affection on Xander. The four original members of the Slayerettes essentially reunify when they combine to fight Adam. Riley is filled with regret at seeing the zombiefied Forrest.

POP-CULTURE IQ:

"It's Must-See TV."
Spike is exulting because Buffy and company have taken the bait and infiltrated the Initiative. "Must-See TV" was the tagline for NBC's Thursday lineup of prime-time shows, which originally included *Seinfeld* and *ER.*

"The Slayer has landed."
Spike informing Adam that Buffy's in the Initiative, is parodying the phrase, "The Eagle has landed," spoken as the lunar module *Eagle* touched down on the moon's surface in 1969.

"The little witch gives her the info and—pop—Alice heads down the rabbit hole."
Spike is referring to *Alice in Wonderland,* a nineteenth-century fantasy novel written by Lewis Carroll (Charles Dodgson). He's anticipating that Willow will decrypt the disks for Buffy.

"Look at little Nancy Drew."
Spike says this to Buffy as she puzzles out where Adam's gone.

"Of course. The Trojan Horse."
Giles realizes that Adam has amassed his demon army inside the Initiative—his followers have been allowing themselves to be captured. The Trojan Horse was an enormous wooden horse containing Greek soldiers; when the curious Trojans brought the horse into their city, the Greeks soldiers emerged attacking and successfully defeating the enemy.

CONTINUITY:

Maggie Walsh's mad plan to merge humanity and demonity is finally revealed. Spike's left with the chip in his head after the destruction of Adam. Forrest, Dr. Angleman, and Maggie Walsh return, though they are reanimated dead. Buffy and company rediscover their original affection for one another after deconstructing their various grievances from "The Yoko Factor." Xander asked Riley in "This Year's Girl" if he had a chip in his brain; turns out it was in his shoulder. The final battle occurs, and as usual, Sunnydale history will not record it.

FROM THE ORIGINAL TELEPLAY:

WILLOW: "I'm scaring you now, huh?"
TARA: "A little. In a good way. It's like a different kind of magic."
Willow and Tara discuss Willow's computer hacking skills in this exchange cut due to length.

WRITTEN AND DIRECTED BY: Joss Whedon. **GUEST STARS:** Kristine Sutherland as Joyce, Amber Benson as Tara, Mercedes McNab as Harmony, David Welles as The Cheese Man, Michael Harney as Man, George Hertzberg as Adam, Emma Caulfield as Anya, Seth Green as Oz, Armin Shimerman as Principal Snyder; with Sharon Ferguson as the Primitive, Phina Oruche as Olivia, Rob Boltin as Soldier.

THE PLOT THICKENS:

After the battle against Adam and his army, Buffy and her friends go to her house to de-tox by watching videos. Riley's off to testify on "the administration's own Bay of Mutated Pigs," with hopes of getting an honorable discharge.

Xander's vote for cinematic release is *Apocalypse Now,* but he has plenty of "chick-and-English guy" flicks in case it doesn't please. But they all fall asleep before the FBI warning is over, and each has a dream that speaks in some way of their personal condition. Each is attacked by a strange, savage woman, seeking their destruction via the same aspect of themselves that they used to enjoin magically with Buffy: Willow's spirit, Xander's heart, and Giles's intellect, or brain.

Willow dreams of being safe with Tara, although they appear, at times, to be in a remote desert. She is getting ready for drama class, and she runs into Oz. Despite the fact that this is her first class, Giles is directing their production of *Death of a Salesman*. Harmony is in it, as a vampire. Buffy is a flapper. Riley is a cowboy. Anya and Xander both appear. The theme of the dream seems to be that Willow has been playing a part and that acting is about hiding. Once the truth is known, she will be punished. Buffy rips off Willow's costume, revealing the outfit Willow wore the first time she met Buffy. Said truth appears to be that deep inside, she's still the frightened, insecure Willow she was back then.

While Oz and Tara whisper about her, Willow tries to present her book report. Xander is bored out of his mind, even when the Primitive attacks her and sucks the life right out of her, both in her dream and in reality.

Xander dreams that Joyce comes on to him, but he ends up in his basement instead of her bedroom. Then he's on a playground. Giles and Spike are on swings, and Spike declares that he's going to become a Watcher. Giles says that Spike is like a son to him. Xander acknowledges that these are both notions *he's* considered. Buffy refers to him as her big brother. Then he's in his ice-cream truck. Anya talks about getting back into vengeance while Tara and Willow, tarted up, kiss each other and invite him to come into the back of the truck with them. Everything is mixed up with *Apocalypse Now* and continually being sent back to his basement. Snyder tells him he's a whipping boy, and there are intimations that his time is running out. In his dream his father taunts him with the knowledge that he'll never get out of the basement; he hasn't the heart for it. Then he plunges his hand into Xander's chest; his hand becomes the hand of the Primitive, and he rips out his heart.

Giles, in his dream, faces the notion of the road less traveled, as Olivia appears pushing a baby carriage. Buffy appears in a childish sundress, urging him to let her have fun at a strange carnival. Spike (in black and white) has hired himself out as a sideshow attraction, striking scary vampire poses as the flashbulbs pop at him. Then they're at the Bronze, where Anya is doing standup. Giles performs a rock opera ("The Exposition Song") and pieces together that the spell they cast with Buffy has released some kind of primal evil. He tries to warn Buffy, but the Primitive appears and slices open his head.

Now it's Buffy's turn. She is standing in her bedroom. Anya, in her bed, urges her to wake up, to no avail. Tara appears, talking to Buffy as the Slayer makes the bed at seven-thirty, recalling that she and Faith just made it. Tara informs her that she doesn't know what she's doing. Buffy begins to look for her friends, and finds her mother living in the wall. She moves on, finding Adam, completely human, sitting opposite from Riley at a glass conference table inside the Initiative. They seem to be creating a new world order. A loudspeaker announces that the demons have escaped; Buffy begins covering herself in mud as she finds herself facing Tara and the Primitive. Tara translates for the Primitive. The woman is the First Slayer. She and Buffy battle furiously, Buffy insisting that she, unlike the First Slayer, is more than rage. Buffy is not alone and she does not sleep on a pile of bones. And she wants her friends back.

The Primitive stabs her over and over—in the enjoining, Buffy was the Hand, the physical vessel for all the magic—but Buffy does not accept that fate. She wakes up—as do the others, unhurt.

After discussing what happened, Buffy goes upstairs to use the bathroom. She tosses off the comment, "Yeah, well at least you all didn't dream about the guy with the cheese…don't know where the hell that came from…."

Of course, they all dreamed about the cheese man.

As Buffy stops on the threshold of her bedroom, Tara, in voice-over, promises Buffy once more that she has no idea what she is, and what's coming.

QUOTE OF THE WEEK:

"I wear the cheese. It does not wear me."

The Cheese Man, with slices of cheese on his head, addresses Giles during his dream.

THE AGONY AND THE ECSTASY:

In the dream, Riley and Buffy may or may not be together; Anya is talking about becoming a demon again, while Xander, who almost sleeps with Joyce, and with Tara and Willow together as well, continues to wind up in the basement. Willow and Tara are together, but Tara reveals that she is not all that she seems. Giles appears to be facing a choice: home and hearth, or something different?

POP-CULTURE IQ:

XANDER: "And I'm putting in a preemptive bid for <u>Apocalypse Now.</u> Heh?"
WILLOW: "Did you get anything less heart-of-Darknessy?"
Discussing the post-battle viewing selections for the evening. *Apocalypse Now* is based on the novella *The Heart of Darkness,* updated to take place during the Vietnam War.

CONTINUITY:

Joyce meets Riley "finally." Riley's future will be based on what Graham and the others testify about the Initiative. As dreams often are, this episode is fraught with threads referring back to past episodes and characters. Principal Snyder even makes an appearance, standing in for Marlon Brando during Xander's "Apocalyptic" nightmare. Willow's real-life decision to take drama represents a giant step forward in self-confidence; in "Nightmares," her worst nightmare was performing in front of an audience. But in her dream, she's the shy, unconfident Willow again, making a reference to Madame Butterfly, which was the opera she was forced to perform in, in "Nightmares." She's also dressed exactly the way she was when she first met Buffy. In Giles's dream, Olivia returns, as does Harmony. Buffy reminds us of Faith's strange conversation with her in "Graduation Day, Part Two," about seven-three-oh, and also about making the bed with Faith—which was actually Faith's dream.

FROM THE ORIGINAL TELEPLAY:

"I think they might be in trouble-danger."
Buffy talks a little wacky to her mom, in this line cut due to length.

From the script, a description of the Cheese Man:
[A skittish, balding, bespectacled little fellow in an old woolen suit. A voice not unlike Peter Lorre's.]

More stage directions:
[And at this moment, as Giles continues to speak, he is suddenly DUBBED INTO FRENCH. We can see him talking, but we can't understand a word any more than Xander can, unless we speak French, in which case la di da aren't we intellectual, I'm not Joe DICTIONARY, ALL RIGHT?]

GILES (French dubbing over): "—the house where we're all sleeping. All your friends are there having a wonderful time and getting on with their lives. The creature can't hurt you there."
XANDER: "What? Go where? I don't understand."
GILES (still dubbed): "Oh, for God's sake, this is no time for your idiotic games!"
[Anya rushes to them, worried. And dubbed.]
ANYA (with the dubbing): "Xander! You have to come with us now! Everybody's waiting for you!"
GILES (dubly): "Honey, I don't—I can't hear you...."
[Anya grabs his arm, starts dragging him.]
ANYA (dubbage): "It's not important. I'll take you there."

| --- | --- | --- |
STRETCH PRINCESS Wind-Up Records—1998's *Stretch Princess*	"Universe"	"THE FRESHMAN"
DAVID BOWIE Virgin—1969's *Space Oddity*	"Memory of a Free Festival"	"THE FRESHMAN"
THE MUFFS Honest Don's—1999's *Alert Today, Alive Tomorrow*	"I Wish That I Could Be You"	"THE FRESHMAN"
SPLENDID Warner-Chappell (not currently available in US)	"You and Me"	"THE FRESHMAN"
CHER Warner Bros.—1998's *Believe*	"Believe"	"LIVING CONDITIONS"
FOUR STAR MARY MSG Records—1997's *Four Star Mary*	"Pain"	"LIVING CONDITIONS"
FOUR STAR MARY MSG Records– 1999's *"Thrown to the Wolves"*	"Dilate"	"THE HARSH LIGHT OF DAY"
PSYCHIC RAIN Warner Bros.—2000's *Spun Out*	"Take Me Down"	"THE HARSH LIGHT OF DAY"
BIF NAKED Lava/Atlantic—1999's *I Bificus*	"Moment of Weakness"	"THE HARSH LIGHT OF DAY"
DEVIL DOLL Label—*Devil Doll*	"Faith in Love"	"THE HARSH LIGHT OF DAY"
BIF NAKED Lava/Atlantic—1999's *I Bificus*	"Anything"	"THE HARSH LIGHT OF DAY"
BIF NAKED Lava/Atlantic—1999's *I Bificus*	"Lucky"	"THE HARSH LIGHT OF DAY"
DOLLSHEAD Universal/MCA—1998's *Frozen Charlotte*	"It's Over, It's Under"	"THE HARSH LIGHT OF DAY"
28 DAYS Festival Music—*Kid Indestructible*	"LA Tune"	"FEAR, ITSELF"

SONGLIST

ARTIST	SONG TITLE	EPISODE NAME
THIRD GRADE TEACHER Third Grade Teacher Music—1998's *Greatest Hits, Vol. 1*	"Ow Ow Ow"	"FEAR, ITSELF"
VERBENA Capitol Records—1999's *Into the Pink*	"Pretty Please"	"FEAR, ITSELF"
PAUL TRUDEAU Kid Gloves Music—*Nu-Clear Sounds*	"People Will Talk"	"BEER BAD"
LAUREN CHRISTY (Not released at time of publication)	"Perfect Again"	"BEER BAD"
ASH DreamWorks—unknown	"I'm Gonna Fall"	"BEER BAD"
SMILE Label—*Girl Crushes Boy*	"The Best Years"	"BEER BAD"
THC (as "SHY") Midnight Music/Brain Surgery Music—*Adagio*	"Overfire"	"BEER BAD"
PAUL TRUDEAU Kid Gloves Music—198X's *Nu-Clear Sounds*	"I Can't Wait"	"BEER BAD"
LUCIOUS JACKSON **(featuring Emmylou Harris)** Capitol—1999's *Electric Honey*	"Ladyfingers"	"BEER BAD"
KIM FERRON Ferronious Punk—1999's *BtVS Soundtrack*	"Nothing But You"	"BEER BAD"
COLLAPSIS Cherry Entertainment/Virgin—2000's *Dirty Wake*	"Wonderland"	"BEER BAD"
PAUL TRUDEAU Kid Gloves Music—*Nu-Clear Sounds*	"It Feels Like I'm Dying"	"BEER BAD"
8STOPS7 Warner Bros.—1999's *In Moderation*	"Good Enough"	"WILD AT HEART"
THC (as "SHY") Midnight Music/Brain Surgery Music—*Adagio*	"Dip"	"WILD AT HEART"
THC (as "SHY") Midnight Music/Brain Surgery Music—*Adagio*	"Need To Destroy"	"WILD AT HEART"

ARTIST	SONG TITLE	EPISODE NAME
JAKE LEE RAU Keltone Records—1999's *Joy*	**"Welcome"**	"THE INITIATIVE"
MOBY BMG—1999's *Play*	**"Bodyrock"**	"THE INITIATIVE"
THAT DOG Polygram—1997's *Retreat from the Sun*	**"Never Say Never"**	"THE INITIATIVE"
FOUR STAR MARY MSG Records—1999's *Thrown to the Wolves*	**"Fate"**	"THE INITIATIVE"
DEADSTAR Festival Music—1999's *Somewhere Over the Radio*	**"Lights Go Down"**	"THE INITIATIVE"
BLINK 182 MCA—1999's *Enema of the State*	**"All the Small Things"**	"SOMETHING BLUE"
SUE WILLETT Monkey Jam Records—*Stories from My Head*	**"Night Time Company"**	"SOMETHING BLUE"
CAMILLE SAINT-SAÉNS BMG/RCA—1992's *Classics from the Crypt*	**"Danse Macabre"**	"HUSH"
THE HELLACOPTERS Sub Pop Records—1999's *Payin' the Dues*	**"Hey"**	"DOOMED"
ECHOBELLY Sony—1998's *Lustra*	**"Mouth Almighty"**	"DOOMED"
12 VOLT SEX Unknown	**"Over Divine"**	"A NEW MAN"
OTHER STAR PEOPLE A&M—1999's *Diamonds in the Belly of the Dog*	**"Then There's None"**	"A NEW MAN"
BLACK LAB 20th Century Fox—1999's *BtVS Soundtrack*	**"Keep Myself Awake"**	"THE I IN TEAM"
DELIRIUM EMD/Nettwerk—1997's *Karma*	**"Window to Your Soul"**	"THE I IN TEAM"

ARTIST	SONG TITLE	EPISODE NAME
LOU REED Warner Bros.—1989's *New York*	"Romeo Had Juliet"	"GOODBYE, IOWA"
NERF HERDER Honest Don's—2000's *How to Meet Girls*	"Vivian"	"WHO ARE YOU"
THE CURE Elektra—2000's *Bloodflowers*	"Watching Me Fall"	"WHO ARE YOU"
HEADLAND Lazy Bones Recordings—*Headland 2*	"Sweet Charlotte Rose"	"WHO ARE YOU"
ROYAL CROWN REVUE Dummy Recordings—1999's *Walk on Fire*	"Trapped (In the Web of Love)"	"SUPERSTAR"
ROYAL CROWN REVUE WITH BRAD KANE TCF Music Publishing—not currently available	"Serenade in Blue"	"SUPERSTAR"
ROYAL CROWN REVUE Dummy Recordings—1999's *Walk on Fire*	"Hey, Sonny"	"SUPERSTAR"
CROONER Kingpop Music	"Parker Posey"	"WHERE THE WILD THINGS ARE"
CAVIAR Available as MP3 at Caviar's web site: http://irenet.net/caviar/caviar.html	"I Thought I Was Found"	"WHERE THE WILD THINGS ARE"
FACE TO FACE Lady Luck Records	"The Devil You Know (God Is a Man)"	"WHERE THE WILD THINGS ARE"
LUMIROVA Lumirova 27—*Lightning Stroke of Persistent Splendor*	"Philo"	"WHERE THE WILD THINGS ARE"
FONDA Top Quality Records—1999's *The Invisible Girl*	"One of a Kind"	"WHERE THE WILD THINGS ARE"
ANTHONY STEWART HEAD (John King on guitar) Originally by The Who (1971's *Who's Next*). Not available	"Behind Blue Eyes"	"WHERE THE WILD THINGS ARE"
ANTHONY STEWART HEAD Originally by Lynyrd Skynyrd (1973's *Pronounced Leh-Nerd Skin-Nerd*). Not available	"Freebird"	"THE YOKO FACTOR"
ANTHONY STEWART HEAD W/CHRIS BECK and FOUR STAR MARY Not available	"The Exposition Song"	"RESTLESS"

CAST PROFILES

Buffy
the vampire slayer

Series Regulars

Sarah Michelle Gellar as Buffy Summers

**"'If you want something done, ask a busy person to do it.'
That's going to be my epitaph."**
— <u>ROLLING STONE</u>, APRIL 2, 1998

KNOWN FOR HER UNSTINTING WORK HABITS, Sarah worked on "The I in Team" despite being very ill with a fever. She burst into hacking coughs between takes, but nevertheless took time to mother co-star Marc Blucas, who was also sick. The question on everyone's mind was if she could make it through to her last day of work.

Of course she did.

Sarah Michelle Gellar has worked nonstop since she was four years old. She was discovered by a casting agent who "found" the precocious child in a restaurant. With no hesitation, Sarah proudly announced her name, age, and full address to the complete stranger. Joss had always been intrigued by the notoriety surrounded her Burger King commercial, because her dialogue required her to mention the competition—McDonald's—unfavorably by name. Sarah was personally included in the lawsuit McDonald's brought against its rival. He enjoyed finally meeting the little girl—now grown up—and after shuffling her around during auditions, realized he had found his perfect Buffy.

Sarah is very close to her mother, who has always supported her career. They struggled during the early years, joking that they ate pasta every night of the week except Fridays, which was Kraft Macaroni and Cheese night. Given her unusual life as a child actress, Sarah felt like an odd duck in school ("prom or audition?"), but all that changed when she transferred to the New York Professional Children's school because all the students had weird schedules, choosing between auditions and the prom, commercials, and shooting TV shows or movies.

Yet she is appreciative of her luck and her success. "I've been so blessed. I should pinch myself" (as quoted in *Scene*).

The Emmy Award-winning actress (for Kendall Hart in *All My Children*), has appeared on the covers of dozens of magazines, from *TV Guide, Mademoiselle,* and *Teen People,* to *Rolling Stone.* One of *People* magazine's Most Beautiful People for 1998, that year she signed to become Maybelline's first celebrity spokeswoman since Linda Carter in the late 1970s. She also received a Blockbuster Entertainment Award for Best Supporting Actress for her role in *I Know What You Did Last Summer.*

In *Rolling Stone,* Alyson Hannigan says of her, "She knows everything. She works so many hours, doesn't

> Sarah first worked with Brad Kane [Tucker] in 1989, on *Girl Talk.* "The Prom" took place ten years later.

have a break, and is still on top of everything." Alyson wonders aloud if maybe Sarah has a chip in her head....(Perhaps Joss will do that next season).

Outside of *Buffy*, Sarah's hosted *Saturday Night Live* twice. She also appeared in the *SNL 25th Anniversary Special* in a skit with James Van Der Beek. Her May 2000 surprise appearance to introduce Britney Spears (who was hosting as well as appearing as the musical guest) caused a stir throughout *Buffy* fandom; the East Coast fans quickly emailed the West Coast fans via the *Buffy* Posting Board, so that they could catch Sarah when the show aired later that night. It happened again later that month, when Jackie Chan guest-hosted.

Sarah has done voice work, as Gwendy Doll in *Toy Soldiers* and in an episode of the *King of the Hill* TV series. She's appeared on the *Tonight Show with Jay Leno*, *Late Night with David Letterman*, and *Regis and Kathie Lee*. She made an appearance on *VH1 Divas Live '99* and at the *MTV Video Music Awards*.

She's also done her share of TV movies, including *Beverly Hills Family Robinson* (1977) *A Woman Named Jackie* (1991). She was in *An Invasion of Privacy* (1983), and *Over the Brooklyn Bridge* (1984) and was credited as Sarah Gellar in *High Stakes* (1989). Her most recent feature films include *I Know What You Did Last Summer*, *Scream 2*, *Simply Irresistible*, and *Cruel Intentions*. She is uncredited in *She's All That*, playing a girl in the cafeteria. The *Buffy* company was filming at Torrance High the same day, and she put in a cameo.

Accolades have followed all the hard work: her Emmy, MTV Awards for Best Female Performance as well as Best Kiss (*Cruel Intentions*), a Blockbuster Entertainment Award for *I Know What You Did Last Summer*, and one of the first annual Teen Choice Awards (for her role on *Buffy*), *TV Guide* awards (including magazine honors such as being named one of *TV Guide*'s "20 Great Faces" as well as the show's innumerable honors at the TV Guide Awards annual ceremony), and magazine awards too numerous to mention.

Despite her incredible work schedule, Sarah still puts time in for good causes such as flying to the Dominican Republic between Seasons Three and Four to work for Habitat for Humanity. Ever since she started working on *All My Children*, she has donated money to charities. She says that her mother taught her to give back, and she does.

As busy as she is, she's an avid reader. She collects antique children's books and she's taken cooking classes. She loves to barbecue and she's a confirmed omnivore, stating, "A little steak, a little hamburger never hurt anybody."

Sarah says of *Buffy*, "The thing is, with this show, you can identify with so many of the characters. You really take an interest in what's happening to each and every one of them. You don't have to be a rebel to be cool."

She's slated to appear in several upcoming films, including *Harvard Man* and *The It Girl*, and of course will continue her role as the Slayer in Season Five of *Buffy*.

Nicholas Brendon as Xander Harris

"Death can really up the ratings!"
—SPECTRUM #17

OF HIS BUFFY CHARACTER, Nicholas Brendon says, "I think he's a kid who's in touch with his emotions." The same could be said of Nicholas, who has managed to stay grounded despite having a short resume before landing a leading role in one of the hottest series on TV. At a recent appearance at a posting board party, he obligingly posed with fans and signed autographs before socializing with his guests and fellow *Buffy* co-stars.

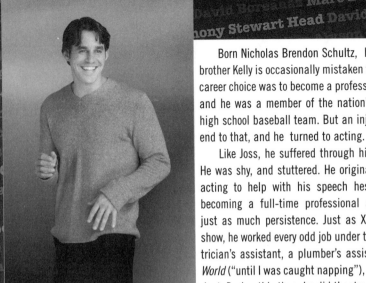

Born Nicholas Brendon Schultz, he is a twin, and his brother Kelly is occasionally mistaken for him. His first career choice was to become a professional athlete, and he was a member of the nation's top-rated high school baseball team. But an injury put an end to that, and he turned to acting.

Like Joss, he suffered through high school. He was shy, and stuttered. He originally started acting to help with his speech hesitation, but becoming a full-time professional actor required just as much persistence. Just as Xander has on the show, he worked every odd job under the sun. He was an electrician's assistant, a plumber's assistant, a production assistant on *Dave's World* ("until I was caught napping"), a script delivery boy, and a pre-med student. During this time, he did theatre work to keep acting. He, (just like David Boreanaz), appeared in a national spot for Clearasil, landed a one-shot appearance on *Married with Children* (1987); a single day of work on *The Young and the Restless* (1993), and a role in *Children of the Corn III* (1994). His frustration level was sometimes almost unbearable as he scrounged for enough loose change to buy a burrito. He even lived for a time in a condemned apartment at the epicenter of the famous Northridge earthquake.

Now, he has the luxury of admitting that his official resume was "exaggerated." He had claimed, for example, that he had had a recurring gig on *The Young and the Restless*. No matter; talent will out: the producers finalized his casting as Xander in a matter of days after his audition.

With the prominence accorded him from his second billing on *Buffy,* work is pouring in. Aside from photo shoots in *Young Miss, Teen People*, and other magazines, commercials for Barq's Root Beer, guest appearances at Buffy Posting Board parties, comic book and media conventions, and interviews in *Rolling Stone*, he is currently starring in the film *Psycho Beach Party,* which has been described by E! Online as "a mix of '60s beach movies and '70s slasher films—with the scares and humor the *Scream* generation thrown in." Lauren Ambrose, who co-starred with Seth Green in *Can't Hardly Wait,* and Kathleen Robertson of *Beverly Hills 90120* also appear. Nicholas's role is entitled "Starcat," a nod to *Gidget* boy Moondoggie.

Though for the record he states, "It's all Joss Whedon," Nicholas has been known to ad-lib on set, as does Jim Carrey, an actor whose work he admires. While WG2 was observing production of "The I in Team," he added, "I loved you!" to the scene in which Spike appeals to Giles and the gang to get the tracer out of his back.

Nicholas, who says Xander doesn't learn, but does experience, has also done his own stunts, including falling down staircases and being set on fire—a feat he shares with James Marsters, who went for a burn of his hand. This all started with an accidental back roll in "Nighmares." He has also made Xander famous for his dance stylings.

When he accepted the award for *Buffy* as Best Genre Network TV Series at the 1998 Saturn Awards, Nicholas thanked his wife—even though he didn't have one. "I'm not married or engaged or even seeing anybody, but I am holding an award. And this is what you're supposed to do."

Nicholas and Kelly are identical; Kelly is often mistaken for his brother on the street. Some young fans even threw French fries at Kelly once when he kept insisting he wasn't Nicky, he wasn't Xander, he was Nicholas Brendon's twin in his own right. For a period of time, Kelly had his hair dyed blond to avert the confusion. On hiatus, Nicholas usually grows a goatee, while Kelly remains clean-shaven, which resurrects the case of mistaken identity. Kelly also worked on *Buffy* for a time as a production assistant. He has a small but noticeable part in an episode of *City Guys*.

258

Pondering the success of *Buffy*, he says, "We're kind of a pathfinder in terms of TV." He tips his hat to Joss and the writers, pointing out that Joss has been nominated for an Oscar, and wonders—as do many critics and viewers—why Emmys for other than technical areas such as makeup continue to elude the stalwart *Buffy* cast and crew. But as he points out, ". . . you just never know what's going to happen in this wacky, wacky, wacky town."

> "Things are so perfect right now in terms of the show that it blows my mind away. It's like, how did I get that lucky?"

Alyson Hannigan as Willow Rosenberg

"We fight the demons. And, you know, we also hang out at the mall."
—TV GUIDE, JANUARY 30, 1999

FLAME-HAIRED ALYSON HANNIGAN is as witty as the character she plays on TV, and just as thoughtful. She was careful to cut out and bring a review to a booksigning. (Which was also the first occasion Todd McIntosh turned her into a vampire. This led to her occasional transformation into "Vamp Willow." She recently told *YM* magazine that the best thing she's done as a TV witch was when good Willow had to impersonate Vamp Willow, dressed up in sexy leather duds.) She includes a sweet smiley face in her autographs. She's partial to animals and children. *E!Online* asked for her professional opinion of the witches in *The Wizard of Oz*, she says, "Glinda had the love of the Munchkins— she rocks!"

Alyson's a seasoned actor. (And a canny one: in her published diary for E!Online of her experiences in the Pro/Celebrity Race at the 2000 Toyota Grand Prix of Long Beach, she writes of her competitors: "Plus, George has one more advantage: No actor in his right mind is going to beat George Lucas right in the middle of the *Star Wars* casting." However, she did.) Like Sarah Michelle Gellar, Alyson began appearing in commercials when she was four years old. Her first acting job was a print ad for Delta, and in the early 1990's she appeared in TV ads for Six Flags, Oreos, McDonald's, and Mylanta.

After her move to California at the age of eleven, success came quickly. She appeared as Jessie Mills in the feature film *My Stepmother is an Alien* (1988). Seth Green had a small role as Fred Glass, Jessie's boyfriend; little did they know then that, nearly a decade later, the duo would portray a couple onscreen again. In between *Stepmother* and *Buffy*, Seth acted on an episode of *Free Spirit*, on which Alyson was a regular (1989). The show dealt with a witch playing nanny to a family.

Other television parts also rolled in. When the television series *The Torkelsons* was revamped into *Almost Home*, Alyson appeared as Samantha (Sam), best-friend-turned-girlfriend to main character Gregory. Sam appeared in two episodes: "The Dance" and "Hot Ticket." In addition, Alyson worked in a 1998 episode of *Roseanne* ("Like, a New Job"), an episode of *Picket Fences* in 1992 ("To Forgive is Divine") as well as an episode of the short-lived *George*, in 1993.

When *Buffy the Vampire Slayer* was morphed into a television series and the scripts were going around, Alyson tried out for the part of Willow, but she was not initially cast. Riff Regan portrayed Willow in the half hour program or "presentation" that was essentially a solicitation piece to sell the series to a network or cable channel. The other main cast members were all there:

Sarah Michelle Gellar, Charisma Carpenter, Nicholas Brendon, Anthony Stewart Head, and David Boreanaz. The only other major difference was the original casting of Principal Flutie.

Once the show was purchased by the WB, the recasting began. Alyson tried to get her foot in the door, again and again. It took over half a dozen auditions before the last round. The final three girls consisted of Joss Whedon's top pick, the WB's pick, and Alyson. She stumbled over some of the 'Net Girl words and technological references and thought she'd blown it.

She got the call about a week later.

Later, Joss Whedon told her that it was her spunk, her energy, her connection with the others that won her the part. Alyson chose to make Willow's innocence just that: innocence. Not coy, not flirty, not faux. She felt the character saw the silver lining on every cloud, and she played it as such. As she told us during an interview, she added a hopeful cadence to her reading of her lines about Xander having stolen her Barbie: "But I got most of it back!"

A devoted animal person, Alyson has a number of small pets—including her beloved Jack Russell terrier, who has spent many a workday in Alyson's trailer—that could fit into the signature backpacks Willow wore back at Sunnydale High. In fact, Jansport backpacks added Alyson to their list of featured celebrities for their "back...pack" two-page ads. On the philanthropy front, she's delighted that her celebrity can help her make a difference: in addition to her 2000 Toyota Grand Prix participation, she has appeared at Make-A-Wish Foundation events, and in the spring of 2000, an ad supporting Breast Cancer research featuring Alyson and other WB actresses began appearing in magazines.

Despite her heavy workload on *Buffy*, she's continued her work in film. For *Dead Man on Campus*, MTV created a special promotion entitled *Cram Session*. The event was a briefing about the *Dead Man on Campus* a few weeks before its premiere in August 1998. Alyson was the hostess, staying in character as Lucy.

In 1999, Alyson played Michelle in the popular film *American Pie*, continuing her trend of playing nerds and geeks. Defending—and defining—Willow, she points out that Willow has the confidence booster of being best friends with the coolest girl in school, even if Buffy is not the most popular. Then she contrasts Willow with Michelle, her character in *American Pie*, who is such a geek that she doesn't even realize it. She also highlights the strangeness of school culture: when she herself was in the band in junior high, band participation did not automatically bestow nerdhood.

She and Sarah Michelle Gellar continue to have a strong relationship, made most visible during Sarah's first guest host appearance on *Saturday Night Live*. At the end of the show, she held up a hand-made sign that said, "I miss you, Aly!" They go for manicures together and Alyson got to spoof Sarah's kiss with Selma Blair on MTV's 1999 Movie Awards.

Alyson also has two movies slated for a 2000 release: *Boys and Girls* and *Beyond City Limits*. The former, starring Freddie Prinze Jr., reteams her with *American Pie*'s Jason Biggs, while the latter includes *Buffy/Angel* actor Alexis Denisof. In *Beyond City Limits*, Alyson tackles the role of a recovering heroin addict.

She's happy with her life and her work, saying "I wouldn't trade this part [on *Buffy*] for anything."

260

Alyson Hannigan appeared with two other Buffy actors in the same Picket Fences episode. PF regular Kelly Connell played Bug Man Norman Pfeister in "What's My Line, Parts One and Two," while Jordan Baker would become Sheila Rosenberg, Willow's mother in "Gingerbread."

Before they were on Buffy, Alyson and, Amber Benson met through a mutual friend at a party. The friend became a witch years later when she joined the cast of Sabrina: the Teenage Witch.

Vamp Willow scolds Vamp Xander for nearly torching her hair with a match in "The Wish." This relays back to Dead Man on Campus, when Lucy's hair catches on fire.

Charisma Carpenter as Cordelia Chase

" . . . [I]t's nurturing and fun and I'm happy."
—<u>PARADE</u>, MARCH 2000

AFTER GRADUATING HIGH SCHOOL, Charisma worked in her father's restaurant, and, later, a video store. Her plan was to fund a college education in preparation for becoming an English teacher.

She moved to Los Angeles the day of the riots of 1992. There, she landed a job at Mirabelle, a restaurant on Sunset Boulevard, where she was encouraged so often to try her hand at acting that she decided to test the waters. She landed several commercials, including one for Secret Ultra Dry. This enabled her to audition and work on her craft with fewer financial pressures.

Following work on one episode of *Baywatch*, she auditioned for Aaron Spelling's new venture, *Malibu Shores* and won the role of Ashley Green. Her screen test for *Buffy* followed a day of work on the primetime soap, and she was an hour and a half late for the producer's meeting.

As we all know, she was ultimately cast as "Queen C," and Charisma confesses now to some trepidation about playing "another bitch," but as her agent gently reminded her: "You have to be well known before you become typecast."

Charisma wasn't in every episode during the first season, but she was considered a main character, with her name in the opening credits. Popular girl Cordelia Chase at first befriended Buffy but disapproved of her hanging with "losers." She was the May Queen, the cheerleader, everything Buffy once was but could no longer be. She stayed on the periphery until the close of the season threw her into the game of good versus evil.

By Season Two, she was in the thick of things, dating Xander and always adding her two cents' worth. Nicholas Brendon told *Spectrum* that Charisma "has great timing with her jokes...and it's nice to work off of somebody like that."

Though she developed a penchant for skydiving that she passed on to Alyson Hannigan, her off-hours are usually taken up by memorizing her lines, doing yoga, and being with her family and dogs. Her grueling schedule requires her to rest and stay focused. As she has remarked, "Dancing comes easy, and acting does not."

When plans for the *Angel* series surfaced during Season Three, Charisma was optimistic and excited about the impending project. "Actually, I'm looking forward to it with open arms and an open heart," she told the *Buffy the Vampire Slayer Fan Club* magazine. She didn't mind the idea of sharing screen time with David Boreanaz, calling him a "really talented actor," and "a wonderful lead actor," as well. She added that on *Buffy*, she didn't have "the pleasure of working with him too often." As one of three main characters, and the only female, she's had more airtime on *Angel*.

Charisma has not actively pursued other acting projects during hiatus, wanting to take time to spend with her family and friends.

> Charisma performed the audio version of the *Buffy* novel, *Immortal.*

> On *Malibu Shores*, Charisma and Greg Vaughan played boyfriend and girlfriend. They were romantically involved once more on the episode "Reptile Boy" when he portrayed fraternity boy Richard Anderson.

261

David Boreanaz as Angel

"'Redemption is difficult,' creator and executive producer Joss Whedon says. 'It takes a long time, and there isn't always a goal in sight. You just have to keep trying to do right, and if you make it easy [in dramatic terms], that's kind of a false hope. The thing about [Angel] is that even when it doesn't look like there's a light at the end of the tunnel, he's going to keep digging, just because that's who he is.'"

—TV GUIDE, OCTOBER, 1999

IT'S WELL KNOWN by *Buffy* and *Angel* fans that David Boreneaz was a virtual unknown when he was spotted by an industry professional walking his dog, Bertha Blue. Marcia Shulman, the original casting director for *Buffy*, and now head of casting for all of Fox TV production, wrote "He's the guy!" on her call log the moment he walked into her office.

He is quite a guy. He's lent his celebrity to causes such as the Make-A-Wish Foundation. In answer to a posting-board question about playing a character who occasionally becomes completely evil, he says "I enjoy playing evil. But the transition was difficult because it was hard watching Buffy cry." He also says that the best part about fame is that he can tell other people how much he appreciates the support his parents have given him. Once, while he was being interviewed on television, they were nearly in tears seated in the audience as he expressed his profound gratitude to them.

Pre-Angelic jobs: parking lot attendant, props department. He never worked as a waiter, which is a typical aspiring actor job.

Inspired by his father, Philadelphia weatherman Dave Roberts, David graduated from Ithaca College's Department of Communications in 1992. However, like Nicholas Brendon and Marc Blucas, he first had dreams of turning pro in his chosen sport—in David's case, football—until an injury sidelined him.

Before he became Angel, he was a virtual unknown. His first acting job was a beer commercial. His largest credit was on *Married...with Children* in one episode entitled "Movie Show" on April 11,1993. After *Married*, his next two roles went uncredited: in *Aspen Extreme* (1993) and *Best of the Best II* (also 1993), and he was "Vampire's Victim" in *Macabre Pair of Shorts* (1996).

But the qualities Marcia Shulman saw in him quickly propelled David from what was supposed to be a one-shot part into the lead in the spinoff series, *Angel*. In Season One of *Buffy*, Angel's popularity promoted him to recurring character status, there to lurk and warn. As things heated up between him and Buffy, he became a Season Two cast regular. At the end of the season, the WB announced publicly that the *Angel* spinoff was scheduled for the 1999–2000 season. In the Season Three finale, Angel bid adieu to his Buffy, but there were three crossover episodes in Season Four, with Buffy and Angel visiting each others' shows ("a logistical nightmare," Joss Whedon notes).

David has landed on the covers of innumerable magazines. He was on *People* magazine's list of The 50 Most Beautiful People for 1999. An unofficial biography of him has been published and he presented at the 1999 *TV Guide* Awards. Yet when in public and surrounded by adoring fans, he remains pleasant and generous, lending credence to his statement, "You define your existence by being truthful to yourself." He visibly brightens when the conversation turns to his two dogs (who, as of this writing, are doing quite well, thank you).

When asked about other work, he points out that he's still trying to find the balance in his life with the grueling pace he already has (referring to it as "strenuous," but adds, "Pressure is something you bring upon yourself.") and he recently turned down a film because he wanted to go to South Africa. He comments, "I learned just to take things for what they are, work hard and be loose."

Words to live—and be undead—by.

Seth Green as Oz

ALYSON HANNIGAN: "What about if you could have lunch with one person, dead or alive, who would it be?"

SETH GREEN: "Somebody who could make a good lunch, I guess."

—AS QUOTED IN <u>TWIST</u>, APRIL 1999

AS WRY AND DROLL as the character he plays on *Buffy*, Seth Ghessel Green was six when he knew acting was what he wanted to do with his life. The place: summer camp. The production: *Hello, Dolly!* Backed by his supportive parents, he landed his first film role in *Hotel New Hampshire* with Jodie Foster.

Since then, the natural redhead has appeared, at last count, in thirty-eight films and TV series as a cast regular, and guest-starred on over two dozen TV shows. As a cast regular on *Buffy*, he still found the time to log on to the Net during his workdays, a practice much appreciated by his large fan following. ("Thank God for ninth-grade typing class!" he wrote on the official Buffy Posting Board). The affable actor is still approachable and friendly, maintaining his composure despite the intense fan interest in him and his work.

An enthusiastic toy collector, he sculpted figures of his fellow cast regulars on *Buffy* for their first Christmas together (raising expectations for the following Christmas, he realized, somewhat ruefully), and wrote a guest column for *ToyFare* magazine before he himself was immortalized in toy form as Scott Evil and Oz. Ironically, his article was about "the hunt" that compels the dedicated collector to drive all over the Los Angeles basin, in search of that elusive figure necessary to round out a collection. That must be easier to handle than wearing the werewolf costumes sculpted for him by Optic Nerve and enhanced by the makeup and hair departments. Of his lupine attire, he wrote on the official Buffy Posting Board: "The suit is still very uncomfortable, but I like being the one in it. It's better than the hair on my skin thing, but still required a very intense eighteen-hour makeup start to finish, high-energy day."

From early appearances in features such as *Radio Days* (1986) and *Airborne* (1993), he continued to garner a lot of feature work (*Can't Hardly Wait, Idle Hands,* and *Enemy of the State,* to name a few), until he found himself in the two Austin powers movies (1997 and 1998.) More features are on the way: Dennis Hopper and John Malkovich share screen time with Seth in the upcoming *Knockaround Guys.* In *Attic Expectations,* Seth portrays Douglas, a mental patient. In *Stonebrook,* he and another college roommate get involved in con games in order to pay off his roommate's tuition.

He became so busy in films that on *Buffy,* Oz left Willow to seek a cure for his werewolf curse. The relationship between Seth and Joss remains very cordial, as when Seth dropped by the lot at Christmas time, a rare comic book in hand for Joss's fabled comic collection. His hair was dyed raven blue-black. Fans of his onscreen persona were likewise delighted by his reappearance in "New Moon Rising" and "Restless." Fans speculate on Oz's fate as Season Five begins production.

In addition to his feature work, Seth has had a long and varied career in TV. Notable TV guest appearances include *The X-Files, Cybill, Mad About You* (in white tails and singing!) and *The Drew Carey Show.* Seth was also a regular on *Good and Evil, The Byrds of Paradise,* and *Temporarily Yours* prior to *Buffy.* You can also hear his voice in various animated series or kids' shows. Seth is the voice of Nelson on *Batman Beyond* (1999-present), Chris on *The Family Guy,* and the title character in *100 Deeds for Eddie McDowd.*.

Of the other two partners in his production company, Breckin Meyer and Ryan Phillipe, he says in *Twist*: "We're all so dedicated, we inspire each other." Inspiration and hard work have equaled success in yet another area of the entertainment business: Disney has optioned a college comedy, *Scorned,* with a story by Seth and a childhood friend, Hugh Sterbakou. The duo will produce the film with others.

Seth's come a long way from so humiliating his prom date with his fashion sense—wearing Converse sneakers with his tux—that she never spoke to him again, to becoming an international TV and movie celebrity. He stays centered, saying of himself that if he weren't where he is today, he'd probably be working in a bookstore, dreaming of becoming a rock star. However, as his taste in seventies music tends toward the *Sesame Street* disco oeuvre, perhaps it's just as well that fate has sent him down another path....

Barely into her teens, Alyson Hannigan spotted Seth while she and her mother were driving into the studio at 20th Century Fox. She cried, "That's the kid from *Amazing Stories!*" They have portrayed boyfriend and girlfriend in two supernaturally-based projects: *My Stepmother Is an Alien* and *Buffy.* Seth also played a student in a classroom in one episode of *Free Spirit,* in which Alyson was a regular.

Before she was Tara, Amber Benson was Stoned Girl/ Stephanie in *Can't Hardly Wait.* Most of her original scenes were with Seth. They share a small photo on the back of the video box. The duo was reunited in "New Moon Rising." Seth's part in the original *Buffy the Vampire Slayer* feature was cut, but a photograph of him appeared on the back of the videocassette rental box.

264

Marc Blucas as Riley Finn

Marc Blucas told us, "This will be short. There's not that much to say about me."

WG2: "Please tell us about how your character started. When you got your first job on <u>Buffy</u>, did you know you were going to be a cast regular?"

MB: "No. I did not. I had originally signed on to do three episodes and there were hints at the hopes of it becoming something more, but that remained to be seen."

WG2: "So you might have been like another Parker?"

MB: "Yeah, I could have very easily been another one-night stand. I guess you could put it that way. But yeah, it started out just as three."

WG2: "When did you find out that you were a cast regular?"

MB: "I guess it would have been the day after the third episode wrap. So it was like on the seventeenth of September, that evening, I knew. Yeah, it made for a great day. I got it at like six P.M. You can't get that call in the morning. You have to wait all day to find out. At least it came on Friday and they didn't make me wait the weekend."

WG2: "Who called you?"

MB: "You know how it goes. It goes through your representation, so my manager did. When I initially got the job, though, Joss called me, which I loved."

WG2: "You were at a barbecue?"

MB: "Yeah, it was a cookout with my friends in Pennsylvania. I just loved the fact that he didn't go through my representation. The fact that he wanted the thrill of giving the gift and getting my reaction. It was great!"

WG2: "Who was the first person you told, once you knew?"

MB: "Well, since I was at a party with my friends [there were about thirty people there], I looked at my best friend who was in the middle of a card game at the time and I didn't want to announce it. He knew I was waiting and I just mouthed it to him that I got it, and he immediately folded. God love him, I hope he didn't have a full house or anything good. But he immediately folded and came over."

WG2: "What are the differences in being a recurring character and a cast regular? How is your life different?"

MB: "Job security! For a short time. In all honesty, there hasn't been much difference with the attitudes on the set. From the day I stepped on here until right now, people have treated me so great and have been so welcoming to me. From the people at the highest end to the people at the lowest end, and I would be on the lower end. But they really have, they've been really, really great. There is not a better job in town right now. I have the best job going!"

WG2: "We were watching your love scenes this morning in the editing bay."

MB: "I didn't go in to look at some of those. What was your opinion?"

WG2: "Wow! The steam was rising off our heads! An editor said, 'I surely wake up early to get here as soon as I can.' She says they're very, very hot. They're beautiful."

265

MB: "Great!"

WG2: "How did you feel doing that?"

MB: "Whether it's that kind of scene or a scene where Sarah and I are fighting a demon, that girl is one of the most professional people on the planet. She has a way of not only setting you at ease but also getting you in the right mental framework. Those can be hard days if you don't approach it with a light tone and even be a little giddy at times, because I'm a hundred pounds heavier than she is and there's gonna be some elbows and some knees in places that are just odd. Be it because you're laying on top of each other, or not to get in someone's light, or be aware of where the camera is. So if you can have fun with it but at the same time not lose your passion and intensity, that's important. And she's been there and she held my hand through the whole thing, literally and figuratively. Hopefully the scenes came out a success. If they did, it's because she gets the drill, not me."

Marti Noxon named Buffy's new boyfriend after Finn, her black Labrador.

WG2: "What's your favorite part of your role?"

MB: "This is gonna sound like I'm trying to be Captain Positive, but you can pretty much be anywhere and do anything if you're around the right people. The cast and the crew that I'm around, they make the day fun regardless of what kind of scene you do, or how intense; or how fun, or how late at night and cold it is, and if you're in a ski mask and night vision goggles that you can't see out of, we have a fun time doing it and that makes your day. The best part about this job is I really feel that whether or not I get killed off tomorrow, I'll walk away with a handful of friends and that's what's really nice."

WG2: "What's something that surprised you about <u>Buffy</u>? What was something that you assumed that didn't turn out to be, as far as your life as an actor goes?"

MB: "This is my first big consistent job on hour-long television, and more than anything else, the speed threw me for a loop for a while. Not in that we shoot seven pages a day. That of course was a new thing. But the speed at how fast relationships are forced or pushed or pulled or just manipulated a little bit, and so that took some getting used to.

"Especially Sarah—Buffy just got out of this huge thing with Angel and then this quickie with Parker, and she's been back and forth a hundred times, and now trying to build something else with someone new, especially a new cast member makes it that much more of a difficult transition on everyone. But I'd have to say the speed of things. The double meaning there. Both the speed at how fast we shoot and the speed at how fast the relationship has to move."

WG2: "What was your very first job you got paid for as an actor?"

MB: "It was the movie <u>Eddie</u> with Whoopi Goldberg, a movie about the New York Knicks. I had just gotten back from playing professional basketball, and I was getting ready to go to law school, when our sports information director where I went to college (Wake Forest University in Winston-Salem, North Carolina) called me and said they're casting a movie in Charlotte, North Carolina and they need a baby-faced white kid that can play basketball and I'm like, 'Hello, I've got one of those requirements. I don't know which one but...' I went down and read for it, and I ended up getting a great part that ended up being changed from a white guy to a black guy. But they kept me on the movie, and I worked for eight weeks on it and just had a very small role but that's where it first got its hooks in me. That was the first one. Then a couple of TV movies followed and then <u>Pleasantville</u> and <u>The Sixties,</u> the NBC miniseries. And then this is by far the best and biggest break that I've had."

James Marsters as Spike

We interviewed James Marsters in his trailer.
He was already in makeup and costume.

WG2: "When did you find out you were going to be a cast regular?"

JM: "Early in last year's pilot season. Maybe May, probably earlier than that, possibly March or April. Sarah convinced Joss that if he wanted me, he should scoop me up before someone else did. I was just about to go in to be seen for <u>Harsh Realm</u> when we finalized the deal. So having worked on <u>Millennium</u>, I was very excited to get back in, to actually meet Chris Carter, which was fun. But I got the better end of the deal here."

WG2: "Was there any kind of change in working style or interactions or anything, between being a recurring character and a guest star and being a cast regular with the rest of the cast?"

JM: "No, the dynamics are exactly the same that they have been before. If anything I am still thinking too much like a guest. I need to understand that I can go and talk to production when I need to. That used to not be my place and I have that entrée now and I need to know that I can use it. My trailer's bigger, but that's basically the only change. It would be frightful to me if I thought that things had changed. I'm proud of my work ethic, and I would hope that would remain constant."

WG2: "Do you have any pets?"

JM: "Yes. I have an old cat who behaves like a kitten, named Zachary. Still gets in fights and chases his tail in the bathtub. Got him in the Bronx at the SPCA. It was the only cat that would not go back in the cage. Scratched the hell out of me!"

WG2: "With Spike there is very dark humor, and his interactions with Dru were always really very funny. But you almost have another layer of humor now because you're so thwarted. Is there anything you're doing differently as an actor to prepare your scenes? When we read it, or when it's on TV, it's really, really hilarious how frustrated he is. Because he is evil, but he can't do anything, and we're all just dying. When you were signed on as a cast regular, did you know this was going to happen to Spike?"

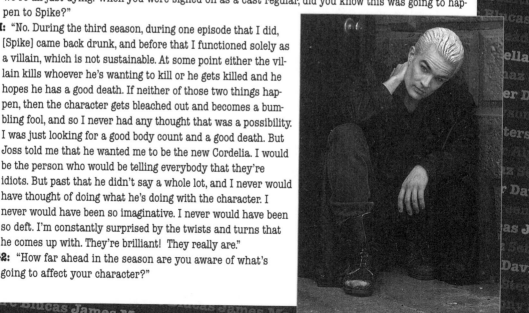

JM: "No. During the third season, during one episode that I did, [Spike] came back drunk, and before that I functioned solely as a villain, which is not sustainable. At some point either the villain kills whoever he's wanting to kill or he gets killed and he hopes he has a good death. If neither of those two things happen, then the character gets bleached out and becomes a bumbling fool, and so I never had any thought that was a possibility. I was just looking for a good body count and a good death. But Joss told me that he wanted me to be the new Cordelia. I would be the person who would be telling everybody that they're idiots. But past that he didn't say a whole lot, and I never would have thought of doing what he's doing with the character. I never would have been so imaginative. I never would have been so deft. I'm constantly surprised by the twists and turns that he comes up with. They're brilliant! They really are."

WG2: "How far ahead in the season are you aware of what's going to affect your character?"

JM: "I'm aware of what we're shooting today. I'm aware of this script this week and past that I don't know anything. I was very relieved to find out that I could fight demons. Fight anybody."

WG2: "As Spike's changed and matured with his tragic love…"

JM: "I don't know that he's matured yet. I think he's still very bitter about that! I think that Spike is an immature vampire. He's an adolescent. At 120 years old he's still quite young, and has only been in one relationship as a vampire. I kept wanting Dru just to grab him and say, 'Spike, I'm with Angel now, grow up! We don't have the luxury of jealousy. Relationships come and go over the course of centuries, and you're just gonna have to get used to that.' So I think that he has yet to kind of get there. I just wanted to go kick Angel's ass—again."

WG2: "Is your workload different since you became a cast regular or is it about the same?"

JM: "It's a bit heavier. In general most of the time in Season Two I would shoot about one day an episode, and I wasn't in every episode. Kind of every other episode, so my days were quite light, and now I shoot three to four days out of the week."

WG2: "Do you have a favorite moment from Season Three? Something that came off really well, that you were really going, 'Yeah I did that right!' or 'That's really neater than I thought it would be when I read this?'"

JM: "I liked lighting my hand on fire. I liked that a lot! I was proud of that stunt! They were rehearsing and we were going through all manner of machinations trying to figure out how to place my hand so a stunt person could come in a do the bit, and I volunteered for it and they were very kind—or very cruel—to let me do it."

WG2: "We know you could feel the heat, but could you feel any pain at all?"

JM: "Oh, yeah! What I discovered is that stuntmen, in fact, get hurt all the time. It's just that they never admit it. Ask a stuntman who's just had his rib broken if he's okay and he will say he's just rosy. So I assumed, well, you know, its one of those gags and nothing can happen and was so cocky about it that I let the burn go too long on both takes, and ended up pretty badly burned.

"I flew off to do a movie in Missouri two days later and showed up on the set with like nine dime-sized blisters all over my hand, which the director loved, because I was supposed to be a workman, and it made my hands look pretty gross."

WG2: "What was the name of the movie?"

JM: "<u>Winding Roads</u>, an independent film. That I've heard nothing about since, so I don't know. I think it's playing a couple of festivals. It might just stay there. I hope not."

WG2: "I was here when they set a stunt woman on fire at the end of the finale of Season Two."

JM: "She probably understood a lot better than I did the length of a burn, about what kind of burns can go long and what kind of burns need to be cut short. I let the burn go long, they cut it out anyway because it was written to be a certain thing, and I was trying to make it more, as we all do all the time. And they always let us do our extra bits and just cut them out, which is exactly what I'd do."

WG2: "What about Season Four? What's a moment so far in this season that you remember or comes to mind?"

JM: "I liked hitting Buffy in 'Harsh Light of Day,' and I liked kissing Buffy in 'Something Blue.' I think you know that you're in the center of things when you're either hitting her or kissing her."

WG2: "Can you tell us anything about this episode, 'The I in Team'?"

JM: "I ended up talking politics with a demon in a car, which I never thought I'd do. I've gotten to work with Tony again. We had two scenes together, which is a delight. He's a fabulous actor, and I pay attention to what he does because I think I can learn a lot from him. You can't say enough about what he does for the show. He's the backbone, I think. They would be hard-pressed to find anything better than Giles."

WG2: "When we came up two years ago, he was taking acting classes, and he said, 'Well I have class tomorrow,' or something like that. That was impressive."

JM: "That is usually the mark of a very good actor, that they never assume that they've made it. And they always know that they can get better so they always do. I unfortunately had such a bad experience with acting training that I have never gone back. Although I recognize that I could probably use it, I would be a terror for an acting teacher."

WG2: "Marcia Shulman cast you in part because you had acting training."

JM: "I've had acting training up to my gills. I did an apprenticeship program in Santa Maria actually, at the Pacific Conservatory, and that was primarily building sets for free and doing small roles with no lines and watching very good older actors work from the first rehearsal to the last performance. For me acting school kind of breaks down into different components, and that doesn't work for me. I get too far up in my own head, and I get too intellectual about it, and I stop paying attention to my instincts. I learn much more not knowing that I was learning anything. I picked it up through osmosis much better."

WG2: "What about the comic book writing? Are you gonna do any more of that or did you enjoy it?"

JM: "I enjoyed writing it very much. Chris Golden was very kind and taught me a lot about what it is to write a comic book, and I'm very glad I did it. I just don't have much time right now. They approached me recently to do another one, and I had to decline just because of time. I didn't think I could really do justice to it."

WG2: "Do you want to direct?"

JM: "Yes. I was just talking about that the other day. I used to have a theater company in Seattle and Chicago and did a good bit of directing there. Directing for film is an entirely different thing, and I'm very respectful of that difference. I would direct a <u>Buffy</u>. Of course, there are people around here that have been doing it all their lives, but some day, yeah. There is a lot to learn before that comes. There is a lot to learn about the visual language.

"I think that I have a strong sense of spacial relationships, what the use of space is on stage and how it can communicate dynamics of a scene just by placement of actors. But that's something you have to have to stage a good play, and I think that would ultimately translate well. I think that I have an instinct toward communicating visually. Certainly actually writing the comic book furthered that, too, because, it is a visual medium. It's really storyboarding a film except the images are stacked and don't flow. I think that I deal well with actors, and I would like to try. I might fall on my face or I might fly, I don't know. Joss did it! He's brilliant. He's a great director."

WG2: "Now that you've moved into the crypt and you're living there with no electricity, I guess you're not used to the niceties."

JM: "No. Spike don't go for luxury. Spike doesn't comb his hair. I don't know how it stays so straight! The fingernails are a good indication. It's an ornament of himself, but he just doesn't care."

WG2: "Is Harmony coming back any time soon?"

JM: "I don't know."

WG2: "Do you enjoy working with her?"

JM: "Very much. Very much. I think she's great. She's been around the show a lot longer than I have."

WG2: "But in a far different capacity."

JM: "Yeah! It's interesting. The two primary things that I thought kind of defined Spike were the fact that he was in love with Dru, and that he liked killing people. Now I'm not with Dru, and I can't kill anybody, and I find that the character is better rounded than ever. So again, kudos to the writers, that they know the character better than I do.

"So the whole thing with Harmony was the exact opposite of Dru. She bothers the hell out of me, but I think that's because I'm in revenge mode more than anything else. I've had my heart broken and I'm bitter and I'm breaking hearts. Poor girl that she was the first one I found. We had a really good working relationship. She's very fun to work with. I would love to have her back."

WG2: "Had you worked with anybody on <u>Buffy</u> before you worked on <u>Buffy</u>?"

JM: "No, I never did. I was pretty new to town when I came on, and had only worked in theater."

WG2: "When you read for Marcia Shulman, the original casting director, did you think you'd gotten the part?"

JM: "No. I felt like I had done my best and so was able to give it up. I only obsess about an audition if I feel like I didn't do my best. That's always really tough, but if I feel like I gave it my best shot, I just kind of give it into the hands of fate and forget about it, frankly.

"The thing is they had their backs up against the wall when they auditioned me. They had been looking for a long time and were scraping the bottom of the barrel and found me. I was new in town, I didn't have a lot of credits and they threw their net wider and I'm very lucky that they came up with me. But I felt great about the auditions. Marcia made me feel so comfortable."

Anthony Stewart Head as Rupert Giles

Tony Head is one of our favorite interviewees. He has wonderful stories and he's simply a delight to listen to.

WG2: "We hear that <u>Buffy</u> is becoming a popular show in England."

ASH: "Everything that I have kind of visualized and hoped, which is basically that <u>Buffy</u> would be a success overseas, has come more than true. It's huge, really huge over there. [At first,] they basically kind of dropped the ball. They put it on after <u>Hercules</u> and <u>Xena</u> on Saturday night, and it died, and they pulled it off midway through the second season. And then the BBC got it with the arrangement that they would show what Sky hadn't shown. And then made a big success of it. They did call on me to do publicity, really reached out, made a sensible decision about programming, which they

then even capitalized on. They put it on at 6:45 on an evening hour, after <u>Star Trek</u>. They edited it. So needless to say, adults who knew about the show started to complain about the fact that they didn't want an edited version. So now it's on twice a week. They repeat at 11:30, 11:45 when people come back from the pub on Friday night. It's brilliant. So now it's building up an enormous audience. Of course then Sky wanted it back, and the BBC had to curtail their transmission, stop transmitting it until Sky had shown all the ones from the second season, and then they were allowed to start up again."

WG2: "So there's kind of a war in the skies."

ASH: "Yes. I just love it because it means that people appreciate the show. I love the show so much."

WG2: "Are you sorry you've never gotten to be a vampire?"

ASH: "I've talked to Joss about it. There was one point when, I think it was the second season, I had a chat with Joss and said, 'I'd love to go bad,' but my girlfriend

pointed out that the role that Giles plays on the show would be missed if you lose that. You know you can trust [him]. There is a sort of calm about Giles, which if the show lost it, it would . . . you couldn't lose it permanently is what I'm saying. I don't know, and yet Joss loves to turn things on their heads and it is conceivable that at some point he would like to make Giles bad. You never know with negotiations and networks."

WG2: "They've figured out a couple of ways to have Willow go vampy, and Xander."

ASH: "But they've done that now. If I was going to do it I'd like to actually have a story arc and actually get into it a little bit. It was very fun being a demon, but if I was going to do a vampire, I think I'd like to have more than an episode to play with just because you want to get in there and muck about and find out what it's like.

"I mean the difference—I think Giles has an enormous amount of remorse about everything. So I think it would be very interesting to play somebody who has absolutely no remorse. That would be fun to play. One of the reasons vampires have always been so cool and so sexy is because there is that kind of 'Wow, how could they get away with not caring?' in taking a life. Not only do they not care, but they celebrate it, which is something that the human psyche doesn't normally allow."

WG2: "In Seasons One and Two, you guys never really discussed the fact that Slayers could not take human lives. And then there's a great bit where Angel is saying to Faith 'I know that now you know what it's like to be like a god, and you've got to feel bad about this or you're lost.' And she basically says, 'I don't care.'"

ASH: "As an actor you want to look at things like this because it makes acting interesting. To play with concepts like this can actually [let you] see how it would make you feel, how you can justify it and how you can make that person—you know it's easy just to play a bad guy but to play a bad guy and make him multifaceted, give him a good side and bad side...Just not make it all black and white. Nothing is black and white. There's a good side and bad side to everything."

WG2: "One of the things that's so interesting about Giles is that you have this sort of a shadowy past that gets alluded to every once in a while."

ASH: "I was glad that Joss gave him that. It's fun to actually play somebody who has secrets, and everybody has secrets, everyone has something somewhere that makes them think, 'I could have been a better person if I hadn't done that.' We all have those memories of things that make you what you are. Giles has got plenty of it. Bless him!"

WG2: "How long did it take you to get all dressed up like the demon?"

ASH: "We started off at four hours. It was immensely enjoyable. Because I did makeup at drama school, I'm always fascinated. It's a piece of art, watching someone do something like that. It's fascinating watching the stages that you go through and watching your whole face completely change.

"There were obviously downsides to it, and there were moments when one would have to come in at three or four in the morning. I just closed my eyes and I'd dose off for a minute and then you'd wake up and go, 'Oh, no, you're green now.'

"But we had such fun and there was a great moment when—it sort of loses something in the translation because I haven't got pictures of it—but there was a point when we were trying to work out, there was a skullcap inside which the horns attached to, the hard part of the cap, and when we first put it on there was nothing to hold it underneath, so basically it would slip as I moved or moved suddenly. Then I'd suddenly get this crease on my brow, and you could see the shape of the skullcap.

"So we sewed some little pieces of plastic on the back of my spandex suit underneath and Velcroed it onto the back of the skullcap so that it held it in place. One of them came undone, and at one point the thing was moving around, impossible to get in to change it to stick it back on because the whole suit was all glued up.

"So I unscrewed one of my horns, and [Todd McIntosh] tried to go in through the top of the appliance. There's a large hole, of about an inch and a half to take the horn, so [his] hands would just about fit in. There was a point when he had his hands in my head up to his wrist and he's struggling; he's got his foot up on the chair where I'm sitting, and he's struggling to get his hand down the back of my head. I got this graphic image of what it must look like with this man's hands sticking in my head. I just cracked up! And he caught it, and we just were falling about— this ridiculous sight of two men, one with his hand in the other one's head!

"So we had a lot of fun. I don't know how those guys on <u>Star Trek</u> do it day after day. One thing that I've said to a couple of people, there are always things that have association: The latex glue that they put on all over your face has a certain smell which by the third or fourth appliance you think 'I don't know if I can do this all my life.'

"And also taking it off because at the end of a twelve-hour day or whatever it was, you just want to get it off and you have to wait. The whole thing takes about an hour. It's gradually taken off with alcohol and thinner. The whole thing was a lesson in the art of putting a demon's head on. It was all about relaxation and patience, and my stunt double hated it. Hated it! I don't think he will ever get into another suit again. He found it very difficult to sit still in it.

"I had thought as I prepared for it, one of the things I wanted to do was to change my walk. Because Joss wanted some part of my face to come through, I wanted my body language to be different and to be bigger and to be more clumsy, so the whole thing would be smashing through doors. And I wanted that sort of heavy footfall feel. A problem with people dressed up in suits is you can see their feet. I wanted to change the outline of my foot.

"So I came up with the idea. I knew that I'm all right on heels because I've sort of leaped around the stage, and for that, for <u>Rocky Horror</u>, they used to have big platforms. I suggested having little ankle boots, little S&M black patent leather ankle boots, pointy toes. I would like to have been on the spiked heel but I think I'd have killed myself very quickly. So I was only on about three inches, but nevertheless, it looked quite cool, and I was able to leap around, I mean I actually had to run from stage level right up to the staircase and I took three steps at a time. It firmed my bottom, I have to say!

"Then Cynthia in costumes sculpted and latexed around the three-inch pump into a hoof, and then we had fur over the top of it, so it has the fur poking out from underneath my leg. It was fun. If nothing else it did exactly what I wanted. It changed my walk completely and made me move differently."

WG2: "'How did you get to be a kid again for 'Band Candy'?"

ASH: "That was interesting because I had two choices. Basically if Giles had [gone] to private school— they tend to get like Hugh Grant, there's still that kind of plum in the back of the throat. I could have gone that way, and I thought about it but I also thought about myself at sixteen, seventeen, and the fact that my father was always correcting the way we talked. And he'd say, 'You'll thank me for this one day.'

"And so needless to say my rebellion was talking a bit more street. Even now if I get into a cab in London, I'll immediately talk, 'Yeah, all right, mate.' I'll immediately switch into what I deem an acceptable way of talking. So I thought about it, and I thought since Giles kind of ran away from it all, that that was the way to go. That was the way he got around being who he was. It was great fun."

WG2: "If you had done the [private] school kid trying for street, it might have been confusing for most of us Americans."

ASH: "That ran through my mind. It's an internal thing, and as long as I can make it organic, it was enough for me to know how I was when I was in my teens. They understood that. They understood that there was something going on but it was still Giles. It was fun.

"I was trying to work out what I was wearing around that time, and at the same time what would be in Giles's closet, because we went through the thing, 'Well, where have you got these clothes?' They have to be in his closet. It has to be something that would be available to him for it to be believable otherwise, 'What, you've gone out shopping?'

"So basically, I don't think anybody would have noticed, but if you look at my jeans they're covered in paint. And the idea was that they were actually painting trousers. Giles had them in his closet, and he uses them to do that, and that came from the fact that I had just been decorating at home and ruined a pair of jeans because I had been painting the walls red, a deep, deep red paint; actually it's a period color and it was all over my jeans. That and a t-shirt and the plaid shirt, it gave you the immediate thing of, 'Oh he looks younger, he looks different.'"

WG2: "Yeah, and then they gave Joyce that coat that you looted."

ASH: "There was at least the excuse that Joyce could have raided Buffy's closet. But basically what they put her in I don't think was a problem. Put her in a miniskirt, she looked great! It was great fun because we talked about how she was when she was a teenager, and who's changed the most and it was very interesting. Our different lifestyles. The different way an English teenager was in the seventies and an American."

WG2: "Such as?"

ASH: "She was talking much more about lying around listening to some albums. And you know, I certainly didn't have a den or a room that was big enough. I go back to where I grew up with my family, and I'm amazed. We cannot fit in it. It's a very small place. It's a little Victorian cottage, and it's lovely, but it's amazing that I and my brother and at one point an au pair grew up in it and my parents grew up in it. You have to move a chair to open the door to get out of the dining room.

"So there wasn't room to lie around and listen to records. I did it all outside."

WG2: "What do you think they would think if they could see you now?"

ASH: "Actually, I've got a studio at home and have an eight-track that was a Christmas present and it has a very confusing logic to it. And when I was first trying to get it going I called up the main company and asked for their help line and it was this guy called Binky!

"And he said, 'I bet you don't remember me,' and I get this a bit. But this guy said, 'I played guitar with you in someone's basement, with Jason and I can't remember who else was in it, and in fact we only did one practice session.' I remembered exactly who he was, we sang the only song that I knew which was 'All Right Now,' by Free. I liked that one so we did that a lot on this one night, and we did it in this bunker under a garden. So yeah, it turned out he's now working for this major corporation on their help line. He helped me."

WG2: "We've been very happy to hear you singing more. How do they do that? Do they record you?"

ASH: "Singing is an odd one. Joss saw me sing a couple of years ago. Because when we first did <u>Buffy</u>, I think it was even in the pilot when I was wondering what the plans were, if it got picked up, what was he planning, and he said he'd love to do an all-musical episode. I've asked so many times, 'So when's the musical episode?' He says 'It's not gonna happen for a while. Not gonna be.'"

WG2: "When we went up there to interview all of you for the first <u>Watcher's Guide</u>, they were talking about that, and we said, 'They just did that on <u>Xena</u>,' and there was a dead silence. I was in Gareth's office, and he said, 'They did?' I'm wondering if that's why it got shelved because everybody was talking about it."

ASH: "Possibly. But you know, if Joss did it, it would be very different. The writers have pitched it to me. They had no idea that I could sing, but they say its Giles's way of retreating into his shell. Basically it's a midlife crisis, and he wants to get back to what he was, find out who he is, and he goes to sing in a coffee bar. And I said, 'That's great.'

"So I was going home at that point, and the script was late and Joss hadn't decided which song I was gonna sing. So I went back with one, which was 'Freebird.' Then they said 'Actually, we'd like you to learn 'Behind Blue Eyes' as well' [for 'Where the Wild Things Are'].

"When I got in on a Sunday, I went to a theater with John King, and he played the guitar on 'Behind Blue Eyes' and I played it on 'Freebird.' I thought of it because I would like to have done it live, but the problem is they have nothing to edit. If you do it live then each take you can't go and see what the tempo is going to be, etc., etc."

WG2: "What do you think about becoming an action figure?"

ASH: "Gee, I can't wait! I cannot wait. It's just, I want it now. They said he was coming out in spring, and he hasn't come out yet. I love Clay's work. I've become friends with Clay and he sent me other stuff that he does and, I think of all the stuff around I think his sculpts are by far the best."

WG2: "What are you going to wear?"

ASH: "I don't know. We were talking about it and basically, he couldn't get a reference for the sort of suit, a forties suit where I wanted Giles to be a little more structured, sort of less 'teddy bear,' less of a fluffy, woolly vest. It was after Jenny Calendar had died so I wanted Giles to be presenting a business-like front to the world. I did talk about having removable glasses, and he said that's a bit difficult in the medium that they work in, so he was talking about possibly having two heads. One with, one without."

WG2: "There is a scene in 'The Zeppo' and you have a huge moment that's off screen and Buffy said, 'That was the bravest thing I ever saw anybody do.' What do you think you did?"

ASH: "Well, there was a moment, it was actually sort of implied that basically in order to distract, because she's being lifted up, I go right into its midst and start screaming at it and whacking it. It could have been more than that, but that was cool enough. Especially if it saved her."

WG2: "Was it hard to do 'Hush' with no talking?"

ASH: "It was extraordinary. It wasn't hard, it was just stretching. It was good fun and the lecture scene was very funny! You just knew you were part of something that was very exciting."

WG2: "As far as the job of being an actor, have you noticed any changes from Seasons One and Two to Seasons Three and Four?"

ASH: "I think back to when we first started, and you know it was a grueling process for different reasons. There were twenty-two hour days and things, trying to get what was on the page on film, and now they're much, much better at knowing exactly what they can shoot. But nevertheless there are still moments. The difficulty is because everything has to go through Joss. When he puts his changes on the script, it just…it puts a shine on it."

WG2: "Can you describe that to us?"

ASH: "I don't know; he just has a feel for people and for what makes people tick. Our writers are very good. I mean I love the way Jane writes for me. But Joss just has that extra edge. His humor is very specific. He knows exactly what he wants. Which for him, it's a curse and a blessing, because he has such a clear view of what works and what doesn't work. So that if he doesn't get it, it's a curse, and if he gets it it's obviously a blessing.

"But I can't put my finger on how he changes it. It just has that little extra shine to them. He will take a scene—it doesn't often happen where he'll reconstruct a scene—but he'll take a scene where the essence is right but it's just not quite working; he'll just change the emphasis of a scene and suddenly it works. But it does mean that everything has to go through that process and consequently sometimes the scripts don't come through until the day before we're about to shoot.

"Writing is not, as you know, an easy process, and consequently, it just puts a different series of constraints on us all—the team—because it's just less time to prepare. But in some ways that makes it exciting. Flying by the seat of your pants.

"From season to season, it's been great fun to play the different beats that Giles has had. He started off as this rigid, pretty inflexible kind of academic and the more time he spends with Buffy, a bit of her has rubbed off on him. Also, with the various changes he's gone through, the emotional changes, it's been interesting to play how that affects him. And as I say, I've been playing his midlife crisis all of this season, which is fun.

"I've not been as heavy in places this season, because part of Buffy's freedom, going to university, is moving away from the adults that have influenced her up to that point. So Buffy has moved away from Giles. I mean I have a fair whack, but there have definitely been episodes where she's done it on her own rather than going to him. So I've had more time to go home [to England]."

WG2: "How did you feel when you got to have a girlfriend again?"

ASH: "That was nice. She's great fun. She's gorgeous. The difficulty is how she fits into it, because she's not a witch or a demon. She's a normal person. How does a normal person fit in other than not fitting in? What's the story there and where do you take that? I pitched an idea involving her. And some part of it may find its way through. She drops in when she's in town, and that's an interesting thing for Giles. Not too much for him to cope with."

WG2: "Had you worked with Alexis Denisof before?"

ASH: "I worked on a wonderful show in London. That's where I met him. We got on really well and it was a glorious production. I went on tour and to the West End with it. Alexis couldn't do it, which was a real bummer because he was just so wonderful.

"In fact, when they said they were looking for Wesley, that they were looking for someone distinctive, I said, 'I think I know the person.' You know, it's very rare that you have a casting department as totally open-minded as we have on <u>Buffy</u>. Amy Britt is quite remarkable in that she doesn't have her little actors that she constantly calls on. She's always, always open to suggestions. The best casting directors always are, because you don't know where you're going to find that person, and Alexis was such a find for the show. We have such fun. I want to go and do <u>Angel</u> because I want to do some scenes with him again. I'm very fond of him. He's a good man."

WG2: "How do you feel about the fact that you have a fan club that keeps track of how many times you've been knocked unconscious?"

ASH: "Somebody's got to! They gave me a [bicycle helmet with] pasta stuff all over it. That's actually one of my lampshades in my trailer. The other one is a straw hat. I went with Alyson to do an autograph signing, and NerfHerder were playing. They're a local band and they had just come back from some tropical resort, and they brought me a straw hat. That's my other lampshade."

WG2: "We like those touches when you'll eat an apple, or you'll stamp some books or do little things while you're talking, and that seems very real."

ASH: "We generally don't just stand and talk to each other. We use the time to do whatever we need to do, and as I say, it's part of the fun of bringing life from outside. It's to make it more human."

Guest Stars

Elizabeth Anne Allen as Amy Madison

**We interviewed Elizabeth Anne Allen a few days
after a Velvet Chain CD launch party.**

WG2: "Where are you from?"

EAA: "I'm from upstate New York."

WG2: "You have a bit of a twang."

EAA: "I think it's just in upstate New York, they have like a lazy Midwestern tongue. Either when I'm waking up or getting tired, I'm probably lazy in my speech."

WG2: "So, we're really curious about your character. Are you coming back?"

EAA: "I'm going to be back next season. Joss has chatted up my people. [laughs] I guess they had a bunch of characters they had to work out, that they had to deal with this season. I had actually done a pilot in Australia. I got wrapped up in that, figuring that out, so I was unavailable for time reasons. It was kinda kooky this year."

WG2: "Everybody wants to know how you feel about cheese."

EAA: "Do you want to know what the funniest thing is? I'm allergic to dairy. That's my standard joke. I love cheese, but I can't eat cheese because it gives me hives."

WG2: "How do you feel about rodents?"

EAA: "I used to have mice, and gerbils, and all those little animals in my house. Which I'm sure was to my mother's dismay. But I loved them. I had tons of hamsters and gerbils and guinea pigs. It was like a zoo at my house."

WG2: "In 'Gingerbread,' Xander comments on Amy's new hair style and color. Was that an ad lib, or an add?"

EAA: "That was definitely an add. When I showed up on the set, I had done an independent feature film, and they had cut my hair off, and they had made it red. And when I walked on the set, they just took one look at me, and they nearly had a heart attack. Joss walked right by me; David Greenwalt walked right by me, and I was like, 'Hi, it's me!' And they're like, 'Oh, my God!' Going dark was my only alternative to being fire engine red."

WG2: "Well, it's interesting, because women change their hair so often, that it's not unusual. Emma Caulfield said she thinks her hair was different for every episode."

EAA: "Especially, I think, we women change our hair so much as it is, much less if you are an actor and they call for characters with different looks. You go from eighties to seventies hair, and from red to dark to my natural color, which is blonde, so it's very odd."

WG2: "How did you get the part of Amy, and who did you tell first?"

EAA: "I had originally tested for the role of Buffy, and I didn't end up getting that role, obviously. And they brought me back in for the role of Amy.

"And it was really funny because I went back in four times, because the director of this particular episode just thought, 'Well, I just don't think she could be mean.' I kept saying to Joss, 'I don't think he knows what he's talking about.' But he had a hard time. After my fourth audition for that character, they finally gave it to me. And the director was great. He said, 'You've proven me wrong.'"

WG2: "Can you tell us any stories you'd like to share about any of the episodes?"

EAA: "Well, 'Gingerbread' was kind of funny, because the day that they put me on the pyre was my birthday. So they said I was a human candle, and when they lit the candle everybody sang 'Happy Birthday' to me."

WG2: "What is your birthday?"

EAA: "November eighteenth. It was a very funny episode. I thought, 'Somebody's sick and twisted out there.'"

WG2: "How close did you get to actual flames?"

EAA: "Pretty close. They have to surround us in it, and it's strange. It's not something that you have a great deal of control over. They always have a guy with fire extinguishers, and there's actually a fireman on the set any time there's fire."

WG2: "We thought it must have been CGI."

EAA: "Well, they do to some extent. But it's a few inches from you, at times. It's kind of scary. Some of your reactions are completely genuine."

WG2: "Could you feel the heat?"

EAA: "Oh, definitely. I mean, they make sure you're okay. There's somebody standing next to you who appears to be an extra but who really is a fire person."

WG2: "Is that one of the scarier things you've ever done, as an actor?"

EAA: "I actually did an independent film which was pretty dark. It's about incest. And there's a few scenes in there which I think were probably the scariest things I've ever done. Just because it's kind of past your emotional limits."

WG2: "Do you have a favorite moment from your tenure so far as Amy?"

EAA: "I actually liked the last episode ['Something Blue'] just because it was so tongue-in-cheek. There were so many people who wrote to me, and wrote to Joss about bringing Amy back. It was so great. Then he called me up, and he said, 'I hope you have a really good sense of humor, but I'd love you to do this thing.' And I just thought, 'Oh, he's going to make everybody so mad. But it'll be so funny.' I just thought it was so much fun to just kind of spoof it. Of course, everybody was like, 'you were nude!'"

WG2: "Were you?"

EAA: "No. Actually, you have on a bathing suit. And they have to stick part of it to you, they double-stick it to you. Tricky."

WG2: "How long did that shot take to film?"

EAA: "I think a couple hours. Not too long."

WG2: "Do you think Amy is aware that she's a rat?"

EAA: "I'd like to think that rats have some capacity to process thoughts. Rather than wake up in a complete stupor two years later, and still think I'm that guy on That '70s Show or something. I'd like to think I know some of the things that are going on. But then again, I don't know. I think some of the things I could have possibly seen…maybe I don't want to hold on to those. I had a couple of people send me letters and ask me if I remember anything from the night Willow spent with Oz."

WG2: "Do you know anything about Wicca in your real life?"

EAA: "I actually did quite a bit of research originally, because I didn't want to falsify what Wicca's about. And Wicca is actually pretty much about the Earth, and what you put out there you bring back. Be careful what you say, because it comes back to you. If you call for judgment, be prepared to receive judgment on yourself. I don't think those are things that people into Wicca would use as lightly as some of the things that we use. It's very serious. They take a lot of responsibility for their actions because it directly affects them. Sort of like instant karma."

WG2: "So did you meet Wiccans?"

EAA: "I did. The Psychic Eye bookstore sent me to a couple people, and through friends I met a couple people, and they're really great people. Real earthy, you know. Not black-wearing goth types at all. Women with careers, and teachers."

WG2: "Can you tell me about any other projects that are coming out?"

EAA: "Well, that all depends on if <u>Then Came You</u> gets picked up. I have an episode of <u>Then Came You</u> on Wednesday night."

WG2: "And you went to Australia to do a pilot."

EAA: "I did, that was fabulous. That was really exciting. I was in Australia for about two months. It was crazy. I had a great time. It didn't get picked up, but every bit of the experience was worth it."

WG2: "What's the strangest place you've ever worked?"

EAA: "I did a film in Tucson, Arizona, and we shot in the airplane graveyard. And it was really odd, because I was in old 747s, these monstrous, dilapidated 747s and jet planes that were just abandoned there. It was called <u>Time Master</u>. It was a kids' film. That was really crazy. It literally felt like a graveyard. I wondered what had happened. Had these planes flown in wars?"

WG2: "Do you have any scars, tattoos, or distinguishing marks?"

EAA: "I have a belly ring."

WG2: "Did it hurt?"

EAA: "Not at all. I actually went with Alyson Hannigan. We went last Fourth of July. That was the goal, getting the belly ring. And we got there, and I think I was the only person who got one. Because Alyson, during the middle of it took one look at me and said, 'Eeeew!' And I said, 'No, you don't say "Eeeew" in the middle of it. When I can't go back.'"

WG2: "So she chickened out?"

EAA: "There were a couple of other girls that were with us, and one did have the intention, and seeing mine she did chicken out. But I don't know if Alyson had the intention to. I was the only one. And I have several scars on my knees, actually."

WG2: "From what?"

EAA: "The day before I did 'Gingerbread,' I got hit by a car. That's why they were kind enough to do some of it sitting down."

WG2: "What happened?"

EAA: "I had parked my car, and gotten out, and somebody came inside the parking lane. It was...interesting."

WG2: "What do you do when you're not working?"

EAA: "I work for a nonprofit organization. I work with this gentleman who runs an organization called the Water Buffalo Club. It's actually an all-men's club, but leave it to a woman to run it. I work with him, and it raises money for abused, abandoned, and neglected children. It's great. They've managed to raise quite a bit of money, and they give it to different charities. They have different events.

"I like doing that. It makes me feel like I'm contributing. So much of what we do is just self-serving, so I think it's nice to do something."

Larry Bagby as Larry

Like Danny Strong, Larry Bagby was mobbed at this year's Posting Board Party. The two actors are very popular with <u>Buffy</u> fans, not only as their characters but as actors and nice guys.

WG2: "Could you tell us a little bit about your background and how you became an actor?"

LB: "I started when I was about twelve years old. We moved from Provo, Utah, out here and my parents were at a career day at our church where they had different booths set up with different careers. They happened to come across this place called Hollywood Film School. That is where I kind of got my start.

"My brother and sisters all went in and did a little screen test. We started just learning a little bit about what the business was. We jumped into some classes there. They had a management company at the time. We signed with a small management company there, and then I got an agent.

"I guess it was the fourth audition I went on, that I booked a low-budget movie that might interest some <u>Buffy</u> people because it is sci-fi. It was called <u>Invasion Earth.</u> It was a pretty cheesy movie, but actually the guy who did the special effects won an Academy Award for his special effects in <u>Aliens.</u> Robert Skotak directed me in that.

"That kind of got my career going. Then I booked a Sizzler commercial after that. That was how I got into the union. Then it just kind of started panning out. I ended up changing representation down the line.

"This is something <u>Buffy</u> people will enjoy. The very first job I ever did on TV, Seth Green was my sidekick. I had worked with him a few times before I worked with him on <u>Buffy</u>. I was like twelve or thirteen and he was about the same. We did an episode of <u>Mr. Belvedere</u>. It was a classic. That was when I first met him. Probably a couple of years later I ended up doing a film with him called <u>Airborne</u>. Then we were reunited once again on Buffy.

"He has been around forever. I saw him in <u>Can't Buy Me Love</u>. Did you see that? He was the little boy. We run into each other all the time at random places. He is a great guy.

"I was just always blown away by how small this world is. Everybody ends up working with each other down the line."

WG2: "How did you get cast for <u>Buffy</u>?"

LB: "After I did <u>Airborne</u>, I did a big movie called <u>Hocus Pocus</u>. I played Ice, the town bully who steals the shoes. I was put up in the cages and stuff. That was a big role for me and opened up some doors.

"Just after I did that movie, I left on a mission for my church for two years to Argentina, learned Spanish. It was the best two years as far as developing my skills as a person, and the spirituality was awesome. Couldn't have been a better two years. Some of the best years of my life. I got married last year. My wife is everything to me.

"But to get to your question, I got back from my mission, and it was actually really hard to get back into things. People didn't know who I was. I looked different. I was a different person. So I got going again. It took a little while. They cast me for one episode, it wasn't a recurring role. It was the Halloween episode. That was the first one.

"I guess they liked me a lot. They liked what I did with the character and they called me and said, 'We know you are LDS [a member of the Church of Jesus Christ of Latter-day Saints, commonly referred to as Mormons. Mormon beliefs do not condone homosexuality.] The point is, it was a character and I thought it was a funny, interesting choice. It actually opened up a lot of doors as far as turning into several more episodes.

"I did that next episode which was 'Phases.' I went in for the character, and this is kind of funny. My name is Larry and the character's name happened to be Larry; it's not like they changed it for me. I even mentioned that when I went in for the audition. 'This part is for me. It is written all over the page here.' They kind of laughed about it.

"I have to continue on with trying to get other work, and I have been auditioning a lot for pilots. I just did a Southwest commercial which will be out starting this week.

"I produced a sci-fi movie with my cousin that is going to be coming out soon. It's at American Film Market right now. It is called Linx."

WG2: "Can you tell me some interesting or funny stories about when you were on the set?"

LB: "It is interesting to see how people are in real life versus their characters on TV. I have a friend who actually knew David from college, so that was kind of interesting. I didn't even know he was a regular. When I first came on I think he just came on board as doing a few more episodes, but he was really nice. They had sushi on set the first day. We did a table read and then had sushi. Seth and I hung out, when we did 'The Wish,' because we had a lot of scenes together. We played basketball and just hung out in his trailer. We played card games and stuff. It was cool."

WG2: "How did you know, when you went to career day and you saw the Hollywood Film School, how did you know that this was for you? Did you have an immediate, 'Oh, yeah?'"

LB: "I always connected with that. My dad was an entertainer. He grew up in a dance band. I loved music. I'm in a band right now with my wife, and we also did a Christian contemporary CD together.

"When I was in elementary school, I loved being in the spotlight. I was the Wizard in The Wizard of Oz in second or third grade. My dad would invite the kids up to sing. I always did my little Michael Jackson impersonation. I love to dance, sing, act. I love to make people laugh.

"That has led to other things. In high school I was in the theater program and the choir program. Any chance I had to entertain, I was there doing it. So when I had the opportunity to be an actor…my mom grew up in West Virginia. Her dream was to be an actress. I think that some of her passion came through me, and she was a great stage mom. She didn't push me too hard, but she knew that I liked it. She would take me on my auditions. She was really supportive. When I was able to drive, I started doing it myself.

"I never lost the passion. As hard as it got. It all ties in. I know that there is a reason for everything. I know there is a reason why I may not be doing another episode of Buffy. Who knows what is in my path? I just know I will keep going and doing all I know. It has always been a passion and always will be. I won't ever retire because it is something I love. I just consider it a blessing that I can support me and my wife for now and eventually I know we will be able to support a family by doing what I am doing. It is just a career, but a fun one."

WG2: "How do you feel when you go to a posting board party and people obviously cluster around you and know exactly who you are?"

LB: "It blows my mind. I can't imagine what it feels like to be somebody of a higher caliber, a star where everywhere they go they get swamped. I just consider it a privilege. I can't believe people actually think I am a star. I would never turn anybody down to sign an autograph or take my picture. I admire people and if I had an opportunity to take pictures of certain people, I would. It is a privilege. I think it is really neat. I am trying to take advantage of the opportunities by just being around and keeping Larry alive, as far as I am concerned."

Amber Benson as Tara

We met Amber after a costume fitting. She was clearly ill, but delighted to be interviewed. "Hush" was scheduled to air that evening for the first time.

WG2: "Tell us what's going on with you."

AB: "I'm Willow's new friend. This is awesome because I love Alyson Hannigan. I knew her before she got the part. I'm kinda shy, I have a bit of a stutter, and I think I'm a nice person. So far I've been nice."

WG2: "We saw your room."

AB: "Isn't it neat?! They did such a nice job. I walk in and I commune with Tara. This room makes me Tara."

WG2: "We were watching the postproduction on Friday night of 'Hush.' Was it hard not to make noises?"

AB: "Well, a couple of times, Alyson and I were breathing really heavy and trying not to talk. Did you see the scary guys? They are absolutely terrifying. They are so nice. It's two guys, I saw them out of makeup finally, and there is no way those are those two guys. There's no way. But they scared the pee out of me."

WG2: "Tell us how you got the part of Tara."

AB: "I went in and read for it, actually, and I didn't tell anybody I was reading for it. I went in and they liked me and they wanted me to come back. It was on a Thursday or Wednesday that I read, and they wanted me to come back the next Monday.

"I was going to be going out of town that Friday, Saturday, and Sunday and I was gonna come back early on Monday. At twelve I talked to my agent, and she said, 'They're gonna bring you in on Monday. Fine. Go. Just be back for Monday.' So we left and we didn't stop until we got to San Luis Obispo, where my dad lives.

"We made a pit stop, got gas and checked the messages, and they were like—it was [from] ten minutes after we left—'Oh, my God, they're having the callback today and they want you to be there today at five.' And of course we were like five hours away at that point and at that point it was already five and there was no way were gonna be able to get back.

"There was nothing I could do. I just had to go and I'm thinking, 'Oh, my God, I'm screwed!' I just had to let it go and leave it in fate's hands. I got a call Friday night; there was a message they didn't find what they were looking for, 'They want you to come back on Monday.'

"It was Halloween weekend and I was hanging out with my sister and I didn't get any sleep. We drove all morning Sunday morning to get back by eleven or twelve. I was just ughhhhhh. 'Whatever happens, will happen, I'm not going to worry about it.'

"So I went in and I read and I was walking out I ran into Alyson Hannigan, and she said, 'I didn't know you were coming in for this. Why didn't you tell me?' You don't want to tell anyone. You want to get it on your own if you're gonna get it. She said, 'I think you're awesome. I'm gonna go tell Joss.'

"She went running in and I went home and I get in and there is a call from my agent immediately when I walk in the door and she's like, 'I just wanted you to know that they want you for _Buffy._'

"And two seconds later while I'm on the phone with my agent, there is a call waiting and it's Alyson and my friend

WG2: "How did you know Alyson?"

AB: "I met her through mutual friends at a party five years ago. It was a long time ago. It was the year she got this, I think, or the year before she got this. She's still into animals, she's just like she was. Still the nicest person that walks the face of the Earth. So down-to-earth and cool."

WG2: "What was your first job you got paid for?"

AB: "The first thing out here was a film called <u>King of the Hill</u> that Steven Soderbergh directed. It was the first thing I really got paid for. I had done plays that I got little money, like a hundred dollars here and there for doing children's theater and stuff. That was my growing-up stuff."

WG2: "Briefly tell me the story of your life. Where you were born?"

AB: "I was born in Birmingham, Alabama. I'm a southern girl. My mom's from Tennessee and my dad is from out here, and they met when they were both in San Francisco. My dad is a psychiatrist and my mom is a psychiatric nurse. He was into hypnosis. All the neighborhood kids liked me and would come over and say, 'Would you hypnotize me?' It was so embarrassing.

"I have a little sister. She's four years younger than me. She kicks ass. She's the coolest person. She's the best present I ever got. She's got blue hair and a tattoo, an eyebrow piercing, and she's very bohemian and artistic and hippie. She's an artist. I was there until I was twelve, and I did a lot of children's theater and that kind of stuff down there. And then we were in Orlando for two years. I went to school across from Universal Studios.

"Then we moved out here when I was fourteen, almost fifteen, and I've been out here ever since. In a nutshell it's sort of my life."

WG2: "When you got the first episode, 'Hush', did you realize that you were going to be recurring?"

AB: "They said it was a possiblity. I wasn't sure what was gonna happen. I prayed and hoped. I thought it would be a really awesome if it would become recurring. These are like the nicest people. They are so cool and the food is really good.

"It's the nicest group of people here. It's disgusting. It's sick how nice they are. You go to some sets, and its just like everyone's crazy and neurotic. Some of them are nasty. They're just doing their job and it's very professional. Here people take the time to come in and are like, 'How are you doing? How was your Thanksgiving? What did you do this weekend?' It's just so nice. I'm listening to Marc [Blucas, while we interviewed him] and nodding yes, yes."

WG2: "So you knew Alyson and Seth."

AB: "I worked with Seth on <u>Can't Hardly Wait</u>. I got totally cut out of it, but I had some cool stuff with him. He's the nicest guy. He's soooo funny! I don't think there's anybody funnier than Seth Green. He is hysterical."

WG2: "Did you ever work with Alyson before now?"

AB: "I never worked with Alyson before. I worked with Lindsay Crouse, though. I worked with her twice actually. She played my mom in <u>Bye Bye, Love</u> when I was eighteen."

WG2: "Are your hopes that this keeps going?"

AB: "I would totally love it. I could stay here the rest of my life. This is so awesome. Joss Whedon is God. That man is amazing. I bow down before the ground he walks on because he he's so cool. He's a special person. When they made him, they broke the mold. That guy is so smart and so awesome and such a nice guy."

WG2: "How many days a week do you usually work?"

AB: "On 'Hush' I worked a lot, but because Joss worked it out that I could do the film, these past two episodes it's a few scenes here and there. Which is totally cool because workload wise, I'm just so beat from two weeks of five in the morning, four in the mornng, three in the morning, getting up. It was so perfect. It's like getting a tease of, just a little taste of Tara."

WG2: "If you see how many lines you have or how much time you're gonna be on the screen, can you kind of figure out how long that's going to take you in prep time at home?"

AB: "Most of what it is on <u>Buffy</u> is memorizing because when you get there it's like they give you time to play and to work on it, and there is a lot of rehearsal time. You get to rehearse a scene at least two or three times before you go in and do it. So for me I memorize it at home. I always read the scripts, of course I'm new to it so I'm studying every script. Going, 'What does this mean and what does that mean?'

"I'm not a TV person, so I've never watched myself. I don't watch much TV but now I'm starting to watch <u>Buffy</u> and reading the scripts and I know what's going on. Someone gave me the <u>Entertainment Weekly</u> guide to <u>Buffy</u>, so I got to read all about what happened. The Buffy-Angel thing, the Willow-Oz thing, the Xander-Anya thing. Oh, I worked with Eliza!"

WG2: "Oh, really?"

AB: "On <u>Bye Bye, Love.</u> She played my best friend and Lindsay Crouse played my mother. Isn't that bizarre? Liza is such a sweetie."

WG2: "You are happy to be here, and you are obviously working in features, and so is there anything lacking in your experience thus far? What would you like to do, what would you like to have Tara do?"

AB: "The first day I got here, I was begging Joss, 'Can I kill somebody?' I just want to take someone out. Just one demon. Just one bad person. Just take one person out. That's all I wanna do. Before I go I just wanna take somebody out.

"I'm really happy with what they've done with her so far. I've enjoyed her. She's been fun. I found out I could stutter, so...."

WG2: "Do you have any pets?"

AB: "I have one cat that lives with me named Benetton. She's a calico. She's the united colors of Benetton and I have two cats that live with my dad. One is named Eurythmic and he's a seal point Himalayan, and I have another cat named Brittany and she's just an alley cat, just a mutt cat. I have a Dalmatian named Penny—Pennsylvania—and she's a big love bug. She sleeps with us. And I have my sister. She's a big pet. Just the three cats and the dog."

WG2: "Do you have any idea if you're gonna be a good or bad person?"

AB: "I think I'm gonna be good. I'd like to be good. I want to take the bad guys out, not be a bad guy. It's more fun to be a good guy, and my grandparents can watch it if I'm a good guy. If I'm a bad guy—they're born again Christians and they live in Alabama—so if I'm a good guy they can watch it, if I'm a bad guy, they can't."

Emma Caulfield as Anya

Emma's sense of humor is wry, just like Anya's, and she sparkled when she talked about her education. The original casting director, Marcia Shulman, once said that the actors who end up on <u>Buffy</u> have to be smart people. We think she was right.

WG2: "Tell us how you auditioned for the role of Anya. How did you find out about the role?"

EC: "Brian Meyers, who is no longer casting the show. Brian called up my representation and said that there was a part on the show, and would I come in and meet Joss. I of course did, I love the show. I found out the same day that I got it. I mean I went in and got it. I was working pretty immediately.

"The role wasn't designed to be anything more than a one-time guest shot and then just sort of evolved from there. I think we got a call like a month later asking if I wanted to come back again. And of course I did, I went back and about halfway through filming that episode it was made kind of clear that they wanted me to come back again, and it just kept evolving from that point.

"By the end of Season Three, the whole vibe was pretty much, 'Well, we'll see you next year,' but without anything formalized. And then I guess when they started up production again in July, I got the call and they asked if I'd come back for sort of an indefinite amount of episodes. They wanted to work me in. They worked me in and about halfway through this season, which is Season Four; they made me a regular. It's been quite an evolution, to say the least."

WG2: "When you found out that you were going to be a cast regular, who did you tell first?"

EC: "I think my sister was the first person to find out because I think she called me on my cell when I was out, and I think I had just gotten off the phone with my manager. She had told me and literally the other line clicked through, and it was my sister. It was one of those things and then it just sort of became a chain reaction at that point. I think most people who found out heard through other people. Everybody told everybody else. It was one of those things."

WG2: "Were you completely blown away, or was it such that you kind of knew, based on the way they were acting toward you, that you were probably going to evolve into a cast regular?"

EC: "I was definitely happy. I was probably more relieved than anything else. I had been working on the show for a while by the time it happened, and it had sort of become my home away from home already. It wasn't like I had no experience with the show. I had already gone through all of the show's growing pains, since I had been there for over a year anyway. So to that extent it was like an added bonus. I mean, doing another pilot or whatever would have been fine, but staying with the show was really what I wanted, so I'm glad it worked out."

WG2: "Do you think the psychology classes you took in college play any part in the way you interpret Anya? Because she's trying so hard to figure out relationships and people?"

EC: Well, having a background in psychology, having taken those classes and trying to basically dissect the human psyche, I don't see how that wouldn't help with any character analysis. The process is very similar.

"But Anya, I gotta say, just comes very easy for me. There's just not a lot of guesswork with her. The most difficult part is not knowing what they want to do with her, and not having that to work with. I wouldn't say I identified with her really, we're pretty different people, but when they humanized her was when I really started to have fun with the character, and there's been nice synchronicity between my take on her and what the writers and Joss want to do with her. Just sort of a nice melding of the minds.

"It's just such a fun character to play. So much of it is in the dialogue, and how can it not come easy to you when someone is writing such great words! Joss created a character that is just so much fun. I don't have to sit and go 'Oh, what am I gonna do with her this week?' She's pretty much out there already."

WG2: "Can you tell me some of your favorite moments that you've had as Anya so far?"

EC: "Every day on the set there is something funny. It's just that sort of atmosphere. Everybody gets along, and it's a very fun place to work. In terms of things that my character's done, scenes that I've really enjoyed doing, a couple stand out; probably the first time that Anya seduced Xander in his basement. That was just so well written and it was well done and it was fun. It was a change of pace for the character to just shift gears. I guess not in terms of how bold she is and how blunt, that's pretty typical Anya, but just to what extent she was willing to go. I thought it was really funny. It was a pretty defining moment for her character at that point.

"I always have fun. Every script I read I'm laughing. Nothing surprises me anymore. The words are so great and the character is just so great. It's impossible not to have fun with her."

WG2: "When you get a script and you start reading, do you have in your mind a mental picture of the way everything is going to look? Or how do you prepare? What do you do?"

EC: "I'm not conscious of it. I never have a visual of what it will look like. I read the script and memorize my dialogue, and then we shoot it and what I think it looks like in my head when I'm actually doing it is never what it looks like once it's completed. Never.

"And again, naturally it wouldn't be like anything else that has been edited, your scene is taken completely out of context and I guess that's what it's like. It's not like doing a play where you have an opportunity to make changes as the performance progresses. You have two hours to complete a thought. You literally go in, you work for however many hours, you know, in this you average like twelve hours a day. You have an actual hour's worth of work and it's very difficult to get any sort of grasp on anything when you work under those conditions. How can you?

"Everything is taken out of context, so I never really get a visual unless something is specifically visual, like the bunny costume. When I read that she had to be dressed up in a full bunny suit, I mean I got an immediate visual of that in my head and what ended up being filmed was by far funnier then what I even had in my head, which was pretty funny. That was another one of my favorite Anya moments. It was just so ridiculous."

WG2: "Was it hot?"

EC: "Hot, yes, it was unbearable. Thank God it was around October. So it was cold outside. We shot a lot of the stuff at night, so that was good. Getting around in it was probably more difficult than actually being hot in it, because the shoes were enormous and I literally had to waddle."

WG2: "It was pretty cute how she stomped around."

EC: "No, I didn't have a choice, it was the only way I could move around. It added to the visual. It was pretty funny."

WG2: "How long did you have to stay in it?"

EC: "I don't remember, all those days seem to meld together at this point. It seems like forever."

WG2: "Would you want your character to have her powers back?"

EC: "I guess for story purposes it would be great and it would be fun to play that, but I hope I never have to go through the whole prosthetic thing again. It's unbearable. I don't know how the Star Trek: Voyager people, do it. I really don't. It's so claustrophobic. I guess some people have a higher tolerance for that than others but after twelve hours I was ready to pull my skin off."

WG2: "How much did your head weigh when you had all that stuff on?"

EC: "I don't know. It seemed like it weighed a ton. I was really uncomfortable, and we shot that in I think August, so it was hot, and then I had the burlap material dress, and it was just a nightmare. Thank God I only had to it once. I don't know that I could do that again."

WG2: "What about your haircut? When did you decide to cut your hair?"

EC: "I cut it off during the summer between Season Three and Season Four. Regretfully. Never again! It's been such a process to grow it out! It's really, really short. I didn't want it short for the character, and they didn't, either. So we had a whole series of different hairpieces trying to find the right one to sort of ride out the wave for a little while.

"And then it finally got to a decent length, and we just decided to go natural. When shows from Season Three re-air, like the prom, and I see how many different hair lengths and hair colors I've had, I mean I've gone through a lot, but I've forgotten just how many. I think I've had a different hair color or something different with my hair every single episode since I've been on this show.

"Probably next season it'll be completely different again. I've been itching to change it, but I haven't done it for continuity purposes. It's like a light kind of goldish, strawberry blond, now it's not quite shoulder length, what can I do come July, maybe go dark again. I can go back to being a dark brunette."

WG2: "Is that your natural tone?"

EC: "Yes. I get bored easily. I'm never satisfied with my hair. I've been that way since I can remember. Since I started paying attention when I was about thirteen or fourteen.

"If you chronicle my hairstyles, the colors for the past ten years it's completely different, I mean I'm a completely different person. I think that really helps for anonymity, because I always get 'she looks just like the girl'—I get that all the time. People standing right there thinking I can't hear them, and it's funny.

"Part of me is relieved, because I can go and do my thing and not be worried about anything. Not that people coming up to you and recognizing you is bad, it's flattering. It's sweet. Most people are really nice. They just say, 'Great job' and they're off doing their thing. But funny, even at the posting board thing, people are like, 'Wow!' It's funny. I'm so used to it I don't think I look that different."

WG2: "Who do you think would win a tactless contest, Anya or Cordelia?"

EC: "Anya! Without any question. Oh, God! Not even a question. 'Orgasm friend.' I mean, who says that? Who talks like that? That's what's great about her. Because it's everything you want to say, but usually don't. She appeals to your base impulses. She is just sort of the Id personified for me, and it's fun to play. It's great. She says things I only wish I could say!"

WG2: "Having been on several teen shows now, how do you feel <u>Buffy</u> compares with other teen shows?"

EC: "I don't think of it as a teen show at all. I think it's been a complete misconception. I think <u>Buffy</u> is the ultimate case in irony. I really do. I think even the name, it's sort of like Joss Whedon has the last laugh on everyone. It's a wink and a nod and I really do think that. It got me, too. I mean when it first aired, I thought, 'I'm not gonna watch <u>Buffy the Vampire Slayer</u>. I mean, how ridiculous is that! This must be so stupid.' And then of course you watch it and it's so smart and clever and understated, and I think the beauty of it is that it doesn't talk down to its audience. It assumes you're smart enough to get it.

"And they leave it alone. I mean the disclaimer at the beginning of the show...I don't know that that's a strong enough disclaimer. Because if I had a twelve or thirteen year old, I wouldn't want my child watching, especially now. I'm surprised. I'm shocked at some of the things that we get past the censors."

WG2: "When you made the little circle and the finger. We were amazed you got away with that! And Buffy with the stake!"

EC: "I don't think it's a teen show at all. Obviously it appeals to teens, and if I were a teenager, I'd be watching it. But the people who make a point to come up to me and say something about the show, they're not teenagers. They're people in their forties.

"I said this before, I do think it's sort of a modern allegory, I really do, and I think the show works so well because they don't treat the situation like it's abnormal. Everything that comes their way is very normal, and that's just life, and they don't camp out the show at all.

"They just play it for straight, and I think that's what makes it so smart. Really, I think ultimately all the characters are good role models for teens. It's a great show, and it bums me out that the Emmy board refuses to acknowledge it every year. It's on every critic's top ten, and so every year they do the plea to the Academy, and they refuse.

"I don't know what their problem is. It's frustrating. I think 'Hush' was some of the best TV I've seen any show do ever. It was a great piece of TV. You don't have to follow the show to understand it. You can just turn it on, and it's complete in and of itself. So smart, so original, it's like, if that doesn't get the show its Emmy nod I don't know what would. It's very frustrating."

WG2: "Do you know what's gonna happen in Season Five to Anya?"

EC: "I have no idea. None. I only just found out what's happening in the episode we're shooting. I'm completely in the dark!"

WG2: "We're really looking forward to seeing what's going to happen with you in Season Five. Most of the time you're paired with Xander and doing your back-and-forth thing, and we think it will be interesting to see them break you out to do your own stories. I mean, it carries very well and you guys work together perfectly, and we're just curious if they're going to give you more of your own kind of world."

EC: "Lord knows there's plenty of avenues they can explore. I mean, where does she live, where does she get her money. What does she do all day? They haven't established her as a student. I think it would be great for Anya to have like a huge penthouse with everything state of the art, stockpile of money and clothing. I mean, if you've been around for 1100 years, wouldn't you?

"Either that or she's the stupidest person on the planet. How could you not have acquired a lot of goodies over the course of 1100 years? But yet she chooses to live with Xander in a basement. Total opulence somewhere uptown, like I just went hysterical! Certainly a lot of material there. Who knows? I have no idea what they have in store for me at all. Completely in the dark."

We interviewed Leonard Roberts and Bailey Chase in their dressing rooms, which were the same ones used by James Marsters and Juliette Landau when they appeared together in Season Two as Spike and Dru.

Bailey Chase as Graham Miller

WG2: "Could you tell us your career from the start? What was your first job, on up to here?"

BC: "Okay, a very brief bio is, I graduated from Duke in '95, moved to Los Angeles. I was out here for close to a year and realized I didn't know anything about acting, so I decided to go back to school and study it. So I moved to London for a year, and I studied over there and learned all about Shakespeare, and it was just an amazing experience. I learned a little bit about acting, and I came back and started working in independent films and had something get into Sundance, and that was really exciting. It was called Cosmo's Tale (1998)."

WG2: "Who directed it?"

BC: "Adam Shankman. It was his directorial debut. Did some guest spots in television, and did a couple of plays and then I got here."

WG2: "So what is it like being on Buffy for you?"

BC: "It's great. It's by far the most fun that I've had working in television. I mean, the crew and the cast, they get along really well and it's a really creative show and we just have a lot of fun. So, it's great."

WG2: "How did you try out for the role?"

BC: "I auditioned for it. They put out a breakdown, my agent submitted me, and I got an appointment and I came in and I preread with Amy Britt and her assistant, and then they brought me back for the producers."

WG2: "What is something that you've gotten to do in this role that you haven't gotten to do before? Anything new?"

BC: "What's really fun is all the Commando stuff. I mean, by day, I'm just a college guy, and a student and we're guys and we hang out, but that's just our cover. And the fun stuff is, you know, our Commando [lives] and our high-tech rifles and weaponry, and that's what's really cool."

WG2: "What would you like the producers to know that you can do that you haven't gotten to show?"

BC: "Well, it's funny. This is the first thing that popped into my head. I can speak. Graham, he doesn't have a whole lot of lines. He's the strong, silent type. But I have a little bit of dialogue tonight, so I guess after tonight they'll know that.

"I was—actually, the other guys were making fun of me. I was making fun of myself the other night because we had this scene, and I didn't have any dialogue. I was the only tired actor that didn't have any dialogue. And I think Joss overheard the whole thing and felt bad, so he threw me two lines. He's like, 'Nah, just go in there and say, like, 'Come on' or 'Let's go,' something like that.

"I don't know if he overheard what we were saying. But then Marc just said they cut that scene out, but it's okay. It's okay. I speak other times, just not very often.

"You have no idea what their ideas are, but it's a great show. I would be very happy if they developed the character more because then I could continue to work on the show. Unfortunately, you know, actors in my position have to take what comes along a lot of the time, and then they get locked in to these long TV deals and they do it because they have to. Whereas, this is a show that I enjoy working on."

WG2: "So, would you consider being on Buffy a good break? A good opportunity?"

BC: "Oh, yeah, it's great. Yeah, I'm proud. I'm proud to work on Buffy, whereas there's some other shows that I've just done for the money that I don't put on my rèsumè or, you know, I don't tell people, 'Yo, you gotta watch this show this night.'"

WG2: "What was your very, very first job that you got paid for?"

BC: "Married . . . with Children. I was a Speedo-clad lifeguard. It was a spring break episode, so they were all in Florida. We were on a set, but it was really funny and they hired a bunch of former Playmates to do a bikini contest in the episode. So it was us three guys in our Speedos and then all these Playboy Playmates in their bikinis. I, of course, was the lifeguard without any lines."

WG2: "What was your next job?"

BC: "It was Baywatch."

WG2: "Do you want to be a comedic actor or a dramatic actor or character actor or leading man?"

BC: "I want to do it all. I want to do more theater, I'd like to do more film, and TV is—There's a lot of great television being done right now."

WG2: "Where were you born?"

BC: "I was born in Chicago, raised in Florida."

WG2: "Do you have any brothers or sisters?"

BC: "An older brother."

WG2: "Any pets?"

BC: "Gauge. He's a yellow Lab. I've had him since college. I had to go in and get lint-brushed earlier because Gauge had slept on my jacket, which is that one lying over there. And I had yellow hair everywhere."

WG2: "Well, we want to thank you so much for talking to us."

BC: "Oh, it was a pleasure."

WG2: "You're going to be in a book."

BC: "I'm going to be in a book. Yay! I made it."

Lindsay Crouse as Professor Maggie Walsh

NOTE: For most of this interview, we interviewed Lindsay in tandem with Mike Stokes of the BTVS Fan Club Magazine. Our thanks to a colleague for his generosity.

**This was the day Adam was going to kill Maggie.
But Lindsay was quite aware that just because someone dies on Buffy,
it doesn't mean they won't be back.**

WG2: "You were born in New York. Did you grow up there?"

LC: "I grew up in New York City. My father was a Broadway playwright."

WG2: "So what you did, do you think it was just kind of a natural thing for you? Were you always around acting and actors?"

LC: "It was kind of an interesting family because even though he was a famous writer of his time, he was not a celebrity-type person. So a lot of well-known writers and actors came in and out of our home, but were treated like friends and whatever. It gave me a sense of confidence and well being around people that I found out later I could have easily been a bit intimidated by, but that was a very nice feeling in my home."

WG2: "Do you remember who some of the names were that came through that you were later impressed by?"

LC: "I remember spending a dinner party as a young girl sitting next to Frederick March, and I had no idea who I was sitting next to. I was sitting next to Fred who was a friend of my dad's, and we had a great time together and he was so magnetic and fun to talk to and never talked down to me. I felt this was my elegant dinner party and my elegant dinner date. It was just lovely and it was just who my father was. He was a humble man and very authentic person and it was a lot of fun growing up in that atmosphere."

WG2: "When did you start acting?"

LC: "I went first into the field of dance. I was interested in music and dance and then, I found that the dance world was sometimes frustrating. Its more restrictive, you perform less, it's really an athletic field where you are constantly, constantly working to keep what you have.

"I began to do showcases way downtown on the Bowery, in terrible little theaters where the audiences consisted of my relatives and someone getting warm.

"They were places were you could really chew the scenery and ask questions, and I think as a dancer I had been ashamed of those questions. I thought if you need to ask, 'What do you do?' or you're doing an abstract piece, 'Who are you? Who are you in relationship to the audience, or in relationship to your fellow dancer'—and I needed to ask those questions, and I realized doing these showcases that those were legitimate acting questions and I decided to go to school.

"While I was performing I was studying with Uta Hagen, who I studied with for a long time and then later on with Sandy Meisner. I had great, great acting teachers. I owe them a lot.

WG2: "Where did you study dance?"

289

LC: "With Alvin Ailey. And with Merce Cunningham. It was a wonderful time in New York. The field of modern dance was really flourishing and even off-off-Broadway was a very vital place, and it fed productions that eventually grew into Broadway shows."

WG2: "Did you hope to join a company?"

LC: "I was really interested in dancing. Dancing was what I wanted to do. I changed my focus. It's a longer story than I need to tell here, but in the middle of it I changed my focus. I had been well educated and I had seen different parts of the world. There were a lot of things that I wanted to bring to what I did, and I felt in the dance world I was stymied doing that.

"One of the things that is great if you become an actor, having been a dancer, is that you really understand how hard you can work. So you're not always complaining. Dancers work really hard."

WG2: "What do you look for now when you take roles?"

LC: "Fun. I look for the fun of it. Even if it's a very serious role or a very tragic role, it's something that there has to be a stimulation to it. Something that fires you up, that fires up the imagination."

WG2: "What did you think when you got contacted for <u>Buffy</u>?"

LC: "It was interesting, because I had a conversation with Joss. I was back in Massachusetts and I was actually out on the water with my cell phone when he called about this. He tried to explain to me who this character was and I must say I was a bit mystified. I said to him, 'Well, I love your show. I'll come and do it. Just point me in the right direction.'"

WG2: "What did he say the character was?"

LC: "He said that she was a scientist, and that she was going to be doing research, and that eventually she might hatch an evil plot but that her front was being a psychology teacher. I tried to get a concept of whether this was a very broad character and he said, 'No, just play her real.' And it just sounded interesting. It sounded like fun and I do love this show. I think there is incredible work on this show."

WG2: "You've been watching for a while?"

LC: "I don't get to watch television very much because I have three children, so school nights we're pretty hands-on at home. But I had seen the show a number of times and I'd really enjoyed it."

WG2: "How old are your children?"

LC: "Seventeen, eleven, and nine."

WG2: "How did you see the character? Even now, do you see her as evil, or just kind of twisted, or totally normal?"

LC: "I feel that this woman, as a psychology teacher, is opposing teaching the standard curriculum, that her heart is really on the cutting edge of science. And I would imagine that she envisions herself as a serious research scientist, who has not received the recognition that she really deserves.

"And that Riley, her teaching assistant, is really the child that she never had, the son that she's proud of, and probably a little confusion there as to whether he's a potential...something, for her. Slightly out of her reach, but she'd like to prevent anybody else, certainly, from being interested in him. So I think she puts herself in direct competition with Buffy there. For his affection."

WG2: "Now that you're done with the show, after about three months, what's your feeling now that you're leaving?"

LC: "Well, I'm very sad to leave this show. When I went to Joss a few weeks ago, I said, 'Joss, what do you think is going to happen, how are we going to develop this character?'

"He gleefully said, 'Oh, you're going to create a monster, and it's going to kill you. You're going to die, it's going to be great.' Well, great for you. I love doing the show."

WG2: "So you didn't know that from the beginning, that this was your fate?"

LC: "No. No, I didn't."

WG2: "What films do you think you're best known for?"

LC: "I think probably for <u>House of Games</u>. That was the first big contemporary part that I played, and I think it had a kind of impact. It was also such a unique film, very special."

WG2: "You were also in the best sports movie ever."

LC: "Yeah, <u>Slapshot</u>. It was a really great one, I loved doing <u>Slapshot</u>. I loved working with Newman. An extraordinary man."

WG2: "You've also done a bunch of guest spots on different TV shows. How does this stack up? Do you have fond memories of other shows?"

LC: "Yeah. I'm queen of episodic television, I think. I love going on all these different shows. What I really like doing, though, is coming back to a show that I've done. Because then I know everyone, I feel comfortable. I feel familiar. You don't have that nervousness of meeting everybody for the first time, and what will it be like, and what's the feeling? You know everybody, so when you come back on a show, maybe even after a couple of years, it's a wonderful homecoming.

"I don't know, it always seems to me you really get a handle more quickly on what you're doing. I just did an episode of <u>Law & Order</u>, and I'd done <u>Law & Order</u> years ago, and it was a beautiful episode, it was just wonderful. And I felt very at home, going back on that show. It was really enjoyable."

WG2: "You come across as a very warm person. Maggie, on the other hand, is not so warm. How do you adapt yourself to do someone who's kind of cold? And also, how do you manage to balance cold with passion? Because you tend to think of passion as having heat."

LC: "Well, of course it's always more fun to play the warmer roles. But what's fun about Maggie is that she's such an extremist. That's fun. And I think she has a vision of what she wants to do. Dr. Frankenstein is sort of a predecessor for her, who I'm sure she admires. Or Einstein, I don't know, she probably has a mix of those. I think she feels that she's testing the boundaries, and I think any human being always feels that they're doing something important, no matter what they are.

"I've always imagined that Maggie treats people like grown-ups, that she doesn't want to live in a world of babies, she doesn't have time for it. So even in her classroom, she treats her kids like grown-ups. And they see her as cruel, or heartless, or demanding, or rigid, or whatever, but she's I think, simply really pulling them up by treating them like, 'Well, you don't get your paper in on time, you're not in my class anymore. How else would you want the world to be?'

"She doesn't have time for playing games. And I think that's her persona. I think she's probably . . . don't know exactly; Joss and I never talked about what exactly drove her to that cause. But I think that human connection is defined in a very different way by Maggie than by most people. And I think the Initiative is her baby, her glory child. Creating Adam. I'm just sorry I don't get to know Adam."

WG2: "Did Joss create the character with you in mind, particularly?"

LC: "You'd really have to ask him. I don't know. I don't know how I'd feel about that, either."

WG2: "He also has a kind of knack for bringing people back from the dead. Would that be something you'd be up for?"

LC: "Oh, I've already told him that. I said, 'You know, I know that death is not the end of anything on this show, so why don't I come back as something else?' Yeah, I've already talked to them about that, so we'll just see. That would really be fun. It's really fun to come back on shows and play different characters."

WG2: "How do you feel about the portrayal of Maggie as an adult on a show that's more geared to the younger portion of the show? Do you feel like she's a rich enough character?"

LC: "You know, a character that comes on a show in that kind of spot that I am in is not going to be a fully developed, three-dimensional character. Just not. I think she's pretty narrowly defined. But I think that's fine. I think on a show like this, each character has its niche."

"The main characters, of course, are growing and going through transformations, and supporting characters are always fairly two-dimensional. They might be real, but they only get to go through certain kinds of things. I think that they've put Maggie on a trajectory towards creating or masterminding something. And being double-sided.

"The thing I like about her, especially in the classroom, is she's no-nonsense, and she seems to be a real teacher. And I think the most complicated situation for her is having Riley fall in love with Buffy. I think finding out that Buffy's the Slayer is kind of a gas, and it's nervous-making and exciting for Maggie to have people on her team. I think she's like a president, you know, she wants a great cabinet underneath her. That's a reflection on her. She claims she's not narcissistic, but I think she did protest a bit much. I think she really would like to fashion the world in her image.

"But I think Buffy puts a wrench in the works there. She's faced with something, a gray area that's difficult to handle. But I like her caustic nature. She's not a mean person, she's just a straight-out scientist. So she's more clinical. It's someone's interpretation that she's mean."

WG2: "We're asking people if there were any special sort of theatrical skills that they would like to maybe show off, but the character didn't allow for the opportunity?"

LC: "Like fencing? I love fencing. I love staff fighting. Theatrical skills, gosh, that's a good question, I don't know."

WG2: "You didn't get much chance to tell jokes."

LC: "You know, I said to Marc, when we first worked together, 'It's so daunting to come on a comedy and be the straight one.' You want to join the fun, but they keep assuring me that Maggie's funny in her own way."

WG2: "What does the future hold for you?"

LC: "I'm glad I don't know, actually. I'm supposed to do a film in January, in Mexico. But we'll see. It's an independent film, and it got moved because of the earthquake and the flooding, so we'll see. I don't know. I would love to do a series myself, and develop a character. Or go back and work in the movies, which is my great love. And to continue teaching. I teach acting, I teach improvisational singing, I teach at a music conservatory in the summer. I love teaching."

WG2: "In the few moments of action that Maggie gets, when she's caught between the werewolves, what was it like? Monsters to the left of you, monsters to the right of you."

LC: "I love it, I love all that stuff. I could do that all day. That's the fun of it. I mean, the stunt people on the show are so fantastic, and the fight choreographers, etc. And coming from a dance background, I'm always saying, 'Can I do that? Can I do that?' I just love doing that stuff. The night we shot that was my date night with my husband. So I brought him along; that was our date night. He could watch me be chased by werewolves."

WG2: "Very romantic. It almost seems to throw you back to pretending, as a child."

LC: "Of course, it's exactly what you got into it for. And sometimes you feel slightly disappointed that there's all this insurance, and safety rules. You long for the days of Lillian Gish, when you could really step out onto the ice floe and there was just a guy with a camera, and you, and a guy with a microphone, and you were making it up as you went along. Those must have been really fun days working in movies."

● ●

David Fury on Maggie Walsh

"IT WAS AN INTERESTING THING because we had not seen, and I don't think Joss had envisioned, Maggie Walsh as being entirely villainous. As opposed to just sort of misguided. And I think she takes a turn into villainy in this single episode ['The I in Team.'] The tricky part was not making it so abrupt, but to kind of make it understandable how she could suddenly become this villain.

"Also—and I'm sure this will be no surprise by the time this comes out—also we can set her up as the great big villain for the rest of the season only to kill her by the real villain. The real villain will rise up and kill her. That's part of the joke of doing it that way. We're setting her up to be the Mayor, for the remainder of the season, but well, she's not, she's Mr. Trick. She's dying, and somebody else is taking over."

• •

Alexis Denisof as Wesley Wyndam-Pryce

**We spoke to Alexis by phone. Alyson Hannigan was in the background, teasing him, and the atmosphere was light and happy.
His accent was clearly American, occasionally tinged with a bit of British.**

WG2: "Are you still working on this season's <u>Angel</u>?"

AD: "No, we wrapped. We wrapped two days ago. We're finished shooting for the season. Although there may be some little pieces, some little pickups and some added voice things that we'll have to do in a couple of weeks, but the bulk of it's done."

WG2: "Are you happy?"

AD: "Well, it's nice to have a break, I must say. It was a very exciting but challenging first season, so I think we're all looking forward to a couple of months off. Just to get recharged for Season Two."

WG2: "Since there are only basically three main characters, is your work load just intense? How do you guys handle it over there?"

AD: "It's pretty heavy, especially for David. He's in almost every thread of the storyline so it's really tough on him. But you're absolutely right; there's just the three of us, so there's a lot of work to be divided between not very many characters. But I love that. I can't complain."

WG2: "How did you get <u>Buffy</u>, and then how did you end up on <u>Angel</u>?"

AD: "I had come over to L.A., I had been living in England, where I had trained as an actor at the London Academy of Music and Dramatic Arts, and came over here on vacation, actually, for ten days with two friends, and we promised ourselves—they were actors, too—we promised we wouldn't look for work.

"Which, of course, is when work comes your way. I got a pilot during that time and stayed on to do the pilot and then that led to more auditions in L.A. I was intending to go back to London—six months had gone by and I had only expected to be gone a couple weeks—and was anxious to go back, and an audition came up for a show called <u>Buffy</u>. I knew nothing about it because it had not aired in Britain. I had no idea that I was going up for this cult, culturally extraordinary show. And really, Wesley was just going to be a couple of weeks.

"Tony was an old pal from England. We had worked together years ago, and so in fact, he is the one who suggested me. I had called him when I was in town just to hang out socially, and they had approached him from the office and said, 'We're looking for

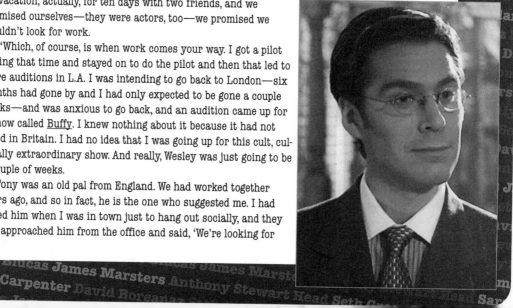

such and such a type part, of Wesley, a Watcher.' And he said, 'I might know of a guy who could do it,' and so he called up and said would I be interested, and I said of course I was.

"And so then I met Joss and the team and we had a meeting and Wesley was invented. Really, he was meant to come in, irritate and annoy Giles and Buffy for a couple of shows, and then be gloriously terminated. That was the original thought behind the character. He was sort of a bookish academic, out of the Watchers Council Training Academy, and was here to shake things up and to get them back onto the straight and narrow.

"But then we found this kind of curious humor in this guy, and it was just too hard to kill him off. Suddenly half the season had gone by and they didn't have the heart to kill him off—which I'm delighted that they didn't—so we broke up for the summer hiatus of Season Three of <u>Buffy</u>, and Wesley was kind of hanging in the air. Joss said, 'Well, we really want to keep him here, it's just how and when to make him part of the community.'

"It was tricky. They already have a very successful and loved and adored Watcher in Giles, so they needed to go to the drawing board and figure out what to do with Wesley. And then I went away and did another movie, <u>Beyond the City Limits</u>, which actually Alyson did as well.

"I went to England and did a TV show there, and then when I got back from that, there was a call from Joss saying, 'I think we found a place for you. How do you feel about joining the team on <u>Angel</u>?' And of course I was thrilled. So we met and we talked about his ideas, and it's just been a wild ride ever since. Demons, fighting and cruising L.A., and darker elements, and here we are looking at Season Two. That's sort of what happened.

"He's obviously been reshaped. Retooled a little. The summer off gave Joss a chance to figure out how to use him in the long-term because the originally conceived character, you know, although lovable in a way, was probably not sympathetic enough to be a long term character. So we needed to give him a little history and a little experience in the world during that break between <u>Buffy</u> and <u>Angel</u> so that when he came back he could be used to expand the show."

WG2: "Was that part of the purpose, during the exorcism episode, 'I've Got You Under My Skin', having the allusions to your father being made?"

AD: "Yeah. I think as we go on we'll learn more and more about him. The idea I think with any successful show, to keep your own interest and the interests of the audience and the people working on it, is to have complicated characters.

"So, yes, that was a glimpse of some of the conflict in Wesley's life, and as we go on, at times he'll provide much needed light relief. His brand of clowning. And at other times you'll see a more sensitive, darker side of his personality, or his troubled past. He's an evolving person which makes it a very interesting, exciting job. None of us are complete, nor are we in life, so in that sense, I think it's partly why the show is so successful."

WG2: "For 'Eternity,' we noticed you had much more of a five o'clock shadow and you were kind of machoed up. Was that intentional?"

AD: "Yes. As I say, you know I think we're all working to keep him as an evolving character, so that there are times when he'll be very rough. He's had a bad night, or he's had a rough ride; in fact some of the shows where Faith comes to town, Wesley goes through very tough stuff. He's being put into a lot of different situations and seeing how to respond. We're trying to do different things with him. I would hate for people to expect him to behave a certain way and then have that be the case. I want him to be a sort of a pleasant surprise—you know, sometimes he triumphs gloriously and other times he gets it hilariously wrong."

WG2: "He definitely has a more serious edge than when he was on <u>Buffy</u>. We're dying to know if it's hard to kiss badly on purpose?"

AD: "Well, I have to say when that script arrived and we'd been having all this fun playing with the chemistry between Wesley and Cordelia, I read that and I kinda laughed hysterically, but then also was struck with terror. Because so often you're asked to create the most magnetic kiss in screen history, but I had never been asked to create a dud.

"So when we came to it, that was one of the most fun days we had playing around with it. It's obviously a very funny scene to play. These two highly charged people kind of coming together and it falls flat."

WG2: "Yeah, which of course none of us expected. That was hilarious! It was just so funny and sad, too."

AD: "It <u>was</u> kind of sad, wasn't it? Kind of a disappointment. But now they've become good friends, which is good. Friends who can bicker but still love each other. So I really like the relationship that we have.

"I mean, I think a lot of people at first were like 'Oh well, they're gonna get together.' I mean I have no idea what will happen in the future, but I think it's been the right choice so far to have Wesley [and Cordelia] partners against crime rather than partners in love. And there's a trust and a comfort and the result of that, that they had sort of an attraction that they had with each other, it gives them an interesting history and an interesting chemistry with each other, I think. It frees them up to really say what's on their minds. I mean, they really tear into each other sometimes."

WG2: "What are the differences in having been on <u>Buffy</u> versus <u>Angel</u>, not so much in your role but maybe day-to-day shooting, maybe something that people wouldn't even think of that might be different from one show to the other?"

AD: "There are some practical differences. <u>Buffy</u> is shot in a self-contained studio where <u>Buffy</u> is the only show. <u>Angel</u> is shot on the Paramount lot where <u>Angel</u> is one of many shows, so there is a very different atmosphere in terms of just simply going to work where one is sort of a universe unto itself. So that's a little different, and there are nice things about both.

"And then also the main difference has been that I think we feel with <u>Angel</u> that we're starting at the ground level with a new show. It's very different than it was for me joining a show in the third season of what was already a huge success. So that was sort of stepping onto a train that was already moving very smoothly and rapidly, and <u>Angel</u> has gone fantastically well, but it's a different feeling. We're creating this new show together, so yeah, I feel the difference.

"And there are fewer of us, as you brought up earlier. There are many more characters in the world of <u>Buffy</u>. It's a little more populated with the regular people week to week, where there are fewer of us regular from week to week and we have more visitors.

"I mean I have loved both. It's a very special, lovely family, and that starts from the top with Joss Whedon and David Greenwalt creating a really wonderful, creative, hard-working environment where people are supported and encouraged so that's been a constant on both sets, and we're all very lucky."

WG2: "Since we have seen you sword fight, do you help choreograph those scenes? Or do you have any input? Do you do many of your own stunts because you have a physical ability?"

AD: "I like to. You know, when I'm capable of it, then I will. Especially if it's a particularly comic one that I want to put a particular touch to, then I will ask to do the stunt. But the fights, yeah, the stunt arranger is very good about hearing any ideas you might have, but they're the real experts in their field."

WG2: "Do you have a specific stunt double? Do you know who he is?"

AD: "I have had this year a wonderful double, Dane Farrell, and he's been superb. Particularly what I have liked about him, he's caught on to the way Wesley moves, and so I've been really happy with him. I had a couple different ones on <u>Buffy</u> last year but this year we kind of settled down to Dane, and yeah, he does some terrific stuff."

WG2: "Do you have any special skills or talents or something that you'd like Wesley to get to do that he hasn't done yet?"

AD: "That's a good question. The thing that delights me about Wesley is sort of when he gets to leave the office and the books and is out in the field. That to me is really fun, because you know, in the office with books he's of course an expert. So it's great fun when you take him out of that environment, and you force him to handle a social situation or a car chase or an argument at a nightclub. You know what I mean, where it shows another side of him that he may or may not be able to handle well.

"I like to think of him as having a very eclectic collection of expertise, a variety of fields, you know. I imagine him taking arcane, obscure courses in strange things, so, you know, conducting chemistry experiments or going off on sailing expeditions or I don't know, some sort of funny archeological things, or you know, suddenly he turns up doing motorcycle tricks or something."

WG2: "What about something that you as an actor can do?"

AD: "I like to scuba dive. Do you think that means they'll give me lots of underwater scenes in the Bahamas?"

WG2: "There ya go. It'll be called <u>Sea Vampire Hunt</u>."

AD: "Rogue Scuba Diver. I am a good swordsman, so maybe they'll do things with that."

WG2: "Did you enjoy working on <u>Highlander</u>?"

AD: "I did. I got a little trip to Paris out of it. Played a very different sort of character. I'm always drawn to things that are a surprise or that I wouldn't expect myself to be doing, or playing, and Wesley falls definitely into that category."

WG2: "Where were you born?"

AD: "I was born in Maryland, a little town on the Eastern shore of the Chesapeake. Salisbury, Maryland."

WG2: "How long did you live in Britain?"

AD: "I lived there fourteen years. I was there when I was teenager. I had grown up mostly in Seattle, and then boarding school in New Hampshire, and then moved over to London right after that. I meant to just go for a year or two and study classical acting. But when I finished that training, I joined the Royal Shakespeare Company and then just started working regularly, and life has a way of creeping up on you. Suddenly thirteen or fourteen years have gone by, and then periodically I would think to myself, 'I should think about going home one of these days, but home has become London now.'"

WG2: "So now are you homesick for England?"

AD: "I do miss it sometimes. I have now realized you can never really know where you'll live or what you'll do with the rest of your life, because it could change at any moment. So having accepted that, I may or may not live in that house that sits there that I own in London, but I love the time that I was there and I do miss things. I miss the newspapers. The real newspapers, not the tabloids. And the TV over there is very good. And I miss June and July, spring.

"There's a lot of things I miss. My friends, a lot of good friends. Thick heavy sweaters and jackets and going inside after it's cold out and having a hot cup of tea. It's funny, it's beautiful weather here in L.A., no question about it, but I do occasionally crave strong seasons."

WG2: "Do you have any funny, interesting, or creepy stories, especially from Season Three?"

AD: "On Wesley's first episode, I was very anxious to make a good impression, and was working very hard, and we had this fantastic monster who was just the size of a bloated walrus, some kind of demon. Giles and I are handcuffed and surrounded by his henchmen, and this superb actor playing that role, which is scaring the hell out of us, and in the middle of the take the little door of the tub that he's in swung open. And this is how the actor gets in and out of the tub and gets into the fat suit, and there before us is from the waist up, this great, enormous, horrific, slimy, bloated demon and from the waist down is this little actor's legs in a pair of shorts. The poor guy was roasting alive in there underneath the rubber suit, but it sort of dashed the moment."

WG2: "And then of course the Cordelia thing. We liked when you first showed up and everybody kept saying, 'Is he evil, is he evil?' and 'Princess Margaret here.' She was pretty cruel."

AD: "Yeah, yeah, she was, but it was very funny. And Alyson and I had a lot of fun at the prom. They were playing a CD or other for the soundtrack for us all to dance kind of sedately to, and everybody was getting bored, and so she snuck a wild Latin salsa song onto the soundtrack, and the whole place just let rip. Wesley and Willow did some dirty dancing not viewed by the public. It's safe to say his glasses flew off and he was never the same."

WG2: "How did you create him? Did you draw from personal experience? Was there somebody you thought of to hang him on?"

AD: "You take a lot from the way a person behaves and their interaction with the people in the scene. It was important to use Giles as the model, because it was important that he be close enough to Giles that it be irritating. That he be irritating. That he be similar but not, at the same time. Obviously when he was first brought in, he was there to kind of get tough with Giles and Buffy, so he thought about what type of personality and behavior would be most loathsome to them.

"And then used the whole Council training as a background. He probably wished himself the head of the class kind of guy, the one who did his homework and kind of was a little bit snotty about it to the other kids, and so just a sort of superficially rather irritating person, who was underneath this soft, fuzzy guy that just really wanted to be liked.

"So now as time goes on we get a chance to shed some of those outer layers and see more of the kid who, like everybody else, wanted to have good friends in school and wanted to clown around and have fun and do well. So that's what how I sort of came about making him. And then in the early days Joss was very clear with notes and saying, 'Well, that's a little too stuffy' or 'Soften that up,' or 'Get tough here with that,' so in that way together you start to mold the person. But a lot of it is just from the ground up. You start creating things, things that work you keep, things that don't work get left behind."

WG2: "Tony said that he is so, so sorry that he ever had Giles stammer cause when he does it's so hard to recreate, to follow. Is there anything that you think, 'Oh, thank God I did X' or 'Jeez, I wish I hadn't done Y?' Or something that is hard to remember that he does, or any kind of a quirk or eccentricity or little point that either you're glad you put it in or you're sorry you ever thought of it in the first place?"

AD: "Well, sometimes I'm sorry I made him so intelligent and clever and able to understand these various demons and historical references that he rattles off with such confidence, because now scripts arrive with paragraphs and paragraphs of stuff I have no idea what they're talking about.

"And I think, 'Oh, God, I've got to somehow make sense of it.' Not only that, learn it. And then I see Angel's response is a grunt and I think, 'Oh, God, if only we could switch once in a while.' But I'm only kidding, it's great fun to play him, and he really just exists now. I don't worry about him too much. Wesley's waiting for me when I get to work. Put on the clothes, there he is."

WG2: "Do you have any other projects in the works besides Season Two of Angel, or is that enough?"

AD: "We've got Beyond the City Limits, and I expect it will be out sometime after your book comes out. And this English program called Randall and Hopkirk."

WG2: "Is that BBC?"

AD: "Yes. A comedy series. I don't know how to describe it. It's pretty unique. Its airing in Britain right now, and I think it will probably come over here."

"But joining a show, it's almost like transferring, being the new kid in school, you know?"

— <u>ANOTHER UNIVERSE</u>, APRIL, 1999

ELIZA PATRICIA DUSHKU was already a full-fledged movie star (*This Boy's Life, Bye Bye, Love, True Lies*) when she stepped into Faith's leather boots during Season Three of *Buffy*. In fact, she was coming back into the business after spending two years as a regular high school student and graduating with her class a month prior to joining the cast. The Bostonian often discusses the support her family has given her, as she pursued acting, dancing, and singing. Her acting career began at the age of ten, when she accompanied her older brother on a commercial audition. She landed the role, and her brpother's agent quickly signed her.

Having come from a grounded and somewhat religious background (her relatives were shocked when Faith had sex with Xander), she displays great sympathy for the character of Faith. Faith lacks unconditional love and support, and her most influential parental authority is a one-hundred-year old villain who aspires to becoming a huge snakelike demon. She's played the daughter of several other actors including Arnold Schwarzenegger, Jamie Lee Curtis, and Paul Reiser. She fondly recalls staying over at Jamie Lee Curtis's house, sleeping in a bed with the households' animals tucked in all around her. "She was a like a mom to me," she remembers.

Eliza's role on *Buffy* was supposed to be a short stint, but actress and character soon won over the cast, crew and audience. Faith became a recurring character for Season Three, returning for four guest shots in Season Four—two on <u>Buffy</u> ("This Year's Girl" and "Who Are You") and two on *Angel* ("Five by Five and "Sanctuary").

Eliza also worked on two feature films in 1999, both of which will open in the fall of 2000: *Bring It On* (formerly titled *Cheer Fever);* and *Soul Survivor. Bring It On* is a teen comedy about competing cheer squads. It stars Kirsten Dunst and has another familiar face, Nicole Bilderbak (the Cordette whose blood gets drained in "The Wish").

Soul Survivor will be a darker piece with characters toying with the supernatural—and ultimately regretting it.

Despite her busy schedule, she still finds time for projects such as Make-A-Wish, vamping with fans (and writers) for pictures and graciously signing autographs and pictures. Knowing Joss's penchant for bringing back characters, and the fact that Faith is still around in Los Angeles, fans may live in hope of seeing more of her—on either *Angel* or *Buffy*—in the new season.

Fab Filippo as Scott Hope

Fab also works using his full first name, Fabrizio.

WG2: "Please describe for us the career path that led you to <u>Buffy</u>."

FF: "I have been working steadily in television and film. I auditioned and landed the part."

WG2: "How much like Scott are you? Would you have dumped Buffy?"

FF: "There was definitely a part of me that is like Scott, or I wouldn't have been able to play him. I think I would have dumped Buffy, because she was keeping such a big secret, and that's not okay with me."

> **"Class Rejector" Award?** In 1992 Fab appeared in a film called *Prom Night IV: Deliver Us from Evil.* He played a character named Jonathan.

WG2: "Please describe the experience of working on the <u>Buffy</u> set. Was it different in any way from other acting jobs you've had?"

FF: "Yes, for me, <u>Buffy</u> was different from most acting jobs because it's an established show with a very large and popular following. The show is successful, and in that regard, everyone working on the show has a sense of achievement and security."

WG2: Has working on <u>Buffy</u> opened other doors for you?

FF: "<u>Buffy</u> opened a few doors for me professionally, and it was a great thing because it got me out there in front of so many people, particularly the viewing audience. I remember standing at an intersection on Sunset Boulevard, waiting for a light to change. A car began to slow down as it passed me, and the person in the passenger seat pointed out the window at me and screamed, '<u>Buffy!</u>'"

Harry Groener as Mayor Richard Wilkins III

It was eerie to have a conversation with "His Honor" that didn't include fearing for our lives. . . .

WG2: "We're just very happy that you agreed to be interviewed for this book. You were huge as the Mayor, and we have no doubt that somehow in the future you will, strangely, come back."

HG: "Wouldn't that be great! I would love to come back. I had such a wonderful time on that set and they wrote such a great part."

WG2: "How did you find that balance? It was so amazing. You were so horrible but you were likeable."

HG: "A lot of that is in the writing. If there was ever a point where I would go a little too evil or a little too sinister, Joss and the other directors would always pull me back and say, 'No, no, no, just make it real nice. Just make it real easy, just make it real nice,' and so it was very clear that Joss's concept of this guy was very specific and clear. It made it really pretty easy."

WG2: "We know that actors have their tricks of the trade and such, so when you say that it was in the writing, specifically, how do you find 'it' in the writing?"

HG: "I don't really know how to answer that. A lot of it is that as you read it you have an idea of how this character is played.

"It isn't so much having to find it like a detective, a lot of it is there already. It isn't as a big a mystery as you're making it out. As you read it you go, 'Oh I see, it's more like that.'

"There is a problem in television and film that you don't have in the theater. In the theater you have so much time in rehearsal; you have four, sometimes five, if you're, lucky six weeks to rehearse a play, and so you have plenty of time to talk about stuff. The actor has time to do research and to do work on a specific character. An extreme example is, you're playing a homeless person, so you go out and you watch some homeless people. You watch how they behave, and you try to understand that behavior and then bring it to the stage.

"Well, you don't have that amount of time in television. You get the script sometimes the night before and so the first and most important thing is, you memorize your words, and then you get out there and you have to make some choices very, very quickly. That's one of the things you learn working on a series, that you have to make choices very, very quickly and you can't get too complicated. The viewer is not gonna see it. You have to make bolder choices, the colors have to be a bit brighter. You can't be too subtle. Of course, there is room for subtlety, obviously, in the Mayor; you can see his treachery, and his demonness can be subtle in ways. He can be threatening in a very subtle way. What's so terrifying about him is it can be innocuous, and he is frightening because he doesn't bare his teeth and have horns coming out his head.

"But you have to make those choices very quickly, and sometimes you say, 'Oh, okay, now there is this scene and they're here doing this and this,' but once you get onto the set the lighting will change it, the camera angle will change how the director wants to shoot the shot. Sometimes the camera is on your feet and you're already talking, and they don't really get to your face until the very last word of the sentence.

"Television is a whole different way of working. It's extremely technical in that respect. You just have to put your faith in the director and let them show you where to go. Now in this situation, there were a number of occasions that I asked, 'Can I do this and can I do this?' And they said, 'Sure, go ahead, we'll put that in.' But sometimes you don't have time to experiment."

WG2: "In terms of a proper rehearsal, it sounds like you don't ever really have one."

HG: "No, you have very little rehearsal. You run the scene, you can ask to run it again and again, but eventually they have to get to work and they have to set it up. So you work the blocking, you say, 'All right, you're going to move from here to here on this line, and then you sit over here and let's try that again, try it again, one more time, all right. Look, you go to makeup and then we'll set this shot up.'

"And we get about forty minutes, and come back, and then you have to do it. And then when you come back you'll find that where you were walking are all these pieces of equipment that you have to maneuver your way around to get to where you have to go. It's a very funny process and it's extremely technical, and the actor has to find a way to be aware of everything, but it has to be peripheral. Your primary awareness has to be on the scene and what you're doing with the character.

"It's very interesting, the two different techniques. But back to the question, sometimes it isn't always on the page. Sometimes you read it and as you get to the scene they decide to change it right there.

"There were times where in the last few episodes of the last season where the Mayor is going to his Ascension, poor Joss. Here is a man who I think never sleeps. He never, ever sleeps and of course he was writing and directing the last two episodes, and there were times when we would simply get a synopsis the night before. You get a synopsis of what the scene will eventually be that you're going to shoot the next day, so you don't even have words. You'd finally get the scenes, so you'd learn it as they're setting everything up, and then while they're setting everything up and getting ready to shoot the next scene, Joss is over in a corner writing the scene that's going to happen after that. It can be kind of nuts! But it all gets done. That's the magic of it. That's the incredible thing, it all gets done. Somehow or other it gets done. The scenes get shot, there is good work that happens, and there is a good spirit on that set. With everybody. Joss, of course, and David; Michael Grossman is a wonderful, wonderful man, wonderful director and it all comes down from the top and that also includes Sarah.

"Sarah is unbelievable, wonderfully talented and a wonderful person and she's been doing it since she was a foot high. She knows everything. She's always prepared; she's always on time; she always knows her words, when there are words to know, she knows everything about every single camera and every single nut and bolt. She knows this business. She's such a nice person, even though we work in a situation that some other actors and directors would find frustrating. It gets done and that's the amazing part. We just have to trust in that. Just be patient and do our work.

"Something that a lot of people don't understand is that the hours really are long. They can be twelve, thirteen, fourteen, fifteen-hour days. And for some people—especially Sarah—that's the norm.

"You learn to conserve your energy. You learn to focus so you know that you have enough energy and that you can do it, you are careful and take care of yourself, and you have discipline. And Sarah and the other actors do. Everybody's just great."

WG2: "What was it like to come back to shoot the video after being gone for a while?"

HG: "It was fabulous to see everybody! It was like a high school reunion! Everybody was so great. They were all, 'Hey, Harry, how ya doing, it's good to have you back,' and it was like seeing really dear friends again. I loved being back. It was good to see Eliza and to play those scenes. It was just really good. It's a comfortable place to be for me. It really is a comfortable place cause they're so supportive. They're supportive and they like the character. Everybody likes the character a lot and so you're doing things, during rehearsal you hear crew people up and around you with booms and things, you hear them laughing and chuckling and all that and that's such great support! It was great to be back. I just wanted to be there longer."

WG2: "Maybe Faith will raise you from the great beyond."

HG: "Well, there's all kinds of ways that he can be brought back. They just have to decide that's what they want to do."

WG2: "The Mayor is so popular. We think because of that affability, and all that kindness, and loving Faith and getting her a cute dress, and, 'The boys are gonna be lining up, the ones that aren't potholes.' What's so eerie about him is that a lot of evil braces itself. It's like it exerts to be evil, like you have to remember, 'Yeah I'm evil, I have forces to fight against.' But the Mayor is obviously so comfortable with his power that he doesn't worry about it. That's what's so scary."

HG: "I was in an acting class where an actor asked, I think they were doing a scene from Shakespeare and he was playing a king, and there was a question, something similar to, 'Well, I don't know how to be a king, how do you be a king, what do you have to do?' And the teacher said, 'You don't do anything, you're the king. Everyone else does everything. Everyone else bows, everyone else defers to you. You don't have to do anything to be king.'

"That's the thing about it, you don't have to be a Snidely Whiplash to be evil. Look at Ted Bundy. Look at that face, I mean look how charming he could be. If he wasn't so crazy and psychotic and if he wasn't a serial killer, under different circumstances he could be very charming, and apparently he was, which is how he got all these women. He could be charming and lovely and he's not a bad-looking guy. But he's an evil, evil, evil man!

"I've played a number of characters where you don't have to scream and yell and all that, you're just bad, and it's extremely terrifying when that happens, because you don't know what's on the inside. The Mayor knew exactly where he wanted to go, and what the end result was going to be. And even when he was thwarted, it was kind of a surprise, but it wasn't tragic. It was 'Oh, well, bummer!' I'm sure there are countless ways to bring him back and it'd be great, but as far as evil is concerned, you don't have to be, you know, 'You must pay the rent, you must pay the rent.' You can be real nice and be just awful!"

WG2: "Maybe that's how it was so effective. Spike has that kind of a mixture."

HG: "They're doing a wonderful thing with Spike. He's a vampire, but he's given certain problems now. The problem that he can't bite. He can't do anything. I think it's just charming, and so Spike becomes more of a friend even though he's got this—it's a love/hate relationship that he has with these people.

"He's become part of it and you can totally believe it if at some point he protects them. He'll find that he kind of likes these people and kind of likes Buffy. You could believe it if that ever happened.

"I love the whole vampire lore, and vampires are capable of many things. They're capable of many emotions. They're not just evil. Vampires can love, they can have terrible tragedies in their lives in terms of relationships. Just like humans can. They go through the same things. They just have these extraordinary other things. But in terms of their relationship to people, they're pretty much the same as humans, and so they don't have to be evil all the time. Angel is an example of someone who has changed his life. So it's possible."

WG2: "We think one of the most chilling bits that you did was when you were talking to Buffy and Angel about their relationship and you were talking about Edna May."

HG: "I love that scene in the cafeteria. It was so cool and so true. The relationship is doomed and they don't seem to understand that, I loved that scene. It was complicated because there were so many people and everybody has to have coverage. The more people you have in a scene, the longer it takes, because every person has to be covered for a line or for a reaction, and that means if you have ten people in a scene that's ten different setups, possibly each person with a different angle."

WG2: "What's your very favorite? Do you have a specific one that just pops out for you?"

HG: "There were a couple really funny scenes with Mr. Trick. There was a scene with Angel in the office that was kind of fun. There were a lot of different sections of scenes that were fun to do and fun lines to say. That scene in the cafeteria was fun because it was the first confrontation with Buffy. And it was the first time that we really saw each other and we dealt with each other. After all that time of being in that office, they'd be off someplace else shooting their scene—and I'd be in my little office and I'd never see them. You'd see the episode as it all came together, but you'd never work with them.

"And then finally, after all this time, I mean I would see Sarah by her trailer or in the makeup trailer or something, and we'd talk a little bit, but you'd never act with them. As it comes down to the wire, you get to get together and see each other. And it was very satisfying to finally get there, and have that scene with her and talk to her and have such great words to say, and have a really good scene. It was just terrific.

"I was usually with the second unit. They have two units. One, the main unit that shoots the main part of the show, and then a second unit that will pick up scenes, like the Mayor in the office or the Mayor walking down the hall. Or a lot of times, the second unit is the unit that goes out and shoots exteriors, you know. And a lot of times I was with the second unit, and they just shot these things, sometimes later in the day when everybody was done. I liked all the things that happened, the knife going through the hand, swords going through the chest."

WG2: "Did you green screen?"

HG: "A lot of that was green screen. Doing the stuff with the hand was very complicated, very different. All different kinds of angles and ways of doing it, and then eventually it had to be shot in front of a green screen.

"And then the sword going through the chest had to be shot a few different ways. They had a thing that was harnessed to me with half a sword connected to it, so that I could stagger back and it be stuck in there, and then you have to do it in front of a green screen.

"In the final episode, where he's at the podium and he starts the transformation, somebody worked on—and it took hours and hours for them to work on—a suit that was supposed to be kind of a break-away suit that breaks as my body expands, like the Hulk. So somebody worked on this jacket, and the jacket had thirty little tiny pieces of fishing line that were attached to different parts of the suit all hanging out of it, that all was supposed to go to four people. It was divided up four ways, two on one side two on the other, and at a certain point they were to pull on these pieces of fishing line and it was supposed to open up the suit.

"So we get to it and we start to set it up; it takes forever to get the little things unwound and separated from each other; it was a mess. And it was near the end of the shoot on the night that we shot it, now this is very funny because we shot where the high school is, of course it is a real high school and people go to that high school. And so you're out there, the shot's near the end of the night, the sun is coming up, we have to get out of there because we can't have it light, it's supposed to be the eclipse, so everybody is rushing to finish it before the sun comes up. 'Come on, come on, we gotta get it before the sun comes up or we'll all be dusted!' So we tried to do as much as we could. We couldn't get the suit tearing, so then we had to do that in front of a green screen. We stand there in front of a green screen and we do it. Now there, it's so technical and very, very specific; you're standing there and the camera is locked, which means it doesn't move with you, so you can't really move that much. You gotta be still. So I'm standing there at the podium and the transformation is beginning to happen and I'm doing whatever it is the hell I'm doing, and these four people begin to pull, and nothing happens. And they're pulling harder and harder, and I'm literally being pulled, and I can't move that much. I'm supposed to stay perfectly still, and they're pulling and pulling and pulling and it's just not working. These four people are pulling at this jacket, and parts of it are ripping and parts of it aren't, and it's just getting stuck, and they're pulling harder and harder and I'm trying to maintain my position. It was hysterical! They finally said, 'Cut!' and burst into laughter. It was just the funniest thing! The thing wouldn't work! It wouldn't fall apart! But it all worked out. They figured it out. But somebody worked for hours to rig it, I mean all that work and it didn't work. And you only had one shot. You couldn't take the time to rig it again.

"I think you see a tiny bit of the transformation at the podium at the school and then they do a digital thing and you see it all happening, but I have enough on the green screen, and they focus more on the face or something. They wanted to give the impression that my upper body was also changing.

"I loved all that stuff, and the head splitting, I thought was a very funny scene. What was so cool is that when they got the head that they were going to use, you only saw the back of the head. The front of the head looked like Charlie Haid. He was on <u>Hill Street Blues</u>. It looked like Charlie Haid's face.

"They had this head and it was all mechanical, and they split it, and the actor sort of timed it, the actor that came toward me with the broadsword had to time it so that the blade came down and the head opened up at the right time. It was just the head and the top part of your shoulders. That's all that little piece was, and it was on a pedestal and it was all mechanically done. It opened and closed mechanically."

WG2: "Is there something you wish you'd done with the Mayor that you didn't do? Was there anything you wish you hadn't done?"

HG: "Gosh, I really can't think of anything. We got pretty much what we wanted with him. The danger is, you don't want to do too much. I always like to put little things in that give you a little idiosyncrasy, that gives you an indication of, or defines a character more.

"There was one scene where I tidy up my office when I'm about to leave, and there's a pen, the pen and pencil set that's on the front of the desk, and I asked Michael, 'Before I go, can I just straighten out that pen?' And he said, 'Yeah absolutely,' and that was picked up on by people. I have heard fans say 'You know, when you straightened that pen, that was so cool!'

"It was something that I thought of that he would do. He would make sure that everything is all tidy and nice and neat and orderly. It was just a little tiny thing that we could take time to do as he was leaving. He just stopped, straightened the pen and then moved on. It was a lovely little touch, and I'm glad that Michael let me do it. I like little things like that, that help define a personality."

WG2: "If you were really the Mayor, do you think it would be easier to control Faith or Buffy?"

HG: "I think it's easier probably to control Buffy. Buffy is a bit more stable. Faith is very much her own person, although their relationship is a very paternal relationship. This was never really talked about, other than maybe it was a child that he didn't have, and that maybe it was a child he had and that died, maybe it was that he finds something in Faith that he wants to nurture.

"I think she does, at some point in another episode, talk about her parents, and she was left on her own, and so she finds in him kind of unconditional love. He wants her to be better. A lot of times he doesn't really want her to change her feelings about things. He likes very much that she's proactive in her career. When she turns evil, he likes that very much.

"He wants her to be better, and he wants her to have confidence in herself, that she is a good person, and that she is beautiful, and he provides a kind of a positive reinforcement for her that she doesn't really have, and she gives herself by what she can accomplish, which is a great deal, as a Slayer.

"But he provides that for her so there is a true affection there, and there's a trust there that is very strong between the two of them. I think he really cares for her and he really loves her, and I think that she deep down inside feels the same way, although they've never said that to each other."

WG2: "Well when she's watching the video and you say something like 'Heck, maybe we made it,' and she gets a real sad smile, she kind of wells up, dreaming of him and dreaming that you're having a picnic and all those things."

HG: "I know, her dream is a very normal dream, isn't it? It's a very nice 'if everything was normal, we'd go out and it'd be my dad and we can go have a picnic and we can talk about stuff and it'd just be a great relationship.' That's the fantasy that she has. She has on the kind of clothes that he wanted her to wear. He wanted her to see that she was also this person, and that she fits very well as someone who can wear a nice lovely feminine summer dress as opposed to the tough leather and boots and all the popular young kids' clothes.

"No, their relationship I think is very special, but he wouldn't want to control her. I think he would have influence over her, and the influence he would use would be one of support, of love. Which she obviously responds to because he knows that she is extremely intelligent, and he knows that she'll get it. If he just is supportive and shows her that he cares, she'll come along.

"He doesn't need to force. He doesn't need to use his power. He doesn't need to do any of that stuff with her. It's not necessary. He just has to show her that he cares and that he will be there for her and that she can rely on him. She can depend on him and that's very comforting.

"What he does basically through love is give her boundaries. Young kids who are a problem, a lot of that comes from not having the correct boundaries and not having a structure, and he provides that for her, you know. And gives her a lot of responsibility, gives her things to do, they are of course killing people, but he gives her a kind of boundary and a place to go for security and structure. And she really responds to that, so if there is any way to control her it would be that way."

WG2: "It just makes him more of a person, a faceted individual character."

HG: "It rounds him out a bit more. That's what I like about Joss, he takes time to set things up and you can round out a character, you can find out about their history and you usually don't get time to do that on television.

"But [TV shows are] classrooms, and Joss also does that in his show. There are wonderful allegories, and moral lessons for young people about how to behave with each other, and what our relationships are with our parents, and how we can empower ourselves as young people. And he does a wonderful job doing that, and he does it with excellent, excellent, excellent writing.

"There are so many friends of my generation and older that watch the show, and they watch it primarily for—well, first of all they love the fantasy, but they also love it because the writing is so good, and they love the tongue-in-cheek quality of it. But they constantly bring up the fact that they love the writing, they love the writing.

"Joss sets the rules, he says, 'This is how I see this show, this is my world that I've created and this is how I kind of want to see it and how I want to tell the story.' And they write those shows and they're just terrific, but there's a lesson."

George Hertzberg as Adam

We interviewed George after a fitting in the costume department. At the time, we had no clue who Adam was, or if he would be important in terms of the show's development. Were we in for a surprise.

WG2: "Where were you were born?"

GH: "I was born in upstate New York. Glens Falls."

WG2: "What's your birthday?"

GH: "November 6. I was raised in Houston, Texas, and I went to USC. I have a Bachelor of Fine Arts degree in Acting from USC."

WG2: "What was your first acting job you received money for?"

GH: "That would be, I think, in high school. I emceed a fashion show for my girlfriend's mother or something. Imagine a few hundred women, and here I was dressed in a costume from a play we'd done. We hosted this whole thing. It was very funny. That was the first gig I was paid for."

WG2: "What was the first school theater project you did?"

GH: "The first one was in kindergarten. 'T'was the Night before Christmas.' I was the father and I was sitting onstage and I had the book, I was the tallest kid, so I had my two best friends sitting in front of me like I'm their father. And I said 'T'was the night before Christmas,' and that's all I said. And then in the end, we sang 'Rudolph, the Red-nosed Reindeer.'"

WG2: "What was your career path that led you here?"

GH: "I was always interested in theater and acting. Even in kindergarten when I did that play. As soon as the play closed, the next day in school I went to my teachers and said, 'When's the next one, when's the next one?' and she said, 'You'll have to wait until fifth grade.' I was upset about that.

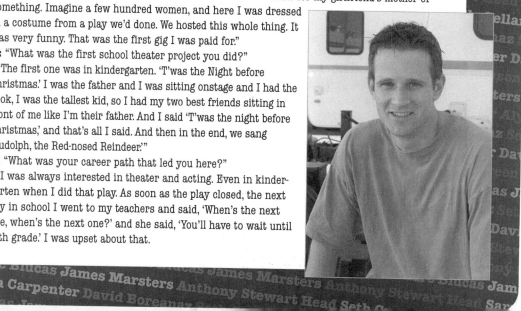

"Then I ended up going to a junior high that had a really good theater program and I did mime and stuff like that, and then my high school was doing shows with twenty-five thousand dollar budgets, which is pretty much unheard of in high school theater.

"We had a lot of great community support, and the families and the parents were very involved and the local businesses were buying seats and blocks of tickets. So when it came time for college and I didn't know what I wanted to do, my mother said, 'You know, you can go to school for theater.' 'Really? Okay.'

"So I went and auditioned at USC and got in and still didn't know what the TV element or film element was going to be, and then I got out and started doing some commercials."

WG2: "What were some of your commercials?"

GH: "Carl's Jr. commercial, Bud Light, Pontiac."

WG2: "And then what happened?"

GH: "While I was doing that I had also managed to do a couple other things, <u>Home Improvement</u>, <u>High Incident</u>, <u>3rd Rock From the Sun</u> so I've done a few things here and there, and just kinda kicking around. Last year I cowrote and executive produced a play at the Stella Adler Theater. I played five roles in it. It ran for six weeks."

WG2: "What was it called?"

GH: "<u>Hardware: a Miracle Play</u>. It was a very funny, original comedy. Although exec producing is a very difficult job. I don't wish that on anybody."

WG2: "How did you find out about this part? How did you read for it? Did you know that it was going to be more than standing up and saying 'Mommy?'"

GH: "I went in and actually was given a monologue of Adam's to do, and it was one of those things. You know what it's like, acting. If you want to do it you have to take the time to do it, and a lot of people don't appreciate it as an art form. I really think it is on every level. You have to really be willing to do it, and it just happened to be that I was lucky and in the right place at the right time.

"I came in and did it, and I left. I was going downstairs and they called me back in and gave me a couple of adjustments and did it again and they liked my choice. I knew that it was recurring when I went in, but I didn't know, I still don't really know to what extent, because recurring is so ambiguous. They don't know, as far as I understand, what exactly they want it to be. All I know is that I'm excited because I have an opportunity to bring a lot of what I want to do to this. I'm so jazzed! It's so awesome."

WG2: "Like what for example?"

GH: "A lot of the demons on the show they have already, they kind of know how they want them to be. I think in a way, not that they don't know how they want this character to be, but I think that I have a little room to bring my own take on it a little. I mean, it's a new character that they are developing here. That's kind of what I mean. Besides I'm grinning from ear to ear.

"I got fitted for a contact lens last week. They had me in four hours of special-effects makeup that day. They had me in a plaster cast from right above my knees all the way up my back. Pretty crazy, but the contact lens was alright. I've never had one in my eye, and they pull out this big thing about the size of a quarter."

WG2: "What does it look like?"

GH: "They just fitted me for a certain type, I'm not sure. It's similar to what the other demons have. I don't know what color they are gonna go with, but that's just the fit and it's gonna be really, really cool. It's so exciting to be in here and to see everybody. So much energy around it. I really wanted to do this."

WG2: "When you look through the contact, what do you see?"

GH: "Your vision comes through your pupil, not through your iris. It just covers the iris and the rest of the white part of your eye; there is a hole in the middle, so all you see is basically a faint outline of the lens. It doesn't really disrupt your vision. You could drive or anything like that. The white ones, those you can't see."

WG2: "Have you actually shot any scenes yet since this episode?"

GH: "The first one is Friday."

WG2: "That is so neat. Your premiere. You must get tired of this question, but how tall are you?"

GH: "I never like to answer that question. Six foot four. I played basketball and put my height to good use."

WG2: "Is there anything so far—we know you're brand new here—is there anything so far that surprised you about this job? Something you assumed it would be like and it's not?"

GH: "Hmm. Other than I guess the level of—I guess the intensity that everybody seems to be—I know everybody's very excited about it. And things I've done in the past, it's been, you know, you come in for a fitting, for example, or you go to get something done, and everybody's going, like, 'Okay. Great.'

"But it seems like everybody is very actively interested to see where this goes. Everybody is putting in so much energy. I guess for me that's so nice to see. It's so exciting. Everyone is so nice, it's just a great group of people to be around."

WG2: "We have no idea what you're going to look like. Do you know what you're going to look like?"

GH: "Yeah, I do have some idea. I know how my face is going to be structured, and stuff like that. I'm just hoping I get to move around. I'm a pretty physical person, I do yoga, and weight-lifting, so I'm very physically active."

Paige Moss as Veruca

Paige's reminder that "only silver bullets kill werewolves" left us wondering if she knows something we don't. If so, we hope Veruca will be back.

WG2: "Would you please tell us how you came to the part of Veruca? Whom did you tell first when you were hired?"

PM: "I put in two different-colored contacts and picked the sexiest outfit I had. I went in to audition and decided this was only going to work if I was willing to let go and have fun.

"So that's what I did, I let go, and she just came out, wolf and all. I got a call back from Joss later that day. The second auditon was different, I actually got to read with Oz! I was excited because we had worked together before, so I thought that would work out in my favor.

"But when I got there Seth was already working with another girl. I immediately started to worry because I wanted to practice beforehand, but we didn't get to! (Actors, we're all so insecure.) It must have worked out for the best, because we had great chemistry in the room, even with all those extra eyes watching! It went great! Seth told me later, when it was all over, Joss picked up my photo and said, 'That's my Veruca!'

"The first person I told was my boyfriend."

WG2: "How did you create the character of Veruca? How much did you draw from personal experience? What do you particularly like about her? What do you dislike?"

PM: "I created Veruca from my lack of confidence. She was the fearless side of me that I wish would come out more! My dog Faux Pas helped too! And my cat Wolf, who thinks he's too good for everyone, I think Veruca related to that. Veruca was sooooo different from most of the parts I play; she was wild and sexy! I love Joss for letting me be different-looking and still be considered sexy."

WG2: "Do you think Oz should have chosen life with you over killing one of his own kind?"

PM: "Yes, Oz and Veruca belong together. They actually had the chance to live out their lives as soulmates. How often does a chance like that come along in a lifetime? Look at Buffy and Angel, and how much pain they are in because they can't be together. Oz and Veruca's bond is something that no one else in the world could share. And remember, soulmates always find their way back home to each other.

"And only a silver bullet can kill a werewolf!"

WG2: "Do you have any funny stories or anecdotes you could share with us about your time on the Buffy lot?"

PM: "My favorite story is when we were filming the morning after Veruca and Oz's first night together as werewolves, in Griffith Park. Oz and I had to wake up in the woods together naked. Well, it was my second day, and I had to wear a thong in front of everyone. Oz was in biker shorts. He saw that they had put me in this tiny underwear, and he changed into the same thing. He said if I had to, he would too. I felt so much better not being alone. Seth is a great person; that was completely unnecessary, but he did it anyway!"

WG2: "Did you work with, or know anyone, in the cast, staff, or crew previous to working on the show?"

PM: "I had worked with Seth before in the movie Can't Hardly Wait."

WG2: "Do you have any scars, tattoos, or distinguishing marks?"

PM: "I have five tattoos and a big scar on my eyebrow. They make me unique."

WG2: "We'd like to hear about your forthcoming work."

PM: "I'm currently working on a slasher film called The Dare Club (or Killer Instinct, they don't know for sure yet) in Pennsylvania, and next up is another film called My Father's House, filming this summer in Baltimore."

Phina Oruche as Olivia

Phina Oruche kindly faxed us her answers, following up with a phone call to make sure we received them.

WG2: "Would you please tell us how you came to the part of Olivia?"

PO: "I auditioned for the part. Amy McIntyre Britt had cast me before in an independent film, so I was comfortable with her. Joss Whedon was in the room, I had no idea who he was because he is so young looking. I remember he gave me an adjustment in my interpretation of Olivia. Thank God I did not know who he was because I could just do my work and not get too nervous."

WG2: "How did you create the character?"

PO: "I created the character as simply as possible. The writing is excellent, so that makes it much easier. I'm from Liverpool, but I wanted her to be from a much more southern part of England, because I wanted more of a cosmopolitan feel. I love Olivia. I don't play people I don't like or can't learn from."

"I especially like the interracial aspect of their relationship, because in England we have less hang ups about that than I have witnessed here, so it was wonderful to create, with no concern about that."

WG2: "What was your experience while working on <u>Buffy</u>? How was it different (or was it different) from other projects you've worked on?"

PO: "The camaraderie on the set of <u>Buffy</u> is pretty amazing. There is also a lightness about things even though the work is specific and serious, the atmosphere does not have to be. I appreciate that."

WG2: "What are some special talents or skills you have that you didn't get to use on <u>Buffy</u>?"

PO: "I am a painter, I have not used that anywhere yet. Though I was able to draw The Gentlemen from the 'Hush' episode."

WG2: "Do you think Olivia should continue her relationship with Giles, even though he deals in the things that go bump in the night?"

PO: "Olivia should stay with Giles, lots of times we go through challenging things. It's easier if someone loves you. If someone is in your corner."

WG2: "Did you work with, or know anyone, in the cast, staff, or crew previous to working on the show?"

PO: "I knew Tony Head [Rupert Giles]; we had studied together before at acting class. I am an admirer of his work. He's a fabulous actor. And then we had also read a play together at one point. We had mentioned trying to find some material to work on for the class, it never panned out. Funnily enough, he wanted to put my name forward but was at home in England, and so by the time he got through to Joss with the information the role had been cast and he trusted Joss's choice. It is a wonderful thing to know that it was meant to be. And quite flattering that he remembered me at the time the opportunity came up."

WG2: "Do you have any scars, tattoos, or distinguishing marks?"

PO: "I have a tattoo on my head; it's a drawing of hieroglyphics of two men praying. It means to 'praise abundantly.' Which I feel is the secret to success; continually praising and giving glory to God. It's tiny and it's covered now by my dreadlocks. But it serves as a reminder. On the left temple, just above the beauty spot that's there."

WG2: "Hobbies? Pets? Superstitions?"

PO: "Yoga, hiking, and swimming. I have two dogs, Calvin and Milli. Calvin's a Staffordshire bull terrier and Milli's a pitbull. I am not a superstitious person. I believe in God and like to start off my day quietly in prayer or in the Word."

WG2: "We'd like to hear about your forthcoming work."

PO: "I have guest spots on <u>V.I.P.</u> and as a life-saving doctor on <u>The Pretender</u> coming this summer; I'm currently shooting a pilot called <u>Fearsum</u> for Fox (which got picked up)."

Leonard Roberts as Forrest Gates

WG2: "Tell us how your acting career got started. What was your very first professional job, and how did you end up on <u>Buffy</u>?"

LR: "My career started when I realized that acting was what I wanted to do. There had been other directions I thought about going in, journalism and law among others, but [I felt an] inexplicable draw to being able to be a part of all those worlds at one time, something magical, and that's what acting seemed to be. The way I saw it, [as an actor] I could be a journalist on Monday and a lawyer on Thursday. I saw it as my all access pass to new people and experiences. It still took the persuading of a friend to get me on a stage when I was in high school, but after that I didn't look back. I applied to The Theatre School at DePaul University, and that's when I felt I was really on my way to making it happen. After graduation I jumped right into the theatre scene in Chicago.

"I grew up in St. Louis, but when I went to DePaul I fell in love with Chicago and stayed. I had had a taste of what L.A. was like when I was part of a showcase with my graduating class. I got a lot of positive feedback from people here, but I just didn't feel it was the place for me at the time. L.A. was a different animal to me, and I felt I needed a little time to find my bearings, so I opted to stay in Chicago. I continued to work in theatre and eventually film and television. I tried coming out to L.A. again and it still didn't feel right. I went back to Chicago and figured when the time was right I would know. The time came in '98. I had a role in the TV miniseries The 60s, my manager was here, and I had an agent. It felt as if everything had fallen into place to allow me to be here on my own terms. I had just been here a year when I auditioned for Buffy. I met Joss Whedon and Jim Contner, who was directing Episode Seven, and read for Graham. Joss asked me to stick around and read the Forrest role. I really didn't think I had a chance. I remember a couple of the guys there were huge. I figured, 'If I was Joss Whedon and needed someone to hunt vampires and demons I'd probably pick that big Marvel comic looking guy.' I had a good time reading both roles, and decided to just leave it at that. I left the stages and went to Best Buy because I still didn't have a sound system in my place. I was in line when I got the call from my manager.

"It's been a really good time. I've never worked on a show like this before. I remember coming back to the stages after I had gotten cast and seeing the Cro Mags from 'Beer Bad' lounging out on the lot. They were reading, drinking coffee, and just hanging out with this intense makeup. I remember thinking, 'This is going to be a wild ride.' It's been a blast, and I'm really looking forward to what Joss has in store for these guys."

WG2: "The Commandos."

LR: "Yeah, I think it's going to be fun. I'm thinking, all my friends with kids and little brothers and sisters, I'm going to call them up and let them know I'm on the show. I call them and they tell me, 'What? No, it's our favorite show.' I had seen it here and there and I really wasn't aware of how big it was. I mean, my first day was the week that I just saw all of these companion guides and fan books and I think Entertainment Weekly came out with an issue that week about every episode.

"It's funny; I live in Hollywood, and I like to swim at the Y. I see guys all the time and we've established this kind of 'Hey, how-you-doing?' relationship and we just pass each other up. One day I'm stretching, and a guy comes up to me, he has this totally different look on his face, and he says, 'You're on my favorite TV show.' And I'm like, 'Huh?' 'Buffy, my favorite TV show, man.' It's great. I thought if anyone does recognize me from the show they will probably be younger girls. I've been surprised that most of the people have been guys around my age. I was in St. Louis and this guy walks up to me and says, 'You're on Buffy. I don't care what anybody says about me I love Buffy, you hear me? I love that girl! How long you been on? How long you going to be on, man? What's going to happen? What about Spike, man? Spike going to be like impotent for the rest of the season, man? What's going on?' All I can say is, 'Well, I don't know. You're just going to have to watch and see.' I'm walking down the street and people are just like, 'Man, you're on Buffy—the GI Joe guy!' So, we'll see what happens."

WG2: "Bailey Chase said he came out here and decided he didn't know anything about acting. He went to London for a year and then he came back. And you came out here and you decided to go back to Chicago for a while and then you came back. And then you both ended up on Buffy."

LR: "I think everybody has their own path and it just works out the way it's supposed to. I'm trying to give myself over to that now. I'm just enjoying the ride. There have been times when we've been on set in our full Initiative gear complete with tasers, rifles, and infrared goggles and Marc would turn to me and say, 'This is like every little boy's dream and it's our job.' That makes it fun. It doesn't even seem like work. My phrase of choice right now is, 'All this and a check.'

"When I first met James, he said, 'How many times did you dream about this when you were nine?' Every day. I was and continue to be a big daydreamer. I enjoy this whole Batman-type thing, you know? We're not so mild mannered college students by day but when the sun goes down…"

WG2: "When's your birthday?"

LR: "November seventeenth."

WG2: "What would you like to do that you haven't gotten to do? What's some talent or skill that you have? Or ability? Bailey said he'd like to let everybody know he could talk."

LR: [big laughter] "I guess he did become the strong quiet one. Forrest, on the other hand, is always running his mouth about something. One day I made a crack to Joss about our college campus wardrobe. Marc, Bailey, and I kind of looked like a boy band. Joss was standing by the monitor and I asked if he was looking for a place to put in our big dance number. We started joking around about what the pitch meeting would be like. 'So the guys have just killed this demon and now…they're going to dance….' I don't know anything they have in store, I really like being surprised. You know, as long as I live, I'd like to stay alive."

WG2: "But just remember. There used to be a character named Jenny Calendar and she was Giles's true love. And Angel killed her when he was evil. She's been back twice since."

LR: "Really?"

WG2: "Yeah, and when they killed her—the day they killed her, Joss walked up to her and said, 'Now, don't forget, I'm the one who brought back Sigourney Weaver in Alien Resurrection. So there's always a way to come back on Buffy. So if you get killed, don't assume you're done'"

LR: "I've been hearing that. Everybody comes back. I'm always flipping through [the new script], I'm like 'Forrest, Forrest, Forrest, Forrest, all right! Made it through.' One day I got [a script] at my door and I picked it up, opened it and it was called 'Doomed.' And I thought, 'We're dead.'"

WG2: "And here you are, and you're in a book."

LR: "All right."

Jack Stehlin as Dr. Angleman

We interviewed Jack Stehlin during lunch at the Santa Clarita location.

WG2: "You graduated from Julliard."

JS: "Yes. I first got introduced to acting at the University of South Carolina, where I went to be a baseball player. I played a little bit of college baseball until I realized that I wasn't going to be able

Forrest did die…and appeared in "Primeval" as an enhanced dead guy.

to make it to the big leagues. That's a harsh realization, but luckily for me I stumbled into acting as an elective course at the University of South Carolina.

"As I got more interested I really decided, 'I'm gonna try to find out where I can really learn how to do this,' so I applied to the major schools after going to the library and checking [them] out. That's what lead me to Julliard.

"I went up to Julliard and auditioned and got in. Graduated in 1982, and then I went into John Houseman's Acting Company, which is a classical repertory company. I spent years and years going to Milwaukee and Boston. I was member of ART, the American Repatory Theater for a few years. I toured the world with them. Worked with all the premier theater directors there. I was very lucky because I continued to work in the theater.

"So about five years ago I decided that I really had to look after the other parts of my dream which was to be part of, I guess, the Hollywood industry. Really what you're trying to do then is just get your work out to more people. I wanted to be involved with bigger things. Television and movies.

"So I've been out here chasing that for the last four years or so. It has been going very well. This past season I did a guest star on ER, a guest star on Judging Amy and I'm on a play-or-pay for a recurring role on a thing called Get Real. Now I'm doing this.

"It's been a good season and things are starting to pick up. It takes a long time to connect. Some people I guess come here right away and they're in. Me, it's been a slow drive. I did other shows as well in these last few years. The Practice, which was a good show that I did, and a couple of movies of the week.

"Also I started a theater company here, which I operate out of the Odyssey Theater over on the west side of Los Angeles. I have a residency there with my theater company, so we do plays there all through the year. I also teach a Shakespeare workshop, which is kind of like when I'm not making money acting, I make money teaching Shakespeare."

WG2: "We know its very, very different to work on TV and film versus theater, and the people who work on Buffy say it's very different working on TV versus features primarily because of the grueling schedules they keep."

JS: "It's really hard work. I guess the typical image of what's going on here is a very romantic kind of fantasy life idea. But I think that people who play leads on television shows work very hard. Especially if you're carrying the show, and you have a big part. You know every week to come up with it and work through it and constantly learning lines, learning twenty scripts a season, wow, in a row. That's got to be really hard. I've never played a lead through many, many shows. I'm looking forward to the struggle. I hope I get a chance to suffer through that."

WG2: "Do you have any idea how you want your character to go?"

JS: "What I sense right now is that it's not a black-and-white thing, and I think that's more interesting to act. It's not just evil. What I'm sensing from the script right now—and I'm trying to get to it, and I'll speak to the director today and maybe learn a little more—I think that it's more fun if you see him struggling to do something that he believes in.

"In my case, in my script here he's going to try and have Buffy knocked off, but she's in the way of something that he feels is more important and she doesn't realize that she's endangering this work that is more important than what she's doing.

"But I think there is a chance to make him not necessarily a bad guy but somebody who is trying to do good work and try to help the world in his way. He becomes kind of obsessed and loses sight of other things.

"I think that's true where you start to believe in what you're doing so strongly that you just must have it that way. I think, I hope, that's the way we'll do it because I think that's more fun and it's just a straight on approach."

WG2: "They usually kind of try to tweak it."

JS: "I think that's a good way to go. So that you have real people, real full-dimension people trying to live their lives instead of just being a bad or a good guy."

WG2: "What do you think of the possibility of working day in, day out in the dark?"

JS: "I like it because I'm ready for that. I was lucky to do the theater and really fall in love with acting and in a very idyllic situation, and I think that's a great challenge to do a show day after day. I'd like to try. So maybe wish me luck and maybe I'll get a show to do that in.

"I think it would be very hard work, but first of all there are realistic things involved. I have a wife and my wife is about to have a baby. I have real reasons to want to work. I'm an actor who wants to work.

"I've been fortunate. Hey, I'd like to make a lot of dough and be part of something. I'd also like to be part, in that way, be part of something to make it good, not just to be there and take the pay-checks. I love to make things good, try to help and make the show good. You have an opportunity to do that in a leading role to really help improve the thing and make it better and better. I think that'd be kind of cool."

Danny Strong as Jonathan

Danny Strong is a funny and considerate guy;
at the request of a friend, he called a fan of his on her birthday.

WG2: "Where were you born? Do you have brothers, sisters, or any other relatives in the industry?"

DS: "I was born on a warm summer's day in Harbor City, California. However I would spend my entire childhood in Manhattan Beach, California. I have an older sister, and a younger half brother. I have no immediate relatives in the entertainment industry (too bad for me). However, I have a distant cousin who is a really great screenwriter that I recently met for the first time."

WG2: "What was your background that led you to acting?"

DS: "I think that I was always interested in acting from a very young age (like seven or eight). I was a movie buff as a kid, and I used to rent movies all the time. I had really odd taste. Chinatown, All That Jazz, and Apocolypse Now were my favorites as a kid—in fact, they still are. Christopher Walken was my favorite actor when I was ten (that just isn't healthy). I started acting in school plays in high school, and I knew this was what I wanted. I was just always drawn to acting. I sort of believe that I was a vaudeville actor in a past life, and that's why I wanted to do it from such a young age."

WG2: "What was your first professional acting job?"

DS: "My first professional acting job was a Doritos commercial when I was fifteen. Dean Cain played my older brother, and I was in the spot for maybe three seconds. My next job wouldn't come for three more years (that sounds like I'm writing my autobiography), when I did the musical Oliver! at the Civic Light Opera of South Bay Cities. I was the Artful Dodger. When I think of my first professional acting job, I think of Oliver! and not the commercial—it was a much more exciting event for me."

WG2: "Please describe your career and how it led you to Buffy."

DS: "Well, after Oliver! I attended the USC School of Theatre and I did a couple of professional plays while I was still a student. I also booked my first role on a TV show, the very powerful <u>Saved by the Bell— The New Class</u>, and a small part in the movie <u>Dangerous Minds</u>, but I was cut out of the film. Then right after I graduated from college, I started landing small roles on various TV shows. One of those was the pilot presentation of <u>Buffy</u>."

WG2: "How did you audition for Jonathan? How did you find out you had the part?"

DS: "Originally, I auditioned for the role of Xander, but I didn't even get a callback for the part (I guess I just wasn't what they were looking for). Then the casting director called me back in to read for some small parts for Joss, and I got the role of Student #2 or something like that. My big line was 'Are you the new girl?' Then they brought me in to audition for some guest star roles during Season One, but I never got the part.

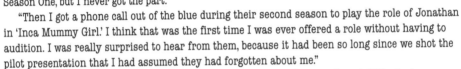

"Then I got a phone call out of the blue during their second season to play the role of Jonathan in 'Inca Mummy Girl.' I think that was the first time I was ever offered a role without having to audition. I was really surprised to hear from them, because it had been so long since we shot the pilot presentation that I had assumed they had forgotten about me."

WG2: "Did you realize you would be on more than once when you first got the role? If not, please describe the process by which your part continued to evolve?"

DS: "I never knew that the role would come back. People hinted to me that it would, but I usually ignore that kind of talk because so often people tell you things that never happen. I'm not really sure how the part evolved. At times they would write him in to the script, and other times I think they would just write something for a random student and decide to use me for it to keep the continuity of the world."

WG2: "How did you feel when 'Earshot' was held back from being broadcast in the U.S.?"

DS: "I agreed that 'Earshot' should have been pulled. It was just too similiar to what had happened, and I think it would have been totally insensitive to air it at that time. I'm glad that it was eventually aired, because I think it's a really wonderful episode. Jane Espenson is a fantastic writer."

WG2: "Please describe how you see Jonathan and how he has changed."

DS: "I see Jonathan as someone who just wants to fit in and be liked. I know that some people see him as a geek or a nerd, but I don't think so at all. I think he's just confused and a bit awkward. He's the kind of guy that it's just going to take him a little bit longer than most to feel comfortable in his own skin."

WG2: "Please talk about 'Superstar.' What it was like to be the star, etc. If you have funny or interesting stories about that or any of your appearances, please share them."

DS: "'Superstar' is one of the best times I've had on any shoot. It was such a beautifully written episode (obviously I'm a big Jane Espenson fan), and I got to do things that I never get to do—especially the fight scenes, I never get to kick ass. It was also cool to get out of the striped shirts and wear some cool clothes for once.

"Unfortunately, I got really sick about halfway through the shoot, so that put a slight damper on the whole thing. In the scene where I croon [to] the audience, I had enough medication in me to kill a small horse. Sarah was going to hold an intervention to get me off of the nosespray, but I kept telling her I wasn't taking it, then I'd go shoot up in my trailer. (God bless Neo-synephrine!)"

WG2: "Do you know what's going to happen with Jonathan in the future?"

DS: "Honestly, I have no idea. He may never return for all I know (but I hope not). No one has said anything to me about returning, so like everyone else, I will just have to wait and see what happens. Hopefully Jonathan will return and have some traces of his 'superstar' alter ego popping up from time to time. That would be wonderful!"

DS: "Anything you'd like to say to your fans?"

WG2: "I can honestly say that I love the fans! This is the first TV show, film, play, or anything that I have ever been a part of that people care so deeply about. It makes such a difference when you go to work and you know that people are going to be excited about seeing what you're doing. Also, some of the fans came to see some of the plays I've done in Los Angeles, and that has really meant a lot to me.

Hey Nancy - What do you think? If you need anything else, don't hesitate to send me a note. Danny

Kristine Sutherland as Joyce Summers

Kristine had flown in from Italy to work in the last episode of the season.

WG2: "We know you've moved to Italy. That must be just wonderful! How long have you been there?"

KS: "We arrived last August, but we are only here for a year. The idea was to come for one school year."

WG2: "Are you just taking the time off when you're there, are you doing any kind of work over there?"

KS: "My husband and I decided to take a year off from work. It had been a longtime dream of ours for our daughter to learn a second language when she was young enough to learn it organically. You know, you talk about something forever and you have endless fantasies about doing it, but you wonder in that quiet place if you really have the guts to do it. One day everything just fell into place and not seizing the moment didn't even seem like an option.

"It was hard for me to leave the show, but here was this phenomenal opportunity that wasn't going to come again. You have to ask yourself, 'If I don't go, will I regret it at the end of the day?' It has been an amazing experience."

WG2: "So you just fly back when you have scenes in the episode and then fly home?"

KS: "Yes. fortunately in terms of what was happening in the show it was an okay time to leave, because with Buffy going to college and everything, for mom to drift into the background isn't so unnatural. When I first went to college I don't think I thought about my mom at all."

WG2: "We really liked when they had Joyce go off for Thanksgiving, and she left to go some place else, and we thought, 'Right on, Mom.' We thought of all those long Thanksgiving dinners and making the stuff and how nice that she just went off to visit somebody and Buffy had to fend."

KS: "Yes. My mom actually did that. I think it might have been my freshman year of college or maybe my last year of high school. My parents were divorced and my mother left. I'm not sure where she went. She left us with the house and my father. And I had to cook Thanksgiving dinner."

WG2: "In 'Band Candy,' when you were sixteen, was that how you were at sixteen, or did you just sort of create a composite of what sixteen-year-olds are like?"

KS: "It was sort of a composite although I have to say that I was not into Burt Reynolds when I was sixteen.

"That was a really interesting episode. I always think that I remember very clearly what it was like to be a teenager, but to actually walk it, talk it, and inhabit it, it was so much more intense than just sitting around remembering what you were like. And it was interesting because I have to say some of it was really fun, and some of it was painful. It brought up feelings that I hadn't even thought about in so long.

"Like the scene with the music, it was that thing of being a teenage girl and wanting to make a connection with the guy and he's into the music, and he's into cigarettes, and he's into the scene, and you want to make a connection with him but you don't quite know how. You're just going along with him because he's leading you into that place. I hadn't even really thought about that so much until we started doing that scene and suddenly all those feelings came back to me of what it was like to be in that given circumstance. But it wasn't until we sat down to really do it that it hit me."

WG2: "Is there anything that you've wanted to do on <u>Buffy</u> that you haven't gotten to do yet?"

KS: "I don't know. One of the things we talked about early, early on was the possibility of an episode where Joyce is possessed and becomes the mother from Hell. And I just thought that would be just really interesting to explore and do but I guess that hit the floor and got cut some where along the line."

WG2: "Are you going to be in Season Five?"

KS: "Yes, as far as I know I am supposed to be in Season Five. I don't know exactly what Joss is preparing, but he always has great and interesting stuff to look forward to."

WG2: "What about 'Gingerbread?' Did that remind you of anything in your own life?"

KS: "No, nothing really in my own life personally. I think the children's death touched her deeply. You know, I think, once you are a mother, you experience children's suffering so personally. So even though it was a spell, there was a lot of her own passion there for getting behind this and doing something. And because of the spell, she felt that what she was doing was the right thing, and needed to be done, and that somebody had to take a stand."

WG2: "Do you have any mythology you've created about how Joyce gave birth to a Slayer? Do you believe there is anything about Joyce that made that be what happened to her? Because we don't really know how the Slayers are picked."

KS: "No, I've actually always sort of seen it as the opposite. That the way I as Joyce see Buffy as the Slayer is sort of symbolic, when you look at your child and realize that they are a totally different person then you are and that they have different gifts and a different calling. It's a separation thing. In this case it's just more extreme and because it isn't just that she's a incredible pianist.

"It's something that has a moral cause behind it and so it brings dual feelings. 'I'm your mother and I'm older and I'm wiser but yet you're my daughter and you're this really spectacular person who's going places and wrestling with things that are beyond what I'll ever have to do in my lifetime.'"

WG2: "How was it different, when Joyce didn't know that Buffy was a Slayer versus now that she knows? Has it made it harder to play her or is it just something that's built into the way you approach your role?"

KS: "It's been much easier, although it was never hard for me as an actress to play that I didn't know that she was the Vampire Slayer. And a lot of people used to say to me, 'Oh, that must be so hard for you,' and I didn't find it hard at all because I think we have a natural built-in mechanism that allows us to deny the things that it's not the right time to see. And I think, a mother, a good mother needs a good healthy dose of that!

"So I didn't find it difficult as an actress to do that, but at the same time, in terms of my relationship with Sarah, it just became so much richer, it opened up so many more possibilities and experiences for my character to move beyond that. Then that whole Season Three was about adjusting to the idea, and get a sense of what she does."

WG2: "And then you even have more layers with Giles because you could be resentful and he wasn't just that nice man who saved you from the barbecue fork or came to visit you in the hospital."

KS: "Right. There's a battle between us somewhat over her, and a sense of a faith on my part, of knowing that she's going out at night patrolling and the kind of danger she's putting herself in. So there's so many more possibilities for me and my character since knowing. So I'm very happy to know."

WG2: "If Joyce could help Faith, what would she do?"

KS: "I think in Season Three, as a mother, I couldn't help but look at Faith and go, 'If she just had a home. If she wasn't living in that horrible hotel, if she had someone to look after her, we could soften those edges.' But I don't think that I feel the same way necessarily after my experience with her this season.

"But in Season Three I think that's what I would have done. Invite her for Christmas, invite her for Thanksgiving, let her come over for a hot meal a couple of times a week. Joyce really liked Faith. She liked her and enjoyed her but the experience of being held hostage by her, I think shattered that."

WG2: "What about if you were a vampire? What if they made Joyce a vampire? Have you ever wanted them to vamp you out?"

KS: "No, I've never wanted to be a vampire! I'm a little claustrophobic. I just have to say I've never wanted to endure the makeup."

WG2: "Can you tell us any kind of like behind-the-scenes story?"

KS: "This wasn't so much of a funny story, but it was really interesting, because when we were doing 'Gingerbread,' the actor who played the demon was so amazing looking. He just seemed so adorable. He was this fabulous guy who'd walked out of a fairy tale, and he was the loveliest, gentlest man. I wanted my daughter to see him because I thought she would get such a kick out of him.

"So I called the baby-sitter, because my husband was working that night, to come bring her and drop her by the set. And I bring her into the room where he is, and the moment that she laid eyes on him she stopped, her body went completely rigid, she dug her heels into the ground and she would not take another step, she was absolutely terrified of him. She just couldn't go near him.

"I said, 'Oh, but honey, he's so nice,' and he talks to her and she could hear that he was a really nice man but she just was so dumbstruck by this towering monster giant.

"I realized that it's because we're adults and we look back on it and think, 'Oh, isn't it great, he's a fairytale monster.' But to her, she's still a child, and so he was like the guy who was going to be under her bed and eat her. She also came to the set when we had all the millions of mummies ['Dead Man's Party'].

"She thought that the mummies were just the best! She wasn't afraid of them at all. She was chatting them up and she was sitting on the curbs with them. To this day she talks about them. She loved the cheerleader from that episode and the guy who had one eye. She still talks about them. It was just so amazing to me that she was afraid of the seven-foot monster but had no problem at all with the dead people!"

WG2: "When you knew that <u>Buffy</u> was gonna come back, I mean when you go to the door in the season opener of Season Three, and you saw her standing there, was it truly for you an emotional moment?"

KS: "Yeah. That was a hard moment because it just sort of came out of nowhere, you know, and was the first episode. It's funny because I remember more after that, you know, when she's finally come home, because it took a lot of preparation. It's pretty amazing thing to imagine what it would be like to spend a summer not knowing where your daughter is. Reviewing their relationship and questioning and worrying and being angry and all that. You can only hope that you pulled it off, but it's such a huge preparation for that moment, to imagine what that summer had to have been like."

"But I think it was the next episode, 'Dead Man's Party', and what I remember so vividly emotionally about that was coming down after her on the stairs, and just getting all of the anger and the upset off your chest."

WG2: "I know that a lot of people are hoping that Joyce has her own story lines in the future not just as "Buffy's mom.""

KS: "I hope so too, and just, you know, the little rumors and whatnot that I hear about Season Five, I'm hoping that will happen more. I think it's part of the natural progression of your relationship with your mother, too. You're seeing Joyce through Buffy's eyes, so what changes is really her perception of her mother. I remember very clearly my perception of my mother through those years, and how it changed, and I feel like the show has very much followed that. As you separate, emerge, and leave home the more you realize that your parent is a person and that they have their own life and their own interests, and somewhere on the other side of college you start the beginning of your real relationship with them.

"As adult to adult they're still your parent, but you've grown up and it starts on a whole different footing."

Harris Yulin as Quentin Travers

When we spoke to Harris Yulin's management, it turned out that he was doing a lot of flying at the time we hoped to interview him. He sent us this fax:

Dear Nancy,

I wasn't aware that Travers had made "such an impact" on <u>Buffy</u> viewers, but am delighted to find it was so. I think it best to present the character and leave the actor shrouded in modest mystery. Most of the questions would have mundane answers. One usually gets a part for instance by someone calling one's agent and sending a script and making an offer, which one accepts or not. As far as asking what I would do that would be different from what Travers did, it's like this: One accepts and attempts to embody the character, so the question is what the character would do, not I. I don't enter into it, except insofar as changing, with the producers and writers, something I think the character wouldn't do, which wasn't the case here. Travers was presented as written.

Again, I'm pleased that Travers interested the viewers and I think I can be so bold as to send his regards to them. It's safe to say, I believe, that Travers himself would be loath to disclose any personal information. Who knows; if the stars are properly aligned, Travers might be seen again.

Sincerely,
Harris Yulin

CREATING BUFFY:
The Production Process

SLIGHTLY LESS THAN TWO YEARS AGO, we took our first drive through the gates of the Buffy lot. It was March of 1998, and we were there to observe three days of production for the first Watcher's Guide. Joss Whedon was directing "Becoming, Part Two." It was the last week of shooting before summer hiatus. This time we were there to observe the last ten days of production of 1999, with plans for more in January.

The first Watcher's Guide covers Seasons One and Two—a season and a half, really, with thirty-four episodes. The new guide covers Seasons Three and Four—two full seasons of twenty-two episodes a season. In the time between 1998 and the end of 1999, Buffy had moved from cult phenomenon to cultural icon. We were curious to see what else had changed since our first visit.

For one thing, a third soundstage has been built. The El Niño Building, so called because it was nothing more than a tarp hastily erected over a pile of lumber and a lot of equipment during the rains, is gone. In its place, Buffy now boasts its own indoor mill.

Two years ago only "our damn alley" and the graveyard served as onsite exteriors. Today Sunnydale's main street has been lovingly crafted into existence, complete with shops, the Espresso Pump, and the Sun Cinema.

At the beginning of the third season Buffy upgraded its film stock from sixteen-millimeter to thirty-five millimeter. Though the finished product is still broadcast from tape, the difference is striking—more depth of field, greater contrast, and a richer look.

The cast has also significantly altered from Season Two to Season Four: Cordelia and Angel are over at Paramount, along with Wesley Wyndam-Price. Oz is on a leave of absence, soon to return. Riley Finn and bad ol' Spike have become cast regulars. Commando Graham just received a field promotion to recurring character status.

There have been changes in the production suite as well. Buffy Executive Producer Gail Berman's New Regency Television has moved, and the offices are now occupied by writers and post-production staff for Angel. As Angel's producer, David Greenwalt has moved from his Buffy second-story office overlooking the executive parking lot and the soundstages, to first-story quarters boasting an enormous and beautiful blue credenza. Mutant Enemy's Director of Development, George Snyder, is also on the Angel side of the building.

Back over on the Buffy side, there is a new Unit Production Manager—John Perry—and a new casting director—Amy Britt. A few people have also enjoyed in-house promotions.

A very few have gone elsewhere. For the most part, familiar faces greet us. As before, our direct liaison to the world of Buffy is Caroline Kallas, and, as before, she makes us feel right at home. In the two weeks of our visit Caroline will provide us with over three thousand pages of material—multiple copies of scripts, breakdowns, schedules, bios, and maps—arrange for our photography coverage, and take us to Todd AO, the famous post-production house, and Digital Magic's P.O.P. (Pacific Ocean Production) facility. She'll drive up and down the Valley to get us to the location shoot, and she'll lend us her office, her phone, and her computer.

We will eat almost two dozen meals with the cast and crew, including their Christmas lunch of lobster and prime rib. We will watch TV with them. And we will watch them make TV.

For this new volume of the Watcher's Guide, we are tracking the creation of an episode from as close to start as we can get, to finish. "Our" episode is lucky thirteen, "The I in Team." It is an episode of firsts—the first time Buffy and Riley make love, Adam's first word, and his first murder.

In this section, we will give a step-by-step breakdown of the making of Episode Thirteen, told mainly in the form of interviews by the folks who make it.

PREPRODUCTION: BEFORE THE CAMERAS ROLL

LIKE MANY TV HOUR DRAMAS, an episode of *Buffy* is shot on an eight-day schedule, with eight days of prep work before the actual shooting. That's the ideal, more generally adhered to at the beginning of the season.

When we arrived to follow the production of Episode Thirteen, the preparation work was all but completed. Only the tech scout and the production meeting remained.

The *Buffy* company is unusual in that there's very little turnover. There's a lot of shorthand communication about how to get things accomplished, with the result that they can move fast and get increasingly ambitious about storylines and production values.

But even the best-laid plans . . . . It was flu season, and a lot of people were getting very sick, even key actors. Fingers were crossed as we marched toward the deadline.

THE TECH SCOUT

AT TEN A.M. ON DECEMBER 6, we walked downstairs from production with Caroline Kallas. Transportation was waiting with a van, and we were all going to Santa Clarita on a tech scout.

When *Buffy* isn't shooting on a soundstage, all the departments concerned with location shooting take a field trip out to the location. Besides Caroline Kallas and the driver, the van loads up with Production Designer Carey Meyer, Art Director Caroline Quinn, Set Decorator David Koneff, Location Manager Ed Duffy, Second Company Grip Gil Valle, and Rigging Gaffer Gus Oliva.

We head up the 405 toward Santa Clarita. As is the common practice in the industry, there are coded, colored signs tacked onto phone poles and street signs to point us in the right direction. Since there are several studios in the area, sometimes our sign was one of two or three fastened onto the same post.

During the drive, everyone's cell phone goes off at least once or twice. The hectic pace of television production is underscored as they quickly answer questions, ask for details, and make additional calls in an efficient, casual shorthand. Everyone's carrying identical phones, like some kind of covert operations squad. Commandos, maybe.

The Lockheed/Legacy complex used to be an actual top-secret facility. It stands atop a slightly rolling hill; in the foreground is a golf course and park. A small ravine to the west will provide the woods where Buffy outmaneuvers Dr. Walsh's Commandos. We approach the security booth and are waved through.

As we pull into a parking space, Director Jim Contner and First Assistant Brenda Kalosh pull up beside us in a separate car. The facilities manager meets us as we troop inside the large building that has already housed the Initiative set before, in Episode Seven, "The Initiative." Stripped bare, it is reminiscent of a large airplane hanger.

Directly across from us rise the metal stairways and catwalks where Buffy and Riley will stand as he shows her the secret underground complex. To the left, Jim Contner, Carey Meyer, Caroline Quinn, and David Koneff survey the area that will become the armory. As Caroline Quinn unfurls a set of blueprints on the clean concrete floor, Carey begins measuring off distances. Caroline grins. "Carey's feet are exactly a foot long," she tells us. It's a common art department joke, but in Carey's case, it's true.

Despite the fact that this is the second time the company is using the facility, everyone is studying the space with great care. David Koneff asks a lot of questions about set requirements—straps on the operating tables, or bolts? Everyone takes a look at the door that will be the high-security entrance into the research area, where the dreaded Room 314 is located (although the door and the room itself are not shot here, but on a soundstage).

Someone calls, "Jim?" to the director. Without a moment's hesitation Brenda Kalosh looks up and says, "Yes?"

We move from inside the building to the exterior, walking along the paved road toward the golf course. Gus Oliva pushes a wheeled gauge that will keep track of how much cable he needs to run from the generators, which will be located in trucks, to the ravine.

At the gently sloping, wooded area, David Koneff takes note of sprinkler heads, errant pipes, and other items that will either be temporarily disconnected and topped off or hidden with greens. The fact that two Humvees will travel across the golf course is duly noted. The company maps out a driving route that will cause the least amount of damage to the turf. They discuss the stunt team's rigging, which will be in the trees.

Despite the fact that it's midday in Southern California, a wind whips up. Brenda Kalosh reminds everyone to dress warmly for the actual shoot. The exteriors will be shot at night, and it will be much colder than it is now.

Finally it's time to leave. Almost everyone present has a meeting to attend. Back in the van the cell phones continue to ring and the calls keep going back and forth. The people in the van talk about various aspects of the upcoming shoot. In the distance the vast amusement park, Magic Mountain, shimmers like a mirage. There are miles to go before we sleep.

JOSS AND THE WRITERS

OCCASIONALLY JOSS WHEDON calls the writers together for a "State of the Union" address. He'll discuss upcoming developments in the series and share thoughts about how to take the characters through various emotional arcs.

Although a lot of what happens from season to season on *Buffy* is planned, there are occasional twists and turns from one week to the next. One-shot characters become series regulars; beloved characters are killed off (or spun off). At the last moment inspiration strikes and everything changes.

As has often been said, the heart of *Buffy* is the written word. As Joss himself put it so eloquently, in Maggie Walsh's lecture on communication in "Hush":

"So this is what it is. Talking about communication, talking about language. Not the same thing. It's about the way a child can recognize and produce phonemes that don't occur in its native language. It's about inspiration, not

the idea but the moment before the idea, when it's total, when it blossoms in your mind and connects to everything, before the coherent thought that gives it shape, that locks it in and cuts it off from the universal. When you can articulate it, it becomes smaller. It's about thoughts and experiences that we don't have a word for."

The writing team for *Buffy* consists of Joss, David Greenwalt, Marti Noxon, David Fury, Jane Espenson, Doug Petrie, and Tracey Forbes.

Marti Noxon, David Fury , Tracey Forbes, Jane Espenson, Doug Petrie, and Joss Whedon (in chair)

JOSS WHEDON, CREATOR/EXECUTIVE PRODUCER

WG2: "With all of this, how do you have a life? Do you have a life?"

JW: "No."

WG2: "Do you care?"

JW: "I do, actually. I remember a life. It was fun! But I've always been obsessive about my work. I do want to live, I want to read and hang out and see my wife, I hear she's really cute! All that good stuff. But ultimately I believe that the only reason that I exist is the work and the only thing that really makes me happy is the work. Although I often wish there was just a little bit less of it so that I could do the work there was as well as I could. Nothing makes me happier."

WG2: "Do you think that the constraints that are imposed on you help or hinder, time-wise, energy-wise?"

JW: "Ultimately, they help, because I think everybody who makes movies should be forced to do television....Because you have to finish. You have to get it done, and there are not a lot of decisions made just for the sake of making decisions. You do something because it's efficient and because it gets the story told and it connects to the audience. And then you've got to do it right and do it fast. I worked in TV before I worked in movies, and I have a better track record at meeting deadlines than some movie writers because you get it done. I think, there is no workshop. There are no "B" movies anymore. I think Roger Corman deserves the life achievement award just because he's the only guy out there still breeding directors.

"There is no training ground. So TV is a good thing. Obviously it has certain pitfalls and rituals that you fall into, shortcuts and whatnot that when you make a movie you want to get out of. But I think the restriction of just having to tell a story to an audience every week is the best thing you could ask for. Ultimately, you want to move on from that. You just want to say, 'Okay, now I want to do something where I have the time to create everything that's in the frame. Everything.' And that's sort of where I'm starting.to be. I'm getting to the point now where I'm like, 'Okay, I've told a lot of stories. I've churned it out.' I just feel like I want to step back and do something where I can't use the excuse of 'I only had a week.'"

WG2: "Do you have any notion of how you're gonna go about that?"

JW: "When I get some free time, I'll write a movie and then I'll shoot it and then I'll edit it and then they'll show it and that's my plan."

WG2: "Will it be a <u>Buffy</u>-related project?"

JW: "I doubt it. I believe this show will probably go on longer than I will go on with it. I mean I'd

O FRONT

shoots Spi

IT LOT

BUFF
XAN
GILE
WILL
SPIK
RILE
ANY
FORRE

MARKS

JY LOT

GRAHAM	W	6:30P	7:30P	REPORT TO NEBRASKA / BUNDY LOT
STUNT COORDINATOR	W	~	6:30P	REPORT TO LOCATION
BUFFY STUNT DBL	H			

love to make a <u>Buffy</u> movie, but it's a complicated thing, and I think there are other voices I'd like to speak with for a while."

WG2: "Will it have supernatural or fantastical aspects?"

JW: "It is entirely probable that it will be somewhat fantastical or supernatural, or at least genre. The sensitive drama still eludes me as a concept. I don't know how to do those. I love fantasy. I love science fiction. I love horror. I love the fantastical elements of something. I don't see any reason to abandon it."

WG2: "What are some movies that are out right now that you're excited about?"

JW: "I know it's [already] on DVD, but <u>The Matrix</u> is my favorite movie that I've ever seen in my life. I saw that movie and it was like I'm just gonna put down my pen and back away and apologize. Those guys know exactly what they're doing. I found that movie to be extraordinarily deep and beautifully realized. I know people don't expect you to say that about Keanu movies, but I don't think I've seen a more intelligent movie in the last ten years. Every line is in place. They really thought that world through. You don't see that a lot anymore. I see a lot of laziness in movies. I still think I see much better work on TV than I do in the movies. Most of the time."

WG2: "What are some of your favorite TV shows?"

JW: "I'm all over <u>The West Wing</u>. I can't get enough of <u>The West Wing</u>. I just want to hear those people talk about stuff. I don't even understand a lot of it 'cause I'm so ignorant."

WG2: "What are you doing today?"

JW: "Trying to break the next story. Watch some filming, although they're in pretty good hands. I'm editing eleven, we're shooting thirteen. We're breaking the story for fifteen, and I've just sent writers off yesterday; yesterday was a lot more crazy than today 'cause I sent them off to do rewrites on shows that have to be done by Friday. So we'll start rewriting them tomorrow, since it's actually kind of a lull day. I'm gonna watch the show tonight."

WG2: "Are you gonna be able to take off any of your vacation time?"

JW: "Starting Friday I'm taking two weeks with no <u>Buffy</u> thoughts whatsoever, although I think I'm gonna work on a <u>Buffy</u>-related comic book just for fun. Sort of tangentially related to <u>Buffy</u>. That's mostly how I relax, is by writing stuff that I'm not supposed to be writing."

WG2: "Is it really is hard to stop?"

JW: "I got the red shoes on and I'm just gonna keep dancing."

MARTI NOXON

We talked with Marti Noxon on the last day of shooting, just after the Christmas party. Though it was the end of a long week, she was relaxed and in a wonderful mood. Her lovely diamond engagement ring is new; her fiancé used to work for Joss.

"So I have him to thank for both my career and my guy," she said, smiling.

WG2: "Last time we were here, you had just found out you were going be a producer. It wasn't even official."

MN: "Obviously they kept me. It's been a continuing kind of experience where Joss and I have just had a real wonderful working relationship together, and David Greenwalt as well, and so I've just been the luckiest girl in the world again.

"This year I got the big office and the assistant and all those crazy things that I only dreamt about. That stuff is amazing, but it's all pretty secondary to the fact that I get to write. That I get to write something I care about and that's so wonderful, and people seem to really enjoy. I'm definitely blessed to be here. I think it's pretty remarkable that I found something like this the first time I got staffed. That's why I say what good fortune."

WG2: "Didn't you have another job offer at the time?"

MN: "Yes. I thought about what I wanted to be doing with my time and I looked at the two programs and I just knew this was closer to my heart. Who knew at the time it was going to become such a phenomenon? It's continued beyond, maybe not beyond anybody's expectations, but certainly beyond mine.

"Recently I was sitting in a restaurant, and I couldn't help overhearing the woman next to me talking about that every Tuesday night her daughter and she cook dinner together and then watch the show. I couldn't help myself. I said, 'I'm writing an episode right now,' because I was working on my laptop. She just looked at me like I was crazy. I had to give her my card to prove that I wasn't insane, and then she was kind of impressed. So that was cool. It's really exciting when you're out in the world and you realize that [Buffy's] really impacting people around you."

WG2: "What are some of the changes that occurred from Season Two to Season Three and Season Three to Season Four?"

MN: "From Season Two to Season Three, I think the show got a little bit darker. I don't think that it was a bad thing, but I definitely think it reflected the seriousness of entering the adult world. The beginning of your shift from 'I'm just a kid, hanging with my high school friends,' to larger issues. We didn't do quite as many high school-centric things.

"We started to play a little bit more with things like 'The Wish.' Every TV show that's on for more than twenty-five minutes does their version of It's a Wonderful Life and this was kind of It's a Terrible Life. And that was really just because we could.

"So, very adult themes and even things like 'The Zeppo,' which I loved. It was an experiment in how can we put what is usually the foreground action in the background and make fun of our conventions. The things we do, the things we rely on and everybody knows they're kind of goofy, but they move the story along.

"I think a lot of the things that we did last year were about finding yourself. Particularly the Buffy-Faith story line. Joss has called the Faith character Buffy's shadow self. Faith was what Buffy would have been without love and support. Without her team. A superhero isn't super unless they have support and love just like anybody else. Those energies and those impulses can be turned to the dark side if you don't have people you care about and values you care about, and those are instilled by community.

"Sometimes Season Three was darker because Faith could go to some pretty dark places. That episode where she strangled Xander—I was like, 'Are we getting away with this?' That was pretty exciting. We were really doing some uncharted territory.

"I think I mentioned this the first time we talked, I hope parents know when to turn the show off. This is not necessarily a show that you should always let your kids just sit in front of and walk away from, because it can get really scary and dark. I thought 'The Wish' was really scary.

"There were also just a lot of really fun episodes. Joss's twins episode was 'Doppelgängland.' I loved the season finale."

WG2: "What about the departure of Angel?"

MN: "That's been a little hard for me. I loved their story line, and people kind of identified me as a person who wrote a lot of that arc. Sometimes that was true and sometimes it wasn't, but I didn't mind being identified as that person. I felt very strongly about their relationship, and I accept

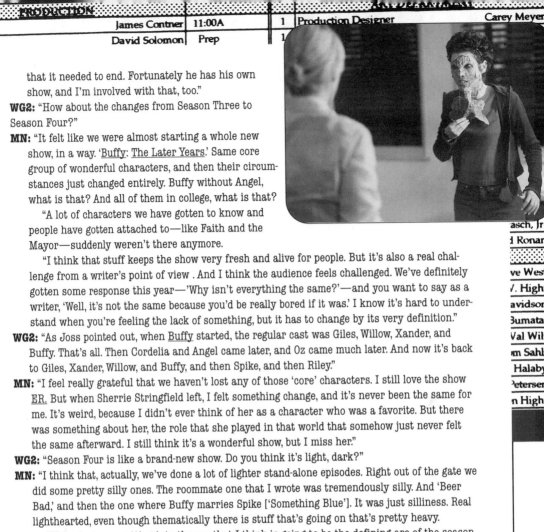

| | | | | Production Designer | Carey Meyer | OC |

CTOR | James Contner | 11:00A | 1 | Production Designer | Carey Meyer | OC
CTOR | David Solomon | Prep | 1

Asst. Di
Asst. Di
2nd Ass
2nd A.D
1 2nd A
Traine
DGA 1
uction S
t Super
ctor of F
era Ope
era Ope
dicam O
AC-A Ca
AC-B Ca
AC-C Ca
C-A Cam
der
l 2nd A(
ef Lighti

that it needed to end. Fortunately he has his own show, and I'm involved with that, too."

WG2: "How about the changes from Season Three to Season Four?"

MN: "It felt like we were almost starting a whole new show, in a way. '<u>Buffy</u>: The Later Years.' Same core group of wonderful characters, and then their circumstances just changed entirely. Buffy without Angel, what is that? And all of them in college, what is that?

"A lot of characters we have gotten to know and people have gotten attached to—like Faith and the Mayor—suddenly weren't there anymore.

"I think that stuff keeps the show very fresh and alive for people. But it's also a real challenge from a writer's point of view . And I think the audience feels challenged. We've definitely gotten some response this year—'Why isn't everything the same?'—and you want to say as a writer, 'Well, it's not the same because you'd be really bored if it was.' I know it's hard to understand when you're feeling the lack of something, but it has to change by its very definition."

WG2: "As Joss pointed out, when <u>Buffy</u> started, the regular cast was Giles, Willow, Xander, and Buffy. That's all. Then Cordelia and Angel came later, and Oz came much later. And now it's back to Giles, Xander, Willow, and Buffy, and then Spike, and then Riley."

MN: "I feel really grateful that we haven't lost any of those 'core' characters. I still love the show <u>ER</u>. But when Sherrie Stringfield left, I felt something change, and it's never been the same for me. It's weird, because I didn't ever think of her as a character who was a favorite. But there was something about her, the role that she played in that world that somehow just never felt the same afterward. I still think it's a wonderful show, but I miss her."

WG2: "Season Four is like a brand-new show. Do you think it's light, dark?"

MN: "I think that, actually, we've done a lot of lighter stand-alone episodes. Right out of the gate we did some pretty silly ones. The roommate one that I wrote was tremendously silly. And 'Beer Bad,' and then the one where Buffy marries Spike ['Something Blue']. It was just silliness. Real lighthearted, even though thematically there is stuff that's going on that's pretty heavy.

"We're just now getting into the arc that I think is going to be the defining arc of the season. Where we reveal the Initiative. I don't think we really surprised anybody too much there. People saw the writing on the wall and that Riley was probably one of them. And the challenge of introducing a love interest for <u>Buffy</u> people are going to accept. I feel that Joss in creating this character has been really, really smart."

WG2: "Are you looking forward to Season Five?"

MN: "I am very much looking forward to next season. I think what's going to happen is going to astound people. I was astounded when Joss told me. I went, 'That is unbelievable!'

"But I know we can do it, and I think it's going to be, again, real brilliance on his part, but I'm getting used to that. I'm getting used to kind of going, 'We are not worthy, I am not worthy.' It's sort of a way of life around here. It's like, how can he think that way? I just keep trying to learn from Joss and all the other talented writers I work with. I just think people are going to be shocked. It's just going to give us so much to work with.

"I don't think Joss is gonna stay with the show forever. I have very mixed feelings about what that means for the rest of us. Part of me thinks, 'How can we ever do this without him? How could it ever be what it is, because it is so much his vision?' There is a real confusion in

326

	OC
	OC
	OC
	OC
	OC
	OC
	OC
	11:00
	OC
	OC
	OC
	OC
	11:00
asch, Jr.	11:00
Ronan	11:00
ve West	OC
J. Hight	per S
avidson	per S
Bumatai	per S
Val Wilt	per S
m Sahli	per S
Halaby	per S
Petersen	per S
n Hight	per S

me about what it's going to be like after he goes. What are we going to do? I do feel like he makes me better. But I also do feel like I have had growing confidence because of how much writing I've done in the past three years. Hopefully you can't help but start to feel a little bit more like...[pauses]"

WG2: "This isn't my last job?"

MN: "You know, I pray God willing this is not my last job. That it's actually not just a fluke. That this time you'll sit and this time you'll have words to put to paper. When I first started here, I really didn't have that confidence. From script to script, I would just panic. I don't panic as much. I still do; I often sit down and think, 'What if it doesn't come?' But there is another little voice that has been growing that says, 'It'll come. It may not always be the best. You may have to work really hard to get it there. Not every script is going to be your best work.' A little voice says, 'I think it'll come.' Something will come.

"I get stuck but I'm beginning to develop some faith that there's something on the other side of that. Because you have to meet a deadline, you learn how to push through that stuff."

WG2: "Our understanding of the process here is that either you are given an idea or you pitch an idea, basically. Then everybody helps you break it, and then you go off and write your draft. When you're collaborating as a writer with another writer after that process, what is the way you collaborate?"

MN: "In our case, like if it's me and David Greenwalt writing the script together, we'll go and take our separate pieces and write separately. And then we'll get together and look at each other's pieces and say, 'Oh, I thought this maybe was gonna happen here,' and he'll look at my stuff, and then we just clump it all together. We don't write together.

"I was never really good at writing with someone else around. For me it's a very solitary thing. I'm sure you could get into a rhythm when you're sitting together and actually talking it through. I know a lot of writers do that, but it's just not my style."

WG2: "Do you think of writing as something that you will do for a certain amount of time, and then you'll move onto something else? Joss said to us, 'Okay, I'm doing all these things, but in my heart I'm a writer.'"

MN: "I hope I write until the day they grab the pen and take it away from me and put me in the ground! Grab the pen from my rigor-mortised hands."

(At this point, Joss came in Marti's office to ask her to come to a meeting. He saw us, smiled and pointed at her, saying, "She's brilliant.")

DAVID FURY

David Fury has a brain floating in a tank and numerous windup toys on his desk. Behind his desk was an enormous, colorful array of his children's artwork.

WG2: "Tell us about your background. How did you eventually end up at <u>Buffy</u>?"

DF: "Well, I was an actor for a number of years, mostly stage actor in New York. Came out to L.A. to go to film school at UCLA, and wound up being drawn back into acting.

"Most of the work I got was in soap operas or one-hour dramas. When things slowed down for me here, I went back to New York, which is where I'm from. I went into stand-up comedy, because it's a perfect opportunity for an actor between jobs to do something, keep themselves out there performing, and found I was reasonably successful. I got invited to perform in all the top clubs, and emceed at several of them, the Improv, and Comic Strip.

"It was around this time that I got involved with a couple of comedy theater groups. One was

GILES	H		HOLD	
WILLOW	H		HOLD	
SPIKE	W	6:30P	7:30P	REPORT TO LOCATION

Manhattan Punchline. It was an off-Broadway comedy theater. Another was Chicago City Limits, which was an improvisational company, New York's top improv comedy group. And through my experience with that I formed my own comedy group, which was called Brain Trust. We performed through the auspices of Manhattan Punchline off-Broadway and had good success.

"And then it came time when I realized I wanted to come back to L.A., now as a comic actor, comedian, and to open up a Brain Trust company out here. And I did that. I produced a show called Mental Cruelty.

"It was an enormous success, couldn't have been bigger, yet I couldn't get anyone interested in me as an actor. I had written most of the show, and people seemed to be more impressed with the writing. I mean, I had a great cast, and everybody got acting work out of it. Because I was the predominant writer, people seemed more interested in me as a writer, wondering what I had, be it screenplays or spec scripts for television. I didn't, not expecting a writing career. Eventually it became obvious maybe I should start working on one.

"Initially, I wanted to sell Mental Cruelty as a possible variety series. I was told at the time by my representatives, the best way to get a show on the air is to put in a couple years on a network sitcom and develop some credibility in television as a writer.

"So I had to watch television, which was something I didn't do, trying to find shows I wanted to write for and I eventually opted for Seinfeld, which had just premiered. It had only just been on the air, but I recognized right away this was a show I had an affinity.

"As I was struggling to write my very first spec script, my girlfriend at the time, Elin Hampton, was onto her fourth. She just kept churning them out; she was very prolific; and she kept saying, 'Maybe we should partner up.'

"And I kept insisting, 'I cannot work with anyone, I'm a lone wolf, I need to write by myself.' And eventually, realizing I would never get through the spec without her, I said, 'All right, let's try it.'

"We wrote a Seinfeld, and it did enormous things for us. The spec was circulated, and we got multiple offers for agents, and meetings on lots of shows. Most of them said, 'You need a second spec.'

"And we wound up writing a spec for Get a Life, the Chris Elliott show. And everyone said, 'It's at the bottom of the ratings, it's not a good spec to write.' And we just thought, 'You know what, we could write something else, but we really want to write Get a Life.' It just seemed to speak to us.

"With those two specs and our comic sensibilities we were treated like the new hot young writers immediately snatched up by Tom and Roseanne Arnold's series The Jackie Thomas Show.

"And from there we went to a number of other shows. Dream On, we did for a season. Then we were offered to run a show after our second year in the business. The John Leguizamo show for Fox, House of Buggin', a sketch comedy show.

After, we came back and did Pinky and the Brain. We were hired to help develop it as a prime-time series, which did not come to fruition, but we did manage to produce a few episodes.

"After that it was around this time that we had two meetings. One was a show called Life's Work for ABC and Disney that was sandwiched between Roseanne and Home Improvement, on Tuesday nights, a twelve-episode order. The other was a show called Buffy the Vampire Slayer, which at that point was a six-episode order for midseason for the WB.

"After meeting with Joss, I said to Elin, 'I think I want to write Buffy the Vampire Slayer. It sounds like the most fun.' And we actually told our agents that of the two, we'd rather do Buffy.

"They thought we were nuts, we were crazy. They said, 'You're turning down a potential huge hit for ABC. It's got a great time slot, it's Disney, it's ABC. It's twelve episodes, not six. It's all of

de and t

OOM
fter

OOM
s Riley

MOVE

spots a

Y PLAYER
le Gellar
ndon
Iead
ugan
ers

3/8 pg

Pg

FRC

5/8 pg

2/8 pg

TION

TION
ATION

ield	ANYA		H	HOLD		
erts	FORREST		W	6:30P	7:30P	REPORT TO NEBRASKA / BUN
	GRAHAM		W	6:30P	7:30P	REPORT TO NEBRASKA / BUN

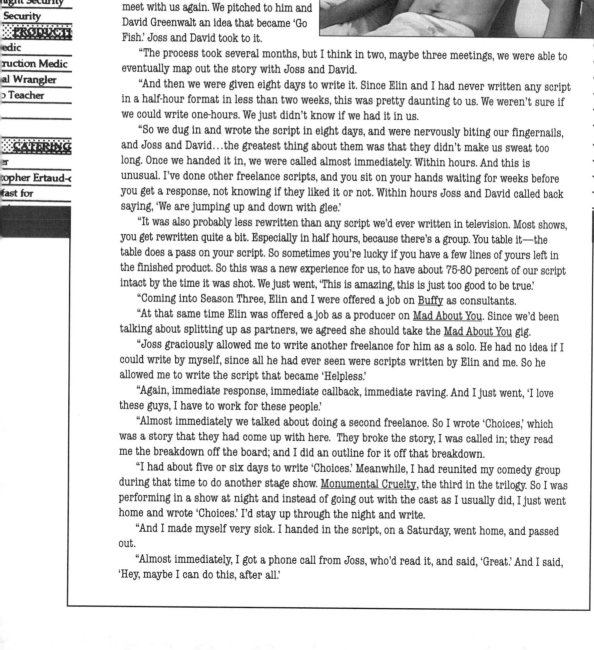

these things, and you want to go to <u>Buffy the Vampire Slayer</u>?' And we said, 'Well, when you put it that way . . . '

"So we opted for the other show, <u>Life's Work</u>, which was cancelled after eighteen episodes, and we know the story of <u>Buffy</u> and how well that did.

"Fortunately, by the time Season Two was coming around Joss was willing to meet with us again. We pitched to him and David Greenwalt an idea that became 'Go Fish.' Joss and David took to it.

"The process took several months, but I think in two, maybe three meetings, we were able to eventually map out the story with Joss and David.

"And then we were given eight days to write it. Since Elin and I had never written any script in a half-hour format in less than two weeks, this was pretty daunting to us. We weren't sure if we could write one-hours. We just didn't know if we had it in us.

"So we dug in and wrote the script in eight days, and were nervously biting our fingernails, and Joss and David...the greatest thing about them was that they didn't make us sweat too long. Once we handed it in, we were called almost immediately. Within hours. And this is unusual. I've done other freelance scripts, and you sit on your hands waiting for weeks before you get a response, not knowing if they liked it or not. Within hours Joss and David called back saying, 'We are jumping up and down with glee.'

"It was also probably less rewritten than any script we'd ever written in television. Most shows, you get rewritten quite a bit. Especially in half hours, because there's a group. You table it—the table does a pass on your script. So sometimes you're lucky if you have a few lines of yours left in the finished product. So this was a new experience for us, to have about 75-80 percent of our script intact by the time it was shot. We just went, 'This is amazing, this is just too good to be true.'

"Coming into Season Three, Elin and I were offered a job on <u>Buffy</u> as consultants.

"At that same time Elin was offered a job as a producer on <u>Mad About You</u>. Since we'd been talking about splitting up as partners, we agreed she should take the <u>Mad About You</u> gig.

"Joss graciously allowed me to write another freelance for him as a solo. He had no idea if I could write by myself, since all he had ever seen were scripts written by Elin and me. So he allowed me to write the script that became 'Helpless.'

"Again, immediate response, immediate callback, immediate raving. And I just went, 'I love these guys, I have to work for these people.'

"Almost immediately we talked about doing a second freelance. So I wrote 'Choices,' which was a story that they had come up with here. They broke the story, I was called in; they read me the breakdown off the board; and I did an outline for it off that breakdown.

"I had about five or six days to write 'Choices.' Meanwhile, I had reunited my comedy group during that time to do another stage show. <u>Monumental Cruelty</u>, the third in the trilogy. So I was performing in a show at night and instead of going out with the cast as I usually did, I just went home and wrote 'Choices.' I'd stay up through the night and write.

"And I made myself very sick. I handed in the script, on a Saturday, went home, and passed out.

"Almost immediately, I got a phone call from Joss, who'd read it, and said, 'Great.' And I said, 'Hey, maybe I can do this, after all.'

"So the implication, once I got the second freelance, was that I would be hired the following season. And in fact I was, as producer of the Season Four. Even though Joss has very graciously commented, 'You've been here since the beginning.'

"So I feel I'm one of the luckiest people in this business, that I've found a home with a boss that I revere and idolize, a genius. I've never had the experience of actually idolizing my boss. So again, I feel very fortunate."

WG2: "When you write, are you frightened by what you write?"

DF: "No, and I love to be frightened. I try to look into the primeval fears we all have ingrained in us, and I try to re-create those. But in re-creating them, I'm still detached from it. I'm re-creating intellectually. And somebody like Marti, and even Joss to a large extent, you know, he feels viscerally, he gets the emotion as he's writing it. It scares him as he writes it. Or Marti writes, when she's writing dialogue between two lovers on the show, she is so caught up in it that it makes her weep. And I think that's what makes it so brilliant.

"I remember one of the first experiences I had with Marti was being on the set with her. She had just written 'I Only Have Eyes for You,' and she wanted to see the scene on the set that she'd written. I happened to be on the set at the same time—this was around the time when I was freelancing for 'Go Fish.' I'd only met Marti maybe a couple of times before. And she started crying on the set, she was watching the scene, and she was all choked up. And I just thought, That is amazing. When I'm looking at a scene of mine, I'm going, 'It's shot wrong! It's the wrong angle! No, you want to get the joke this way.' But Marti's able to lose herself in the scene. That's a gift I hope to, if I can't ever actually gain, at least emulate. So I study her, I study Joss. They're the most emotionally ingrained in the series and the characters."

WG2: "When you watch episodes you haven't written, can you—"

DF: "Oh, I cry. I weep. I weep at other people's episodes, absolutely. I watched 'Amends' from last season. It moved me so much when Angel was talking about, 'You don't understand, I'm not sorry about the person I became when I was a vampire; I wasn't that good a guy before I was a vampire.'

"He was talking about his wasted life, and I was crying like a baby. I'm moved often by the show.

"The only down side of being a part of the show is, I see these things coming too soon to allow them to affect me as much as they used to. To be a part of 'Wild at Heart,' when we bid Oz goodbye, when he breaks up with Willow, which is a great, great scene that Marti wrote, it's wonderful, it's gut-wrenching. But I was so a part of it that by the time I saw it on TV, I didn't weep, and I should've. I mean, I felt like, Oh, this is great. But I wasn't weeping. 'Amends,' since I wasn't around for that, I was able to get caught up in it.

"Other episodes have moved me tremendously. Actually, 'The Prom,' when Buffy is given her Class Protector thing, gets to me. Again, that was all before I was really a part of the show. Now that I am, it's harder to become emotionally connected to it."

"[For Buffy,] you need something interesting and phlebotinous. You've heard that phrase, right?"

WG2: "No."

DF: "Phlebotinin is our little catchword for 'What's the supernatural element of the script?' What's the phlebotinin? Let's say—this is not a story—Buffy's regressing to childhood again. What demon or supernatural thing makes her do that? It's like a McGuffin. It's a catchphrase like McGuffin. Everybody has their own spelling. Some people think it's PH, some people think it's F. Phlebotinin. That's just our little catchphrase."

WG2: "When you read a script that you haven't written, and then you watch the episode, is that what you see when you read the script? Does it match in any way?"

DF: "Rarely does it ever, except when Joss directs his own scripts. Or when David Greenwalt directs his scripts, and I've read the script before seeing the episode. I usually see [on the screen] what I saw in my mind's eye. But when I'm reading other people's scripts, directed by other people, I rarely see what I saw on the page. It's a whole different thing.

"That's the thing when you get to direct your own material. You really trust the way it's laid out, you trust the picture that's presented on the page, and you present it that way. So Joss obviously, when he writes he's very specific, and he means what he writes. He writes it and he shoots it; it's there."

WG2: "What are your work habits like?"

DF: "My work habits are horrible. Writing, to me, is a very, very, very difficult thing. And I'm a big procrastinator.

"They've gotten better. There's a book that's helped me a lot, called Bird by Bird [by Anne Lamott]. I don't know if you've ever heard of it. It's about writing; it's about dealing with writer's block. The premise being, 'bird by bird.' She's talking about her brother, who had to do a report on birds for school. Lets the deadline go; it's the night before it's due; goes into a total panic—'I can't do this.'

"The father, who is also a writer, sat down with him, and while the boy was freaking out— 'How do I do this report now, I have to hand it in tomorrow'—the father just calmly said, 'Bird by bird.'

""Meaning, forget about the whole project, forget about the big picture. Just do a bird. That's all you focus on. Just do the bird. One bird. And it's the getting through the little part, okay, I'm just gonna focus on one bird. That's all I have to do. Then when you're done with that, you go, boy, that wasn't that painful. Okay, do another bird.

"The other analogy she uses is, you have a big project due, a script, a screenplay, a book, whatever. Imagine a window, a postage stamp-sized window. And that's all you're going to do today. You're going to do this little part. This paragraph, this opening paragraph of your book, that's all you're going to do. And remember, when you do it, and you're finished with it, it's going to be crap. It's going to be horrible. Nobody puts something brilliant down on the page. All the great writers have to get through them. You have to put it down first. You'll make it good eventually. The point is, get through.

"It actually helped me enormously. I was going through severe writer's block. Not wanting to do anything. And once I got into this mindset of being able to not look at big pictures, not look at 'I have to write a screenplay,' but 'All I have to do is write the first couple of dialogues. First two pages, where I know basically what's going to happen, and that's all I'm going to worry about.' There's a gratifying feeling of accomplishment after doing it and succeeding in that minimal deadline. And eventually, before you know it, it's done.

"I found it hugely, hugely helpful in terms of getting through it. And it's helped me with, again, the task of writing one-hours, which was at one point a daunting task that no longer daunts me. I used to have to write linearly. I used to have to plow through any script linearly. And I find I can't do that anymore, and I find it's good that I can't do that. Because I find myself skipping around now to things that I know I can write, like, gee, I know this part later, let me go ahead and write that part. I know exactly how that run should go.

"Eventually I'm putting these little puzzle pieces together, and I wind up with a script afterward. That's a new process in my writing, that I've only been doing for the past year. There was a time when I'd start writing at page one, and by page five or six, I'd start getting like, I'm dragging myself, it's getting hard, I'm trying to move through it. Just finish the first act, kind of thing. Eventually I realized I don't have to write that way. And being able to skip around actually helps me to get excited again. Because I won't be bogged down in 'how do I write this scene?' I'll

GRAHAM	W	6:30P	7:30P	REPORT TO NEBRASKA / BUNDY LOT
STUNT COORDINATOR	W	~	6:30P	REPORT TO LOCATION
BUFFY STUNT DBL	H	HOLD		

be like, 'well, there's a scene I know how to write, I'll go enjoy writing that.' And that fuels everything else."

WG2: "For people who are aspiring, do you recommend them taking seminars, or reading certain books?"

DF: "Reading is always a huge, huge thing. If you're writing spec scripts for television, read a minimum of five scripts for the show you want to write. If you can read five scripts, you're as prepared as you need to be. You don't need to read ten, and I recommend reading five rather than reading three. Five somehow is always the magic number for me. By the time you've read the fifth script, everything is so ingrained in you of how to emulate the voice of the people doing it. I mean, that's a really big deal. And you'll get your format from reading those scripts. I don't think you have to learn structure of writing for television. People take television writing classes to learn what a script looks like. Reading five scripts will give you the idea what it looks like."

WG2: "What is the thought behind writing a spec script for a show you don't expect to work on?"

DF: "You always have to write a spec for a show you love, period. No one should ever write a spec because they think people want to read that spec. Saying, 'Oh, everyone wants to read ER specs, so I better write ER even though I don't really watch the show.'

"Wrong. Pick the show you're passionate about. What rarely happens is getting hired on the show that you wrote the spec for. But what they see is somebody who can emulate the style of a show, the quality of a show, and put a huge amount of their heart into it.

"The reason it's very hard to get a job on the show you wrote the spec for, is for every story that gets written, there have been dozens and dozens of stories we've talked about. So in other words, your idea is probably a variation of something we've already done, so there's nothing fresh about it. And we're gonna be picky about voices, because we feel like we know the voices so well. So if somebody says a line, and we know they would never say that line, we've already colored our opinion of it.

"But if we see it's a show we respect, say, The Sopranos or something—we love The Sopranos—we get a Sopranos spec here, we read it. We're not going to be picky about it because we're not thinking of Sopranos stories. We're going to be much more forgiving.

"What you're doing is saying, 'I can write a quality show, I can emulate a show.' You read it, and if it seems professional, you think, 'that person can write.' That's all you need. But it's always—there's the subjectivity of reading something that you're already working on, saying, this isn't as good as something we would have turned out, or it's as good—even if it's as good, it's not enough to say, 'let's hire this person. We could do this ourselves, we need somebody who's going to come up with something fresh. We're not gonna get a sense of it from somebody writing a spec for Buffy.'"

WG2: "How many people, would you say, are full-time employed writers in television?"

DF: "Oh, I don't know. I haven't a clue. It's very tough. All of us who have the privilege of having a job in the industry just should be thanking whoever their God is. Thanking their lucky stars that they are here, because there are so many very talented people who are not. They just haven't had the breaks we've had."

WG2: "Well, you know, they say opportunity only knocks."

DF: "Yes. You have to have the stuff to back it up."

ATIONS: Condor placement, ITC
DUCTION: sc 18-Binocular FX in Post
L LABOR: 2 X Addl Grips; 1 X Addl Electricians

JANE ESPENSON

We interviewed Jane Espenson on the Initiative set in Santa Clarita. She was enjoying the shoot and had no objection to sitting in a corner of the Lockheed/Legacy facility, on cold, hard concrete. She kept an eye on the production for us, so we would know when to stop talking while a take was being filmed.

WG2: "Can you tell us your career path?"

JE: "Sure. I was in graduate school studying linguistics at UC Berkeley, and I found out that you could submit a script to Star Trek: The Next Generation without an agent. I wrote three of those and sent them in, and they called me and invited me to come and pitch.

"I didn't know what pitch meant, but I started flying down from Berkeley every couple of months and pitching stories at Star Trek. And they bought one story and one premise. It was enough to get me a beginner agent.

"I met a few other people who were doing the same thing, and one of them told me about the Disney Writer's Fellowship. So I wrote a Seinfeld spec, and submitted that, and got into the Disney Writer's Fellowship. So then I moved down here, and Disney put me on my first show, which was Dinosaurs. I was there for the very tail end of it. It had already been canceled. But I was free because I was being paid for by the Fellowship, so I worked on Dinosaurs for like two months.

"Then I was thrown another Disney show, Monty. It was Henry Winkler and David Schwimmer. I did that for a while, first season.

"I did a few other sitcoms, and ended up on Ellen. I spent a year at Ellen, the very last season of Ellen, and from there I came to Buffy.

"All the shows I'd been on up to that point had either been shows that only went one season, or shows that had had a long run, but I was on the final season. So Buffy was my first second season ever. I'm really enjoying that.

"Between the sitcoms I wrote a freelance episode of Deep Space Nine, and a Nowhere Man. Nowhere Man is no longer with us. So I was very happy to have an actual Star Trek episode with my name on it.

WG2: "What's it called?"

JE: "The episode was called 'Accession.' It had a Quark scene in it, so I got to write for Armin Shimerman on several different shows. I also got to write for Jack Plotnick, who played the deputy mayor [Allan Finch] this year. He was Peter's boyfriend Barrett on Ellen. It's very cool. You work in this town long enough, you write for everybody twice.

"I was doing sitcoms, but I had started in drama. Buffy was my very favorite show. I thought, 'That would be a good place for me.' I have strong joke-writing skills, but I never enjoyed the pressure and pace of a sitcom room.

"I thought drama would be a good place for me to explore, as Ellen was ending. So I told my agent, 'Let's try to put me on a drama.' I'd written an NYPD Blue spec. He sent in one of my produced Ellen's and my NYPD Blue spec. I got a meeting based on that, and I got hired here at Buffy.

WG2: "How do you get started pitching and breaking a story?"

JE: "Well, it's a weird process. It's very strange. The room is very different than a sitcom room— all my previous shows were sitcoms, where the room is even more vulgar than this room. This room is…lots of craziness, and you feel very free to throw out even very bad ideas. You won't be actually punished for them, although jokes may be made if it's a particularly cheesy idea.

"There's a lot of joking around, there's a lot of talking that isn't about the story, that's sort of the stuff you need to do. You talk about everything, you make every stupid joke you can think of. There's a lot of poking fun at everyone's personalities. It's almost like a talent show in there. Tracey [Forbes] won a lip-synching contest once, so it'll be, 'Let's make Tracey lip-synch.'"

WG2: "So, are you pitching at that point?"

JE: "No, this is when we're trying to break the story. Pitches are much more solitary, organized, focused things. For pitching stories, you have like a session alone with Joss, and you just say, 'Here are some ideas I have for episodes.'

"We also use the word when we're all sitting in the room trying to break a story, and you say, 'I've got an idea I want to pitch,' or 'That thing that Doug just pitched, that sounded good to me.' So we also use it to mean when you're just making a suggestion for an element of a story."

WG2: "So when you're breaking a story, how much of a thumbnail do you have for that?"

JE: "Sometimes it can be very sketchy. Sometimes it can be more detailed. Usually it doesn't come off a pitch. 'Beer Bad' did. Tracey pitched that at her job interview. I pitched 'Band Candy' at my job interview. But usually it's either Joss has a great idea, or he says, 'Given what's happened so far, and what's going to happen in the future, this episode has to be about the following thing.'"

WG2: "So then you flesh it out? For example, if it's going to be about Giles's bad past, you say, 'How about if he turns into a demon? Why would he turn into a demon?'"

JE: "Actually, that one is interesting. You're talking about 'A New Man.' We really wanted to do a story about Giles feeling alienated. We usually start that way, from the emotion, and then we say, 'Okay, what's the metaphor for it?'

"So we did not start with 'Giles turns into a demon.' We started with his emotions, and we had specifically sort of marginalized the character earlier in the season so we could get to him feeling alienated. So everything that happens is really done for a reason. Sometimes it's a reason that only Joss knows, but it's remarkable how far ahead he has planned—not events, in some cases, but just emotional places for the characters to be. A lot of the times it's events, too."

WG2: "So when you're breaking the story out, is there a certain technique? Do you try to get a high and low point for each act?"

JE: "The act breaks is where you start. At the end of each act, which is going to be its emotional high point. You want to make sure the audience comes back after the commercial. So usually we don't write anything on the board, we just talk for a long time. It can be anywhere from an hour to three weeks. At some point Joss will say, 'Oh, I'm beginning to see a story here. If this is about Giles feels alienated, and we're going to have Giles turn into a demon, then he should turn into the demon at the end of Two.'

"We knew Episode Twelve would have Buffy's birthday, because it always does, so we knew that was a good way to get Giles feeling alienated early.

"At some point Joss just said, 'Okay, end of One. Ethan steps out.' He pitched that moment exactly as it appears in the script. He had that whole thing completely in his mind. That was our first-act break.

"Second-act break, okay, he's a demon. Third-act break, Buffy says, 'He killed Giles. I'm going to kill him.' So that we have that Giles heading for the ultimate danger moment as we head into Act Four.

"So it's the moment in which Joss lays those three moments down, the ends of Acts One, Two, and Three—at that point you're actually very close to writing things up on the dry erase board. But not until then. We never start writing anything up there until Joss has decreed the act breaks.

"That's the very first step. He never comes up with the act breaks until he's figured out the emotional arc. We talked a lot about alienation, what it's like when your father has a breakdown, what it feels like to be old. Exactly what are Giles's concerns, is his concern more about his career, is his concern more about does Buffy love him anymore?

"He and Olivia had just had that interesting conversation at the end of Ten, so we thought, does he get a call from Olivia that she's not coming back? We had a lot of elements to play with. We had originally thought that this episode might contain a lot of Xander, because they have both been on parallel courses this season. So we thought, should it be Xander's life goes up as Giles's goes down, or should they be in twin declines, or does the Xander stuff not support Giles at all?

"So we talked about all sorts of different avenues. We ended up with the shape of the demon and then that the redemption for Giles comes when Buffy sees him and recognizes him. And that's what sort of brings him back. It doesn't solve all his problems. He's still not as central to Buffy's life as he used to be.

"But he knows that she knows him; she saw him; she values him. She was ready to kill the demon, not just in her normal demon-killing way but with specific revenge in her heart. 'You killed Giles.' So we had to have all that before we could even start thinking about what happens in each scene.

"Let's imagine we're breaking Act Two now. What would happen next? What other beats have to be played? Where's Buffy? What else is happening? Big long discussions, writing things up, erasing them, moving them around, arrows all over the place."

WG2: "What is a beat?"

JE: "A beat is smaller than a scene. A beat is sort of the smallest unit of action in the story. We usually talk about beats in terms of the emotion. You might say something like "Let's do a beat where Ethan's trying to pick up the waitress, because that will also plant the phone number that we're going to need to get later, but it also sort of highlights the way he and Giles feel useless and rejected at this point in their lives. And then we can do a beat of them reminiscing.

"It's an emotional moment or a moment of action in a story. The smallest step in a story.

"Eventually, the board's all full. Then Joss rereads it and says, 'Okay, that looks like a story, and these scenes are all right.' And unlike many shows, that story usually sticks. All those beats stay."

WG2: "Do you next prepare an outline or a beat sheet?"

JE: "A beat sheet, when you have time you do both. A beat sheet is much shorter, about half as long, and it simply says, 'Interior Bronze, Willow and Buffy talk. Willow expresses sadness that Oz is leaving.' It's just a few sentences for each scene. Outlines are almost always fourteen pages long and contain much more detail.

"This far into the season it's just an outline. But you have one dry-erase board full of information that does not equal fourteen pages' worth of stuff. There's a lot of work to be done by the writer, in terms of suggesting some jokes that might go in this scene, laying out attitudes that were left sketchy on the board, the order in which things happen within the scene is sometimes a little vague, you know, 'At some point in this scene we'll find out that Willow has a secret.' That sort of thing. And you have to decide where it all goes.

sc 18- Trace
IR/MUFX: sc
scs 20,21,22
22pt-shoot o
RIC: condor
: Condor plac
N: sc 18-Bind
R: 2 X Addl G
UIPMENT: V

SET
INT LOWELL
INT ELEVATC
INT SEWER T
T SHOOTS
INT CRYPT
INT COMMON
INT BUFFY/M
INT TARA'S D
INT XANDER'

335

.OCATIO
E 3

E 2

E 1
,

E 3

,

INT INITIATIVE(#12)	3/PT	0,8,ATMO	8/8 pg	D	LUCKHEED, SAN
INT INITIATIVE	25PT,12PT,10,9,43PT,A33	1,6,8,11,D1,D2,ATMO	6 pg	D	
EXT WOODS	2	1,6,8,9,10,C1,C2,X,1X,9X,10X,A	1 4/8 pg	N	
		TOTAL	8 2/8 pg		

"Then you get notes from Joss on the outline, which can be big or can be small, and then you're sent out to write a first draft. When there's a luxury of time that takes two weeks, but now it can be as short as five days. That would be unusually short. Usually if there's that little time, like if there's three or four days, you absolutely split it up between writers, so that everyone only takes a chunk.

"You turn in the first draft and you get a second set of notes from Joss. You write a second draft. If there's time you write a third draft. Then Joss takes it and does his own pass at it. So everything goes through him. There's not a line that he has not approved and there's not a story that has not largely been, not just influenced by him, but really pitched by him. Most of the stories really come from him."

WG2: "When you pitch an idea, and then you go into this very collaborative situation, is the writer who pitched the idea who does the beat sheet, the outline, and the drafts?"

JE: "Yes. And the person who wrote that first draft, that's the person whose name is on the episode. In sitcoms, very frequently not a word is left of what you wrote, or there's not even time to write a first draft so you write it in the room with everyone, writing line by line, with twelve people, and you just pick a name when it's done."

WG2: "Explain the hierarchy of writing titles."

JE: "Staff Writer's the lowest. Then you become a Story Editor. You have exactly the same duties; there's no editing of stories. Then you become an Executive Story Editor. And the joke is that you give the Story Editor assignments, but in fact you do exactly the same thing that you do when you're a Staff Writer. And there's nothing executive, and there's nothing about stories, and there's no editing.

"Then you become Co-producer, which is where I am now. The joke is 'co means not.' A Co-producer is technically not a producer. And Producer, Supervising Producer, Co-exec Producer, and an Executive Producer, which is what Joss is. And these don't all have to be filled. We don't have a Story Editor."

WG2: "Is this promotion based on amount of work, number of years?"

JE: "Longevity, yeah. Number of years, pretty much."

WG2: "Tell us about your episodes."

JE: "The ones I've written were 'Band Candy,' 'Gingerbread,' and 'Earshot,' last year. And this year, 'Harsh Light of Day,' 'Pangs,' 'A New Man,' and then one to be named later, that I haven't done yet. I also did the 'Rm w/a Vu' episode of <u>Angel</u>.

"'Band Candy' was my pitch. And 'Earshot' was out of something I pitched. I pitched a bunch of stuff that Joss didn't like, and then I said I had one other idea which is, someone uses psychic ability to cheat on a test, but I couldn't get a story out of it.

"[David] Greenwalt said, 'That'd be interesting if you were cheating on a test, and instead you heard someone say "I'm gonna kill everybody"' I said, "Huh." And Joss said, "Okay, that'd be your second-act break." And as soon as he said that, I said, "Okay, I've got a story." So that sort of came out of my pitch.

"'Harsh Light of Day' was just assigned to me. We were talking about what would happen at Thanksgiving, and Joss said, 'You know what would be cool on Thanksgiving would be if we fought an Indian.' So 'Pangs' was his.

"Marti, Greenwalt, and Joss had been in a meeting talking about something completely different. As they walked out of the meeting, Greenwalt said, 'While we were in there, we thought of an idea for Giles. We think Giles should have a breakdown. It sounded like something you should write.'

"Giles doesn't have a breakdown; the story ended up migrating away from that. So I went off and thought about breakdowns and stuff. The rest was set down without Joss. We came up with

Giles turns into a demon, pitched it to Joss, who didn't like it the way we had configured it, but came up with a different approach to him turning into a demon. We had configured it more like <u>The Fly</u>, where it was a more gradual transformation that Giles went through alone. And Joss thought he should wake up in the morning and already be a demon. So even when it's your own pitch, Joss finds a way to put a twist on it and make it special.

"But in a way that's sort of the progression you go through on this show. You would think that as you got more established you'd start pitching more story ideas, but it's kind of the other way around. It's the newer writers who generally write the stand-alone episodes, so they need to pitch ideas. And it's more like as you feel more secure in your job, you start being trusted with the arc episodes, and you don't need to pitch those because you're filling in the next thing that's going to happen. So you actually pitch less. I haven't had a pitch session with Joss this whole season. Last year I had a bunch where I went in."

WG2: "Now, how did you get the idea for 'Gingerbread?'"

JE: "'Gingerbread' was not my pitch. 'Band Candy' was. On 'Gingerbread,' though, I added Hansel and Gretel. That was not in what I was given. When I went out to write the outline I put Hansel and Gretel in it, and it sold. I was very happy with that. Because you take a chance when you write something like that."

WG2: "What did you use as inspiration for 'Band Candy?'"

JE: "I looked back recently at the original sheet that I brought to my job interview. The log line that I pitched was 'teenagers think it would be great to see their parents as they were at their own age.' It would sort of cut them down to size, but in fact it's really frightening. And then I pitched a story which had to do with Joyce and Giles drinking—it was coffee, at that point—that made them younger.

"And as we all talked about it Joss was interested in it, particularly because Giles was who he was when he was a teenager. In my original conception, Giles and Joyce went off to raise the demon that became the danger, but of course that means the demon can't show up until quite late in the script. So Joss's way of bringing in Ethan and the demon already pre-existing, Lurconis, helped very much."

WG2: "How did you nail the jargon for 'Band Candy' so well?"

JE: "I just used the teenspeak of my own childhood, pretty much. I actually saw someone criticizing the episode, saying, 'How come no matter how old the characters are they all talk like they grew up in the seventies?' It's because I did.

"You identify so much with the teenagers on this show as you're writing it, that I was thinking of Joyce and Giles like my parents. So my first thought was, okay, they grew up in the fifties. Then I realized, 'Oh, my God, no, they're closer to my age than my parents' age. So I'll write them as if they were teenagers when I was a teenager.'

"I hadn't realized that Snyder was older than them, or I might have written Snyder a little differently."

WG2: "Do the writers watch very much production?"

JE: "No. I actually did for 'Band Candy,' because I was not included in as many story meetings last year. So I was free, and I went down and watched them shoot almost every single scene of 'Band Candy.' I haven't had a chance to do that since.

"I would have loved to watch them shoot 'A New Man,' with Tony in the demon outfit and everything. My favorites are the episodes with lots of jokes, because of all my years of sitcom training. I'm always kind of startled when I see a joke that I wrote on TV, and I wasn't there to see it get shot. You always see everything get shot on a sitcom because you go down to the stage Friday night and you watch it. You watch it with the audience. Here you write them and then you see them on the air. It's very strange."

337

TRACEY FORBES

During the first day of location shooting on the Initiative set, Joss showed up with the writers in tow—David Fury, Doug Petrie, Tracey Forbes, and Jane Espenson. (Marti Noxon had stayed behind to work on a script.) Someone murmured, "Oh, it's so nice to see the writers on set. They don't get out much."

Joss was amenable to the writers being interviewed during their set visit, but requested that they stay nearby in case of a "writer emergency."

WG2: "What could come up that Joss would say, 'Tracey, quick! I need you right now!'?"

TF: "Well, it's the fast-approaching Christmas break, in two days, and Doug Petrie has to be writing his episode, which is Episode Fifteen, over Christmas break, and we haven't broken it yet. So we're trying to break it with every second Joss has free."

WG2: "You guys basically get back and start; there's no transition, right?"

TF: "Yeah, we're prepping one right now we'll start filming as soon as we get back, and Doug's will be into prep as soon as we get back, so he'll be working over Christmas."

WG2: "Define 'breaking a story' for us."

TF: "Well, it starts in general discussions about where the characters are emotionally at this point in the season. Sometimes we're breaking a stand-alone episode, which is fairly disconnected from the others in terms of the season's arc, but mostly we start by talking about emotions and themes and metaphors that we want to deal with, with Joss and the rest of the five of us in a room. And then we work out emotional arcs for Buffy and other characters in the episode.

"On a big whiteboard in Joss's office, we begin breaking the story down into teaser and four acts, and then within those acts, seven to nine story beats. We always do this with Joss and any writer who is available to work on it. Anyone who isn't working on the breakdown is probably off writing their own script at the time.

"While we're breaking, often a lot of jokes are thrown around the room, a lot of neat moments that don't necessarily get written on the board. But whoever's writing the script is taking notes. We work from the general to the more specific, scene by scene.

"Then whoever's writing that episode goes off and writes an outline, fleshing out all the beats that we discussed, filling in any gaps there might be, and showing how things would play out."

WG2: "For the most part, scripts credit a primary writer, but we've seen a couple of episodes where there's maybe even two or three people credited as the writers. How does a collaborative effort differ from the work of a sole author?"

TF: "Sometimes two writers, or even three writers, will divide a script up. One person will take the teaser and Act One; another will take Two and Three; maybe someone else will take Four, because we need it faster. I think Jane had a shared credit with someone, because the story was pitched by a freelancer or someone who pitched an idea. We wanted to use it, and Jane ended up writing it."

WG2: "How did you get started in writing, TV writing in particular?"

TF: "It would probably start with always having enjoyed writing as a child. My brother bought an 8mm film camera and decided he wanted to make movies. I was ten and I had a couple of cousins who were like ten and eleven.

"My brother would make up these short, three-minute stories, and he would film us acting in them. We would make some costumes, make some laser guns, and shoot something in the garage. We probably have five or six of these. I think that's what really started me on this path.

"My brother went on to study television in school, and was always very good about including me in whatever he was doing. So I ended up studying the same thing in university as he did. I guess that's how I got started—through my brother."

WG2: "What about your first sense of story? What sorts of things were you exposed to as a child, and do you still read now?"

TF: "As a child I did read a lot, and I was read to a lot. I'm in the last twenty pages of <u>A Little Princess</u>, a children's novel. It was one that passed me by as a child, and recently Joss said that it was his favorite book. I thought, 'I'm gonna have to go back and read it.'

"Next on my list, Marti recommended <u>High Fidelity</u> by Nick Hornby. And over Christmas everybody is reading the <u>Harry Potter</u> books, so I'm hoping for the first one in my stocking."

WG2: "How did you get to <u>Buffy</u>?"

TF: "I just moved to L.A. in May to take this job. Prior to that, all my life I'd been working in Toronto, Canada. In Toronto I worked on a couple of series: <u>Psi-Factor: Chronicles of the Paranormal</u>, and another sci-fi series.

"My agent moved from Toronto and joined an agency in LA. And I made it clear to her I wanted to come down and work on a really cool show down here. She set up a bunch of meetings for me. I met with <u>Buffy</u> in February or March. I got here on the third of May and I started work on the tenth of May [1999]."

WG2: "Did Joss read some of your scripts from the Toronto shows?"

TF: "Yes. First he read an <u>X-Files</u> spec, which started out with George Snyder at <u>Mutant Enemy</u>. And then I believe it went to Marti and then Joss, and maybe David Greenwalt. After I met with them, they called my agent to say, 'We'd like to see some more work of hers.' We sent an <u>Ally McBeal</u> spec that I had, and an episode of <u>Psi-Factor</u> that I wrote. And then a week and a half later or so, I had an offer to come down. That was around the end of March. And so very quickly my boyfriend of nine years and I planned a wedding, we got married, we sold our condo in Toronto, we bought a car, and we drove down. That was a big transition."

WG2: "Did you actually pitch any <u>Buffy</u> story ideas in that process?"

TF: "I had two meetings. One with George Snyder first, and then two days later with Joss, David and Marti. My first meeting, with George Snyder, he went over with me—very sweet of him—how to pitch a story in ways that they would respond to. Talking about, what was the <u>Buffy</u> of the pitch, essentially her emotional arc. What used to be a high school metaphor but is now a college metaphor. And the monster. <u>Buffy</u> stories essentially have those three elements.

"So I went away, and for two days I thought of a bunch of ideas that had those three elements in them. When I met with Joss and David and Marti, I pitched a few ideas. My first one, we talked a bit about it in the interview, and then they decided it wasn't going to work. My second one was a bomb, nobody liked it. My third one is the one that became the first script that I wrote here, which was 'Beer Bad.' My pitch was, Xander gets a job at the college pub and serves beer that turns intellectuals into Neanderthals. That was the essence of that."

WG2: "What was your sensation the first day on the set when they were filming 'Beer Bad'?"

TF: "I was overly cautious about where I stood, where I sat. The first time I went down, I went down with Joss. We had been up in his office breaking a story for an episode down the road, and he was going to go down and watch rehearsal. He said, 'Do you want to come?'

"We went into the studio. I was sort of

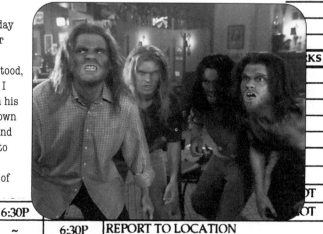

hanging back, and he of course was right up front doing his thing, showing the actors what he would like, and watching rehearsals.

"He pulled me right up onto the set and told me, 'This is your episode. You should be watching whenever you want.'

"It was tremendous of him to make me feel as comfortable as possible on the set. After that, every spare second I had I was on the set watching. And they were really great about coming right up and giving me headphones so I could listen to the dialog."

WG2: "Hearing your words."

TF: "Oh, yeah. What a thrill that was."

WG2: "What character do you have the most fun either creating situations or dialog for?"

TF: "I enjoy writing Willow. Her voice came the easiest of all the voices for me to write."

WG2: "How do you feel like you're fitting in with the camaraderie of writers on this show?"

TF: "They've all been extremely welcoming, actually. They tease me constantly about my oots and aboots, and ehs, and strange words I use occasionally. Since my transition coming down here was such a large move, I expected to be really homesick. It really helps being happy and having work and really liking the people that you work with. And having my husband here helps a lot. And my little dog. But I can't tell you how much it helps to look forward to coming to work every day."

WG2: "Americans tend to be very ethnocentric. We tend to think, 'well, we all know McDonald's and the Gap, everybody does.' <u>Buffy</u> is rife with pop culture type references. Is that something that comes easily to you? Or are you trying to catch up there?"

TF: "I don't notice it as much in writing for <u>Buffy</u> as much as I notice it in the room where we sit and break stories and tell jokes and everything. Whereas they all have an education in American history and American literature, I chose to study Canadian literature."

WG2: "Not many Margaret Atwood references in an episode."

TF: "I do notice a difference there. But in terms of the writing, I listen to the radio, I watch TV, I think I get by okay in the <u>Buffy</u> universe."

WG2: "What types of personal experiences, if any, do you find yourself bringing to the scripts? Do you remember, oh, I had these types of experiences in college, or as a—not significantly younger, but somewhat—younger person?"

TF: "Well, in terms of 'Beer Bad,' it kind of speaks for itself. But actually I didn't have that kind of experience in university. I didn't go out drinking a lot. In terms of 'Something Blue,' my husband and I did plan our wedding in four weeks, so there was a lot to draw on there. And also, at the time, Doug Petrie was planning his wedding, so he was a resource for that script."

WG2: "What's your next episode?"

TF: "It may be Seventeen or Eighteen I really don't know what it will be yet."

WG2: "So some of it is who has a specific idea, and some of it's just working with who has what workload, and who's available to take a certain episode?"

TF: "Yeah. We generally go in order, and sometimes for various reasons people will get shifted around. Someone will be working on an <u>Angel</u>, or like Doug and his wedding, working around that. As it goes, I'll be two from now. Looking forward to it. I'm trying each time to come a little closer with my first draft of the script and hoping—trying to make Joss's workload a little lighter when he finally does a pass on it. I hope I can bring it close for him."

"Not this year, anyway. I'm really concentrating on <u>Buffy</u>, and I think that's enough for me right now. It's a very particular world to get to know, a lot of backstory."

WG2: "Some of the staff and crew have talked about public awareness of the production process today being different than ten, twenty years ago. People are aware that Sarah and Alyson are not the orig-inators of their lines. Are you getting feedback about things you've written that people have liked?"

eld	ANYA	H	HOLD		
rts	FORREST	W	6:30P	7:30P	REPORT TO NEBRASKA / BUN
	GRAHAM	W	6:30P	7:30P	REPORT TO NEBRASKA / BUN

TF: "I am online, and it's fantastic. So many shows are on the air, and for so many of them, their fan base focuses around their stars. Buffy is one of the few shows where the fans really recognize the writers, and the work at every level that goes into telling these stories. Sarah and Alyson and Nicky and Marc and everybody are extremely popular, and everybody loves them.

"Yet you go online after an episode, and the fans are extremely excited to have a writer there. They ask you questions about how you came up with things, and compliment you on your lines, and it's really wonderful. We're very fortunate to be on a show where they acknowledge us."

WG2: "So what does the future hold?"

TF: "Future for me? I really don't know. I love working on Buffy, and I have a hard time seeing past this right now, because I'm enjoying it so much. So that's sort of where I am, just very happy in the present."

DOUG PETRIE

Doug Petrie (pronounced "Pee-tree") was among the contingent of writers who accompanied Joss to the Initiative set. We also interviewed him in his office, which was filled with toys and comic books. Doug is delighted to have written a number of Buffy comic books for Dark Horse.

Doug told us about how his wife and he were extremely burnt out and desperately needed a vacation. They flew to Hawaii and collapsed—only to be called in the middle of the night: their house had burned down. They returned home to a lot of wreckage, and they called in a company that specializes in restoring items suffering from smoke damage. To Doug's dismay, many of his most treasured comics were destroyed.

WG2: "Please tell us about your career, and your early life, and where you were born."

DP: "I grew up in beautiful Great Neck, Long Island, and had a very happy childhood there. At an early age I confused myself with Batman. My parents had to actually sit me down and say to me, 'you are not Batman.' My mother made me a cape with the serrated edges, and I wore it all the time. At a very early age—the TV show was on when I was really little and very impressionable, and the first song I could sing was the Batman theme, and I was convinced I was Batman. When my parents explained to me that I wasn't, I was like, uh-huh, uh-huh. I humored them."

WG2: "You knew that it was really your secret identity."

DP: "Yeah. I was like, 'that's cool. You go ahead and make yourselves feel better thinking that I'm not Batman, but in fact I am.' I'm still working that out.

"Sure, it's great. So that's pretty much my childhood, was being Batman. Did a lot of drama in high school. I was in a lot of plays, I was acting in a lot of plays, I directed a couple of plays, had a very active theater community."

WG2: "Where did you go to college?"

DP: "I went to college at William and Mary in Virginia. I went there for four years, studied English, and didn't like the acting program a whole lot. Didn't like the actors. There was an ego-to-talent ratio that was out of whack. And after being with these really great actors in high school and then going to college and seeing these people who thought they were really good, and they weren't, I didn't know what to do with myself.

"But there was a great writing program, and you could write one-act plays and have them produced at the school. So I wrote, you know, like between a dozen and two dozen over the course of my years at school. I wrote a lot of very bad one-act plays. Just awful, awful plays. And then by the end, they weren't good but they sucked less. That was my guarantee to the audience."

342

WG2: "What were some of your titles?"

DP: "The Dust Bowl. Crash. Crash sounds like a Buffy title, actually. Those are the only ones I remember. They were terrible. The Wall. Not to be confused with the Pink Floyd album. It was just as pretentious, but not as good. It was a terrible play. So I wrote a bunch of plays, and then when I got out of college I was going to go to Chicago to study Improv with Second City. That was my big dream.

"And a friend of mine called and he had gone to Harvard, and he said, 'Instead of being broke and miserable and alone in Chicago, why don't you be broke and miserable with your friends? Come to Cambridge.'

"So I did. I moved up to Cambridge and stayed there for six months and I met a large group of friends who were then forming the Cornerstone Theatre Company. They were recently graduated from Harvard, and they were starting a company that was going to get in a small van and travel around the country and produce classical plays, in small communities, in small towns across America, but rewrite them. And have community members act in them along with the company actors, but rewrite them so they took place in the town where we performed them. So in Marmouth, North Dakota, population of 180, we did the Marmouth Hamlet. As if Hamlet had always taken place in Marmouth, North Dakota. And it ends with a shootout, and the line, 'There is no king in Denmark, but an errant knave,' became 'There is no king in Denmark, but a horse's rear end,' and huge laugh. We were sure the audience thought we were making up 'Something is rotten in the state of Denmark.'

"Then I got a job writing for 'Entertainment Watch' for VH1. It was just thirty-second spots. Our boss had this thing, where everything had to end in the same rhythm, where it had to go, da da da da da da—da da. It was really horrible.

"But we had a lot of fun. We started writing stuff to see if they'd put it on the air. And they would. It was just totally light, light, lightweight stuff.

"I got a job writing for a game show called Clash that was on HA! TV before there was the Comedy Channel. There was the Comedy Channel and there was HA! TV and they merged and became Comedy Central. It was cool because we were all really broke, and pretty young, and we all went on to be writers for The Simpsons, and Saturday Night Live.

"It was before any of us made it big. It was actually a really funny game show. Then I wrote promos for Nick at Nite TV Land. It was launching Superman, and I had a really bad cold in the summer, and I watched a hundred episodes of Superman in a row, which was a lot like tripping.

"We came up with this one ad that I loved: "Criminals of Metropolis, you know that beating Superman means staying in shape. That's why you need the Jimmy Olsen thirty-minute workout." And we just showed criminals beating the crap out of Jimmy Olsen. Every episode, Jimmy Olsen—he's like the Giles of the Fifties, one shot and he goes down. So we made this loop reel of Jimmy Olsen getting knocked out about twenty times in twelve seconds. And that's the Superman thirty-minute workout. So that was a lot of fun.

"I moved on to write for a Nickelodeon TV show called Clarissa Explains It All. That was my first time getting in the Guild. They called me and they said, 'Do you want this job?' And I was really struggling at that point. 'I finally just got a job, what do you pay?' When they told me what Guild minimum was, I said, 'I'll be there.'"

WG2: "What is Guild minimum?"

DP: "This is like eight years ago, it was $1800–1850 a week. That was just huge money to me, and still is really nice money. So I jumped on it, and went back and forth between Orlando, Florida, and New York City. They shot it in Universal in Orlando.

"It was fun, overall, and the person who first said, 'You should hire this guy,' is now my wife. Alexa Junge, who wrote for Friends for years. In utter despair I wrote a spec script of Parker

Lewis Can't Lose, which was a show I just loved, and everyone said, 'You'll never get anything writing a Parker Lewis. You don't know what you're doing.' Alexa, who I had never met, read it, and she went to her boss, who was running the show, and she said, 'Tell me this guy's available to work on the show and tell me he's single.'

"So the agent who told me, 'You won't get anything writing this Parker Lewis spec' couldn't have been more wrong. I get into the Guild and I got my wife, so you never know. Write what you like is the lesson.

"So I wrote for Clarissa, and then did that for two years, got fed up with Florida, couldn't do the long commute to Orlando, central Florida. So I'd had my fill. I really liked writing for Clarissa. It was a really fun show. You got to be smart, and you got to be goofy, so I liked it.

"Then, I had a long and torturous audition as a writer for Saturday Night Live. It was my life-long dream. I was sending them material. It was the funniest material I've ever written in my life, and after eight months of back and forth, they said, 'Sorry, we can't hire you.' So I was just heartbroken, and figured there was nothing left in New York City. I always wanted to be a moviemaker, so I packed up—I had a lot of money for the first time in my life, and I thought, 'put your money where your mouth is. You wanna make movies, pack up.'

"I stayed in San Francisco for a month, just to kind of figure out what I wanted to do, and I came to Hollywood for four days. I'm friends with Amy Brennerman, who's in Judging Amy, and she was then in Casper, directed by [her now husband] Brad Silberling.

"My second day in Hollywood I went to a party on a houseboat where I met Jim Carrey and Cary Elwes. My third day in Hollywood I was on the sets of Casper, being ushered around the sets of this giant Steven Spielberg-produced movie at Universal.

"I couldn't believe how cool Hollywood was. I thought every day was gonna be like this. So it was very clear, move to Hollywood. So I did. And I haven't had a day like that since.

"I came to Hollywood, wrote some spec scripts that no one would read. I wrote a spec script that again, everyone told me not to write. It was for a science fiction show that was in its second season; it was just starting an audience; it was called The X-Files.

"A couple of agents asked, 'What is this show, why are you wasting your time?'

"Then Nickelodeon showed up and I got a job writing the movie Harriet the Spy. It was one of my favorite books as a kid. It was hugely influential in my becoming a writer. When they hired me they had a bunch of scripts and they were going to start shooting in six weeks or lose the option. The director Bronwen Hughes and I just got together and we just wailed on it, and wrote it in about ten days. Just threw out every script and wrote it in about ten days. And they basically filmed what I wrote. Less than a year later it was in theaters.

"So I moved here Fourth of July weekend of '94, and two years to the day after I moved to Los Angeles I had my name on a movie screen. It made me really happy.

"Then I spent about a year or two in development land, because now you're a writer, you know, and kind of going through being the ball in the pinball machine of Hollywood, just getting bounced around. There were a lot of ups and downs, and I was very dedicated to making movies. A lot of my friends wrote for TV, and I didn't want to write for TV at all. I was very aggressive about that. And my then-agent, who's still a really good friend of mine, said, 'Do you want to meet Joss Whedon for the TV show Buffy the Vampire Slayer?'

"I knew that Joss Whedon had written Speed, which I just loved. I said, 'Yeah, I want to meet the guy who wrote Speed.' And we met and hit it off in a huge way. We really liked each other. We both talked about the Star Wars rerelease, and how we hated the fact that they changed the movie so that Han gets shot at, before shooting Greedo in the bar. So basically we were two eleven-year-old geeks talking about comic books and Star Wars for about an hour.

the love

taped

y

VE TO FRO

s and shoot

YERS
lar

RONT

REMA

GILES	H		HOLD	
WILLOW	H		HOLD	
SPIKE	W	6:30P	7:30P	REPORT TO LOCATION
BUFFY	W	10:30A	11:30A	REPORT TO LOCATION

"When I saw that there was a movie called <u>Buffy the Vampire Slayer</u>, I had to see it. I was colossally disappointed, and I bored the hell out of all my friends going, 'With a title like <u>Buffy the Vampire Slayer</u>, it should have been this and it should have been this. You know, you should have teen sex, you should have great jokes, you should have great karate fights, it should be a really cool movie.' They had no idea what I was talking about. They said, 'You went to see a movie called <u>Buffy the Vampire Slayer</u>. Of course it's terrible.' I was like, 'No, it should be great.'

"I was really frustrated about that, and met with Joss when we talked about it. And then he said, 'So, would you be interested in writing on staff?' And I was like, 'Yeah, I guess' [said very unenthusiastically]. So he didn't give me a job.

"After I met with him, I watched 'The Pack.' That was the first episode I watched. And I sent him a little <u>Creature from the Black Lagoon</u> postcard saying, 'Man, that episode rocked. Hope there's a place on the staff for a guy like me. Your pal, Doug.'

"We kept in touch. Even though I wasn't on staff, I wrote a couple of outlines for episodes that never made it. One was a baby-sitting episode, where Buffy baby-sits for a baby that's not human. It turns out the father is really evil. It was pretty cool. We went pretty far with it and realized it won't work. There were a couple of reasons it couldn't work. Then there was another one, a mirror episode, where the girls' bathroom mirror in Sunnydale High comes alive, and it becomes kind of this little embodiment of vanity, and it pulls Buffy in and steps out, so it's like doppelganger Buffy, bad Buffy. And she's the living embodiment of vanity, and she goes around being a lot like Cordelia. That was a lot closer to a real live <u>Buffy</u> episode.

"But that also didn't get made.

"I had to meet with Joss and David, and we had a great time, and they would take me onto the sets and we'd come up with these great ideas. And it was always really fun. And they'd say, 'We're not gonna make your episode, but we like you. Keep coming back.'

"In the spring of '98, this hot TV hiring season was coming. Alexa was saying, 'You really should think about <u>Buffy</u>.' But I'd say, 'Maybe, but what about movies?'

"And then they said, 'Would you like to join the staff?'

At first I was very coy. 'Well, I could do a couple of days a week.' They said, 'No, you jerk.'

"After a week of hemming and hawing, I thought, 'You know, that's a really good idea.' So I did. And I'm so glad I did. It's been great. It's definitely been the best job I've ever had.

"I always wanted to do a TV series or a movie that's much like the Marvel Comics I read growing up. And the thing about the seventies was that, when you said you read comic books, a lot of people got a picture of something unrealistic, and kind of broad and stupid. The thing about Marvel Comics was they had this really smart, New York-based stable of writers, who weren't writing for kids, they were writing for college students. As a thirteen- or fourteen-year-old, you were let into an adult world.

"Especially <u>Spider-Man</u>—when Gerry Conway was writing it and Len Wein was writing it and Ross Andru was drawing it—it's very much like <u>Buffy</u>. Emotionally the guy's a mess, but he's got these superpowers that help him, and everything's a metaphor. I've always very, very strongly felt—and this is why I'm so frustrated with a lot of the fantasy movies, or action-adventure—that if you're going to go to a fantasy place, you have to ground it emotionally as much as possible. You have to really sell the audience: 'No, no, this is really happening.'

344

"In the best sense, Buffy and Spider-Man have this huge overlap. What's interesting about Spider-Man is that he's incredibly vulnerable, and Peter Parker's love life is constantly a mess. He can stop the end of the world, but he can't get a date. That's where that guy lives, and it's really fun. So you're playing out both. Buffy is just this huge opportunity to explore all of that. Couldn't be more fun."

[At this point, David Fury walked by. Doug asked us if we knew that David provided the voice for the pilot in the opening of The Raiders of the Lost Ark.]

DF: "Jock."

WG2: "Jock. In the opening scene of Raiders of the Lost Ark. And he said—"

DF: "'Come on. Show a little backbone, will ya? Oh, that's just my pet snake, Reggie.'"

WG2: "Get out!"

DP: "That's him."

CASTING

AMY BRITT, CASTING DIRECTOR

We met Amy Britt in her spacious office in the *Buffy* production complex and we began by asking her to describe the casting process.

AB: "Ideally, we get the scripts close to the first day of prep. With Episode Thirteen, we finished yesterday. That's when we cast Dr. Angleman.

"Sometimes they have scripts in the can, and they can pass them on to us pretty early, even though they will go through many rewrites. Story-wise, the characters are pretty much what they're going to be. With Episode Thirteen, we originally got an outline, which gave us a heads-up."

WG2: "When did you get it?"

AB: "It might have been right before Thanksgiving. And then we got a script Friday, I think. So that was a decent amount of time.

"I wait for the script to come in so I have dialogue, but the outlines [alone] are extremely helpful to me, because they give me at an idea. I know I'm not the end of the line. Wardrobe, hair, makeup—all those people are sweating bullets until they get hold of the actor. They're just waiting for a person. They can't even start to guesstimate sizes, types of build—anything like that—until we have it cast.

"The character of Adam has heavy prosthetics and specialty makeup. When we were casting, they were still deciding how much of his face would be covered or uncovered. But we had to get an actor immediately in order to get him in front of the camera before the year 2000.

"In Episode Thirteen, all we're going to see of Adam is at the very end of the show. He kills Maggie, and has one line. 'Thank you, Mommy.' [Note: It was shortened later to just one word: 'Mommy.']

Christine Yammine, Amy Britt, and Lonnie Hamerman

And you cannot tell the range of an actor from that line. So Joss wrote a monologue [for the actors to use at audition] that will most likely appear in some form, probably rewritten a little. It could be next episode, it could be two episodes from now.

"That happens a lot in casting—having a character introduced in a brief way, then having to find some bit of material to judge their talent, whether they're right for the role or not. So we did that last week, and got lucky, and had about eight actors in. We picked one [George Hertzberg] and were very happy, and sent him to makeup.

"In terms of auditioning, actors come in different echelons, basically. There are actors who will come in for a one-liner; and actors who won't come in for anything but a guest-star role in an episode, which would be somebody who's not in the recurring or series regular cast, but has the biggest story line.

"While the outlines point me in the right direction, I usually have to wait for the script to know what pool of talent I'll be pulling from. Sometimes it winds up becoming very last-minute. In television, schedules are really important because in an eight-day period, everything has to happen. All the elements have to fit into the period. The same goes for the writers, and every other department."

WG2: "How did Lindsay Crouse get cast?"

AB: "We were searching for Maggie Walsh for a while. It was hard to find the exact right fit. She's an incredibly intelligent, straight-shooting woman with a bite, but you have to like her. We met a lot of people, and we weren't quite nailing it.

"In the first episode she was only in one scene, in the lecture hall. We didn't feel like we had Maggie by the time Episode One was shooting. So we continued the search, found Lindsay, hired her, and then shot it all out in Episode Three. [In other words], we shot the scene to be inserted into Episode One while we were doing Episode Three. And it was worth the wait, because she turned out very well."

WG2: "How did you become a casting director?"

AB: "Well, I was at college in D.C., at American University. I was studying international PR, and enjoying it. When I was a junior, I read an article in People magazine about Jane Jenkins and Janet Hirshenson, who are high-end film casting directors. The movies that were cited as their recent credits, When Harry Met Sally, Parenthood, all sorts of stuff like that, were some of my favorites. I've always been a huge movie fan, a huge television fan, and especially a fan of actors. I was never an actor, never got involved in it, but really always knew who was who and just had an affinity for actors.

"The thing that made me read the article in People on them was I remembered seeing their names all the time in the opening credits of films. So when I was flipping through, I saw their names. 'What do these people do anyway? Just sit around and meet actors?' Which is a lot of what we do, obviously. It's a little more complex than that, but it is a truly enjoyable profession if you like people.

"That was when I was a junior, and senior year came along. I was graduating and I thought, 'I'll give L.A. a year, I'm gonna go try this casting thing out.'

"I got out here and picked up the yellow pages, found the Casting Company, which is the name of Jane and Janet's company, and wound up getting a job with them a couple months later, just through calling them. I worked for them for over five years. I started as a receptionist, went through being an assistant for one, and then the other; and then they promoted me and I was casting projects under their roof.

"About a year and a half ago I left and started a company with two other women. And I was lucky enough to get this job. It's just been amazing here. It's a great group of people to work with. My company has an office up on Sunset in West Hollywood, which I was reluctant to leave when I first got this job. That was the one drawback in my eyes, coming out here and being away from my partners. But I love the environment here. It's a little Buffy compound. You basically don't leave here during the day. You know everybody, everybody's really friendly, and it's just a wonderful place to work."

WG2: "You cast for Buffy and Angel. Do you cast for anything else?"

AB: "I don't right now. Mainly throughout the season I do this exclusively. It's more than a full-time job. A couple months ago I did some U.S. casting for this Irish film that Jim Sheridan is producing. He did In the Name of the Father, and My Left Foot, stuff like that. He has a company called Hell's Kitchen, and they needed to come stateside to explore some name actors.

"So it was something that I could feasibly do concurrently with a schedule like this. Because the producers and directors are only in town for pockets of four days. Four days here, then a couple weeks later four days, couple weeks later four days, and that was it. But otherwise, I can't do anything else except during hiatus.

"And I'm more than happy with it. There is a challenge in finding people who have the right humor for the show. This is an hour drama, and while there's a ton of comedy in it, it's not 'budump-bump.' It's not that easy or formulaic."

WG2: "What was the most interesting casting decision for Episode Thirteen?"

AB: "Actually, I would have to say the character of Adam. Maggie, Forrest, Graham, and Tara were cast this year and are recurring characters. So there are really only three people outside of recurring and regulars [in Episode Thirteen].

"Adam is this Frankenstein-like monster comprised of other demon, robotic, human, cyber-netic parts. A scary guy. But the beauty of the show, besides the tongue-in-cheek aspect, is that the choices are always interesting. The only thing about George Hertzberg, who's playing Adam, is that he's tall. He's six-four. We wanted to cast somebody tall. But he is seemingly an all-American, midwestern type of guy. Kind of fair, blondish hair, blue eyes, and a very pleasant face.

"His appearance is going be so imposing between his height, and what they're going to put him in, but this is a guy we're going to want eventually to have some affinity for. We can't just see him as an evil being. He is evil to the core; he should scare us with his actions; but there's also innocence. Like the Frankenstein monster, you realize that they're only doing what they know. Or what they've been programmed to do. These aren't born creatures, these are creations.

"George's approach on the material is pretty light. He's looking out at the world for the first couple times, speaking for the first time, and then he does something that you realize, wow, he's truly dangerous."

WG2: "How do you keep current on the one-line actors?"

AB: "I depend on workshops for those. I have ones that I prefer, where I find more talent than others.

And they're not restricted to one-liners. I met an actor, Andy Umberger, who has been D'Hoffryn on our show. I met him in a workshop. He did that character on Buffy the past two seasons ['Doppelgangland' and 'Something Blue'], then did an entirely different guest spot on Angel.

"There are usually about twenty-four actors, and it's a cold reading workshop, a little seminar. You meet the actors, give them scenes, match them up; they do the scenes, which I sometimes

---

sc 18- Trace
R/MUFX: sc
scs 20,21,22
22pt-shoot o
RIC: condor
Condor plac
N: sc 18-Bin
R: 2 X Addl G
IIPMENT: V

SET
INT LOWELL
INT ELEVATC
INT SEWER T
T SHOOTS
INT CRYPT
INT COMMON
INT BUFFY/W
INT TARA'S E
INT XANDER'

OCATIO
E 3

E 2

E 1
,
E 3
,

INT INITIATIVE(#12)	3/P1	6,8,ATMO	6/8 pg	D	LOCKHEED, SAM
INT INITIATIVE	25PT,12PT,10,9,43PT,A33	1,6,8,11,D1,D2,ATMO	6 pg	D	
EXT WOODS	2	1,6,8,9,10,C1,C2,X,1X,9X,10X,A	1 4/8 pg	N	
		TOTAL	8 2/8 pg		

critique, and then there's a question-and-answer period. You kind of get a sense of them. A lot of times they're people who are brand-new in town, have little or no credits in terms of television or film, have come out of the theater school, and/or have done plenty of stage. They need to meet casting directors. There are also established actors who are continually expanding their network, which is very smart.

"For actors, it's this vicious cycle, where you can't get an agent without tape, but you can't get tape without getting on a show. And you can't get a show without having an agent. So this kind of closes the gap between actors and casting directors.

"We depend on so many different sources, but we release breakdowns a lot. They go out to the agents, who submit their clients. A workshop provides such a better screening process for me than sitting down with a stack of fifty pictures. Sometimes there are fifty, sixty, seventy pictures submitted for any given role. You have no idea who half of these people are.

"And that's a crapshoot, right there. It's just, okay, pick ten faces you like and hopefully one of them can do it. As opposed to 'I've seen these people do much more complex material in workshops. I know what they can handle.' And then with everything else, I just watch TV, watch movies, read magazines, talk to agents, do generals. But I love doing all those things."

WG2: "Did you learn anything new, working on Thirteen?"

AB: "Another big thing, with casting, is who goes [with whom,] whether it's aesthetically or the style of their acting, the way they're going to balance each other. Especially if it's a family or something like that. Even if it's two doctors working together, you do think about 'Okay, we've got a duo here, it's not just every man for himself.' You have to keep it in mind."

WG2: "Were you a horror fan in any way before you started this?"

AB: "I wouldn't say classic horror, but definitely suspense. Love it. The scariest movie to me ever is <u>The Silence of the Lambs</u>. The way I felt the first time I watched it, I just remember crawling out of my skin and loving every minute of it. Just dying in the theater."

WG2: "Is there any part of your job that's especially hard?"

AB: "Deadlines. I come from a film-casting background, and there is a big difference. I mean, the turnover. Especially when you're doing two series concurrently, because that divides your time. But it's really easier than doing two separate shows, like most people would be doing. Because we share Joss, and David, and Marti.

"And there're all those common links. They're very respectful that there's another job to be done. Most people, when you divide your time, you divide your time. And here, it's built that way so that everything gets done. It's difficult, but it's not insurmountable. It's kind of nice. It's nice to be busy.

"On a film you have up to three months for casting. You get your foot in the door and start working at the beginning of preproduction, and that's usually three months before principal photography. Granted, you see a lot more people. In television, time is a big issue. I don't like the concept of settling. With Joss, I just aim to please; I want to do my job really well.

"Keep looking until [Joss] says, 'Stop, I'm done, I don't want to see another person for this role.' And then you still, until you actually hire the person, kind of have it ticking in your mind, in case. You never know when you're going to have a conversation, or be flipping through something, and say, 'Oh, my God, I didn't think about that person. Wow, that's the person.'

"Now you always have to make sure that somebody else thinks that's the right person, because it's really not about the casting director's choice, it's presenting choices."

WG2: "To whom do you present? And do you present everybody, including extras?"

AB: "No. I do all the speaking roles, and extras do all the nonspeaking roles. Every once in a while I'll cast a nonspeaking role if it has a considerable amount of direction. Because there are

KILEY		W	10:30A	11:30A	REPORT TO LOCATION
ANYA		H	HOLD		
FORREST		W	6:30P	7:30P	REPORT TO NEBRASKA / BUNI

nonspeaking roles who turn around, see a vampire, and have a long shot of terror. That person you probably want to cast. Because that's actually harder to do sometimes than five lines. But in general I do all the speaking roles.

"The bigger roles go to Joss. He likes to be involved with anybody who's going to be in more than one episode, anybody who is a major guest star, has a lot to do. But he also trusts his team. Which means the director is present, which I think is different. I don't know that all television programs are like that. [Here] the director is a part of the process, and their opinions are listened to. And what I've heard around the industry is that it's not always the case. Ultimately, Joss is the end of the line. Whatever he says goes. But here the directors are an integral part of the process.

"For this show Marti is usually second. If Joss isn't a part of the casting session, then Marti comes with the director, maybe the writer. It's really about putting like a little buffet in front of them, and them going, 'Hmm.' They all have different opinions, and then they sit with their session notes and everybody gives their opinion. 'Well, I saw this, and didn't we say in the tone meeting that this is what we were looking for in this character.'"

WG2: "If you lump together all the meetings and everything, how many days of preproduction per episode would you say there are?"

AB: "Well, it's a pretty strict schedule. It's eight, because they have to start shooting. That is the official preproduction time. Right now we're in prep for Fourteen. But then again, if in the next episode, there's a character that's going to have a three-episode arc, I would have been told about that way before prep, ideally.

"There's just a lot to get done in eight days. Not just the eight days of shooting; it's getting everybody on the same page to start shooting.

"This floor [the production office complex] feels like a giant dorm hall. Everybody pops in and says hello to each other. If you're waiting for something to come in, you can go sit on somebody's couch and chat for a while. It's just a nice environment. Personalities are a big part of this work environment, and everybody getting along well."

WG2: "Which is amazing, given the stress level. Or given the pressure."

AB: "I think it all boils down to time. There just are not enough hours to do everything at a nice, luxurious pace. So that's when everybody gets tense and patience runs thin. And that definitely happens here, but the result isn't screaming terror. Being verbally abusive just doesn't happen."

WG2: "One of the production staff told us, 'I'm salaried for twelve-hour workdays, but I usually stay longer.' People work so hard in television."

AB: "Yes, they do. Take a look at the actors on this show…Sarah works her butt off and is really good at what she does. She's always prepared. All of them are. But being Buffy and being in the majority of the scenes and working almost every day of the schedule—it's rare that she's not here. When you're trying to cast someone to play opposite her, you have to have somebody who is a pro. Because she's really good. And she deserves to have people around her that inspire and challenge her."

ECTOR	James Contner	11:00A	1	Production Designer	Carey Meyer	OC
ECTOR	David Solomon	Prep	1	Art Director	Caroline Quinn	OC
					ia Ruskin	OC
					Starlight	OC
					l Koneff	OC
					ustafson	OC
					ngblood	11:00
					th Cuba	OC
					Wilson	OC
					ly Kelly	OC
					Eriksen	11:00
					asch, Jr.	11:00
					d Ronan	11:00
					ve West	OC
					V. Hight	per S
					avidson	per S
					Bumatai	per S
					Val Wilt	per S
					m Sahli	per S
					Halaby	per S
					Petersen	per S
					n Hight	per S

Left margin labels:
Asst. Di
Asst. Di
2nd Ass
2nd A.D
'l 2nd A
A Traine
l DGA 1
duction S
ot Super
ctor of F
era Ope
era Ope
dicam O
AC-A Ca
AC-B Ca
AC-C Ca
C-A Cam
der
l 2nd A(
ef Lightii
350

THE COSTUME DEPARTMENT

CYNTHIA BERGSTROM, COSTUME DESIGNER

The offices and workrooms of the costume department staff are grouped around a middle section where racks and racks of clothes are hung. Each character has a section. Buffy has her own rack.

We cut to the chase and asked Cynthia about her third- and fourth-season design and shopping habits for the Scoobs and other assorted Sunnydalians.

WG2: "Let's talk about how you dress the characters. What about Buffy?"

CB: "Buffy's look has changed. Her character is definitely stronger. She's no longer hiding who she is. She is the Slayer, she knows that she's the Slayer. It's not necessarily a job for her anymore. It is her way of life, and she realizes that. But there is still some playfulness to her in the way that she dresses, and some femininity.

"I think definitely the way she dresses is an outlet for her, considering that she's saving the world on a daily basis. So she can really play upon her wardrobe. She'll wear any of the fashionable looks that are out there. Her skirt lengths have dropped. Her colors remain anywhere from the brighter tones, the rich jewel tones, Indian- or Moroccan-influenced colors to deeper darker blacks and browns. It just depends.

"But I always give her something interesting about her wardrobe. Jewelry, or I throw a Pashmina on her. They're wonderful, it's the finest cashmere that you can get. They're wraps. They're cozy. Now they're making skirts out of Pashmina. So she's got a few of those. But I am using a lot of skirts wherever I can. Giving her that playful girly image. She's still very eclectic. Lots of different patterns and faux animal prints."

WG2: "What about Xander?"

CB: "Xander, he just cracks me up. I love his character. He's just kind of there. He's either in his uniform of the week, depending on what job he has, or he's in very casual baggy pants with maybe a tighter fitting T-shirt and either tennis shoes or Adidas slides. Very laid back."

WG2: "Anya?"

Cynthia Bergstrom (seated), Lori DeLapp, Leslie Miller, Kathleen B. Mussehl, and Nickolas Brown

CB: "Anya's interesting because she is an ex-demon, but she does know how to dress. It's like 'Okay, where did she get her fashion sense?' She's been around for 1100 years. I'll do anything from a tight little capri with a trimmed cuff and a tight slim-fitting sweater to looser, more flowing skirts, and I keep her colors a little bit on the darker, muted side. I like to do a little beadwork with her. Things that are more of an old-world flavor but in silhouettes of today."

WG2: "Kind of like Jenny Calendar at the end?"

CB: "Sort of, but a lot more casual and a lot more funky."

WG2: "What about Giles?"

CB: "Giles has changed quite a bit. He is no longer the three-piece suit guy. He's wearing nubby, loose knit sweaters, corduroys, and jeans. I'm not sure where he's going, but he's got a new love interest who visits town every once in a while. He is just sort of exploring himself, I think.

"Olivia, she's an enigma. We don't really know who she is. I give her sort of a soft Euro look. She shows her figure nicely, with lower-cut necklines and funky jewelry. She's a hipster.

"Spike's still Spike. He does get a new shirt only because he accidentally shrunk his when he washed it at Xander's. But he's still in his black jeans, black T-shirt, black leather coat. But it was fun putting him in his cutoff shorts and Hawaiian shirt for one episode.

"The Commandos just needed to be sleek and simple and definitely camouflage because they're usually out in the woods. I didn't want a lot of accoutrements, [because] they've got to fight—and it's more physical combat unless their taser guns get the demon right away. So it's more for mobility than anything else."

WG2: "Where are you shopping?"

CB: "I shop both Fred Segal in Santa Monica and Melrose. I shop a lot with Abercrombie & Fitch and Anthropologie. Barney's New York, Saks, Neiman's. I have a tendency to like the smaller, more boutiquey stores where you can get things that you don't necessarily find everywhere."

WG2: "I noticed you had some Urban Outfitters."

CB: "Love Urban Outfitters. That's a good look for Anya and Tara."

WG2: "What's a Buffy store?"

CB: "Definitely Saks and Fred Segal."

WG2: "What about Willow?"

CB: "I get a lot of her stuff at Anthropolgie. Xander is Fred Segal. They're so zany. Giles is sort of like your Territory Ahead, Bloomingdale's kind of guy. Riley, I actually get a lot of his stuff at Urban Outfitters and the Gap. Very basic. Lindsay Crouse's civilian clothes—Bloomingdale's."

WG2: "Faith?"

CB: "I did a lot of wholesale through Betsey Johnson and some shops on Melrose. And Fred Segal as well."

WG2: "Where did you buy for the Mayor?"

CB: "He was mostly Fox Rentals."

WG2: "Just business suits."

CB: "Yes, conservative."

WG2: "What about Larry Bagby and Jonathan?"

CB: "Larry was a J. Crew kind of guy. Jonathan was like Gap and Structure. Harmony's a great character to work with. Her stuff comes from Fred Segal as well. Sometimes I'll find things at Saks and Curve on Robertson. Actually another is Vin Baker."

WG2: "Have you had any historical scenes?"

CB: "Not any historical this year. I'll look to medieval or renaissance looks for some of the demons. I make a lot of the demons. We definitely have more demons this year than vampires."

WG2: "What are your three most looked-at reference books?"

GILES	H	HOLD		
WILLOW	H	HOLD		
SPIKE	W	6:30P	7:30P	REPORT TO LOCATION
RILEY	W	10:30A	11:30A	REPORT TO LOCATION

CB: "Definitely anything that has to do with period costumes. I have a book that's called <u>The History of Men's Fashion</u>, which is an awesome book. I love that. Books from one of my college days, <u>The History of Fashion</u> and <u>The History of Art</u>. I will look at old paintings, some of the masters, to get ideas. Sometimes photography books. I soak up just about everything. Sometimes I'll just rent movies because of the costumes. It's amazing where you get ideas."

WG2: "What's something that surprised you this season? Something you made that came out really well or something that you got to make or buy that you've always wanted to work on?"

CB: "I think my favorite was the Gentlemen from 'Hush.' I just loved the entire completion of their look. That was one of the simplest, but it was such a statement. They were so eerie. I loved the footmen, their servants in the floppy straitjackets. It was such a great look.

"Joss asked for [the servants] to be in straitjackets, and I thought 'What am I gonna do with their sleeves?' I actually cut the sleeves down and took off the buckles, because they had to fight and the buckles would hurt in the fight. And then we reattached the straps so we had some floating. I thought that was really eerie, and I know I've definitely seen that somewhere, like from some old, old film when I was a little girl. And I just thought it was the best thing for the bottoms was just black pants.

"Then I took these shirts, just these regular button-down shirts, but I rounded the collars instead of having the regular pinpoint collars to give it more of a vintage look. I did that for The Gentlemen and for the servant guys. The footmen were almost like downgrades of The Gentlemen. The costumes started out the same, and then they got the straitjackets. But The Gentlemen just needed to be elegant.

"Everyone's talking about 'Hush.' But Thirteen's going to be great, too. We have Adam, who's the new character. He will definitely be fun to work with. His costume is just military garb, but it's modified. He's gonna have all these special things. He has a CD player coming out of his chest. There'll be some sort of computer circuitry and metal. It'll turn out very cool."

WG2: "How involved are you with special makeup effects and prosthesis and latex suits, and how do you coordinate with those other departments?"

CB: "Anything that is done with latex or is a prosthetic, that's all done through Optic Nerve and the special-effects department, and I just do the clothing part. When it gets into, like with Adam's costume, the computer circuitry or the leg brace, then props comes into play. So we all work together as a team. It takes a lot of communication."

> The costume department sent a buyer to Maya on Melrose to pick up a selection of silver hoop earrings for Eliza Dushku.

THE ART DEPARTMENT

CAREY MEYER, PRODUCTION DESIGNER

The art department creates the visual look of Buffy's world, from the demonic dimensions of the lower worlds to Joyce Summers's cozy kitchen. The soft-spoken head of the department is Carey Meyer. We met in his office, which is still a tidy profusion of maps, color circles, blueprints, and a drafting table.

WG2: "We're focusing on the production of Episode Thirteen. So can you tell us anything about what's going on right now in Thirteen that's different? Or that highlights the production process for you?"

(Marginal/bleed-through text from adjacent pages:)

352

e and t

JOM
ter

JOM
Riley

MOVE

spots a

PLAYER
e Gellar
ndon
ead
igan
rs

eld

rts

3/8 pg

pg

FRO

5/8 pg

2/8 pg

TION

TION
TION

ANYA	H	HOLD		
FORREST	W	6:30P	7:30P	REPORT TO NEBRASKA / BUN
GRAHAM	W	6:30P	7:30P	REPORT TO NEBRASKA / BUN

CM: "We are still developing the Initiative. We're going back out to the location that we shot once before for the underground Initiative, which is, you know, a huge underground facility with a large operating pit. And I'm excited because we're going back to this location which is, I think, a really good-looking set. We've done a lot of interior Initiative work at another facility closer to town, and it just does not look as good. It's a lot of brick and it's just—not as interesting. So I'm excited that we're going back and sort of reestablishing, you know, a much bigger, broader look with the Initiative. And it also looks like we'll go back there for Episode Fourteen as well.

"We're sort of extending the whole idea and look of the Initiative as well with the new set on stage, which is Room 314, which is where we find Adam, the new villain now that Maggie Walsh will have died at the end of Episode Thirteen."

WG2: "Let's talk about Season Three. Were there any unusual sets or sets that changed markedly in the last season of high school?"

CM: "Well, from Season Two to Three, we really developed the exterior Sunnydale Street and the Sun Cinema and, you know, highlights of that were in the Christmas episode where we snowed it in.

"And then, of course, near the end of last season Buffy and Faith had the huge fight from Faith's apartment out onto that rooftop, and which sort of tied us all into the Sun Cinema and the exterior Sunnydale Street. And that was kind of fun because it wasn't something that was really scripted, it was something that we just sort of developed and organically came together in terms of a connection between sets. I had a concept that we would try to tie these together, but was unsure exactly how that would really come to fruition.

"But fortunately it did. So when we built Faith's apartment, I placed, outside the window, a miniature of the Sun Cinema and the street, just to tie her into Sunnydale, so that we kind of would know where we were instead of just putting a generic translight out there and saying she's sort of anywhere in Sunnydale. I really wanted to place her in a specific spot.

"And then, near the end of the season, Buffy and Faith have the fight and they go crashing out the window onto a rooftop. I built the rooftop onstage and placed another miniature outside the rooftop, which was of a scale in between this miniature and the full scale. I built a quarter-scale sign and Sun Cinema where Faith falls off the edge of the rooftop. That was all done onstage, and the Sun Cinema is there in the background. And it's a different scale miniature. And then we cut to her falling down onto the back street, you know, where the truck drives by and she falls into the back of that and it goes on off. That was all done on the Sunnydale street.

"I don't think often we get to really tie together the environment so cohesively, which, for a designer, is a really fun thing. My job, I always feel, is to not just create the environments that we shoot in or that the show is, but also have as much of a cohesive and tied-together environment as possible. Just so that you feel like you are in a place that is real as opposed to just random little bits. And as much discontinuity as we have from episode to episode, it's really fun to be able to, over the course of fifteen or twenty episodes, find some sort of thread that really ties it all together."

WG2: "Moving to the fourth season, when everything was new, who conceived of using UCLA as a template?"

CM: "Joss did, really. It was always something that had been talked about since Season Two, really. You know, it was always, 'UCLA

G. Victoria Ruskin, Stella Starlight, Carey Meyer, and Caroline Quinn

is such a beautiful campus.' We'd always talked about going there, and we always knew it might be a problem to shoot there."

"We shot a lot of stock footage of UCLA, to establish a scene, and then we cut in tighter to cover a scene at the Braun [complex] where you have red brick and you have lots of beautiful trees that sort of give you a campus feel."

WG2: "David Koneff, the set decorator, said that this season for him is about trees."

CM: "It is. Yeah, 'cause the college campus is so much more lush and green and beautiful, and so not only are we spending time in graveyards in Sunnydale, but now we're on sort of exterior campus where you really want to get the feel of large quads and large green areas.

"And then also, sort of a gimmick or a thread that the writers keep using to get us from Point A to Point B is taking us through the woods to get to someplace. Or something happens in the woods. I think it's 'cause you have a campus and then you have a Sunnydale community and what's in between? I guess the woods tend to crop up as the obvious place to go that still may be campus, but still sort of Sunnydale. It's just a generic enough space that anything can happen. So David has been very busy creating woods this season."

WG2: "And Caroline Quinn says she doesn't want to have to design any more crypts. She's tired of crypts."

CM: "Well, crypts are just the vernacular of the show. We'll never get past that. Crypts and vampires are sort of synonymous with each other."

WG2: "When you started designing the individual sets for the campus, did you have any college memories of your own?"

CM: "I suppose. I mean, I always thought of those spaces that you walk through to get from one class to another, where kids were hanging out between classes and just killed some time. And so you try to find a spot that was always sort of humming with activity but that you were able get some peace and be able to sit down and do stuff.

"That's really why I wanted to create the commons area, which is just a nice, wide open space that gives us as much scope and scale onstage as possible. We could shoot onstage but still feel like we had a large environment to shoot in. You know, outside the window is a sort of a quad area, so you really feel like you're almost outside, but you're not really. And it's a big enough space that you really do get some scope. Like this season we've even had people throwing Frisbees in it because it's large enough to really get some flight of a Frisbee. And so it gives you nice depth for lots of different scenes. It's a generic space, but it's got some nice arches and things."

WG2: "The Rocket Cafe is really cool. And that octagonal—"

CM: "The atrium. That was purely Royce Hall and the library and everything; it's just such a beautiful structure that I always knew I wanted to try to do something with brick and Spanish tile, in order to kind of bring that element into it. And so we went there for the first episode. I'd known for a while that I wanted to do that stuff, so last season I was researching materials and looking for things that I would try to develop the look with. I didn't have it designed, but I knew in my head what I wanted to do. Structurally, we used a very similar layout as what we'd had for the first three seasons, the high school. You know, the hallway and the lecture hall are all the same structure as the old hallway and the library. And, actually, if you go in the lecture hall and you look up, the ceiling is almost the same ceiling from the library.

"The atrium just sort of developed out of a way to connect the lecture hall to the hallways, as well as, again, to give us another space that does a similar thing as the commons to give us an outdoor feel. You know, because there's a skylight and there's a tree in a planter there, and you feel like it's a place where somebody would just sit down for half an hour and read a chapter in a psych book or whatever while they're waiting for class to start. And it's played out that way. It's a really fun set, and I was really happy with it. Unfortunately, I don't feel like we've gotten the use out of that set that maybe everybody had hoped for."

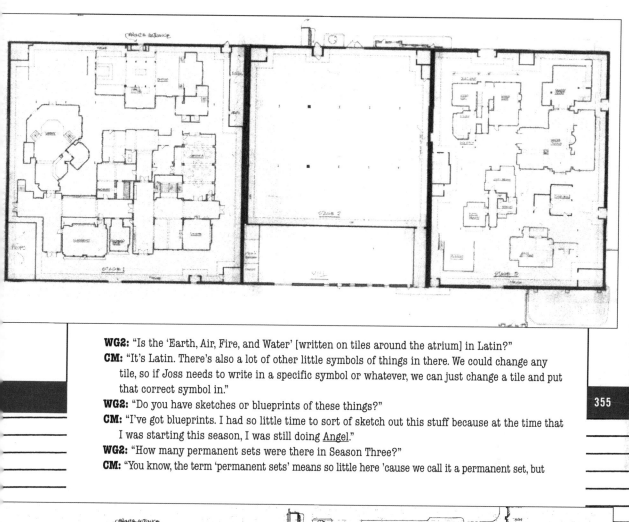

WG2: "Is the 'Earth, Air, Fire, and Water' [written on tiles around the atrium] in Latin?"

CM: "It's Latin. There's also a lot of other little symbols of things in there. We could change any tile, so if Joss needs to write in a specific symbol or whatever, we can just change a tile and put that correct symbol in."

WG2: "Do you have sketches or blueprints of these things?"

CM: "I've got blueprints. I had so little time to sort of sketch out this stuff because at the time that I was starting this season, I was still doing Angel."

WG2: "How many permanent sets were there in Season Three?"

CM: "You know, the term 'permanent sets' means so little here 'cause we call it a permanent set, but

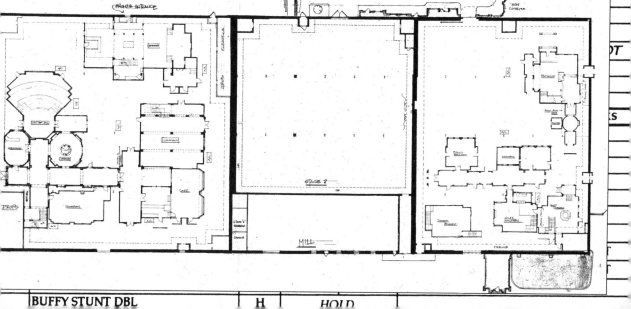

BUFFY STUNT DBL | H | HOLD

we'll rip it down at the drop of a hat and build something else. But we do have permanent sets. We've got the lecture hall, the hallway, the atrium—those are all really one set. And then you have the commons and the Rocket Cafe, which is all really one set, but it's sort of two permanent sets. You've got Xander's basement. Buffy's dorm room. The hallway. And, of course, Giles's place."

WG2: "And exterior."

CM: "And exterior, which is new this season. Since we didn't have the library anymore, and obviously Giles is an important character, we needed a place for them to be that wasn't the library. So we decided that Giles's place was going to be a more prominent set this season. And since it's such a small set, we wanted more places to be. So we created that little courtyard outside it.

"And then we have the Lowell House, which is Riley's cover. And then permanent sets other than that, well, of course, the Braun. And, you know, the graveyard and the exterior Sunnydale Street and the alleyway. And I suppose that's it in terms of permanent sets."

WG2: "Was there anything in Season Three that was a shock to you? Or something that was particularly challenging or fun?"

CM: "No, none of it's a shock. It's all challenging and a lot of fun. The last couple episodes of Season Three were really fun in that not only what I was talking about before, but also that, we got do a lot of physical effects, with the mayor-snake man, you know, tearing out the fountain courtyard where we built the clock tower for another episode.

"We built the clock tower for 'Earshot.' We built it on top of the school actually, and then built an interior set. And then, knowing that we might need it again, we left it up there and secured it. And then not knowing that we would blow it up necessarily, but knowing that we maybe needed another shot on it or whatever, we decided to leave it. And then Joss, obviously, came up with his finale. And we were going to blow up the front of the school, originally. We wanted to have a huge explosion at the front of the school, but there was a host of problems with that. One being that we would have to do it pretty much all digitally because there's four huge pine trees [at the Torrance High School location]. There was nothing we could do to really protect them, so in the end, we decided, well, we just can't blow up the front of the school.

"Joss really wanted it, which is why we did a smaller close shot where the front door of the school blows up, which we did with a series of effects, one being a small fireball actually shot practically in front of the school. But then we also built a façade of the school which we shot against black and actually blew it up and then matted—not really matted, but we just did a double exposure of the two elements so you actually see some elements of the school sort of blowing toward you. They just doubled them together to give us the sign, you know, that says Sunnydale High and the front doors, so you really knew where we were. But then the big explosion happened in the fountain courtyard, which was a lot of fun to conceive of."

WG2: "Okay, so maybe Season Three for you is about breakaways?"

CM: "What would Season Three be? I guess Season Three for me was about really trying to incorporate more elements together to create a look really, not just creating a town, but really trying to create, be involved with all the digital effects and all the physical effects and all the different elements. Really trying to bring all those together and add to them in terms of miniatures, just trying to harness all those things together to create as much diversity for the show as possible. And, again, this season, we're just trying to expand on that as much as possible. Little effects shots that are just little tiny inserts."

WG2: "Like what?"

CM: "Well, like this season we did a miniature of Buffy's dorm building when Spike falls out the window. Well, I say miniature but, you know, that building was actually sixteen feet tall. So when I say miniature, they're not like little tabletop miniatures. They're sort of quarter-scale build-

OOM
le and t:

OOM
fter

OOM
Riley

MOVE

spots ar

Y PLAYER!
le Gellar
ndon
Iead
iigan
rs

/8 pg

3/8 pg

pg

FR(

5/8 pg

2/8 pg

TON

TON

RILEY	W	10:30A	11:30A	REPORT TO LOCATION
ANYA	H	HOLD		
FORREST	W	6:30P	7:30P	REPORT TO NEBRASKA / BUN

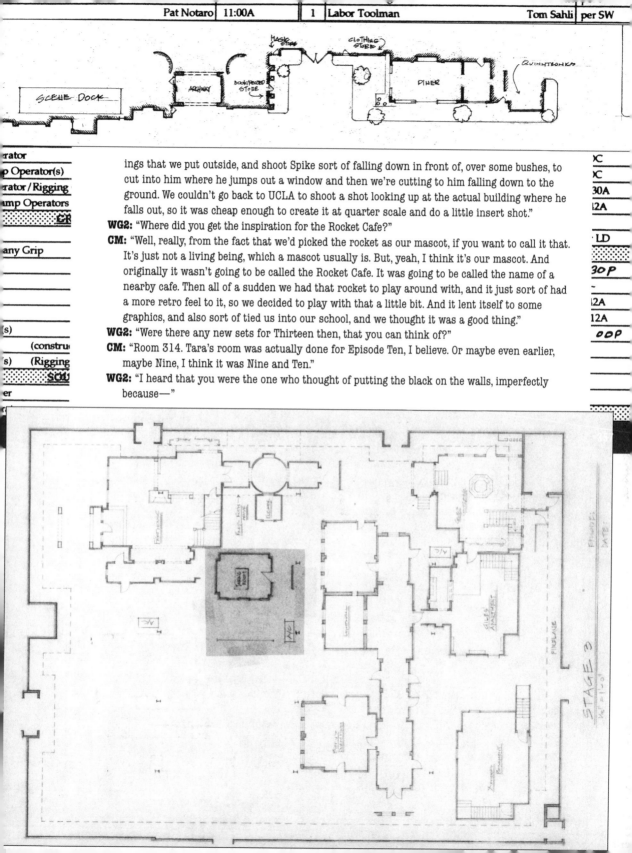

ings that we put outside, and shoot Spike sort of falling down in front of, over some bushes, to cut into him where he jumps out a window and then we're cutting to him falling down to the ground. We couldn't go back to UCLA to shoot a shot looking up at the actual building where he falls out, so it was cheap enough to create it at quarter scale and do a little insert shot."

WG2: "Where did you get the inspiration for the Rocket Cafe?"

CM: "Well, really, from the fact that we'd picked the rocket as our mascot, if you want to call it that. It's just not a living being, which a mascot usually is. But, yeah, I think it's our mascot. And originally it wasn't going to be called the Rocket Cafe. It was going to be called the name of a nearby cafe. Then all of a sudden we had that rocket to play around with, and it just sort of had a more retro feel to it, so we decided to play with that a little bit. And it lent itself to some graphics, and also sort of tied us into our school, and we thought it was a good thing."

WG2: "Were there any new sets for Thirteen then, that you can think of?"

CM: "Room 314. Tara's room was actually done for Episode Ten, I believe. Or maybe even earlier, maybe Nine, I think it was Nine and Ten."

WG2: "I heard that you were the one who thought of putting the black on the walls, imperfectly because—"

358

CM: "Well, you know, in the script, Joss'll write something down or whoever, Marti or one of the other writers, will write something down. Joss said he wanted it to be a black room, and that's all he wrote. But I didn't want to just paint it black 'cause I just thought it would look too perfect. I just wanted it to look as though she had sort of worked on her room randomly. And so I just took this little room that we had and added some elements to it and then just had it rolled so you could still see the roller marks and things.

"And then I came up with the whole concept of putting the constellations on her back wall. She's created a whole diorama of constellations. You can see I like to play with the physical elements, you know, the constellations and, of course, the Earth, Wind, Air, Water in the Atrium. It's fun to just throw those things in, 'cause the show deals with those sorts of things so much. I just put it into the set so that maybe it would get used. Or since things do develop and they're sort of beyond our vision at the moment, it's fun to just throw those things in and then maybe Joss'll see it and he'll write it into the show.

"Which is a similar thing to what happened outside Faith's window, where they fall out onto the rooftop, and all of a sudden we're falling into the Sunnydale street. If I hadn't placed the Sun Cinema outside her window, who knows? We probably would've done the same scene, but we wouldn't have been falling into Sunnydale. Which is maybe not a big deal to a lot of people.

"But for me, it's fun to try to connect all that stuff. And, again, it's like the constellations. I had a hint that Tara is going to be an important character with Willow this season, or near the end of the season anyway. Joss didn't come right out and say what he wanted, but I knew that he had something in his mind, and it was an important character, and she had a specific look.

"So we didn't want just any old dorm room, which is easy to do. I knew that he, somewhere back in college, had been in somebody's room that he liked, and knowing that she's a witch and Willow's a witch and, you know, you're just dealing with the sort of astrological stuff. So we just developed that whole back wall of constellations, and then we put in the Christmas tree lights in the major axes, x-y-z axes, of the universe.

"So if you walk in there, you'll see that the Christmas tree lights create not so much a grid, but a box in three dimensions. So you're within a grid, or you're within a universe. The constellations are on a wall, and then, with chalk, she's been sketching in behind the constellations, which are raised off the walls. We put screws into the wall in the form of constellations and then tied metallic string between them and then put little glow-in-the-dark stars on some of the major stars in the constellations. Then on the wall behind, which is black—it's almost like a chalkboard—she took chalk and she's been drawing in the romantic symbol or the romantic sketch of what the constellations were.

"She's very much in her own world. She doesn't really associate with anybody very well at all. She's very shy. She's opening up to Willow, but obviously she's sort of been stuck in her room. She's just completely in her own world. When Joss said he wanted it to be black, I thought I kind of knew where he was going, and so we created that, and he walked in and just laid on the bed and said, 'Ahh, this is exactly what I wanted.'

"So that's kind of fun. You know, it's just a tiny little set and it's not like it took a lot of money or anything. But it's fun to hit the nail on the head sometimes and really get it right."

WG2: "Where did you build the cabin in 'Homecoming'?"

CM: "Right out in the parking lot. We built the woods and the cabin, and blew it up."

WG2: "So there's been a lot of blowing things up."

CM: "This show is about blowing things up, I think. We blow a lot of stuff up. Especially since Season Three. When we got the beat sheet, we're like 'What? What? What?' Amazed. 'They're actually going to do that?' Then we did it, we just actually blew it up."

WG2: "David Koneff said that when he was lying on one of the school rooftops it [lifted] from the shock."

CM: "I was there, too. We were both sitting right next to each other. It was on a building just on the opposite side of the courtyard."

WG2: "Of the real high school?"

CM: "Yeah. It was about two hundred feet away from the explosion, maybe three hundred feet. And, literally, I felt like I was off the rooftop for a second. I was sitting cross-legged, and I just felt poomp! I just felt like I bounced up. And it was a couple times, and there were several concussions from some, because they had, you know, they had twenty explosions in there and like maybe four or five quite large ones."

WG2: "Did it break windows or anything?"

CM: "We broke a couple panes of glass, and that was really about it."

WG2: "So we guess Torrance is kind of ticked."

CM: "Yeah, they don't really want us back."

CAROLINE QUINN, SET DESIGNER

We talked with Caroline Quinn in the sprawling conference area located on the second floor with all the production offices. Her lovely British accent was still intact, as were her patience and sense of humor.

WG2: "Tell us a bit about what it is you do in your job."

CQ: "I work with Carey Meyer, and he basically comes to me with a script outline and says, 'We need to create this set, this set, and this set.' Sometimes he has definite ideas of what he wants, and sometimes I go away and think about it and see what we can come up with.

"Sometimes it's sets we've already had, and I've got to pull them out of storage and get them set up again. So I guess it depends on the situation. It just evolves fairly quickly, and we have to get it done. We have to get it done pretty fast."

WG2: "When we talked to you last time you were talking about how much you enjoy working on the library set. How did you feel when it went away?"

CQ: "The library set had had its day. Everyone was sick of it. It was nice to see it go away and bring something else to the set. So then we spent all this energy and time on the new school, the new college, which is good."

WG2: "Have you noticed throughout the seasons how much shorthand everybody has started using amongst themselves? Has it gotten so such that you barely have to speak to each other sometimes?"

CQ: "Definitely. It's just like you start a sentence and you go, 'Okay, right,' and you go away and you don't need to finish the sentence. It's the good side of working for so long with the same people. You pretty much know what your job is and you know what the other person is thinking or what they're going to do and how they're going to go about it. If you feel like you don't understand or they think you may not understand then you know that it's time to talk more."

WG2: "When you were working on Thirteen, is there anything that was new?"

CQ: "Room 314 and the hallway outside is all new. We based it on these lab cell sets that we had. It was all designed with these two-foot square tile walls, and just all very clean and white, and that came about because the floor of the room we used at Lockheed was all that tile. It was a computer room or something before, so they had this false floor that you could lift up, and it was all these tiles. We ended up just building out sets to match exactly with that tile so everything was this white tile."

the love

d taped

E TO FRO

and shoot

ERS
ar

GILES	H	HOLD	
WILLOW	H	HOLD	
SPIKE	W	6:30P	7:30P	REPORT TO LOCATION

WG2: "Is it easier to take an existing set and transform it, or to build a new set from the ground up?"

CQ: "It's a lot easier to build from scratch. You have the total freedom of doing what you want where you want. When we're revamping one set into another set, then a) it's not as creative because you pretty much are limited, and b) it's quicker for construction, but then they have to sort of fiddle around and change things that are already there, where it is always easier for them to just build it new. It does save time, obviously, and money when we revamp a set. It's just not as creative. You're stuck with a footprint, and you can't really change it that much."

WG2: "One of the things we're surprised about is sometimes the rooms, when we go on the sets, are so much smaller than they look, and sometimes the rooms are so much bigger than they look. Buffy and Willow's dorm room on the set is enormous so they can move the cameras and do lots of things. Are there some tricks of the trade to make a big space look smaller, or, like the lecture hall, to make it look a lot bigger when you see it on TV?"

CQ: "Sometimes, like in the Rocket Cafe and in the cafeteria last year that's gone, we just used tiny tables to make them look bigger. Instead of having a big table where it would seat eight people, we just have little three-foot tables that sit four or five, so that helps. Sometimes it's more to do with, if a set is one big square, it's hard to do anything with it. If you start breaking it up, you can change how it looks with headers and stuff, so it looks like it's more enclosed.

"I know when we designed Buffy's dorm room, we purposely designed it big because the crew always had a hard time in Buffy's bedroom because it was so tiny. So we designed a lot bigger dorm room that actually was bigger than it is now. We designed it a lot bigger, and it was too big. We tried to design it big enough so we wouldn't have a problem shooting in there, so then we actually lopped off about thirty percent of it to make it small enough."

WG2: "In the Lowell House sets there is kind of an old Ivy League feel to the way it's dressed. How did the initial idea for the whole configuration of the college, or the actual sets, the spaces themselves, come about?"

CQ: "We didn't want it to look like it was a new model. We wanted definitely to give it an older feel. Sunnydale is an old established little town in California somewhere. We used the college of UCLA, a lot of their interiors. I think it was Powell Library we shot on the first episode."

WG2: "Did you actually shoot in the library?"

CQ: "Yes. All that tile work is actually directly taken from there and all the brick and everything. Using Braun for exteriors, that's all brick as well."

WG2: "When you took down the high school and put up the college, were there any major changes? The configuration is still pretty much the same."

CQ: "Yeah. I guess the biggest thing was converting the library into the lecture hall. Apart from that there was no real huge change. More superficial."

WG2: "When you create a new room or a new space, what's the major consideration? Is it the budget? The look? How easy it will be to shoot? Is there one overriding factor? When you look at a script or you look at Carey's ideas and you think, 'Okay I have to create these sets,' what's the most important thing that you keep in mind when you're doing it?"

CQ: "For us, it's usually all of the above. Everything is like, 'Okay, we don't have that much money, we have certain amount of time to do it in,' and if there's a lot of pages being shot in this scene, if it's a big scene then we'll obviously put more money and effort into it. If it's a tiny little scene, and it's just basically shooting one wall, or if it's a set that's more than just a room, if it's a crypt, which we have a lot of obviously, or more interesting sets, then obviously we can think more about coming up with something fun."

WG2: "About Spike's crypt. He does not clean up, I noticed. Angel kept the mansion really nice.

Right now the crypt is a little barren, I suppose because he's moving in. Are you guys going to dress it as you go?"

CQ: "I guess that depends on where the scripts take us. He's not somebody who has any possessions. He's kind of on the run. I suppose it would just depend on how much time we spend in there, and if he really does seriously take up his home there."

WG2: "What does the family name [Frawley] on the back refer to?"

CQ: "Those were actually mausoleums that we have lifted from previous sets, so that has nothing to do with Spike. No, it was just a name I came up with; it sounded kind of old and it was cleared with the legal department."

WG2: "How did you pick the dates?"

CQ: "I think there were all nineteenth century, a little bit of early twentieth century, and I just wanted to maybe make it a hundred or so years old. You can't be too old because it is Sunnydale, after all."

WG2: "Of Season Three and Season Four sets, what is your favorite?"

CQ: "Season Three, it would probably have to be the mansion. Of the Season Four permanent sets, I guess I would have to say Lowell House, just because it was a change for us to do a nice house, as opposed to a funky crypt or whatever."

WG2: "What is something that you would like to design that you haven't done for the show?"

CQ: "Can I say what I wouldn't like to design again? Crypts. I don't know, I think more modern stuff would be fun. Like when we did Ted's house, he was stuck in the fifties and he had this little case-study type house. That was good because that was different. More sort of stuff that's maybe 1950s, 1960s would be fun."

WG2: "Can you think of something that you designed and you imagined what it would look like when it was finished; then when it was dressed, it was a complete shock or total surprise?"

CQ: "That happens all the time! Well, sort of, I'm exaggerating. There are times but I can't think of what at the moment. I can't think of anything specific that really jumps out. Usually there is always something that is like, 'Well that didn't quite come out as I thought it would, but it looks good anyway.' Something big like the street, the back lot, that we obviously designed piecemeal, and I guess I didn't expect it to come out so well on film. It all was designed in bits. We'd do a couple of façades there and a couple of façades there."

WG2: "Most of it has sort of an older look. Is there any particular time period that it's sort of reminiscent of?"

CQ: "Deco, I guess it's meant to be. We just looked through tons of books, and we wanted to come up with a real sort of middle-America feeling, where it just doesn't look like the West Coast. It doesn't really look like the East Coast, it just kind of just sits there. Just a typical Main Street, USA. But it was really fun to design because we rarely do exterior buildings; it's always inside something, so it was really good to be able to, especially when you have time."

WG2: "We noticed the Carey's Sporting Goods?"

CQ: "Meyer's Sporting Goods. There's a Quinntronics. We have a lot of fun naming the signs after our families. When you're thinking of names, you want to pick something that is going to be kind of fun. We've got Decker Hardware, which is my married name. We've got West Brothers Construction and that's Steve West, our construction coordinator.

"We're always having to think of names of anything, from candy bars to buildings. The last band name—it was a fictional band, usually they are real bands, but I guess this sort of fictional band came in because it was the episode when Veruca comes in. We had a name and it was something like Shimmy, and for some reason we couldn't use it. This was the last minute, and we had to think of a name really quickly because we had to make some artwork for the bandstand that night to shoot the next day, and there were myself and two other people in the Art Department.

ghting 7		light	per SW
T		amel	per SW
Board		nillo	per SW
perator		pson	per SW
perator			
perator		trom	OC
perator		app	OC
mp Op		nthal	OC
perator		sehl	10:30A
Lamp (		own	9:42A
p		liller	per LD
npany (			
rip		ttosh	5 30 P
		Ellis	~
		esne	9:42A
		Noe	10:12A
rip(s)		ndon	6 00
rip			
rip(s)			
Mixer			
perator		ney	

We wanted to make it something similar 'cause Marti had chosen this name originally, so we came up with Shy, and it was like this is a really bad name then it cleared legal, and that's what we're left with."

WG2: "When you're building a set, do you think it looks more interesting to have some up and downs, or is it easier to film if it's flat?"

CQ: "Definitely more interesting if it has some little steps up, and we just have to make sure that they can be pulled out of the way easily. Or if they can't be pulled out of the way, then there's enough room in the set where they can work around them."

WG2: "What's another story about names?"

CQ: "The Lucky Pint. Carey wanted it to be a Chinesey bar, one of those hokey bars that has a Chinese flavor. There is a real place called the Good Luck Bar, something like that. So Eve and I sat down and came up with Lucky Pint, and said, 'Okay, Lucky Pint it is, and the design of it has got the 'Lucky,' and then hokey Chinese writing, and then 'Pint' is normal, and this little black shamrock next to it. It's this weird Irish-Chinese bar."

DAVID KONEFF, SET DECORATOR

David Koneff was extremely tired the day we interviewed him. He'd been running flat out for days. The next time was saw him, early in the morning after a late-night wrap, he was more energized. Later, we saw him back out in the cemetery with his crew. And his trees.

David Koneff knows a lot about trees....

WG2: "Could you tell us some interesting things about decorating the sets? For example, from the end of Season Two to now, what is different about what you've been doing?"

DK: "Every season is completely different. You don't realize how different it's going to be until you start shooting, and suddenly you realize that there is a pattern forming. For me, I guess it has to do with what's happening in the script because I'm dressing all the sets.

"Season Three, if you had to sum it up in one word, it was pipe. We started that during Season Two but it really became out of control during Season Three where just about every set that we had involved pipe. We were dressing pipe into subterranean rooms and caves and grottos and sewers and different mechanical works, and so it became all about warehouses and pipe.

"Season Four is all about trees. It's all about plants. We spend a lot of our time outside in wooded areas, and no matter how wooded they are, they always want more. It's never woodsy enough for <u>Buffy</u>. We tend to spend a lot of time and energy trying to come up with new and different ways to make the same spaces look different using plants. For those people who are interested in doing what I do, it's a greens job. Set decorators and art directors usually put their heads together and discover what it is they want, a forest, a park, a wooded glade or meadow or whatever, and the greensmen will come in and tell us what materials they would use to do it.

"But since we don't have a greensman, I go out and do all that. With the help of the director and the script and Carey Meyer, our production designer, we come up with different ways of doing it. Then I go out and shop for it. Consequently I've learned the Latin names of many plants that I'll never ever use in real life. It's kind of like algebra."

WG2: "What kinds of trees do you use?"

DK: "I use a sumac for cut brush. The grips use the cut brush for putting in front of the lights to dapple the light onto the set. But I also use it to build my own trees. We'll rent a stock tree, a stock tree being a tree that was probably on somebody's front lawn that they didn't want anymore, and

362

wanted it taken away, so they cut it down to its bare bones until it's between twelve and sixteen feet tall and has a sixteen or eighteen foot spread on it, and then you'll get two dozen pieces of cut brush like sumac or oak and you'll nail it onto it and rebuild your own tree."

WG2: "Why do you do that instead of getting your own tree?"

DK: "Because you can't normally get trees that big that are alive. A tree that was that big would be in a ten- or twelve-foot box. But these trees are cut off at the bottom and nailed and plated to a rolling four-foot stand, and that can be forklifted onto our cemetery or around the lot. I just base it out with some plants and it looks real.

"What people see every week are usually silk plants, or live plants that are staked down to the ground that are sitting in five-gallon black pots or ten-gallon pots, and we just base it all out with other plants to make it look like its actually growing into the ground. Which is actually what I'm going to do today. In about ten minutes I have to go outside and finish doing a forest for Episode Thirteen.

"This show has forests that have been fifty thousand dollars, forests where we've had greens-men actually come in and build the forest for us because it was just too big for us to do. And then this is our simple little thirty-five hundred dollar forest. We have one tree that we paint, actually. We have our own stock tree. We bought it last year and for every episode where we were doing a forest or a park or a cemetery, we would have to get brand-new cut brush for it, fresh brush that wasn't dead and nail it onto it."

WG2: "Tell me about Tara's bedroom."

DK: "Joss gave me certain information about Tara's bedroom. He said the walls were black, and that she was a slight outcast, and I knew that she had witch ability. So I figured that maybe, like all people who feel as if they don't fit in, no matter how angry they are about not fitting in or not being a part of the regular group, and how much they dislike the regular group of people, they probably want to be a part of the regular group of people. So her room was black, but there were elements of her room that I thought maybe subconsciously told us that she wanted to be differ-ent than who she was, and blend in a little bit better with who she thought was supposed to be a regular crowd. Little did she know that'd she'd get in with a crowd that was far from regular."

WG2: "What are some of the touches?"

DK: "Someone commented to me about a month ago about the pictures of women in her room. I thought these two or three pictures of women were people that maybe she in some ways secretly aspired to. Artistically they were very pretty pictures, just pastoral scenes with a semi-nude Rubenesque woman. I thought it was just a pretty picture in a nice antique frame; and I thought that maybe she would find it a pleasing picture. But her room is very bohemian. It's a dorm room that she's completely taken over.

"It's the kind of room that I wouldn't mind having in my house as a getaway room. I thought it was a nice warm room. I didn't know if she was going to be a good character or bad character, but she's someone who I thought probably had a lot of things going on."

WG2: "Do you find that when you're trying to dress a set do you like this, it seems almost like you made some choices unconsciously?"

DK: "Sure, I make unconscious choices all the time. You have to do that. Decorators are masters of rationalization. But sometimes that gets in the way and slows down the process of shopping for things that you have very little time to shop for. So the pace of the show dictates that you trust your judgment, and you sometimes have to spontaneously go for something and hope it's the right effect. I would say about ninety percent of the time we're pretty right, and then Joss or someone else or a director or Carey or even my crew will tell me when I've gone off the deep end and done something wrong."

INT INITIATIVE(#12)	3/P1	6,8,ATMO	6/8 pg	D LOCKHEED, SA
INT INITIATIVE	25PT,12PT,10,9,43PT,A33	1,6,8,11,D1,D2,ATMO	6 pg	D
EXT WOODS	2	1,6,8,9,10,C1,C2,X,1X,9X,10X,A	1 4/8 pg	N
		TOTAL	8 2/8 pg	

WG2: "What would be an example?"

DK: "Joss thought that my idea of what Riley's room was all about was wrong, and that was a set that I overrationalized. It was a set that I said, 'Well, Riley lives in Lowell House.' Lowell House isn't really a fraternity, but it's some sort of building on campus where people from this group live for the most part, and I thought that since Lowell House has such a long history—we've kind of given them this fake history of being around for a hundred years—I thought that characters like Riley would do their time in college for four years and then move on. And the furniture would be the same furniture that had been around for, not quite a hundred years, but had been around for a while.

"Joss wanted more of a mix of the old and the new, and he was exactly right. That was one of those sets where I had very, very little time, and I had to make some quick decisions, and I didn't have time to really think about it, and my judgment wasn't quite right."

WG2: "When you say very, very little time what are you talking?"

DK: "Sometimes I only have one day to shop a set like Riley's. I'll have to shop, and we'll have to put it on a truck the next day, and have to dress it that same day for the following day so I'll shop it on a Monday, we'll pick it up on Tuesday, dress it on a Tuesday and it will go in front of the camera on Wednesday. Sometimes we'll do what they call 'tag and drag,' and I go through the prop houses and the trucks follow me wherever I go and they pick up the stuff and we dress it the same day."

WG2: "How much stuff do you actually purchase? Do you go out and purchase things or do you always rent?"

DK: "We have enough furniture to fill four houses here. I've bought a lot of furniture. I buy a lot of stuff. When we know we have a character that's going to be around for a while I'll buy it or put it on a permanent rental so that we can keep it for the whole season so it isn't so labor intensive."

WG2: "How did you get the idea for how to dress the inside of the Espresso Pump?"

DK: "Carey wanted it to be a former gas station, so that's why the waiters and waitresses are dressed like carhops. So we built the furniture out of cars. I went to a place, Memory Lane, and bought some car parts and had them all chopped up and turned into sofas and chairs and tables and shelf units and things like that."

WG2: "What does your house look like?"

DK: "I have an eighty-five-year-old Craftsman. I'm just getting started decorating. I'm still waiting for my chairs to get here. I ordered a couple of chairs, and I'm still waiting for them from Civilization. Civilization is a place I do a lot of shopping at. It's in the old Helms Bakery Complex in Culver City. They've been fantastic for four years. I've furnished Buffy's house from Civilization and a couple other sets. They have really good eclectic, homey, warm, inviting furniture. Some of the furniture in Lowell House I got from Civilization.

"Getting back to where you get inspiration from…not only inspiration but guidance from, Joss is a little more after-the-fact because I think he trusts us to do our job. Carey is during the fact or just before the fact rather, and my crew is while we're doing it. I will give them all the pieces necessary to dress a set for me since the union doesn't allow me to touch anything. My guys have to put everything in place, so they become as intimate with the furniture and the pieces as I do, and sometimes even more because they'll dress a set and undress a set over and over and over. So if its not a permanent set but a set that we bring in often enough, they'll know the furniture better than I do."

WG2: "So a set decorator is more like a designer of a set, whereas a dresser is the person that actually places things."

DK: "I tell them where to place everything, but a lot of times I won't have a whole lot of time to tell them all the different places that I want things. I'll breeze through a set when I know all the set dressing is there, I'll rough it all in with them and they'll go into the Gold Room, and they'll find some things that they like that they think are appropriate, that fit the needs of the set that I've shopped for.

"And they'll add some things and they'll subtract some things and they'll say, 'I didn't think that this quite worked.' And I'll go back and I say, 'Well, I kinda do think it works, but maybe it doesn't work there, maybe we should put it over the bed; how do you like this? Don't you think that works great?' 'Yeah, I think that works great! Do you really think that this person would have this?' So that conversation is the conversation that I would have with them, but it could also be the conversation that they're having with each other. Hopefully they're as interested in it as I am."

WG2: "What's the Gold Room?"

DK: "The Gold Room is where we keep all the set dressing that we own."

WG2: "Where do you get all the statutary for the crypts?"

DK: "Monterey Art. In El Monte. It's worth the drive. They produce a large amount of work for us. All of our plaster work comes from them. Everything."

WG2: "Buffy and Willow's dorm room. What did you do to make it different from when Kathy left?"

DK: "When Buffy first moved in, she was really out of sorts and wasn't fitting into the college life, so I didn't think that her room would be any more inviting than anywhere else on campus. So I really didn't decorate that much of her room, and to be honest I've never really been satisfied with where her room has gone. Her side of the room and Willow's will always be a work in progress because I've never quite gotten it."

WG2: "Were you more satisfied with their rooms when they lived at home?"

DK: "No. I liked Willow's room. I liked what I did with Willow's room sometimes. There were some times when I was happy with Buffy's room at home. I liked Joyce's bedroom. I liked Xander's room. I like Xander's basement. I don't think Xander's basement is like your typical TV teenage set, which is maybe why I'm not completely satisfied with Buffy and Willow's dorm room because it seems so typical and so predictable.

"I really liked what we did with Oz's room. I thought that I was helping him express his character there. But I think you could probably ask anybody in my crew, and I don't think any of them would really truly enjoy it. I think Buffy and Willow's rooms are probably their least favorite set."

WG2: "What's your favorite set?"

DK: "I liked the Chinese bar that we just did. It was a really simple set to do and it dressed itself and all the elements were there all at once, and I thought it had a really nice look to it.

"I don't really have any favorite sets, but when I watch movies and whether I know who the decorator is on it or not, I have a pretty good idea of who the decorator is. On feature films as soon as you know who the designer is, you usually know who the decorator is, because they usually go hand in hand with one another.

"People have certain recognizable styles, and you try not to think about it when you're watching it, but every once in a while someone does something so good that you're absolutely blown away by it. It's like this tiny little epiphany that you'll have that you'll think that this person had this moment of absolute clarity, where something that they saw was absolutely perfect for a scene and even though it has nothing to do with the actor's speaking or anything, it just fit perfectly into the scene. It's just a moment of absolute brilliance, so that's why I say that there is no favorite set, that I take pleasure from finding a little corner in the room that's a really precious little moment. There are favorite little moments in dressing each set."

WG2: "Give me a specific."

DK: "We're dressing a little forest outside, and I decided to get a dead log to put on the set. It wasn't something that I could really afford but something that when I saw it, I wanted it, so I got it. Then I got a stump for it, and then I knew that I had a couple of funny little Japanese pine trees that grow horizontally, so I plopped a couple of those and that's my little happy moment for myself. My little satisfaction moment for that set.

"You just get little moments where you'll suddenly base an entire set off of one chair that you find, or a piece of stemware or a candleholder or a couch, and all of a sudden the entire set gets built around that.

"Or you have real moments of pleasure where you walk into a set, and you find a set dresser who you thought maybe lacked a little inspiration, found a huge amount of inspiration and put together a beautiful set that you didn't have to do anything to, they found their own pieces for it and they put together the puzzle for me. Those are pleasurable moments."

WG2: "You do so many crypts—do you get tired of the crypts?"

DK: "Yes, very."

WG2: "Are you going to add stuff to Spike's crypt as time goes on?"

DK: "I added two more statues. In Episode Fourteen Spike is living inside one of the sarcophaguses, or he's hiding in one of the sarcophaguses, underneath this dead Victorianesque woman, to hide from the Initiative people."

WG2: "What was it like when you guys blew up the library?"

DK: "We got it wrong. We had to keep doing it, because Joss couldn't tell it was a bomb. So we had to do it twice. We shot the explosion after the company had wrapped for the season. We reshot the bomb. There was almost no library there whatsoever. The entire set had been struck except for that little portion that you saw when the demons look at the library.

"Blowing up the school was fun. It was a twenty-hour day. I drank so much coffee that I could smell it coming out of my pores. We stayed there all day just to watch them blow up the courtyard. When they blew up the courtyard, I was lying on top of the roof of the Administration Building a hundred yards away, and I was lifted off the Administration Building when it exploded. The shock wave rolled out of the fountain quad and the Administration Building was one of these buildings that's up on stilts and underneath it were all the bike racks. The shock wave rolled out of the fountain quad and expanded when it got out of the fountain quad, and then got collapsed underneath the Administrative Building, and it pushed the Administrative Building up, and literally my whole body lifted off the roof of the Administrative Building. It was really weird. And then we had to wrap it all up that night.

"We had to strike it all out of there. We had to be completely cleaned out of there that night because we knew they'd never let us back. What else did we do in Season Three? I liked Faith's apartment a lot.

"We turned this water pipe in Faith's apartment into a boxing bag. Just like they did in Rocky. Her [first] place was really, really depressing, and I liked her new place because I liked her drapery a lot. We hand-made her drapery and we grommeted it with aluminum grommets and we had chains holding all the panels together; Stella built those for me. Stella built the comforter for me, too.

"The vampire mansion I liked. Then it became a set that I hated after a while."

WG2: "Because you were bored with it?"

DK: "A little."

WG2: "What about the prom?"

DK: "The prom was a lot of fun. You felt so close to being at the end of the season, that the prom felt like the prom. It felt like you were getting ready for the prom, and it was a fun set to do because you had that feeling of anticipation for the end of the season, just like you would the end of the school year.

"But what made the prom really fun for me was that I got a call from this woman in Arizona who was prom committee chairman for her daughter's high school. She called me right as I was in the middle of the prom, and she asked me where to go to get stuff. I thought it was just completely kismet that she would call me at that moment. I think she only had three or four hundred dollars, but there I was spending six or seven thousand dollars on our prom. So I felt bad. [But] it was a real pleasure to talk to her. She was sweet! It wasn't that she was a bad planner, I think she didn't see it going anywhere, so she took it over and tried to make it happen., to make it more of an event."

JOHNNY YOUNGBLOOD, ON-SET DRESSER

We met with Johnny Youngblood in a carpeted, paneled room behind the Intiative set at the Lockheed facility.

Portions of the floor had been covered with thick brown paper pads to create pedestrian walkways, thus preserving the facility's carpeting. The room grew dark as the sun set. Beyond the door Drs. Walsh and Angleman conducted the nefarious secret business of the Initiative.

We began by asking Johnny how he got to *Buffy*.

JY: "It started with a phone call. The set decorator [David Koneff] had been looking for an on-set dresser, which is what I do. It's a little more specialized because you're with the camera, as opposed to the other set dressers who ride on the truck and bring all the furniture in. I'm there to move that stuff around as things change, because things change.

"So my specialty, as it's developed over the years, has been on-set dressing. David kept getting my name. And he said, 'Who is this guy Johnny Youngblood? How come everyone keeps recommending him?'

"So he called me, and we interviewed, and it turned out that the show that I had come from—it was a show called Relativity—was also a Twentieth Century Fox show. Relativity had just gotten cancelled. So when I went in for the interview, I saw some guy carrying a box, another set dresser, and my handwriting was on the side. I recognized it as one of the boxes that I had packed up a month before on Relativity. So all the set dressing from Relativity ended up on Buffy.

"And so in a way, I came with the set dressing. And that's how I ended up on the show.

"How I ended up staying on the show is just because the people are so nice. And David lets me be creative, and be more than just a pair of muscles. So I came on the second season, the first season was just a half season, so I came on the first full season, and I've been on ever since. And I'll stay on as long as it goes, as long as I'm welcome."

WG2: "Can you talk about changes you've noticed from season to season? From Two to Three, for starters?"

JY: "Second season we were really cutting corners. It was still about not spending the money, and making a little go a long way. Season Three was fun. We started building bigger sets. Better-looking sets. We got to do Joyce's bedroom, third season. We got to do Faith's apartment. We got to really do some nice, creative sets as opposed to, you know, a high-school classroom. There's just so much you can do.

"Then with the Mayor, and Spike coming on—all these great things happened in the third season, that just made it even more fun to work on.

"It's kind of weird watching the direction that the writers and the creators sent the characters

367

GILES	H	HOLD	
WILLOW	H	HOLD	
SPIKE	W	6:30P	7:30P	REPORT TO LOCATION

in order to continue it on, but college is great. My parents were both college professors at the University of Miami, so I grew up on a college campus. I'm very comfortable on a college campus. And even though we don't shoot on a college campus now, you know, we have the sets on the stage that are very college campus-y, and I enjoy that. Whenever we're in a classroom and there's a chalkboard, I get to think about what the scene is about and then what's the class about, and I'll do a little research and figure out what to write on the board. For me, that's a blast, because I get to create something, and it's real. So that's something I really enjoy about this season."

WG2: "We were on the college set looking at all the flyers and stuff posted everywhere. Is that something made up by you?"

JY: "Most of it, if it's typed, with graphic design and all that, chances are we absconded it from somewhere. My boss went to UCLA at the beginning of the season, and saw what kind of stuff they have up. Then we'll get a box of paperwork that's just papers, with printed stuff on it. We'll go through that and find things that are applicable.

"But then what we'll do with flyers is, on the day, depending on what set we're on, I'll take a blank piece of paper and write 'Do you hate your roommate and want to switch?' and an extension. Or when we shot in the laundry room, and I made up a sign that says, 'Do you hate doing your laundry? Why not let me do your laundry?'

"Because I went to college for so long, I remember that people are always selling something. It's always handwritten stuff. I always carry a set of colored pens so I can create little signs on the day. The stuff that's just shapes can be anything. If we're going to see it and be able to read it, I like it to be a little more appropriate for the thing that we're shooting.

"I'm a musician. That's what I grew up doing. And my job allows me to contact bands and get artwork from bands. There's a band called Widespread Panic that just has great artwork for our show. I found them the first season I was on here. I had some friends who had a band in Athens, Georgia, and Widespread Panic is from there. They went to University of Miami, and they were students of my dad in the Music School.

"I got ahold of them and I said, 'Hey, I'm doing this show, send me some artwork, let me see what you have.' Turns out their style for their artwork is very Gothic, it's very dark. It's about monsters, it's about angels—it's just very fantastic, very <u>Buffy</u> appropriate. So I started getting their stuff, and it works out perfectly.

"Now they're big fans of the show, and all their fans are fans of the show. They'll watch it to see their posters come on. There are other bands whose artwork I'll see, and I'll really like it, so I'll go about finding the record company and getting artwork. So that's something that I get to do that I enjoy."

WG2: "Do you have to get some kind of permission to show that?"

JY: "Generally, by the bands sending you the artwork is giving you the clearance. I always ask, and sometimes if I'm not talking to the person I'm sure is in charge, I'll say, 'You know what, fax me a letter that says '<u>Buffy the Vampire Slayer</u> is cleared to use our stuff.'

"I work with some surf companies for artwork, and stickers, because we do a lot of stickers, kids' notebooks, the lockers—we had lockers in high school, and that was all about stickers. Not so much now. But I get stuff from them, and that's fine. These are people that I'll deal with down the line. Going to another show, I'll say, 'Hey, it's Johnny Youngblood, I'm on another show,' and they'll blast out another package of stuff. They love it. And it's fun.

"I have a job that's fun, and it pays well, and it's as good as it gets."

3/8 pg

Pg

FRC

5/8 pg

2/8 pg

R

TION

TION

TION

ANYA		H	HOLD		
FORREST		W	6:30P	7:30P	REPORT TO NEBRASKA / BUN

Operators		11:00A	1	Music Coordinator	John King	OC
Operators	Matthew Pope	11:00A	1	Editor	Regis Kimble	OC
Operators			1	Editor	Nancy Forner	OC

Coordinator-Di

tion Manager
Location Manag
tion Asst.
nan
e
ecurity
night Security
Security

PRODUCTI
edic
truction Medic
al Wrangler
o Teacher

CATERING
er
topher Ertaud-c
fast for

WG2: "How did you make the transition from school to the film business?"

JY: "When I was in my last year of my film program, I got an internship with this boom operator, and I became a soundman. And so I was working in the business while I was finishing my English degree. I was already working, doing commercials, little things in Miami. So I worked as a soundman for a year, but I found myself working in low budget, and I was making such little money, and I was having to fight for it. It was just not a pleasant environment.

"I finished a low-budget movie in Orlando in December of '93 and went back to Miami. A guy I knew from college called me. He knew that I had worked my way, supporting myself, through school with all kinds of jobs. He had a prop-assisting job on Wendy's commercials. But he was moving into animation.

"So he called me. He said, 'Can you cover me tomorrow? It's an emergency. Five A.M.'

"I showed up and they were building a kitchen set for a Wendy's commercial. I had built kitchens before, as a cook and as a construction worker. So I was like, 'Oh, I know how this goes,' and I just started moving stuff around.

"Then the Wendy's people came in—Dave Thomas—and looked. They had done kitchens before, but they said, 'Wow, this looks like a real kitchen.' So it was like I landed kind of where I belonged. Because set dressing takes a little from every experience. You know, college campuses, you do those. You do commercial buildings. I understand construction, I know what a construction set should look like. All those things come into play.

"So when I started doing art department, it all fell together. And the way the Wendy's people are, once you work for them, they want you. It's a family. Dave Thomas likes to know everyone on the crew by name. I worked for them for four years. I moved out here, and they still called me. They'd fly me to Miami, give me a car, and every job they'd give me a raise. They do a lot of commercials.

"So that was my entry into the business. Out of school, into low budget, almost out of the business, and then it was that one phone call saved me. And then when I came out here, I didn't know anyone, really.

"I had a handful of résumés; I'd see a film shoot going; I'd say, 'Here's my résumé.' The fourth or fifth time the guy was about to crumple it up, and then he said, 'Oh, you've done some big commercials. Why don't you go talk to our production designer?'

"The first guy I met there said, 'Will you work for fifty bucks?' What else did I have? I said, 'Sure.'

"He said, 'All right, come in at six A.M. tomorrow.' And I showed up. By lunch he said, 'I'll give you a hundred bucks.' And by twelve hours into the day, he said, 'You know what, you guys are doing such a good job, I'm gonna go home. I'll give you two hundred bucks for the day.' And I became his guy, doing commercials and music videos.

"I was told early on, at one of my jobs, that every job you do should turn into three more jobs, if you do your job right. So that's pretty much worked out for me. If I meet someone on a job, chances are they're going to call me later.

"But now I have at least three or four people that I can call. And it's weird getting on a TV show for this many years. I'm working for one guy; I keep having to call these other people. 'I still exist, I still want to work for you, I just have this steady thing going.'"

WG2: "Have you done feature films?"

JY: "My first one, which I got into the union on, was called <u>House Arrest</u>. I was a prop shopper on that. It was a kids' movie, so I shopped for all the tools. I was on props on that, and then I needed work and I was still struggling, so I started doing greens. I met a greensman. I worked for about six months doing just greens: shuffling trees, digging holes, and that's brutal work. I did a movie called <u>Spy Hard</u> as a stand-by greensman, which is basically on-set greens. That took us through the O. J. trial and all that.

"Then I did a movie called <u>The Long Kiss Goodnight</u>. It was with Geena Davis and Samuel L.

369

CTOR	James Contner	11:00A	1	Production Designer	Carey Meyer	OC
CTOR	David Solomon	Prep	1	Art Director	Caroline Quinn	OC
					a Ruskin	OC
					Starlight	OC
					l Koneff	OC
					ıstafson	OC
Asst. Di					ngblood	11:00A
Asst. Di					th Cuba	OC
nd Ass					. Wilson	OC
nd A.D					ly Kelly	OC
1 2nd A						
Traine					Eriksen	11:00A
DGA 1					asch, Jr.	11:00A
uction S					d Ronan	11:00A
t Super						
tor of F					ve West	OC
era Ope					/. Hight	per S\
era Ope					avidson	per S\
licam O					3umatai	per S\
C-A Ca					Val Wilt	per S\
C-B Ca					m Sahli	per S\
C-C Ca					Halaby	per S\
-A Cam					Petersen	per S\
ler					n Hight	per S\
1 2nd A(						
f Lightii						

Jackson, directed by Renny Harlin. They shot most of that in Canada, but when they came back to town, I worked up in Solvaang for a couple weeks.

"And then this summer I did a movie called Picking Up the Pieces, starring Woody Allen and Sharon Stone. It's an independent movie directed by Alfonso Arau, who did Like Water for Chocolate, and A Walk in the Clouds.

"If I can do a feature in between seasons, it usually works out well. Oh, I also did Cruel Intentions, with Sarah. I did that between the second and third season. I did on-set dressing, and regular swing gang.

"That's what they call the regular set dressers, the swing gang. I think it's just a loose term; you're just kind of always moving around. It's fun, it's a different world because you're just working with a bunch of buddies, and you have music playing, and you're joking around. There's no pressure, really. There's no camera around.

"But I've always kind of enjoyed watching the process a lot closer than...just being swing gang gets kind of boring and monotonous, because you don't really see the purpose of it. You just do it and you walk away. Whereas to do on-set, you're really watching the pieces come together.

"I didn't grow up as a film buff or anything like that, so when I got my film degree, it always intrigued me, the way things come together. I mean, these directors and script supervisors who understand how coverage, and how all these things work, blow me away. There's so much to be learned there. And I guess because of my many years in college, the learning, I just love to learn. So it's like I'm constantly learning it, understanding it."

WG2: "On this particular episode, are there any special set dressing challenges that you're dealing with?"

JY: "Well, we're about to go outside in these forests, there's a couple of fights out there. You know, it's a challenge working in the elements, in that we have stuff hidden all over the place, and I have nothing but plants. So the challenge for me is to take the plants I have and hide everything. We call it hiding our sins. There are lights, our stunt pads.... If someone's fighting, there's a pad somewhere. And we're constantly hiding things.

"You said 'challenge,' but I never look at it like that. It's just part of the day, you know, it's like, we have all the tools to make it work.

"Plus, being that it's our fourth year, we kind of have it down. We know what to expect. We're always pulling sets apart, and the challenge sometimes will just be, how am I gonna get this piece through that door? The challenge a lot of times is just to work within the space that we have. As far as set dressing challenges, I think we've crawled beyond the challenges.

"My boss has challenges sometimes because the writers will give him sketchy information or whatever, and he'll have to just take the ball and run with it. We walk on the set, and as much as they have tech scouts, or the directors tell us, 'We're gonna be looking at this, we'll be looking at this,' on the day, it changes. So the challenges are really in the moment. And we work it out. We move a couple things around. What do they always say, 'Steal from Peter to pay Paul.' And it all works out well, you know.

"You're always compromising. Whenever we're in certain sets that are supposed to be grungy and dirty, my boss loves leaves on the floor. He just loves the look. The sound man hates leaves, because people walk on them and they crunch. So my boss will come to me and ask me to put down leaves, and then the sound mixer will comes to me and asks me to sweep up the leaves. I'll go on in and I'll crunch all the leaves down, so they're already flat. And then I'll have to walk the sound mixer over, and I'll say, 'Look, there's a leaf here, but it's a quiet leaf.'"

370

In "Pangs" a sconce in Giles's living room was replaced by a little window specifically so an Indian could shoot an arrow through it.

THE PROP DEPARTMENT

EDWARD J. BORASCH JR., SET PROPERTY MASTER

The prop room is located in the same warehouse as the sound stages and the mill, just behind the strip of reserved executive parking spaces. Each object a character picks up, from Veruca's hamburger to Buffy's crossbow, the IV in Faith's arm to the rose that Willow and Tara levitate, is a prop.

WG2: "Tell us how you got your start in the business."

EB: "In 1990 I was living in Florida and a film crew was shooting at a location near my apartment. I walked over to the set and watched them for hours. That's when I realized for the first time that I wanted to do this as a career. I just had to figure out how to get started.

"I thought if I drove up to the Universal Studios guard gate at the soundstages they would just let me in. It doesn't work that way. On my third try in two weeks I told the guard (a different one had been on duty each time) that I had a casting session and he [let me in].

"I found my way into the production building and knocked on every door. I told whoever was there that I wanted to work in the film business and would work for free, I'd sweep floors, whatever! After I got pushed out of four or five doors, I went to the elevator to head up to the second floor. A woman was on the elevator with me and asked if I was an actor. I said, 'Yes...I am an actor.' She said, 'Good! Follow me.' We got out and I followed her to a conference room. We went in and about fifteen to twenty people with scripts in front of them looked up and the woman said, 'I have your detective for you.'

"They said, 'Do you act? Are you [in the Screen Actor's Guild]?' I said, 'No SAG card' in a stuttering voice. I was feeling put on the spot to say the least. They said, 'That's okay, we don't have any lines for you at this time. Just be here tomorrow at seven A.M.' Within twenty minutes of sneaking onto the Universal studio lot, I got hired to be a principle extra on a cop show called Super Force. That was my foot in the door and it gave me a chance to schmooze with the departments that could hire me.

"After a month of bugging everybody on set, the Lead Man of the Set Dressing department said he would give me a shot. And within two weeks I was hired as a Set Dresser, which then moved me to On-Set Dresser and eventually into the Prop department."

WG2: "What is the difference between a Set Dresser and somebody in Props?"

EB: "A Set Dresser is part of the Set Decorating department. They take the vision and orders from the Set Decorator or Lead Man and bring in all the furniture, rugs, lamps, desks, couches, and so much more. They make the set ready for filming.

"A Prop person gives what is scripted for the character to touch or handle in any way. Certain props have to be created for the story, which is very specific and detailed. Props would need to

GILES	H			
WILLOW	H	HOLD		
SPIKE	W	6:30P	7:30P	REPORT TO LOCATION

be shown to the Production Designer and, once approved, get shown to the director for final approval. You need to have a few options to show; never have just one.

"There's a lot of coordinating that has to be done. The actor wants the prop a certain way and the director wants it a certain way, and you do your best to meet in the middle and make everybody happy. A lot of special prop fabricating is involved in doing <u>Buffy</u>. The head of the Property department, Randy Eriksen, does all the designing and creating of <u>Buffy</u>'s props. When we are filming an episode, Randy is designing and fabricating the props for the next episode.

"Sometimes when we are filming, [a prop we've created based on the script] would need to be bigger or smaller or have something added to it—and it needs to be done in three minutes, because the camera and actors are waiting. That's when the challenge is on to think fast on your feet to give them what they want. I always have to be watching and thinking when I'm on set. So much is happening and you need to anticipate what the director and the actors are going to want and have it ready. That's why I love what I do! I get to be creative and challenged and have a lot of fun doing it.

Dave Ronan, Assistant Property Master

"In the two seasons I've been with <u>Buffy</u>, I've gotten to know the characters and the actor, who play them. I enjoy anticipating what the actors are going to want, prop-wise, in the scene. A lot of the small hand props you see with the actors are a part of their characters' personalities. Most of those props are not scripted in the scene. For instance, Giles's teacup and writing instruments, Willow's computer and wicca trunk, Buffy's stakes and crossbow."

WG2: "What is something Buffy likes to have?"

EB: "I know she likes to have props that are easy to handle, that would not encumber her movements and cause a distraction. In Season Four Randy wanted to make Buffy's stakes a little shorter and more streamlined so they look like they would hide in her outfits better. The new stakes were easier to carry and fight with. I think [Sarah] liked them."

WG2: "You make a lot of mystical stuff, but it's very heavily based in reality. Are there any tricks you use to avoid making the mystical stuff look bogus or fake?"

EB: "We use a lot of paint. Arts and crafts comes into play a lot with that. In preparing for Willow's wicca trunk, Randy went to Chinatown and Koreatown to find little herb and spice stores that sell things you would not find in your local store. He would buy very strange looking seaweed, roots, and powders.

"What we try to do is go on the odds of how much of this is out there, how many people really would have something like this. [But even] if the odds are really rare, we might not change the look of the prop. It can be a unique looking prop that will be perfect for the scene and for the actor."

A TOUR OF THE PROP ROOM

BUFFY'S CROSSBOW HANGS ON THE WALL. Her Class Protector parasol—in two parts—sits atop a gray storage container beside a familiar large wooden cross. Several tiny bride and groom figures sit on other shelves. On the large worktable are scattered the huge "Vampyre" book—which weighs mere ounces—nasty-looking knives made of rubber, runestones, and other *Buffy* paraphernalia. Boost Bar wrappers and the Hershey's chocolate candy bars they covered sit within temptation.

There are gallon bottles of prop blood, a jar of plastic rat eyes (created by Optic Nerve for "Lover's Walk," they are plastic balls with dots on them), and the rubber rat that is Amy Rat—"just your standard rubber rat"—are casually displayed. Atop the African mask from "Dead Man's Party," a rubber bat has made a nest of flowers.

The locking devices that bolt the demons to the operating tables in the Initiative complex were fabricated by a high-tech company for the prop department.

The wall farthest from the door is lined with red plastic bins. Each is labeled. Their contents include:

KITCHEN TOWELS AND SHEETS ✦ PAPER BAGS ✦ QUIET BAGS ✦ LICENSE PLATES ✦ ZIPLOCK BAGGIES ✦ SLINGSHOTS ✦ RILEY'S AND SPIKE ✦ BUFFY'S PERSONAL PROPS ✦ XANDER'S PERSONAL PROPS ✦ GILES'S PERSONAL PROPS ✦ GILES KITCHEN ✦ WILLOW'S ✦ WILLOW'S ROOM ✦ TALISMEN ✦ CHALICES ✦ PENTAGRAMS ✦ HERBS & SPICES ✦ COLORED SAND ✦ ROPE ✦ INCENSE ✦ VOODOO & BLACK MAGIC ✦ CANDLES ✦ CHEMISTRY GEAR ✦ RESTAURANT ✦ SHACKLES ✦ KNIVES, RUBBER & REAL COFFEE CUPS/JARS ✦ BACKPACKS (2 bins) ✦ ROCKS ✦ CHAIRBACKS ✦ BIG CROSSES ✦ GIRLS' PURSE STUFF ✦ STUNT/RUBBER STAKES ✦ STAKES ✦ EYEGLASSES/SHADES ✦ 3-RING BINDERS ✦ SCHOOL FOLDERS ✦ TEXTBOOKS (several bins) ✦ MEDICAL (several bins) ✦ SNACKS ✦ DOLLS & ANIMALS ✦ JOYCE/MOM PERSONAL PROPS ✦ GAFFER'S TAPE ✦ EXPENDABLES ✦ PAPER & ELECTRICAL W/ASSORTED TAPES ✦ MAGAZINES ✦ GYMBAGS & PURSES ✦ DAYPLANNERS ✦ SKETCH BOOKS ✦ FABRICS ✦ TOWELS ✦ TOILETRIES ✦ RESPIRATORS ✦ BOOZE BOTTLES ✦ CELL PHONES/MISC PHONES ✦ FAKE HAND PROPS ✦ FLASHLIGHTS ✦ CANDLEHOLDERS & LAMP OIL ✦ EYE & EAR PROTECTION ✦ SCIENCE STUFF ✦ PILLOWS ✦ SPORTING BALLS

THE CONSTRUCTION DEPARTMENT

STEPHEN L. WEST, CONSTRUCTION COORDINATOR

WG2: "Were you here when you had that building outside, the El Niño building [see Watcher's Guide, Vol. 1]?"

SW: "That was my El Niño Building."

WG2: "You must feel pretty spiffy now having an indoor room."

SW: "It's very nice to have an indoor mill to work in. We got it last year. We build all the sets in our mill, and we have locations that we go out on and we prefab everything here."

WG2: "How many people are in the department?"

SW: "We have twenty with painters, plasterers, and the laborers that we carry, and the prop makers. We make all this stuff, so we don't have to go out on location."

WG2: "How do you make everything look so old?"

SW: "We use foam and the plasterer puts his plaster on it and the painters do their number on it and everything looks the way it should be."

WG2: "What's the hardest thing to build?"

SW: "I don't think we've had that yet."

WG2: "What's the easiest thing to build?"

SW: "The easiest thing we had to build was the airplane fuselage we turned into the sewer on Stage Two and we've used that for numerous sets since then."

WG2: "How many sets do you construct per season, swing sets and the more permanent?"

SW: "Every eight days we have a new episode, and we usually get six to eight sets per episode. Which is quite a bit, but they've never had to wait for us yet."

WG2: "Before you had Soundstage Two, when you guys had only One and Three, was it real hard to build things around here?"

SW: "We had the El Niño building, so we built a lot out underneath that until the Fire Department made us take it down."

WG2: "Is that what happened? It was kind of cool coming out here, and there was like this pavilion of wood. Did you build the exterior street?"

SW: "Yes, that was ours. Gareth got the money for that somehow, and it saves them a lot of time going out on location and saves them a lot of money."

WG2: "What visually, or in any way, what has been your favorite set in Seasons Three or Four?"

SW: "I liked building the street and I like the new college. The lecture hall. They don't use it enough. And I like the new frat house."

WG2: "Very cool and elaborate. How long have you been doing this?"

SW: "I've been in the industry since 1976. My first show was Airport '77. I've worked as a prop maker and a foreman for different coordinators, and finally decided I didn't want to hammer nails anymore and I would rather be on the other end. I had to take a test to become a construction coordinator."

374

WG2: "What are some of the other shows or features you worked on?"

SW: "I was in St. Martin on Speed 2 for six months as an effects diver. I've worked on some of the Jaws movies. Lot of TV. Back to the Future 2 and 3. I did a lot of TV in my early career. I worked on Alice and WKRP. The earlier ones; I hadn't done TV for quite a while. I've stuck to features, [but] the industry has kind of gone sour for the last two or three years and TV's been the popular thing to get into. Canada has taken a lot of our work."

WG2: "Has there been any significant difference in the way you work or the things you work on from Season Two to Season Three that you can think of?"

SW: "We've done a little bit more of our permanent buildings to keep [the company] on the lot, and stop them from going on location so much. We did the ['Hush'] clock tower out at Universal; we did some exterior work and some signage out there. It's a lot of fun to go on location. But I also like it when the company's gone, and we're here working on the sets."

WG2: "That way they can leave you alone! How do you make the brick look so real?"

SW: "We get different type of brick products from different vendors depending on what the production designer is looking for. The painters do their thing on it and the plasterer ties every thing in."

WG2: "How many hours a day do you work?"

SW: "We usually work ten hours a day, five days a week. It's usually eleven and a half for most crews but I think it's a waste of money actually, that last hour and a half, so we work ten and get everything done then."

LOCATIONS

ED DUFFY, LOCATIONS MANAGER

Ed Duffy nearly fell out of the helicopter that was filming the aerial shots for the opening credits of the prime-time soap *Dynasty*. He just smiles enigmatically when pressed for stories about *Melrose Place*.

WG2: "How did you get this job?"

ED: "I started off being a production assistant for a small company that used to do a lot of TV movies and things like that. Then I moved into a production supervisor job at another small company that also did lots of TV movies.

"I was in a position to hire a lot of people, and so I hired a lot of location managers for all the shows that we did, and I was looking for a job and a friend of mine was doing Paper Chase, the series, over at Fox. And he said, 'Why don't you come over and do this, because it's real easy, we just go to USC once an episode.' So I went over there, and I just sort of fell into it. At the time [the idea of] location manager was sort of in its infancy. The city was not quite as jaded; the permit process was a lot simpler. A lot of things were simpler. So it's sort of grown along with all the problems. Basically this is my first year on Buffy. I was doing Melrose Place for the last five years. Before that I did Moonlighting and Dynasty. Those are the bigger series I've done. I got here based on the fact I knew Gareth, who is the producer, previously."

WG2: "Did you work together?"

ED: "Very briefly, at Paramount. He remembered me, and there are some people at Fox who are friends of mine. Bruce Margolis, who is one of the executives, used to be my assistant; so we're pretty close. So I sort of knew that Buffy's position was becoming available, so I pursued it a little bit and that's how I got here.

GRAHAM	W	6:30P	7:30P	REPORT TO NEBRASKA / BUNDY LOT
STUNT COORDINATOR	W	~	6:30P	REPORT TO LOCATION
BUFFY STUNT DBL	H		HOLD	

"Basically my job is to read the script or outline, whatever we have; sort of ascertain what we are going to be doing on location and what we need to do in the studio, and try to come up with different ideas and places to make that happen. And make sure I get everybody there, places to park, permits, police, fire, maps, anything connected to the location, contracts, insurance. And I get that all sewed up; and I'm there on the day to make sure everything gets taken care of the way it's supposed to."

WG2: "When you look at a script, do you already have a steady set of places that you think of first?"

ED: "Well, sort of. I mean, I've been doing this for twenty-two years, so I have quite a few things in the back of my head. Most major places that you shoot in Los Angeles, I've shot. Quite a few things that you sort of tuck away in there that you remember and then say, 'You know, that would be a good spot.'

"And then you try and ascertain whether you can actually take a production company to a place like that, and how easily you can get in and out of it. Because we're usually on a pretty tight schedule. We usually have only twelve or fourteen hours to shoot, and so if it's something involved, I usually won't mention it. I usually sort of hold it back unless I get really in trouble. You know, they ask me for suggestions, they have ideas, too, and we just put them all together and try to come up with the best plan.

"The thing we're dealing with right now is the Initiative, which is something that took us a long time to figure out where it should be. We weren't quite sure what it was, and it needed to be a very big space, and we couldn't decide whether I was looking at actual NASA properties and Boeing properties and Hughes Aircraft properties and things like that. But we were realizing that most of that was a little too hard for us to get in and out of, because of security clearances and things like that we'd never have time to get. So that's how we ended up where we are.

"Another big part of this year is the campus that she's going to, and that became a very involved process too. We started with UCLA, which is our prototype of the campus. We ended up shooting there the first episode, and it was pretty difficult moving around it and just getting clearances and being able to do it on a regular basis. It just took too much to do, so we wound up shooting where we do shoot, which is an office complex actually. The Braun Company used to be there. It's still called the Braun Complex, but they moved to Texas years ago."

WG2: "We've been to the UCLA campus a lot, and we thought all the exteriors were still at UCLA."

ED: "Right. That's what we were trying to do, we needed to come up with something that looked older, in brick, and the right feeling. So it's worked out pretty well for us."

WG2: "In the first episode, when they shot at UCLA, were there real students in the shots?"

ED: "That was an interesting thing. In the first scene we shot there, we were supposed to have shot that on a Saturday. Because of scheduling problems, we ended up having to shoot that on a Friday. And that Friday that we had to shoot it, we pushed back a couple of weeks because <u>Angel</u> pushed back a couple of weeks and we were trying to match.

"That Friday was also initiation day for the incoming freshman and we were shooting Bruin Walk, which is the main area where all these freshman were meeting that day. So we had two hundred kids there and they had eight hundred kids there and we couldn't quite ascertain who was us and who was them, and it became a pretty interesting day. It was quite amazing."

WG2: "Did you just put up signs that said, 'If you are here you'll be on TV?'"

ED: "Uh-huh. And besides them, there was also construction of a building going on right about ten feet behind us, so that was pretty interesting. That was a big day, and we got through it, but it wasn't easy. Of course all these freshman were very interested in <u>Buffy</u> and very interested in Seth and Alyson, and we couldn't figure out how to keep them away from them, because we didn't know who was us and who wasn't, so it got pretty involved."

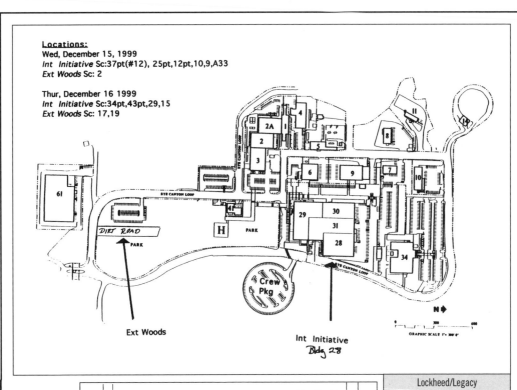

Locations:
Wed, December 15, 1999
Int Initiative Sc:37pt(#12), 25pt,12pt,10,9,A33
Ext Woods Sc: 2

Thur, December 16 1999
Int Initiative Sc:34pt,43pt,29,15
Ext Woods Sc: 17,19

Ext Woods

Int Initiative
Bldg 28

Lockheed/Legacy

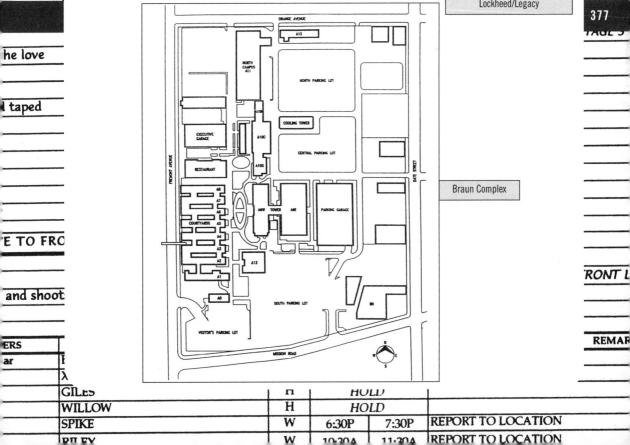

Braun Complex

he love

taped

E TO FRO

and shoot

ERS

RONT L

REMAR

ar				
	λ			
GILES	H	HOLD		
WILLOW	H	HOLD		
SPIKE	W	6:30P	7:30P	REPORT TO LOCATION
RILEY	W	10:30A	11:30A	REPORT TO LOCATION

WG2: "Have there been many other exciting things like that?"

ED "Well, there's other things that have happened. Mostly our biggest things happened there at UCLA those couple of days, because we had quite a few kids that were extremely interested and knew more about <u>Buffy</u> than a lot of people on <u>Buffy</u>. There were some people that knew every single writer. Knew what they wrote, what they did, every director, and were just totally just connected to the whole thing.

"Seth was very much talking to all of them, so there was one point where we actually broke for lunch and we moved inside a lecture hall, and Seth stayed there through his whole lunch hour and signed things and talked to every single person until they were done talking to him. That was very nice, and we had people from <u>The Daily Bruin</u> there trying to do interviews. It was interesting. We haven't really run into anything like that since because I got wise right about then and realized that I needed to keep us a little more insulated. So I've been able to do that. Sometimes it's not possible, but so far I've been able to do it."

WG2: "Do most of the facilities you deal with have experience with being used as a location?"

ED: "Most of them do. A great deal of them do. There aren't too many places in town that haven't been shot. And the ones that don't want it usually had it a couple of times and they couldn't handle it. It's hard to find something that hasn't been [used]."

WG2: "In Season Three or Four, you went back to Rosedale Cemetery."

ED: "Our cemetery isn't quite that large, so if it's something big or something like that, then we would go back there."

WG2: "Do you have any idea of how many days in a season you go on location?"

ED: "We usually go out two days an episode. Three of the episodes this year we've gone out three, and then for the Halloween episode we only went out one, for the frat house."

"The exterior of that place was quite difficult actually, because it had to be a place that looked like all the windows would disappear and the doors disappear. And it was all night work, so we were there in a neighborhood until about two or three in the morning, and that was another situation where we had planned on trying to be done by midnight.

"Right across the street from where this house was, was a Brothers retreat house. And these Brothers, all their windows were right behind us, and they knew we were going to be there, and they knew we'd be finished about twelve-thirty because we had to get their permission. But what I didn't know was that they don't close their curtains and their windows, so they couldn't go to sleep because we had the place all lit up. They had curtains on the windows, but for some reason—I guess they wake to the sun coming up—they couldn't shut their curtains. It was quite of a little bit of an ordeal. I felt very bad, but we were there, and there was nothing much I could do. They used to own the property that we shot, as a matter of fact, but somebody else owns it now.

"We had to make the door disappear, so we had to build a whole piece that went on the inside of the door. It was a little involved. Initially we didn't realize that was going to happen, 'cause we were looking for a place that sort of went along with the look of UCLA, so we were trying to find something older, in brick. By the time we got the script and had already picked this place, we realized that somehow at one point Giles takes out a buzz saw and cuts into it. So it was gonna be hard to do that with brick, so we ended up having to build a whole fake piece to make that work."

WG2: "Do you approach very many private residences? Are people in Los Angeles fairly jaded about it?"

ED: "In certain areas. It depends on where you go. The nice thing about <u>Buffy</u>, it's basically small town. So most of the areas I go to aren't a mansion or aren't Encino or Cheviot Hills or something like that, so it's pretty good."

WG2: "What was something that was unusual in Episode Thirteen?"

RILEY	W	10:30A	11:30A	REPORT TO LOCATION
ANYA	H	HOLD		
FORREST	W	6:30P	7:30P	REPORT TO NEBRASKA / BUN

THE SLAYER

AND HER FRIENDS

LAGOS

VERUCA

AYER
AT HEART"
DY) #1

APPRO

Sketch for Willow's Homecoming dress

Buffy as Little
Red Riding Hood
Halloween Costume

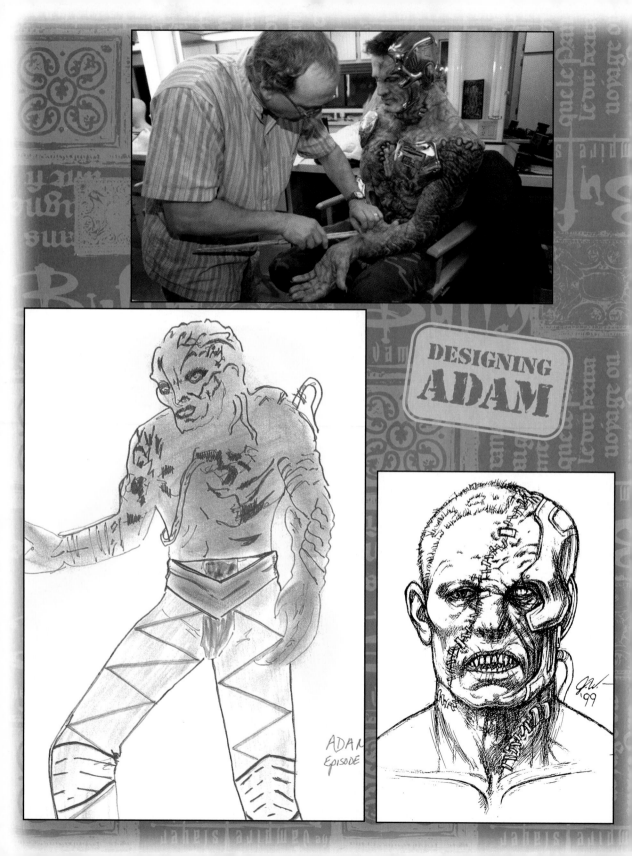

DESIGNING ADAM

ADAM
EPISODE

ED: "The thing that we're going to be doing is we have some neighborhood scenes that we have to shoot, that we're actually gonna shoot right outside our gate, which we have never done. We've been working on that."

WG2: "The cast for this episode is pretty small. Does that make your job with transporting things considerably easier?"

ED: "Transportationwise, everybody transports themselves pretty much. So my biggest challenge is to make sure that they can figure out how to get there. And that can be pretty odd sometimes. Especially when we go to some place like Alhambra, because most people don't know where that is. It's not a place that you travel to. Just getting off the freeway and trying to find the right street can be hard."

WG2: "Is it always the same something else?"

ED: "Yes. So I'm not saying what that is."

WG2: "What about if there are surprises, like mud? Or does anything like that affect you?"

ED: "Well, some things do. Rain affects us because sometimes if it rains, we can't go out. A lot of times rain doesn't hurt us because we're usually a pretty gloomy show, so that's not usually a problem. But there are things that affect me. We'll run into construction zones sometimes that we didn't expect. We'll run into certain things like that, that just pop up, or we'll run into another film company half a block away."

WG2: "There was something about Colonial Drive at Universal Studios?"

ED: "We were there on Joss's last show ['Hush']. That was a very interesting show because we knew we needed a small town. So we ended up going around looking for more than the town we have on our back lot, so we went to all the small towns around here.

"But then once we got the outline, we realized that these people actually have to float through the town, and the only way to do that was to actually construct giant cranes with wires that have to be erased, that go all over the streets and everything. So we had to go to some place that we could do that. It was gonna be impossible to shut down an actual town, and there was also a clock tower involved that we didn't know about, so we had to actually go there, we had to build the clock tower because we didn't like the one where it was. For one thing we wanted to have some residential streets around it, so we went up to Colonial Street [at Universal Studios], which is actually a little residential street that has a business section at the end. There is a church at the end, and we built the clock tower on top of that. Trying to get Universal at the last minute and getting it all worked out was very difficult, but they were very accommodating and they got us in there. At the same time Angel was shooting just below us two days earlier, so they were there, too, shooting a whole bunch of stuff on European streets. That was interesting."

WG2: "What's your average length of day?"

ED: "If we're shooting on location, for instance, last week we had a situation where Giles became a demon. So last Friday I think we started at eight in the morning with his makeup. The crew call was at eleven and we finished at one-thirty in the morning. So by the time the trucks and everything got out of there, it was about three in the morning. That's a very long day. So it's a very painstaking thing."

KELLY HARRIS, LOCATIONS ASSISTANT

Kelly Harris was bundled up on the Initiative set. It was quite chilly inside the cavernous building. She wore a headset and calmly surveyed the action as Sarah Michelle Gellar rehearsed in light clothing beside Marc Blucas. Both actors were by then quite ill, and they would take advantage of the time between takes to cough.

379

Kelly and her boss, Ed Duffy, came to *Buffy* from *Melrose Place*. Hailing from Ohio, Kelly has a degree in Films and Radio; while in Cincinnati, she began working in locations scouting for such prominent film directors as Jodie Foster and John Sayles.

At the invitation of a friend, she came out to winter in L.A., with only one suitcase and a garment bag. While visiting the office of a friend in the industry, a producer asked her if she wanted a job.

"And I never went back to Cincinnati," she says with a laugh.

● ●

LOCATIONS, LOCATIONS, LOCATIONS:

Oz's House . . . . **LOS FELIZ, CA**

Oz & Veruca wake up in woods. . . . . **GRIFFITH PARK**

miscellaneous woods near Cedar Grove . . . . **LOS FELIZ, CA**

Alpha Delta Fraternity House ("Fear Itself") . . . . **LOS ANGELES, CA**

U.C. Sunnydale including Dean's House. . . . . **BRAUN COMPLEX, ALHAMBRA, CA**

Dream World, ("Living Conditions"), U.C. Sunnydale, Royce Hall Colonnade,
Powell Library, Murphy Sculpture Garden, Ackerman Plaza,
Bruin Walk . . . . **UCLA CAMPUS, WESTWOOD, CA**

Buffy Dorm Exterior . . . . **FRANZ HALL, UCLA**

The Initiative Complex,
campus woods. . . . . **LOCKHEED/LEGACY, VALENCIA, CA**

Interior Old Mission,
Old Cultural Center ("Pangs") . . . . **SAN FERNANDO MISSION, MISSION HILLS, CA**

Town of Sunnydale, Bell Tower
100 Universal City Plaza, ("Hush") . . . . **UNIVERSAL STUDIOS, UNIVERSAL CITY, CA**

Giles's apartment building exterior . . . . **LOS FELIZ, CA**

● ●

OPTIC NERVE

We spoke with Greg Solomon of Optic Nerve, the company that does the latex masks, suits, vampire prosthetics, and contact lenses for *Buffy*. From Adam to Tapparich, they've done all the demon work that appears onscreen. They also provide the icky bits and pieces you occasionally see on this gore-low show: decapitated heads, arms, and the occasional bowl of human eyeballs.

Greg was eating breakfast in the vast warehouse that served as the company dining hall during the Santa Clarita location shoot. He had just delivered parts of the Adam outfit to Makeup Department Head Todd McIntosh.

WG2: "How did you get into the business?"

GS: "I started out, about twenty-six, twenty-seven years ago, doing theatre makeup. And a person I knew back then had done makeup for some movies in the thirties. She took me under her wing and showed me a few things about makeup. I learned the basics of makeup, highlight and shadow, laying crepe wool beard and things like that, and I just really took to it. I loved it. I started studying it on my own, and through the years I did community theater whenever I could. I never looked at it as something I could make a living at."

WG2: "What was your day job at the time?"

GS: "I was in construction for a while, had my own contracting company, actually. So I'd always worked with my hands, always did creative things. And then finally I decided one day to go ahead and make the jump, try to do this as a living.

"I just started knocking on doors. I got a little job here, a little job there, in special makeup effects. Actually, I did quite well right at the beginning. I was kind of surprised. I worked with Stan Winston for my first job. I worked there for four days. But it was great. I was really happy.

"My second job was with Rick Baker, and that lasted two years. So I was pretty thrilled with that. And then I hopped around to different shops from there.

"One nice thing about working at Optic Nerve is that I've finally gotten into a shop that deals mostly with makeup effects. We don't do that many mechanical effects or model making or large props that a lot of the other shops do. It's mostly back to my first love, which is prosthetics.

"And then they offered the supervising job for Buffy for this season. So far it's worked out well. Once I catch up on my sleep I'll be fine."

WG2: "When you watch movies, can you sit back and relax, or do you always watch analytically?"

GS: "I always get caught up in a movie, even movies that a lot of people don't like. I enjoy a movie for what it is. I like to be transported to different places, different situations. I like just basically to be entertained, that's all I ask for in a movie. And if they entertain me, that's great, it's a good movie.

"One thing I enjoy about Buffy is that I was a fan of Buffy before I ever worked on it. I enjoyed the first movie that they did. And then when they started making the TV show I really got into it. I'd love to see them produce another movie now, with the characters that they have now, and the actors."

WG2: "What's your normal work schedule?"

GS: "Well, we like to say that we work from nine to six every day. But ever since the episode 'Hush,' we've been very, very busy, because every episode after that has been intensive as far as the work load goes. This one [Episode Thirteen] has been our heaviest.

"The Giles demon ['A New Man'] was a big episode, too. They were very specific about what they wanted with it, and sometimes that causes us to fall behind on our schedule because there are so many changes. You know, we get to a certain point, and it's 'we want this different,' and so that causes some late nights, but that's TV schedule. That's what happens."

WG2: "How do you go about matching somebody's concept once it shows up?"

GS: "Normally our art director, John Wheaton, is given some information and some feedback about what they're thinking about. They'll have a very brief description in the script about what the demon is, or whatever the character is."

WG2: "We've seen some scripts that just say, 'These guys are really scary.'"

O FRONT

IT LOT

d shoots Spi

MARKS

BUFF
XAN
GILE
WILL
SPIK
RILE
ANY.
FORR
JY LOT

GRAHAM	W	6:30P	7:30P	REPORT TO NEBRASKA/BUNDY LOT
STUNT COORDINATOR	W	~	6:30P	REPORT TO LOCATION
BUFFY STUNT DBL	H		HOLD	

GS: "Exactly. Like this next one coming up, for Fourteen, is 'a rough-looking demon.' That's all we know to go by. But luckily, on that, they did give us a little bit of an idea of what they wanted, so we'll be able to come up with something I'm sure. Because it's more of a minor character.

"But normally John [Vulich] will take the brief description, make a few drawings, submit them, they'll say 'okay, we like this, but want this a little bit different.' We'll get some feedback, usually from Joss, through Marc Alpert, and we'll make some changes. Normally we don't have to make too many alterations before we come up with something that they like."

WG2: "So at this stage John Wheaton is doing drawings?"

GS: "Yes. He does all of our design work. He's also a sculptor and a painter. He sculpts most of the main characters, such as the face on the Adam demon. He also helped sculpt the body, and helped paint it, as well. It's definitely a team effort. John Wheaton gives us the input as to color schemes, and directions as to how to go. We also get input from John Vulich as well. And one way or another, we get to a point where everybody's happy."

WG2: "How do you determine what level of prosthetic you're going to use? Is that determined by the script? By how mobile the character has to be?"

GS: "There are a lot of different factors involved. It depends on how much they're seen on screen, if they have dialog—that determines what their teeth are going to be like, if they're going to have to talk with false teeth in their mouth. How much they interact with other characters, how long they're going to be on screen, and also budget. What are we budgeted for for this certain character? Sometimes we have to change things, or reuse some existing pieces, like gloves, in order to try to get the budget down."

WG2: "With the concept of Adam being assembled from other demons, did you do any recycling? Not necessarily of actual pieces, but of demons that you have come up with before?"

GS: "Not on him, no."

WG2: "He's pieces of brand-new demons."

GS: "Yes, he definitely is. One of the arms he has is the Polgara demon, which is also featured in this episode. The suit itself is a suit that we've used in the past, but we altered it and changed it, so it's hopefully not recognizable."

WG2: "What's your normal amount of lead time? Did you have a little extra time with Adam?"

GS: "Yes, we had quite a bit more time. We had about two weeks to put him together, which is about twice as much time as we normally have. But there's probably about three times as much work on this one as most of them.

"Normally we'll create just a head, which would consist of a cowl piece and then a face to go on top of that, for any new demons that are featured. But on this one, there's a full body—well, it's an upper torso body. Full arms. We created new hands for him. And a cowl and a face piece, as well as the armor plating, which goes on him as well.

"There's an armor breastplate, where they said, 'We want to see an A drive on that.' What we made will be duplicated and used as an insert shot where the actors actually take a disk and put it into him. It'll appear like it's going into him."

WG2: "Do you bring the actor into the shop to fit it to him?"

GS: "Yes, we do. Normally what we like to do is get the actor ahead of time, as soon as they cast him. And then we bring him in and we do a life cast, on his head and shoulders. On George, our Adam demon, we life-cast his head and shoulders and his whole upper torso, from the thighs up. Separately we also cast up his hands and arms.

"Because we had so many new pieces to create for him, and since he was going to be a main character throughout the rest of the season they wanted him to be new and special. Luckily they scheduled him into the end of the shooting schedule, which helps us a lot."

WG2: "Once you get all the finished products here do you ever have to go back to the shop to redo or retrieve something, or do you rely on your relationship with Todd [McIntosh] and the makeup crew to adjust anything that gets here?"

GS: "Normally once it gets to set it's pretty much used as it is. TV schedules don't allow too much for taking things back and tweaking them. It would be that way for a feature film, where you'd have the luxury of doing a makeup test. We're doing one today, but for a feature it would be a week or two before it plays, instead of the day before. Any changes they ask for today, we'll be doing overnight tonight. Hopefully there won't be too many."

WG2: "Is there any type of monster that you're particularly fond of, that you keep hoping the writers find a way to fit in the show so you can do the prosthetics?"

GS: "I'm too busy trying to get them what they do want. In fact, we've had conversations in the shop about this, we've tried to think, okay, what have they not done on Buffy? They've done zombies. Adam is like a Frankenstein monster. They've done wolfmen, werewolves, fish monsters."

WG2: "They haven't done Phantom of the Opera yet."

GS: "But there was the first roommate, in college, who had a half face. When the face pulled off, when I finally saw that on camera, I was going, 'Yes, it worked.' That was one of the first episodes that I supervised, and it was the first episode we really had something that was kinda tricky. And when I finally saw that, I was very happy with myself. Hopefully Adam will be the same experience."

WG2: "What sort of things are the trickiest?"

GS: "Any time you have something other than just something that you glue onto the face, it becomes more problematic. In this case, with Kathy, we had to create an appliance that looked like there was skin torn off and a demon face underneath, and then have her own likeness on top of that. So getting all that put together and having her own likeness fit just right and everything, and have the illusion that the face is coming off, takes a bit more. But it's also the most rewarding kind of thing, when you see something work well like that."

"The 'Hush' episode, also. When I watched that, I was very happy with the way they turned out, and how creepy they looked."

WG2: "What are the difficulties of creating stuff that has to stay on people during action sequences?"

GS: "A lot of times in a script there's really no indication as to how major of a fight any of these demons get into. Sometimes we don't read into it quite right, and we have these big old horns on a demon, and she ends up doing these major backflips, and flying into walls, and things like that. It's like, 'oops.'

"A lot of times if we make things like horns out of something very rigid, we have problems with them. So we started making them out of a flexible material with an armature inside of them that will bend, so that if they do get hit, it just bends the horn. It doesn't break off. And we've had much better success with that."

WG2: "When you have someone who is undergoing a transformation, how do you determine how many pieces you're going to make, how many stages we're going to see? Like Oz the werewolf, for example."

GS: "In the case of Oz werewolf, it's funny how he has transformed from the first time we saw him. At first we used a fully mechanical head. I think they only used that the very first time. Then they decided to go to a more natural look, using more facial prosthetics rather than a mechanically operated head. It worked out very well.

"As for the transformations, it depends on how the script reads, and it depends on budget. For

| RECTOR | | James Contner | 11:00A | | 1 | Production Designer | Carey Meyer | O |
| RECTOR | | David Solomon | Prep | | 1 | Art Director | Caroline Quinn | O |

							a Ruskin	O
							Starlight	O
							l Koneff	O
							ustafson	O
							ngblood	11:0
							th Cuba	O
							Wilson	O
							ly Kelly	O

every transformation they do, if they want to see stages of transformation, there's CGI involved. Then there are different stages that they need to actually see on set, where he goes from human to partway to a little further. The makeup working with the CGI has to all come together for the transformation.

"Every time they want to show the full transformation, it becomes very expensive. So they will usually write in one transformation like that in an episode. And then the other transformations, if he transforms other times in the episode, they just do it in cuts. They will come back to it instead of showing it with CGI. And then, boom, he's a wolf. It's a lot simpler. But they want to have the production value of seeing a complete transformation at least once.

"I've been in the business now for over twelve years, and there are still things I'm learning. <u>Buffy</u> is a very good chance for me to learn more, hopefully without causing too many problems as I learn. It's a very rewarding show to work on."

							Eriksen	11:0
							asch, Jr.	11:0
							d Ronan	11:0
							ve West	O
							. Hight	per
							avidson	per
							Bumatai	per
							Val Wilt	per
							m Sahli	per
							Halaby	per
							Petersen	per
							n Hight	per

PRODUCTION: CAMERAS, ACTION!

THE PRODUCTION MEETING

The Production Meeting for Episode Thirteen is scheduled for four P.M., on December 7. About a dozen long tables abutt each other, forming a square. One of the production assistants puts out steno pads, legal pads, pens, and pencils, and a large variety of snacks and beverages. There is always plenty to eat in the production offices.

Generally, a department head or senior member of each department attends Production Meetings. The invitees for this meeting include:

Diego Gutierrez, *Assistant to J. Whedon* | **Marti Noxon,** *Supervising Producer* | **David Fury,** *Producer/Writer* | **James Contner,** *Director* | **John Perry,** *Unit Production Manager* | **Marc Alpert,** *Production Supervisor* | **Cathy Carr,** *Production Coordinator* | **Brenda Kalosh,** *1st AD* | **Edwin Perez,** *Production Accountant* | **Carey Meyer,** *Production Designer* | **Caroline Quinn,** *Art Director* | **Craig Davidson,** *representing the Construction Coordinator* | **Cynthia Bergstrom,** *Costume Designer* | **Cindy Rosenthal,** *Costumer* | **Gil Valle,** *2nd Company Grip* | **Ed Duffy,** *Location Manager* | **Kelly Harris,** *Assistant Location Manager* | **Brian Wankum,** *Post Production Coordinator* | **John King,** *Music Coordinator* | **David Koneff,** *Set Decorator* | **Gustav Gustafson,** *Leadman* | **Eric Parker,** *Best Boy Electric* | **Gus Oliva,** *Rigging Gaffer* | **Bruce Minkus,** *Special Effects* | **Greg Solomon,** *representing Special Effects Makeup (Optic Nerve)* | **Jeff Pruitt,** *Stunt Coordinator* | **Robert Ellis,** *Transportation Coordinator* | **Loni Peristere,** *Visual Effects (Digital Magic)* | **George Snyder,** *Mutant Enemy (Director of Development)*

Brenda Kalosh presides over the meeting. It's like the last team strategy session before the big game. All the departments have been prepping for the new episode—in some cases, for a couple of weeks—designing and building new sets, creating and acquiring costumes, casting actors, renting equipment, obtaining various permits, and so on. Now the director, Jim Contner, needs to make sure everyone is on the same page…so to speak.

Every person present has a copy of the script. Brenda quickly reads the breakdown of each scene. Anyone who still has a question about something asks it now. David Koneff wants to know if the Boost Bars Xander will be selling in this episode come in different colors. The director tells him they come in boxes. How many boxes? How big? Does he want chips and soda for the poker scene?

Brenda reminds Transportation they'll need the Humvees. Maggie Walsh will need a stopwatch to time Buffy. The Commandos will wear balaclavas but no infrared goggles (there is a moment—extremely brief—of joking about whether the word is balaclava, or baklava).

Every time extras are indicated, Brenda spells out how many—five Commandos; forty students in the Rocket Cafe. The director asks if the company has a stock shot of the cemetery during the day. For Spike's crypt scene, David Koneff asks the director if he wants lit candles. Mr. Contner says, "Yes." He asks locations to ask for them.

Props is told to have a couple containers of blood for Spike. Brenda notes that Scene A6, in which Buffy and Riley are being viewed on the security monitor, will be shot on video. Then she asks why the "spying POV (point of view) is being omitted." The writer, David Fury, answers that it's to maintain the secret for just a little longer.

A little further on in the script, Mr. Contner asks David Fury a couple of quick questions. Satisfied, he reports to Brenda, "All is clear."

During the first shot of Adam, Brenda wants to know if he has two arms yet. David Fury says, "Best if you don't show it." The director supplies the answer: "We'll shoot with a sheet high up over his shoulder."

David Koneff asks if he can use a big operating lamp for that scene, and Contner replies, "Good idea."

For the scene when Anya pulls Xander toward the dance floor, Brenda asks, "Do we need playback dance music?"

Brenda reminds props that they need a bunch of pagers. For the Bronze scene, she reminds them to tent the door. Then, during the scene where Dr. Angleman briefs the troops on the Polgara demon, Gareth Davies asks, "Brenda, is Mason working more than one day?" Brenda tells him no. Mason's not in the Bronze scene.

In the scene where Buffy, Riley and the rest of their team are patrolling in the woods, the stage directions state that Buffy is wearing "all sorts of gear" over her clothes. Brenda wants this spelled out. David Solomon suggests a web belt. After some discussion, they decide on a retractable cable and a black belt with pouches. Brenda underscores that they do *not* want to see Buffy with a gun. That means a total of four taser riles, some infrared binocs, a walkie-talkie, a net, and a telescoping baton.

Later on, when the Commandos are shooting at Spike, Bruce Minkus wants to know if the director wants a flash or little puff of dust?

A discussion ensues about how to show the Polgara demon's arm skewer. The director and Gareth Davies settle on an insert of the arm.

For the love scene, Brenda announces, "Body makeup and all that naked stuff."

The meeting progresses, still going rapid-fire. Will Riley need a glass of water for his pill? Is it more manly to swallow it dry? What about clamping the Polgara's stump? Cynthia Bergstrom points out that Buffy's been in the same clothes for most of the entire episode. Could she have a change? Hair needs to remember about the static-electricity scene. When Buffy's blaster is shown to be defective in the sewer, Bruce Minkus will need to provide "practical" (that is, real) sparks. When the Warrior Demon is electrocuted, he must provide "practical" smoke.

the love

d taped

y

VE TO FRC

s and shoot

YERS
lar

GILES	H	HOLD	
WILLOW	H	HOLD	
SPIKE	W	6:30P	7:30P	REPORT TO LOCATION

RONT

REMA

Brenda notes that they need to discuss the demon's death scene with Jeff Pruitt.

Brenda delivers the news that there's no crane available the day the director wanted to get a certain shot. "I was hoping to get a little mood," he says. After some discussion, they rearrange the shooting schedule to take advantage of the day they have Condor cranes.

The last major item is how to best portray Maggie Walsh's death. "What about rotoscope?" "Do we want a practical bone?" "CGI?" "How about a bone on a plate?"

"What's she wearing?"

It's decided to go with the plate.

"That's it," Brenda says, and the meeting slams to a finish.

It's time for the actual shooting. We observed on-set shooting whenever we could, as the production offices and the soundstages are less than a minute's walk from each other. We also observed the location shooting on December 15 and 16.

Most of us have seen behind-the-scenes shows that detail the step-by-step process of filming a movie or a TV episode. Still, it's a thrill to hear Director James Contner yell "Action!" and watch Xander and Anya sitting on Giles's couch just before Spike bursts in, demanding that the good guys circle the wagons. Here is the scene, reprinted from the actual shooting draft, dated December 7, 1999.

SCENE 23 INT. GILES'S APARTMENT—MORNING

Giles finishing pouring himself a cup of tea and moves into his living room.

GILES: "I don't know how many more ways I can say I'm not interested."

XANDER AND ANYA are there on the couch. Several boxes of Boost Bars rest on the coffee table.

XANDER: "Try one. Check these flavors: Cherry berry, maple walnut, almond licorice—"
ANYA: "Ew."
XANDER [forced smile]: "Anya, we don't say "ew" in front a potential customer."
ANYA: "Just skip this part and tell him you want money to buy me pretty things. He'll understand."
GILES [a resigned sigh]: "Very well. The maple walnut."
XANDER: "An excellent choice."

He hands a bar to Giles who tears it open, looks at it for a moment, then takes a bite. After a few beats of chewing, he stops and looks at Xander.

GILES: "Please leave my home now."
XANDER: "It's the gritty texture, isn't it? Maybe you're a cherry berry fellow."

He reaches for it as, suddenly, there's a desperate POUNDING on Giles's front door. Giles quickly moves to answer it. He unbolts the door, but before he can open it—BOOM!—Spike bursts in, covered in a plastic car tarp.

ANYA	H	HOLD		
FORREST	W	6:30P	7:30P	REPORT TO NEBRASKA/BUN
GRAHAM	W	6:30P	7:30P	REPORT TO NEBRASKA/BUN

SPIKE: "Close the door!"

XANDER: "Spike? You may wanna give up these morning jogs."

SPIKE: "Soldier boys are out in force. Been trying to get 'em off my scent, running 'em in circles, but they keep coming."

Giles, Xander and Anya share a look.

GILES: "And how is this our concern? Being that you expressed a desire to have nothing more to do with us."

XANDER [to Giles]: "Spike said that? About us? Well, now, I gotta tell you...that hurts."

SPIKE: "Yeah, awright...whataya want me to say? I need help. [to Giles] And no cheek from you."

Giles doesn't say a word. Spike throws off the tarp and shows them his wound.

SPIKE (cont'd): "Look. Buggers shot me. In the back."

Giles eyes Spike's bleeding shoulder for a moment.

GILES: "Remind me. Why should I help you?"

SPIKE: "Because...you do that. You're the goody-good guys. You're the bloody, frickin' calvary!"

GILES: "You can come up with a better answer than that. Why should I help you?"

Spike thinks. Then...

SPIKE: "Oh! 'Cause I helped you. When you turned into a Fyarl Demon. I helped you, din' I?"

GILES: "Out of the evilness of your heart?"

SPIKE: "Hell, no. I made you pay m—[pauses, getting it] You right bastard...."

With an aggravated sigh, he reaches into his coat and slaps a handful of crumpled bills into Giles's outstretched hand.

SPIKE: "It's all that's left. Spent the rest on blood and smokes. [muttering] Which I'll never see again."

Giles pockets the money. Spike looks at the others.

SPIKE (cont'd): "Well, come on. Circle the wagons. Tend to the wounded here. No time for layabouts."

Director Jim Contner thoughtfully provided us with portable headsets so we could listen to the dialogue. With the sensitive sound equipment available, the actors can speak in very natural voices, which is not always audible at any sort of distance. First the master shot is filmed, which shows all the actors in

387

the scene head-on, like at a play. Then different angles of each actor are filmed, called "coverage." For example, Xander's lines spoken while the camera is trained on Anya with Xander facing away from the camera, or over Giles's shoulder, etc.

After the line "That hurts," Nick Brendon once pointed at James Marsters and said, "I loved you!" The crew quietly chuckled, but the actors stayed in character until the director called, "Cut." Then everyone burst into laughter. The line wasn't used in the broadcast version, but it was very, very funny.

This is what the actors and crew do, day in, day out, until the episode is completed. Then...they begin the next one. It's a very grueling existence. Workdays of from twelve to sixteen hours are not at all uncommon. And that's not including the time the actors need to spend learning their next set of lines.

Another scene we closely observed was Scene 11, in which Tara and Willow talk in the commons. Tara offers her her family heirloom doll's-eye crystal. This scene was interesting because there were a lot of extras in it. Once their actions were "blocked," or laid out, they repeated them endlessly with each take. It was fascinating to watch them acting casual. Some extras make a living from extra work and have no higher aspirations, but many are hopeful actors themselves. It must be difficult not to look at the camera, hoping to be noticed.

THE EXTRAS

CHASE FERGUSON AND LENIN LORA

We interviewed Chase and Lenin as they were waiting to be called to the set. They were both attractive young men, well-spoken, and happy to tell us the ins and outs of extra work.

Extras really do register with Central Casting, and they call the hot line in the evening to find out what the various production companies need for the next day. Chase gets a lot of work because he fits the look of a "college-age, all-American boy." Lenin told us that he's trying to take some time off to get some new headshots, "but you get hooked in."

Some extras work because they want to become SAG actors. Others literally work for the food. On that score, Buffy's pretty lavish, they told us. "They try to give you all the bumps"—meaning, the company usually "rounds up" to the next-higher rung of compensation in terms of money or amenities in accordance with the Central Casting requirments.

The second-second assistant director is in charge of extras, who are referred to as "background." At the second-second's discretion, s/he may hand out SAG vouchers to extras who perform some kind of distinctive action or speak a line, in the event that the union-specified number of SAG members didn't show for a particular day of background work. Once an extra collects three of these vouchers, he or she may be permitted to join the union.

. . . .

Here are some pay rates for extras:

Union. . . . . $96 a day for the first eight hours

Non-union . . . . $46 a day for the first eight hours

After sixteen hours . . . . "golden time," which is double

Professionals, such as EMTs . . . . $115 a day

Stand-ins . . . . $115 a day

. . . .

CATHY CARR, PRODUCTION COORDINATOR

Cathy's desk faces the large-ringed clipboards hanging on the opposite wall that archive the call sheets for the season.

WG2: "Please tell us what your job entails?"

CC: "It's always a hard question to answer, because production coordinator encompasses so much. I kind of look at the production office as this great big sieve that everyone pours everything into, and we sort through it and either do what we need to ourselves with it or distribute it to others, get it to the person it needs to get to.

"Daily jobs—we handle all the distribution, so that's all the paperwork, all the scripts, all the schedules, all of that sort of thing [that] we are in charge of getting to all the cast, all the crew, the network, Fox, the studio, all over everywhere.

"Also, the departments come to me and say, 'Okay for this we are gonna need extra, we're gonna need a crane, we're gonna need a dolly, we're gonna need an extra camera body, we're gonna need an operator,' etc., so I get all that ready to go.

"I'm kind of one step ahead of everyone else just because it's necessary. Like what they're shooting actually today up in Santa Clarita, I've already dealt with two days ago. And I'm already on to Monday when we come back from hiatus: What are we going to need?"

WG2: "How many people are on your staff?"

CC: "There's me—I'm the production coordinator; then Lisa Ripley-Becker is the assistant production coordinator. We have three PAs—production assistants."

WG2: "Do PAs tend to stick around very long?"

CC: "Not necessarily. Because a PA job is kind of a stepping stone. The turnover rate is higher because it's your jumping point. People do that to kind of figure out what they want to do and go on to something else. It's not really a career-type position."

"We're also in charge of the call sheets which, as I'm sure you've probably learned by now, is everyone's work order for the day and the next day. All the scenes we're gonna shoot, everybody's call times, all the equipment we need, everything is on that one sheet of paper. So we're in charge of copying and distributing those when they're ready as well as the production report, which is what tells you what actually was done for that day. It's the follow-up to the call sheet. It's the reality of that day. So we know how much film was shot, how many pages were shot, if there were any setbacks, accidents. We're in charge of getting that to other people and the contracts over to Fox so that the actors can get paid. So all that paperwork from the script notes, the sound reports, the camera reports; all that stuff is sitting on my desk in the morning.

"We follow up on everything in the morning. We have to make sure the editors get the script notes, the camera reports, and the sound reports so that they can start cutting and putting everything together. And then accounting gets the production reports so that they can start budgeting the actual cost of the day. It's just a lot of that sort of thing as well as the odd requests. We get those."

WG2: "Like what?"

CC: "Marc Blucas won the football pool that we do every week. We do the football squares. So Marc won one week and wanted to do something special for the crew. So we had the Java bus come out—he bought out the bus—and so I made all those arrangements for him.

"On other shows it's been things such as, 'I need an acupuncturist on the set.' Trying to find one that will make a house call is a difficult thing. [If] any of the cast members aren't feeling well or need to be seen by a doctor, I have to make those arrangements and have the doctor actually come to the set to see them. Things like that.

"Like today: 'Where do I get a muffin basket?' Just any kind of general question comes to me. Exactly. If I don't know the answer I can find out the answer. I have a good network of other friends in the business so I can ferret it out.

"It's different from other shows I've done in the fact that a lot of the crew has been here for three or four seasons. They've been here almost the entire time, so everyone knows the idiosyncrasies and what it takes and how to get it done, so it's really a pleasure for me that everyone does their job so well. It makes my job that much easier."

WG2: "How did you get started?"

CC: "I came out here with no real plans, lived in Texas and kind of decided I needed a change and moved out here, was fairly young, got a job as a PA. Did that on two shows and started working for a producer as an assistant, then was an assistant coordinator and then started coordinating. I've been very fortunate. The nature of the business is just very up and down and you never know what is going to be next or where your next job is, but I've been very lucky.

"It's hard to describe the job. It varies from show to show. The first month you're feeling it out and how much of this do you have to do and are you expected to do that. It's part of what I enjoy about it. It changes.

"Another thing we do is make sure the Humane Society has the script, in case they have to send a person out and observe the episode when we have animals in it. If we have kids, we have to have a teacher and a welfare worker, which are usually one and the same, but we have to make sure we follow all the guidelines for SAG for minors."

WG2: "How do you organize things?"

CC: "That's a big part of the job, just being organized I write everything down [in a notebook], because no matter how good your memory is, something is gonna slip because you're just bombarded with things constantly. I just write everything, write a little box next to it, when I'm done I check it off and then move on. When I was an assistant, I worked with a coordinator who would take scrap paper, and she would write everything down. And then she would put a little circle

---

Leonard
Bailey C
Jeff Prui
Sophia (
Chris Sa
Jacob Cl

STAND
UTILITY
UTILITY
(C)=CON
TOTAL

LL DEP,
PS: sc 24
DEPT/S
IAL FX:
EUP/HA
TUMES:
ERA: sc
P/ELECTR

RT TO NEBR
RT TO NEBR
RT TO LOCA

RT TO NEBR
RT TO NEBR

SKA/BUNDY
SKA/BUNDY
SKA/BUNDY

ts,taser rifle

ATIONS: Condor placement, ITC

DUCTION: sc 18-Binocular FX in Post

L LABOR: 2 X Addl Grips; 1 X Addl Electricians

of Photography

Operator-A Cam.

Operator-B Cam.

n Operator

Cam.

Cam

Cam

am

AC

SETLIG

nting Technician

oard Operator

erator

erator

erator

erator

p Operator(s)

erator/Rigging (

amp Operators

ER

around it and then write another thing, and so there was this whole spider web of things and she would cross them off as she did them. Everybody's technique is different."

WG2: "What do the PAs do?"

CC: "They spend a lot of time on the road. They put a lot of miles on their cars. They're driving to and from and in between. The transportation department on show is really great, so they do a lot. You make a daily run to Fox and the WB. If actors aren't working, if some of the cast aren't working that day and they need the script, we have to get it to them."

WG2: "What about fan mail?"

CC: "David Goodman—he's our script coordinator—he ends up with a lot of the fan mail. He'll post things on the wall by the kitchen."

WG2: "Do you have a lot of cross-pollination with the production coordinator on <u>Angel</u>?"

CC: "Elyse Ramsdell's been great just 'cause she was here last year. They left to do <u>Angel</u> and they've been great. I can call them up with things and say, 'How did you do this before, where can I find this?' It's a lot of keeping track, but everyone here is very good and strong at what they do. It's quite easy for me, to be honest with you. It's still busy, it's still crazy, but not really as much so as I've experimented before."

JEFF PRUITT, STUNT COORDINATOR

Jeff is married to Buffy's stunt double, Sophia Crawford.

WG2: "Please tell us about the fire stunt in [Buffy's dream sequence in] 'The Prom.'"

JP: "It's what we call a full burn. It's just your basic burn."

WG2: "And Sophia did it? How did you feel about that?"

JP: "Fine. The only problem we had was, we were outside and the wind was blowing the wrong direction. So when we did it, the effects guys tried to put a fan under it to keep the wind off of her face, because what happens is we have protection all around—we have gel on the face and we have protection underneath the wedding suit. But if the wind blows, the flame wraps around and it goes up your nose or in your mouth, and then it will really burn you badly, so that's what we were watching for.

"I had to watch the wind, and when the wind kicked up and blew the flames up toward her nose I had to cut it. So we stayed ten seconds. We would have gone like twenty seconds if the wind had blown the other way. She had to stand perfectly still. When you see people on fire in full burns, normally you see them moving around; they move forward and it keeps the flames away from their face."

WG2: "Were you nervous?"

JP: "No. Because I had myself and two of my top stunt guys. They are really excellent burn guys, and we did all the protection for it, so I wasn't concerned."

WG2: "Tell me some of the doubles you've done in Seasons Three and Four."

JP: "On Buffy I've played a vampire a few times, and doubled Xander and Spike, driving and fighting, and sometimes I just jump out there."

WG2: "You were actually on camera for the season premiere, and you opened a door."

JP: "Oh, yeah, Joss just said, 'I want an innocent-looking guy, a guy who is a nice guy that you would trust opening the door. Pruitt, you look like the guy.' So he told me to stand there and open the door. No stunt, but it was funny, because all the stunts I've done on the show, no one knows about—but that one time I opened a door, they saw my face clearly. They all know me from that."

WG2: "Does anything unusual happen in Episode Thirteen?"

JP: "So far we did the ratchet and the air ramp off the hill, and then we did the wire gag with Buffy flipping off the hill and landing, and then she does a quick little combination to a couple of the guys. We were really, really rushed because they were behind shooting the acting scenes earlier in the day, so we just had a couple of quick takes on everything. We hardly moved the cameras at all."

WG2: "Obviously there are episodes that have more action or stunts in other episodes. Can you quantify stunts? Can you say how many stunts there are in an episode, how many things you plan for?"

JP: "Usually we have three fights in an episode. Often in the opening teaser we'll have a fight. They're scattered throughout the show, and then something bigger storywise at the end. It varies, but there are little stunts scattered throughout the show and usually two or three fights.

"I just try my best to make each fight a little different. Sometimes we're locked into certain sets and locations and certain actors and people, so I try to just find a way to make something new happen. There has to be a different way of ending a fight, or some different combination. It can't be exactly the same, even though the circumstances are similar. It's harder to do in the graveyard, because the graveyard is exactly the same all the time. So we have to go out there and with no special rigging, with no special equipment, we have to make something that looks a little different from the previous week. I have to think carefully about that. [Jeff showed us storyboards from Episode Thirteen.]

"This is from the other night. Episode Thirteen. Here you see Buffy comes through this gate, she looks, and she's got a weapon that Maggie has given her, and Maggie has rigged it so that when Buffy tries to fire it, it shocks her. So she comes to here, we see two demons are coming, it shocks her so the gun needs to land over here, because this is water and at the end of this fight (this is the sewer looking overhead), this is like a little platform in the sewer and this is open.

"She leaps down and kicks the two guys and does all of this fight that I have choreographed out. And I had to change it a little bit here because it was too long and involved, so I had to cut it in half. Sometimes that will happen and Joss will come down and say, 'No, no there's no time for that, we've got to cut it,' so I'll pick places and cut it in half."

WG2: "Do you have a favorite fight or favorite stunt so far in Seasons Three and Four?"

JP: "I enjoyed 'Beer Bad.' The fight at the beginning teaser, that was fun. The Spike fight that we did in 'Harsh Light of Day.' I loved the Buffy and Faith fights that I did in Season Three."

WG2: "How long does it take you to get ready to do a fight?"

JP: "I usually come in thirty minutes before. I choreograph the fight thirty minutes before the stuntmen get there. I show the stuntman and Sophia the fight, and we practice the fight for thirty minutes. Then I send them off to makeup. Then the crew and the director arrive, and I tell them what we're gonna do and they light the set. Then when the actors come and the stuntpeople come, usually we do the fight with the stuntpeople, and then we find spots that we put the actors in."

WG2: "That's all the practice you need?"

JP: "Yeah, just thirty minutes, because I have really good stuntpeople. Normally what I do is just pick what the important things are in the story, like what happens at the end and what happens at the beginning, and then where there are pieces of dialogue that I have to fit in. Then [I] choreograph the fight around that to make whatever the intention is happen."

WG2: "How do you recuperate?"

JP: "When we're on the show we don't really have much time. It's like I'm always coming back and forth to the show and [Sophia's] always recuperating from previous work and then she has a day or so, twenty-four hours to heal up before she does the next fight. So she's usually covered in bruises from head to toe. She never really heals up until the end of the season.

"What usually happens is she gets pretty beaten up so that by the time we're at right now, where we are, hiatus, she's completely burned out and she needs to rest. So I won't let her do anything over Christmas except take a break, and then when we come back she's all charged up again. Then we make it until the end of the season. At the end of the season she's completely beaten up. At the end of the second season she had the broken finger and all that stuff. She's usually like that all throughout the season. Some kind of injury all the time."

SOPHIA CRAWFORD

Depending upon the location, it is sometimes possible to rig an area for shooting one day, and leave the rigging in place to be used again the following day (or night). But if the location is too public, the stunt team must take all the rigging down the same day and store it in the van. After tonight's stunts—expected to finish around midnight—the team will have to take the rigging down. Sophia estimates it will take about an hour.

Sophia runs down the list of stunts for tonight's shoot:

SC: "First of all, Forrest's double, Eugene Collier, will be doing a ratchet back from the middle of the hill onto some pads. It's a pretty fast ratchet. And after that, Dave Huggins will be doing an air-ramp from the top of the hill onto the pads. Then I will be doing a front somersault from the hill to the ground in between the guys. When I land, we'll do a short fight combination. Then I turn the guy around, he gets tasered, and the headlights come on, and that's the end of the scene."

> Sophia Crawford played a vampire in one episode in Season Two, with Kendra. That was the week that Sarah went to do *Saturday Night Live* for the first time.

WG2: "Who is Dave Huggins doubling for?"

SC: "He's doubling for Graham. And then we have two ND stunt guys here tonight who'll be in balaclavas, you know, being two ND commando guys that we'll fight, too."

WG2: "What does ND mean?"

SC: "ND means nondescript. It doesn't mean they're not worth anything. They're great. But they're not a particular double."

WG2: "What was it like to do the fight scenes between Buffy and Faith?"

SC: "Faith's more animal-like and Buffy is more of a martial-arts expert, so when we fight together, our styles are compatible. And Karen Shepherd [Eliza Dushku's stunt double] has so much determination and so much aggression that when she comes at you, when we're rolling, you'd better be prepared. But that's what I love about her, though, because sometimes when two women fight, they might be a little bit gentle with each other, like, 'Oh, I don't want to,' you know. But with Karen, man, no way. No holds barred. She's really great."

WG2: "What do you do to train for your stunt work?"

SC: "Well, I get a good workout here. But aside from that, we have a gym at home now, which is really cool. Built the gym up. I have three heavy bags. I have a really tall heavy bag, I have a guy—a man dummy—and I have a short bag. And I rotate those three bags.

"The guy is really good because when you hit a hand, his other one comes around and you have to dodge it. It's a really cool thing. We've got it out in the backyard. We dressed him up. We put rain gear on him because we didn't want him to get wet. It looked like there was a man in the yard, it was really funny.

"Basically my training at home consists of that, swimming, and I use focus mitts for contact. Also I put two pound ankle weights on and I use two-pound dumbells, and I do shadow boxing and kicking in the mirror."

WG2: "Tell us about this episode."

SC: "We had a fight two days ago, with the demons. One of the guys that we had in the demon mask had an allergic reaction, to the latex. So we had to replace him today with another guy. And that's never happened before.

"But you know, he probably will work in the suit, but what we have to do is make sure he has a mask on, something between the latex and his skin. Because he's perfect for demons; it's not like he's gonna lose a job, no way."

WG2: "What makes one perfect for demons?"

SC: "Big! You gotta be big. He's like six-five and built, you know, but also capable of doing stunts. It's one thing to be big and built, but it's another thing to be able to move and do reactions, to be able to do the stunt work."

WG2: "I would think you would want to be small to be a stunt person."

SC: "Well, yeah, it's great to be small and nimble. But when Buffy's fighting demons, we want the opponent to look really fierce. She can't fight little guys. She's got to be fighting big demons."

WG2: "Is it hard to see in a mask like that?"

SAFETY NOTICE   IMPORTANT   READ THIS

There are covered, below-ground pits on all of the three stages on the Buffy lot. As well, there are covered pits in the exterior "graveyard" grass areas. Operation of heavy equipment (lifts, condors, etc.) in these areas is potentially dangerous. Check with your foreperson for the exact location of these hazards before operating such equipment on the stages or on the grass areas. Some pits are marked in yellow over the area of the hole, but some are located within active sets and the pit cover is not different from the surrounding floor color. The grass areas are especially hidden and difficult to spot.

RILEY	W	10:30A	11:30A	REPORT TO LOCATION
ANYA	H	HOLD		
FORREST	W	6:30P	7:30P	REPORT TO NEBRASKA / BUN
GRAHAM	W			REPORT TO NEBRASKA / BUN

SC: "Very hard. I guess they kind of just get used to it, you know. You can see. They [the Warrior Demons] didn't have any nose holes. They could only breathe through their mouths. But they do it—this is what they do for a living. They're used to it, they're trained, and they love it.

"Sometimes when the guys have really awkward mouths, they can only have food through straws. One guy, you know, snake boy, that episode ['Reptile Boy']? He had to have a mirror to see where his mouth was. It was the funniest thing. But you know, the demons this year have been great. I mean, they're always great. Todd [McIntosh, the head of makeup] always does such a splendid job, they always look really good. And scary. The Gentlemen [in 'Hush'], they were so scary. That was a good episode."

WG2: "How was it fighting the weird crazy guys, the ones who looked like they had straitjackets on?"

SC: "They did have straitjackets on. Actually, I'll let you in on a little secret. When I did my fights with them, we had to tie the flaps that were hanging down up a bit because they kept slapping me in the face. Sometimes we have to do that when there's a lot of wardrobe that's hanging down because it could hit me or Sarah."

WG2: "It has to be cool to be you because you almost always win the fight."

SC: "Yeah, but sometimes Buffy really takes a beating before she wins. I feel it, too. I have bruises all the time."

WG2: "Then do they haul you off to makeup and say, 'Can we look at how big that bruise is so we can make one on Sarah?'"

SC: "It's funny because in the summertime, I do need to do that sometimes. I have to cover my bruises with makeup because Buffy wears, you know, cooler clothing. When it comes to the winter, we always have big jackets and trousers, so we never have a problem with hiding bruises. But yeah, plenty of them. Lots of Tiger Balm and everything like that, as well, for aching muscles.

"The injuries this season have been very minimal. Ro got his nose broken in one episode, and that was about it."

WG2: "What was you scariest stunt this season? When they set you on fire?'"

SC: "When I did the burn in the wedding dress? That was great. That wasn't scary at all, I actually really enjoyed that, had a good time with that. I actually haven't had a scary stunt yet. I really haven't had a scary moment. Not yet. This season's been great. You always get an adrenaline rush before you go. Even with stunts that you've done a hundred times over and over, you always get that little bit of adrenaline rush. But that's part of the reason why we do it."

• •

STUNT DOUBLES

BUFFY ➝ Sophia Crawford • **GILES** ➝ Eddy "Doogie" Conna • **XANDER** ➝ Kevin Foster; previously Mark Wagner, who went to Cirque du Soleil • **SPIKE** ➝ Steve Tartalia/Eddie Braun • **ANGEL** ➝ Mike Massa • **WILLOW** ➝ Michelle Sebek as Vamp Willow/Jennifer Badger • **RILEY** ➝ Brian Machleit • **ANYA** ➝ Jennifer Badger • **FORREST** ➝ Eugene Collier • **GRAHAM** ➝ Dave Huggins • **OZWOLF** ➝ Lee Whittaker • **HARMONY** ➝ Sophia Crawford • **KATHY** ➝ Karen Shepherd • **FAITH** ➝ Karen Shepherd • **TAPPARRICH** ➝ Scott Schwartz • **SUNDAY** ➝ Gloria O'Brien • **WESLEY** ➝ various • **CORDELIA** ➝ Jennifer Badger

• •

	James Contner	11:00A	1	Production Designer	Carey Meyer	OC
-TOR	David Solomon	Prep	1	Art Dir	Quinn	OC
					uskin	OC
					rlight	OC
sst. Di					oneff	OC
sst. Di					afson	OC
nd Ass					blood	11:00A
nd A.D					Cuba	OC
2nd A					Vilson	OC
Traine					Kelly	OC
DGA 1						
ction S					iksen	11:00A
Super					ch, Jr.	11:00A
					Ronan	11:00A
tor of F						
ra Ope					West	OC
ra Ope					V. Hight	per SV
cam O					avidson	per SV
C-A Ca					Bumatai	per SV
C-B Ca					Val Wilt	per SV
C-C Ca					m Sahli	per SV
A Cam					Halaby	per SV
er					Petersen	per SV
2nd A(					n Hight	per SV
Lightii						

DAVID GREENWALT, CONSULTING PRODUCER

We met with David in his new offices on the *Angel* side of the building. New suites, new furniture—things certainly have changed since we interviewed him for *WG1* two years ago.

WG2: "So when you were doing Season Three in preparation for the Angel spin-off, what kind of choices did you make about Angel's character? Did you shade him differently before he was spun off?"

DG: "We knew he would leave at the end of the year. That's really what we went into the season knowing, that he would have to leave. And we knew that he and Buffy would suffer greatly with each other during the year but would come to, eventually, a mutual conclusion of how and why this is a thing that could never be."

WG2: "How did Spike come back to Buffy and stay?"

DG: "Joss, I believe, was [thinking about] 'how do I make Spike a part of the Scooby Gang in a cool, believable way?' And I think part of that feeling was the absence of Cordelia. Who's going to fill that vacuum? The Dr. Smith from Lost in Space is back in the show. And he came up with this notion that Spike has been captured by the Initiative and has had this chip implanted in his head that prevents him from doing violence on humans.

"I just thought what a great idea that is. You can have so much fun with this guy. He can hate everybody, he can do all kinds of neat things, but he can never hurt anyone. Which eventually will keep them from killing him. There's no need to kill a helpless thing. And he's a wonderful actor and we had fun. He came to Angel in Episode Three this year.

"He is a Cordelia-like character in that he can say and do anything. Obviously he's a villain and she's not, but there's a similarity in the larger-than-lifeness to both of them.

"There's also the character of Anya on Buffy, who turned into such a wonderful running character. And she was someone who guested in a show I directed called 'The Wish.' [She] turned out to be a really neat, interesting character. Again, another character who's sort of blunt and speaks their mind, not completely of this world."

WG2: "Most [of our interviewees] have been telling us that their impression of the different seasons is that One was just the heady excitement of being on, Two was light and funny, Three was very dark, and then this season is lighter again. Do you agree with that?"

DG: "You're asking the guy who's down there digging coal. Is it different today than it was yesterday? For me, it was, 'Is this little show going to make it? Oh, this little show has become a great big hit.'

"You know, you gotta come to work, you gotta break stories. It was wonderful to be associated with a hit and it was wonderful to be on a show that people got and that critics got the way it was intended, that people didn't confuse or confound or hate it. And so all that part is wonderful.

"If things get too unbelievably dark, I start whining and saying, 'bring in the clowns, where's the dancing fun?' And Joss would say, 'Okay, we're not going to make Buffy suffer in this episode, we're not going to make her cry this time.' And, inevitably, we would end up finding the stories are more interesting when she suffered and went through some thing. They had more resonance to them.

"The thing I love about this show is, one week it's farce and one week it's tragedy and you never know what you're going to get on the show. A lot of times, we make one look like the other. So you never know quite exactly what you're going to get, which I like. But I think Season Four has been like a whole new show in a way. And I felt that Joss wrote and directed a brand-new pilot for the opening episode. She had found her way and felt somewhat comfortable in her high-school world finally, and now she was little girl lost in the big world of college again and she wasn't that big noise in that world.

"I loved the way he shot it. She was always little in the [frame]. You emotionally felt every-thing just visually from the show. But you know there's some big stuff coming, so maybe Season Five will be not so much dark or light as epic, but there's all kinds of goodies coming. I don't feel the show in terms of dark and light. I just feel the show in terms of good and bad."

WG2: "What's your favorite episode?"

DG: "Boy, I loved 'Ted.' 'Stepfather One.' I think the big soul-changing episodes. I'm thinking mostly of the big Joss Whedon episodes, 'Amends,' 'Hush,' and 'Becoming.' The ones where people just had to suffer. When Oz left Willow. When people had to suffer these unbelievable changes.

"And then the wonderful farce ones, 'Zeppo,' 'Dopplegangland.' 'Ted' was probably half farce and half tragic. 'My mom's dating a guy I know is a creep.' I loved 'Gingerbread,' the idea of the town thinking the girls were witches and all the mothers tying up the girls and willing to set their kids on fire.

"They almost all move me in some way. You know, they're breaking one now about Jonathan that I just love ['Superstar']. I'd kill to direct that show. I'd give anything to direct that show 'cause I think it's going to be so unbelievably funny."

WG2: "So, with your move to Angel, how do you and Joss interact?"

DG: "I say, 'Hey, quit messing around with that show, your other show, and come here and help me on mine.' And I try to get him down here as much as possible to help us break stories. And then he weighs in, he watches cuts, he reads scripts, he does everything he's been doing on the other show, only more so. It's been a long year. We've done well. We got a lot of scripts in the bank on Angel. That's helped us get through the year."

WG2: "If you could have anything you wanted, what would you want?"

DG: "The ability to break a story really easily. A little magic tool that allows you to let go of things, not hold on to things and worry about things. I pretty much have the thing I want, which is great work-ing conditions with great people, and I have a terrific show full of people that I like. And I've been doing this for twenty-five years and that is not the way it happens every day."

WG2: "Do you have as much time to write as you want?"

DG: "No, I don't. In a way, I'm doing both more and less writing on Angel. I'm doing a lot of rewriting."

WG2: "What's your preference?"

DG: "My preference is to be writing, but rewriting is fun, too. They'll have different aspects of them, but when it's necessary to write, I can squeeze the time in. It's two jobs, you know. One is a producer job, the other one is a writing job, and somehow I have to do both."

the love

d taped

E TO FRC

and shoot

ERS

RONT

REMA

GILES	H	HOLD		
WILLOW	H	HOLD		
SPIKE	W	6:30P	7:30P	REPORT TO LOCATION
RILEY	W	10:30A	11:30A	REPORT TO LOCATION

GARETH DAVIES, PRODUCER

We saw Gareth on a regular basis throughout our visit. His office walls are still covered with headshots of the cast and guest stars, and there are red dots on the ones who have been killed. Harmony has a little bat on hers. Gareth also had a rogues' gallery of demon sketches stretched along one wall.

WG2: "Please tell us about Seasons Three and Four?"

GD: "It all blends into one after a while. It's weird with this business because you concentrate on something for a very short space of time, so some people become an expert in something very shortly. Your mind, it becomes compartmentalized."

WG2: "We just watched 'Hush' downstairs. It was amazing."

GD: "Oh, you did. That was commonly known as 'the miniseries' to me. Joss comes in that door and says, 'Oh, ah, did I mention I have this little thing that I need?' 'No you didn't, Joss.' 'Ah, could I get it?' 'What's it for?' 'Oh, for Episode Ten. The miniseries.'

"I think it came out very well. I took it home, saw the rough cut, went in the next day and said, 'You're totally forgiven, it was absolutely worth every penny.' Yes, it's extremely good."

WG2: "What was the little thing that he had to beg for?"

GD: "Oh, I don't remember. It's like, 'There's a couple of new optical effects I need....' Well, optical effects are always the stake to my heart because they're always expensive? Or it's 'Could we have another little flying piece?' Or 'You know I need this piece, which is just one shot....But it is a company move to another location sort of thing.' Actually it was a great experience—particularly now that it's over.

"It's also fun watching it with the crew who made it. Frequently they don't see the show, because on a Tuesday night at eight o'clock, we'd have to be finished at seven o'clock for them to get home. Sometimes they get home and see a little bit of it. We've got a policy here, at lunchtime we show it. If they want to borrow a cassette, they can take it home.

"But, when you're working in the business, and work long hours, you don't want to really go home and watch television. So it always amuses me on a Tuesday to go down there and watch them rather than watch the film, and I see the reaction."

WG2: "When the heads [of The Gentlemen] blew up the room just erupted in cheers. It was so funny."

GD: "The lemon curd. That's what it reminded me of, lemon curd. With The Gentlemen we did them three different ways. You didn't see their feet, so Bruce [Minkus], special effects, who is quite amazing, talked about doing something so simple, and yet it worked so well.

"He built a little square platform with a center slot in it and wheels on the corners and a bar coming up so that they could stand on it. Depending on whether he would have to pull or push, it would be one of his guys with a cable tied to the front who is pulling them this way and the camera would be just above their feet, so in that big shot there were four of them done that way and two of them were literally flying. That was two ways of doing it and then in the dormitory Bruce put up a track, almost like a curtain rail, up top, and they were flown on a cable."

RILEY	W	10:30A	11:30A	REPORT TO LOCATION
ANYA	H	HOLD		
FORREST	W	6:30P	7:30P	REPORT TO NEBRASKA / BUN

WG2: "Does anything else come to mind?"

GD: "At one point, basically they walk into the school, and they know there is something going on [in 'Doomed']. They come to this hall, and they see three demons with the open Hellmouth, and a big fight ensues, and basically the last demon jumps into the Hellmouth.

"And they realize that will be the end if he does, so Buffy jumps in after them. The way we did it was we have a blue screen, we had her stationed, and then the camera was zooming in on her. The other day we did the Hellmouth, which is basically a tunnel which she is flying toward. So Carey built this tunnel, like it's a mine shaft, and then we put the camera the other way, and went zooming this way. Then we mapped the two so it will appear that she is falling down through the tunnel.

"There are various ways of doing this stuff. It's very true that sometimes the simplest way is the best way. Sometimes we get overly complex and then we look at the end result and think, 'Ugh, that didn't work that great.' Then we do things like putting them on PVC pipe and say, 'That's terrific.' Mind you, it's been easier this year."

WG2: "Why?"

GD: "Largely because we've all hung together. Normally when you do a show, there is a tremendous turnover of people, and here there basically isn't. People come to our production meeting and don't know how the hell we do it because we say very little. It's just to make sure we've covered all bases, in case something falls through the cracks, or spelling out who was going to do something. But basically it's shorthand."

WG2: "We went to that meeting and we couldn't tell what people were talking about."

GD: "It's not that we necessarily haven't talked about it or anything. It's like in props, they say, 'Which taser is this,' or 'Which blaster is this?' 'It's the big taser,' or whatever. 'Is this Digital Magic's work or is this practical?' 'No, this is Bruce.' It really is very much a shorthand. And that's made life much easier."

WG2: "We're amazed at all the activity."

GD: "The thing that happens every year with every show is scripts. You start off the season with a certain number of scripts in hand. But you burn them off very quickly. Also because with our show, the problem is that Joss is involved in everything.

"We've discussed this many times. The studio would like him to do other things, but the way he does shows, there is only one way. And on occasions when he's let go for a day or so, he's never really happy with what happens. He's so full of vision, and sometimes he's not good at explaining that vision to you, or he thinks he has and he really hasn't.

"We had a script when we started shooting the current one. We all thought it was a pretty damn good script, and then a couple of days ago a bunch of blue pages dropped on my desk, which are revisions, and I thought, 'Why is he rewriting this scene?' Then I read it and he just tweaked it a little bit, but it became so different. The scene that we originally had was fine, but boy, this is so much better. He did it again yesterday.

"It's frustrating from a production point of view. The danger with production always is, this is not about money, it's not about saving money, it's nothing about that. It's always the end product on the screen, and if a late change improves that end product, I always think if we can afford it we're gonna go and do it. Some people in production don't think like that. But with Joss, if he ever makes a change, it's invariably a quantum leap better."

WG2: "Why is he so quick? People were talking about problems you had, or surprises, like Seth leaving. Is that part of it, or is that just a skill you acquire as you move through being in television production or film production?"

GD "It's a skill you need in television, that's for sure. In Joss' case frequently the problems that arise make something better. I can think of the instance when we had to lose Sarah to go to

399

		James Contner	11:00A		1	Production Designer	Carey Meyer	OC
CTOR		David Solomon	Prep		1	Art Director	Caroline Quinn	OC
CTOR							a Ruskin	OC
Asst. Di							Starlight	OC
Asst. Di							l Koneff	OC
2nd Ass							ustafson	OC
2nd A.D							ngblood	11:00A
2nd A							th Cuba	OC
Traine							Wilson	OC
DGA T							ly Kelly	OC
uction S								
t Super							Eriksen	11:00
tor of F							asch, Jr.	11:00
era Ope							l Ronan	11:00
era Ope								
dicam O							ve West	OC
C-A Ca							V. Hight	per S'
C-B Ca							avidson	per S'
C-C Ca							Bumatai	per S'
-A Cam							Val Wilt	per S'
ler							m Sahli	per S'
2nd A(							Halaby	per S'
							Petersen	per S'
f Lightir							n Hight	per S'

400

Saturday Night Live, and they came up with a story of turning her into a rat. Sometimes it really is the mother of invention. It really does make you think hard about your job, or what you're going to do, and I can't think of an instance where we have been hurt by it.

"Another case in point is, last season the plan was to do an episode with Spike and Drusilla coming back. We couldn't get Drusilla, as she was doing a feature somewhere. So they rewrote the whole thing just using Spike. It was a huge success. Spike is now with us permanently, and that's the reason why. So to me it just turned out wonderful!

"Joss never says a lot of what he has planned for the future. I think part of that is that he wants to keep all his options open."

WG2: "Of Season Three, what was something that you will keep as a good memory?"

GD: "The most excitement I got—and also the biggest nightmare—was this sequence, which is the final show ['Graduation Day, Part Two'].

"The scenes in the breakdown, which to me are the easy scenes, are the ones I tend not to watch at home. But the nightmare scenes, the scenes that require all these people to be firing flame-throwers and flaming arrows and have lots and lots of people and lots of stuntpeople and then lots of stunt doubles and people in prosthetics all the time, those are the bits that I eagerly watch at home. It was certainly the biggest challenge because we also had huge amounts of CGI with the Mayor and all that."

WG2: "What's something that stood out in this first half of Season Four?"

GD: "Definitely Episode Ten.

"The interesting thing also is the way young girls respond to Buffy. I've had letters which say— one specific one I can remember because I knew the little girl's grandmother, who told me about the problems that they have had within that family. And this little girl wrote to me and said, 'Buffy gives me such strength. It gives me the strength to get through a lot of problems I have in my life.' And it so happened I knew about the problems, although she didn't know I knew.

"But it was interesting, the fact little girls feel empowered by Buffy. I've never been on a television show that has had that sort of impact before."

MARC ALPERT, PRODUCTION SUPERVISOR

Marc remains the unofficial production historian; any time anyone couldn't answer a question, they said, "I'll ask Mark."

WG2: "Please tell us what you do and how you got to this job?"

MA: "Last season I was promoted to the title of production supervisor. Prior to that I worked as Gareth's assistant, and essentially as production supervisor, I'm still an extension of him.

"I got the job from Janie Kleiman, who is our vice president of production over at Twentieth Century Fox TV. After Joss and David Greenwalt finished the presentation pilot, they were look-ing for a place to do the show, for stage space, [and it was] very difficult to find some in L.A. at that time. I was on a show called Space Above and Beyond, which had just been canceled, and they came and looked at the stages and hated them.

"Janie found this spot, which at the time was just an empty, run-down warehouse and this building which was completely empty, hadn't been occupied in years. It was a mess. They decided this space would work for them. Jamie hired me to come on and work with Gareth, oversee the construction of what we now call Stage 1, which was essentially just a tin shed filled with a lot of junk and a whole bunch of holes in the wall.

"So I came on to set things up. We had sound engineers in, and then contractors; we built Stage 1, and I opened up the offices, had the phones put in, set all the offices up, and when that was done I was thinking I was just going to walk away and go somewhere else. Janie suggested I work for Gareth.

"I thought at the time, 'I'll give it a shot and if I like it, I'll stick with it. Four years later I'm still here working with him. So I liked it.'"

WG2: "You were his assistant and now you're a production supervisor."

"I get into everything from [handling] cast matters to working with the AD's in scheduling and working with him. While the AD's are still in action and one is prepping the show and the other is shooting, we'll get a copy of the script ahead of the AD, who will be prepping that next episode. So Gareth and I will break it down and look at the elements of it and see if there is anything unusual in it that we need. I'll deal with casting matters in terms of scheduling actors' availability.

"I'm the liaison between Warner Bros. and their publicity department and our show. So any publicity matters usually come through me first. You can imagine with this show there is a tremendous amount of publicity that it generates and a tremendous demand for our cast to do absolutely everything. Usually they're very good at weeding out what is worthwhile and what isn't.

"The worthwhile stuff will then come to us, and we'll try to do our best to make it work. We'll see whether or not in this episode Sarah can go to New York for three days to do <u>Letterman</u>, go do all these other talk shows—and it's a question of taking the script and seeing whether or not there are three days' work to be done without her.

"If not, we'll go to Joss and he'll have the writer do a rewrite and make it work. Everything the WB has come to us with in that sense has always been worthwhile, so we'll make it work. It makes it a little more difficult on us, but we understand and realize the importance of the publicity, and we'll schedule it and we'll make it happen."

WG2: "Tell us about 'The I in Team.'"

MA: "There will be a considerable number of extras. Usually when we use a lot of extras is when we're shooting in the school and the campus. When you need to fill the lecture hall or the campuses. Here you'll have a bunch of additional military types so they'll be commandos and you'll have some scientists, and the cast for us is actually a pretty good number of regular cast. Anya, Maggie, Forest, Graham, and Adam who will be new to us. I think we're all pretty excited about him. I think we're all excited to see how he's gonna turn out.

"As he's the new bad guy, we're spending a tremendous amount of time and resources on him to make him look that way. He probably doesn't know where the character is going or how important it is; maybe he does, but it's going to look incredible. We hope! A lot of my job is working with John Vulich and his Optic Nerve Studios in terms of getting the drawings and going over the concept of the themes with him after Joss comes up with it, and then being the liaison between Joss and Optic Nerve throughout the whole process. Make sure the designs are coming out as he wants it."

BUFFY THE VAMPIRE SLAYER
Episode #P4ABB13: "THE I IN TEAM"
ADAM #10 (FULL BODY)

the love

d taped

'E TO FRO

and shoot

ERS
ar

GILES	H		HOLD	
WILLOW	H		HOLD	
SPIKE	W	6:30P	7:30P	REPORT TO LOCATION

JAMES A. CONTNER, DIRECTOR

James A. Contner took a break during the Santa Clarita location shooting to talk to us. We were outside; it was late, cold, and windy, but he appeared to take everything in stride as the scene was lit for the next shot.

WG2: "You're a very constant presence on <u>Buffy</u> and <u>Angel</u>. How many have you done?"

JC: "I did one the second season, four last year, that's five, and this is my fourth one this season, so that's nine. And I'm doing two more, so I've done eleven. And I'm doing four <u>Angel</u>s. I've done three already."

WG2: "Please tell us how you got started in the industry, and then how your jobs led you to <u>Buffy</u>?"

JC: "I started out in a camera department as an assistant cameraman and worked my way up to be a cinematographer. I shot mostly feature films and sort of broke into television as a cameraman on shooting <u>Miami Vice.</u> I decided when I was doing that, that if I was gonna get away from features and do television, I thought I'd try to parlay my way into directing. Which I was able to do on a series, another Michael Mann series called <u>Crime Story</u>, which I shot the first season.

"Then from there it sort of took off. I sent my reel around and started getting more and more work. I did a lot of work with Stephen Cannell, who was very, very good to me. I did a lot of <u>21 Jump Street,</u> some other shows that he was doing at the time.

"What led me to <u>Buffy</u>? Caroline [Kallas] had a lot to do with bringing my name up. I remember they sent me the pilot the first season, and I think they were interested in me. They'd seen my work, were interested in me working on the show then, but I had about three years where I was doing primarily movies of the week and wasn't doing much episodic directing. So when Season Two came along they asked me to do one episode and it turned out very well."

WG2: "Which one was it?"

JC: "It was 'Bewitched, Bothered and Bewildered.' The one where all the girls fall in love with Xander. It was a Valentine show and it was very funny.

"Last year, because that worked out so well they offered me four shows. Joss was very happy with them. This season they pretty much made me exclusive to them. I was very flattered because what appeals to me on this show is that the writing is very unique to television. There is a cadence to it and it has its own dialogue, which took me a while to figure out because I'm not of that younger generation. Which is also flattering that I'm not the young, hip director that one would expect to be associated with the show. But I do get it, and so things have worked out well in that direction."

WG2: "Is there a certain cadence to the way you shoot <u>Buffy</u> that would be different from another show? Is there a <u>Buffy</u> technique, style, or signature?"

JC: "Yes and no. We're always looking for unusual and different angles in order to shoot. The nice thing about the show, what also appealed to me when I first started, it sort of has an old-fashioned style. Joss wasn't demanding that we had to shoot everything in close-up. He loves very wide angles, so we try to get a really good wide shot that is interesting and we move the camera a lot on the show, which a lot of shows do."

WG2: "Is it a two-camera show?"

JC: "It's not always a two-camera show, but we are afforded the luxury of shooting two cameras quite a bit on this show. We are also given the Steadicam quite often and the Technocrane, which a lot of shows won't

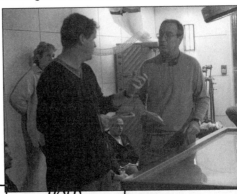

ANYA	H		*HOLD*		
FORREST	W	6:30P	7:30P	REPORT TO NEBRASKA / BUN
	W	6:30P	7:30P	REPORT TO NEBRASKA / BUN

spend the money for. Today we're using the Technocrane. So we're able to get a lot of interesting movement because of that. Going from extreme low angle to a very high angle. Because we're dealing with a lot of fights, a lot of drama in this show, those types of movements, [by] using a crane or a quick move on a Steadicam, we're able to heighten the drama quite a bit."

WG2: "Do you have a particular kind of script you like? Do you like heavy action, do you like the comedic ones?"

JC: "I like the shows that are a nice balance between comedy and action. You can almost get too much action. Although I'm sure the fans like the action-packed shows. Sometimes they are very difficult to shoot. We've done some really big fights. I did one on the last episode—Episode Eleven—where Buffy has to battle three demons who are trying to jump into the Hellmouth as sacrifices, and it's not just Buffy fighting, but it's Willow and Xander and Spike, so it was quite a big fight."

WG2: "What do you get the most satisfaction out of when you're directing a <u>Buffy</u> episode?"

JC: "I like good drama and real honest emotion, which this show gets a lot. It's also a very emotional show with the characters. Especially Buffy, who has gone through so many metamorphoses over the years. I like those scenes. I like the scenes that are really humanistic and show real compassion and real emotion."

WG2: "Is there a significant difference in the way you approach directing an <u>Angel</u> episode over a <u>Buffy</u> episode?"

JC: "They sort of have different styles. The lighting is different. I approach each show depending on the content of the script a little different anyway. I kind of try to treat each scene as its own entity. Depending on what emotion or comedic or dramatic elements we're trying to capture, it [changes] how I would shoot it. Comedy is usually funny in a wider shot and in drama you want to get tighter. It also will affect my lens choice, where a lot of times to really make the character central, I use a very long lens and sort of obliterate the background so it's almost in limbo, so the audience only focuses on what the actor is doing.

"In a different situation, not quite so dramatic, you may want to see the surrounding a little more and see what's going on, especially on the campus shots. You want to see a lot of activity. You might not use quite such a long lens or get in closer with a wider lens to the actors, so the background also becomes as important—but not more important—than the actor."

WG2: "What kind of cameras do you use?"

JC: "We use Panavision cameras, 35mm. The first two seasons were 16mm."

WG2: "Can you tell the difference?"

JC: "If you see it side by side you could. I don't think the average audience would know the difference but I think people who work in the industry can certainly see it. It's a different grain structure, it's a different contrast, especially because we do so many CGI effects. They were having to shoot those in 35mm anyway, so they were carrying a 35mm. You need the larger negative in order to work. You lose in generations the more you composite and the more optical work you do, although all the optical work now is computer-generated."

WG2: "What kind of prep do you do when you get the script?"

JC: "I first read through it a couple of times. I break it down, each scene, figure out what props I need, what special set dressing, what effects we need to do in that scene. I do pretty much the basic, general stuff because immediately we have to get all those different departments working on putting those elements together. Then we scout the locations, we pick the locations, we take all the department heads out there, and then once all the nuts and bolts are taken care of, I start working on the emotional parts of the scene. You know, what the actors need to be doing, what emotion they need to be telling the audience or giving the audience in any particular moment. How they're relating, what is the story they are telling in that particular scene.

		PRODUCTION				ART DEPARTMENT		
RECTOR		James Contner	11:00A	1	Production Designer		Carey Meyer	C
RECTOR		David Solomon	Prep	1	Art Director		Caroline Quinn	C
M							a Ruskin	C
Asst. Di							Starlight	C
Asst. Di							l Koneff	C
2nd Ass							ustafson	C
2nd A.D							ngblood	11:
d'l 2nd A							th Cuba	C
A Traine							Wilson	C
dl DGA T							ly Kelly	C
duction S								
pt Super								
							Eriksen	11:
ector of F							asch, Jr.	11:
nera Ope							d Ronan	11:
nera Ope								
adicam O							ve West	O
AC-A Ca							. Hight	per
AC-B Ca							avidson	per
AC-C Ca							Bumatai	per
C-A Cam							Val Wilt	per
der							m Sahli	per
dl 2nd A							Halaby	per
							Petersen	per
ef Lightii							n Hight	per

"I like to work with a shot list in my prep. Each day, at the end of every night or day that we shoot, I go home and sit at my computer and I break each scene down to know which shots I need in order to tell the story most efficiently; and what's going to capture each element, each emotion to tell that story as best as I can."

WG2: "Do you and [Director of Photography] Michael Gershman have a shorthand now?"

JC: "Yes, we work together very well. He knows how I shoot, and I know how he shoots. It is a good shorthand, and he comes up with very good suggestions. He knows the show since he does every episode, and I'm in and out. He's very helpful, and his work is terrific."

WG2: "Do you prefer location shooting or stage, being on the set?"

JC: "I like a combination. I think [with] these shows, you need to have a certain amount of permanent sets in order to make your days be cost-efficient. I originally started in New York in the business. The first fifteen years, pretty much most of our work was location work until the middle seventies. When the studios started to come back to New York, we started to do more and more studio work. I like location work. I like being out."

WG2: "Are you working on anything else?"

JC: "I'm doing one episode of <u>Charmed</u>. I did two of them last year."

WG2: "What is a full plate for a director?"

JC: "Basically, because there are twenty-two episodes, and a director can only do every other episode because he has to have prep time and then shoot, figure eleven shows a season, which is what I'm doing. I could do eleven and maybe a pilot or maybe a movie of the week if I wanted to work without stopping at all."

WG2: "Do you find directing satisfying?"

JC: "When all the elements come together and work, it's very satisfying. When you know you've nailed the scene and the actors have nailed it and you've shot it how you envisioned it and everybody hit all the right notes, it's very rewarding."

404

BRENDA KALOSH, FIRST ASSISTANT DIRECTOR

Brenda Kalosh is the First Assistant Director (1st AD) on the odd-numbered epsides of *Buffy*. Alan Steinman is the 1st AD on the even-numbered episodes. "The I in Team," being Episode Thirteen, was Brenda's.

During the long, grueling day (and night) of location shooting, Brenda ran the set for Director Jim Contner. If anyone called, "Jim?" she answered, "Yes?"

WG2: "What is your job description, other than 'everything?'"

BK: "On the best days it's like being a camp counselor, trying to get everybody to play baseball at the same time. On the worst days it's like being a cross between a dentist and a deviant psychologist. It's my job to schedule the show and to run the set—to try to get everybody to do what they're supposed to do when they're supposed to do it, without a lot of pain and agony.

Paula Smith, Robert Skidmore, Brenda Kalosh, Athena Alexander, and Grace Liu

"When I get a script, I generally, I break it down into all of its elements, all the different scenes and all the cast and the props and the effects and whatever we need for a scene. Then I put the scenes in the most logical order, based on a variety of things—on actor availability; if we have a special demon makeup and when that can be done; when sets can be built; and what needs to be done on location. Night work comes at the end of the week. It's like putting a puzzle together.

"And then my second AD takes those fairly broad strokes and translates them into a daily log. That becomes the call sheet and lists everything that's needed for the day. With the help of the different departments, the second AD determines what time somebody needs to come in for make-up to be ready at a certain time, and so forth. So it's a real sort of community effort on the part of ADs and the crew to make each day work as painlessly as possible."

WG2: "And you don't have a lot of time to put that all together, because you only get the script a couple of weeks before you start shooting."

BK: "We're supposed to have eight days of prep and eight days of shooting, and ideally you get the script for those eight days, but I plead the fifth."

WG2: "But the eight days of prep are also shooting days."

BK: "For the other first AD. While one's prepping, one's shooting, and vice versa. There's one staff of second ADs, the second—the key second [Athena Alexander], the second-second, [Paula Smith] and a DGA trainee [Robert Skidmore] . They do all of the episodes, and don't ask me how they manage to do that. If I had to do it every day I'd die. I at least get a little break—I work mortal hours for eight days, as opposed to our sixteen, seventeen hours [during shooting]. Door to door, I'm talking."

WG2: "What is your background for coming into the business, and what is the process that brought you to Buffy?"

BK: "I was lucky enough to get into the Director's Guild Training Program. It takes four hundred days to get into the DGA, and the Training Program is designed to provide you with on-the-job training, with those four hundred days. There's a testing and an interview process that you have to go through to get into the program. It's offered every year, and it takes about two years to get your four hundred days. Otherwise, people go the PA [production assistant] route, which is a little more difficult because you can't work in town [doing anything for which there is a union position available], and it gets complicated."

WG2: "That must be a pretty competitive field—a lot of people would want to do the Director's Guild training."

BK: "Yes, it's hard to get into the Training Program. Out of, I don't know, they get upwards of three thousand applicants per year, and they take in as few as half a dozen people to fifteen people. So it's kind of lucky to get in. It depends what they're looking for. I guess they're looking for people who can think on their feet, who can assume a leadership role....I was a high-school teacher, so it kind of prepared me for this. I do the exact same job now, from lesson plans through to baby-sitting. Same kind of thing. I just don't get to give them report cards.

"But it's the same sort of thing. The only creative outlet for the AD on the set is to do the backgrounds [direct the extras]. The first AD is the director's right hand, so you can help—it goes in varying degrees. A lot of directors don't want your help at all, in terms of shots, and what a scene may call for. But some directors let you kind of dabble a little bit in putting together shots, suggesting things. It's a middle-management kind of thing, is what I do."

WG2: "And is that an end goal? Is this what you want to do, or is this a step along the way?"

BK: "Assistant director's generally a step along the way. There's a certain age limit on assistant directors. The older you get, the less you get hired as an assistant director because of the work hours, and the pervasive thought in the industry that young people have more energy and more enthusiasm.

the love

d taped

E TO FRO

and shoot

ERS
ar

RONT

REMA

GILES	H	HOLD		
WILLOW	H	HOLD		
SPIKE	W	6:30P	7:30P	REPORT TO LOCATION

"So my logical progression is to go from assistant director to unit manager, to producer, or stay unit manager forever and ever. Very few assistant directors become directors. There are a few. We're sort of channeled more into the business end of things, you know, the nuts and bolts, than the creative, unfortunately. But I know of several ADs who have made it to director, and have made a career out of directing. I can't think of anybody in features who's done that, but in television it happens.

"I am here to be everybody's mother and everybody's mothah—you just decide which one you want me to be at any given moment. Because I can do both. I think I actually told that to Gareth in the interview, too, but I'm not sure."

WG2: "You're the queen of continuity and organization."

BK: "Yes, I am the superior mother, as opposed to Mother Superior. I don't know how the crew relates to male ADs, if they consider them a father figure or what, but a lot of times I think that they—particularly the cast, being young—see me as kind of a mom. Which is fine. Whatever works. Whatever makes them be quiet from time to time, and pay attention. Like I said, same job as high school teaching. Same job."

WG2: "What was your first job after you finished your trainee period?

BK: "Out of the training program, my first job was a feature called The Morning After. Sidney Lumet directed, and it was Jane Fonda, and Jeff Bridges. I've done a lot of things, because I've been doing this for fifteen years now, so you figure, with some exceptions, an average of a couple of shows per year.

"Mm-hmm. I became a first AD in '92, and I've done a few TV movies. I worked on Dr. Quinn, Medicine Woman for three years. Then I did a few TV movies. I occasionally still do TV movies over hiatus. And I've done Buffy for the last four years. But as a second I did . . . it's probably not very nice to say, but a lot of times when things go wrong on the show and we're looking at, you know, rubber fingernails flying everywhere, and we have a delay to glue them back on, I think to myself, 'Oh my God, my career used to consist of Mississippi Burning and Steel Magnolias. Now I'm gluing fingernails back on rubber-faced vampires.'"

"But sometimes I'd rather glue fingernails back on rubber-faced vampires, because it's more fun."

WG2: "On this particular episode, what are the main challenges that you face?

BK: "Christmas vacation is a big challenge. To try to make everybody pay attention on our last three days before two weeks off. It's just the usual. It's a lot of off-camera angst about things being ready when they're supposed to be.

"Right now, we've got two sick actors. Sarah [Michelle Gellar] is sick and Marc [Blucas] is sick, and it's crossing your fingers that they make it through what we need them to do.

"It's all boring stuff. When I listen to myself talk about it, it's like, God, so boring. I'm not doing the exciting stuff. Although not many people on a film set get to do the exciting stuff.

"It's like getting paid to play out in the backyard, a lot of times. I can't think of anything more fun to do. Especially on a show like this, where you get into silly situations. You know, guys in rubber suits and taser guns that don't really fire.

"I did a show once that had little creatures, monsters, in it, that were fun fur-covered bowling balls that would attack. It was Critters II. I don't know if you ever saw it. We laughed like crazy, off the set—just off camera, everybody was dying because there are fifty guys throwing fur-covered volleyballs at the cast. You can't do that working at a bank. As far as I know."

OM
and t

OM
er

OM
Riley

MOVE

pots ar

PLAYER!
Gellar
don
ad
gan

/8 pg

3/8 pg

pg

FRO

5/8 pg

2/8 pg

R!

TON

TON

RILEY		W	10:30A	11:30A	REPORT TO LOCATION	
ANYA		H	HOLD			
FORREST		W	6:30P	7:30P	REPORT TO NEBRASKA / BUN!	

		1	Labor Toolman	Tom Sahli	per SW
		1	Labor Gang Boss	Baha Halaby	per SW
		1	Laborer	Erik Petersen	per SW

ROBERT SKIDMORE, DGA TRAINEE

Always on his feet, one finger pressed against his earphone, "Skid" was a walking directory of where everyone was at any given time.

WG2: "You're Robert Skidmore, the DGA trainee."

RS: "Feel free to call me Skid, please."

WG2: "Skid. Can you tell us how did you get to this position at Buffy as a DGA trainee?"

RS: "Basically, the training program is run jointly by the Alliance of Producers, who negotiate all the union contracts, and the Directors Guild of America. Together they set up a separate board that becomes a training program. What the training program does is, fifteen people are selected each year...."

WG2: "How many applicants?"

RS: "I believe it starts with an application process and a written test, about nine hundred people take it. Eight hundred to a thousand or so, at two locations, here in L.A. and also in, I believe, Chicago. And from that, from the written test and the application materials, about a hundred and fifty folks are selected to do a group assessment program where they basically observe some group interaction skills, some writings and essays and such things. From that, it proceeds to an individual interview stage, board style, where the people ask you questions, and then from that they make the final selections. Of course, you started with so many people, so many qualified applicants, a person has to feel very fortunate to be selected. Those fifteen folks are then enrolled in the program. Besides some orientation and some monthly seminars and such, we are assigned, through the training office, to shows. And different television shows and movies and pilots, movies of the week, will request a trainee, the tradeoff being that I can do union work, I'm union sanctioned, but my wages are substantially less than they pay a fullscale assistant director. So, consequently, I'm learning and there's an understanding of that, that I'm in the training process, and at the same time I'm assisting with the show as much as I can. Four hundred days of work qualify you for union membership. The other route would be to work non-union shows and earn those four hundred days on my own. I'm very fortunate to be in the training program."

WG2: "So how many more days do you have left?"

RS: "This is my second show. We do them in approximately fifty-day chunks. So I have just over a hundred days. So another year and a half or so before I've done it."

WG2: "So when you're finished, will your employment goal be second AD?"

RS: "I will be eligible to join the Directors Guild as a second AD. Probably my first job will be as a second second, but the union doesn't make a distinction between key second and second. Those are just more of responsibility levels in the show. If I've done my job well, ideally then people will recommend me and hire me when that time is up."

WG2: "What have you learned or what is your experience on Buffy as opposed to your first show?"

RS: " My first show was Party of Five. The two biggest things about Buffy that have been most interesting from an AD perspective, and to be a trainee, have been the prosthetics, our monsters, our vampires and demons. Not only the excitement of how that works and was part of the plot, but also from a planning perspective—the time it takes to put these people together, how we coordinate their schedules, extended lunch periods and such for these people with our normal cast.

"And the action sequences. What's interesting on this show specifically is that I think it's still a smartly plotted and interesting show with fun characters, and these additional elements for me have been really exciting."

WG2: "Do you want to be in features or television? Do you care?"

RS: "I don't think there's anyone in this business who wouldn't want to be in features, or wouldn't say so if asked. The fact of the matter is, at this point, since I have no input on where I go, I'm just enjoying the sampling I can get. I'm going to The West Wing next. That's going to be a different kind of show from the two I've done before, another that'll hopefully be an interesting experience. And after that, who knows? Within my four hundred days, I'll do at least one feature; I'll do at least one segment on location out of L.A.—that's the goal anyway, that's the training program objective. Some people do more or less than that combination. Which means hopefully I'll be a good AD by the time it's done."

WG2: "So there are only fifteen DGA trainees at one time?"

RS: "In any given class, and there are really two classes at work at one time 'cause there's the fifteen ahead of us. It takes about two years to complete, and they select these fifteen every year. The application process started up again in October. The test will be in January. And by next May, I will be the senior class and there'll be fifteen new folks coming in after us."

WG2: "Do you have an undergraduate degree?"

RS: "Yes, I have an undergraduate degree. If you don't have an undergrad degree, there are ways of getting work equivalent, but that's a basic minimum for the program."

WG2: "Do you have to have a film degree?"

RS: "No. In fact, mine is in ethics, politics, and economics. I graduated back in '93 from Yale. Had some other life experiences before moving to L.A. just about a year ago to get into this business. I spent some time in the military, that was my time in between, for five years, and came out here. I had about nine months of set work, but in fact the essays were in no way referencing film. They're more just about life experiences and challenges and such. And the written test was an aptitude test, you know, dealing with math and verbal and problem-solving and creativity, these sort of things. Mostly my degree is good for bar conversations, and I flip through Newsweek and understand a little backstory. But I opted not to go in that direction myself. I don't regret it at all. There are other aspects of this business that interested me, and that's why I'm here now. I would like to be on my way to be a first assistant director.

"First assistant directing doesn't lead to directing or anything on the creative side. It generally leads, as you're probably aware, to production management. John Perry is where I would go on my career path. The interesting thing about this industry is, you meet so many people in so many different walks. Who knows who I'll know and what opportunities might be available for me? For now I'm focused on this.

"But I see in five years, being a good marker for looking back, seeing where I am. I plan to be an AD, maybe first in line and maybe not. It just takes a lot of days to get to first. And either I'll be enjoying this enough to continue or perhaps have some other opportunities in the writing or directing part of the industry."

WG2: "Do you work twelve-hour days?"

RS: "I work sixteen-hour days, mostly. I average about eighty a week on this show. Party of Five was about the same on hours, maybe a little less. I'm told The West Wing is maybe a little more. It's not, obviously, the hours that attracted me, but this is an exciting part of the industry and I think that all of this, all the people and the equipment, the time and the scheduling and everything that goes on behind, the idea of it all combined to create a moment on the screen, something creative—you know, it's all invisible behind it. That is actually what excited me—that's why I'm in this position."

MICHAEL GERSHMAN, DIRECTOR OF PHOTOGRAPHY

We interviewed Michael Gershman during a break in the shooting of Scene Eleven of "The I in Team."

WG2: "So, okay, this the Commons. What are you shooting right now?"

MG: "We're shooting a scene between Willow and Tara. This is just a little scene where Tara wants to get together with Willow and Willow explains to her she's sorry, she has other plans. This is the normal setup for us with the majority of the light being motivated by exterior sunlight sources."

WG2: "When you shoot at the Lockheed facility, it's so enormous, do you break it up into different pieces?"

MG: "No, we pretty much light the whole place and then go ahead and isolate the scenes and give them special lighting for the scene. I use a lot of the existing lights that are in there. There are fluorescents overhead. I use those to create a basic ambience, and then we bring in our own units, and just kind of punctuate the overhead with spots of hard light."

WG2: "Usually, when people get that fluorescent stuff on, they look so awful."

MG: "The fluorescents there are so high that they're just really an ambient light, and then I use special lights that are fluorescent film lights, called Kinoflos. We match the overall quality, but these are controllable. I can put them where I want them, and we can match the quality of the fluorescents, but they look nice."

WG2: "Since we talked to you last—it was two years ago—you've done all of Season Three and half of Season Four. How many times have you directed since then?"

MG: "I directed one episode last year, and I just completed my first episode this year. It's a learning process for me. I have much more respect for the directors that come through here. It's a hard job. This is the hardest show around for a director, because you've got the humor, the comedy, you've got the horror factor, you've got all the makeup considerations, you've got all the special mechanical effects, the ones we do on the set. You've got all the special visual effects, the ones we will do later. Then there's also Joss's vision, and his vision can be very specific, and we're all trying to realize that vision. And so it makes it very difficult. There are just a lot of elements to combine and there's never been a show that I've done that's as difficult a show as Buffy is. We like to think that we make a little mini-movie each week, each episode. We try and give it the kind of production values that you'd give to a motion picture."

WG2: "Tell us about your episode from last season and then your one from this season."

MG: "They're totally different episodes. There are much more comedic overtones in my episode this season, where my episode last season was a very serious episode about the Faith character trying to bring Buffy to the dark side, and Buffy resisting it. You know, thinking about succumbing but resisting it. And so it was not the typical Buffy, it was a much more in-your-head kind of Buffy. Whereas this year I've been able to play a broader physical humor with Tony in a demon suit, and so I enjoyed this one more than last year.

"And my next one that I do, I get Faith back again, so I'm excited about that [Episode Fifteen, 'This Year's Girl']."

WG2: "Of the three that you've done overall, which one is your favorite?"

MG: "The first one ['Passion']. I read the script, and I just saw each frame in my head. I knew exactly what it was—I just knew exactly what I wanted to do and was able to execute easily. It just came together real easily for me. As a matter of fact, after I did the first episode, I thought, 'Oh, this directing thing's pretty easy.'

"Then I did my second one, and I went, 'Oh, my God, was I mistaken. This is really hard.'

"And after this last one ['A New Man'], it is hard. Next to Joss's job, the job of the director is the toughest job here. You know, the only saving grace is that the directors get a little break in between.

"As a cinematographer I do so many shows every year—all twenty-two. So, it's day after day after day we're here. And because I'm the head of the technical crew, if any of these guys are having problems, it always comes to me. You know, 'This department isn't working with this department.' It may as well be an office, I mean the same things happen."

WG2: "In terms of the way you're working as a D.P., is there any difference between second season and third season, and third season and fourth season? Did you say, 'Okay, the look should be...or we should light different ways now or...'"

MG: "The way I always approach it is to make it interesting. What's it going to take to make it interesting? What kind of shots can we do to make it interesting? How does the lighting keep it interesting? What kind of stage can I set for the characters? It's all about giving the characters, the actors, a stage to work on."

WG2: "The last time we interviewed you, you were talking about lighting the Bronze, and you said that one of the things you liked about Buffy was that there didn't have to be logic to the lighting."

MG: "There's a logic, because I have to be somewhat logical in my job capacity in order to do this and make this work all day long.

"But the idea is that there are no rules. You can use your imagination. If you've got to shoot a television show, this one is great because all the things that make it difficult also make it fun because you're solving problems all the time.

"It's not cut and dried. It is demons. It is makeup. It is special effects. It is mechanical effects. It is comedy. It is drama. It is horror. You have all those elements, and not too many shows can do that. So I play with it. You can look at it and say, 'Oh, okay, we'll make this pretty. Okay, we'll make this....' I can bring light from places I wouldn't normally. If this were a courtroom drama, it would be different. It'd have to be more conventional."

WG2: "When you did 'Anne,' the first episode of Season Three, and they go to hell and have all those fires and stuff burning, how did you do that?"

MG: "I thought to myself, 'How do we make it look interesting? Well, we want it dark. It's a huge set. I can't light the whole thing. I want darkness, but I want highlights in there. I want things to draw your interest and pique your interest and make your eye go to certain places.'

"So that motivates the decision on where the lights go. What do I want to see here? Okay, dark, dark, dark, light, ahhh. I want somebody to look and try to see there. You know, go from the light to the darkness and darkness to the light.

"You want to control the aspect of the viewer, what they look at. Within the physical demands of the set, there's only so much you can do. It's also figuring out how to do it in two days. It's figuring out how to come up with a scheme that will work so that we can get the amount of work we need to do in the time allotted."

Operators
Operators
V18...
Coordinator-Di...

ion Manager
Location Manag
ion Asst.
an

curity
ight Security
Security
PRODUCT
edic
ruction Medic
al Wrangler
Teacher

CATERING
r
opher Ertaud-c
fast for

WG2: "When you direct, is there somebody else taking over the director of photography [duties]?"

MG: "Yes. For my last two shows [as director], it's been the gentleman who is normally our second unit director of photography, Ray Stella."

WG2: "What's the longest to set up for?"

MG: "You mean the length of time? What takes the most to light? Generally, a shot that travels. You know, we had the second season or the third season, I don't recall which, we had a shot that started in the library, came down the school hallway, came all the way down the hallway and into the lounge, and with five pages of dialogue during the whole scene. Started behind the counter of the library and came out. It was a Steadicam shot. And I think it took three hours to light. But we got five pages in one scene once we started shooting."

"A scene like that where you have so much dialogue over such...you're covering so much ground, those are the ones that are most difficult.

"I couldn't do what I do without the support of the people around me. Alan Easton. Tom Keeffer, who's the key grip. Paul Theriault, Mike Klaskin, and Chris Strom."

BRUCE MINKUS, SPECIAL EFFECTS COORDINATOR

We interviewed Bruce Minkus in tandem with Mike Stokes from the *Buffy the Vampire Slayer Fan Club Magazine*; again, our thanks to a colleague for working with us.

BM: "My job is basically mechanical effects, and anything that interacts with the computer graphics guys. So any time something has to fall over, move, blow up, or whatever, even though it's tied in with the computer guys, we do the physical part, and they add in the other parts."

WG2: "How much time do you get before they tell you what you're going to have to be doing?"

BM: "Not as much as we'd like. We'd like to get the scripts earlier, but we don't. Some shows we're definitely under the gun."

WG2: "So what do you do? Do you work with pyro?"

MB: "Yes, all the pyrotechnics, all the mechanical stuff. All the basically physical stuff. Wind, rain, fire, snow. Smoke. Any of that."

WG2: "Tell us a little bit about when you blew up the school in 'Graduation Day.'"

BM: "I think the surprise to that school was its age. I think that part of the building was [built in] 1915, somewhere around there. It's the oldest school in Torrance. It's a historical monument."

WG2: "So you blew up a historical monument."

BM: "We're sorry. The trouble with it was there were no building codes back then. So we were surprised to find out that all the roof joists were just two-by-fours. Which wasn't enough to handle the load of the explosives. So the whole roof had to be trussed up. Basically all of our stuff was floating over the top of the real roof. We had to take it to the bearing walls, which were about every twenty, thirty feet apart. So that turned into a big pain, to do that."

WG2: "What was your career path to get to Buffy?"

BM: "I started in the business in the mid-seventies. And back then it was very regimented, how you went through effects. You had to start as a prop-maker, and then you worked for so many years, and then you went into what was called the prop shop. And then you had to work there for so many years, and log hours. It was very regimented, the studio system back then. So the effects guys were on the shows and we were in the prop shop; we had to build the stuff, and then we'd go out with it. With our gag and the effects guy who did the show.

411

"They don't do that anymore. Now you can pretty much just be an effects guy if you know somebody. It's easy now. And then from there I got into the real special effects. Doing my own shows and stuff."

WG2: "What other shows have you worked on?"

BM: "I did Aaron Spelling television shows for years. And then I decided I was tired of doing television, so I went to work for some pretty big names in the effects world, in features, Michael Lantiri, and Tommy Fisher. I worked on Back to the Future 2 and 3, and Jurassic Park, True Lies, Terminator 2. On Jurassic Park I was the second unit coordinator, so I met Steven Spielberg. I went to Poland and did Schindler's List with him, was the coordinator on that."

WG2: "Do you work on set most of the time?"

BM: "Today, there's three of us. Today Matthew is on the set doing smoke. He's our on-set, so if anybody has little on-set problems to be fixed, they go to Matt and he handles that. And then whenever we do any kind of effects, then we're usually all there. I try to be there for everything, basically. I think that's why we're as successful as we are, because we're always all there."

WG2: "When a stunt person's set on fire, is that your province?"

BM: "Yes."

WG2: "When Angel is imagining he's married to Buffy, and Buffy goes up in flames—is that Sophia?"

BM: "That one was Sophia. What stunt handles is the gel and stuff, and what we're responsible for is the fire."

WG2: "And then was there also a dummy?"

BM: "There was a dummy. Did we ever actually film that? I don't think we did."

WG2: "What are the challenging things for you?"

BM: "The schedule is the most challenging thing we have on this show. It's a lot of basic stuff. They can be pretty creative, these writers."

WG2: "With snow and things like that, what are the secret recipes? Is it corn flakes?"

BM: "No, it's not corn flakes. The stuff we use now is called BioSnow, and it's cornstarch based. Plastic snow looks the best, but it's also the biggest cleanup problem. So if we can use plastic snow, we do. If it's possible to clean it up, like on the back street there or on stage, we use plastic snow.

"Outside, on the last Christmas show we worked, we snowed on San Pedro, and we snowed everywhere. We use the BioSnow for that, because it's not a cleanup problem. It just disappears the next heavy dew, or rain or whatever, it's gone. So we like that.

"And then for the snow on the ground, for the dressing, it's all foam. So all the background on that show was foam. All the ground snow and all the dressing on the trees was foam."

WG2: "What kind of cleanup is involved with that?"

BM: "Hose it down. Actually, at Universal, the cleanup was to leave it. Because once it all dissipates, once it turns back into nothing again, you can hose it off. But if you're hosing the foam down and someone catches it going out of a storm drain, even though it's totally biodegradable, it's a big deal. So cleanup on that is basically to walk away from it, which we like a lot. We can do that kind of cleanup."

ia Ruskin	OC
Starlight	OC
l Koneff	OC
ustafson	OC
ngblood	11:00
th Cuba	OC
Wilson	OC
ly Kelly	OC
Eriksen	11:00
asch, Jr.	11:00
d Ronan	11:00
ve West	OC
V. Hight	per S
avidson	per S
Bumatai	per S
Val Wilt	per S
m Sahli	per S
Halaby	per S
Petersen	per S
n Hight	per S

412

WG2: "What's been your biggest project, on <u>Buffy</u>? The Mayor?"

BM: "That ['Graduation Day, Part Two'] was probably the biggest single show. Joss's shows are always big. The first show that season ['Anne'] was pretty big, when we had the hell set. That was kind of a big one. We had big pots of fire, and liquid on fire. This last one, the one with the floating men, 'Hush,' that was a lot of rigs for floating. We flew them on wires down the hallways, and we flew them on tracks. We had a lot of floating track we laid down.

"We had carts for them that they stood on. Kind of like a roller coaster thing. We had guides, front and back. And we would just lay a track down. The biggest problem with TV is the schedule. They've got a lot of work to do every day and not a lot of time to do it. So we always try to find the quickest way to do something. And that turned out to be 3/4 inch PVC pipe on the floor. It bends really tight radiuses, and we'd just screw it down in whatever way he wanted to travel. We'd just kind of pull them through it, and they'd float through the thing. It was simple."

WG2: "Do you do that a lot, just figuring out strange ways to do things?"

BM: "All the time. We always try to find the simplest way, because that's usually the fastest. And we're simple people. So we always look for the simplest way. Sometimes there is no simple way, but we hunt for it if there is."

WG2: "What's the funniest thing that's happened so far?"

BM: "I think the funniest thing that's happened was James Whitmore's show, when it was very simply written in the script that the ground had to move. She [Buffy] had a cat, that she buries, and then it becomes a demon cat. And it was a very simple thing, we just had to have the ground undulating. And then they were gonna cut to the cat.

"And we had a four-by sheet of plywood, with kind of a set-piece on it, and we had the real cat climb up through a hole. So that was all very simple. And then James decided that he wanted to see the cat burst through the dirt, out there on location. He decided that about six in the evening, the night before we went out there. So we rigged up, a little stuffed kitten's head. And we stuck it on a piece of Laxan rod, because Laxan bends really tight tubes, and then we bent a piece of copper tubing, and stuck the head on the end and buried the whole thing under the ground. So as the ground moved, we could force the Laxan and it would force the head up. And if you twisted the Laxan it would kind of move its head around.

"So Leo was doing the head, and I think I had a paw that was coming up, too. And he did one or two too many twists and didn't realize it. So it was covered with dirt, and when it popped up it shook its head really fast, and it was crystal white on this dark dirt ground. I think it did about four revolutions. It was the exorcist cat. It popped its head out really quick and sprayed all the dirt off. And there it was, crystal white, looking at the camera."

WG2: "Can you go through your top stunts that you've done?"

BM: "Well, blowing up the school was nice. I wished they could have used more of it. They only used about twenty percent of what we did. The timing was bad because of the [Columbine] thing. I would say a good eighty percent or more of the school blowing up was cut out. But that was a fun show. And the whole thing going down the hallway.

"We had an earlier episode, and we had a bloodsucking machine that we built ['The Wish']. We had a machine that had arms that reached over, and big needles that drove into a girl and sucked all her blood out.

"Because we didn't have much time and it turned out to be a much more elaborate thing than we thought it was going to be, we were right on the wire getting it to work. We were working on it while they were shooting other scenes around it. We had no test time, we just wheeled it in and pretty much hoped it worked. And we lucked out on that one.

the love

d taped

E TO FRO

and shoot

ERS
ar

GILES	H	HOLD		
WILLOW	H	HOLD		
SPIKE	W	6:30P	7:30P	REPORT TO LOCATION

RONT

REMA

"And the snow. I think the snow scene on the Christmas show ['Amends'] was a good-looking show. I think those were our best ones. 'Hush,' I think that was a nice one too. Those were our four best."

WG2: "What kind of education background did you have going into this?"

BM: "I started right out of high school, basically. A neighbor of mine worked in the studios, and in the seventies things were booming. It was kind of one of those things you got thrown into. There's not really any college—it helps to have kind of an idea of basic, common-sense engineering. I think-common sense helps out the best of anything, with this. We probably overbuild stuff—if you were an engineer you would probably not overbuild stuff as much as we do. But we like it to go in and work, and not have to fool with it, so we tend to overbuild, I would say. Overcompensate."

Leo Solis, Bruce Minkus, and Matthew Pope

WG2: "What are you working on today?"

BM: "Paperwork. That's the other thing we have to do a lot of. And we'll start breaking down this next script today."

WG2: "How big a staff do you have?"

BM: "Myself and two. Leo Solis and Matthew Pope. And then we'll hire—for instance, blowing up the school, I think we had eight guys or so. Eight extra people, full time. It's not uncommon to have a fourth or a fifth guy on a busy show."

WG2: "What's been the most dangerous stunt you've done?"

BM: "Any time we're working with pyrotechnics, or fire. We do some big fire scenes on stage, and these stages aren't really conducive to it because the ceilings are so low. That's a problem. There's lot of sprinklers, and they're low. So it took us a while to get a feel for how much fire we could do, and for how long, without popping the sprinkler heads. Fortunately we've never done that. But I think any time we're in those situations, where the sets are always small, and they always want as much fire as they can get, I think those are times when we really have to keep our heads up and pay attention. You do things the same always, and that pretty much keeps you from getting hurt. Never change anything; that's our rule. If you do it the same every time, it'll always work."

HAIR AND MAKEUP DEPARTMENTS

Todd McIntosh, the head of the Emmy Award-winning *Buffy* makeup department, took a few moments out of his third consecutive eighteen-hour workday to begin the session.

Todd sat in one of the canvas-backed chairs arranged in a loose semicircle stage right of the vast Initiative set. Over Todd's shoulder, Riley gave Buffy her first view of the vast underground complex.

Todd's counterpart in the hair department is Michael Moore; like Todd, he is quick to praise the individual efforts of his staff while emphasizing the friendly, teamlike working atmosphere of the *Buffy* set.

Todd began by assessing the changes that have taken place since his interview in the first *Watcher's Guide*. The makeup department's workload has increased even with the addition of two staff members, and it's often still a scramble to get everything done.

Leonard
Bailey (
Jeff Prui
Sophia (
Chris Sa
Jacob Cl

STAND
UTILITY
UTILITY
(C)=CO
TOTAL

LL DEP
S: sc 24
DEPT/S
IAL FX:
EUP/HA
UMES:
ERA: sc
/ELECTR

RT TO NEB
RT TO NEB
RT TO LOC

RT TO NEB
RT TO NEB

SKA/BUNDY
SKA/BUNDY
SKA/BUNDY

ts,taser rifle

ATIONS: Condor placement, ITC

UCTION: sc 18-Binocular FX in Post

L LABOR: 2 X Addl Grips; 1 X Addl Electricians

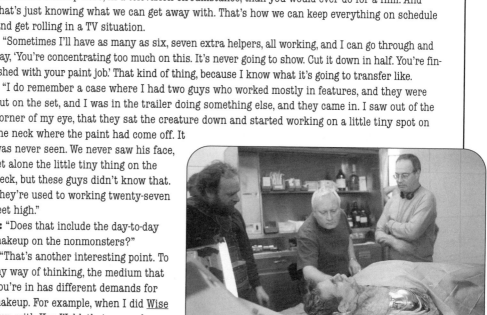

TM: "We used to have scripts that would come out with seven vampires, and by the time we got around to shooting, it was down to three. Now we have seven, and they add two more, and a couple stunt doubles."

WG2: "Does that constitute a 'makeup emergency?'"

TM: "There are no emergencies. Well, there are, but that's a part of the joke. Doing television is all about being able to handle those emergencies. That's the whole thing. You're never prepped entirely; you never get enough time. It's all about what you can pull out of your hat to make it work. And get it on set on time.

"There are a few times where we've had to change things because it wasn't exactly what Joss had in mind, but that's not even an emergency. When you've done the thing and you've shown up on set and someone says they want to change it, you change it. That's what we're here for.

"There have been a couple of times that we've ended up taking a little bit of extra time to repaint something or brighten it up. There was a demon this season, at the beginning—the group from 'Living Conditions,' that were a natural brown umber color, and they didn't really show up. So we ended up just quickly brushing them with pumpkin orange color to bring out the texture. It worked. I liked it. But that's it. That's what we do, on-feet thinking. Last-minute adjustments."

WG2: "How close is what you apply to the final product translated onto film once you put it under the lights?"

TM: "Everything goes down two or three values, especially if it has any blue in it. We do a lot more theatrical makeup here, in a television circumstance, than you would ever do for a film. And that's just knowing what we can get away with. That's how we can keep everything on schedule and get rolling in a TV situation.

"Sometimes I'll have as many as six, seven extra helpers, all working, and I can go through and say, 'You're concentrating too much on this. It's never going to show. Cut it down in half. You're finished with your paint job.' That kind of thing, because I know what it's going to transfer like.

"I do remember a case where I had two guys who worked mostly in features, and they were out on the set, and I was in the trailer doing something else, and they came in. I saw out of the corner of my eye, that they sat the creature down and started working on a little tiny spot on the neck where the paint had come off. It was never seen. We never saw his face, let alone the little tiny thing on the neck, but these guys didn't know that. They're used to working twenty-seven feet high."

WG2: "Does that include the day-to-day makeup on the nonmonsters?"

TM: "That's another interesting point. To my way of thinking, the medium that you're in has different demands for makeup. For example, when I did <u>Wise Guy</u>, with Ken Wahl, that was a drama

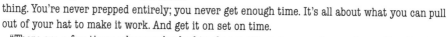

cop show. There was very little makeup, we kept everything down, and if they started to shine a little bit, it wasn't a big problem.

"For a show like Buffy, which is part comedy and part horror, we went the opposite direction. I keep the makeups in what I call a comedy style makeup. Everyone looks good. They look clean and polished and powdered. We do have more makeup on the actresses, particularly, than we would normally have in a regular straight drama. But that has more to do with the nature of the show than with how it reproduces in film."

WG2: "When they film a morph to vamp take, how many applications of makeup do you have to go through to makes the transition?"

TM: "You're going to laugh. This is my fourth year on the show and I can't answer that question.

"We've been improving the morphing procedure every season. Often, what we've got is one day of green screen. Which means that you'll see the actor in normal face, and in vamp face, on the location, and we'll either film that in two different days or we'll film it in the same day, and they'll find something else to do while I switch the makeup."

WG2: "When a creature is called for in a script, but has never appeared before, is it your job to have the final product match Joss's vision?"

TM: "That's correct. But I get my time to talk to Joss, and to talk to the ADs about what happens in the production meetings, and to coordinate between Optic Nerve and the actual filming. That's what I do. I'm the clearing house for information there. They all talk to me, I double-check, I check with the lens tech what color the lenses are going to be, check with the wardrobe about what they've styled.

"Sometimes Optic Nerve prepaints things if they're really big. Sometimes they just send it to me blank, and it's my job to create that on the day. We're very symbiotic. We're good friends, I've known John Vulich for many years now, and we work very well that way together. We have sort of almost a shorthand. We know where we're going; we all know the same products; we're all using the same techniques."

WG2: "When you have a show with as many action scenes as Buffy, is there a lot of touch-up?"

TM: "It's constant, like a little anthill. We're just climbing over the creatures all the time. That involves mutual cooperation among the set costumer, the hair department, Optic Nerve, and me. Sometimes when the creatures come in full suits, makeup's not prepared to be able to maintain those suits, and the situation is actually a crossover between costume and Optic Nerve. So Optic Nerve sends a representative. Then we do it together as a team."

[Todd gestures to the two Warrior Demons from Episode Thirteen. They are large, lumbering creatures dressed in raggedy brown robes. Watching them eat a lunch of turkey with all the trimmings earlier in the day was awe-inspiring.]

TM: "We have several styles of demons. These guys are a pull-over-the-head mask, basically. They're really not required for any articulation, or to do anything that's meant for close-up. They're very simple. Pull the mask over the head, glue around the eyes, glue around the mouth, blend it with some color and they're done.

"We also have a more complicated demon version, which is a cowl appliance, and then a face that gets glued over the top of that and blends into the cowl. Sometimes the cowl blends into the suit. That takes longer and is much harder, more detailed work.

"And then we have what are more in the style of character makeups. Appliances are over-lapped and laid on an actor. The Gentlemen would be an example of that, in the episode that just aired last night ['Hush']. That's the most labor-intensive."

WG2: "We're following the production of 'The I in Team.' Please tell us about the demons in this episode: Warrior Demons, the Polgara Demon, and then there's Adam, who's turning into a big feature player."

TM: "Well, again it's all been predicated on the time restrictions and what Optic Nerve has to do. Obviously the Adam creature, since it's going to run for a long time, has to be very well designed. They've had a lot of lead time, but that time has been used sculpting the body and face. That is a huge task.

"So while that's going on, production had to figure out what's going on with the rest of this. The two Warrior Demons are pull-over-the-head masks. They were done very quickly, very get 'em out there and get 'em done, because they are not featured.

"The Polgara Demon is one of the cowl and face types, so he will be a little bit more detailed. As of yet, I haven't seen the drawings on him, so when we do him tomorrow it'll be the first time I'm seeing this stuff, just like you. And we'll detail it as we go along.

"The one thing that they did that I wasn't expecting is throw a makeup test for Adam in. Since he works on Friday, they want to see him Thursday, so I know have two full demons to do, when I didn't plan for that. Which means that we have to bring in more people. Extra help will take care of the other demon and I'll do the Adam creature, and then we'll film him on Friday. So really, the two that are coming up, I can't tell you what they look like. I've seen videotape of the sculpture for Adam, but I haven't actually put it on yet, and I have to see what they've done with the paint job on the body.

"And naturally the arm on Adam matches the Polgara demon. So I have a general idea of what he's going to look like, but we're all going to see it tomorrow."

WG2: "Tomorrow is back here, right?"

TM: "Yes, we're out here on location. We have two permanent trailers assigned to the show. During the first year, we had one small one. Second year, we had the small one plus a second one that was casual. Then we bumped up to a really nice trailer, and last year I was able to put one on permanently as a second trailer. So we drag both of them around when we can. And we'll do all the tests in the second trailer so that it's calm and clean and separate from the day's chores in the other trailer."

WG2: "So there's always only one location that's being shot, you guys never have to divide and conquer?"

TM: "Oh, no. I've had as many as three different units going at once. We just send everything out from those trailers to the different sets. In fact, that's a real juggling job, when you have to man each set so that there's someone there watching, plus have enough manpower to get each of the actors done and all of the creatures done.

"Then there might makeup changes, because one unit will be doing morphs. So you'll start in clean face, then clean them up, and then put the vamp face on and send them back out. Meantime, first unit is doing one episode, and the other unit is doing scenes from another episode. So you have to watch the continuity on all three as well."

WG2: "Have you found yourself catching any continuity mistakes?"

TM: "It doesn't happen all that much. We have one standard makeup for most of the actors, and it changes a little bit here and there if the script demands it. If you're going out for a dinner party, or going to the prom, or something like that, then we do something different. For example, Alyson Hannigan has one standard makeup that I establish at the beginning of the year, and it stays that way for the whole season. So that really works to our advantage; they can just walk from one episode to another and not have to worry about changes."

WG2: "When you're doing appearances at conventions or whatever, is it hard to remember the specifics of something you did two years ago?"

TM: "I get a lot of Internet questions. 'What eye shadow did Sarah wear in Episode Twelve?' I try and keep records, but we're moving pretty fast in there. The thing is that, if you're working with a set of tools because that's your craft, you're probably more familiar with them than most people. So I

: sc 18- Trace
AIR/MUFX: sc
scs 20,21,22
22pt-shoot o
RIC: condor
: Condor plac
ON: sc 18-Bin
R: 2 X Addl G
UIPMENT: V

Y|SET
INT LOWELL
INT ELEVATC
INT SEWER T
IT SHOOTS
INT CRYPT
INT COMMO
INT BUFFY/M
INT TARA'S D
INT XANDER'

.OCATI
E 3

E 2

L 1
,

E 3

,

INT INITIATIVE(#12)
INT INITIATIVE
EXT WOODS

3/PT	6,8,A1MU	6/8 pg	D	LOCKHEED, SA
25PT,12PT,10,9,43PT,A33	1,6,8,11,D1,D2,ATMO	6 pg	D	
2	1,6,8,9,10,C1,C2,X,1X,9X,10X,A	1 4/8 pg	N	

TOTAL

do remember what bases I've used, I do remember what eye shadows I've used, in general. Within two or three colors. It's easy enough to keep track of that kind of thing. But I must say that these four years are starting to blur together now."

WG2: "You mentioned the Internet. Do you look in on that at all?"

TM: "Yes, it's been wonderful. The producers, and the makeup artists, and one of our grips are online all the time, and that's a shocking change in how the general public interacts with us. With the advent of <u>Fangoria</u>, <u>Cinefantastique</u>, and <u>Cinefex</u>, there are a lot more people ready and able to interact with us than there ever were in the past. And the Internet is their great opening. I'm on that posting board when I can be. It's very, very hard for me to have the time, you know, with my turnaround. But when I can, I'm there, and I'll talk to them, answer any questions that they want.

"The funny thing is, our craft, what we do for a living, is really labor intensive. You go into it knowing you've got those hours to put in, it's really hard work. And people will ask me on the Internet how to get into it, or they have an interest in makeup, what to do? And in various stages of learning for themselves. I will always say the same thing. I've said it for four years now. Send me five photographs of your very best work. I'll critique them. I'll tell you where I think you're standing and give you some direction. Not one person, in five years, has ever followed through.

"I would love to help someone in that way. And I would love to do that as a regular thing. But no one ever responds to it. Professionally, I'm willing to help anybody. Maybe someone will respond from reading this."

WG2: "What's the average amount of time that a cast member is going to be spending sitting in a chair?"

TM: "We always allow two hours [for vampires]. [For other creatures], I schedule according to the pieces Optic Nerve sends me. They'll list all the pieces and I'll say, okay, that's a five-hour job. And we're usually right on time.

"But then after the first time you've done a particular creature, it starts getting quicker and quicker, because you know the shortcuts. And every makeup is touchy; it has to be modified. Nothing goes on perfect the first time. You learn that you have to cut a little channel in the nose, you have to do this little thing, to customize it every time to the actor. After that, it gets quicker and quicker, till you can cut a five-hour makeup down to two hours, two and a half hours, if you know where you're going with it."

"We also have different levels of glue. If I know an actor is just going to stand there, or they're going to be morphed and the makeup is going to come right off, I use a very light glue that comes off with soap and water".

WG2: "Have there been any particular characters or monsters that you really just enjoy doing?"

TM: "I have to say, anything that is character-driven is much more interesting to me than the big masked demon things. For example, The Gentlemen. And the werewolf makeups. The transformational stage makeups on Oz were so much fun. And demon makeups that have a face appliance that blends into skin, like the torn-off face on Kathy in 'Living Conditions.' Those are the really fun jobs to do."

WG2: "Tell us about your department."

KILEY	W	10:30A	11:30A	REPORT TO LOCATION
ANYA	H	HOLD		
FORREST	W	6:30P	7:30P	REPORT TO NEBRASKA / BUND

TM: "This year I'm credited as makeup supervisor. By our union rules there is no such thing. You would call me department head. But my credit reads makeup supervisor.

"Under me is Robin Beauchesne, who I have known for fifteen years. We did <u>Masters of the Universe</u> together. I trust her implicitly, and she is wonderful at everything. She can do a beauty makeup, right through to the most complicated demon makeups. And that's what I look for in my department. I need flexibility. Again, we're in television, and you can't just specialize.

"The other makeup artist on our show is Douglas Noe. He also comes from a wide experience of dealing with beauty makeups on a street level, selling cosmetics for Maybelline. Then he worked into film and into prosthetics, and he has that wonderful balance of being able to do a great beauty makeup and paint anything in a monster makeup. He just has a natural gift for it.

"So Robin and Douglas are my support team, and between the three of us we just balance the show. Because the members of my department have changed a little bit, it sort of worked out this season that I'm doing the older cast members, the ones who have been with us for all four seasons, and Douglas and Robin juggle all the new cast members. And then as far as the monsters go, we toss them in whichever direction we feel like. You know, if Douglas just came off a show where I gave him most of the monsters and needs a break, then Robin will do them, and Douglas will do the straight makeups. And I step in and balance that as well.

"And the fourth member in our makeup department is Brigette Myre-Ellis, and she works with Sarah. It was a mutual decision that someone needed to be there for Sarah all the time. And I was starting to get so overwhelmed with all the rest of it."

WG2: "At the end of the day, when the actor has to take the makeup off, do you help them do that, too?"

TM: "Absolutely, that's a major part of our job. Some shows have a second team of makeup artists that come in just for removal. For the most part I try and keep all of our people to remove the makeups that they put on. You know how it went on, what the glues are and how it's going to affect the actor's skin, so you do the removal. We're there for the whole day. The glues that we use are so strong, that if you tried ripping the mask off or pulling it off, you could tear the skin. And even when we do our very, very best, we sometimes end up with little tears. There are a number of professional line solvents that we use. And again, if there are amateur makeup artists reading this article, I have to say be very careful about all of the glues you use. You have to make sure everything you use is FDA approved for working on skin. Our main adhesives are medical adhesives. One is silicone based, and the other is acrylic based, and they're used for colostomy and real prosthetics, people who have replacement pieces, to hold them on, so they are very strong."

[At this point, more of the Hair and Makeup Departments joined us.]

TM: Todd McIntosh, **MM:** Michael Moore, **DN:** Douglas Noe

TM: "Our department head of hair is Michael Moore, and his second is Gloria Casny. We have a fairly full department now, and it certainly keeps us hopping. One of the things about having a good hairdresser in the spot of department head was someone who knew wigs, could handle the stunt double stuff, and was also creative enough to be able to do monster wigs and the strange things that might come up. Like say a werewolf. And Michael has a ton of stage experience,

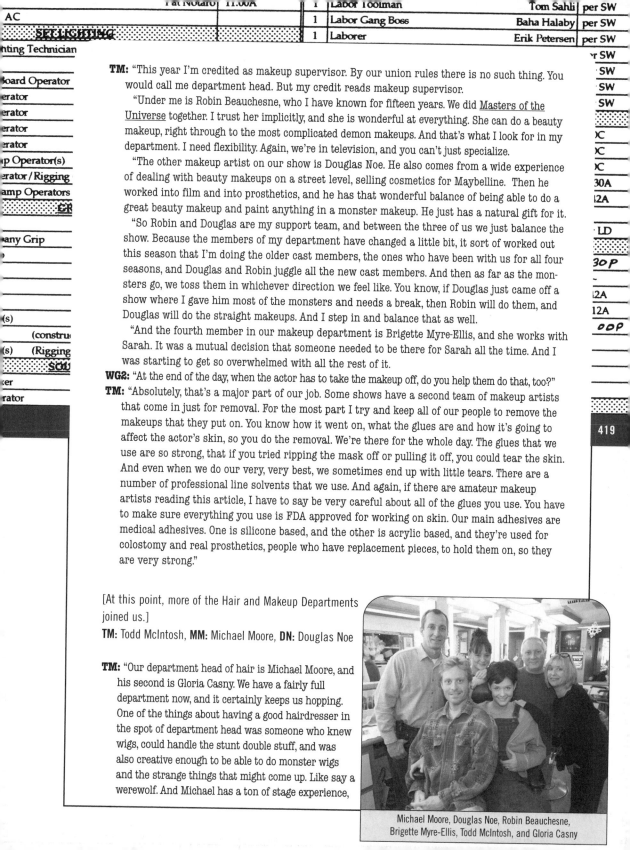

Michael Moore, Douglas Noe, Robin Beauchesne, Brigette Myre-Ellis, Todd McIntosh, and Gloria Casny

CTOR	James Contner	11:00A	1	Production Designer	Carey Meyer	OC
CTOR	David Solomon	Prep	1	Art Director	Caroline Quinn	OC

which is really a wonderful help. I guess advice to anyone wanting to get started would be to go to the theater and get some advice in theater wigs and makeup. You can always tone down to what you need for the other media. But that's the best training ground. So we have a terrific team—every one of them, the top I can find.

"Hair and makeup teams work together very, very closely, obviously. Our works are sort of connected. And Michael also has training in makeup, which helps us a lot as well, so that he knows what my problems are and I know what his problems are, and we can mesh that way. He's also, because of his many years in the theatre, very inventive, and will often come up with ideas that will help me, because he's dealt with stuff like that. It's really wonderful."

WG2: "If you're working on something where the elements seem very blended, how does that work? For example, once again, werewolf makeup. You're doing appliances, you're doing makeup, you're doing hair—everywhere."

TM: "It's another one of those things where there are so many elements to it, but each person involved is so good at their one thing that we do come together. For example, we put the prosthetics down, and then the suit is a completely different entity, and I have a wonderful wig maker, a makeup artist that I use all the time who's been terrific. He took samples of the suit home and made the wig, and neck pieces, and face blender pieces, to match the suit. So there's a relationship between him and the suit makers at Optic Nerve.

"So Michael and Gloria put the wigs down, and between the three of them they all dress it together, and he helps dress the hair into the suit, and the suit person is there to maintain it, and we all three are watching."

WG2: "How is it determined what the main character's hair and makeup will be? I know you said you have a basic makeup that you've established. How do you know, okay, we want to do a certain thing with her hair for the scene, leave it loose, put it up…how is that determined?"

MM: "Well, if they're going to the Bronze, we'll try to do something a little special, make the hair kick out a little more, ornaments….With Alyson in particular we've been doing a little thing this last season because of the breakup with Oz—she's showing some of her apathy toward life in general right now by not dressing herself up. Occasionally, though, we do try to make her perkier, a little fun, and we're hoping to kind of break out of that, start doing more, starting probably the next episode or so."

"You'll also notice if you watch, from the first season to the current season, Alyson's makeup has shifted, and it's done on purpose. She went from no makeup to a little bit more makeup to a stylized makeup that maybe her friend Buffy might have come up with with her, or Cordelia's influence might have come in, to this year where she has a very distinctive make-up on, and it's a little bit different than it has been before. She's coming more into her own as an adult. We've done that purposely over the seasons. It's a great advantage to do a show from beginning to end, because you can look long-term like that."

WG2: "How do you deal with, if an actor either changes hair for a different work, or just for fun? Is that something that you have to compensate for later?"

MM: "A perfect example is Oz. When I came in last year, I had pictures of him and he's this color. But he's coming in now and he's this color, so we have to keep him this color. For the movie he did, the <u>Austin Powers</u> movie, he had his hair dark with chunks of blue in it. We couldn't keep him with that, so really the only thing we could do was make the blue chunks black with temporary color, because he had to go back to the movie to finish that up.

"Now one of our characters that actually Joss had a lot to do with the decision on was because Tara, Amber Benson, comes in with about three inches of roots and this bleached-out hair. So it's, do you fix her hair? Do you make it look right? But what he chose was to make it more the character. And what we did was instead of correcting it, we went the opposite direction. We put dark streaks into the light. So you look at it and you don't really know what it is about it, but it's different than what you'd see in most hairstyles."

WG2: "What about the fight scenes—do you usually have to do a series of makeup?"

DN: "Like cuts and bruises? Usually it's minimal. Most of the time it's just after-effects. During a fight there's very little you do—they're so fast-paced usually."

WG2: "Have you ever had to go back and do clean face makeup on an actor who got banged up accidentally in a fight?"

DN: "Oh, yeah. Oh, yeah."

TM: "Did you tell them about the times that a foam latex mask gets torn, and you have to repair that? These are fun, too."

"I think it goes back to what we were saying about TV. Sometimes you're forced into creativity because you don't have the time to think about it, and be methodical, and plan it. Because it comes at you so suddenly, that's the exciting part. In that regard it's a lot like theater. Curtain goes up at five after eight whether you're ready or not. Moving at a fast pace is probably one of our worst nightmares, and our best teacher, forcing creativity. We fight it and we hate it and yet we appreciate the fact that it makes us really work hard."

"I think probably as you're watching how it goes on you're getting the same impressions most people do when you come to set and you look at all these people, and here's someone reading a newspaper, and here's someone lazing back in a chair over there—it looks like chaos, but in actual fact it is very close to the military. Everything is so organized.

"What I was leading up to is, Brenda is an example the way we interact with every other department is so precise. She gives us time estimates, we have things ready on time, and all that pressure is underneath all of this. We sit back and we joke and we have time to talk to you and we run and do our little thing and have a cup of tea and read our magazines, and under the undercurrent, the web that's holding it all together, is the time structure. And the AD's telling us when things need to be done and what's going to happen and anticipating that."

WG2: "Can you give us an example of something creative you did, maybe spontaneously, and then ended up loving?"

TM: "That's a terrible question to ask a group of artists, because we're all our worst critics."

MM: "I wasn't terribly happy with Willow's prom hairdo last year, but I literally had ten minutes to do it, and I was hoping for forty-five minutes to do prom hairdos. We had disaster day that day—we had torrential floods, we had last-minute things where they were taken away from us.

"So when she sat in my chair to get her hair done, they said, 'You got ten minutes.' So everything was out the window, and it was like, 'Well, let's see what this...' And as I was doing the twists and stuff, she started laughing and giggling and having a good time with it, so I felt it was somewhat of a success, although it wouldn't be what I had planned and it wouldn't be what I would do with enough time."

the love

d taped

E TO FRO

s and shoot

YERS
lar

GILES	H	HOLD		
WILLOW	H	HOLD		
SPIKE	W	6:30P	7:30P	REPORT TO LOCATION
RILEY	W			REPORT TO LOCATION

RONT

REMA

BRIGETTE MYRE-ELLIS AND LISA MARIE ROSENBERG

Brigette and Lisa Marie work together in a trailer near the other hair and makeup trailers. The prosthetic for Buffy's neck scar where Angel drank from her was tacked on the wall.

WG2: "Could you tell us what your jobs are?"

LMR: "I do Sarah's hair."

BME: "And I do Sarah's makeup. I started Season Two as a Day Playing makeup artist."

WG2: "Could you tell us, Lisa Marie, how your career path was that you ended up at Buffy?"

LMR: "Well, I did Sarah on I Know What You Did Last Summer, in North Carolina. And then we came back and I was on another show, and then it turned out that she was going to get personals third season. And then she contacted me and asked me if I was interested in coming and being her personal. And that's how I landed here on Buffy, third season."

WG2: "How many different hairstyles has she had since you were here?"

LMR: "Some episodes we'll do seven different hairstyles just in one episode. Last year we did a lot more styles. She was still in high school. It was a lot more trendy. A lot of fun things with a lot of ornaments, a lot of up-dos. This year we're taking her a little bit more sophisticated. It's her first year of college. Just more of a classic look instead of the more trendy look."

WG2: "What are some of the considerations you have to have when you're doing her hair?"

LMR: "If she's going to be doubled, how the hairstyle's going to work for her double. If it's a fight scene, are we going to be outside. Is she wearing a jacket, what's the neckline of her wardrobe, what set we're going to be on. If it has to be a scene where later in the episode, she's walking to her bedroom and she's in her pajamas. Where is that hairstyle that we started, during the day, going to end us in the evening? That kind of stuff we have to take into consideration. But I'd say the biggest consideration is what we're going to do for fight episodes, when she's doubled. Did Michael tell you they both wear hair extensions?"

WG2: "Now how did you get into doing hair?"

LMR: "I started as a makeup artist, and everyone said, 'If you can do both, you'll work so much more.' And so I went to hair school, and then there's so many more makeup artists than there are hairdressers, and I always got called to do hair, and then finally I got a call to do a show doing hair. And the show went union, so I was like, 'Well, I guess hair's my calling.'"

WG2: "And how did you end up doing makeup, Brigette?"

BME: "My mother was a makeup artist before me. She taught me all she knew. I think I was about fifteen when I worked on my first commercial."

WG2: "Do you use mostly professional makeups, or is there any kind of makeup you use that we could buy?"

BME: "We do use Maybelline. Definitely. Sarah is a Maybelline girl."

WG2: "What are some of the considerations you have to take into account when you're making her up? Like filters, or lights, or day or night?"

BME: "This is my third year here, so I know how the lighting is and I know how Michael works.

BRIGETTE MYRE-ELLIS' MAKEUP TIPS
If you aspire to Buffy-level beauty:

1. Drink LOTS of water.
2. Blend, blend, blend.
3. Don't pick! Keep your hands off your face.
4. STAY OUT OF THE SUN.

422

and t

OM
ter

OO
Ri

M

pots a

PLAYER
e Gellar
don
ead
gan
rs

eld

erts

3/8 pg

pg

FRC

5/8 pg

2/8 pg

F

TION

TION

TION

		H	HOLD		
	ANYA	H	HOLD		
	FORREST	W	6:30P	7:30P	REPORT TO NEBRASKA / BUN
	GRAHAM	W	6:30P	7:30P	REPORT TO NEBRASKA / BUN

Like Lisa Marie, I do have to take into consideration if she's going to be doubled. For most of the season, we had a scar on her neck from <u>Angel</u> biting her last season. Now that's gone. That's taken until now to go away. That was a consideration, we always had to make sure that was on the double."

WG2: "Do you tint her eyelashes, or does she wear false eyelashes?"

LMR: "She has really long eyelashes."

BME: "She has amazing eyelashes. Those are totally hers. And Maybelline Great Lash."

WG2: "She seems very pink."

BME: "Yes, I keep her very rosy-looking. That's kind of her thing. She's got these cute little rosy cheeks, and that's just Buffy. Buffy always looks pretty, cute and perky."

WG2: "For just regular makeup and hair stuff, how often do you guys do touch-ups?"

BME: "She has the most amazing, amazing skin. I go in maybe every other to every third take."

LMR: "She's super careful and conscious."

BME: "She's really good about not touching her face."

LMR: "Like she would prop her pillows up in her trailer and lay like that, unless she's really not feeling good. Then she'll say, 'I'm gonna lie down,' and she'll totally let us know. But she's really careful."

BME: "Which is really great."

LMR: "We love it."

WG2: "In the morning, how long does it take her for her hair and makeup, usually?"

BME: "We're pretty fast. I think we have her done in forty-five minutes."

LMR: "Total. She comes in with wet hair, and she walks out that door forty-five minutes later ready to go."

BME: "We've really got it down to an art. But that's just from doing somebody with great skin, and doing the same face for two years."

LMR: "She's usually on the phone for business."

BME: "Or reading the paper."

WG2: "What constitutes an emergency for you? Does she ever come out of a fight scene with bruises or anything that you have to cover?"

BME: "A few nicks on the hands or something. We just throw NuSkin on there and send her back out. She's a tough girl."

WG2: "What's NuSkin?"

BME: "You can buy it at any drugstore. It's like a liquid bandage. You just throw it on there, and it stops the bleeding. She's tough. She puts up with a lot.

"You just never know what they're going to do with a sci-fi show. It's like, 'Oh, you know what? She's going to turn into a Cro-Mag.' We're like, 'Okay.' You just never know."

LMR: "We have wigs, we have falls, extensions, any kind of cuts, bruises, prosthetics, all that stuff. Blood. We keep it in here. We're ready to go."

WG2: "Do you have any hair tips that you could impart?"

LMR: "A lot of people who blow-dry their hair straight, they like it to last for more than a day or two. And it gets a little oily at the scalp, or if you've had a rough night's sleep it gets a little sweaty. Take a little bit of baby powder and a cosmetic sponge, and just section off the hair and put a little bit of powder in there, you'll get an extra day out of your blow-out."

WG2: "How long is your average day?"

BME: "We probably have the funkiest hours of anybody."

LMR: "We have fun ones, though. Like yesterday, we only worked about four hours. But on Monday we did sixteen hours. When she works, we work."

WG2: "Did you two know each other before?"

BME: "We worked together like eight years ago. We didn't even figure it out until we had been working together for a while."

TRANSPORTATION

ROBERT ELLIS, TRANSPORTATION COORDINATOR

We interviewed Robert Ellis where he was most comfortable—sitting in the back of one of the fleet of trucks for which he is responsible. He has an extensive background in the film business through his family.

WG2: "Can you tell us sort of how you got into this line of work, and how you became associated with this show?"

RE: "I got into this line of work twenty-one years ago, right out of high school. My father, Joe Ellis, started me in the business. He was a production manager; he actually did the first season of <u>Buffy</u>. He figured transportation suited my personality the best. I think he probably figured I wouldn't get enough surf time in if I was a camera operator—then I couldn't leave the set.

"I flew to Colorado and worked on Matt Dillon's first picture, called <u>Over the Edge</u>. After that film I went to Paramount Studios, and got all the days in that were required to get into the Teamsters Union. I worked on various projects like <u>Little House on the Prairie</u>, <u>Urban Cowboy</u>, <u>Mork and Mindy</u>, a little <u>Happy Days</u>, <u>Laverne and Shirley</u>-type stuff. It was a great time. There were a lot of cool things happening.

"It was a little different then. Now, you're required to have all the licenses to drive everything. Back then, you could get in by what was like a chauffeur's license. Basically you had to be qualified as a bus driver. They didn't have the same regulations they do now. The Department of Transportation has huge, strict standards for our department.

"I drove forklifts, you know, for rigging stages, rigging all the catwalks and the lighting stuff for <u>Little House on the Prairie</u>, and whatnot; drove little lot hooties that carried set dressing furniture for all the sets. We'd go down underneath the studios, where it was just miles and miles of endless couches, and tables and lamps. And then we'd go around to the sets and dress those. I would occasionally drive a large truck out to location.

"Basically, I ended up driving a lot of stars and a lot of directors. That just seemed to suit the way I was, kind of younger and more apt to make some shakes in the morning for them, or go out and make a food arrangement, and keep their trailers clean. I was fresh in the industry, really eager to please people and do

424

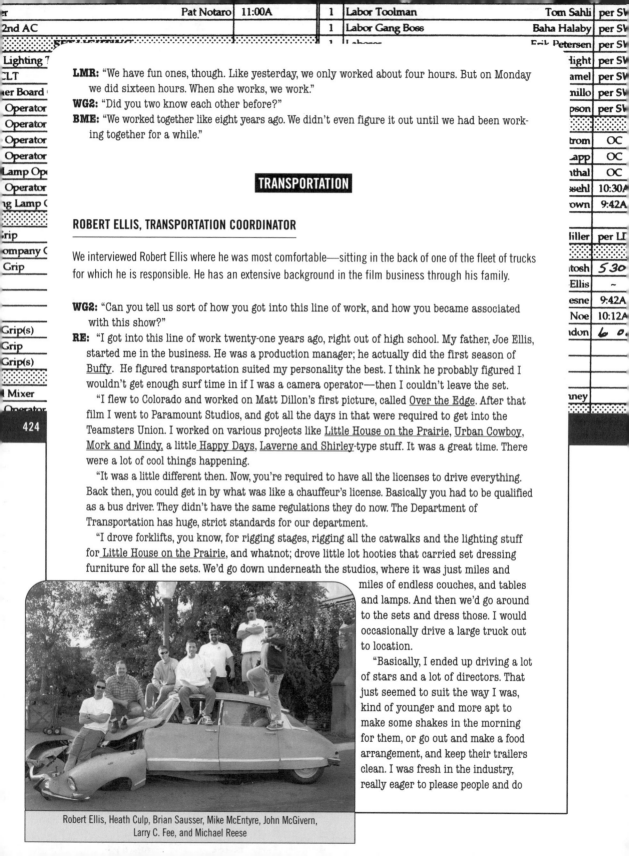

Robert Ellis, Heath Culp, Brian Sausser, Mike McEntyre, John McGivern, Larry C. Fee, and Michael Reese

well. My brother and my sister are also both in the industry, so I kind of had a little family reputation to uphold. Drove a lot of good actors, lot of good directors.

"I did a lot of television in the early eighties. I got hooked up with Stephen Cannell. I started on a pilot that we all were thinking, 'This is goofy.' And it was called <u>The A Team</u>. And it ended up, you know, part of history.

"Then we did another pilot that was kind of goofy. It was called <u>Hunter</u> and <u>that</u> ended up as part of a long-running television series.

"After a while, I worked on <u>Matlock</u> and <u>Jake and the Fat Man</u>. For the first four years I was captain on <u>Matlock</u>. I worked for a guy, Jim Antuez, who used to be John Wayne's driver. He filled me full of the best hints about when you start up a picture, going around and meeting people in the auto parts stores, and meeting tow truck drivers, and all your suppliers. You hand them your business card and tell them, 'Hey, I'll give you all the business, just give us a good deal on stuff. And I will direct everything I can to you, if you just give this company a break.' Which I still do.

"I went down to Mexico on vacation again, and Susan, my sister, called me and said, 'Hey, I'm doing this television series called <u>Buffy the Vampire Slayer</u>.'

"I thought, 'Oh, weird.' When I was into rock and roll, somebody came out with a song about Buffy from <u>Family Affair</u>. It was a satirical song about Buffy. And I thought, 'Buffy, oh, that's a name we always called, like lame, you know, Buffy or Barney.' And I thought, 'I gotta do this thing.' I cut my vacation short and came back to interview.

"And that was a great season. My dad worked on it, first season, but he retired. Subsequently I've met quite a few production managers on the show, and it's been a really good run of great people.

"One of the production managers last year, Kelly Manners, ended up going to produce <u>Angel</u>. So Gareth and Kelly, the last week or so of <u>Buffy</u> pulled me in the office. Kelly said, 'I'm going to do <u>Angel</u>,' and Gareth said 'We'll be here at <u>Buffy</u>, and we both want you to work for us. What are you going to do?' I looked at them and said, 'I'm doing both.'

"Basically I spread my crew from <u>Buffy</u>. I took two guys and Frankie [Thomas, Angel transportation captain], put 'em over on <u>Angel</u>.

"When we need something from <u>Angel</u>, a <u>Buffy</u> driver can go over and get it. When I need something from <u>Buffy</u>, an <u>Angel</u> driver will go get it. Subsequently, we kept our group small.

"Our relationship with the cast has been incredible. We're the first ones there in the morning. If [an actor] goes in their trailer and they need something, a heater, water, something's not on, or something needs to be done, or they need something, our drivers take care of it. The cast members go into their homes, which are their trailers, and if they're not happy in their home, they're not going to be happy on the set.

"Some transportation coordinators will disassociate themselves from the cast all together, just stay out of their way because they're afraid if they don't keep them happy, their jobs aren't going to last. I go the other way. I'm right in their face, first thing: 'How're you doing, Bob Ellis, transportation.' I'll tell them, 'I'm at your service, we'll do anything you need. You forget to turn your gas off at home, you need your bracelet you left, we're there.'

"And likewise, we do that for the crew, too. Flat tires, broken cars—we're taking them down to get them repaired. These people don't have time to leave the set. Drivers can leave. So part of the value of our department is that we take care of the crew, from their home to their work, and back. Occasionally we'll go out and buy some fresh snacks to bring them, you know, some cappuccinos. In this day and age, they have cappuccino machines on the set, but they didn't used to. So it was really nice to go out and get a dozen cappuccinos and bring them back to the set.

"When we did our first hiatus, I did a film with Kirstie Alley, and Brigette Myre was her makeup artist. It was called <u>Urban Legend</u>. I brought her on the set of <u>Buffy</u> the second season.

425

She knew one of the makeup artists, and she started day-playing for <u>Buffy</u>. By the third season they requested her.

"The producer, Gareth, was so considerate. He asked us if working together would affect our home life [by then we were married]. We pulled it off great.

"Another big part of <u>Buffy</u> and <u>Angel</u> is the picture cars. I'll give [David Greenwalt and Joss Whedon] choices, so I've had a slight creative impact on the cars. The bottom line is what Joss wants. And I know that when he says, 'I want a car for Giles,' I'm not going to go out and get him a racy BMW or a cargo van.

"I showed him all these—unfortunately—incredibly rare cars, that we've ended up sweating, and literally pushing them into shots sometimes, because we have cars that they don't make parts for. Citroens. Things like that. So we totaled Giles's car in the last episode [Episode Twelve, 'A New Man']. We all stood up and clapped. In fact, the guys from <u>Angel</u> who used to work on <u>Buffy</u> came to the set just to watch it get destroyed because we were happy."

WG2: "What about Xander's Bel Air convertible? When he was Car Guy."

RE: "He loved that part of his image. Some of the cast have a say in what part of their image is, and he loved the car. And he also liked to have a little surf image, so we supplied him with a couple surfboards as set dressing, so they put him in his basement, put a few stickers on. After the first season, I gave Joss a life-sized surfboard with the <u>Buffy the Vampire Slayer</u> logo on it. He flipped, he loved it, he put it in his office. Everybody was telling us about it."

WG2: "On this particular episode, how many vehicles do you have working?"

RE: "We've probably got about seventeen pieces of equipment. We've got seven cast trailers. Three makeup and hair trailers. And we've got seven or so heavy duty trucks, semis and things like that. So I'd say seventeen at the minimum. On and off we bring on extra vans and extra pickup trucks, as needed. Because we're filming here today, but tomorrow we're prepping another area, so there's a whole other crew.

"Off production I've probably got four trucks running all the time, with construction and set dressing. Construction uses a smaller type of truck, and set dressing uses a large truck. And they're pretty much a show on their own. I don't communicate too much with those drivers. They take their direction from the construction coordinator, or from the set decorating department."

WG2: "And what about on Episode Thirteen?"

RE: "On the show, I've got two Humvees, and we've got these three little white electric carts, and that is what we have on this show. <u>Buffy</u> is a light picture car show."

WG2: "Well, they're only twenty minutes from the Bronze, and they didn't drive much in high school."

RE: "Exactly. And fortunately, Buffy's mom had a brand new Chrysler, you know, the Jeep that we got from Chrysler. I have a great connection with Chrysler. They give us free vehicles whenever we need newer-looking vehicles."

WG2: "You've had a great life."

RE: "They always call transportation the backbone of the industry. We're the ones who carry. Can you imagine, tomorrow morning we have to be somewhere at six A.M. All this stuff has to move. All this stuff has to have fuel. All this stuff has to get there safely. And there's millions of dollars' worth of equipment here. And drivers are a part of the crew, but we're always away from the main shooting crew.

Leonard
Bailey (
Jeff Prui
Sophia (
Chris Sa
Jacob Cl

STAND
UTILITY
UTILITY
(C)=CO
TOTAL

LL DEP,
S: sc 24
DEPT/S
IAL FX:
EUP/HA
UMES:
ERA: sc
/ELECTK

RT TO NEB
RT TO NEB
RT TO LOC

RT TO NEB
RT TO NEB

SKA/BUNDY
SKA/BUNDY
SKA/BUNDY

ts,taser rifle

ATIONS: Condor placement, ITC
DUCTION: sc 18-Binocular FX in Post
LABOR: 2 X Addl Grips; 1 X Addl Electricians

PROPERTY

"It's like set dressing. They dress an unbelievable set, and then the company comes in and just tears it apart, shoots it, films every angle, moves this and moves that. And occasionally people will say, 'Wow, what a great job these guys did, what a great set.' But they go so unrecognized, construction and set dressing. I've driven for set dressing before, and spent days and weeks dressing sets, and all of a sudden you see this whole invasion come into this thing and just like use it all, and you're like, 'Nobody's turning around and telling me what a great job it is.' And there's a lot of it, so we pat ourselves on the back quite a bit."

THE VEHICLES OF BUFFY:

GILES → 1963 gray Citroen Coupe DS Wagon • **OZ** → 1974 Ford Econoline Van (originally in zebra pattern, now blue) • **CORDELIA** → red 4-door Chrysler Cirrus; "Queen C" license plate • **CORDELIA's DAD** → red 2-door convertible Chrysler Sebring with black top • **XANDER** → Uncle Roary's blue 1957 Chevy Bel Aire • **JOYCE:** green Jeep Cherokee Sport • **SPIKE** → 1963 black DeSoto • **SUNNYDALE POLICE CAR** → 1991 Ford Crown Victoria • **ANGEL** → 1973 rusted brown 4-door Impala (as driven on *Buffy*)

LUNCH & AN EPISODE

WHENEVER THERE'S A NEW EPISODE airing on the WB on Tuesday night, the cast, crew, and staff get to watch it first. The lunch hour is extended an extra thirty minutes, "on the house."

The TV is large and surrounded with black baffles. It's set into a corner of the lunch room adjacent to the desserts—today, cheesecakes and apple pie. The episode was "Hush."

The room was buzzing as crew and staff brought in their trays, department members sitting together. Extras approached shyly, and were invited to join groups at tables. People who usually ate at their desks came in, often to choruses of greetings, and soon the place was packed. The atmosphere was giddy and up, like that of the opening night of a highly anticipated movie.

When the lights went down and the teaser began, everyone cheered. Then they hunkered forward, watching closely. The familiar *Buffy* theme music came on, eliciting another round of cheers.

The episode was on and running. People sat back, clearly enjoying themselves; occasionally members of departments murmured to one another, usually chuckling, infrequently groaning. During the sequence in the bell tower where Riley sees the shadows of the evil Gentlemen as he stands in the street, voices yelled in chorus, "Yo! Athena!" which is the name of the second-second director. The stunt scenes got cheers. At various points in the episodes, applause, chuckles, or quick, quiet conversations broke out.

When the episode was over, there was a rousing round of applause, laughter, and cheering. A few people turned to us and said, "Well, what did you think?" It was obvious they were expecting a positive answer.

Meanwhile, chairs slid back and chatting colleagues carried away their empty trays. "Hush" was all but forgotten as everyone got back to business. Within a couple of minutes, the lunchroom was nearly deserted.

It was time to resume work on Episode Thirteen.

POSTPRODUCTION: EDITING AND PREPARING THE EPISODE

SPOTTING SESSION: "DOOMED"

We were invited to watch the spotting session for Episode Eleven. This is a viewing of the episode to date, with particular emphasis on editing, sound, and music. Composer Christophe Beck would begin work on this episode after the session.

The session took place in a large room in the production offices complex, the fourth in a row of editors' workrooms. Just past it is the office presided over by David Solomon, the producer in charge of post-production, and Brian Wankum, the post-production supervisor.

Assistant Editors Marilyn Adams and Golda Savage work out of the viewing room, as does Post-Production Assistant, Tamara Becker. Lining the wall farthest from the door are these season's episodes encased in video cassette boxes, as well as multiple copies in cardboard banker's boxes.

In attendance were: Music Coordinator John King; Todd AO Sound Effects Supervisor Cindy Rabideau; Assistant Music Editor Fernand Bos; Composer Christophe Beck; Post-Production Assistant, Tamara Becker; Assistant Music Editor Tim Isler; Sound Effects Editor Mark Cleary; Producer David Solomon, who directed the episode; Post-Production Supervisor Brian Wankum; Editor Mike Marchuin; and Executive Producer Joss Whedon.

The session got underway. On the couch, Joss handed the remote to David Solomon and said,"You have the con."

The reprise lasted for thirty-six seconds, featuring the two-shot on Buffy and Riley from the end of "Hush," where they sit in silence.

"Hey, first time no music in the reprise," Chris Beck observed.

"Don't worry. I'll give you challenges," Joss answered.

They watched the show, nods of recognition and soft chuckles at various places not always humorous or noteworthy to outside observers. Joss was clearly in charge. When the earthquake rumbling began, he

Regis Kimble, Adrian Casas, Nancy Forner, Brian Wankum, David Solomon, John King, Golda Savage, Michael Kewley, and Marilyn Adams

said, "Come in clean on the earthquake. We don't want to give it away." In another scene he commented that a character was coming off as too angry, and that the delivery of the dialogue should be toned down.

At the Porter Dorm earthquake party scene, he said jokingly, "Look. It's how old people think kids party." Later, when Willow realizes she's been lying next to a dead student, he mused, "That's actually gross. We haven't done anything gross for a while."

Later, he turned to David Solomon and said, "Big 10-4 on the cut."

They watched a fight sequence. "She's been giving us some pretty good kicks lately," Joss said approvingly. He began inventing dialogue to accompany the fight. "Just pitching," he mock-apologized to the others.

At that point Seth Green, sporting a head of very black hair, walked in with a bagged and boarded comic book. Joss leaped happily from the couch. They slapped hands and hugged. Seth held out the comic, explaining that he had come by to give it to Joss, and hoped it was something he didn't have.

Joss excused himself and the two went into the hall to chat briefly. Some people took advantage of the break to get something from the snack area. John King sang softly, "It was something in the air that night, the stars were bright, Fernand Bos," to the tune of the ABBA song "Fernando."

Joss quickly returned, and the session resumed. At intervals, Joss would look at Chris Beck and make a gesture. Chris would nod and make a brief comment, and they would both continue to watch. After three years of working together, they had their own shorthand.

At Xander's comment about "Mayor Meat," everyone chuckled in unison.

After the tape ended, the group broke up into twos and threes and began going over details. In an industry where time is money, everyone stayed on target and kept their focus.

REGIS KIMBLE, EDITOR

The editor's workrooms are usually dimly lit, if at all. There's a microphone next to Regis's bank of computer screens for actors to use to record "wild lines." Wild lines are bits of spoken dialogue not synched up to an actor's lips onscreen (called ADR, or looping).

WG2: "How many days do you have to do your edit?"

RK: "Well, they shoot for eight, and we usually have probably like three—sometimes less, sometimes more—but approximately three days after they finish their last day's dailies. Once they start shooting we have to wait for their stuff to arrive. But that's for our cut. Then the director will look at it. Then after that it's off to the producers, then after that it's off to the studio and network."

WG2: "When you're editing a scene, are you as the editor choosing if it's a master shot, or a close-up, or an over-the-shoulder that gets used? Is that your province?"

RK: "You basically go for the angle that's going to tell your story the best, and it's our job to figure out what pattern we want to show them. There's a million ways to do it. After working on a show for this amount of time you sort of get to know what they're expecting, the style they like."

WG2: "What kind of style do they like?"

RK: "It's an interesting show as far as, there is a lot of contrast. Like here [Buffy and Riley in a close-up where she tells him she's 'ready.' They step into the Initiative elevator.] you expect to drop out to a wide shot and find the two in a situation quite different than what you end up in, and so there's your contrast. So you're in this particular spot you're just trying to play their innocence and tension and his attentive-ness, and then you realize that it's over a completely different set of circumstances."

WG2: "How much footage do you have to work with, usually?"

RK: "Various directors will print more—different shows, when there's a lot of action quite often you'll get a lot of footage. And it also depends on how many characters are in the show, but it averages probably around nine hours for one hour of show."

WG2: "What was your career path that led you here to Buffy?"

RK: "I started as a P.A. Then I became an apprentice on the pilot of <u>Matlock</u>. Then by around Season Seven I started cutting for them, after I had been assisting for a while. I assisted on many different projects. A thing called <u>Tanner 88</u> for Robert Altman. A show for HBO, and the Paul Simon <u>Graceland</u> concert shot in Zaire.

"Then I started cutting <u>Matlock</u> and started working on <u>Legend</u> with Richard Dean Anderson where he was a writer in the <u>Old West</u>.

"After that I moved on to <u>The New Adventures of Flipper</u> for Samuel Goldwyn, Jr. They shot the first two episodes in Florida and then moved the whole thing to Australia, but we cut it in Hollywood. That was crazy because you had twenty hours of underwater footage of dolphins and various things going on, so you'd have to cut these elaborate sequences of dolphins doing things that were supposed to be interesting. I think that show is still going.

"I think I came here from <u>Flipper</u>. In between I've done a show called <u>119</u> with Paramount. I was one of three editors on that. I also cut a pilot for them called <u>Seven Days</u>."

WG2: "Did you do the <u>Buffy</u> presentation?"

RK: "No. David Solomon did the presentation. I did the <u>Angel</u> presentation. I've been with <u>Buffy</u> since the beginning of the series. I came on as the third editor."

WG2: "Can you explain briefly what an editor does?"

RK: "If you consider the first day of production, we don't have any dailies that day, obviously because they just started shooting, so our day really starts editorially on day two of production.

"It's interesting because it changes from project to project in some ways. Sometimes you're trying to hone in on exactly what your director is trying to accommodate and what your writer is trying to get across. And then sometimes when you have an executive producer who basically writes them all, you're taking what the director does and trying to manipulate it into what he wants.

"Joss definitely has a different take on humor. You have to get up to speed with the way it's written, and the way you cut it to make it come off as it's written."

WG2: "Basically, how do you know what picture to pick?"

RK: "Usually you judge what angle you're going to be in for the performance that's coming out of it. And what will sometimes happen is you'll start in a certain angle and you'll know by say, line five, the performance was really great in say angle 'B.' So what you have to do is, you have to choreograph how you're going to start and how you're going to go from cut to cut so that when you get to line ten you are able to accommodate that particular take.

"It's sort of like a house of cards, where you start off with a certain pattern, so that you can

3/8 pg

Pg

FRO

5/8 pg

2/8 pg

R

TION

TION

TION
·TION

	ANYA	H	HOLD		
	FORREST	W	6:30P	7:30P	REPORT TO NEBRASKA/BUN
	GRAHAM	W	6:30P	7:30P	REPORT TO NEBRASKA/BUN

end up at a specific place in the film. And sometimes that can change, and then out of surprise you almost have to start over completely, because everything was shuffled to get to that spot. Its basically gauged on performance and telling the story, because it's no good to have everything in close-ups if no one can see what they're doing with their hands. So you have to show them both."

WG2: "Can you take maybe the first half of one shot, and edit in the second half of another shot?"

RK: "You do that all the time. Basically you read where you're coming from, you read the scene you're working on, and you read where you're going to. And you've read the whole script, so you know what the subtext is, and what's important to each character as you're going along.

"It's funny because you might see something in dailies and you say, 'Ah, that's great, and I'd really love to be able to use that,' and sometimes once your scene is cut that particular moment doesn't really apply anymore, because the scene is not about that. But that's just part of the deal, and you just have to weed through it and continually massage it into telling the story. So you'll steal pieces from anywhere you can."

WG2: "Once you cut it, does it become a new entity?"

RK: "It's funny, I've worked with different producers that have the idea that what's written is different from what's shot is different from what's cut. But I think that Joss knows the script so well that he'll get word-specific. He'll say, 'She's supposed to say 'was' instead of 'were.'' They write it the way they want to see it. Once you get into changes sometimes you can't do the things they're asking, and it's not like they compare what you've done from what they've asked you to do. They might down the road say, 'Hey, did you ever try that?' And you could say, 'Yeah but the angle doesn't exist,' or 'There was a camera bump.' There're a million reasons why you can't use something. There're always ways around it you could try, but sometimes you can't."

WG2: "Tell us something that was especially hard to do?"

RK: "'The Zeppo' was a really hard episode. On that particular episode, it was a very fine line between what was going to be funny and what was going to be horrific. It was the treatment of Xander, especially when he confronts his nemesis at the end, in front of the bomb. There was a conflict of how to interpret Xander at that point, where he was supposed to become comfortable in the fact that he was okay with sacrificing himself for his ideals and friends. So that was an interesting lesson to work on. They had to re-shoot some stuff for that."

WG2: "What about this season?"

RK: "'Hush' was pretty interesting to work on because of the lack of dialogue."

WG2: "Did anybody blow it? Did they forget and speak?"

RK: "No, none of the actors did. I mean, it's really hard to take a punch without grunting and stuff, so there's always going to be some noise. The actors were pretty amazing. They all hit it."

WG2: "How many hours a day do you work here?"

RK: "It depends. The first few days, depending on how much footage you're getting, can be just your usual eight-hour days. But then what will start to happen is, as more and more footage comes in, you start going over what you've already cut and it starts to get into, fifteen-hour days. You start getting crazy, and then right before you show it to them, you have to add all your music and sound effects, that are temporary, so you have to find soundtracks that seem to work with the story. Some places, that's no big deal, they don't care what music you throw in there. But here they really like to get a sense; basically you're cutting for how you think it should go on the air."

MARILYN ADAMS, ASSISTANT EDITOR

Marilyn Adams and the other assistant editor, Golda Savage, told us about an excellent book written by Barbara Clark, who is in charge of *Buffy* foreign distribution [*Guide to Post-production for TV and Film: Managing the Process*, by Barbara Clark and Susan J. Spohr; Focal Press: 1998].

WG2: "What was your career path that lead you to <u>Buffy</u>? How did you become an editor?"

MA: "I went to UCLA Film School many, many moons ago, and I worked in film. I never worked in video. Then I had two kids, so I took eight years off. When I left we were on flatbeds on film, and when I came back we were on Avids [computer systems], so I had to go with an editor that I had worked with before I took a leave of absence. Trained on it for four months, and then his assistant got another job, so he was able to bring me on. If it hadn't been for that, I would probably still be unemployed, because it's very difficult to get your first job on an Avid, especially with no experience. That was <u>Dark Skies</u>.

"So I did that season of <u>Dark Skies</u> and then it got canceled. That editor went onto a different show, and couldn't take me because they already were staffed with assistants. Then I started looking for work, and I knew a couple of the people here because I had done a pilot in this building. I interviewed and was fortunate enough to get the job."

WG2: "What is your favorite part of <u>Buffy</u>?"

MA: "The writing. I think it's really good writing. It's really funny. I think it's really good for kids, and for teenagers especially, that have all this angst and questioning. I have a teenager, and I think it's really almost like a public service on that level."

WG2: "What does the editor put into the cut?"

MA: "We put everything in. It's word by word. I was going through the script this morning, and started making a list of the different temp sound effects that we'll need for this specific show. We're gonna need this stock, and then we're gonna need ADR, Additional Dialogue Replacement, so he [Regis Kimble] can include that in the cut. Just trying to go through and make note of things like that."

WG2: "What about the special effects?"

MA: "I order those. The editor designs them generally, but again that's to the script. This script, we have a lot because we have the Initiative we're dealing with now. They wear a lot infrared glasses, or night-vision glasses or something, so the whole thing will be toned green.

"We've also got these head-cam things, so there'll be all those monitors and stuff, so they're gonna have to shoot stuff ahead. In this script also, there's the camera in Riley's bedroom, and then we see all the monitors, and see Maggie watching Buffy and Riley in his bedroom, so in this particular script there will be a lot of playback stuff. Not generally, but yeah, this one is very heavy on that."

WG2: "What are some things that you guys looked ahead to and said, 'Oh we've got to make sure we keep aware of that?'"

MA: "Generally what I get—which I haven't gotten yet this time, but this is an example from the last show—they have a visual effects meeting, and they'll determine how many visual effects are going to be made. And they'll make a bid sheet together from that, and then I'll get this list and these are all the visual effects that we have to have in this show. It's keeping track of details like that, of stock of various things that we're going to need. I have to talk to John King

432

The current season is kept in the dailies room in banker's boxes. Successful shows require lots of storage. The entire show is stored in the production offices in a large, very cold room. The cassettes are stored on shelves from the actual library set. When Episode Eleven of Season Four ("Doomed") was shot, they stole a shelf back and destroyed it.

"Rubber lips"—actors whose mouths just can't seem to synch up during ADR (looping).

downstairs, who's our music coordinator, if we're going to be in the Bronze and we're going to have a source cue that we're going to need, and then he tries to find something that's within budget."

WG2: "What's a source cue?"

MA: "If the radio is on. If there's a band actually playing, then I've got to have that piece of music up here so the editor can cut to that. So when I go through the script, I'm looking for all those kinds of things that I need ahead."

CHRISTOPHE BECK

We began by asking the *Buffy* composer how he knows what to do once he's been to a spotting session.

CB: "[Episode Thirteen] is something like my fortieth or forty-first episode of the show. There are certain things that we always do, and there are certain things just from having done this so many times that I know Joss will want in certain places. For example—and this is a really basic example—but any time there is any kind of demon or vampire that just pops out suddenly, we will want to sting that with a big, sort of slap-you-in-the-face, with the music. It sort of gooses the audience there a little bit. If a fight ensues—I don't think we have ever done a fight without sort of pulse pounding action music.

"Occasionally, like at the end of 'The Wish,' which is all slow mo, it gets a little bit more surreal. 'The I in Team' has a fight sequence that is intercut with Buffy and Riley having sex for the first time, that is played with a slightly trippy electronic music. I did not write that piece and I had very little to do with choosing that piece. Very often if they know that what they are doing is stylistically very different from the rest of the show, they will try to find something that they can license and put in there...which in this case ended up working. In the case of Buffy and Riley sparring in the episode before this one, it did not work, and I ended up replacing what they were hoping they would license with something different that Joss liked better.

"Also, the end of 'Wild at Heart,' with Oz leaving Willow. They looked for weeks for a song. Ultimately nothing quite gave Joss the satisfaction he needed and the emotional range he needed there. So at the last minute I sort of came in and, I guess, did some kind of a rescue job. But apparently everyone was happy with it."

WG2: "Creatively speaking, do you need to feel the way the music is going to be or can you sort of plug in and go at it with what you would call a more objective level? For example, when Oz leaves Willow, did you feel sad when you composed the music?"

CB: "The answer is yes. It doesn't happen with every scene. It only happens with the most affecting scenes, obviously. But a scene like that or the end of 'Amends,' with the magic snowfall, or Buffy and Angel's wordless goodbye at the end of 'Graduation Day, Part Two.' Scenes like that, that are really special and that really have a lot of emotion in them to begin with, that is really when I am loving my job the most. When I can sort of create a piece of music that goes under the scene and just completes the experience. In the case of Willow's utter misery, you know, I was right there with her."

WG2: "Is there anything particular to Episode Thirteen that was in some way challenging?"

CB: "Challenging and different, yes. Because Joss was busy directing and Marti [Noxon], who, recently in any case, is sort of taking over more of a Jossian role when Joss is not around, also was not available at the spotting, so we spotted basically on our own. That is always a little bit scary. This was the first time actually since Joss was directing that Marti gave me notes on the music, and Marti was really the one at the mix, sort of running things.

"We were plunged into this, like you were saying before....How do I know what Joss will like? Well, when you do forty episodes, you just know. At least mostly. I will never be 100 percent sure. But with Marti we were just sort of plunged into this and we had never really done this before. There were some notes she gave me that I don't think I addressed exactly the way she would have liked me to and I think that Fer [Bos] was kept pretty busy, sort of saving my butt. Getting it to where Marti was happy. But that, more than any kind of creative aspect, was the most challenging part of that episode, just getting to know someone new to work with.

"From a creative standpoint that particular episode was one of my favorites of the season, just because there are so many plot twists and it is so cool. From a musical perspective, there was not much for me to do besides just sort of hide in the background and give a little push here and there, but there wasn't really much storytelling for the music to do as much as story supporting."

WG2: "How did you come up with the Riley/Buffy theme?"

CB: "By the seat of my pants! That was in the middle of 'Hush,' actually. I don't generally get clued into the long-term plan for these things, so I didn't even know what the future of Buffy and Riley was. My first pass at that particular scene where they kiss for the first time was a little restrained and played as much to the situation around them and the creepiness of that, as it did to their blossoming love.

"Joss really wanted a strong romantic statement there. When he heard that scene, he told me he really wanted to play the moment as romantically as possible, with still an acknowledgment that they are in the middle of something that is bigger than they are, but still mainly romantic....So that is sort of what I went on, and then my second attempt seemed to work nicely.

"That theme is very difficult to reuse. It has an epoch quality to it that just seems too big any time I try to use it again. Even when I do a really delicate version of it on piano, it doesn't quite have the resonance that I was hoping it would have. So we may try to come up with something new. Although I just realized that there is a place in Episode Fourteen where it will work fine, so it will be coming back."

WG2: "In 'Anne,' Buffy gets a phone call and she says 'Hello, hello?' and you cued us that it was Angel calling her from Los Angeles."

CB: "Oh yeah, that was a great idea. That was Joss's idea."

WG2: "A gift for the fervent fans."

CB: "He even said that at spotting. It was such a clever little touch that he did to, sort of, have the tiniest little crossover between the two episodes. It seemed only natural to have music. He said, 'Yeah, we will do that for all the Internet fans out there.'

Close Your Eyes
(Buffy/Angel Love Theme)

Music by
Christophe Beck

434

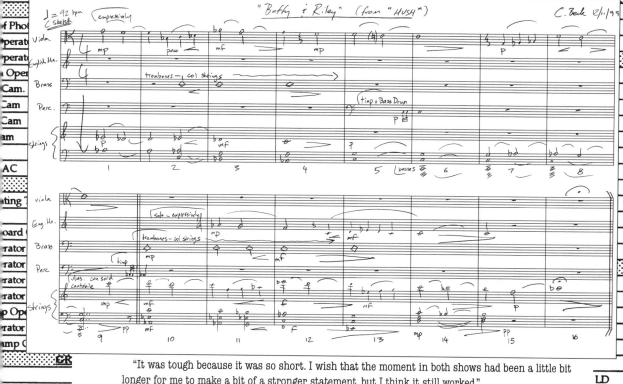

"It was tough because it was so short. I wish that the moment in both shows had been a little bit longer for me to make a bit of a stronger statement, but I think it still worked."

WG2: "Do you know ahead of time about how much music you are going to compose?"

CB: "I don't know until I sit down and watch the episode. But once I sit down, it is easy to tell, until Fer actually sits down and adds it all up, I don't know the exact amount, but I can probably guess to within a couple of minutes, how big a show it is. The shows have been pretty reliably consistent in the amount of music—about nineteen, twenty minutes."

WG2: "How long do you have to do that?"

CB: "Usually a week, although sometimes when things get pushed back, which is often the case when Joss is directing, things get slowed down a little bit. It can be shrunk to four to five days. I think that is the case, actually, on Episode Fourteen."

WG2: "How do you compose? What is your procedure or your protocol?"

CB: "I sit down at my computer and my samplers and my synthesizers and everything is set up so that I have very quick access to virtually every instrument in the orchestra. I look at the scene and 98 percent of the time, I have an idea before I am done watching the scene for the first time. Generally writer's block is not a problem for me. If I have to come up with something, I always can. It may not be the greatest thing in the world, but it will be something that at least does what it is supposed to do.

"Whatever that idea is, it might be just a rhythmic idea. It might be just a color. It might be a particular sound that is very unusual. In the case of a sensitive scene, it will most likely be a melodic fragment. In the case of a creepy scene, it will most likely be some kind of texture, some kind of odd combination of colors. Then I will just sort of go with it.

"The technology makes it very easy to try ideas out with picture. The picture is essentially running digitally off the same computer that I am recording the music into. The show is constantly going on, on my TV monitor while I am writing. So it is very easy to try different ideas."

WG2: "Are you able with your system to create very new sounds or do you stay within a range for Buffy?"

436

CB: "Yes and no. Not maybe in the sense that you are talking about. With a real orchestra your palette is virtually limitless. There are techniques and experiments that you can try with a real orchestra: when you have the interactions of eighty or ninety great musicians doing maybe some very odd things with their instruments, but still you have just this gigantic palette to play with. With the black boxes I have in my studio, I can simulate a subset of the range of expression you can get with an orchestra and a small one at that.

"When you are using samples, you are actually triggering recordings of musicians playing their instruments, but you are triggering them from a keyboard and you are triggering the same recording every time, so for example, repeated notes on certain instruments will very quickly sound very robotic and electronic. If you don't have the right kind of sounds to do repeated notes, then there will not be a lot of repeated notes in my compositions. So there are these sort of arbitrarily imposed limits on the range of expression I can get when it comes to emulating an orchestra.

"One of the advantages I do enjoy is, I have very easy and quick access to sounds that an orchestra could never produce, sounds that don't sound electronic, but they really are created electronically. For example, one of the things you can do with a gong is take a super ball and rub the gong with it and you get this sort of very ethereal otherworldly groaning sound. It has been used to great effect in film music with orchestras for a long time.

"What you can do with a sampler is take that same sound and play it half as fast or twice as fast and end up with a totally mutated version of the same sound that you could never get in the real world and that sounds totally different from the original piece of material that was recorded. But that is just as evocative and probably, in the case of it being played twice as slow, becomes ever more menacing.

"So that is the kind of thing that you can do with electronic manipulation that you can't really do with a real orchestra, and it doesn't really fall in the category of simulating an orchestra but mostly in the area of the creepy cues."

WG2: "Both the sound effects editor and the costume designer said that they were starting to need fresh ideas to clothe and make voices for demons. Do you run into that problem, finding new ways to make things sound?"

CB: "I am constantly looking for ways to keep things fresh. One of the things I am always on the hunt for is new sounds. The currency that we all deal in is sounds. They are very expensive and they take an enormous amount of man hours to create well. It is a very niche market, but there are companies that make orchestral sounds. I do a lot of creating of my own. For example, I was unsatisfied with certain cymbal rolls that for some reason seemed to be woefully underrepresented in all the major orchestral libraries. So I bought a cymbal and some drumsticks and recorded a bunch of my own. Things like that.

"For 'Fear, Itself,' I used an electric cello, plugged him in through my wacky effects processors and put flangers and delays and reverbs and all kinds of stuff on it. We just sort of spent several hours making the weirdest sounds we could think of. Then I loaded those into the samplers, and I have them at my disposal to slip them in wherever I feel it is appropriate. So generally when there is a show that is truly inspiring, like 'Fear, Itself' was, like 'Hush' was, then the first thing I will think is how I can make this different from anything I have done for the show before.

"That is one thing I love about working with Joss on <u>Buffy</u>. He loves it when I do that. I have never been told 'This doesn't sound like <u>Buffy</u>,' 'This is really different,' and 'Do what you normally do.' On a score like 'The Zeppo,' sort of hyperactive fiddle and Latin percussion. I couldn't imagine it in any other episode of the show except for that one. It seemed to work great. It is great to be able to have the opportunity to stretch like that. In a lot of other TV shows, you give them something different and they freak out.

"Because I do an episodic television show, I am forced to repeat myself constantly but I hate it. I am always looking for ways to not repeat myself. But my palette in music is a little bit larger, I would guess, than demon growls. I can see why someone making up all those demon growls after fifty, sixty episodes feels like they have pretty much exhausted the possibilities."

WG2: "How often do you use real instruments?"

CB: "But most every episode has at least a live woodwind, and some have live vocals, string instruments, cello, viola, violin. I have brought in a French horn occasionally. Percussion occasionally."

WG2: "How do you make that decision?"

WG2: "Do you do a lot of other things during hiatus?"

CB: "I do a lot of other things all the time. I happen to be doing a film now, but the good thing about this particular film is that I am scoring it over a period of four months. It is really the kind of thing I can do in between episodes, there happened to be a week where there was not an episode, so I had a week off. I took advantage to work a little on the movie. It's called <u>Cheer Fever</u>. Eliza Dushku stars in a supporting role. It is a cheerleading movie with Kirsten Dunst and Eliza."

WG2: "What are your work habits? Do you work at night? Do you have a schedule?"

CB: "Right now my wife is out of town and my schedule changes completely. I revert back to my college ways, which is a progressively later getting up and later working. I basically got up at ten-thirty this morning because I was up until three. But when my wife is around, which is really most of the time, happily, it is like ten to eight. I don't work insane hours, but I rarely take days off. I don't even know what to do with myself on days off."

JOHN KING, MUSIC COORDINATOR

John King's office is downstairs in the *Angel* complex. There are bookcases filled with CDs, and more CDs on his desk. And more CDs elsewhere. He's a happy man.

WG2: "Could you tell us how you ended up at <u>Buffy</u>? What was your career path?"

JK: "It was a winding one. I had started out in '92 working for friends in a restaurant 'cause I had just gotten out of film school and I moved out here. I didn't know anybody. It was hard to get a foot in the door if you didn't know anybody.

"A friend of mine got me into a commercial production house as a PA. Then I started doing set PA work, moved from the office to the set. I did that for a couple of years, and then moved into the camera department. I was second assistant camera. I did that for about a year, and after that I kind of got burnt on the whole production thing altogether and got a desk job at Disney in the music publishing department. I was producing and writing some things on my own while I was on that job because it gave me the freedom and time to do that, whereas production kind of limits your time and availability to do your own projects.

"After that, I went back to production and worked with a friend in set dressing and did that for about half a year. Just doing music videos, commercials, and a couple of TV pilots.

"Then, I had a friend who worked here, Brian Wankum, who's the post coordinator—he was originally the post PA here. He gave me a call and said, 'Look, I've been moved up, would you care to come work here in post?' And I've always wanted to get into post-production, so I started middle of the first season as a post PA.

"I guess I came in around Episode Six of the first season, 'The Pack.' There I was just doing the

GILES	H	HOLD	
WILLOW	H	HOLD	
SPIKE	W	6:30P	7:30P	REPORT TO LOCATION

post PA work, and because there were songs that needed to be found, Brian and I both took that on because he didn't always have time to be looking for songs. He had coordinating to do. So in my spare time I would look for music and try to find something that would work for the show.

"And by the Season Two, the music got really heavy. Music became like another character in the show. Brian was actually helping me the first two seasons finding music. Season Two was pretty exciting. A lot of new characters were coming in, and there were a lot of events for music. And they had asked me if I would mind taking over that position, the music.

"The backlash was, I still had to do the post PA stuff. I was working two jobs at once, and it was rather difficult when you had to be at one place and yet you had a deadline for something else. So it was fun but chaotic in the second season.

"And then came the third season, where it was the same deal, but I now had the official title of music coordinator instead of post PA, but I was still doing both jobs. So that was even more chaotic, and the music was even heavier.

"Now this season [Four] it's been extremely heavy. It's probably the heaviest in music that the show's ever been. I think in the half-season that we've done, we've pretty much combined enough music to equal up both Seasons Two and Three. It's a pretty extensive list of stuff.

"This year they also gave me Angel, because Angel's a new show, and since I was, I guess, pretty much keyed into the Whedon sound, they wanted to give me a shot on this and make it full-time.

"So now I'm working full-time on both shows, and no longer doing the post PA work. And I like it. It's fun."

WG2: "What is the Whedon sound?"

JK: "It changes from one cue to the next, but there's always some kind of emotional level there. The songs have to fit the scene. A lot of TV shows will tend to just take the biggest hit they can and just needle-drop it into the show wherever they can and crank it up really loud. So it's almost like, 'Okay, here's story, story, story, and now a hit song by Third Eye Blind.'

"A lot of shows are doing that now and it's not really a trend that we started, but it's kind of something that I think Buffy had made popular.

"The songs should not take away from the scene. They should enhance it. The actors are [taking the emotional level up] themselves. But the song just kind of emphasizes that and just pushes it just a little further to grab you. And the fans of the show remember that. I mean, name one of the songs, and they can tell you the exact scene, who was in it, and what was the scenario.

"It's because the songs have that emotional tie to the scene that the fans relate to it better. They can buy the Buffy soundtrack, and listen to the song and say, 'Oh, I remember that part.' But if you're just going to throw a song in there at random and say, 'This is a hit, let's put it in there,' people aren't going to care. I mean, they can turn on the radio and listen to that song."

WG2: "Can you elaborate on how you pick music?"

JK: "Say in the script, it reads 'hip and somewhat ethereal music fills the room from the stereo as Willow appears to speak in incantation.'

"Well, usually when it comes to something like that, I wait until the editors have cut the scene so I can look at it, see the room, who's in it, what would they be listening to, what the atmosphere calls for.

"Same with the Bronze; you know, are people dancing? Are they not dancing? Are they just hanging out or not? How many people are there? If it's crowded, I make it a bit up tempo; if it's not so crowded, kind of low key. If it's vampires listening to music, it's usually edgier. It depends on what character would be listening to what.

438

OM
e and t

OM
er

OM
Riley

OVE

ots ar

PLAYER
Gellar
on
ad
an

d

ts

/8 pg

3/8 pg

pg

FRO

5/8 pg

2/8 pg
R
TON

TON

KILEY	W	10:30A	11:30A	REPORT TO LOCATION
ANYA	H	HOLD		
FORREST	W	6:30P	7:30P	REPORT TO NEBRASKA / BUND

"Like Giles, for instance, Giles is always a hoot to get music for. When someone comes over to his apartment and you're always wondering, 'What is he listening to now?' The last time we used David Bowie from back in 1970 off his Space Oddity album. It was a rare song called 'Memory of a Free Festival' that not many people are too aware of. In 'Band Candy,' we had him listening to an old Cream song, 'Tales of Brave Ulysses.'

"We used a number of unsigned bands last season, too. We had Mad Cow, Darling Violetta, who is also doing the theme song for Angel. They did an on camera appearance.

"I knew Darling Violetta through members of Four Star Mary, and they sent me a CD [Bathwater Flowers].

"And it turns out that Joss went to see Splendid and Darling Violetta was opening up for them."

WG2: "Do you actually take submissions?"

JK: "Oh, yeah. I go to shows. I'm like an A&R guy. I go to clubs and events. If someone says, 'Oh, you gotta go check this band out,' I'll go check 'em out. And sometimes that band will be exactly what I'm looking for, or won't exactly fit into the Buffy vibe, but there'll be a band on afterward."

WG2: "What is the Buffy vibe?"

JK: "It's really hard to describe. It's all about—I think lately it's about coming of age, you know, discovery, love and loss, and change. I think that's been a big theme in the show lately, change. If you listen from Season One until now, the music has changed immensely, it has progressed. The music matures as the characters mature, or at least that's what I've been trying to do, trying to slip in more mature stuff. Sometimes it gets by and sometimes it doesn't because you still want to keep that fun-ness about it."

WG2: "So if somebody wants to send you music to listen to, can they?"

JK: "Yes, but they need to send it to me at the Twentieth Century Fox address. P.O. Box 900, Beverly Hills, CA 90213. I am looking for a lot more unsigned artists, with good recordings, of course, to use in the show, not just on camera. I mean, I try to save those—the unsigned bands—for the on-camera stuff when they occur because, one, they're the ones who need the exposure. And number two, we like to give it to them.

"We really like to help these bands out. I mean, that's partially what the charm of the show is about, and Joss is very aware of that. We like to expose people to new music. And, I mean, why should we put music on there that you can turn on the radio and hear in heavy rotation?"

WG2: "Who found Nerfherder [the theme music]?"

JK: "Submissions. They sent a demo on a cassette; it was very rough. It was Perry from Nerfherder just doing a little Casio thing and guitars. But Joss liked it and they went in and recorded it. And there it is. It just encompassed the whole attitude of the show. It was young, hip and trendy, but in the coolest way."

439

DAVID SOLOMON, PRODUCER IN CHARGE OF POST-PRODUCTION
BRIAN WANKUM, POST-PRODUCTION COORDINATOR

The first time we visited with them, Producer David Solomon and Post-Production Coordinator Brian Wankum were taking a short break from long hours of mixing "Hush" at Todd AO. The world-famous post-production facility is striking; as you negotiate the winding, carpeted staircase, you walk down and around a waterfall punctuated with rocks and glass brick.

We went to the snack area in the foyer, sitting at a circular table. Other clients came and went, some greeting David and Brian and asking how things were going.

WG2: "At what point do you start the post-production process? What are the components of post-production?"

DS: "We start as soon as the script's written. Just like all the other departments. We go through and find out the things that we're going to need. Mostly, for us, it's visual effects, special sound effects, playback on the set, either sound or picture. If it's picture, we have to rent it or shoot it. If it's sound, we have to get the soundtrack for it, the music for it. We spot where we have to buy visual effects, or visual effects that we can make on our own, in the edit bay. So, like all the departments, we wait for the scripts to come out and we start to break them down immediately."

WG2: "How much time do you usually have, between the time you get the script and the time you must be finished?"

DS: "Well, you know it varies from show to show. Being post and all, we measure it from the time we finish shooting the episode to the time it, say, delivers to the network. It's usually about four weeks."

BW: "Usually, but it can be as short as two weeks."

WG2: "This episode is 'Hush?' Are you on schedule?"

DS: "With this? No, we're behind. But we'll make it. We always do."

WG2: "Brian, what is the difference in your job and David's job?"

BW: "Well, let's see. David's definitely heading up all of post, and I'm handling everything that is not what an editor does, not what an assistant does. Post-production coordinator is the name, so coordinating post-production."

WG2: "What is the hardest part of your jobs?"

DS: "Ever-changing schedules."

BW: "The logistics of fitting all the various elements into the time that we have. That changes all the time. And sometimes you have to wait to get an answer on something."

WG2: "Is there a way to tell, or to shorthand, when you're prepping an episode, how to save yourself some time in post-production?"

DS: "Just things that sound expensive on paper, sometimes there's an easier way to do them, and that's where the advance planning comes in. A lot of times it's easier to, say, shoot something on a green screen than it is to create it from whole cloth, to start over. Or some things that sound like very complicated effects turn out not to be.

"In the particular case of Joss's episode tonight, there's a scene where these guys' heads explode. And everybody talked about, we're gonna do this on a blue screen, or do this thing or do that thing, and all we did was made wax heads and put little bombs in them and exploded them right on the set. And used spaghetti and yellow paint for brains. It was pretty cool. Looks great."

WG2: "Was Episode Ten ['Hush'] unusually challenging?"

DS: "You know what, it's just such a good episode that we all worked much harder on it. I don't mean that as a line. It's actually true. And you will see what I mean when you see it.

"It's also different because there's no dialogue in it, so there not only has to be better than average music but way more of it. And better than average sound effects but way more of them. Because they're all filling the gap and keeping the story going. So that's the big challenge for that one, for us."

WG2: "Besides being indicative of a noise, what is the purpose of a sound effect in the making of a TV show or a film?"

DS: "Well, it keeps the scene alive, and keeps it real all the way through. And in cases where we replace the dialogue, all the sound goes away. But <u>Buffy</u> specifically has lots of demons and fights and they don't involve you unless they have movie sound effects in them, which are generally larger than life."

WG2: "Do you have a mental scale or even a written standard of about how much amplification, or larger than lifeness?"

DS: "Larger than life's not just volume, it's quality. Punches would never sound as loud as they do on TV. Nothing sounds that well-defined in real life. We're storytelling, so we have to go a little above and beyond."

WG2: "Can you tell us some anecdotes about any of the episodes from Seasons Three and Four? Something that was a challenge, something that was funny, something that went wrong, something that you were extra resourceful about?"

BW: "I have one that's my favorite. I saw it in the quiz book [<u>Pop Quiz: Buffy the Vampire Slayer</u>] that just came out, they had a thing, 'What song was Spike singing at the end of Episode Eight?' And he was singing 'My Way,' but not just any recording of 'My Way.' He was singing what was supposed to have been the Sex Pistols' version of 'My Way,' but we couldn't get the rights to that for whatever reason, so he was actually singing along to the Gary Oldman recording of 'My Way' from the <u>Sid and Nancy</u> soundtrack,which we were able to get the rights to. And I don't think anybody knows that."

WG2: "Does it make a difference to you in post-production how much is shot on a stage and how much is shot on location? Is it more work for you?"

DS: "Minimally. When you get on a stage it's harder for them to mix the dialogue because it's harder to hear outdoors, but we have a great sound man so that's not really a problem anymore."

WG2: "You don't have to name names, but are there some actors that you just know have to loop more than other actors?"

DS: "Tony. I'll name names. Because, as he describes it, his character stutters. He created a character that has a stammer. And every time he comes in here to loop he says, 'I'll never have another character that stammers again,' because it's difficult for him. When he starts off on a sentence and then he realizes he's gone somewhere else, he wishes he had never begun this character like this. But that was his creation, so, yeah. He tends to loop a little more.

"And a lot of people can't understand English accents, go figure. True. Other than that, everybody has about the same amount of looping. You know, they don't have much anymore."

WG2: "Brian, tell me how you got to your position."

BW: "Actually it's a funny story. Marc Alpert called me, when Joss and David Greenwalt were moving into their offices, and the building was completely empty and had no phones. So it was Joss and David Greenwalt, and Gareth was getting ready to move in soon, and I heard that there was some-

GRAHAM	W	6:30P	7:30P	REPORT TO NEBRASKA / BUNDY LOT
STUNT COORDINATOR	W	~	6:30P	REPORT TO LOCATION
BUFFY STUNT DBL	H	HOLD		

body named David Solomon moving in at some point. But we had a card table and we're ordering furniture and phones and things like that. So basically my first job on <u>Buffy</u> was moving boxes. Eventually I was organizing all the box movers, and then the rest was history."

WG2: "So what is your day like?"

BW: "It's different every day. Sometimes it has a lot to do with paperwork, the credits, that the spelling is right of everybody's name in the credits, that all the bills get paid, and bad bills don't get paid, and things like that. That everything's in the show that needs to be in there. That when we first do the online—David said it's beautiful, but there're still problems with it, like dirt and hair and things like that that need to be spotted. Those things get painted out. The same way like you were talking about, a boom shadow or something like that. Like odds and ends, all the odds and ends and little details."

DS: "Post is thousands and thousands of little details. We're the last people to touch the film. When we're done with it, it airs. That's it."

BW: "That would probably be the most distinctive thing that I do. I'm the last guy to watch it, actually. Even when all these guys are done, they go and they put the final picture together with the final sound, and I go to that, and about one out of four times there's one or two last little details…."

WG2: "Do you add some kind of an ambient noise to the background?"

DS: "Yes. There's always a background going. Whether it's light wind, light traffic, crickets, birds, dogs, sprinklers. Something. It's always some little thing."

WG2: "Can you think of anything that you will do in Episode Thirteen?"

DS: "The bone coming out of Maggie's chest will be partially practical, on the set, and partially a 3-D animated effect. Bruce Minkus, who does the practical special effects, will put a device inside her shirt to make it poke out a couple inches."

WG2: "Is that called a plate?"

DS: "It is called a plate. And that'll make her shirt look natural and normal sticking out when we optically paint a stake coming through her."

WG2: "Now why were they wondering, at the pre-production meeting, if she was going to be wearing a sweater?"

DS: "Just a different look, you know, if she was wearing a thin silk blouse you might see the plate through it when it's in a resting position. And a sweater has natural places for something to poke out without worrying about how the shirt would rip."

WG2: "So actually a sweater would have been easier."

DS: "Sweater would have been easier for us, but a shirt'll make a better sound when it rips, so six of one, half a dozen of another, you know."

WG2: "So that's right, you make all kinds of gooshy, splattery, yucky sounds."

DS: "We do. And the network hates us for that, but we do it anyhow because we like it. We're an eight o'clock show, and we try not to be too gross, but sometimes it's fun. They leave us alone when they're demons or bad people, but humans they have a problem with. We don't kill that many humans, though."

WG2: "Can you tell us a little bit about morphing?"

DS: "Morphing is something we would rather not do, but we do. It's where one character becomes another, when a human becomes a vampire or a person becomes a werewolf. We actually had an Indian become a bear one time….

"We shoot the scene on the set normally, up until the person or thing needs to change. Then they go get in or out of the makeup and

THE SWEET SOUND OF DEATH

Four sounds are mixed together to create the sound of a vampire dusting:

1. a reverse scream
2. a "whoosh-by"
3. an animal growl
4. a flame-thrower burst

come back an hour later and continue. And then we take them and put them in front of a blue screen, and try and light it the same and recreate where we were. We shoot both the A side and the B side. The nonmorph and morph. Then we do it in the computer. The whole thing's done upstairs by Digital Magic, frame by frame. I shoot all [the second unit scenes]. Scenes that we didn't have time to do, or we didn't have the right things to do it then. Or an actor wasn't available, or the special effect thing wasn't made yet. For some reason or another that didn't quite fit in the [shooting] schedule, we do that on a whole 'nother day. And that's generally a mishmash of little bits and pieces of things. Parts of scenes, inserts, doohickeys, whatever got left out. It all eventually gets done."

WG2: "How do wires and rigs get painted out?"

BW: "I tell somebody at Digital Magic where the stuff is that has to get done. If the wire is here in this frame and it's here in the next frame, they take a clean piece from one frame, and they paint the clean piece over the piece with the wire in it. So they steal from other frames, or recreate, or find a clean frame of something and put it over the top of where either the dirt or the wire or whatever is.

"It's like digitally patching stuff. Just patch it up and put something that you want to see where there was something you didn't want to see."

WG2: "Has dusting vampires changed significantly?"

DS: "Dusting sort of gets better every season. You see the bones a lot more."

WG2: "Well, when we worked on the first Watcher's Guide, Gareth told us it was $5,000 a dust. Is that about still what it is?"

DS: "Same. We don't let them go up, no matter how much more we ask of them."

WG2: "What's the most expensive effect you've ever had?"

DS: "The snake from last year. The Mayor snake. But, with the exception of that and a few minor exceptions, the show is not really about the visual effects. It's about the characters and the comedy and its general Buffyness. It doesn't live or die on the effects, I don't think."

WG2: "How often do you use puppets?"

BW: "I remember the hyena in Season One ['The Pack'] was a puppet. And then we had a Mayor puppet that we didn't use very much of. It was just kind of reference for the 3-D people. Oh, the Hellmouth monster is all a huge puppet."

DS: "Yes. And the skeleton from the Halloween show was a puppet that took four guys, I think, to make it work. Very sophisticated. It was nice."

WG2: "In the last two years, have they set very many people on fire?"

DS: "No. You know, we set Sophia on fire for the prom episode last year, in a big wedding dress. Who else burned? Absalom, we actually had burning. But I can't think of anybody else we really burned."

BW: "We had Spike's hand bursting into flame, facedown drunk."

DS: "That was pretty funny. I liked that."

WG2: "Do you digitally put in very much fire?"

DS: "No, we really don't. We did for the burning Buffy in the wedding gown, but other than that, it's practical and sometimes it's enhanced digitally."

BW: "If you're too close to somebody, but there definitely has to be fire in the scene, then they put some licks in the foreground in front of them."

DS: "And we burned the entire set in 'Beer Bad.' Actual furniture, on fire for many hours. Everyone was in smoke masks, all day long. And dozens of firemen standing by, just in case."

WG2: "We were writing down interesting tidbits in the call sheets, and one was that you had to have a fire marshall present because you had burning pumpkins. Jack-o'-lanterns."

BW: "I think if you have a Thanksgiving dinner with candles on the table, you have to have a Fire Marshall. Any kind of fire. I don't know if you light somebody's cigarette, whether if that counts."

DS: "We are very safety conscious."

WG2: "So you morphed a bear."

DS: "We morphed a bear. Did you hear about Bonkers? Bonkers, who was supposed to be a ferocious, man-killer bear, really was about the sweetest puppy dog of a bear you ever saw in your life."

"And Bonkers' specialty is bouncing. So Bonkers would get on his feet and just start to bounce up and down, and then just become airborne with a big grin on his face. When Sophia was doubling Buffy and she was supposed to be in there fighting him, she waved her knife around to try and get him agitated, and he just thought she was waving and he just waved back with this big stupid grin on his face. He was a really sweet bear, but he was not a man-killer, that's for sure. I shot all the Bonkers and coyote stuff. The coyote hit his mark on the first take, took his look exactly where he was supposed to, and we put him back in his cage and he went home. One take. Two minutes."

THE MIXING SESSION

On Wednesday, January 26, Producer David Solomon, head of post-production, began the final mix of "The I in Team" at Todd AO Studios. David told us that the average time to mix an episode is about twenty hours; we joined him on Thursday and watched the last nine.

As we entered the offices of Todd AO, David made us known to the security guard/concierge. Stage 4 is *Buffy*'s permanent mixing suite.

Two Fairlight consoles of three bays each face the large viewing screen. Kurt Kassulke, Adam Sawelson, and Ron Evans staffed the front console. Todd AO Special Effects Sound Coordinator Cindy Rabideau, David, and Fernand Bos sat at the back console.

David had a list of fixes on a standard legal pad. "Fer" was equipped with his computer, mixing board, and a second screen at right angles to the large screen on the back wall of the suite. Behind Fer the connecting door to the projection room was propped open, but the projectionist was only audible on the intercom.

As the group settled in after a two o'clock lunch break, Cindy offered to show us around Todd AO. She took us upstairs to meet Chris Reeves, who is the dialogue editor on *Angel*. Occasionally he works on *Buffy*. Later we would meet Dan Tripoli, who is his *Buffy* counterpart.

Chris explained that he takes the dailies, which are supplied to him on digital audio tape (DAT), and uses a Fairlight mixer to clean out the noise and smoothe out the sounds that make up human speech. He tries to match up the ADR (looping) with the output from the picture editor, which has been done with AVID. He then lays out the dialogue on a single track so that the sound-effects editor has the other tracks to work with. He has a maximum of five days per episode to encode and process every single syllable in the show.

Chris worked for five years on The *X-Files*. The main difference for him between *X-Files* and *Angel* is that *X-Files* went on location a great deal. Location is always harder for dialogue editors, because of unpredictable extra noise. *Angel* is a heavy set show—that is, shot on soundstages.

"Many of the exteriors are shot on the Paramount lot," he added. Exteriors are harder to shoot when they actually are outside, as opposed to built on a soundstage. But the walls at Paramount dampen the traffic and other noises.

Our next stop was effects editor Mark Cleary's office. Mike Marchain, who is second in command, was hard at work in a adjacent room.

Mark told us, "*Buffy* is a sound person's dream. You have otherworldly sounds—monsters and demons, and Willow's magic. I can use cool winds, ambience. And the fight scenes are the best. There's never a dull moment."

Mark illustrated the process of designing sound for a fight scene by first showing us the scene in "The I in Team" where Buffy fights the Warrior Demons in the sewer. The original soundtrack was in place. We could hear the grunts of the stunt team, including the very recognizable voice of Sarah Michelle Gellar's stunt double, Sophia Crawford. Fake battle-axes clattered as they fell to the ground. Bodies slammed into wooden panels painted to look like stone.

Mark removed all the sound, then ran the scene with complete silence.

"Now he'll build up the sound," Cindy explained. "He can pull up twenty-four tracks, and use more if he wants."

Using an editing system called Protools, Mark started with background sounds—air and water drips. Then he layered on sound effect after sound effect—the whir and activity of the Initiative's underground complex; computer noises; battle noises; the beeping of Buffy's heart monitor, including, later, the flat line. He added the heightened sounds of punches, body slams, and the clang of weapons.

As he was demonstrating, two men appeared in the doorway to say hello to Cindy. They were members of the loop group, there to record "efforts." Efforts are the grunts, shouts, exhalations, and other noises the on screen characters make. The original efforts performed by the actors during filming cannot be used because they don't sound real.

So, in essence, the loop group provides "grunt doubles." None of the "oomphs" or "arghs" uttered by Giles, Willow, Spike, or any of the other actors is actually made by that actor—except for Sarah Michelle Gellar.

"She came in one day and made an entire reel of efforts for us," Cindy said. "Buffy's so distinctive that we had to have Sarah."

It was a member of the loop group who provided the scream in "Hush."

The loop group also records the *Buffy* "Foley"—new sounds created by people in a special room, who are copying the movements of the actors as they watch the projected footage. Footsteps are often Foley'ed, for example. The Foley sounds are digitally recorded and added to the sound library Mark Cleary has at his disposal.

With the fight scene completed, Mark moved to a scene in which the Commandos don civvies and walk through Sunnydale. "Everything except the dialogue is manufactured," he told us as he added in a lawn mower, an offstage car horn, birdsong, footsteps, a bike whizzing past, and so on. "Nothing you hear is real, except for the dialogue."

445

GRAHAM	W	6:30P	7:30P	REPORT TO NEBRASKA / BUNDY LOT
STUNT COORDINATOR	W	~	6:30P	REPORT TO LOCATION
BUFFY STUNT DBL	H		HOLD	

He went on to discuss one of the most challenging areas of sound-effects work for *Buffy:* demon vocals. "We marry human screams and grunts with animal growls," he said, "and we're running through the animal kingdom." In other words, it's getting more challenging to create new voices for new demons.

In addition, the demon vocals often have to cut through big music cues. "So we need big guttural sounds."

Mark started out as a driver at West Productions, a job he secured as a result of his father, Kevin Clearly. The elder Cleary was a prominent mixer. Through the driving job, Mark got his foot in the door. He cut Foley for *L.A. Law* and *Picket Fences.*

Both he and Cindy cut cartoons such as *Speed Racer* (the new version), *Teenage Mutant Ninja Turtles, James Bond Junior,* and in Cindy's case, *The Jetsons.* Kevin Burns, an ADR (looping) mixer at West, who was the mixer for the first two seasons of *Buffy.* Cindy was on *Law & Order* before *Buffy.*

After our tour, we returned to Stage 4. Music Editor John King—referred to by others in the room as Chun King—had given Fer a note that a song played in the background of a scene Bronze needed to be replaced. The musical number originally slotted had proved to be too expensive to use.

A quick discussion provided an alternative. That matter solved, they resumed watching. In unison everyone noticed that a "wild line"—a piece of dialogue spoken off-camera by an actor—did not match with the on-screen dialogue of the same actor. It was delivered at a different volume, tone, and rhythm, and sounded odd.

The front row went into high gear. As they began adjusting the line, David picked up one of several newspapers and industry magazines. The actor's voice got louder, softer, warmer, fuller, thinner.

One of the guys said, "David, you listening?"

"Not till you get closer," he replied, grinning faintly as he turned the page of the newspaper.

In the end, no one was satisfied with the match, and David felt that the scene would play better without it.

"Dump it. Onward," he said firmly.

The process of augmenting the illusion of reality continued. There were different kinds of phone rings to select; the volume of various "efforts" to modulate; bringing up a background noise or making it quieter.

If a new or different sound was required, Cindy got on the phone to Mark Cleary, upstairs. From his vast library, he would fill the request.

After about an hour and a half, Producer Marti Noxon came in with J. D. Peralta, her assistant. David showed her what they had so far, taking more notes as he watched. She gave him the notes Joss had asked her to pass along, as well as some of her own, and he read off his own list. They began to discuss the placement of a section of Chris Beck's score. Bos called Chris. Marti called Joss for his input, Fer made some adjustments, and, satisfied, they continued.

At one point they experimented with the vocals of the Warrior Demons, diminishing, then subtracting, the chittering sound of a rattlesnake. They added a footfall to "fill a hole." They experimented with a vari-

	ANYA		H		HOLD	
	FORREST		W	6:30P	7:30P	REPORT TO NEBRASKA / BUND
	GRAHAM		W	6:30P	7:30P	REPORT TO NEBRASKA / BUND

ety of beeper sounds. A long discussion ensued about creating a "small sustaining suspense sound" to enhance "the impact of the sting"—i.e., when the audience realizes that Maggie Walsh is spying on the couple.

At eight-forty that evening the mix was finished. A copy would be messengered to the network in the morning so that they could watch it. David's mind turned to other matters. He found it interesting that when he directed Episode Eighteen, he would go on location in Camarillo, in the abandoned insane asylum. He reminded the staff that a guest star in an upcoming episode couldn't sing, and that they would need to find "someone to do that for him." Also, a song, and clearance for that song.

Everyone gathered up their things and bid each other good night. Offering to drive us back to our car, Cindy Rabideau led us back upstairs. Chris Reeves, the *Angel* dialogue editor, had left. Tom Tripoli, the *Buffy* dialogue editor, now sat in front of the same computer, settling in for a night's work.

A FINAL WORD: THE FUTURE

GEORGE SNYDER

We felt that George's summation of his work helping to protect Joss's vision was an excellent way to end our section on creating *Buffy*.

GS: "I met Joss when I was working for Sandy Gallin. Gail (Berman) introduced me to Joss, when they had approached him about doing a pilot based on the series, and he said to me, 'Have you ever done a TV pilot?' And I said, 'No, I haven't,' and he said, 'Well, neither have I.' We just hit it off.

"It was going to be a temporary thing for me, and we shot the pilot and it was just something interesting. I said, 'You know, you want some cute little twenty-one-year-old blond assistant,' and he said, 'Sounds great, but I think my wife will like you better.' And we just laughed and had a good time and did the pilot.

"Then he said, 'Are you the High Plains Drifter—are you gonna take off?' Because I was writing, and I thought I would do other things, and he said, 'If it gets picked up, why don't you stay?'

"At the time that the show got picked up by Fox, Alien Resurrection went into production, also a Fox project, and it made sense for Fox to make a deal with Joss. An overall deal for features, television, animation to write, direct, produce pretty much anything he wanted. And so the company was born and he had to have a company logo, so he drew one himself.

"And he said, 'Now you can be my director of development,' and I was like, 'What's that?'

"Well, turns out, it's pretty much anything that he wants me to do. I'm the one that sort of keeps our relationships with agents for writers and directors. When scripts come in to Joss they come to me to read. Last staffing season, I think the final tally in terms of scripts sent to us was something in the vicinity of six or seven hundred scripts. So I read, well, most of them....

"The mandate from Joss is to find writers who understand what he does, directors who understand what he does. Always with an eye open, as in the past, to future projects like Angel and potential future projects which we may develop once we move on to other things, whether it be television or animation or features. We have a number of projects in development. But obviously our primary focus is Buffy and Angel."

WG2: "Do you want to or can you talk about any potential future projects?"

GS: "There are about thirty projects that are Joss's ideas or Joss's scripts that he would like to develop, or projects that are just pitches. Last season he was directing and he came out—they were doing a lighting change and I ran into him downstairs—and he said, 'You know, I've got this idea.' And we'd walk around the building, walk around our stages, and he'd pitch this idea and he said, 'What do you think?' and then go back in and direct.

"He's always way ahead in terms of things he'd like to be doing, things he's thinking about, and we take those and run with them. Do the research when research is necessary, pitch ideas to the studio when it seems appropriate. We've explored a couple of things that we've set aside for now.

"The hardest part is that no one works in this business like Joss. His method doesn't leave a lot of room to do a whole lot else. But he's a young guy and there's going to be a time long after Buffy and hopefully we'll be all around to pick up some of these projects we've toyed with.

"And then there's just day-to-day. There's the cast and crew jackets, for instance, there are the charity events that he does. There are the requests of his time. Everything from speaking engagements, to meetings, to pitches and projects from outside writers and producers. He's approached with specs that people would love for him to produce. So all of that has to get funneled through somehow and just to keep abreast of what's happening, what's going on, trying to keep the whole thing moving along. Joss is an industry in and of himself.

"But we've kept small. Joss said, 'I don't want a bunch of executives sitting around making paperclip sculptures because there's nothing to do, because I'm too busy with Buffy. However, there are people who need to get to me, I need to know about things. I need to keep abreast. I need to know who the writers are out there. I need to know who the directors are. I need to stay on top of all this, and so I need people doing that.' In addition to keeping track of the M&L, keeping track of the show, keeping track of Sarah's schedule, keeping track of this stuff. It keeps us occupied.

"People always ask what he's going to do next, and that's a good question, because Angel and Buffy together is really an awful lot. It keeps us occupied. And the question is how much can he do in addition to what he's already doing."

WG2: "Or how much can he let go of what is being done now."

GS: "Right. And what we do is try and find those writers, find those people who get what he's doing. It was very hard in the beginning. When we staffed our first season, people would send, you know agents send samples, and they sent Tales from the Crypt and they sent Sabrina and then later on, we got Dawson's Creek specs and we got Felicity specs, and it was hard. They're different kinds of shows. As the show aired and we developed a fan base, now people can come in and say, 'I've seen every episode, I get it and this is what I think. This is what I would do.' It makes our job a little easier."

WG2: "Conversely, by that very fact you have a lot more to read through, though."

GS: "And that's easier said then done. Being this close [to the show], you begin to see it from a different perspective. [For instance], Buffy is our hero. And that's hard.

"Joss said a long time ago, when we were talking about the show and why it was difficult finding people who got what he was trying to do, 'You know, I really am an ultra-feminist. It's hard for people to accept a beautiful woman who is powerful. Beautiful women tend not to be very bright. Powerful women tend not to be very beautiful.' And I said, 'Well, there's Xena,' and he said, 'And Xena's a fantasy.' Xena is couched very clearly in fantastic terms. She doesn't exist.

"And of course the strength of Buffy lies in its adherence to a strong reality. I think a lot of people want to dismiss Buffy, and need to, because ultimately she is a threatening figure. She threatens our deeply held notions about beautiful people. Funny, pretty women are stupid. The blond bimbo. And powerful women are plain—at best.

"I think the beauty of it is the number of levels that <u>Buffy</u> works on. I've read a number of <u>Buffy</u> specs that have come from agents, and I'm always struck by how much harder it is to tell our stories than people realize. Our writers can work on so many different levels. And I get to appreciate how deeply the reality can be embedded within the stories.

"That males can be vulnerable. That women can be empowered. That the world is not always a safe place. Dangerous ideas. Sometimes I get overly protective of Joss, and I have often been frustrated at what seemed to me people's unwillingness to see what he was trying to do.

"I have wanted to protect him from criticism, the adverse fan mail, because again, so many of us feel it's just the nature of the man to feel protective of him. I believe in him completely. I have never had the experience that I've had to say, 'Ah, come on, Joss, that's crazy,' or 'Oh, come on Joss, that won't work,' and been right. Everything that he has wanted to do has only made the show better.

"And this is not a situation where you get to do whatever you want. There are constraints. There are restrictions. There are the practicalities of trying to do this, what we're doing, in eight days with studio execs and network execs who are like, 'Can you do it for cheaper? You can't have that. You're not gonna be able to that.' And believe me, they have been nurturing, which is a curious word to use with studio and network execs, but they have been nurturing to us.

"Nonetheless this is a business, and my role has had to be to try and fend off the worst. But I am occasionally the one who's had to go to him and say, 'They don't want you to do this,' or 'This is what they want to do,' and try and steer a middle course through it.

"But I have never had the experience that what he wanted was not better, and for the better of the show. But it's hard to do, and it always upsets me when I see people say, 'Oh, how could he have done that? And I would underscore that this is a business, after all.

"I remember once we were out in the cemetery, the real cemetery before we built our own, and we were walking along and looking at all the stuff that gets built, and he got on the topic of popes and how popes commissioned art and how Michelangelo didn't just walk in and say, 'I'll do this to this ceiling and it will be fabulous.' In fact, it's an oddly shaped room, it's a bad design. It had a lot of flaws built into it, and he made it work. It was a commission. Joss is a consummate artist in being able to make what they want work and still remain true to his vision. So you feel protective. You want him to be able to do it."

WG2: "When something comes in, do you have a sense of, 'Joss would like this, or this is nowhere near anything Joss would be interested in?'"

GS: "I can't predict and I don't pretend to predict one hundred percent. You do, over time, get a sense of the kinds of things he likes and I find that I've got a pretty good record on saying, 'Yeah this is good. I think he'll like this writer. I think he'll like that. I think he'll like this music.'

"I think this is what John King will tell you too. John and I have worked together over the years saying, 'Is that end-of-the-show music? Is that Buffy 'Oh, I miss Angel' music? Is that 'We're at the Bronze and having fun' music? Is that 'Oh, poor Willow' moment music or not?' You can pick them. The writers, too. I've been pleased that there have been, in the samples that I forward to him, people's work that he has said, 'Yes, I think this is good.' But to some extent the job is being a marriage broker. Because it's about a relationship, and I'd love to be able to say if it's on the page that's all that matters, but in fact it's a relationship. As you've seen. An intense relationship that is about many, many subtle variables.

"I'll tell you one of my favorite things that happened early on that really taught me a) how he did the job and b) how much work this was gonna be. It was our first season and we did not have the company, it was just the two of us. He kept going down to the set and I kept needing him to come upstairs and talk on the phone and do things, and I was just overwhelmed

449

the love

d taped

VE TO FRO

s and shoot

YERS
lar

RONT

REM

GILES	H	HOLD		
WILLOW	H	HOLD		
SPIKE	W	6:30P	7:30P	REPORT TO LOCATION

and I was frantic and people used to say, all of George's extra lines are pre-set to 911. It was just frantic!

"We were working around the clock, and we got to the episode entitled 'The Pack,' and we knew the director, we had a gorgeous cast. That's the episode the writers came in and said, 'We think we ought to do an episode on gangs.' And Joss said, 'Oh, please, that's great, but let's not do one of those afterschool specials, 'Gangs are Bad,' and they have shaved heads and have bad tattoos and who would want to hang with those kids?' He said, 'Let's do something interesting.'

"But anyway, so there we are frantically busy, working around the clock, going to wardrobe, going to editing, going to all this stuff. We had just gotten off the ground and he said, 'I need to go down to the set.'

"So we walked down to the set and it was a very simple scene. It was a tracking shot where there is a fat kid sitting, a pack of kids walk by him and they say something mean about him being fat, they pass by Buffy and Buffy observes that these kids are pretty mean. And we walk down and the director said, 'This is how it is set up, it's just a simple tracking shot, we just follow with the pack of kids,' and Joss looked and said 'No.' He said, 'The fat kid is sitting by himself, there is a pile of candy wrappers in front of him and he's eating a Snickers.' He said, 'Get rid of the junk food wrappers, get rid of the Snickers, give him a piece of fruit, and give him some friends.'

"And he turned to me and said, 'Now do you understand why I have to be everywhere and watch everything?'" And of course just in those notes, unscripted, but just in those notes he transformed the scene from a simple cliché. Because if you have a fat kid eating a piece of fruit with his friends, the whole tone is changed—it's not his fault he's fat, see?

"Broadcast Standards and Practices—my first hurdle is to get a script to them to vet it for their big concerns—sex and violence. As they read they have to try and decide for themselves how bad it's going to look. Generally, it's interesting. The policy has been we can do anything to demons. You can do anything to monsters and demons you want. They get very nervous, however, when it's mortals, humans and of course especially when it's children. You can imagine one of our most difficult episodes was 'Gingerbread.' Despite the transformation of those children into a demon, they were very concerned that we would open an episode with dead children. Not a good thing to open an episode with."

WG2: "What about the night that Buffy slept with Angel for the first time?"

GS: "We had to go through several versions of that particular scene in order to get the one we actually aired. They would have been happy had we not seen anything.

"It was extremely problematic to them. Buffy was technically underage, and it didn't quite play with them that Angel was 243 years old and dead. They wanted a safe sex message, which seemed inappropriate to the scene, and we had some negotiating to do.

"It's not been entirely clear to me, but I think there is a sense, and I think this is to Joss's credit and its kind of funny, it's the very success of what Joss does that makes the task more difficult. I think there is a clear perception that <u>Buffy</u> is more real. That therefore it's more powerful. Therefore it's more dramatic, it's more sexual, it's more violent."

RILEY	W	10:30A	11:30A	REPORT TO LOCATION
ANYA	H	HOLD	
FORREST	W	6:30P	7:30P	REPORT TO NEBRASKA/BUND

SET LIGHTING
hting Technician

Board Operator
erator
erator
erator
erator
p Operator(s)
erator / Rigging
amp Operators

any Grip

(s)
(constru
(s) (Rigging

ker
rator

r SW
SW
SW
SW
)C
)C
)C
30A
12A

LD

30 P

12A
12A
OOP

451

"Because there's a perception of the depth and integrity of the storytelling. And you can see how in someone else's hands a teenage girl who goes to bed with a vampire would be a scene played for laughs. Pure comedy. The fact that those scenes can be so powerful is the testament to Joss's ability but it also makes our job much more difficult. When his characters die, people really care; and it is a testament to the success of Joss's writing ability that he creates characters that we care about. And one of the main rules of his work, which I've heard him say time and time again, is that you go for the dark, you go for the pain, if there is no contrast between light and dark, if it's all gray, you can't care. You've got to kill the one you love. You've got to go for the pain. Otherwise there is no hero's journey.

"Because when it's funny, it becomes funnier. When it's bright, it becomes brighter, because we come out of the darkness. If you don't have contrast, it becomes a muddy gray. But that makes it problematic all the way around. Because we snapped Ms. Calendar's neck, and they really didn't like that! She was human. To kill a human is a bad bit.

"Well, the network found it difficult. Because it is a challenge to kill real people. So that's something that has to be dealt with. As you know we had an episode pulled, because there was a gun ['Earshot']. Back to 'The I in Team,' that's the first thing I have to worry about—is that we get the Broadcast Standards and Practices clearance [regarding the death of Maggie Walsh], and that will not end until we get to a final cut."

WG2: "Have you had any reaction yet to the love scenes between Riley and Buffy in 'The I in Team?'"

GS: "There is concern, what they call a caution. The problem is, we are intercutting the fight with the bed scene, and intermingling sex and violence is always problematic. So we'll see. And I'm sure they'll negotiate and it will be fine. I need to say, their trust in Joss's work is significant. They trust him. We have a history now. They know better than they did the first season when it was like, 'And you're going to eat the high school principal? You're gonna eat the pig?' Of course we got more mail about the pig than we ever did about the principal. Nobody complained we ate the principal but they were really offended that we ate the pig."

WG2: "Did you get any caution about the death of Lindsey Crouse?"

GS: "No. Except for the penetration shot, that it not be too violent. Anyway, that's the first thing to worry about. The second thing is to basically see that all our bases are covered. That Joss's schedule continues. What's gonna be happening while this is shooting. Where is Joss? What's he going to be doing? What needs to get done? His schedule.

"Like now the big concern is making sure everybody gets out of here and off to their hiatuses. Their various hiatuses. Joss is going to want to get away, so is there anything we need to do before they finish shooting this episode?

"So you end up looking at sort of the bigger picture. Are there any writers that he can read, that he could take with him? Can we talk about any of these other projects?

"And don't forget the concern is that while we're on this episode, the rest of the world doesn't stop. We're prepping the next. Where's that script? When is Joss going to get to

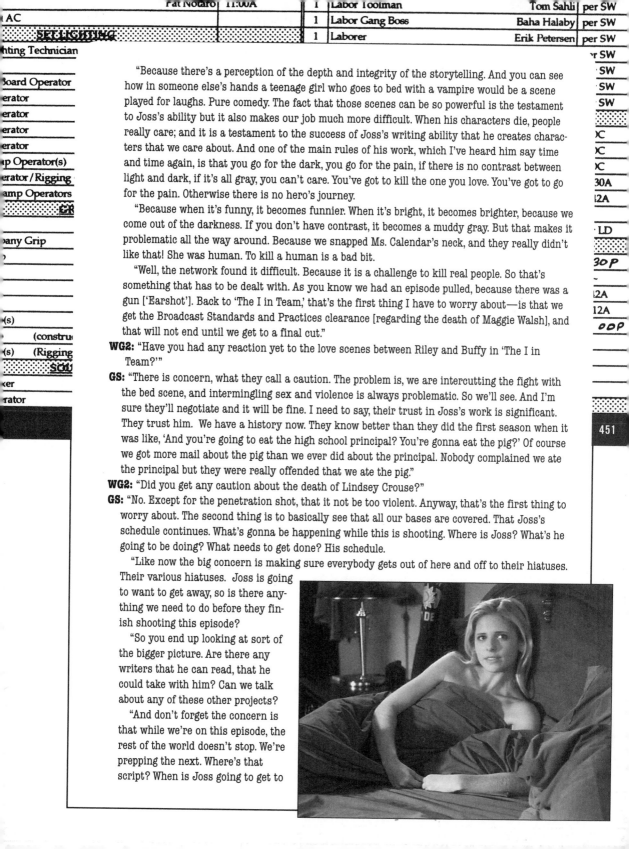

that script? So you're always working on two shows at least. Much as you're having the opportunity to sort of follow one through, the rest of us are all following this one plus the one they're prepping, plus of course, don't forget the two for <u>Angel</u>. The one they're shooting, the one they're prepping, and the ones that are gonna come after these two.

"And when we get back in January where are we, and is there going to be time to do some of the meetings we need to do then? That's sort of all tied to the episode . . . and when is he gonna do the mix? When is he gonna find time to do the editing on the previous episodes? That's the hardest part I think in television. Unlike features you can never be just on this and then when we're finished with this we'll look at something else. You're keeping several balls in the air at once."

WG2: "Do you have a life outside of this?"

GS: "Who needs a life outside of this? Tomorrow night I'm having a group of people over to watch 'Hush.' A bunch of people. Joss often does, and I often will go to Joss's, but this time I've got too many people who want to watch, so I'm doing a group. It's the best kind of job to have. These are my friends."

THE BANDS OF Buffy the Vampire Slayer

TVT RECORDS RELEASED *Buffy the Vampire Slayer: The Album* as *Buffy* entered Season Four in the fall of 1999. The album contains a compilation of music that suited the show's sensibility and that of its musical directors. Like a good college radio station, the music of *Buffy* manages to mix established classic and popular rock with relatively obscure bands for a sound that is cutting edge without being inaccessible. It also manages to work equally well in evoking moments from the show (who can hear the Sundays' "Wild Horses" without thinking of Buffy and Angel at the prom?) and existing as an eclectic slice of the musical life of the late 1990s. It also reflects a range of music beyond the gothic and occult that the casual observer might associate with the show and its supernatural themes.

• •

The majority of the music on the album has been used on the show, including:

"Buffy: the Vampire Slayer Theme" performed by Nerfherder
The featured version is the one from Season Two.

"Already Met You" performed by Superfine
Season One: "Teacher's Pet"

"Strong" performed by Velvet Chain
Season One: "Never Kill a Boy on the First Date"

"It Doesn't Matter" performed by Alison Krauss & Union Station
Season Two: "When She Was Bad"

"Transylvanian Concubine" performed by Rasputina
Season Two: "Surprise"

"Pain (Slayer Mix)" performed by Four Star Mary
Season Two: "Bewitched, Bothered, and Bewildered"

"Charge" performed by Splendid
Season Two: "I Only Have Eyes For You"

"Close Your Eyes" score by Christophe Beck
Season Two: "Becoming, Part Two"

"Pain (Slayer Mix)" performed by Four Star Mary
Season Three: "Deadman's Party"

"Virgin State of Mind" performed by k's Choice
Season Three: "Doppelgangland"

"Wild Horses" performed by the Sundays
Season Three: "The Prom"

"Pain (Slayer Mix)" performed by Four Star Mary
Season Four: "Living Conditions"

"Lucky" performed by Bif Naked
Season Four: "The Harsh Light of Day"

"Nothing But You" performed by Kim Ferron
Season Four: "Beer Bad"

"Teenage FBI" performed by Guided By Voices
Season Four: "The I in Team"

"Keep Myself Awake" performed by Black Lab
Season Four: "The I in Team"

"The Devil You Know" performed by Face to Face
Season Four: "Wild at Heart"

The remaining songs on the soundtrack include: **Garbage's "Temptation Waits,"** Hepburn's **"I Quit,"** and **Furslide's "Over My Head."**

. . . .

The music of *Buffy* appears in the background of scenes for dramatic impact, appears in recorded form as an integrated part of the characters' lives, or can be part of a "live" performance by fictional or real bands, usually in the Bronze. *WG2* spoke with members of several bands, including Nerf Herder, who are responsible for the theme song, and Four Star Mary, who provide the music behind Dingoes Ate My Baby, as well as other bands who have appeared on the show as…bands!

Santa Barbara band **NERF HERDER** was formed in 1994 by singer-guitarist Parry Gripp, drummer Steve Sherlock, and original bassist Charlie Dennis, and now includes Pete Newbury on bass and guitarist Dave Ehrlich. Nerf Herder's fans respond both to the band's driving guitar lines (displayed to advantage in the *Buffy* Theme) and to the humor and wit in their lyrics. The band's name comes from a line in *The Empire Strikes Back* where Princess Leia calls Han Solo a "half-witted, scruffy-looking nerf herder." George Lucas may never have more precisely defined a "nerf herder," but if the band is anything to go by, it must mean a neo-punk-pop commentator on popular culture and its foibles. The band has also appeared on the MTV show *Loveline* and had a song "Don't Hate Me Because I'm Beautiful" included in the movie *BASEketball*. As of mid-2000, the band had released two albums, one eponymous and the recent *How to Meet Girls*. More information about the band can be found at their web site: **http://cahnman.com/nerfherder/**

WG2: "Were any of you fans of <u>Buffy</u> before your association with it?"

PG: "We all watch <u>Buffy the Vampire Slayer</u> religiously. We were associated with it before it was on the air. I actually saw the original movie and bought the soundtrack because of fellow Santa Barbara-ians and local friends Toad the Wet Sprocket."

WG2: "How were you contacted by the show?"

PG: "Joss called me at my family's orchid nursery. I'm not sure how he got the number. I think that some of the cast members had come to see us, maybe even him. One funny thing is that after Joss and Co. picked our song for the theme, I had to meet with the sound editor (I'm not sure if that's her real title) from the show. She was this funky lady who invented a game about <u>I Love Lucy</u> (she no longer works for the show). Anyhow, when I told her I didn't read music she said, 'Oh, no, you can't do this!' And then she told me that our song sounded 'just like incomprehensible noise!' Despite that, she was actually very nice, and the whole thing worked out great."

WG2: "What sort of impact has your experience with <u>Buffy</u> had on increasing the band's exposure?"

PG: "We've gained a lot of fans from the show. A whole bunch from Europe, too. It's been great for us, even though I think most people don't even know we do the theme. Maybe we can get them to retitle the show <u>Buffy the Vampire Slayer, the show with the Nerfherder theme</u>. Probably not...."

WG2: "What does the future hold for Nerfherder?"

PG: "Well, if Willow gets her own show, we would really like to do the theme song. Other than that, we will be touring all over the country supporting our new CD, <u>How To Meet Girls</u>. We'll be on the road, and we will be playing the <u>Buffy</u> song every night!"

FOUR STAR MARY is the band behind the music of the fictional Dingoes Ate My Baby. Oz's band started as a throwaway line in the pilot episode, but then was fleshed out by Seth Green and the other actors, and given a true rock sound by the members of Four Star Mary in about a dozen episodes during the first four seasons. FSM's members include Steve Carter on bass, lead vocalist Tad Looney, Chris Sobchack on drums, David McClellan on guitar, and Michael "Zu" Zufelt on guitar and backup vocals during the band's original association with the show. Their music is a true collaborative effort, resulting in lyrics that stir the heart and mind set to alternative rock music which moves the body. John King first included FSM's music in Season Two:

"Inca Mummy Girl"; the actual band members were never viewed by the *Buffy* audience until Season Four: "Restless." For more information, visit the band's web site at **http://www.fourstarmary.com/**

WG2: "What can you tell us about Four Star Mary's background?"

SC: "There's an interesting 'kinship' between <u>Buffy</u> and Four Star Mary. Both the show and our band are an interesting mixture of 'light' and 'dark.' In <u>Buffy</u> the juxtaposition is between the often humorous dialogue and situations, placed within the 'dark' context of vampirism and dealing with various forms of ghoulies. In Four Star Mary it is the combination of upbeat, energetic instrumentals and melodies with the 'dark' situations and monologue of Tad's lyrics. The show and the band manifest similar underlying ironies. I think this similarity between <u>Buffy</u> and Four Star Mary is one of the main reasons that so many <u>Buffy</u> fans have become Four Star Mary fans."

WG2: "Were any of you fans of <u>Buffy</u> before your association with it? How were you contacted by the show?"

SC: "As with most relationships, it all started at a party! Music Editor John King was at a party being thrown by my girlfriend. I put one of our tapes in the stereo, and he heard it and asked me , 'Hey, who is this?' The rest is sorta history at this point. Some people might be interested in the following trivia though: Most bands who are used or appear on <u>Buffy</u> appear as themselves performing at the Bronze. For example, John also liked our roommates Darling Violetta, so they ended up playing in the Bronze during an episode when all the adults start acting like kids ['Band Candy']: This was the kind of thing that John had in mind for Four Star Mary. However, what John didn't know was that Joss had planned right from the start to have one of the shows' characters be <u>in</u> a band! So when Joss heard our tape, he thought we sounded right as the source music for Dingoes Ate My Baby and Oz, respectively. John was initially worried that we would be mad about having our songs 'lip-synched' instead of us being <u>on</u> the show, and tried to talk Joss out of it. Luckily, Joss wouldn't be swayed. As a result, we've had more music used on the show than any other band! In addition, we got to meet Seth Green [the actor who plays Oz] and make fun of him for not being able to play guitar! (Seth is one of the funniest people you will ever meet in the world!) Naturally, the next season, Seth called up and asked Zu to come down and coach him on the set." [See sidebar]

WG2: "You commented on the similarities in tone between Four Star Mary and <u>Buffy</u>— has the show inspired any music for the band?"

SC: "Yes and no. After Season Two, we were informed that the show 'needed more music' from the band. This prompted us to go into a studio and record several of the songs which ended up on <u>Thrown to the Wolves</u> (our second CD). However, none of the songs were written <u>for</u> the show. Indeed, what is really ironic is that we have no contact with the writers or really even the music supervisor, until John (the supe) calls up and says, 'Hey, I'm using such-and-such song for a scene. You gotta problem wit dat?' (big smile) We're never on the set except in extraordinary circumstances, like when Zu went down to coach Seth."

WG2: "Do you work together with the music director to decide on a song, or does he already know what he wants 'Dingoes' to perform?"

SC: "Actually, I think it is important to point out: some bands <u>have</u> tried to write songs specifically for the show, and have submitted them to John. The <u>Buffy</u> universe is not vampire-centric. It's not even centered around <u>Buffy</u>, except in a dramatic sense. So any music <u>written</u> with the show in mind, kind of by definition doesn't work for the show's purposes. Does that make sense? I mean, obviously, providing score to support dramatic elements of scenes is a different proposition. But songs which are supposed to be a realistic part of the environment, they need to be their own thing. It's like, you're not going to see an extra on the show walk through a scene wearing a <u>Buffy the Vampire Slayer</u> T-shirt, right? 'Nuff said."

WG2: "What sort of impact has your appearance on <u>Buffy</u> had on increasing the band's exposure?"

SC: "Huge. We're constantly blown away by how many people manage to find out that we're the band behind the band, so to speak. I mean, <u>we</u> have to sit there and freeze-frame and search, and sometimes <u>we</u> can't find any screen credit! So how do these kids find out about us? It's amazing."

WG2: "Do you have any theories on why today's TV audience is familiar with Four Star Mary, not just Dingoes Ate My Baby, as opposed to the audiences of shows like <u>The Partridge Family</u>?"

SC: "Oh, well, let's not forget: David Cassidy made <u>huge</u> amounts of money as a musician/singer. He was, at a certain level, the real deal. Now, Seth's situation was much more like the Monkees, a bunch of actors told to <u>act</u> like musicians! Of course, The Monkees <u>became</u> musicians and, via the performance of songs written by others for them to perform, had several Top Ten hits! I think the actual answer to your question is the Internet and publications like <u>The Watcher's Guide</u>, which make information available and give props to the people in the background working to produce the show."

WG2: "Did Four Star Mary play at previous Posting Board Parties, or just the 2000 one?"

SC: "Four Star Mary played the Season Two cast party at the El Rey, the Posting Board Party '99 preparty at the Holiday Inn in Hollywood (the old Revolving Restaurant room! <u>Very</u> cool!), and this year's Posting Board Party. We also played 'Viva Las Buffy,' a Halloween party organized by the Las Vegas contingent of the Posting Board crew, which was the <u>longest</u> show we've ever played (i.e., we played something like twenty songs, including a cover of 'Bloodletting' by Concrete Blonde!)."

WG2: "What does the future hold for Four Star Mary?"

SC: "Fame. Riches. Hookers. Jail. The usual rock-star stuff. Except we plan to skip the drugs."

"ZU'S BIG DAY OUT"

I CAN START WITH ALL THE FOOD. There is food every five feet, it seems. Everyone chilling down with some frosty frappuccinos, pretzels, pastries, and anything else with a high sugar content. To start the day, if you can call it that, at 3 P.M. is not most people's morning, but when you are shooting an outside night scene, it kinda needs to be dark. I start around two, having a late lunch with John King, the music supervisor, then spend the next hour or so touring around the production offices of *Buffy, Angel,* and Mutant Enemy, making the rounds with John meeting all the people that make the show happen.

It's four, and I'm told that Seth is waiting for me down at the set, so I grab my guitar and head out. The crew has already started blocking the first scene of the day when I walk into the Bronze. Seth yells from the other side of the room, and we exchange greetings loudly. We are both immediately told, 'We are working people, keep it down!' I'm on the set thirty seconds, and I'm already being told to shut up!

Seth has to finish blocking the scene, then we retire to the college student union set. We sit around and talk about what we have been doing for the summer, etc. The second AD comes in and announces: "Seth, we need you on the set," so off he goes for a while. In the meantime I have picked up one of the magazines in the student union and begun reading: It's a 1991 issue of *Cosmo*.

I start to show Seth the parts of the song ("Dilate" off of our new CD, *Thrown To The Wolves*) that he'll be playing, and I just tell him to put his hands around here on the guitar neck, and jump up and down, and it will look cool. He insists that he wants to actually *learn* the parts so it can look as real as possible. I teach him the chorus of the song. Then Seth tells me that he never even touched a guitar before he started the show, and he has now gone out and bought one so he can practice. He is picking up the chords pretty quickly. Then he starts talking about how he always wanted to introduce a song (in his heavy Bono accent): "We wrote this song in Johannesburg when we heard little Steven playing...." We both start laughing hysterically....although Seth actually does a real good Bono impression.

We finish learning all the parts of *Dilate* we think he needs to know for the scene, then we start jamming this Green Day song he knows. It's one that I haven't heard before, and he says he has the CD in his dressing room, so we go out to his trailer and he's blasting the last song off the *Nimrod* CD, rocking out with some mean air drumming. I suggest, 'Maybe Oz should have been the drummer in Dingoes?' On the counter in his trailer he has some *Austin Powers: The Spy Who Shagged Me* flyers from Japan. We start wondering how they translate "Shagged Me" into Japanese. I think that it probably said "the spy who was horribly disrespectful to me."

Finally off to the set to film the performance part of Dingoes and we do take one. After spending all that time learning the song, it doesn't look right because Four Star Mary has two guitarists and Dingoes has only one. I tell him were going to have to change his part because it doesn't look like it's matching the song. He looks a little worried, but I tell him to just put his hand up higher on the guitar neck and pick individual strings instead of strumming. We are all back by the monitors watching the second take, and this time everyone is saying that it looks a lot better. I walk out onto the set after the take and worship his air guitar prowess with the double "rock-out" hand gesture (if you don't know what this is, go find an old Scorpions or Def Leppard video!), which makes him bust out laughing. He is relieved and they do a couple more takes with a hand-held camera before finishing the scene.

Seth thanks me for coming down and helping him out and gives me his number so he can come and see how Four Star Mary plays the song. I'm packing up my stuff, and he asks if I'm staying for dinner. "Sure I'll meet you there." I proceed to get lost trying to find where everyone's eating and end up going home hungry.

Fade to black . . .

Roll credits . . .

The end.

THE EXPOSITION SONG

IN THE SEASON FOUR FINALE, "Restless," Joss Whedon wrote "The Exposition Song," which Giles (Anthony Stewart Head) sings in the story. Basically his dialogue, about what is going on, was put to music. He is accompanied by Chris Beck and the members of Four Star Mary, for once not performing as Dingoes Ate My Baby.

Steve Carter relates the experience of working with Anthony Stewart Head and crew on "The Exposition Song":

SC: "Let me explain the Four Star Mary/Chris Beck aspect a little for you! Tony starts to talk to himself ... hen he starts to sing to himself ... and then, wandering about on to the stage area ... it's a <u>rock opera</u>!! Well, not quite. However, Tony does have a <u>great</u> set of pipes. So, when about two bars into his 'exposition' Chris Beck plays a pickup on the piano, Tony kicks up the volume a bit. Then Chris S., Zu and I (representing three fifths of Four Star Mary) kick out the jams for a bit of Queen-esque rock dramatacism, supporting some <u>very</u> funny lyrics!

"Half of the backstory here as I understand it is that Joss was just fooling around with Tony and the script at a read-through and said, 'Hey, you should <u>sing</u> this!' ... which apparently quickly led to a 'Hmm ... and haven't Chris Beck and the Dingoes been invisible for far too long?' type epiphany, which led to a bunch of hurried phone calls and a hastily scheduled recording session, followed by a midnight taping. Yes, Chris Beck and Zu, Tad, Dave, and Chris all show up <u>on screen</u> in this scene of the episode (Tad is playing my bass in the scene, thus allowing every 'member' of Four Star Mary to be represented. I had to be in Boston during the taping)."

WG2: "Who wrote the music to accompany Joss's words?"

SC: "Chris [Beck]. And jeez, he's just disgustingly talented. Very annoying. I say we pants him!"

WG2: "How was this experience different from the usual Four Star Mary/'Dingoes' experiences?"

SC: "Well ... we've <u>never</u> recorded something <u>for</u> the show per se. They've always just picked up our songs 'as is.' Plus ... well ... we write our own songs, and Tad has less hair than Tony!"

DARLING VIOLETTA started with Los Angeles native singer and songwriter Cami Elen and southern guitarist Jymm Thomas performing around Los Angeles as a pair of acoustic musicians. The addition of regular members Atto Attie on bass and Steve McManus on drums resulted in the band as it exists today. Darling Violetta's style combines various modern rock sub-genres like pop and psychedelic rock to result in their unique sound. Darling Violetta has released two independent albums, *BathWaterFlowers*, and *The Kill You EP*. The Season Three *Buffy* episode "Faith, Hope & Trick" featured the band performing "Blue Sun" and "Cure" in the background in the Bronze. The band's Web site includes a diary of their experiences filming on the *Buffy* set in August 1998. Their journal reveals their encounters with the cast, crew, and catering, as well as transportation, technical, and wardrobe issues. It is a fascinating and funny chronicle of the difference between being a band performing live for an audience, and the movie magic that makes it seem that they are playing for the Bronzers. Following their successful *Buffy* encounter, Darling Violetta went on to compose and

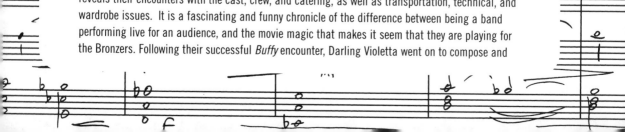

perform *Angel*'s theme song. They continue to play a variety of live venues in Southern California and contribute music to other media projects as well. To learn more about the band, visit their Web site at **http://www.darlingvioletta.com/darling.htm**

WG2: "Were any of you fans of <u>Buffy</u> before your association with it? How were you contacted by the show?"

CE: "Well, funny enough, we share rehearsal space with Four Star Mary (the band who provides music for Dingoes Ate My Baby) and Steve Carter, their bass player, passed our music along to John King, the music supervisor for both shows (although back then, <u>Angel</u> was not around yet). We didn't hear anything for a long time, and I actually forgot about it. Almost a year later John called and said they had an upcoming episode that he thought our music would be perfect for that also called for the band to be playing in the Bronze. He said the creative team would be having a meeting to discuss whether we would be on or not. A couple of days later John called again and said 'Okay, you're in, and we're shooting Tuesday.'"

AA: "And I think Joss had seen the band live months before by accident at the Martini Lounge in Hollywood one evening when we were playing with Splendid and we made an impression."

SM: "John mentioned that when he brought the music in for the episode, Joss said something like, 'Oh yeah, I've seen them before.'"

JT: "We all were aware of <u>Buffy</u> before our involvement with the show, but once we were involved with the show, I started regularly taping every episode (we rehearse on Tuesday nights). Through the official <u>Buffy</u> posting board, I have made friends with people who let me catch up on episodes I had missed. I am now what you might call a rabid fan and have become involved with the <u>Buffy</u> online community. I think being a fan helped when we were asked to submit ideas for the <u>Angel</u> theme, because I really knew what was going on with Angel's character and I had a good sense of what to shoot for with the theme music."

CE: "We were asked to play the preparty for this year's 'Posting Board Party' in Los Angeles at the Key Club, and I must say the <u>Buffy/Angel</u> fans who were in attendance made up one of the most boisterous, energetic, appreciative crowds we have played to. I told them, 'We feel the love!' They were singing along with all the songs, screaming, and basically made us feel like we were headlining the Forum!"

SM: "Playing the pre-Posting Board party was a blast. Afterward we had a chance to meet an awful lot of the crowd when they came downstairs to buy CDs. We signed most of them, took lots of pictures with them. They're a great bunch of people, these Bronzers, and we hope to play for them in their hometowns this year."

WG2: "What sort of impact has your appearance on <u>Buffy</u> had on increasing Darling Violetta's exposure?"

CE: "We are constantly stunned and amazed by the amount of e-mails and letters we get from people all across the globe who have been turned on to us through <u>Buffy</u> and/or <u>Angel.</u> Being involved with both shows has definitely been a way for us to reach people who may never have heard of us otherwise, and who have now become some of our most loyal fans."

JT: "Our appearance on <u>Buffy</u> led directly to our landing the <u>Angel</u> theme and it's very cool to know that millions of people all over the world have been exposed to our music via the shows and the Internet."

SM: "We definitely get a lot more hits on our web site! And I've noticed that because we've been on <u>Buffy</u> and <u>Angel</u>, people are more willing to investigate the rest of our catalog."

AA: "So you could say some doors have opened for us...."

CE: "That were deadbolted and chained before!"

WG2: "What does the future hold?"

JT: "We'd like to sell millions of records and sell out world tours all the while perfecting our recipe for lentil soup!"

CE: "We do have plans for a U.S. tour and are starting to work on our next as yet untitled record. We'd like to do more television and film work as well."

SM: "Getting on the road is high priority, and I'd like to continue to experiment with our music to see what other places we can take it."

AA: "More of the best things in life...the unknown."

VELVET CHAIN, like many bands, was formed from the shifting, kaleidoscope components of several earlier bands. Lead vocalist Erika Amato is a talented actress as well as a musician, focusing her high-energy personality into the smooth conduit for the band's powerful atmospheric and stylized songs. She formed the core of Velvet Chain in 1993 with Jeff Stacey, who is the driving creative force behind both the lyrics and music as well as the bass player. Stacey also serves as remix artist and producer on their albums. Velvet Chain's sound defies categorization; descriptions resulting in a mish mash of a string of musical stylings fail to convey the smooth manner in which they have assimilated the best attributes to result in a truly unique sound. When their second album, *Moody Grove Music*, was released in mid-2000, supporting band members included drummer Brett Chassen, guitarists Arif and Brian Reardon, keyboardist David Fraga, and "DJ Swerve," aka Mark Murray. For more information on the band, visit **http://www.lama.com/velvetchain**

WG2: "Were you fans of <u>Buffy</u> before your association with it?"

EA: "Actually, no, because we were on it when it was still in its very first stages. We were asked to be on the show way back in 1996, when they were first shooting the show. One of our fans here in L.A. (Brian Wankum) was involved with the show, and brought our demo CD <u>Groovy Side</u> [out of print], in to Joss Whedon, who totally liked us and wanted to use us on screen in addition to just using the songs. (That's us playing in the Bronze while <u>Buffy</u> and Owen are dancing....) They called us and asked us if we'd like to do it. No one had ever heard of the project yet, and we weren't even sure it would be picked up. I believe ours was only the third episode ever shot, although it was the fifth to air. ('Never Kill A Boy on the First Date') We shot the show in June of 1996, and it finally aired on March 31, 1997. Little did we know it would do such good things for us!"

462

WG2: "What sort of impact has your experience with <u>Buffy</u> had on increasing the band's exposure?"

EA: "It has had enormous impact. We were always popular here in L.A., but being on the show has given us a national and even international audience we could only reach in a limited way [via the Web site] before. After the show so many more people had heard of us, and then they got turned on to the music, and the word continued to spread from there…and now with the soundtrack, that exposure has just continued to grow. It's great."

WG2: "What years did Velvet Chain play at the Posting Board Party? What year did Seth Green join you?"

EA: "We actually played the cast/crew wrap-party in 1998, at the end of their second season, which was cool, and that's how we met Seth. He ended up playing the <u>Buffy</u> song with us at one of our local L.A. gigs that summer, which was a riot, and was witnessed by pretty much the whole cast, who all came to see if he'd blow it! [laughs] Joss, Anthony Stewart Head, Alyson, Nicky, and of course Seth were at the show. "We played the Posting Board Party in both 1999 and 2000. Seth played with us at the 1999 Posting Board Party, and would have repeated his performance this year if he'd been in town, but sadly, he wasn't."

WG2: "Who really answers the Diva Icon's e-mail?"

EA: "Mostly I do, but sometimes it's Jeff."

WG2: "What does the future hold for Velvet Chain?"

EA: "As Madonna once said, 'World domination!' Just kidding. We're releasing our latest CD, <u>Moody Groove Music</u>, in April, and we're very excited about it. Maybe it will get picked up by a major label, maybe it won't, but we don't really care. We're just thrilled with the work, and we can't wait for our fans to check it out! Also, we're almost done with the video for the song, 'Beyond Time,' which we will be premiering at our CD release party at the Key Club in Hollywood. It's coming out great, and we're pretty optimistic about the exposure it will garner us. Who knows? We could even end up on <u>Buffy</u> again, which would be extremely cool."

With their mature soulful lyrics and thoughtful instrumentation, **bellylove** sometimes sounds like more than a pair of musicians. Lead singer and song writer Toni Garcia and bass guitar player Lisa Black not only are solely responsible for bellylove's sound, but also do most of the writing, production, and distribution of the band's materials through their own label, Bad Boy Kitty Records. Bad Boy Kitty Records has produced two albums for bellylove since the band formed in 1997, an eponymous first album and *Xipe Totec*. For more about this self-sufficient band, visit **http://www.bellylove.com**

WG2: "Were you fans of <u>Buffy</u> before your association with it?"

TV: "My mother is a huge fan. She was so excited, as were we."

WG2: "What were some of the memorable moments from your time on the set?"

LB: "Eating lunch with the cast in the commissary, I remember Alyson came up and sat right next to me like she was an old friend. I like her; she's a very down-to-earth person, I really liked her in <u>American Pie</u>. Also Nicholas Brendon was so un-Hollywood. He was just willing to chat and spoke so highly of his twin brother."

TV: "Meeting Seth Green was quite memorable for me, as well as the way the filming went. It only took like three takes, and they made us feel really good."

WG2: "What sort of impact has your appearance on <u>Buffy</u> had on increasing the band's exposure?"

LB: "We gained worldwide exposure and received many wonderful compliments from people. Plus our CD. sales from the show put us in the black."

TV: "We have sold CDs all over the world and the United States which was really cool and we wouldn't have done that yet."

WG2: "What does the future hold for bellylove?"

LB: "I'd like to get a boxer puppy some day."

TV: "Fame and fortune! Top Ten songs and a lot of fun!"

Before the band's *Buffy* appearance, **LOTION** earned a place in cultural trivial pursuit as the band with liner notes written by notoriously reclusive author Thomas Pynchon (*Gravity's Rainbow*). This East Coast "college rock" band thrives on enthusiastically punching out multiple guitar chords and catchy pop rhythms while occasionally commenting on the material side of the business via their art. Band members Rob Youngberg, vocalist Tony Zajkowski, and guitarist William Ferguson draw on their media and marketing skills in promoting the band. Like most of the bands of *Buffy*, Lotion has fans who insist that the only way to experience the true impact of the band is in a live performance. For more information, visit **http://www.ilovelotion.com**

WG2: "Were any of you fans of <u>Buffy</u> before your association with it?"

Lotion: "Yes. While making our third album, <u>Telephone</u>, we would fill up the down time eating Chinese food and watching videos. Rob brought a tape of most of <u>Buffy</u>'s Season One he had made and turned us all on to the show. After that, all four of us were anxiously awaited Season Two."

WG2: "How were you contacted by the show?"

Lotion: "On a whim (you know how whims are) Rob and his girlfriend (not Thomas Pynchon) sent a copy of our new album as soon as it was done. We knew they played pretty cool music on the show, so maybe they'd play ours. They responded by saying they really wanted to use the single 'Blind For Now' from our last record [in Episode fifteen of Season Two, 'Phases'] and asked if we could be there (L.A.) three weeks later to play the song on the show. We were like, 'Wha?' and they were like 'Yee-ah!' and we were like, 'Doy!' and they were like, 'Shee-ya!' and we had no idea what 'Shee-ya' meant, so we booked four tickets for LAX just in case.

"We're from New York, so going to L.A. is already like being on a movie set. It's January and it's T-shirt weather. Arrived on the set at 8:00 A.M., and we're in high school again. There was nothing going on for the first two hours so we just roamed around the hallways of Sunnydale High, chilled in the library, set up our amps and drum kit onstage at the Bronze, sat on <u>Buffy</u>'s bed, kicked the tires of Giles' Citröen, stole a card from the card catalogue the Library, and put Lotion stickers on about every fifth locker. We ate three food services meals, which probably sucks after a few days, but the first day is great. We got our own trailer. And we hung with Alyson H. and her puppy. Rob got his hair done sitting next to Charisma C. Even Sarah posed

for pictures with us, high kicking at the camera. We gave out a bunch of Lotion T-shirts. Fooled around a bit with Anthony Stewart Head and Seth Green. We got to pick out whatever clothes we wanted to wear from wardrobe, and a group of young Gen-X-looking L.A. type kids were herded into the Bronze for our big scene. We ran through the song about four times, Tony lip-synching away, Bill stomping and biting his lip, Jim trying a few phony windmill chords, Rob softly tapping the cymbals, the cameras catching all the splendor. Then we shot the werewolf part, the director crying 'Wolf!', the playback stopped, thirty girls screaming and everyone running for the exits, the band grabbing their guitars and scooting offstage, over and over about ten times. All in all a pretty good day for some <u>Buffy</u> fans."

WG2: "What sort of impact has your experience with <u>Buffy</u> had on increasing the band's exposure?"

Lotion: "None that we can tell. It was more for us. Although we did have people e-mailing us telling us how many times a Lotion sticker was seen on each subsequent show. The next season they used another song, 'West of Here,' this time from our new album, after Oz's band's set at the Bronze. We're pretty lucky."

WG2: "What does the future hold for Lotion?"

Lotion: "Another record, and eventually our own sitcom."

Companion to Dingoes Ate My Baby, Bronze band **SHY** from Season Four exists both in the fictitious realm of the Buffyverse and the real world. In the real world Shy is composer and arranger George Shimeal aka George Sarah's band THC/The Hard Core. For the purposes of the show, The Hard Core's electronic dance music was arranged into something approaching a popular music sound, and Sarah played the part of Shy's keyboard player behind lead singer Veruca (Paige Moss). Sarah is a veteran of the Los Angeles music scene, and the music of THC has been included in half a dozen feature films, as well as on *Angel*. For more information visit **http://www.dungeonkids.com/THC/**

WG2: "How were you contacted by <u>Buffy</u>?"

GS: "I had been aware of <u>Buffy</u>, its music and the involvement of various bands before being contacted by the show. A mutual friend brought THC's music to the attention of the music director. The Episode Two of <u>Angel</u> also features a THC song, 'Girlflesh'."

WG2: "How did the writers fit Shy and THC together?"

GS: "The writers were listening to THC when working on the episodes in which 'Shy' appeared ('Beer Bad' and 'Wild at Heart'). They worked to match Paige Moss as Veruca to THC, rather than creating the character and asking me to match the music to their concept. Everyone on the set was warm and friendly. I even had a chance to interact with Seth Green, who is a music fan."

WG2: "How did you feel about the cast and characters' reaction to the band and its performance?"

GS: "They were very receptive and seem to have an appreciation for electronic music, so it was really great to be a part of a group of artists that shared a mutual respect for one another."

WG2: "What sort of impact has your experience with <u>Buffy</u> had on raising your profile, especially since you do other pseudonymous work?"

GS: "The appearances on the shows had a very positive impact because of the very loyal and well-informed fans."

ROYAL CROWN REVUE has been swinging for years, and swung its way to "Superstar" as Jonathan's backup band. Band members Eddie Nichols (vocals), Mando Dorame (tenor sax), Bill Ungerman (baritone sax), Scott Steen (trumpet), James Achor (guitar), Veikko Lepisto (bass) and Daniel Glass (drums) spent the nineties building their reputation as leaders in the revival of swing sounds complemented with other styles to form "retro swing." This sound is dedicated to the musical scene of the golden age of swing, but grows and develops from it. Royal Crown Revue has released five albums in ten years, and shows no signs of stopping. To get the latest on Royal Crown Revue, visit "Club RCR" at **http://www.rcr.com**

WG2: "How were you contacted by <u>Buffy</u>?"

DG: "We were contacted because many of the cast members and producers were fans of the band. I think they also wanted a swing-type band for the show, as one of the characters became a loungy kind of superstar."

WG2: "How did the taping work with the cast and the band?"

DG: "Great, no problems. Very professional, but typical television craziness. We had to be on a plane to Vegas by 6 P.M., and therefore had to leave the studio by four-thirty if we were to make our flight. The crew was also taking their dinner break at four-thirty, so if we didn't finish our portion by then, we'd have missed our flight. We had arrived on set at 10 A.M., so we didn't think there'd be any problems finishing on time, but there we were at four-fifteen, still waiting for our scenes and sweating! We filmed our entire sequence from four-twenty to four-thirty and had to haul ourselves to the airport."

WG2: "What does the future hold for Royal Crown Revue?"

DG: "More albums, opening new international markets like Australia, Europe, and Japan, where there are many maniacal fans who've waited years to see the band."

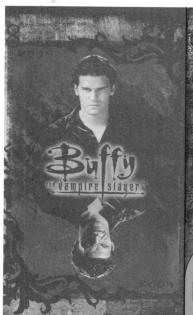

MERCHANDISING

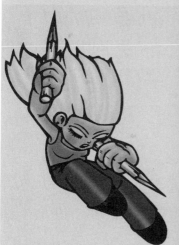

BUFFY THE VAMPIRE SLAYER FANS faithfully watch the show. They discuss it in person or via electronic methods. Fans gather together for marathon viewings and season finale parties, and take every possible advantage of opportunities at conventions and other gatherings to meet the cast and crew of the show. And, they buy the merchandise.

Licensed merchandise items not only give members of the established fan base substantial, physical mementos of the show they already love, they also serve to draw new viewers. Action figures, comics, novels and video games all cater to collectors who are looking for quality products in their area of specialization, whether they are familiar with the source product or not.

How extensive is the array of items one could possess? A dedicated U.S. fan could spend less than a dollar for an official *Buffy* lollipop to hundreds of dollars for a letterman's jacket or collectible statuette. Read on for an overview of the array of products.

Blue Grape Merchandising, Inc. offers the most basic, natural item of appreciative fans everywhere—character T-shirts and sweatshirts. They have produced shirts with images of the characters and iconic references to the show since late 1997, when *Buffy* entered its first full season. The shirts are composed of a balance of images provided by Fox and in response to customer requests. Recent examples include a reproduction of the "Welcome to Sunnydale" logo, and a "Sunnydale High Class of 1999" shirt featuring photos of Willow, Oz, Buffy, Xander and Cordelia. Through the end of Season Three, the most popular images were of Buffy and Angel, although the fans' quest for new items means that newer images are always the most popular. The shirts usually retail for around $17.00, and can be found in a variety of specialty and gift shops.

Dingbats has provided *Buffy* fans with a chance to admire their favorite characters every second if they so choose. The Los Angeles company has made *Buffy* watches and clocks since early 1999, launching its second line in June of 2000. Their timepieces featuring Buffy and Angel are sold in specialty stores and through on line vendors. They were very popular during the 1999 holiday gift season, retailing for between $19.99 and $29.99. In October 2000, Fossil will be offering a trend watch that retails for approximately $28.00. The watch will be packaged in a black microfiber, drawstring pouch with beadwork appliques. They will also offer a Limited Edition watch that comes in a beautiful oval jewel box that will retail between $65.00 and $95.00. And Cedco manufactured calendars for one's wall, desk, desktop, or locker.

Buffy and her friends can be found in all their three-dimensional glory in a selection of materials and sizes. Clayburn Moore has forged the strong reputation of Moore Action Collectibles through his ability to balance the art of a detailed, articulated action figure with the options fans want in accessories—crossbows, stakes, daggers, etc. All figures are available to their club members (www.mooreaction.com), in specialty comic and popular culture outlets and range from $10.95 to $15.95 per figure.

In 1999, Moore Action Collectibles made four general *Buffy* action figures available, as well as a set of "exclusive" variants. The first series included a Season One Buffy in jeans and a black leather jacket, with shoulder-length hair, Angel in human face, Willow with long hair and white top, and the Master. The rare variants included Buffy with black pants and blue jacket (MAC Collectors Society), "Prophecy Girl" Buffy in a formal dress and brown leather jacket (Wizard), Angel in vamp face (Diamond) and Willow in red jeans and blue top (Another Universe).

The second series figure assortment calls for a Season Two Buffy, Cordelia, Giles, Oz, Spike, and Xander. The proposed exclusive line will include Cordelia in her cheerleader outfit, Giles in his Halloween costume of sombrero and serape, Oz with werewolf head and hands, and a vamp-faced Spike. These items should be available between September and December 2000.

As much as manufacturing will allow, the action figures' clothes are based on costumes the characters have worn in the show. Moore works from videotapes, photos and magazines as reference for each character. A great amount of thought goes into the case assortment based upon which figures the MAC team believes will be most in demand. With the first series, demand for the Willow figure exceeded expectations because of the extraordinary sculpt and Alyson Hannigan's appearance in *American Pie*. Action figure fan Seth Green (also incarnated in plastic by McFarlane Toys as "Scott Evil" from *Austin Powers*) has shared his input on the likenesses, as has Moore's personal friend Tony Head. Moore's work is causing *Buffy* fans to collect this series whether or not they were action figure collectors before, and is even drawing them to other sculpts of his, like comic's "Lady Death" and "Witchblade."

A huge assortment of two-dimensional merchandise is available. Advanced Graphics, "the Home of Cardboard People," produced an approximately life-sized cardboard stand-up figure of Buffy in August 1999, and produced Angel to keep her company in the fall. Buffy and Angel do not come with a voice box feature like some other Advanced Graphic items. The figures retail for around $30.00, and can be purchased in specialty and gift shops to decorate fans' work cubicles and homes.

Online monster pop culture retailer Another Universe (www.anotheruniverse.com) offers most of the *Buffy* merchandise described here, as well as an original print of Buffy and the Master by renowned fantasy artist Julie Bell. First available in December 1998, the print sells for $24.95 unsigned, or $99.95 signed.

Inkworks produces the *Buffy* trading cards, collections of images from all the seasons that invoke the most memorable characters and moments. All of the trading card sets contain randomly inserted cards autographed by members of the *Buffy* cast and crew. In addition, foil treated uncut mini press sheets of the puzzle sets are available.

Season One, produced in the fall of 1998, included subset cards with "Giles's Secret Library," "Slayer Speak" and "The Beastiary" in the primary assortment. Its scarce "chase" (not related to Cordelia) card sets included a nine-card puzzle of "The Chosen One, " a six-card collection of weapons forming the "Slayer Kit," and a very spe-

cial and rare die-cut coffin-shaped card with directions on "How to Kill a Vampire." Season Two, released in the Winter of 1999, contained a continuation of "The Beastiary;" the chase card sets were the nine card puzzle of Buffy and Angel and their "Dark Destiny," six cards with romantic couples, entitled "Love Bites," and another die-cut coffin which opens to reveal "How to Lose Your Soul." The Season Three set was released in the fall of 1999, and contained more monsters in "The Beastiary," as well as chronicling "The Dreaming," "Willow's Spells & Whistles,"

members of "The Watcher's Council," and graduation shots of the "Class of 1999." A nine-card foil puzzle of "Graduation Day," six miniature "Sunnydale High Yearbooks," and a die-cut reproduction of a Claddagh ring with a Buffy and Angel wedding image in the heart made up the chase cards for this set. Season Four trading cards will be released in fall 2000, but to satisfy demand, Inkworks issued a set titled "Reflections—The High School Years" in June 2000. This collection reflects on the Buffy gang's years spent at Sunnydale High School and is printed on high-quality canvas card stock for a more artistic effect. The chase cards include a nine-card puzzle entitled "Portrait of a Slayer" featuring Buffy, her high school friends and Watcher, and a six-card set called the "Slayer's Journal."

Inkworks also produced a set of several dozen 4x6-inch photo cards between their Season Two and Season Three card sets. The set covered the variety of characters' appearances in the past seasons, and included a chase set of six foil-stamped cards. In addition, Inkworks has produced two special collector's albums. In the end of 1999 the company produced a different but equally desirable product: a set of three jewel-toned collector bears. In the first bear set, the royal purple Buffy bear is embroidered with her name and a stake, emerald green Willow bear has the Wiccan symbol from "Gingerbread," and the sapphire blue Angel bear's chest has a two-color representation of his Claddagh ring. Individual card packs retail for around $3.00 to $4.00, while the bears and the uncut sheets retail for about $10.00 in specialty stores. The president and much of the staff at Inkworks are fans of the show, and their enthusiasm is reflected in the products. Because the products are produced for the collectors' market, most of them sold out upon release and can only be found now on the secondary market.

At-a-Boy of Hollywood not only produces thirteen wicked photographic magnets, mostly of the individual characters, but also four durable pocket mirrors. The mirrors (which ironically include two images of the nonreflective Angel) and magnets are both generally available for less than $5.00.

A fascinating assortment of products from key chains to glassware and ceramics to denim and leather jackets is handled by longtime licensee Creation Entertainment. Objects available in specialty and gift stores can be as inexpensive as a $3.99 key chain with a classic shot of the original cast to a $299.00 serious investment in a quality leather jacket. Middle ground items include dozens of cast photos ($5.99 retail); new images are released as often as possible to keep up with fan demand for their favorite characters with up-to-date hair and fashions.

Mehndi Body Art's temporary tattoos and iron on images offer the creative Buffy f an dozens of ways to make a very individual statement about their favorite show. The tattoos are primarily black and silver designs like a coffin outline with a cross and Buffy's iconic "B" in the center. The iron-on images include some unique photo images featuring Buffy, as well as designations like "Slayer," "Angel," and "Wicked." They can be found in specialty and gift shops for around $6.00 a piece.

At A Glance produced three images for Buffy wall posters: "Buffy," "The Group" (Season Four's continuing regulars), and "Beep Me" (as in "If the Apocalypse comes, beep me"). The posters retail in a variety of outlets nationally, usually for about $5.99.

Fans enjoy watching their favorite episodes multiple times: they prefer the chance to do so without commercial interruptions or the tape wearing thin. Fox Home Entertainment so far has provided two sets of VHS assortments of Buffy. Each tape sells for about $9.95, and they are available everywhere videos are sold. Selected episodes from Season One include "Welcome to the Hellmouth" and "The Harvest," "The Witch" and "Never Kill a Boy on the First Date," and "The Puppet Show" and "Angel." The Buffy and Angel Chronicles from Season Two contain "Surprise" and "Innocence," "Passion" and "I Only Have Eyes For You," and "Becoming, Part One," and "Becoming, Part Two."

Fox Interactive will release the Buffy the Vampire Slayer interactive adventure game for playing on Sega

Dreamcast, PlayStation and the PC in spring 2001. A Nintendo Gameboy version is also in development. The game, which retails for around $70, allows fans the ultimate *Buffy* experience: a player can be Buffy as he applies her powers of slaying, martial arts, enhanced senses and healing ability to ridding the world of evil. Familiar allies in the game include Angel, Xander, Cordelia, Willow, Oz and Giles. Locations like the late Sunnydale High School, some of the cemeteries, the Summers'es home and the Bronze add to the experience. Fox Interactive enhanced the verisimilitude of the game by working with *Buffy* stunt professionals Jeff Pruitt (Stunt Coordinator) and Sophia Crawford (SMG's stunt double) on the game character's fighting moves. In a spring press release, Fox Interactive explained its motivation behind acquiring the rights to the show's characters. Karly Young, Director, Worldwide Brand Marketing stated, "Of all entertainment properties available today, *Buffy the Vampire Slayer* is the franchise that gamers have been asking for. Now's our chance to give gamers the opportunity to live out their own *Buffy* adventures anytime they feel the need to kick some serious vampire butt." Some of Fox Interactive's previous creative efforts include *Aliens vs. Predator, The X-Files* and *The Simpsons Cartoon Studio.*

Fans eager to resemble the vampires and demons on *Buffy* can turn to the creative folks at Cinema Secrets. Cinema Secrets makes prosthetics and latex masks available on their Web site and through specialty retailers which can transform any fan grrl or boy into a reasonable fascimile of characters including Angel, Spike, Drusilla and the Judge. Their Web site (www.cinemasecrets.com) includes an icon for "what you need to create the effect," an optional instructional video, and categories ranging from "Witches, Devils and Werewolves, Oh My!" to "Industrial Accidents" and "Impalements." Their prosthetics are available in both latex and film quality foam material, and range from $10.00 to $40.00.

Fans who can't get enough *Buffy* stories during the television show's regular season have two alternatives for their "*Buffy* fix." Dark Horse Comics editor Scott Allie shared some insights into their projects. The "*Buffy*" comics launched with a variety of talented writers in September of 1998; summer 2000 saw regular writer Doug Petrie penning "*Buffy*: Ring of Fire," and Joss Whedon writing a future Slayer series is in discussion. Products include the *"Buffy the Vampire Slayer"* series of single-issue monthly comics, an *Angel* series of single-issue monthly comics, and a *Buffy* Annual in the summer. The monthly comics are available with art or photo cover choices in specialty stores and on newsstands for $2.95. Original trade publication "The Dust Waltz" was sealed in the "Supernatural Defense Kit," which also contains a cross, a Claddagh ring, and a vial of holy water for $19.95. The "Origin" story incorporated and smoothed out the disparate elements between the 1992 film and the television show. Differences in production schedules mean stories in the comics run about a year behind those on the show, but the time delay prevents contradictions. Editor Allie explained the biggest benefit to comic book format over film media, "We have an unlimited special effects budget. I can blow up Main Street, Sunnydale; I can have an eighty-foot bug, or a giant flying bird swooping down on the kids. Try that on TV and it'll blow the year's budget." The disadvantage? "We always know that the TV show is the real thing, and we're just icing on the cake."

Another source for more *Buffy* tales is Pocket Books. Pocket Books first published the movie novelization of *Buffy the Vampire Slayer* in 1992. The continuing series based on the television show was launched in the fall of 1997. The fiction line is a mix of original storyline novels and novelizations from certain episodes. Pocket Books currently publishes six adult titles and six teen titles per year, in addition to hardcovers, poster books, postcard books and trade paperbacks (such as the one you're holding!). Prices range from $4.99 to $22.95. All of the books are still in print and available everywhere books are sold.

Readers can keep their places in their *Buffy* books using tassled bookmarks or a "shapemarks" available from Antioch Publishing. They can record their impressions of the novels in journals or diaries, and keep important information on their wallet cards with features like a "Sunnydale High library card," or "Willow's List of Internet

Sites." Antioch's catalog includes door hangers, mini-bookplates and stickers. All of their items can be found in bookstores or general stores, and retail from $1.50 to $9.99.

Buffy lunchboxes and cloth wall scrolls are offered by Palisades Marketing through comic book and other specialty stores. Playing Mantis has a license to release die-cast cars and model kits through gift shops and hobby stores; figures should be available sometime in 2001. Alpha Polishing provides a variety of costume jewelry including hair clips, necklaces, rings, and earrings to specialty and gift stores. Clothing from CPI International can be found in The WB stores and in catalogs. C&D Visionary creates a variety of portable fan items like patches and magnets for specialty stores. The WB Studio Stores distribute *Buffy* baseball caps from Paramount Headgear, as well as the board game and puzzles issued by Hasbro in the summer of 2000. The Signature Group makes both headwear and mugs, available in specialty stores. European candy makers have wrapped their Chupa Chupa lollipops with special stickers of the *Buffy* characters. And *Buffy* candy bars from True Confections will also be available soon.

The best licensed periodical for fans curious about news on the show, cast, or products is the product of the official *Buffy the Vampire Slayer Fan Club*. The *Buffy* magazine was pitched by editor Mike Stokes to the publishers of MVP Media group, whose 'zines and fan clubs include *Cinescape, Dawson's Creek, The X-Files,* and *Wicked*. It launched in the fall of 1998 at the beginning of the show's third season. Four issues of the glossy, slick 'zine ship during the eight-month television season, and three variants are produced of each issue. Two different photo covers are released for single issue purchasers, selling on newsstands or comic stores for $5.95; members of the fan club have a special cover with the more rare of the photo covers and the fan club's logo, but no cover blurbs. They also produce a yearbook during the summer hiatus, recapping events of the previous season and looking ahead. The yearbook has a different binding, and retails for $9.95. While back issues have been available for order, many are

increasingly rare or sold out. The magazine has a close working relationship with the *Buffy* cast and crew to balance the fans' need for up to date information against the need to preserve information about plot twists and significant events. Interviews have appeared with most of the cast and crew, and Todd McIntosh has contributed articles on makeup. Special Fan Club merchandise is available to members, and selectively to the general public, through the magazine or their web site at **www.buffyfanclub.com**. While MVP Media will select from licensed merchandise available from existing vendors, vendors of their own choosing create much of what they make available.